# Encyclopedia of African American Business

# Encyclopedia of African American Business

## Volume 1
### A–J

## EDITED BY JESSIE CARNEY SMITH
### Millicent Lownes Jackson, Consultant
### Linda T. Wynn, Consultant

Greenwood Press
Westport, Connecticut • London

**Library of Congress Cataloging-in-Publication Data**

Encyclopedia of African American business / edited by Jessie Carney Smith ;
consultants : Millicent Lownes Jackson, Linda T. Wynn.
    p. cm.
  Includes bibliographical references and index.
  ISBN 0–313–33109–X (set : alk. paper)—ISBN 0–313–33110–3 (v. 1 : alk. paper)—
ISBN 0–313–33111–1 (v. 2 : alk. paper)  1. African American business
enterprises—United States—Encyclopedias.  2. African American businesspeople—
United States—Encyclopedias.  I. Smith, Jessie Carney.  II. Jackson, Millicent
Lownes.  III. Wynn, Linda T.
  HD2358.5.U6E53 2006
  338.7092'396073—dc22      2006002866

British Library Cataloguing in Publication Data is available.

This book is included in the African American Experience database from Greenwood
Electronic Media. For more information, visit www.africanamericanexperience.com.

Library of Congress Catalog Card Number: 2006002866
ISBN: 0–313–33109–X (set)
      0–313–33110–3 (vol. 1)
      0–313–33111–1 (vol. 2)

First published in 2006

Greenwood Press, 88 Post Road West, Westport, CT 06881
An imprint of Greenwood Publishing Group, Inc.
www.greenwood.com

Printed in the United States of America

The paper used in this book complies with the
Permanent Paper Standard issued by the National
Information Standards Organization (Z39.48–1984).

10 9 8 7 6 5 4 3 2 1

In recognition of
African American entrepreneurs
for their vision, endurance,
and notable contributions to the world of business;
and to my father, James A. Carney, an early entrepreneur
and my inspiration for this book

# Contents

# Entry List

Henry "Hank" Aaron
Robert Sengstacke Abbott
Advertising Agencies
Advertising and Marketing
Archie Alphonso Alexander
Clifford Leopold Alexander Jr.
Paget Alves
American Savings and Loan
  League
Wally "Famous Amos"
  Amos Jr.
Association of Black Women
  Entrepreneurs

Barbecue Establishments
Don H. Barden
Edwin C. Berry
Jesse Binga
Black Banks: Their Beginning
Black Business Development and
  the Federal Government
Black Business Development in
  Missouri
Black Businesses in Large Cities:
  A History
Black Corporate Directors
  Conference
Black Fund Managers
Black Press: Newspapers in Major
  Cities
Black Retail Action Group
Blacks in Agriculture

Booker T. Washington Business
  Association
Ruth Jean Bowen
Richard Henry Boyd
Sheila Bridges
Andrew Felton Brimmer
Brotherhood of Sleeping Car
  Porters
Todd C. Brown
Dorothy E. Brunson
Thomas J. Burrell
Roland W. Burris
John Edward Bush
Business Ownership in Select
  Academic Institutions

Cardozo Sisters
Albert Irvin Cassell
Catering Industry
Centers for Entrepreneurship in
  Academic Institutions
Chambers of Commerce and
  Boards of Trade in the
  1920s and 1930s
Debra Martin Chase
Leah Chase
Kenneth Irvine Chenault
Robert Reed Church Sr.
Citizens' League for Fair Play
Alexander G. Clark
Coalition of Black Trade
  Unionists

Daniel C. Cochran
Marie Therese Coincoin
Virgis William Colbert
Donald Alvin Coleman
Kenneth L. Coleman
Colored Merchants'
  Association
Sean "Diddy" Combs
Conferences and Studies on
  the Negro in Business: The
  Early Years
Conferences on African
  American Businesses
Ward Connerly
Consumer Cooperatives
Nathan G. Conyers
Edith W. Cooper
Corporation of Caterers
Credit Unions

Calvin Darden
Edward Davis
Erroll B. Davis Jr.
Thomas Day
Suzanne de Passe
Charles Diggs Jr.
Don't Buy Where You Can't
  Work Movement
Frederick Douglass's Business
  Enterprises
Dr. Dre (Andre Young)
Joe L. Dudley Sr.

## Entry List

E-Commerce and the African American Community
Economic Boycotts and Protests
Kenneth "Babyface" Edmonds and Tracey Edmonds
Elleanor Eldridge
William Ellison
Evern Cooper Epps
Eta Phi Beta Sorority, Inc.

Faith-Based Entrepreneurship
James Conway Farley
Melvin Farr
Fashion Industry
Federal Records for African American Business History
Federation of Southern Cooperatives Land Assistance Fund
Food Service Industry
Barney Launcelot Ford
James Forten
Ann M. Fudge
S. B. Fuller
I. Owen Funderburg

Edward G. Gardner
Marcus Garvey's UNIA Enterprise
A. G. Gaston
Karen Patricia Gibbs
John Trusty Gibson
Bruce S. Gordon
Berry Gordy Jr.
Earl G. Graves
Sylvester Green
Grocery Store Enterprises

James Francis Haddon
Elliott Sawyer Hall
Marc R. Hannah
Carla Ann Harris
Lowell Hawthorne
Darryl B. Hazel
Ellenae Henry-Fairhurst
Alexis M. Herman
Alonzo Franklin Herndon
Dennis Fowler Hightower
Jesse Hill Jr.

Casper A. Holstein
Christine Moore Howell
Catherine "Cathy" Hughes

International Black Women's Congress

Maynard Holbrook Jackson Jr.
O'Shea "Ice Cube" Jackson
Thomas "T. D." Jakes
Earvin "Magic" Johnson Jr.
Eunice Walker Johnson
John H. Johnson
Robert L. Johnson
Caroline R. Jones
John Jones
Quincy Jones
Vernon Eulion Jordan
Marjorie Stewart Joyner

Kid/Teenpreneurs: Business Leaders in the Making
Don King

Thomy Lafon
Lunsford Lane
Ronald N. Langston
John Anderson Lankford
Dorothy R. Leavell
Debra Louise Lee
Spike Lee
Legal Defense and Educational Fund
Byron Eugene Lewis
Delano Eugene Lewis
Reginald F. Lewis
William M. Lewis Jr.
Alfred M. Ligon
James Bruce Llewellyn

Paula Madison
Annie Turnbo Malone
Julianne Malveaux
Bridget "Biddy" Mason
William G. Mays
Jewell Jackson McCabe
H. Carl McCall
Renetta McCann

McKissack and McKissack Architects and Engineers, Inc.
Calvin McKissack and Moses McKissack III
Frank Mercado-Valdes
John Merrick
Lightfoot Solomon Michaux
Minority Businesses in Major Cities
Minority Enterprise Development Week
Aaron McDuffie Moore
Rose Morgan
Cecilia Antonietta Mowatt
Eddie Murphy
Isaac Myers
Woodrow Augustus Myers Jr.

John E. "Jack" Nail
James Carroll Napier
National Afro-American League
National Alliance of Market Developers
National Association of Black Accountants
National Association of Black Owned Broadcasters
National Association of Black Women Entrepreneurs
National Association of Investment Companies
National Association of Minority Contractors
National Association of Negro Business and Professional Women's Clubs
National Black Chamber of Commerce
National Black Farmers Association
National Black MBA Association
National Black United Fund
National Negro Business League

Berry O'Kelly
Hazel R. O'Leary
E. Stanley O'Neal

# Topical Entry List

## Academic Institutions

Business Ownership in Select Academic Institutions
Centers for Entrepreneurship in Academic Institutions

## Advertising

Advertising Agencies
Advertising and Marketing
American Savings and Loan League

## Agriculture

Blacks in Agriculture

## Biographies

Henry "Hank" Aaron
Robert Sengstacke Abbott
Archie Alphonso Alexander
Clifford Leopold Alexander Jr.
Paget Alves
Wally "Famous Amos" Amos Jr.
Don H. Barden
Edwin C. Berry
Jesse Binga
Ruth Jean Bowen
Richard Henry Boyd
Sarah Breedlove. *See* **Madame C. J. Walker**

Sheila Bridges
Andrew Felton Brimmer
Todd C. Brown
Dorothy Edwards Brunson
Thomas J. Burrell
Roland W. Burris
John Edward Bush
Cardozo Sisters
    Elizabeth Cardozo Barker
    Margaret Cardozo Holmes
    Emmeta Cardozo Hurley
    Catherine Cardozo Lewis
Albert Irvin Cassell
Debra Martin Chase
Leah Chase
Kenneth Irvine Chenault
Robert Reed Church Sr.
Alexander G. Clark
Daniel C. Cochran
Marie Therese Coincoin
Virgis William Colbert
Donald Alvin Coleman
Kenneth L. Coleman
Sean "Diddy" Combs
Ward Connerly
Nathan G. Conyers
Edith W. Cooper
Calvin Darden
Edward Davis
Erroll B. Davis Jr.
Thomas Day
Suzanne de Passe

"Diddy." *See* **Sean "Diddy" Combs**
"P. Diddy." *See* **Sean "Diddy" Combs**
Charles Diggs Jr.
Frederick Douglass. *See* **Frederick Douglass's Business Enterprises**
Dr. Dre (Andre Young)
Joe L. Dudley Sr.
Kenneth "Babyface" Edmonds and Tracey Edmonds
Elleanor Eldridge
William Ellison
Evern Cooper Epps
Ellenae Fairhurst. *See* **Ellenae Henry-Fairhurst**
James Conway Farley
Melvin Farr
Barney Launcelot Ford
James Forten
Ann M. Fudge
Samuel B. Fuller. *See* **S. B. Fuller**
S. B. Fuller
I. Owen Funderburg
Edward G. Gardner
Marcus Garvey. *See* **Marcus Garvey's UNIA Enterprise**
A. G. Gaston
Karen Patricia Gibbs
John Trusty Gibson
Bruce S. Gordon

# Topical Entry List

Berry Gordy Jr.
Earl G. Graves
Sylvester Green
James Francis Haddon
Elliott Sawyer Hall
Marc R. Hannah
Carla Ann Harris
Lowell Hawthorne
Darryl B. Hazel
Ellenae Henry-Fairhurst
Alexis M. Herman
Alonzo Franklin Herndon
Dennis Fowler Hightower
Jesse Hill Jr.
Casper A. Holstein
Christine Moore Howell
Catherine "Cathy" Hughes
"Ice Cube." *See* **O'Shea "Ice Cube" Jackson**
Maynard Holbrook Jackson Jr.
O'Shea "Ice Cube" Jackson
Thomas "T. D." Jakes
Earvin "Magic" Johnson Jr.
Eunice Walker Johnson
John H. Johnson
"Magic" Johnson. *See* **Earvin "Magic" Johnson Jr.**
Robert L. Johnson
Caroline R. Jones
John Jones
Quincy Jones
Vernon Eulion Jordan
Marjorie Stewart Joyner
Don King
Thomy Lafon
Lunsford Lane
Ronald N. Langston
John Anderson Lankford
Dorothy R. Leavell
Debra Louise Lee
Spike Lee
Byron Eugene Lewis
Delano Eugene Lewis
Reginald F. Lewis
William M. Lewis Jr.
Alfred M. Ligon
James Bruce Llewellyn
Paula Madison
Annie Turnbo Malone

Julianne Malveaux
Bridget "Biddy" Mason
William G. Mays
Jewell Jackson McCabe
H. Carl McCall
Renetta McCann
Calvin McKissack and Moses McKissack III
Frank Mercado-Valdes
John Merrick
Lightfoot Solomon Michaux
Aaron McDuffie Moore
Rose Morgan
Cecilia Antonietta Mowatt
Eddie Murphy
Isaac Myers
Woodrow Augustus Myers Jr.
John E. "Jack" Nail
James Carroll Napier
Berry O'Kelly
Hazel R. O'Leary
E. Stanley O'Neal
Clarence Otis Jr.
Anthony Overton
Harry H. Pace
Henry Green Parks Jr.
Richard Dean Parsons
Robert Paschal and James Paschal
Frederick Douglas Patterson
Charles V. Payne
Philip A. Payton Jr.
Heman Edward Perry
Charles E. Phillips Jr.
Joseph Alphonso Pierce
Winston Pittman Sr.
Myrtle Stephens Potter
Ernesta G. Procope
Barbara Gardner Proctor
"Puff Daddy." *See* **Sean "Diddy" Combs**
"Puffy." *See* **Sean "Diddy" Combs**
Franklin Delano Raines
Antonio "L. A." Reid
Sylvia Rhone
Linda Johnson Rice
Norman Blann Rice
Roy S. Roberts
David Ruggles
Herman Jerome Russell

Patricia Russell-McCloud
Frank Savage
Alan Shaw
Joseph Jacob Simmons III
Russell Simmons
Naomi R. Sims
Norma Merrick Sklarek
"B" Smith. *See* **Barbara "B" Smith**
Barbara "B" Smith
Paula A. Sneed
Charles Clinton Spaulding
David L. Steward
Leon Howard Sullivan
Percy Ellis Sutton
Lucious (Lou) Switzer
Vertner W. Tandy Sr.
Susan L. Taylor
John W. Thompson
Gloria E. A. Toote
Dempsey Jerome Travis
Lloyd G. Trotter
Sheila Vaden-Williams
A'Lelia Walker
Antonio Maceo Walker
Madame C. J. Walker (Sarah Breedlove)
Maggie Lena Mitchell Walker
Lloyd David Ward
Carl H. Ware
Augustus Washington
Booker T. Washington
Regynald G. Washington
Sarah Spencer Washington
Barbara Mae Watson
Damon Wayans
Paul Revere Williams
David Augustus Williston
Oprah Winfrey
Sylvia P. Woods
Andre Young. *See* **Dr. Dre**
Alfred W. Zollar

## Booking Agencies

Theater Owners Booking Association and the Entertainment Industry

xiv

# Topical Entry List

# African American Business Leaders by Occupation

## Abolitionists

Frederick Douglass. *See* **Frederick Douglass's Business Enterprises**
James Forten
John Jones
David Ruggles
Augustus Washington

## Accountants, Actuaries

Roland W. Burris
Jesse Hill Jr.

## Activists

Frederick Douglass. *See* **Frederick Douglass's Business Enterprises**
Marcus Garvey. *See* **Marcus Garvey's UNIA Enterprise**
Earvin "Magic" Johnson Jr.
Don King
Julianne Malveaux
Maggie Lena Mitchell Walker

## Actors

O'Shea "Ice Cube" Jackson
Eddie Murphy
Damon Wayans

## Advertising Executives, Agents

Donald Alvin Coleman
Caroline R. Jones
Byron Eugene Lewis
Barbara Gardner Proctor

## Architects, Building Planners

Albert Irvin Cassell
John Anderson Lankford
Calvin McKissack and Moses McKissack III
Norma Merrick Sklarek
Vertner W. Tandy Sr.
Paul Revere Williams
David Augustus Williston

## Artisans

William Ellison

## Artists—Painters, Portraitists

James Conway Farley

## Artists—Woodcarvers

Thomas Day

## Arts Patrons

A'Lelia Walker

## Athletes

Henry "Hank" Aaron
Melvin Farr
Earvin "Magic" Johnson Jr.

## Authors, Writers

Wally "Famous Amos" Amos Jr.
Richard Henry Boyd
Earl G. Graves
O'Shea "Ice Cube" Jackson
Thomas "T. D." Jakes
Julianne Malveaux
Patricia Russell-McCloud
Barbara "B" Smith
Susan L. Taylor
Gloria E. A. Toote
Dempsey Jerome Travis

## Automobile Industry Executives, Dealers

Nathan G. Conyers
Edward Davis
Melvin Farr
Elliott Sawyer Hall
Darryl B. Hazel
Ellenae Henry-Fairhurst
Frederick Douglas Patterson
Winston Pittman Sr.
Roy S. Roberts

# African American Business Leaders by Occupation

## Bankers, Bank Founders, Executives

Jesse Binga
Richard Henry Boyd
Todd C. Brown
Roland W. Burris
I. Owen Funderburg
Frederick Douglass. *See* **Frederick Douglass's Business Enterprises**
A. G. Gaston
James Francis Haddon
Carla Ann Harris
William M. Lewis Jr.
James Bruce Llewellyn
Anthony Overton
Heman Edward Perry
Norman Blann Rice
Maggie Lena Mitchell Walker

## Barbershop Owners, Operators, Workers

Alonzo Franklin Herndon
John Merrick

## Beauty Industry Officials

Joe L. Dudley Sr.
S. B. Fuller
Edward G. Gardner
Marjorie Stewart Joyner
Annie Turnbo Malone
Naomi R. Sims
A'Lelia Walker
Madame C. J. Walker (Sarah Breedlove)
Sarah Spencer Washington

## Beauty Salon Owners, Operators

Cardozo Sisters
Marjorie Stewart Joyner
Rose Morgan

## Bibliophiles

Aaron McDuffie Moore

## Booking Company Executives

Ruth Jean Bowen

## Booksellers

Alfred M. Ligon

## Broadcast Executives

Catherine "Cathy" Hughes

## Casino Owners, Operators

Don H. Barden

## Charm School Officials

Barbara Mae Watson

## Civil Rights Leaders, Activists, Workers

Archie Alphonso Alexander
Clifford Leopold Alexander Jr.
Richard Henry Boyd
Alexander G. Clark
Barney Launcelot Ford
James Forten
Earl G. Graves
Jesse Hill Jr.
John Jones
Thomy Lafon
Lunsford Lane
Julianne Malveaux
Leon Howard Sullivan

## Chemists, Chemical Company Executives

William G. Mays

## Civic Leaders

Edward G. Gardner
Herman Jerome Russell
Carl H. Ware

## Columnists

Julianne Malveaux
Susan L. Taylor

## Communications Industry Executives

Thomas J. Burrell
Delano Eugene Lewis

## Community Activists

Robert Reed Church Sr.
Isaac Myers
James Carroll Napier
Alan Shaw

## Composers

Quincy Jones

## Corporate Executives

Kenneth Irvine Chenault
Virgis William Colbert
Evern Cooper Epps
Ann M. Fudge
Dennis Fowler Hightower
E. Stanley O'Neal
Richard Dean Parsons
Myrtle Stephens Potter
Franklin Delano Raines
Frank Savage
Paula A. Sneed
Lloyd David Ward

## Cosmetics Company Officials, Founders

Joe L. Dudley Sr.
S. B. Fuller
Rose Morgan
Anthony Overton

## Economists

Andrew Felton Brimmer
Julianne Malveaux

## Editors

Eunice Walker Johnson
Susan L. Taylor
Augustus Washington

## Educators, Educational Administrators

Richard Henry Boyd
Andrew Felton Brimmer
Albert Irvin Cassell
Suzanne de Passe
Dennis Fowler Hightower
Marjorie Stewart Joyner
John Anderson Lankford
Berry O'Kelly
Hazel R. O'Leary
Joseph Alphonso Pierce
David Ruggles
Norma Merrick Sklarek
Augustus Washington
Booker T. Washington
David Augustus Williston

## Engineers

Archie Alphonso Alexander
Joseph Jacob Simmons III

## Entrepreneurs, Business Leaders

Henry "Hank" Aaron
Clifford Leopold Alexander Jr.
Wally "Famous Amos" Amos Jr.
Don H. Barden
Ruth Jean Bowen
Richard Henry Boyd
Sheila Bridges
Albert Irvin Cassell
Debra Martin Chase
Robert Reed Church Sr.
Alexander G. Clark
Marie Therese Coincoin
Kenneth L. Coleman
Sean "Diddy" Combs
Ward Connerly
Joe L. Dudley Sr.
Kenneth "Babyface" Edmonds
  and Tracey Edmonds
Elleanor Eldridge
Melvin Farr
Edward G. Gardner
Marcus Garvey. *See* **Marcus
  Garvey's UNIA
  Enterprise**

A. G. Gaston
John Trusty Gibson
Berry Gordy Jr.
Earl G. Graves
Lowell Hawthorne
Ellenae Henry-Fairhurst
Alexis M. Herman
O'Shea "Ice Cube" Jackson
Thomas "T. D." Jakes
Eunice Walker Johnson
John H. Johnson
Robert L. Johnson
Don King
Lunsford Lane
Reginald F. Lewis
James Bruce Llewellyn
Annie Turnbo Malone
Julianne Malveaux
William G. Mays
Jewell Jackson McCabe
H. Carl McCall
John Merrick
Lightfoot Solomon Michaux
Aaron McDuffie Moore
Isaac Myers
John E. "Jack" Nail
James Carroll Napier
Hazel R. O'Leary
E. Stanley O'Neal
Anthony Overton
Henry Green Parks Jr.
Charles V. Payne
Heman Edward Perry
Ernesta G. Procope
Barbara Gardner Proctor
Linda Johnson Rice
Roy S. Roberts
David Ruggles
Herman Jerome Russell
Frank Savage
Russell Simmons
Norma Merrick Sklarek
Barbara "B" Smith
Percy Ellis Sutton
Gloria E. A. Toote
Dempsey Jerome Travis
Lloyd G. Trotter
A'Lelia Walker
Antonio Maceo Walker

Madame C. J. Walker
  (Sarah Breedlove)
Carl H. Ware
Augustus Washington
Booker T. Washington
Oprah Winfrey

## Entertainment Agents, Entrepreneurs

Ruth Jean Bowen
Robert Paschal and James
  Paschal

## Farmers, Planters

William Ellison
Augustus Washington

## Fashion Industry Executives

John Jones
Reginald F. Lewis

## Fashion Show Producers

Eunice Walker Johnson

## Film Producers, Production Executives

Debra Martin Chase
Suzanne de Passe
Spike Lee
Eddie Murphy
Damon Wayans
Oprah Winfrey

## Financial Industry Executives

James Francis Haddon

## Financial Journalists

Karen Patricia Gibbs

## Food Industry Officials, Founders, Owners

Todd C. Brown
Leah Chase

## African American Business Leaders by Occupation

Lowell Hawthorne
Reginald F. Lewis
Clarence Otis Jr.
Robert Paschal and James Paschal
Barbara "B" Smith
Regynald G. Washington
Sylvia P. Woods

### Fund-raisers

Delano Eugene Lewis

### Furniture Industry Executives, Owners

Thomas Day

### Government Officials (Federal)

Andrew Felton Brimmer
Alexis M. Herman
Ronald N. Langston
Delano Eugene Lewis
Joseph Jacob Simmons III
Barbara Mae Watson

### Government Officials (State, Local)

Roland W. Burris
Hazel R. O'Leary
Norman Blann Rice

### Health-Care Officials/Workers

Aaron McDuffie Moore
Woodrow Augustus Myers Jr.
David Ruggles

### Hotel Owners, Operators

Edwin C. Berry

### Humanitarians

Joe L. Dudley Sr.
A. G. Gaston

### Insurance Company Executives, Founders

A. G. Gaston
Sylvester Green
Alonzo Franklin Herndon

Jesse Hill Jr.
John Merrick
Aaron McDuffie Moore
Anthony Overton
Harry H. Pace
Heman Edward Perry
Ernesta G. Procope
Charles Clinton Spaulding
Antonio Maceo Walker

### Interior Designers, Executives

Sheila Bridges
Lucious (Lou) Switzer

### Inventors

Marjorie Stewart Joyner

### Investment Bankers, Consultants

Franklin Delano Raines

### Investment Company Executives

Daniel C. Cochran
Edith W. Cooper
James Francis Haddon
Carla Ann Harris
Vernon Eulion Jordan
Charles V. Payne

### Labor Union Activists, Officials

Isaac Myers

### Lawyers

Clifford Leopold Alexander Jr.
Paget Alves
Roland W. Burris
Kenneth Irvine Chenault
Elliott Sawyer Hall
Maynard Holbrook Jackson Jr.
Vernon Eulion Jordan
Debra Louise Lee
Reginald F. Lewis
James Bruce Llewellyn

James Carroll Napier
Hazel R. O'Leary
Harry H. Pace
Richard Dean Parsons
Gloria E. A. Toote

### Manufacturing Executives

Lloyd David Ward

### Marketing Executives

Thomas J. Burrell

### Media Executives, Entrepreneurs

Dorothy Edwards Brunson
Sean "Diddy" Combs
Catherine "Cathy" Hughes
Quincy Jones
Renetta McCann

### Merchants

Berry O'Kelly

### Midwives

Bridget "Biddy" Mason

### Models

Naomi R. Sims
Barbara "B" Smith

### Morticians

Charles Diggs Jr.

### Motivational Speakers

Wally "Famous Amos" Amos Jr.
Patricia Russell-McCloud

### Music Producers, Publishers, Promoters

Suzanne de Passe
Quincy Jones
Harry H. Pace

Antonio "L. A." Reid
Russell Simmons

## Newspaper Publishers/Editors

Robert Sengstacke Abbott
Frederick Douglass. *See*
    **Frederick Douglass's Business
    Enterprises**
Anthony Overton

## Organization Founders, Officials

John Edward Bush
Bruce S. Gordon
Vernon Eulion Jordan
Jewell Jackson McCabe
Sheila Vaden-Williams

## Philanthropists

Robert Reed Church Sr.
Virgis William Colbert
Joe L. Dudley Sr.
Casper A. Holstein
Eunice Walker Johnson
John H. Johnson
Marjorie Stewart Joyner
Don King
Thomy Lafon
Reginald F. Lewis
James Bruce Llewellyn
Annie Turnbo Malone
Bridget "Biddy" Mason
John Merrick
Aaron McDuffie Moore
Berry O'Kelly
Herman Jerome Russell
Dempsey Jerome Travis
Madame C. J. Walker (Sarah
    Breedlove)
Maggie Lena Mitchell
    Walker
Sarah Spencer Washington
Oprah Winfrey

## Photographers

James Conway Farley
Augustus Washington

## Physicians

Woodrow Augustus Myers Jr.

## Policy Bankers

Casper A. Holstein

## Political Activists, Leaders

Richard Henry Boyd
Robert Reed Church Sr.
Ward Connerly
Barney Launcelot Ford
James Carroll Napier

## Political Advisers

Franklin Delano Raines

## Politicians

John Edward Bush
Charles Diggs Jr.
Maynard Holbrook Jackson Jr.
John Jones
H. Carl McCall
Percy Ellis Sutton
Gloria E. A. Toote
Augustus Washington
Booker T. Washington

## Popular Culture Executives, Moguls

Sean "Diddy" Combs

## Public Servants, Officials

Archie Alphonso Alexander
James Bruce Llewellyn

## Public Utility Officials

Erroll B. Davis Jr.

## Publishers, Publishing Executives (books, magazines)

Richard Henry Boyd
Earl G. Graves
John H. Johnson
Dorothy R. Leavell

Linda Johnson Rice
Susan L. Taylor
Dempsey Jerome Travis

## Rap Artists

Dr. Dre (Andre Young)
O'Shea "Ice Cube" Jackson

## Real Estate Developers, Brokers

Don H. Barden
Jesse Binga
Barney Launcelot Ford
A. G. Gaston
Thomy Lafon
John Merrick
John E. "Jack" Nail
Philip A. Payton Jr.
Dempsey Jerome Travis

## Record Industry Officials, Performers, Producers

Dr. Dre (Andre Young)
Kenneth "Babyface" Edmonds
    and Tracey Edmonds
Berry Gordy Jr.
Quincy Jones
Harry H. Pace
Antonio "L. A." Reid
Sylvia Rhone

## Religious Leaders, Evangelists, Ministers

Richard Henry Boyd
Alexander G. Clark
Thomas "T. D." Jakes
H. Carl McCall
Lightfoot Solomon Michaux
Leon Howard Sullivan

## Screenwriters

Suzanne de Passe
Damon Wayans

## Singers

Carla Ann Harris

# African American Business Leaders by Occupation

**Slaves**

Lunsford Lane

**Songwriters**

Kenneth "Babyface" Edmonds and Tracey Edmonds
Antonio "L. A." Reid

**Sports Promoters**

Don King

**Technology, Computer Industry Executives**

Donald Alvin Coleman
Kenneth L. Coleman
Sylvester Green
Marc R. Hannah
Charles E. Phillips Jr.
Alan Shaw
David L. Steward

John W. Thompson
Alfred W. Zollar

**Telecommunications Officials**

Paget Alves
Bruce S. Gordon

**Television Executives, Network Executives, Journalists**

Don H. Barden
Karen Patricia Gibbs
Robert L. Johnson
Debra Louise Lee
Paula Madison
Frank Mercado-Valdes

**Television Hosts**

Barbara "B" Smith
Oprah Winfrey

**Television Producers**

Damon Wayans
Oprah Winfrey

**Theater Owners, Producers, Managers**

John Trusty Gibson
Earvin "Magic" Johnson Jr.

**Traders**

Elleanor Eldridge

**Transportation, Shipping Company Executives, Shipbuilders**

Calvin Darden
James Forten
Isaac Myers

# Preface

Researching and writing on African American themes is both rewarding and challenging. A special challenge comes with determining the best and most logical way to present the findings so that readers who are knowledgeable in the field will gain fuller insight into trends in African American business and those who are barely knowledgeable will learn with ease. While some aspects of African American culture such as literature have broader appeal, clearly business is an area that affects everyone. And for African Americans who have experienced, and continue to meet, the challenges of a society that has yet to remove all vestiges of racial segregation, this work will contain information on African American business that helps to define their lives.

This encyclopedia is designed as a user-friendly guide to all readers who seek to know more about African American business developments. To determine what focus the work should take, the editor conferred with African Americans who are business educators, business leaders, corporate executives, researchers, students, librarians, and information specialists. Special concern was given to consulting librarians and information specialists, for they are the ones who are called to address the information needs of all groups. Two primary advisers/consultants assisted the editor in making the final selection of topics. Space limitations made it necessary to limit the number of entries; consequently, the reader should not expect to find every conceivable topic or an exhaustive list of biographies.

This encyclopedia includes a variety of topics and ideas that may spur one on to further study and exploration. The topical arrangement is alphabetical; some topics are broad—for example, "Black Banks: Their Beginning"; others are specific—such as the "Booker T. Washington Business Association." A specific item is listed according to the most logical arrangement for that item; for example, "Frederick Douglass's Business Enterprises" is arranged under the D's, while "E. E. Ward Transfer and Storage Company" is arranged under the W's. The arrangement also includes organizations and movements, such as the Colored Merchants' Association and the "Don't

Buy Where You Can't Work" movement. Interspersed throughout the topics are entries on well-known African American women and men business leaders, such as entrepreneur Marcus Garvey, automobile dealer Melvin Farr, hair-care magnate Madame C. J. Walker, and television personality Oprah Winfrey. There are also lesser-known black entrepreneurs of an earlier time, including hotel operator Edwin C. Berry, banker Jesse Binga, furniture maker Thomas Day, and theater owner John Trusty Gibson. Timely topics, such as "E-Commerce and the African American Community," and topics of concern to America's black youth, such as "Kid/Teenpreneurs: Business Leaders in the Making," are included as well.

All entries, which are signed, were written by scholars with a connection to educational institutions. Each entry concludes with a list of sources. The reader is encouraged to consult these references for additional information.

Where appropriate, blind entries are provided to guide the reader to the actual listing for an entrant; for example, popular culture mogul Sean "Diddy" Combs, who has assumed various names from time to time, is actually listed under "Combs"; blind entries include "P. Diddy," "Puff Daddy," "Puffy," and his current assumed name, "Diddy." Similarly, rapper "Ice Cube" is referenced to O'Shea "Ice Cube" Jackson.

Bold references appear throughout the work; thus, terms, individual names, and so on, that are themselves entries in the encyclopedia are bold-faced when they first appear in an entry. If a cross-reference is boldfaced in an entry, it does not appear as a "see also" reference.

To further facilitate use of the information in this encyclopedia, special lists are provided at the front of the book: Entry List, Topical Entry List, and African American Business Leaders by Occupation. The Topical Entry List gives broad headings in alphabetical order, under which various topics are further grouped, alphabetically arranged. The topical head "Academic Institutions," for example, includes entries "Business Ownership in Select Academic Institutions" and "Centers for Entrepreneurship in Academic Institutions." "Biographies" is another heading and provides an alphabetical listing of individuals who are entries in the encyclopedia. Other headings include "Booking Agencies," "Boycotts and Protests," "Businesses," the "Food Industry," and "Organizations," among others. The final section, "Women," lists the entry "Women and Business," although the reader should realize that information on women is scattered throughout the encyclopedia.

The African American Business Leaders by Occupation list is likewise alphabetically arranged by occupation and includes headings such as "Abolitionists"; "Activists"; "Architects, Building Planners"; "Artisans"; "Authors, Writers"; "Corporate Executives"; "Engineers"; "Entrepreneurs, Business Leaders"; "Food Industry Officials, Founders, Owners"; "Philanthropists"; "Politicians"; "Publishers, Publishing Executives (books, magazines)"; "Record Industry Officials, Performers, Producers"; "Religious Leaders, Evangelists, Ministers"; "Technology, Computer Industry Executives"; "Television Executives, Network Executives, Journalists"; and "Traders". Those businesspeople whose various occupations place them in more than one category may be listed under two or more categories.

The encyclopedia's illustrations were chosen carefully; they include tables, photographs of people, and images of early black businesses, such as the North Carolina Mutual Life Insurance Company's office building and Poro College Building, where hair-care magnate Annie Turnbo Malone operated her enterprise. The inclusion of older images not readily seen in published sources was deliberate: They illustrate the rich and colorful early history of African American enterprise. Similarly, the tables include historic as well as contemporary statistical information on business, employment, banks, and other topics covered in the book. The encyclopedia concludes with a Selected Bibliography, which will facilitate further study on African American business, and the About the Contributors section, which provides a brief biographical note on each scholar who contributed to this book.

This chronology of African Americans tells the story of their contributions in the area of business. It is hoped that this encyclopedia will inspire users to continue their exploration into this aspect of African American culture.

# Introduction

The *Encyclopedia of African American Business*, though restricted in size and coverage, gives an overview of the black business community and black business leaders in America from the first quarter of the eighteenth century to the early twenty-first century. Its purpose is to help bridge the information gap in the field, identifying such data as might be useful in educational and business arenas.

While this encyclopedia's primary concern is with African Americans in business, it must be emphasized that blacks had been involved in business long before they were brought to America as slaves. In their mother country Africa, blacks had seen their own people work as traders. When they reached America, many did not lose their will to be entrepreneurs—they lost only their opportunity. Even the plantation economy demanded artisans and craftspersons to operate, and blacks had roles that went beyond planting, hoeing, and reaping. In urban settings the enslaved worked at such jobs as artisans, musicians, and dressmakers; they enhanced or developed skills that would be economically useful to them once they were freed. Some were allowed to hire themselves out and earn the money needed to purchase their own freedom and that of their families. Many free blacks did become entrepreneurs. They were seen in almost all southern cities working as barbers, butchers, mechanics, and artisans. Some even manufactured furniture, pottery, and bricks. Both slave and free blacks produced materials for the local markets. Some maintained restaurants and hotels. The fine caterers of antebellum America, the fashionable dressmakers, and the hairdressers—most of whom worked outside the South—were black.

Those black-owned enterprises that survived the slavery period succumbed to the changed business requirements that came during the industrial age. Business operations had to be efficient, thus calling for a positive response to the requirements for modernization. Black businesses during slavery were, for the most part, located outside the South and involved skilled trades, such as blacksmithing, painting, plumbing, and shoemaking.

As noted, catering and hairdressing were also popular, as were barbering, hotel and restaurant management, and several small enterprises. While a few businesses catered to blacks, most did not and for survival—if nothing more—fit their enterprises into the whole economy instead. A separate black and white economy could not coexist; however, in time, black leaders encouraged self-help activities in an effort to strengthen the black economy and weaken ties with the white economy.

Historians found, however, that almost as soon as the first settlers came to America, they constructed laws to discourage black entrepreneurship. From the end of the Civil War to the modern civil rights era, whites drove blacks out of their trades. Even those cited earlier that slaves had practiced and dominated so well were later closed or severely curtailed. Fortunately, black businesses found other ways to survive. Many were born out of churches and fraternal societies and aimed to provide essential needs that blacks could not find otherwise. From these businesses—the fraternal societies in particular—came banking and insurance companies that clearly strengthened the black economy. The Freedman's Savings and Trust Company, popularly known as the Freedman's Bank, established March 3, 1865, to serve the financial needs of blacks, was penetrated by the white banking business and, of course, led to black's mistrust of the banking industry when the bank failed. That the reasons for failure lay outside the black community was hardly acceptable to the black community. The failure rate of banks during this period, however, appears to have been no greater for blacks than for whites.

Some business historians suggest that the slave society shaped those businesses that blacks entered early on. The successful early businesses were primarily those that whites chose not to operate, thus leaving opportunities for blacks to become shoemakers, draymen, and liverymen. The *Encyclopedia of African American Business* embraces the activities of black entrepreneurs, documenting when and where blacks owned and operated their businesses. The biographies, articles, and statistical tables given here document black business development and illustrate the occupations of blacks during various periods in history. For example, Table 28 shows that, in 1863, blacks owned twelve types of businesses, which included bakery, catering, dressmaking, fish and oyster, and sailmaking. By 1913, however, blacks owned seventy-two types of businesses, which included automobile service and garage, architecture, banking, bottling and soda water-making, drug store, electrical, employment bureau, haberdashery, hotel keeping, insurance, jewelry, printing and publishing, real estate, stationery, undertaking, and wood and coal.

As African Americans began to take a fuller share of American prosperity, they also played a larger role in shaping the economic development of the black community. By no means, however, has the gap between white and black wealth and economic influence been bridged; rather, blacks are simply more visible in far more economic arenas than they were in the past. Economic progress continues to lag behind improvements in civil rights.

After the Civil War the South's economy was decidedly segregated by race. Whites refused to patronize black businesses, and certainly after 1873 few black businesses in the South survived. Those that continued or emerged after that time had black clientele, and black businesses as a whole remained relatively small. The transition into the industrial age was difficult for the small, black entrepreneurs who had little capital and limited management skills—both essential to survival. This encyclopedia draws on a continuing tradition of assessing the role of blacks in economic endeavors. For example, one cannot overlook the important work of W.E.B. Du Bois and Atlanta University. Du Bois edited the proceedings of various Atlanta University conferences, specifically its conference on "The Negro in Business" (1899). The university was concerned with the extent to which blacks were entering into business life and thus devoted its fourth annual conference to that theme. The statistics, reports on various enterprises, and recommendations for strengthening black businesses have been important to the economic development of the black community.

In 1907, Booker T. Washington published his seminal work *The Negro in Business*. Rather than give statistical accounts of black business enterprises or a detailed and consecutive history of black business development, he reports on many successful blacks and what they have done in the field. The aim was to encourage increasing numbers of young blacks to seize the opportunities open to them in the business field. Washington was well positioned to publish his work. In 1900 Washington became a founder of the National Negro Business League (NNBL) (renamed the National Business League in 1966); it became a key organization among black businessmen. His activities with the National Business League often put him in contact with black entrepreneurs or would-be entrepreneurs. He had traveled the country and noted the number of black men and women, often in remote districts or small towns, who were engaged in various lines of business. Their lives and work document black business history during this period. Persons included in his findings were engaged in such occupations as agriculturalists, bankers, caterers, hotel keepers, inventors, journalists, manufacturers, newspaper owners, realty company operators, town builders, and undertakers. As well, his book gives accounts of black entrepreneurs whose work had made them highly visible.

The scarcity of published information on African American people in the field of business and topical issues related to black business development both in the United States and in some foreign countries has been partially remedied by the important *The Negro Yearbook*, under different editorships and published by Tuskegee Institute (as it was previously known) in Alabama from 1912 to 1947. Much credit for the establishment of the publication is owed to Booker T. Washington, educator, the school's president, and a founder of the NNBL. The yearbooks give statistical information, biographical information, topical essays, and data on then-timely topics that relate to business history. The early yearbooks document the NNBL's importance to black business development and the effects of World War I on business activity that peaked in the 1920s. It was at this time that building and loan associations, insurance companies, banks, real estate agents, chain stores, steamship lines, and other enterprises came on the scene.

Black businesses increased rapidly during much of the first half of the twentieth century, particularly during what was called the golden age, or up to the 1930s. Many of these businesses, however, followed new lines and still served segregated markets. During this time the black real estate market emerged, and blacks built hotels, theaters, homes, office buildings, and other facilities and financed them through black banks and loan associations. Transportation, leisure, and entertainment enterprises were seen as well, often in response to segregated facilities and sometimes facilities not available to blacks at all. Blacks, for example, built their own railroad lines, municipal transportation systems, summer resorts, car rental companies, automobile repair shops, and automobile manufacturing companies. These businesses are documented in *The Negro Handbook*. Still an important source for historical accounts, *The Negro Handbook* was published variously between 1942 and 1966. It is considered a useful source on aspects of black business for the periods when the work was published; for example, the 1966 edition, published by Johnson Publishing Company, discusses "The Negro Market" and includes lists and assets of black banking institutions; savings and loan associations; funeral and burial insurance companies; and limited life, mutual aid, assessment health and accident companies. Other statistical data on banks and on the black economy are given as well.

African American organizations are not to be disregarded in the development and promotion of black business leaders and their work. Their involvement has been seen, for example, in the work of the Association for the Study of Negro Life and History (ASNLH), later known as the Association for the Study of African American Life and History. ASNLH discussed the subject of blacks as entrepreneurs at a special session held during its annual meeting in Washington, D.C. in 1925. The association abandoned an early idea of conducting a much-needed survey of blacks in business and instead collected data for other studies, such as the economic activities of blacks since the Civil War. The data revealed interesting, important, and useful facts that shed light on blacks as businesspeople. There are limitations in the results; for example, data failed to indicate which businesses that appeared to be controlled by blacks were actually owned by whites. Data were also restricted to blacks in independent businesses "without going into its ramifications," the report said.

Thus, the report, published as *The Negro as a Business Man* by J. H. Harmon Jr., Arnett G. Lindsay, and Carter G. Woodson (1929), discusses blacks as local entrepreneurs, developments in black banking, and the development of insurance companies. While the study shows that blacks took an early interest in establishing banks and savings institutions, such as the True Reformers Bank in Richmond and Binga State Bank in Chicago, insurance companies were the more prosperous black business enterprises among the race. Black insurance companies helped to perpetuate the segregated economy that was seen early on. Many white-owned companies refused to insure blacks, and if they did so, premiums were decidedly higher for blacks than for whites. Among those black insurance companies discussed in *The Negro as a Business Man* are Standard Life Insurance Company in Atlanta, the first old-line legal reserve corporation organized among blacks; and North Carolina Mutual Life Insurance Company in Durham, which would become the nation's largest black-owned insurance company.

Among the classic publications on African American business is Abram L. Harris's *The Negro as Capitalist: A Study of Banking and Business among American Negroes* (1936). The results of a study, the book covers a variety of topics, including the rise of capitalism, the accumulation of black wealth prior to 1860, the economic base of the black middle class, and black banks. Added to this is Vishnu Oak's proposed three-volume series titled *The Negro Entrepreneur*; each volume approaches black business from a different perspective. Titles in the series are *The Negro Newspaper* (1948), *The Negro's Adventure in General Business* (1949), and *Negro Insurance and Banking*. The scope of the second work is broad and includes business ventures popular in the late 1940s, when the work was completed.

Atlanta University and the National Urban League combined their interest in studying business and business education among blacks and on February 1, 1944, launched a study that ended on February 1, 1946. Joseph A. Pierce, of the Atlanta University faculty, directed the study and published the results in *Negro Business and Business Education* (1947). The study examined only those businesses owned and operated by blacks. The study reported on issues or operations, such as banking, consumer cooperatives (including the Colored Merchants' Association), life insurance companies, building and loan associations, and problems of business education training among blacks. As seen throughout studies and reports of black business operations, the racial climate of the nation played an important part in making black businesses necessary as well as in causing their demise. Results of the investigation gave Atlanta University information that it needed to go forward with a proposed graduate School of Business Administration to serve the needs of blacks and the business community. The National Urban League and its local branches gained information to make their services more valuable to the nation and to enlarge job opportunities for blacks. Cooperating black institutions were to be linked with their communities so that they would be positioned to identify community needs and to render better service to those communities. Clearly, activities that followed this investigation helped to shape the development of black business and business education around that time.

As late as 1971, when John Seder and Berkeley G. Burrell published *Getting It Together: Black Businessmen in America*, they found that information about successful black businessmen of that period remained incomplete. They mirror other findings, showing that, during the 1920s, thousands of black businesses were founded, many of them banks and insurance companies that survived the Great Depression and were operational in the 1970s. Some are still operational. As black businesses emerged rapidly—many short-lived—the investigators were hard put to keep up with their contributions. But they stressed an important fact—the need to interview the business leaders to gain deeper insights into their lives than had been previously known and published.

Recent and important newer studies, histories, and accounts geared to black business development have made great strides in identifying trends from the 1790s through the 1990s, giving biographical sketches as well. These include John N. Ingham and Lynne B. Feldman's *African-American Business Leaders: A Biographical Dictionary* (1994). The 123 biographies included in the work contain detailed and comprehensive information up to the date of publication. The authors cast their net widely, covering leaders in a broad range of southern cities, major northern centers, and the Far West. Coverage of leaders in some areas was incomplete, thus necessitating further research.

The most recent and comprehensive work on black business is Juliet E. K. Walker's *The History of Black Business in America: Capitalism, Race, Entrepreneurship* (1998). With this work, Walker took the field of black business information in a new direction. Using hundreds of primary and secondary sources, she traced black business development from the 1600s to the 1990s, giving accounts of the work of slaves and free blacks, then the work of black entrepreneurs later on. Stories of black millionaires, early automobile manufacturers, and others dispel the myth that black businesses were always small, unproductive, and unsuccessful.

Juliet Walker was not done with her study of African American business development. She continued her scholarly and comprehensive work in the field with the publication of the *Encyclopedia of African American Business History* (1999). Its purpose, as noted in the introduction, is "to illuminate the historic continuity of black business in America from the colonial era to the post–civil rights era and to underscore the diversity of black business activities, from slavery to freedom." Walker points out a primary flaw and omission in black business scholarship: It remained on the margins of the scholarly exploration of the African American experience. An important information source, the work gives over 200 entries on African American business experience from the 1600s to the 1990s and includes biographies, topical issues on black business history, and business participation in certain industries.

A smaller but more recent work is Rachel Kranz's *African-American Business Leaders and Entrepreneurs* (2004). Kranz acknowledges an issue that the former Association for the Study of Negro Life and History noted in its report in 1929, stating that "the world of black business is becoming ever more white-dominated." Following the trend of larger enterprises to acquire smaller ones, companies such as Motown Records (founded by Berry Gordy Jr.), Wally Amos's Famous Cookies, *Essence* magazine (now owned by AOL Time Warner), and Russell Simmons's Defjam records (and later his clothing line Pfat Farm) are examples of black-founded enterprises that have become either wholly owned by whites or almost so. BET (Black Entertainment Television), though not discussed in the book, is another example.

Although the entries in *African-American Business Leaders* are limited to some 165 entrants, some of the entrants identified are women about whom too little has been said.

For students and scholars interested in primary research materials on the subject of this book, including data relating to a wide variety of enterprises from one- to two-person operations such as barbershops and beauty salons to multinational operations, we have included a discussion of Federal Records for African American Business History. These records are available at the National Archives and Records Administration (NARA) headquartered in Washington, D.C. and NARA II in College Park, Maryland. Regional record centers located throughout the United States are useful as well. A guide to such records is the publication *Black History: A Guide to Civilian Records in the National Archives* (1984). Among the bureaus, branches, and/ or divisions represented in the records are the Department of Commerce (under President Franklin D. Roosevelt's administration); it was during this period that records relating to black businesses multiplied. Records of the Division of Negro Affairs, located in the Office of the Secretary of Commerce, are important for information on insurance companies, lending institutions, conferences on blacks in business (1940–1953), architects, real estate agents, journalists, hair-care producers, funeral directors, and other topics. Other insurance companies, New Deal agencies, World War II agencies, the black press, Office of War Information, and so on, are represented in the records as well.

Historically Black Colleges and Universities (HBCUs) are represented here for their work in developing entrepreneurial programs. Examples are the Center for Entrepreneurship and E-Business at North Carolina Agricultural State University in Greensboro, and the gender-conscious program at Tennessee State University in Nashville, the Women's Institute for Successful Entrepreneurship. Useful sources for these data are reports from the programs published in newsletters and, of course, write-ups in journals.

The work of the African American press, covered in this work as an essay, cannot be overemphasized as a vital source of information on black business leaders and the development of black businesses. It was that press that preserved black history when mainstream publishers, presses, and journalists failed to recognize its worth, gave no credence to developments in the black community, and found no market in disseminating the news from black people. From the antebellum newspapers, including *Freedom's Journal* founded in 1827, to the present, that press has advertised black businesses, such as heat-cleaning and sewing, and products that targeted black people, such as hair-care products that Madame C. J. Walker manufactured later on. Many of the entries included in this encyclopedia use information from newspapers such as the *Afro-American*, *Chicago Defender*, and the *Pittsburgh Courier*. Long-standing journals such as *Crisis* (publication of the National Association for the Advancement of Colored People [NAACP]), *Opportunity* (official publication of the National Urban League), and *Southern Workman* provide a wealth of information on black businesses and document the lives of many black business leaders. Black popular publications, such as *Jet* and *Ebony*, join the scholarly ones in casting the net even wider and deeper, sometimes supplying details otherwise overlooked. For the business field, *Black Enterprise* magazine has been, and continues to be, the chief source of current information, whether statistical, biographical, or simply newsworthy highlights.

Along with articles and sketches on well-known business leaders, journals such as *Black Enterprise* and *Ebony* include in their monthly publications emerging black entrepreneurs—people to watch. These journals almost always identify blacks promoted to top positions in corporate America. *Black Enterprise* recognizes people and businesses by naming them "Entrepreneur of the Year," "Advertising Agency of the Year," "Auto Dealer of the Year," or "Industrial/Service Company of the Year." Such ranking preserves an important part of history and at the same time recognizes the current leadership among black entrepreneurs.

Perhaps the decade of the 1960s ushered in a new approach to journalism by mainstream publishers as they began to give coverage to the black community, including business leaders and business developments. Along with such highly recognized newspapers as the *New York Times* and *Washington Post*, papers that in the past had given more than passing recognition to the black community, papers of major cities in the South expanded their coverage. Examples are the *Atlanta Journal/Constitution*, the *Charlotte Observer*, and the Memphis *Commercial Appeal*. Popular mainstream journals, such as *Time* and *Newsweek*, and more specialized ones, such as *Business Week*, have helped document African American business developments.

African American business developments are recorded also in the stories that slaves told. Later, some of these narratives were published individually or collectively. This occurred despite the restrictions that the American slave system placed on those who labored under bondage. Some slaves were known to excel in business and at times to earn enough money to buy their freedom as well as that of their families. Such experiences are included here in several overlooked works. One may note with interest the use of the slave narrative (a source not to be overlooked) for biographical information. As examples may be cited nineteenth-century entrepreneur Lunsford Lane and his *Narrative of Lunsford Lane, Formerly of Raleigh, N.C.* (1842), and three slave narratives by Frederick Douglass—*My Bondage and My Freedom* (1845), *The Narrative of Frederick Douglass* (1845), and *The Life and Times of Frederick Douglass* (1881). Lane, of Raleigh, North Carolina, sold smoking tobacco that he and his father processed and used the profits to purchase his freedom. Among his various notable deeds, Douglass headed the Freedman's Bank in 1874. Other slave narratives tell of successes in such businesses as cabinetmaking and grocery store ownership and in various enterprises. Increasingly biographical information on African American business leaders is made immediately available to researchers, whether they are in academia and seek to fulfill assignments for term papers or are part of the general public with a need to fill. The sources update the field of biographical works since William J. Simmons published his seminal work *Men of Mark: Eminent, Progressive, and Rising* (1887), Monroe A. Majors issued his *Noted Negro Women* (1926), and Hallie Q. Brown brought out her pioneer work on black women, *Homespun Heroines and Other Women of Distinction* (1926).

It was not until 1992, however, that the first major contemporary work on black women's biography was published. At that time the editor of this encyclopedia published the first of her series of works on women, *Notable Black American Women*; Book II was issued in 1996, and Book III in 2003. Coverage extends to early black women entrepreneurs such as former slave and pastry chef Quaimo, former slave and tradeswoman Elleanor Eldridge, and banker Maggie Lena Mitchell Walker, as well as to contemporary black women entrepreneurs such as entertainment booking agent Ruth Jean Bowen. Added to that set is this editor's *Notable Black American Men* (1999), where entries span the gamut from early furniture manufacturer Thomas Day to current corporate executive Kenneth Irvine Chenault. In recent years, scholars have published reference works on African Americans that provide biographical information on business leaders and business educators. Such works are comprehensive in the subject areas included and yet are important for the purposes of this encyclopedia and the whole field of business. One example is Rayford W. Logan and Michael R. Winston's *Dictionary of American Negro Biography*, published in 1982. As well, there are Darlene Clark Hine's two-volume set *Black Women in America: An Historical Encyclopedia* (Carlson, 1993) and the three-volume second edition of her work (Oxford University Press, 2005). In addition to biographical data, there are discussions on women in business.

In 2004 editors Henry Louis Gates Jr. and Evelyn Brooks Higginbotham added to the biographical references on blacks by publishing *African American Lives*, to be followed by a forthcoming multivolume *African American National Biography*. There are other important biographical sources continuously published, such as *Contemporary Black Biography* and *Who's Who among African Americans*, and the mainstream publications that have increased their coverage of blacks, such as *Current Biography*, *Who's Who in America*, and *Who's Who in Commerce and Industry*. The multivolume *American National Biography*, published in 1999, is a good example of the increasingly comprehensive coverage of African Americans in standard reference works. While the earlier *Dictionary of American Biography* was mostly concerned with white men, its contemporary successor covers women and blacks far more inclusively.

Interviews serve well as a means of gathering information; they give firsthand accounts, help clarify errors of fact that have been published, and preserve a long-standing tradition in the African American community. Some of our writers have included personal interviews with subjects, whether by telephone or in person. This is demonstrated in the entries on restaurateurs Robert and James Paschal and real estate executive Cecilia Antonietta Mowatt and in the interviews with owners and operators of roadside stands.

Researchers also benefit from the immediate access to information that online searches provide. There are Web sites for organizations, individuals, businesses, and so on. For example, the history of the Citizen Trust Bank in Atlanta and the history of the Federation of Southern Cooperatives Land Assistance Fund are both available online. There are also online biographical sources, such as *Handbook of Texas Online,* and articles on the current Afro-American History Conferences held at Tennessee State University in Nashville. No current history of African American business would be complete without the inclusion of information on e-commerce and technology. We have provided that here in the entry "E-Commerce and the African American Community." Biographies of those black leaders who have made, or are making, important contributions in the area of technology are scattered throughout the encyclopedia.

Finally, repositories of primary resources are essential for gathering data that may or may not be available in published sources. Those in various state libraries and archives, archives in academic institutions, and papers of historical societies are among this group. Fortunately, some of these institutions will respond to online requests without charge or provide additional and indepth research for a fee. Special African American Collections are another essential source; those at the Woodruff Library at Atlanta University, Fisk University, the Moorland-Spingarn Research Center at Howard University, and the Schomburg Center for Research in Black Culture, New York Public Library, are among the comprehensive collections available. For example, Fisk has the papers of the McKissack and McKissack architectural firm as well as those of James Carroll Napier, a subject in this encyclopedia and a founder of Citizen's Bank in Nashville—one of the oldest continuous African American banking institutions.

There still remains a great need for scholarly investigation in the field of black business. For example, there are African American business leaders who are in high posts and about whom, regrettably, little has been said. Equally important is the need to know the entrepreneurs at other levels— those who pioneered, who made a way when there appeared to be no way. Various pioneering business ventures have often set the stage for the visible big-time operations that followed. Within the limits imposed by our current knowledge, this work tells the story of accomplishments from before the arrival of blacks in this country to the present hour. That history is sad, colorful, exciting, fascinating, eventful, unbelievable, and yet incomplete.

# Encyclopedia of African American Business

# A

## Henry "Hank" Aaron (1934– ), Baseball Legend, Entrepreneur

"Hammerin' Hank" Aaron became an international sports icon in 1974 when his 715th home run broke Babe Ruth's long-standing all-time home run record. By the end of Aaron's twenty-three years in major league baseball in 1976, he had hit 755 home runs—a number unsurpassed for more than three decades. After retiring from the playing field, Aaron became a vice president for the Atlanta Braves, the team on which he had played for twenty years. That position made him the first African American in top-level management of major league baseball. Though Aaron's baseball career was marked by a number of historic firsts, it also was marred by racially motivated slights and hostility. Over the years, the home run king has spoken out against racism in baseball, supported civil rights initiatives, and contributed to efforts to improve life chances for African American youth. He also has become a savvy businessman with holdings that include a number of thriving fast-food restaurant franchises and a group of successful car dealerships.

Henry Louis Aaron was born during the Great Depression on February 5, 1934, in Mobile, Alabama. He entered the world the day before the thirty-ninth birthday of reigning Home Run King Babe Ruth. Aaron's father Herbert worked as a dry dock boilermaker's assistant and tavern owner to support his wife Estella and their eight children. When Aaron was eight years old, his father bought land on the outskirts of town in Toulminville and built a home for his family. Though poor, the Aarons were among the few black homeowners in the community at a time when Jim Crow laws and practices often restricted life chances for African Americans.

Aaron developed a passion for baseball early in life. As a child, he swung a homemade bat at bottle tops, fashioned baseballs by wrapping nylon stockings around old golf balls, and spent hours hitting them with a mop stick. Sometimes he would repeatedly throw a ball over the roof of his house and swiftly run to the other side to catch it before it hit the ground. Aaron decided to become a major league baseball player at fourteen after his father took him to hear a speech by his hero Jackie Robinson, the black player who integrated major league baseball in 1947. Young Aaron prepared for his future by playing softball on a Mobile recreation department team prophetically called the Braves.

Then, in 1951, Aaron caught the eye of the Black Bears, a semiprofessional African American baseball team based in Mobile. His mother gave him permission to play shortstop with the team during their Sunday home games. Aaron finished high school at the Josephine Allen Institute in Mobile in 1952 in spite of being preoccupied by baseball. The Indianapolis Clowns, one of the best of the remaining Negro League teams, snatched up the eighteen-year-old to play shortstop that same year. The scrawny kid from Mobile with the strong, swift, cross-handed bat swing soon attracted the attention of major league scouts. The Boston Braves signed him up in the middle of the 1952 season. The right-handed batter corrected his grip as he played for the club's farm team in Wisconsin. Aaron was voted the Northern League Rookie of the Year by the end of 1952.

In 1953, the year the Braves moved to Milwaukee, Aaron's performance with the club's farm team in Jacksonville, Florida, also paid off: At nineteen, he was named Most Valuable Player in the South Atlantic (Sally) League. At the end of the season, Aaron married Barbara Lucas, a Jacksonville college student. The couple soon became the parents of a baby girl they named Gaile.

The twenty-year-old family man got his big chance to play his first major league game during the 1954 season when he replaced the Braves' injured left fielder. He hit a home run on his very first turn at bat. Over the next two decades, he built one of the most amazing careers in major league baseball history. He hit a minimum of twenty home runs each season from 1955 to 1975—a record thirty homers in fifteen of those seasons. "Hammerin' Hank" Aaron became the league's Most Valuable Player in 1957 and later that year led the Braves to a World Series victory.

Life for Aaron was good but far from perfect. He faced racism every day. The racial slurs hurled at him from the stands stunned and hurt him. While on the road, Aaron and fellow black teammates could not stay in hotels with their white teammates because of Jim Crow laws and practices. The quiet, dignified baseball player once had to hide in the woods of Covington, Kentucky, to elude a posse of police cars pursuing him because he rode in a car with a white teammate, the teammate's wife, and sister-in-law. The white press often portrayed the slugger as a slow-witted character with natural talent rather than as a skilled, disciplined, and purposeful player.

Aaron rarely lost his temper in public after such personal outrages, but throughout his career, he publicly spoke out in the media against segregated training camps and continually called for the hiring of African Americans for coaching and management positions on major league teams. He also became a stalwart supporter of the National Association for the Advancement of Colored People (NAACP).

Paradoxically, after Aaron went to Atlanta with the Braves in 1966, he experienced both his greatest popularity and most frightening confrontations with racism. By 1970 he had become the first player to amass 3,000 hits and over 500 home runs. Fans applauded when he stepped onto the field. He began the 1971 season with a three-year contract at $200,000 a year, making him the highest paid player in baseball. He ended the 1973 season just one home run short of Babe Ruth's record.

However, as thousands cheered him on, Aaron received hundreds of letters from all over the country warning him not to usurp the Great Bambino as the all-time home run king. Though Aaron's marriage to his wife Barbara dissolved during this period, he was the proud and protective father of four children. He hired a bodyguard and welcomed the help of local and national authorities in the face of death threats against him and his family. Undercover Federal Bureau of Investigation (FBI) agents in Nashville, Tennessee, protected Aaron's oldest daughter Gaile, a student at Fisk University and the target of a kidnapping attempt. By the fall of 1973, Aaron's concern also extended to his new wife, Atlanta educator and television personality Billye Williams, and his seven-year-old stepdaughter Ceci.

In spite of the dangers, Aaron went on to tie Babe Ruth's record and then exceed it before a cheering crowd of more than 53,000 fans during the Brave's opening game in Atlanta on April 8, 1974. Aaron played his last two seasons in major league baseball for the Milwaukee Brewers. By the end of his career in 1976, he had established a dozen other major league baseball records, including most games, at-bats, total bases, and runs batted in (RBIs). He also had earned three Gold Gloves as an outstanding defensive outfielder and played in twenty-four All Star games. Aaron was inducted into the Baseball Hall of Fame in 1982 for his lifetime of achievements.

Aaron returned to Atlanta in 1977 after new Braves owner Ted Turner appointed him vice president of player development. That position made Aaron the highest-ranking African American in major league baseball management. He has since served on the Braves' board of directors and as senior vice president for the club.

In the early twenty-first century, the retired slugger is a successful businessman. He owns Church's Chicken, Popeye, and Krispy Kreme franchises in Atlanta and Charlotte, North Carolina, all under the umbrella of his 755 Restaurant Corporation. Additionally, Aaron is chairman of the board of the Hank Aaron Automotive Group, Inc., which includes BMW, Jaguar, and Toyota dealerships. The automotive group was number 38 on the *Black Enterprise* list of the top 100 auto dealerships for 2004.

Aaron's philanthropic activities include the Hank Aaron Chasing the Dream Foundation, which he cofounded with his wife Billye Aaron to provide opportunities for children to develop their talents. In 2002, George Bush awarded Aaron the Presidential Medal of Freedom. In 2005, the NAACP Legal Defense Fund awarded him the Thurgood Marshall Lifetime Achievement Award. The organization also has established the Hank Aaron Humanitarian in Sports Award.

## Sources

Aaron, Hank, with Lonnie Wheeler. *I Had a Hammer: The Hank Aaron Story*. New York: HarperTorch/HarperCollins, 1991.

Binford, Minter A. "Hank Aaron." *The New Georgia Encyclopedia.* http://www. georgiaencyclopedia.org/nge/Article.jsp?id=h-739.

Stanton, Tom. *Hank Aaron and the Home Run That Changed America.* New York: Perennial Currents/HarperCollins, 2005.

Sykes, Tanisha. "Power Hitter: Baseball Legend Hank Aaron Scores Big with His Import Dealership." *Black Enterprise* 34 (June 2004): 160–162.

*Clarissa Myrick-Harris*

# Robert Sengstacke Abbott (1868–1940), Newspaper Publisher and Editor

Robert Sengstacke Abbott was the founder in 1905 of the *Chicago Defender*, which became one of the leading African American newspapers in the United States. A very astute businessman, he was persistent, frugal, shrewd, and skilled in gauging his potential customers. After initial struggles, he achieved substantial success by 1917, when he became a promoter of the great migration of blacks from the rural South to the urban North. At his death he left control of the paper to his nephew, John H. H. Sengstacke (1912–1997), who turned the paper into the *Chicago Daily Defender* in February 1956.

Abbott was the son of Thomas Abbott and Flora Butler Abbott. His father, who was then running a grocery store on St. Simon's Island, Georgia, died in 1869, and his mother moved back to her native Savannah. In 1874, his mother married John Hermann Henry Sengstacke, and the couple had seven children. Five-year-old Abbott took the name Robert Sengstacke. He attended Beach Institute in Savannah, Clafin University in Orangeburg, South Carolina, and then Hampton Institute. During his years at school he faced color prejudice due to his own dark complexion. At Hampton Abbott sang in the Hampton Quartet, finished a printing course in 1893, and completed his academic work in 1893.

In 1897 at the age of twenty-eight, Abbott moved to Chicago to pursue a law degree, which he earned from Kent College of Law in 1899, using the name Robert Sengstacke Abbott. After attempts to establish a law practice elsewhere, he returned to Chicago and found work as a printer. In May 1905, he published the first issue of the *Chicago Defender*. This was the fourth black newspaper in Chicago at the time. The paper nearly failed, but the support of his landlady, Henrietta Plumer Lee, enabled it to survive. In 1907, the paper had a press run of 1,000 copies, and Abbott increased its success by his first campaign—against the concentration of vice in the black community.

In 1915, Abbott began to publish an eight-column, eight-page, full-size newspaper, which was on its way to becoming a national paper. He launched his "Great Northern Drive" campaign, urging blacks to move to the North and reporting frankly on conditions in the South. This aroused intense anger among southern whites, but by the end of 1918 circulation was about

180,000 copies, reaching 230,000 in 1920, with at least two-thirds sold outside Chicago. In 1929, Abbott launched the first well-financed black magazine, *Abbott's Monthly*, but it failed to survive the financial stresses brought on by the Great Depression and ceased publication in 1933.

The *Defender* ran into problems during this time also but had returned to profitability by 1933. One effect of the financial squeeze was the firing of the white printers working for union wages in the paper's black-owned printing plant, which had been a first for black newspapers when it opened in 1921.

Abbott married twice. The 1918 marriage to Helen Thornton Morrison ended in divorce in 1933. In 1934 he married Edna Denison. Neither marriage produced children. Abbott was generous to his many relatives and especially fond of his nephew John H. H. Sengstacke, whom he trained to take over the *Defender*.

In 1923, Abbott had had to deal with financial irregularities due to faulty bookkeeping and named Nathan K. Magill managing editor. Magill was financially astute but lacked Abbott's flair in understanding the readers' interests and needs. For example, Magill opposed the efforts of railroad porters to unionize. Since the distribution of the paper depended a great deal on the cooperation of porters, Abbott had to intervene. Magill's tightfisted money management benefited the paper, but Abbott felt he had to fire him during the 1930s because of new financial irregularities. His nephew, John Sengstacke, joined the paper as a replacement.

Abbott experienced multiple incapacitating health problems during his final years. He was diagnosed with tuberculosis in 1933. His eyesight became so bad that he could no longer read. He was unable to go to his office for long periods of time, and by the time of his death, he was almost completely confined to bed. He died of tuberculosis and Bright's disease on February 24, 1940, and his nephew took over management of the *Defender*.

Two landmarks of John H. Sengstacke's career were the establishment of the paper as a daily in 1956, the year he also acquired papers in Pennsylvania (*Pittsburgh Courier*), Tennessee (*Tri-State Defender* in Memphis), and Michigan (*Michigan Chronicle* of Detroit), and his foundation of the National Negro Publications Association in 1940. Sengstacke served several terms as president of the association. The success of the papers did not continue to the end of his long tenure as changing economic and social conditions challenged black newspapers. At his death in 1997 the circulation of the *Defender* had plummeted, and the Michigan weekly was the sole paper to show a profit. In addition, the estate faced large inheritance taxes. The *Defender*'s audited circulation in 2002 was 1,629 daily copies in place of the 230,000 of its peak years in the 1950s. The sale of the paper was delayed by family disagreement, but Real Times LLC acquired the papers in 2003, named Roland S. Martin executive editor, and undertook the task of rebuilding.

Robert Sengstacke Abbott was a very successful newspaper publisher and made the *Chicago Defender* into one of the leading, if not the leading, African American newspapers. His successor, John H. Stengstacke, built on this success to turn the paper into a daily and maintain its strength and stability for many years. Abbott worked very hard and possessed great business acumen and, equally important, an understanding of the basis of his paper's appeal to its readers.

*See also*: Black Press: Newspapers in Major Cities

**Sources**

Fitzgerald, Mark. "'Defender' Editor: Revenue, Circ Up in Last 5 Months." *Editor & Publisher*, January 17, 2005. http://www.editorandpublisher.com/eandp/news/article_display.jsp?vnu_content_id=1000760435.

———. "The Revival of the Black Press in America." *Editor & Publisher*, November 26, 2004. http://www.editorandpublisher.com/eandp/search/article_display.jsp?vnu_content_id=1000727192.

Ingham, John N., and Lynne B. Feldman. *African-American Business Leaders: A Biographical Dictionary*. Westport, CT: Greenwood Press, 1994.

Johns, Robert L. "Robert Sengstacke Abbott." *Notable Black American Men*. Ed. Jessie Carney Smith. Detroit: Gale Research, 1999.

Logan, Rayford W., and Michael R. Winston, eds. *Dictionary of American Negro Biography*. New York: W. W. Norton, 1982.

Minor, Michael. "Defender Prepares Its New Offensive." *Chicago Reader*, January 24, 2003. http://www.chireader.com/hottype/2003/030124_1.html.

Ottley, Roi. *The Lonely Warrior*. Chicago: Henry Regnery, 1955.

*Robert L. Johns*

# Advertising Agencies

Black-owned advertising agencies, firms created to target African American consumers, were a new concept in the 1970s. They became novel in the 1980s, and by the 1990s, they had forged a niche in the marketing business. Currently, large general marketing agencies are in a race to buy into them in order to reap the huge profits the ethnic market has to offer.

In previous years, black-owned agencies faced the problem of convincing major advertisers to take the ethnic market seriously. This is no longer the case. The hip-hop movement of urban music, dance moves, lingo, and fashion has spread to the international market, causing general marketers to be lured to the urban market. This has heightened mainstream competition for the urban market, and the entire industry has become engulfed in change.

By the end of the twentieth century, African American–owned agencies had begun to discuss mergers with large general marketing firms. Finally, the huge general marketing firms realized that they needed more than just the input of the agencies; they needed the agencies themselves.

Mergers and alliances with black agencies and other minority-owned groups are becoming popular with mainstream agencies. The first agency to join the merging trend was the Burrell Communications Group, a Chicago–based advertising agency whose clients include Coca Cola, Kellogg's, and McDonald's, among other large companies. In 2000, the Burrell Company, listed as number 3 on *Black Enterprise*'s Top 100 Advertising Agencies list, sold a 49 percent share of its business to the giant French agency Publicis, one of the world's largest media service conglomerates. Publicis was just starting to begin a major expansion into the U.S. market, and the two shared a common vision for the future. It only made good business sense for the two companies to form an alliance. The Burrell Company kept the larger share of 51 percent, and the partnership has proved to be beneficial for both companies. The merger has allowed them to offer clients a broader range of marketing communications services. Another minority advertising agency that has joined the partnership trend is Spike, an agency owned by African American filmmaker **Spike Lee**. Lee announced, in a December 1996 article in *Jet* magazine, that he was forming an alliance with marketing agency, DDB Needham to form Spike DDB. Lee became creative director and supervises the daily operations while DDB Needham performs non-creative services, such as strategic planning, research, media planning and buying, and accounting. Those black-owned agencies that have not yet joined the merging trend are contemplating the move. Also, many general marketing agencies are searching for minority firms who can provide valuable experience with niche advertising.

Many business leaders are skeptical of such mergers. Some feel that black agencies are being pushed aside by mainstream agencies that are racing to get a large portion of the ethnic market business. They believe the black agencies are becoming victims of their own success because they have revealed the potential of the African American consumer market, and now white advertisers are using them to bring in their profits. Skeptics also believe black agencies are fighting for the right to market to the very market they helped create.

Some small black-owned agencies have been accused of allowing the big companies to exploit them. In one such incident, some individuals in the industry attacked the integrity of Spike Lee, owner of Spike DDB, number 8 on *Black Enterprise*'s Top 100 Advertising Agencies list in 2004 (Table 1). They called Spike a setup guy and accused him of allowing the white conglomerates to exploit him. Now a large number of independent black-owned agencies are collaborating with general marketing agencies. Traditional minority agencies that are joining the merging trend describe themselves as integrated urban culture market communications companies and see themselves as no longer competing against other black-owned agencies but as competing with anyone doing lifestyle advertising. In order for general market agencies to stay competitive, they must choose between partnering with African American agencies marketing to urban audiences or lose their business completely.

Like their larger competitors in the advertising business, the majority of the black-owned advertising agencies have reaped big financial rewards by partnering with general marketers. Some agencies have adjusted to their new status as a partnership, while others have pondered such unions. All marketing agencies appear to be preparing themselves for the effect that having a more

# Advertising Agencies

**Table 1.** Top Advertising Agencies

| This Year | Last Year | Company | Location | Chief Executive | Year Started | Staff | Billings* |
|---|---|---|---|---|---|---|---|
| 1 | 1 | Globalhue | Southfield, MI | Donald A. Coleman | 1988 | 180 | 400.000 |
| 2 | 2 | Carol H. Williams Advertising | Oakland, CA | Carol H. Williams | 1986 | 165 | 350.000 |
| 3 | 4 | UniWorld Group Inc. | New York, NY | Byron E. Lewis | 1969 | 117 | 220.798 |
| 4 | 3 | Burrell | Chicago, IL | Fay Ferguson/ McGhee Williams | 1971 | 131 | 190.000 |
| 5 | 5 | Compas Inc. | Cherry Hill, NJ | Stanley R Woodland | 1991 | 54 | 170.000 |
| 6 | 6 | Muse Communications | Los Angeles, CA | Jo Muse | 1995 | 50 | 60.000 |
| 7 | — | Fuse Inc. | St. Louis, MO | Clifford Franklin | 1997 | 22 | 53.396 |
| 8 | 7 | Equals Three Communications Inc. | Bethesda, MD | Eugene M. Faison Jr. | 1984 | 40 | 50.000 |
| 9 | 10 | Matlock Advertising & Public Relations | Atlanta, GA | Kent Matlock | 1986 | 30 | 48.700 |
| 10 | 8 | Spike DDB | New York, NY | Dana Wade | 1997 | 45 | 45.000 |
| 11 | 9 | Anderson Communications | Atlanta, GA | Virgil M. Scott | 1971 | 16 | 41.500 |
| 12 | — | Images USA | Atlanta, GA | Robert L. McNeil Jr. | 1989 | 40 | 41.300 |
| 13 | 13 | E. Morris Communications Inc. | Chicago, IL | Eugene Morris | 1987 | 36 | 37.000 |
| 14 | 11 | SWG&M Advertising Inc. | El Paso, TX | Robert V. Wingo | 1983 | 38 | 36.700 |
| 15 | 14 | RJ Dale Advertising & Public Relations Inc. | Chicago, IL | Robert J. Dale | 1979 | 20 | 35.500 |

*In millions of dollars, to the nearest thousand, as of December 31, 2004. Prepared by B. E. Research. Reviewed by the certified public accounting firm Edwards & Co.

*Source: Black Enterprise* 35 (June 2005): 168. Published by permission.

diverse society will have on their business. J. Melving Muse, owner of Muse, Cordero, Chen and Partners, the most highly sought after multicultural advertising agency in America, says the future is in having a fully diversified firm to perform the integrated marketing services that clients want. He believes that in order to be successful in today's urban market, agencies need to provide more than standard advertisements containing African Americans. Muse also believes that without merging with the larger general marketing agencies, black-owned companies lack the ability to provide the additional services that are needed. He says the black firms that cannot provide the full-integrated services that are needed will find themselves nonexistent.

According to black business leaders, another problem facing blacks in the advertising business is that the black leaders of the industry's largest agencies are aging. Others agree that the number of blacks entering the field is declining. Therefore, in order for African Americans to be representatives of the African American population in the area of **advertising and marketing,** they must be recruited.

The alliance of black-owned advertising agencies and larger general marketing agencies enables the agencies to offer integrated marketing and to reach various markets, including the highly profitable urban audience. This is a growing trend and could account for the success of marketing agencies in the future.

*See also*: Thomas J. Burrell

**Sources**

Earl Graves Ltd. *Black Enterprise*'s 2004 Top 100 Advertising Agencies List. July 2004. http://www.blackenterprise.com/BE100s.asp?Source=Ad04.

Gite, Lloyd. "Breakthroughs for Black-Owned Agencies." *Black Enterprise* 31 (June 2001): 21.

Hayes, Cassandra. "Media Meltdown." *Black Enterprise* 30 (June 2000): 179–184.

Moss, Mark R. "B. E. Advertising Agencies: The Battle for Urban Markets." *Black Enterprise* 31 (June 2001): 187–191.

Smikle, Ken. "The Future of African-American Advertising Agencies Is as Clear as a Blank Piece of Paper." *Target Market News* (July 2004): 1.

"Spike Lee Forms Ad Agency with DDB Needham Worldwide." *Jet* 91 (December 1996): 35.

VNU Business Media. "The Marketing of Hip-hop Culture." *Adweek* (2003) (Special Advertising Section): 1–4.

*Sharon McGee*

# Advertising and Marketing

For nearly a century mainstream advertisers failed to see the potential for huge profits that marketing to African Americans could produce. They had always moved cautiously toward including African Americans as a targeted market. It was not until 1916 that African American consumers were seen as a specific advertising market. The spreading of hip-hop culture (urban music, dance moves, lingo, and fashion) to the international market alerted general advertisers to the true profitability of the African American consumer.

In the 1930s, national studies were conducted to better understand African American consumers. Reports from the studies revealed the overwhelming spending power of African Americans as a consumer group. This prompted the emergence of a systematic means of advising advertisers and manufacturers about ways to advertise to the African American consumer and the addition of African American marketing consultants to the staffs of mainstream advertisers in the 1940s. The United States had also begun to recognize African Americans as a consumer group. As a result, census data on the comparison of black and white spending habits was kept.

During the 1950s, companies were afraid to sponsor African Americans for fear that it would cause a hostile southern market and whites would no longer purchase their products. It was during this time that Nat King Cole, an extremely popular African American singer with several number-one hits, was unable to continue his highly rated television variety show despite good ratings. Scenarios like this occurred simply because of the fear that racism would cause large companies to lose profits.

By the late 1950s, and early 1960s, African Americans became known as consumers who sought status and prestige by purchasing leading brands, and numerous articles and trade publications described African Americans as such. Despite general advertising agencies' knowledge of the brand consciousness of African Americans, little changed in the marketing industry. One of the strategies advertising agencies used prior to the 1960s was the use of black models possessing straight hair (natural or chemically processed), light complexions, and Caucasian features in ads. Civil rights advocates rallied for changes in the attitudes and strategies used to market to African American consumers, but it was not until the 1960s that any publications, including African American publications, used advertisements in which Negroid features and the natural Afro hairstyle were featured. This trend did not last; by the 1990s, publications were once again using African American models with Caucasian features.

## IMPACT OF CIVIL RIGHTS GROUPS

Some of the work of civil rights activists proved to be successful. After feeling the powerful jolt of the civil rights movement, some large corporations began to target African American consumers. Some of the most successful marketing campaigns were those advertisements featuring African American causes and characters. Some successful advertisements in radio used the voices of African Americans, familiar and unfamiliar, to reach the African American consumer. The monetary strength of the African American consumer was once again revealed to advertisers in the 1970s. Statistics showed that African Americans comprised a mere 11 percent of the population but made up a whopping $30 billion a year in consumer spending. However, mainstream advertisers refused to integrate advertising campaigns for fear that the white market may become alienated. In order to learn the white market's perception of integrating African Americans into advertising, mainstream advertisers conducted studies. The results showed that there were no negative effects when black models were used alone or with white models. Results also revealed that when blacks were used in main roles in advertisements, there was a slight negative reaction by highly prejudiced white students. However, African American viewers clearly favored these advertisements. Although whites revealed that the integration of African Americans in advertisements made little difference to them, the amount of advertising dollars used to target African American consumer groups remained insufficient in the 1980s. At this time, most in the marketing business believed that African American consumers fit into one of two groups, those who were unable to purchase national brands and those who desired to purchase the brands that wealthy whites purchased.

Research results in the 1980s mimicked the results of the 1970s concerning the profitability of the urban market. It was found once again that while African Americans constituted a small percentage of the population, they represented huge profits for marketers. It was also found that they consumed a higher percentage of several products than other consumers. For example, African Americans consumed over one-third of all the hair conditioner and over one-fifth of the chewing gum sold in the United States. Although it was found that there were several ways to target African Americans from all segments of the community, there were some easy targets that seemed to be common to all African Americans: All segments of the African American community were heavy viewers of off-network reruns of shows featuring predominantly African American casts, they listened to African American radio stations, they purchased African American magazines, and they watched African American people when they appeared on television.

## TARGETING THE AFRICAN AMERICAN MARKET

A big mistake that mainstream advertisers made when targeting African American consumers in the mid-1980s was when they began targeting the Latinos with Spanish ads and assumed that African American consumers were being targeted when they reached out to all other English-speaking consumers. Marketers failed to remember that African Americans needed to be targeted in a distinct way, and not doing so caused them to lose enormous profits. Mainstream **advertising agencies** failed to realize that although the Hispanic population was growing faster and oftentimes outnumbered the African American population, the African American population remained the bigger spenders in the consumer market. General markets also learned from marketing studies that the vocabulary and common traits used when advertising to white consumers did not apply to African Americans. They again found that they were not targeting African Americans effectively when the Ford Motor Company commissioned the Uniworld Group, the largest African American–owned advertising firm in the United States, to perform research to help them to better understand the African American market. The results revealed that the top ten television shows viewed by African Americans were different from those watched by the general market consumer. General marketing companies also learned that African American consumers of different socioeconomic levels should be targeted in different ways. Mainstream advertising agencies were stunned when they realized that they were trying to reach the African American consumer in the wrong way. It was information such as this that made large advertising agencies begin to change the marketing strategies that they had been using for years to target African American consumers.

In the extremely competitive market of the late 1990s to the present, large advertising companies began to ask African American advertising firms, advertising agencies created to target African American consumers, to partner with them. They wanted the African American firms to reach out to African American consumers in creative ways, and together they (the large general marketing agency and the African American firm) could offer full-service advertising, such as special events, promotions, community relations, community outreach, and public relations. They believed the full-service marketing style, sometimes known as integrated marketing, would cover everything necessary to successfully reach the urban market. Also, just as they had learned in the 30s, they realized that they must attain an understanding of African American consumers in order to acquire the huge profits that could be gained from this market, so they are asking the African American firms to provide statistical research on black consumers. It is no longer the day when companies ask African American advertising firms to simply place standard-issue advertisements in media regardless of the location and lifestyle of the consumer. General marketers are finally beginning to realize that the multicultural population is steadily increasing, and in many instances, multicultural consumers outnumber the white population, and failing to target cultural lifestyle needs could mean the loss of huge profits.

The end of the twentieth century began a trend of African American–owned agencies talking merger with large general marketing firms. The huge general marketing firms recognized that in order to reap large profits from the urban market they needed more than just the input of the black-owned advertising agencies; they needed the agencies themselves. Mergers and alliances between black-owned agencies and large general marketing agencies are becoming popular. Now a large number of independent black-owned agencies are collaborating with general marketing agencies. Traditional minority agencies that are joining the merging trend describe themselves as companies that are integrated into the urban culture communications market and that target this market by offering a fully integrated service. It is believed by many in the marketing business that in order for general marketing agencies to stay competitive, they must choose between partnering with African American agencies marketing to urban audiences or lose their business completely.

Like their larger competitors in the advertising business, the majority of black-owned advertising agencies have earned significant financial rewards by partnering with general marketers. Some agencies have adjusted to their new status as a partnership, while others have pondered such unions. All marketing agencies, it seems, are preparing themselves for the effect that having a more diverse society will have on their business.

One thing that has held true for nearly a century is that although African American consumers constitute a small percentage in the nation, they remain a highly profitable market. Since hip-hop culture has reached the international market, marketing agencies find that they must provide the necessary integrated services to appeal to the urban market.

**Sources**

Dates, Jannette L. "Advertising." *Encyclopedia of African-American Culture and History*. Ed. Jack Salzman, David Lionel Smith, and Cornel West. New York: Macmillan Library Reference USA, 1996.

Gite, Lloyd. "Breakthroughs for Black-Owned Agencies." *Black Enterprise* 32 (September 2001): 21.

Hayes, Cassandra. "Media Meltdown." *Black Enterprise* 30 (June 2000): 179–184.

Moss, Mark R. "B. E. Advertising Agencies: The Battle for Urban Markets." *Black Enterprise* 31 (June 2001): 187–191.

Smikle, Ken. "The Future of African-American Advertising Agencies Is as Clear as a Blank Piece of Paper." *Target Market News* (July 2004): 1.

Washington, Frank. "Going for the Green." *AAOW Magazine*, October–November 2001. http://www.onwheelsinc.com/AAOWMagazine/2001_octnov/pg22.asp.

*Sharon McGee*

# Archie Alphonso Alexander (1888–1958), Engineer, Civil Rights Leader, Public Servant

The large-scale construction jobs that Archie Alphonso Alexander built between 1927 and 1955, such as highways, municipal power and sewer plants, bridges, viaducts, and apartment buildings, earned him a reputation as one of the most successful African American entrepreneurs and architectural engineers in the country. He overcame discouragement from being denied employment with white architectural firms in his native state Iowa, owing to his race; worked as a $10-a-week laborer; and in 1941 began his own engineering company, A. A. Alexander, Inc. He moved beyond his initial small-time clientele and in 1917 joined forces with Alexander & Higbee, Inc., and in 1929 with Maurice A. Repass to become Alexander & Repass, finally winning contracts worth $3.5 million.

Alexander was born in Ottumwa, Iowa, on May 14, 1888, the son of janitor and coachman Price Alexander and Mary Hamilton Alexander. He had eight brothers and sisters. When he was eleven years old the family moved from their community of poor blacks and whites to a small farm on the outskirts of Des Moines. The father became head custodian at the Des Moines National Bank, then regarded as a prestigious post for a black man. Archie Alexander attended Oak Park Grammar School and Oak Park High School, graduating in 1905. While it was uncommon then for a janitor's son—black or white—to undertake higher education, he was determined to do so. He held part-time jobs, secured some financial assistance from his parents, and attended Highland Park College for one year and the Cummins Art School, both in Des Moines. In 1908 Alexander entered the College of Engineering at the State University of Iowa, now the University of Iowa, in Iowa City. The only black student in that college, an engineering professor at the college warned repeatedly that in that day's society a black should not hope to succeed as an engineer. Alexander ignored the warning and continued to support himself by working part-time. He excelled academically and joined the all-black Kappa Alpha Psi fraternity; he also became the first black member of the varsity football team where he was a star, earned a letter in three years, and was given the title "Alexander the Great." He received his Bachelor of Science degree in 1912 and in 1921 took coursework in bridge design at the University of London. In 1925, Alexander received a degree in civil engineering from his undergraduate college, and in 1947, Howard University awarded him an honorary doctorate in engineering.

Anxious to practice engineering, immediately after receiving his undergraduate degree Alexander applied for employment with every engineering firm in Des Moines but was rejected. The warning of the engineering professor at the State University—that a black engineer could not hope to succeed—loomed large. But his attraction to the field led him to work as a laborer in the steel shop of the Marsh Engineering Company, where he earned twenty-five cents an hour. By 1914, he had moved up to $70 a week and was in charge of bridge construction in Iowa and Minnesota. He resigned in that year and established his own engineering company, A. A. Alexander, Inc., a modest firm that attracted few bidders; it also served minority clients. In 1917, he entered a partnership with white contractor George F. Higbee, with whom he had worked at Marsh. The new firm Alexander & Higbee, Inc. specialized in large projects such as bridge construction, road construction, and sewer systems. Higbee died in 1925 as result of a construction accident, leaving Alexander to carry on alone. In 1927 Alexander received a contract from his alma mater, the University of Iowa, to construct a $1.2 million central heating and generating station along the Iowa River. The next year he completed two other projects for the school—a power plant and tunnel under the Iowa River to pipe steam, hot water, and electricity to the other side of the river where the campus extended. During the four years after Higbee's death, Alexander built bridges and viaducts—his specialties—as well as apartment buildings and sewage systems.

Alexander added a junior partner and his second white partner in 1929—former football teammate and college classmate Maurice A. Repass—to form the team Alexander & Repass. In 1929 as well, the firm successfully bid for a City of Grand Rapids contract to build a $1 million sewage treatment plant the next year. They went on to complete projects in nearly every state, including the Loup River Power Plant in Columbus, Nebraska, in 1933. By then the firm felt the sting of the Great Depression and, though highly successful, began to struggle to keep the business alive. They laid off workers, and the partners took on small jobs themselves, such as repairing sidewalks and streets and handling miscellaneous jobs. Around this time white contractor and road builder Glen C. Herrick, who was prominent in Des Moines, hired the firm to help develop a canal system in Nebraska. Herrick assisted the firm further by financing a number of projects.

In 1935 Alexander & Repass took on another major project when they designed and built the Union Pacific Railroad Bridge that crossed Nebraska's North Platte River. The firm was hired for other projects in Iowa, including the Des Moines River Highway Bridge over the Des Moines River, the Des Moines Sewage Disposal Plant, the East 14th Street Viaduct over the Des Moines River, and the Fluer Drive Bridge over the Racoon River in Des Moines.

World War II efforts brought a need for various construction projects. One of these was for an air field at the U.S. Army air base located in Chewhaw, Alabama. Alexander & Repass successfully bid for the project and built the 99th Pursuit Squadron Air Base and Pilot Training School. The site is historically significant as the training site for the Tuskegee Airmen, the all-black elite air force unit that trained under a federal program at Tuskegee Institute (now University) in Alabama.

## DESIGNS TIDAL BASIN BRIDGE

In response to the federal government's need for new projects around Washington, D.C., the firm opened an office there and successfully bid on what became perhaps its most notable but not its largest project. Alexander designed the Tidal Basin Bridge and Seawall, a granite and limestone structure also known as Independence Avenue Bridge. It is especially prominent during Washington's Cherry Blossom Festival held each spring. It is estimated that 160 workers were employed to build the $1 million structure. Other projects that Alexander & Repass built in Washington included the K Street elevated highway and underpass from the Francis Scott Key Bridge to 27th Street, NW, and the $3.5 million Whitehurst Freeway that runs along the Potomac River bypassing the Georgetown section. The Whitehurst Freeway was then the largest of its kind in the country. In 1955 Alexander designed the Frederick Douglass Memorial Estate Apartments in the Anacostia section of southeast Washington, also built by his firm. While Alexander was awarded other contracts, his role as designer for these projects is undocumented.

A lifelong Republican, Alexander was active in party politics. In 1932 and again in 1940 he was assistant chairman of the Iowa Republican State Committee. His support of Dwight D. Eisenhower and the Eisenhower-for-president movement, along with his support of the Republican Party, garnered him an appointment in 1954 as governor of the Virgin Islands. A man with an imposing appearance and commanding personality, Alexander was blunt, outspoken, aggressive, dogmatic, paternalistic, undemocratic, and difficult as a taskmaster. This served him well as a businessman but not as a governor. He alienated the easygoing islanders, who in addition to opposing his personality and administrative style accused him of cronyism due to his developing business interests in South America and the Caribbean. Nor did he endear himself to the legislature. Eighteen months after his appointment, Alexander, now in declining health, was pressured to resign his unsuccessful appointment. He returned to Des Moines.

Alexander's personality and business acumen gave him stature in the black community, both in Des Moines and in Washington, D.C. In Des

Moines he was board member of the Colored Young Men's Christian Association, head of the local National Association for the Advancement of Colored People (NAACP), and a member of the local Inter-racial Commission. He had witnessed the ugly tentacle of racism in 1944, when he and his wife fought a restrictive racial covenant, bought a sizable home in Des Moines's fashionable white neighborhood, but witnessed a cross burning on their front lawn. His worked to improve racism and civic matters. He was a trustee at Tuskegee Institute and Howard University and in 1934, at the request of the Haitian president, joined a team that investigated Haiti's potential for economic development. His recognitions included the Harmon Award in 1926 for achievements in business and the NAACP's Spingarn Medal in 1934 as the second most successful black American entrepreneur.

Alexander died in Des Moines of a heart attack in 1958 and was survived by his wife, Audra A. Lindzy of Denver, whom he married in 1913. Their only child, Archie Alphonso Jr., died in his early years. Alexander left a trust fund for his wife; upon her death, most of his wealth would go to the University of Iowa, Tuskegee, and Howard University for engineering scholarships. The three institutions each received $105,000 in 1975.

**Sources**

"Bridge-Building Team." *Ebony* 4 (September 1949): 59–60.

Bullock, Ralph W. *In Spite of Handicaps*. New York: Association Press, 1927.

Lufkin, Jack. "Archibald Alphonse Alexander (1888–1958)." *African American Architects: A Biographical Dictionary 1865–1945*. Ed. Dreck Spurlock Wilson. New York: Routledge, 2004.

Obituary. *Des Moines Sunday Register*, January 5, 1958.

Wynes, Charles E. "'Alexander the Great,' Bridge Builder." *Palimpsest* 66 (May–June 1985): 76–86.

———. "Archie Alphonso Alexander." *American National Biography*. Vol. 1. Ed. John A. Garraty and Mark C. Carnes. New York: Oxford University Press, 1999.

*Jessie Carney Smith*

# Clifford Leopold Alexander Jr. (1933– ), Attorney, Businessman, Civil Rights Activist

Clifford Alexander Jr. is known as a force in the leadership for civil rights for minorities and women. As a result of his efforts, the definitions of what constitutes discrimination in the workplace were clarified, and the Equal Employment Opportunities Commission established more comprehensive and tenable guidelines by which to work. He was instrumental in women and minorities gaining entry into the media workplace and directed investigations into allegations of job discrimination in various industries. Alexander has served under four U.S. presidents: John F. Kennedy, Lyndon B. Johnson, Richard M. Nixon, and Jimmy Carter. He has served in a leadership position with Dun & Bradstreet, he served as foreign affairs officer of the National

Security Council, he established his own consulting firm, and he was the first African American to be appointed secretary of the army.

Alexander was born on September 21, 1933, in New York City to parents who believed that education was an integral part of life and who provided him with both administrative and humanitarian models. His father, a native of Jamaica, worked at a YMCA branch in Harlem and as a bank manager; his mother, a native of Yonkers, worked for New York City's welfare department, served on a mayoral commission that strove to improve race relations in the city following World War II, and became the first African American representative in the Electoral College. Thus, he was encouraged in his academic pursuits and to use his talents for the betterment of the conditions of humanity. He attended Ethical Cultural School and Fieldstone School. Following Fieldstone, he matriculated at Harvard University, where he excelled both academically and socially. Alexander was elected president of the Student Council, was the first marshal of his class and a talented basketball player, and graduated cum laude with a B.A. in 1955. After graduation, he entered Law School at Yale University to pursue a professional degree, one that would allow him to be independent. In spite of the rigors of the program, while there he worked for Mutual Life Insurance Company, where he headed the Complaints Department. In 1958, he received his LL.B. from Yale University Law School; enlisted in the New York National Guard, where he served with the 369th Field Artillery Battalion at Fort Dix, New Jersey; and ended his military stint in 1959.

In the year he left the military, he was admitted to the bar and became assistant district attorney for New York County (Manhattan). In 1961, he became executive director of the Manhattanville Hamilton Grange Neighborhood Conservation Project, where he was responsible for enforcing city codes relating to apartment dwellers. He oversaw over 3,000 violations during a nine-month tenure. This job ended in 1962 when he became program and executive director of Harlem Youth Opportunities Unlimited (HARYOU), and he practiced law in New York City.

Due to his work and his contacts formed throughout his academic and professional career, he was recommended to and subsequently asked by President John F. Kennedy to serve on the White House staff as foreign affairs officer of the National Security Council. Following Kennedy's assassination in 1963, he became the deputy special assistant and counsel to President Lyndon B. Johnson. In this capacity, he advised President Johnson on civil rights issues (1963–1969) and was influential in the passing of the Civil Rights Act (1964) and in the increase in the number of African Americans serving in national government posts. Because of his efforts in the Johnson administration, the White House was accessible both socially and politically to more African Americans. Alexander's stance on opportunities for African Americans and his previous work record, both in and out of the White House, led to President Johnson appointing him chairman of the U.S. Equal Employment Opportunity Commission (EEOC) in 1967, a post he held until 1969.

Under Alexander's leadership, the commission was restructured and expanded the training and productivity of the regional offices; thus, there was an increase in workers, size, cases, issues being addressed, and accountability. One of his thrusts during his tenure was investigation into job discrimination in a variety of industries with varying results. As a result of two public hearings (New York and Los Angeles) that pointed up discriminatory actions in media-related positions, the first African American was hired on television network news; there were major efforts to include representative minorities on the professional staff of newspapers; and other areas followed suit in an effort to include minorities in the workforce. Questioned about their actions were corporations such as WBC, CBS, and ABC. One of the major challenges he faced was sensitizing employers to the need for providing opportunities for minorities and women. The tone and attitude toward discrimination and the recognition of the need for the White House to support EEOC shifted following the election of Richard Nixon; there was even an accusation that employers were being harassed about job discrimination. Alexander resigned his position in 1969.

He returned to the private sector and the practice of law in Washington, D.C. in the firm of Arnold & Porter (1969–1975); he left this group to join the law firm of Verner, Lipfert, Bernhard, McPherson & Alexander in Washington, D.C. (1975–1976). During this period, he was the host and coproducer of his own Washington television show at WMAL-TV, *Cliff Alexander—Black on White*; and he made an unsuccessful bid against Walter Washington for the position of mayor of the District of Columbia in 1974.

In 1977, he resumed government service when President Jimmy Carter appointed him secretary of the army, the first African American to hold this post. His duties involved managing all army affairs including training, operations, administration, preparedness, and developing and managing the army's annual budget. The assignment was fraught with challenges: the racism in the army, the need for increased professionalism, the need to make the all-volunteer army more viable, and the need to include minority businesses in awarding contracts. Alexander's experience with the EEOC made him an ideal choice in the confrontation of the challenges posed by the army. He served as secretary of the army until 1981 when President Ronald Reagan took office.

Following his stint in the government, Alexander formed Alexander & Associates, Inc., a consulting firm to work with Fortune 500 companies and other businesses on their inclusion of women and minorities. Even though progress had been made, he recognized the fact that discrimination still exists. It is just more sophisticated and requires strategies different from those of the 1960s and 1970s. In 1999, Dun & Bradstreet Corporation chose Alexander to oversee its operations and its search for a permanent chairman and chief executive officer. In this capacity, he oversaw the company's division of its two operations into two separate companies: Dun & Bradstreet Operating Company and Moody's Investors Service.

He has served on the board of directors of such corporations as American Home Products Corporation, MCI Worldcom, and IMS Health Mutual of America; as director of Wyeth; and as nonexecutive chairman of Moody's Corporation (retired in 2003). Throughout Alexander's career, his championship of minorities and business acumen have been recognized with such awards as the Ames Award, Harvard University (1955); Frederick Douglass Award (1970); Outstanding Civilian Service Award, Department of the Army (1980); and the Distinguished Public Service Award, Department of Defense.

Alexander married Adele Logan (1959), a former high school classmate, a writer, and a teacher. She is the author of *Homelands and Waterways*, which was nominated for a Pulitzer Prize (1999) and in 2000 won the Black Caucus Literary Award of the American Library Association. They have two children: Elizabeth, a poet, and Mark Clifford, a law professor.

**Sources**

"Clifford Alexander." *Contemporary Black Biography*. Vol. 26. Ed. David G. Oblender. Gale Group, 2000. Reproduced in *Biography Resource Center*. Farmington Hills, MI: Thomson Gale, 2005. http://galenet.galegroup.com/servlet/BioRC Document Number: K16060011628.

"Clifford L. Alexander Jr." *Who's Who among African Americans*. 18th ed. Gale, 2005. Reproduced in *Biography Resource Center*. Farmington Hills, MI: Thomson Gale, 2005. http://galenet.galegroup.com/servlet/BioRC Document Number: K1645500090.

Williams-Jenkins, Barbara. "Clifford L. Alexander, Jr." *Notable Black American Men*. Ed. Jessie Carney Smith. Detroit: Gale Research, 1999.

*Helen R. Houston*

# Paget Alves (1955– ), Telecommunications Company Officer and Lawyer

Paget Alves is president of Strategic Markets for Sprint's Business Solutions division. Most recently, Alves was named head of the board of directors of West Greenwich, Rhode Island. He has been an innovator in the telecommunications industry for more than twenty years. His biggest coup is the changing of Sprint and the cell phone industry from a sales-driven business to a customer-oriented market-driven industry.

Alves was born and raised in White Plains, New York. After completing high school, he studied at Cornell University, where he earned a bachelor degree in industrial and labor relations. He continued on at Cornell, earning his Juris Doctor in 1982. Alves's career has been marked by many firsts; but he is best known for transforming telecommunication businesses from sales driven to customer driven.

Fresh out of law school, Alves became a law clerk at IBM. He held the position until 1986, when he was appointed IBM's area counsel. He stayed at IBM for an additional two years. In 1988 he joined Murata Business Systems as its general counsel. Murata Business Systems is the U.S. distribution company for Murata Machinery, Ltd., a privately held Japanese corporation that manufactures cell phones and fax machines. He ultimately became executive vice president and chief operating officer, the highest position an American may hold at Murata.

In 1996, the Sprint Wholesale Services Group hired Alves as vice president and general manager of Reseller Services. In only eighteen months, he developed a comprehensive customer service program. In the process he transformed Wholesale Services from a sales-driven team to one that was market oriented—the rationale being that it is not enough to just make sales; the market should be analyzed, then Sprint should develop the products and services that people/businesses need. The year 1997 was a banner year for Alves and Sprint. Sprint's Wholesale Services division saw a 25 percent increase in growth. As a result, Alves was promoted to president of the Wholesale Services division.

In 1999 Alves was listed in *PhonePlus* magazine's the "So Most Influential People in Competitive Long Distance." An avid golfer, this was the year he played with Tiger Woods at the Sprint International Pro-Am in Castle Rock, Colorado. In addition, Alves joined the floundering Austin, Texas–based Voice Over IP company Point One Telecommunications as chief executive officer and president.

Despite his best efforts, Point One filed voluntary bankruptcy in August 2001. Alves left the company later that same year. Alves's next move was to join Centennial Communications in 2002. He stayed less than a year, resigning in February 2003 for personal reasons. In November 2003, Alves rejoined Sprint as one of two vice presidents of the newly reorganized Sprint Business Solutions Strategic division. He continues to work for Sprint in Kansas City.

In addition to conquering the telecommunications industry, Alves is involved in his two favorite activities. He is an avid golfer and a fitness buff. Weighing in at approximately 150 pounds, Alves can bench over 300 pounds. In addition, he is active in his community. Past activities include being cochair of the Kansas City United Negro Fund. While in Dallas, he served on the boards of the Family Guidance Center and the Presbyterian General Health Services. He is married and has three daughters.

Alves is a prime example of how one man can change an entire industry and yet take the time for family and to give back to the community and those less fortunate than himself.

**Sources**

Alumni Office/Cornell Law Association. *Alumni Class Notes—July 2000 Forum.* Cornell Law School. http://www.lawschool.cornell.edu/alumni_new/class%20notes/class700.htm.

———. *Alumni Class Notes: November 1998 Class Notes.* Cornell Law School. http://www.lawschool.cornell.edu/alumni/class%20notes/clas1198.htm.

———. *Alumni Class Notes: November 1999 Class Notes.* Cornell Law School. http:// www.lawschool.cornell.edu/alumni_new/class%20notes/clas1199.htm.

Karp, H., and C. Hayes. "The Strategy of a Shadow Warrior." *Black Enterprise* 11 (June 1998). http://search.epnet.com/login.aspx?direct=true&db=f5h&an= 638322.

"Point One Telecommunications Appoints Former President of Sprint Business Services Group, Paget L. Alves, to Chief Executive Officer and President." *Cambridge Telecom Report.* Business and Company Resource Center. June 26, 2000. http://galenet.galegroup.com/servlet/BCRC?vrsn=149&locID=umd_umes& ste=5&docNum=A20630178.

Sprint. "Key Executives." 2003. http://www3.sprint.com/PR/CDA/PR_CDA_Execu tive_Profiles/1,1572,,00.html.

Titsch, B., Jr., and K. Henderson. "The 50 Most Influential People in Competitive Long Distance." *Phone+.* November 1998. http://www.phoneplusmag.com/ articles/8b1cover.html.

"Unmasking Telecom's Unlikely Heroes." *Phone+.* November 1999. http://www .phoneplusmag.com/articles/9b1cover.html.

Whigham-Desir, M., and R. D. Clarke. "The Top 50 Blacks in Corporate America." *Black Enterprise* 30 (February 2000): 7. http://search.epnet.com/login.aspx?direct =true&db=f5h&an=2704910.

Whispers. *Inter@ctive Week* 7.24 (June 19, 2000). http://web9.epnet.com/Delivery PrintSave.asp?tb=1&_ug=dbs+f5h+sid+D03DBF3E77DE.

*Anne K. Driscoll*

# American Savings and Loan League

The American Savings and Loan League (ASLL), a thrift institution trade organization that primarily represents minority-owned savings and loan associations, was established on November 12 and 13, 1948. Its role was to assist in improving the acute housing situation among African Americans by exploring the possibilities of new construction and to devise plans for adequate mortgage financing of homes and housing projects for African American occupancy. At the time, thirteen associations were members of the league, whose objectives included expanding their program of service to all minority groups by forming additional associations operated by African Americans.

Originally known as buildings and loans, savings and loan associations like the ASLL first appeared in the 1830s. They encouraged working-class members to practice economical spending and to work together in order to achieve the goal of home ownership.

ASLL leaders pushed regulators to make it easier for blacks to own as-sociations and to create positions within the Federal Home Loan Bank of Boston (FHLBB) to focus on the minority housing issues. Although the FHLBB agreed with the ASLL's position that there should be more minority thrifts, its support was limited. The chairman of the board of the FHLBB believed that African Americans should help themselves in becoming homeowners and emphasized that strong groups with a reasonable likelihood for success and strong community support should establish new thrift groups. In order to prevent any new savings and loans (S&Ls) from causing problems with the Federal Savings and Loan Insurance Corporation (FSLIC), the chairman felt that it was inappropriate for minimal capital requirements to be lowered to make it easier for minorities to organize thrifts. Since blacks generally had had only minimal access to capital, the position of the chairman was not beneficial to the ASLL. In 1961, the FHLBB board realized that its actions did not support its rhetoric concerning its support of minority thrifts. A report was then submitted to the Commission on Civil Rights by regulators, conceding that the growth in new minority S&Ls should be attributed to the national civil rights movement. The FHLBB still maintained that it too had been supportive of minority thrifts, and it felt that the fact that the increased approval rates for blacks exceeded that of whites was proof of its support.

In the 1960s, despite the expansion of the work of existing associations, ASLLs were unsuccessful in working with federal regulators in increasing the number of minority-owned thrifts. Through the years, some S&Ls grew immensely, but many remained small. At the time of the establishment of Carver Federal Savings and Loan in New York City in 1949, its subscribed capital was $225,000, and its cash value was $15,000. By 1963 its assets had grown to over $24 million. All of the largest black-owned thrifts were located in California. The largest, Trans-Bay Federal, was located in San Francisco and had more than $74 million in assets. Los Angeles had four black-owned thrifts, which controlled nearly $154 million in assets. Throughout the nation, thirty-four African American thrifts held more than $400 million in total assets.

The American Savings and Loan League is affiliated with America's Community Bankers (ACB), a national trade association providing services and support for progressive community banks that are devoted to strengthening America's communities. The ACB, whose office is located in Washington, D.C., was formed on June 1, 1992, under its original name Savings & Community Bankers of America. The name was changed to America's Community Bankers on January 29, 1995.

According to a 2003 report from the Federal Financial Institutions Examination Council, African Americans are still denied home loans more than twice as often as whites when applying for home loans at American Savings and Loan Associations. Loan records suggest that there is a lending gap so pervasive that often high-income blacks are rejected at the same rate as low-income whites. Loan records also indicate that redlining—withholding loan funds in an area because of race—continues and may have grown worse since the 1980s as federal regulators decreased enforcement of fair-lending laws. During the period from 1993 to 1998, denial rates for all ethnic and racial groups increased considerably.

It is evident that thrift organizations, such as the American Savings and Loan League, are still much needed in our current society. The use of these organizations has made it possible for many Americans, including African Americans, women, and ethnic Americans, to realize the dream of home ownership.

*See also*: Black Banks: Their Beginning; Real Estate Industry

**Sources**

Dedman, Bill. "The Color of Money: Blacks Turned Down for Home Loans from S & L's Twice as Often as Whites." *Atlanta Journal-Constitution*, January 22, 1989. http://powerreporting.com/color/53.html.

Federal Financial Institutions Examinations Council. "Reports—Nationwide Summary Statistics for 2003 HMDA Data Fact Sheet." July 2004. http://www.ffiec .gov/hmcrpr/hm_fs03.htm.

JPL Networks. DocLoan: "Free Loan Advice and Financial Information." http:// www.docloan.com/loans/terms/A.

Mason, David L. *From Buildings and Loans to Bail-Outs: A History of the American Savings and Loan Industry, 1831–1995*. New York: Cambridge University Press, 2004.

*The Negro Yearbook*. 11th ed. Tuskegee, AL: Tuskegee Institute, Negro Year Book Publishing Company, 1952.

U.S. Department of the Treasury Office. Office of Thrift Supervision. Index to the OTS Glossary of Terms. http://www.ots.treas.gov/glossary/gloss-a.html.

*Sharon McGee*

# Wally "Famous Amos" Amos Jr. (1936– ), Business Entrepreneur, Author, Motivational Speaker

Born on July 1, 1936, Wallace (Wally) Amos Jr. will ever be associated with chocolate chip cookies and baking. At age twelve when his parents Wallace and Ruby Amos divorced, Amos moved from his birthplace in Tallahassee, Florida, to live with his mother's sister in New York City. Aunt Della taught him how to bake his favorite chocolate chip cookies, developing his interest in cooking and his dream of becoming a chef. Amos attended Food Trades Vocational High School but dropped out to join the U.S. Air Force. He was discharged in 1957 after earning his GED (general educational development) equivalency diploma.

Amos enrolled in a secretarial training program at a New York City business school while working as a stock clerk at Saks Fifth Avenue. At Saks, his competency was rewarded with an appointment as manager of the supply department. With the added pressure of a growing family, and the realization that further advancement at Saks would be difficult, Amos searched for other opportunities. In 1961, excited about the possibility of working in show business, he took a job in the mailroom at the William Morris Talent Agency in New York City. There, Amos advanced quickly through the ranks from mail deliveries to the secretarial pool to the music department and upward to become the first black booking agent at a major theatrical agency. Amos worked directly with or supported popular talents of the day such as Simon and Garfunkel, Dionne Warwick, Helen Reddy, and the Supremes. The change in music from rock and roll to hard, psychedelic rock, coupled with personnel changes at the agency, caused Amos to rethink his future with the firm. In 1967, after six years with the agency, he quit to start his own talent agency, based first in New York and later in Los Angeles. Unfortunately, Amos was unable to attract successful performers to keep his business profitable. In 1968, he became a personal manager for Venture Records, booking clients on television and variety shows. Amos continued freelancing in show business for another six years, part of the time with his own artist management firm, Wally Amos and Company.

Amos had dreamed of becoming a chef ever since he first tasted Aunt Della's chocolate chip cookies. For years, he had baked and shared chocolate chip cookies with friends who had raved about them, even encouraged him to sell them. In 1975, armed with a business plan, he secured $25,000 in financial backing from show business friends. Amos believed that his new product deserved celebrity status, but being short on funds, he used his talent agency experience to his best advantage. He traded cookies for advertising time at a local radio station, then celebrated the opening of his business on Sunset Boulevard in Hollywood with a huge party. Amos also capitalized on his nickname "Famous," calling his new commercial venture the Famous Amos Chocolate Chip Cookie Company. It was the first black-owned cookie retail business. Amos succeeded in turning an old recipe into a winning one with his moist, chewy cookies. Within the next two years, Amos branched out in the West to Tarzana and Tucson. On the East Coast, a contract with Bloomingdale's and production plants in Nutley, New Jersey, and California helped to move the business to a full wholesale operation. Selling to department stores such as Jorgensen's, Bloomingdale's, and Macy's provided the recognition and prestige that allowed the business to branch to additional locations in California, New York, Chicago, and Hawaii. Famous Amos Cookies, with the help of the media, became nationally prominent, selling cookies in upscale stores like Nieman-Marcus that appealed to the gourmet crowd. Amos became known as "the face that launched a thousand chips." As personal manager for his company, Amos became his own promotion billboard with his "Friends of the Cookie" corporate symbols, a straw Panama hat, embroidered shirt, and the ever-present kazoo around his neck.

Amos's decision to move to Hawaii in 1977 proved to be more advantageous for his personal life than for his business. Although he appointed friend and manager Sid Ross as the president of the company, Amos's absence affected the efficiency of the business. The company enjoyed ten years of relative stability, with annual sales reaching more than $10 million in 1982. However, fierce competition from established cookie makers Nabisco and Keebler and new companies Mrs. Fields and David's saturated the market with brands of premium and fresh-baked cookies. By 1984, Famous Amos no longer cornered the gourmet cookie market. The company began to suffer heavy financial losses due to forced expansion and high overhead. Desperate for new investors, Amos sold a majority interest to Bass Brothers of Fort Worth, Texas, for $1.1 million in 1985. The expected turnaround was not immediate; Famous Amos changed hands four times from 1985 to 1988. The new owners tried unsuccessfully to license similar products such as ice cream, candy, and soda with the Famous Amos brand name. Amos attributed his losses to his lack of business acumen. He had the vision, grit, and resourcefulness, but as an entrepreneur, he was not equipped to handle management and financial problems. Amos signed a noncompete clause and left the company in 1989 with a salary of $225,000 a year plus expenses.

In 1991, Amos, determined to duplicate his earlier success, formed Wally Amos Presents Chip & Cookie, to sell cookies, dolls, apparel, and related merchandise. The Portola Group, the new owners of the Famous Amos Chocolate Chip Company, sued him for trademark infringement in 1992. With a new marketing strategy of selling to vending machines and warehouse clubs, Famous Amos had moved from near bankruptcy to become the number one in the vending-machine cookie retail business. The company did not want its product confused with any others carrying the Amos name. Product sales, which had been climbing steadily, now reached over the $70 million mark, surpassing Nabisco's Oreo. The legal agreement allowed Amos the use of his name and likeness on promotions but barred him from use on any products.

In 1992, Amos formed the Uncle Noname (pronounced no-nah-may) Cookie Company to sell cookies but later changed to low-fat and sugar-free muffins. Uncle Noname was Amos's creative wordplay on his legal situation with the Famous Amos Chocolate Chip Cookie Company. From his home in Oahu, Hawaii, Amos presided over two new ventures, Uncle Wally's ultra moist muffins, which evolved from Uncle Noname, and his Florida-based company, Aunt Della's Cookies, chocolate chip and other flavored gourmet cookies. Amos is the spirit and force behind marketing his products, which he promotes to vending machine and supermarket businesses and club warehouse stores. His companies grossed $18 million in 2002. A bakery in Long Island, New York, employed more than 100 people. Amos has successfully turned the loss of his company and, in a sense, his name into new life. He believes that life is all about the future and not the past. Amos attributes his success to his enthusiasm for life and his love for the products in which he has an interest.

The Famous Amos Company was sold in 1998 to Keebler, a subsidiary of the Kellogg Company. Surprisingly, in 1999, Amos returned to the company as its spokesperson, and in 2000, on the company's twenty-fifth anniversary, Amos became the official "director of cookie fun" to promote the brand name. Pleased with the new association, Keebler granted permission for Amos to once again use his name and face. He changed Uncle Noname to Uncle Wally's. In 2001, the Kellogg Company bought out Keebler Foods.

Wally Amos, inventor of the original "Famous Amos" chocolate chip cookie, has come full circle. He has written five books recounting his remarkable experiences, offering sage advice, and sharing his witticisms on life. From 1977 to 1980 he participated in the annual Macy's Thanksgiving Day Parades. In 1980, Amos's panama hat, Indian-style gauze shirt, and his cookies were selected by the Smithsonian Institution to be enshrined in the Business American exhibits collection of the National Museum of American History. Along with an honorary citation from the Horatio Alger Association, Amos received the Small Business Entrepreneurial Award for Excellency in business ownership and entrepreneurship from President Ronald Reagan in 1986. Amos uses his fame to promote literacy. He is the spokesperson for the national organization Literacy Volunteers of America. Amos is also a board member for the National Center for Family Literacy, a post he has had since 1979. In 1990 he received the National Literacy Honors Award from President George Bush. He travels the country, promoting literacy at libraries and conferences and giving motivational lectures on how to overcome adversity while keeping a positive attitude. This is the kind of work that brings the pioneer of the gourmet cookie a sense of satisfaction, being, and purpose.

*See also*: Black Businesses in Large Cities; Food Service Industry

**Sources**

Amos, Wally, and Camilla Denton. *The Man with No Name: Turn Lemons into Lemonade*. Lower Lake, CA: Aslan Publishing, 1994.

Amos, Wally, Eden-Lee Murray, and Neale Donald Walsch. *The Cookie Never Crumbles: Inspirational Messages for Everyday Living*. New York: St. Martin's Press, 2001.

Amos, Wally, and Leroy Robinson. *The Famous Amos Story: The Face That Launched a Thousand Chips*. New York: Doubleday, 1983.

"Famous Amos Chocolate Chip Cookie Company." *Leading American Businesses: Profiles of Major American Companies and the People Who Made Them Important*. By Michael Burgan. Farmington Hills, MI: UXL/Gale/Thomson, 2003.

"Wally Amos." *Leading American Businesses: Profiles of Major American Companies and the People Who Made Them Important*. By Michael Burgan. Farmington Hills, MI: UXL/Gale/Thomson, 2003.

"Wally Amos Jr." *African American Almanac*. Detroit: Gale Research, 2003.

*Janette Prescod*

# Association of Black Women Entrepreneurs

Established in 1985 within Los Angeles's hotbed of black entrepreneurial expansionism, the Association of Black Women Entrepreneurs (ABWE) was founded to address mounting frustrations associated with female and minority marginality in the corporate world. To counter the trend, ABWE has grounded itself in providing networking workshops, mentoring relationships, and pertinent information sessions to help black women establish independent and economically viable enterprises.

As president of Corita Communications—an educational business consulting firm—and as a long-standing instructor of business administration at California State University at Northridge, Dolores C. Ratcliffe, current president of ABWE, possesses the skills and vision to help provide aspiring black women entrepreneurs with the practical tools to succeed. In addition to her tasks as proprietor, educator, and trade organization leader, Ratcliffe has inspired many through writing as well. She wrote *Women Entrepreneurs Networking and Sweet Potato Pie: A Business Survival Guide* (1987) as an outgrowth of ABWE's objectives. Accordingly, at its fifth national conference in 1989, ABWE focused its energies on the prospects of national and international entrepreneurship in the 1990s.

Specific agenda items covered at the conference included limited risks in franchising opportunities, practical management strategies, and approaches to financial discipline. In the case of franchising opportunities, Ratcliffe and Detroit-based **National Association of Black Women Entrepreneurs** (NABWE) president Marilyn French-Hubbard both concluded that the transition from the corporate world to owning one's business could be facilitated more fluidly through franchising since the infrastructure of the company is established and does not have to be re-created. Historically, black women have faced obstacles attracting seed funds to launch projects and securing contracts from purchasing agents. ABWE has assisted in neutralizing this pitfall by filtering professional contacts and business information to help members propel their respective services into able and interested clients' hands. Moreover, Ratcliffe is quick to point out the need for black women to adapt their corporate skill base to the entrepreneurial world and systematically devise mechanisms for sustained success.

An immediate service afforded to ABWE members is the SOS Call Line, which serves as a troubleshooting contact point in which members can reach the Los Angeles headquarters twenty-four hours a day and discuss problems associated with getting their businesses off the ground. According to Ratcliffe, the most consistent complaint stems from prospective lenders' pervasive stereotypes and connotations of black women as high risks and potential liabilities owing to insufficient experience. She also points out that most cases in question are overtly discriminatory because the women involved have demonstrated good credit and substantial home equity. Yet the perils of biased lending persist.

Not to be dismayed by societal constraints, Ratcliffe and ABWE have continued to navigate through limitations and offer programs of empowerment. Primarily through mentoring of local black female business owners in the Los Angles area, Ratcliffe has helped countless numbers take their businesses to higher heights. Letitia Wright, host of the *Wright Place* television show, represents this category. Wright was chosen in May 2005 to participate in ABWE's WIN-TEC program—a program whereby a select few small businesses interact through organizational initiatives in an effort to broaden their existing bases and expand their overall niche. As an appointed member of Los Angeles County's Office of Small Business Advisory Board, Ratcliffe has used her behind-the-scenes insight while providing continuous advice on increasing opportunities for small business procurement.

For twenty years ABWE founder and president Dolores Ratcliffe has remained at the fore of the movement to encourage black women's business ownership; support the showcasing of black women business owners; offer professional development, training, and technical proficiency; and provide accessible microloan programs. With members on its corporate board representing Walt Disney Productions, AT&T, Miller Brewing Company, Southern California Gas Company, the Northrop Corporation, and the Southern California Edison Company, ABWE has solidified its role as the preeminent power networking organization of Southern California representing the combined interests of black women entrepreneurs. With this in mind, in *New Age Media Concepts*, Ratcliffe holds firm to her belief: "When you hear the words how dare you succeed? Smile to yourself and say 'That's not what I believe.'"

*See also*: Women and Business

**Sources**

"Association of Black Women Entrepreneurs Selects Dr. Letitia Wright for 2005–2006 WIN-TEC Program." *New Age Media Concepts Online*, May 21, 2005. http://press.namct.com/content/view/1279/9.

Thompson, Kevin D. "Black Women in America Starting Over." *Black Enterprise* 19 (August 1988): 58–61.

Whigham, Marjorie. "Networkers Focus on Entrepreneurship." *Black Enterprise* 20 (November 1989): 31.

Zev Yaroslavsky Press Release. March 30, 2000. http://zev.co.la.ca.us/PressReleases00/033000ratcliffe.htm.

*Uzoma O. Miller*

# B

The history of the barbecue establishment in this country is inextricably tied to the history and culture of the African American community, particularly in the South. Although traditionally these businesses have been small, varying from a roadside stand to a sit-down restaurant, they continue to serve as a source of income for the owners and as a cultural icon for African Americans.

In the Senegambia region of West Africa, open braising of meat was common practice. Slaves who arrived in colonial South Carolina came from the West Indies and may have practiced open braising techniques as a part of their African heritage. In *Smokestack Lightning*, Lolis Elie notes that the African influence is often downplayed, but it cannot be denied. "Barbecue, more than most American foods, has come to be inextricably tied to African American culture," he notes. As we know it today, "barbecue is also the product of the blending of techniques," he says. It differs by region; for example, in the East most barbecuing is done with pork, while in the West it is done with beef. As Anglo-American, Hispanic, African American, and other cultures mixed, the hybrid culture that resulted included barbecue.

Native Americans and black slaves taught early colonists how to cook or barbecue whole hogs; then barbecuing became an important part of American culture, particularly in the South. After the Civil War, barbecue was prepared for special occasions. As well, a community gathering or a big festival was often called a "barbecue." It follows that, during this period, the cooks who served the white community in the South were black. To Burt Feintuch, who wrote for the *Encyclopedia of Southern Culture*, barbecue was a way of cooking as well as a way of "serving the result." *Barbecue* referred to "meat cooked slowly over embers" and kept moist by a basting sauce. Central to the black identity in the South early on was barbecue. In fact, the food was so popular that roadside stands became the Old South's first restaurants. In time, however, whites in the restaurant business had an advantage over blacks: They were able to meet the requirements that new urbanization set forth. With their limited funds, owners of the small, black businesses were unable to meet the sanitary regulations that were imposed in the late 1800s and into the 1900s. As well, blacks still cooked their barbecue over a hole in the ground—a pit—a procedure that was unacceptable to health officials.

Region, rather than race, affects the way the food is prepared. In North Carolina, for example, the barbecue tradition is to cook the meat until it falls apart; then it can be pulled into shreds and served. In some sections of the state the meat is chopped. Regardless of the form of the final product, a vinegar and hot pepper sauce is used. Contents of sauces used in other regions will vary, as will the cut of meat, whether shoulder, loin, or ribs. In contrast, the black east Texas barbecue tradition, as well as in the state's majority culture, beef, which is in abundance in the state, is used rather than pork. In the Old South, whites have held huge barbecues in Texas for civic and other gatherings. Thousands of people have attended and whole herds of cattle been slaughtered; however, the traditional black culture was preserved owing to the fact that the cooks were black.

Nick Spinelli found that barbecue remained on the East Coast and in southern states for some time before spreading across the country especially to cattle and rail towns. "African Americans—knowledgeable in cooking the less meaty and less desirable cuts of meat—migrated to the northern and western states" and took their cooking tradition with them. Thus, cattle and rail towns picked up the tradition.

Since barbecue is a part of the African tradition, it follows that the African American community would continue to practice this cooking technique. In time, barbecue became commercialized and a means of income for black people. Barbecue establishments became prevalent in practically every African American community of the South. An early entrepreneur in the field was Henry Perry, who in 1970 opened Kansas City, Missouri's first barbecue restaurant. Later the business became known as Arthur Bryant's.

Barbecue restaurants were especially popular during the mid-twentieth century, and many of these were small black businesses. Some may have been established and flourished owing to a long-standing community legend that only blacks could cook "real" barbecue. Joseph A. Pierce, who in 1944 surveyed black business, suggested that blacks should build on this legend and reenter the barbecue business because of its potential as a profitable undertaking. Barbecue businesses in the African American community have developed from a simple shack in the community; cooking styles varied from one region to another. In time, the establishments grew in size and popularity and attracted considerable business from whites. Despite the rigid racial segregation that existed in the South, whites always had the freedom to shop and eat where they chose; many chose to do so at black establishments, particularly the barbecue stands.

During the 1950s and 1960s, black-owned Martell's barbecue establishment, located on the outskirts of Greensboro, North Carolina, operated a racially segregated restaurant: It seated and served white patrons in a dining area but required African Americans to use the drive-in window. Whites had other choices. Gary D. Ford notes in *Encyclopedia of Southern Culture* that "whites, in a strange reversal of Jim Crow traditions, made stealthy excursions for take-out orders" in the black barbecue establishments. This was seen early on at Cromwell's Barbecue (Phoenix City, Alabama), Archibald's Drive-In (Northport, Alabama), and The Spare Rib (Greenville, Texas). In Nashville, Tennessee, businesses such as Maxwell's on Charlotte Avenue (now closed) and Mary's on Jefferson Street had no segregated seating practices. Nor did Shakey's on 14th Avenue North (also closed); like many other barbecue establishments, however, all patrons, regardless of race, were served from a stand-up window. Two barbecue establishments of national acclaim are found in Kansas City, Missouri—Bryant's and Gates'. In 1926, Arthur Bryant founded Bryant's Barbecue, and George W. Gates founded Gates' old Kentucky Bar-B-Que in 1946. Gates offers a variety of barbecue foods, including chicken, beef, turkey, and his speciality—ribs. Both establishments are famous for their sauces and ship nationwide. In Arkansas, Lindsey's, founded in 1955 and located in North Little Rock, is an example of a family business handed down to a descendant of black African Methodist Episcopal (AME) bishop D. L. Lindsey. In recent years, Sim's Barbecue, founded by Allen Sims and managed by his nephews, was said to have the best barbecue in the state. These small, black barbecue establishments are examples of those that proliferated throughout the South in the 1950s and 1960s.

The current trend toward showcasing all aspects of African American culture is seen in various festivals and celebrations throughout the country. Among such celebrations that promote local culture as well as local barbecue traditions is the W. C. Handy Blues and Barbecue Festival, a week-long activity held each June in Henderson, Kentucky. The festival promotes blues, bands from across the nations, and feasts of barbecue, red beans and rice, and other items from local vendors. Although for a time racial divides prevented them from entering, blacks have also preserved their barbecue traditions by participating in the Memphis in May 1982 festival's barbecue cook-off contest and other sizable barbecue cook-offs in Georgia and Texas.

Notwithstanding the influences of Anglo, Hispanic, and Native American culture on barbecue traditions, the barbecue establishment remains an important influence on the economic development of the African American community.

*See also*: Food Service Industry; Roadside and Street Vending

## Sources

Elie, Lolis Eric, ed. *Corn Bread Nation 2: The United States of Barbecue*. Chapel Hill: University of North Carolina Press, 2004.

———. *Smokestack Lightning: Adventures in the Heart of Barbecue Country*. New York: Farrar, Straus and Giroux, 1996.

*Encyclopedia of Southern Culture*. Ed. Charles Reagan Wilson and William Ferris. Chapel Hill: University of North Carolina Press, 1989.

Feintuck, Burt. "Foodways, Geography of." *Encyclopedia of Southern Culture*. Ed. Charles Reagan Wilson and William Ferris. Chapel Hill: University of North Carolina Press, 1989.

Ford, Gary P. "Barbecue." *Encyclopedia of Southern Culture*. Ed. Charles Reagan Wilson and William Ferris. Chapel Hill: University of North Carolina Press, 1989.

Pierce, Joseph A. *Negro Business and Business Education: Their Present and Prospective Development*. New York: Harper and Brothers Publishers, 1947. Reprint, Westport, CT: Negro Universities Press, 1971.

Spinelli, Nick. "True Barbecue." *Prepared Foods* 170 (July 2001): 69.

*Jessie Carney Smith*

# Don H. Barden (1943– ), Entrepreneur, Venture Capitalist, Television Executive, Real Estate Developer, Casino Owner and Operator

Don Barden's love for a challenge goes hand in hand with his flair for risk taking. Taking chances and leveraging profits are proven strategies for Barden as evidenced by his phenomenal success. Barden Companies Incorporated, with its diversified portfolio of businesses, including casino gambling, real estate development, and international trade, is one of the top minority firms in the country.

Barden, an entrepreneur venture capitalist, seemingly possesses an uncanny knack for being in the right place at the right time. He was born in Inkster, Michigan, on December 20, 1943, the ninth of thirteen children. His parents, Milton and Hortense Barden, were hardworking people who raised their children with the same work ethic. In high school Barden played quarterback on the football team and was also a captain on the basketball team. He completed one year of college at Central State University in Wilberforce, Ohio, but had to drop out after his freshman year in 1963 due to lack of funds. He settled in Lorain, Ohio, working in a variety of jobs including one with the American Shipbuilding Company.

In 1965 Barden used his $500 savings to open a record store, his first venture into the entertainment business. The lessons he learned running Donnie's Record Shop served as preparation for future business ventures. He honed his skills at selling and promotion and also learned public relations. From the start, Barden never let his businesses stagnate but kept moving to the next opportunity. He expanded his record business into booking shows, promoting artists, and even creating a new record label. His entrepreneurial spirit and intrepid determination willed him to forge ahead. In 1968, he sold his record store and opened a public relations office. However, public relations and advertising were slow to produce the level of financial rewards Barden expected. Eager, proactive, and on the lookout for new opportunities, he entered the real estate arena, beginning with a contract to provide housing for the U.S. military. Barden formed Waycor Development

Incorporated in 1988 to continue buying, selling, renting, and developing properties to meet supply and demand. Although he made some very profitable real estate investments throughout the 1970s, not all of his ventures proved to be successful.

At the same time he was working in real estate, he also anchored the local news and hosted a weekly talk show for a television station in Cleveland, Ohio. A partnership to publish a weekly entertainment newspaper, the *Lorain County Times*, folded after two issues. Undaunted, Barden secured financial backing to continue publishing the paper until it was sold five years later. All his public ventures—newspaper publishing, television broadcasting, relations with the local chamber of commerce and other community groups—inevitably propelled him into the political arena. He was elected to the Lorain City Council, where he served for two terms from 1972 to 1975, as the first African American councilman. A later bid for a Senate seat in the Ohio legislature proved to be more elusive.

In the 1970s, when the cable television entertainment business was expanding from high- to middle-income consumers, Barden envisioned a market for cable in the often overlooked urban black communities. Through negotiation, he was able to forge a deal that opened 4 percent interest of the cable television franchises to black ownership. Barden's 2 percent interest in each franchise earned lucrative benefits for his new company Barden Communications Incorporated, which became one of the first African American companies to be a major player in the cable industry. In 1981, Barden Cablevision of Detroit won the franchise to bring cable television to mostly black communities in Michigan, first in the town of Inkster and later Romulus and Van Buren Townships. In 1983, amidst a storm of controversy, he won a fifteen-year contract for the Detroit cable franchise. The contract was completed in partnership with the Toronto-based Maclean Hunter.

Envisioning endless possibilities in casino gambling, Barden sold his interest in Barden Cablevision to Comcast in 1994, garnering over $100 million. This capital provided the funds to enter the gaming business with his first venture, the *Majestic Star* riverboat casino in Gary, Indiana. His national casino company, Barden Companies Incorporated, is an African American first. He later rebuilt the *Majestic Star* into a riverboat-casino complex. Barden's dream to build a casino in the city of Detroit was defeated in a 1997 ballot after he was unable to garner support from the mayor. Another joint proposal with Michael Jackson for a theme park on the waterfront gained even less favor and was abandoned.

Barden's aggressive business style and high-risk nature had not yet enticed him into the automobile business despite his Detroit-based roots. It was the international auto business rather than the domestic market that attracted his attention. Unexpectedly, the president of Namibia opened the door for Barden to gain a foothold in the international business market. In 1997, he brokered a deal with General Motors (GM) to sell GM vehicles to Namibia. Under the contract with the Namibian government, his new company, Barden International, constructed an auto manufacturing and processing facility in the African country, employing locals to retrofit the American-made vehicles from left-hand to right-hand drive. Barden foresaw that the Namibian opportunity might open the door to other international ventures, or at least provide a stream of retrofitted vehicles to be exported to other African countries.

Barden Companies Incorporated is ranked among the largest African American companies in the United States. Barden has broken new ground with his successes in communications, real estate, cable television, and casino gaming. In 2001, in an unprecedented gamble, Barden acquired from bankruptcy court three casinos in Las Vegas, Tunica (Mississippi), and Black Hawk (Colorado) formerly owned and operated by Fitzgeralds Casino. In addition to being the first African American to own a national casino company, he is also the first with ownership in the Las Vegas area. He continues to place heavy bets on the entertainment industry while developing new products and services. In 2002, he announced new additions to his company, Barden Entertainment and Barden Technologies, which he anticipates would operate a national network of digital video jukeboxes. Barden Technologies is also developing new touch-screen voting machines. Barden has not abandoned the hope of entering the Michigan casino business. In 2004 he filed applications to operate local horse tracks in locations in and around Detroit and is lobbying for others in Maryland and Pennsylvania. In particular he wants to build and operate a horse track with slot machines, a racino, north of Detroit Metropolitan Airport. Barden projects big profits from these new markets.

Barden has not abandoned the hope of entering the Michigan casino business. In 2004 he filed applications to operate local horse track locations in and around Detroit. His dream is to build a racino, a horse track with slot machines, north of the Wayne County Detroit Metropolitan Airport. Barden projects big profits from the racino market and lobbied heavily for legislation in Michigan, Maryland, and Pennsylvania. Thus far, Pennsylvania is the only state with a racino law. Although the state is yet to approve new gaming licenses, Barden's group has already proposed a seventeen-acre site with casino, riverfront promenade, and restaurants. Lawmakers in Michigan opted to increase casino taxes instead of authorizing racinos. Further, any gaming expansion must be placed on a ballot to be approved by voters. Barden continues to expand his gambling empire. In 2005, he bought the Trump Casino–Hotel riverboat in Gary, Indiana, for $253 million. It will be fittingly renamed the *Majestic Star II* as it is a dock mate of his first acquisition, the *Majestic Star*.

Barden's foresight, wisdom, flexibility, and ability to capitalize on business opportunities with rapid growth potential have singled him out for national recognition including a recent Trumpet Award. Many speculate that he will reenter the political arena in the near future. He has served as a campaign fund-raiser for both Representative Richard Gephardt and President Bill Clinton. If the opportunity is presented at the right time and the stakes are high, there is no doubt that Don Barden will throw his hat in the ring.

*See also*: Black Businesses in Large Cities: A History; Real Estate Industry

**Sources**

Bray, Hiawatha. "Wired for Success." *Black Enterprise* 22 (June 1992): 134–140.

Dingle, Derek T. "Don H. Barden: The Barden Companies." *Black Enterprise Titans of the B.E. 100s: Black CEOs Who Redefined and Conquered American Business.* New York: John Wiley and Sons, 1999.

Gupte, Pranay B. "Detroit's Gift to Namibia." *Forbes* 162 (October 1998): 112+.

Hughes, Alan. "The House Always Wins." *Black Enterprise* 23 (June 2003): 126–128, 130, 132, 134, 136.

LoDico, John, and Rebecca Parks. "Don H. Barden: Business Executive." *Contemporary Black Biography.* Vol. 20. Ed. Shirelle Phelps. Detroit: Gale Research, 1999.

Smith, Eric L. "Barden's Excellent Adventure." *Black Enterprise* 28 (May 1998): 74–82.

*Janette Prescod*

# Edwin C. Berry (1854–1931), Hotel Owner, Caterer

Recognized as a leading black businessman and hotel keeper in the late nineteenth and early twentieth centuries, Edwin C. Berry first owned a restaurant and later built and operated a hotel in Athens, Ohio, that was deemed one of the finest available. Although his clientele was primarily white, he served whites as well as blacks.

The son of free parents, Berry was born in Oberlin, Ohio, on December 10, 1854. In 1856, when he was two years old, the family relocated to Athens, Ohio, where school facilities were available for blacks. To help support themselves, the Berrys took in boarders.

Young Edwin Berry attended the Athens public schools, and later, when the new school opened, he studied for a short time at Albany Enterprise Academy. Albany was an early example of an educational institution in this country founded, owned, and operated by blacks. When his father died in 1870, Berry, then sixteen years old, dropped out of school to help provide for his mother and his eight younger siblings.

As he sought employment, Berry walked ten miles away, to Athens, Ohio, where he was hired in a brickyard for fifty cents a day. The bricks were to be used for constructing the state mental hospital. Berry became so skilled in a short time that his wages increased to $1.25 a day; now he could provide more for his family. He continued to work in the brickyard during summer months, but in winter he worked as a delivery boy or store clerk. These were difficult years for the economy, so Berry seized as many opportunities as he could to earn more money. For example, when other youngsters spent some of their money on the traveling circus, Berry made the circus profitable for himself. He set up a refreshment booth that earned more money for him than the brickyard paid. He also sold refreshments for various excursions on the train and elsewhere.

For a while, Berry worked in Parkersburg, West Virginia, as an errand boy in a dry goods store. There he earned $10 a month and sent $8 of it to his mother each month. He also worked as a waiter in an ice cream parlor and developed an interest that would affect his life from 'then forward. Berry returned to Athens, and from 1868 to 1872, he apprenticed himself as a cook in a local restaurant and developed a profession of catering. So efficient was he as caterer that the customers of his employers demanded his service. He decided that, as a caterer, he would do better for himself than he did for his employer's customers.

He married his schoolmate, Mattie Madry, of Pomeroy, Ohio, on October 18, 1878; her parents also had been slaves. The couple set up housekeeping in one room. His interest in establishing a business for himself never waned, but he had neither the capital nor credit to do so. Meanwhile, Berry had been paying his in-laws $3 a week for his wife's board. Mattie Madry persuaded her parents to allow Berry to divert the money into "business capital." In 1888, Berry left his employment in the local restaurant and, with his elder brother and $40 in capital, started a business known as Berry Brothers. He bought out his brother and continued the business on his own. His restaurant was successful from the start, and by 1880 he purchased a lot for $1,300. As soon as he paid for the lot, he borrowed $1,000 from a farmer friend and put up his first building, which became a part of Berry Hotel. Berry continued to prosper for fourteen years; this required him to seek various locations to support the thriving enterprise.

In 1892, Berry borrowed $9,000 from a farmer friend, mortgaged his building, and expanded his business by building the Berry Hotel, a twenty-room facility, next to his restaurant. It, too, was immediately successful, requiring several additions over time to meet patrons' needs. Later on he expanded to fifty rooms served by an elevator and equipped each room with a closet and bath. Although his clientele was predominantly white, he served blacks as well. According to **Booker T. Washington** in *The Negro in Business*, he had a deep sense of loyalty to his race and would rather lose customers than be "disloyal" to black people. Berry Hotel, which grossed $35,000 annually, was known for its fine meals and the precision care that was given to the guests. The hotel is credited with having in each room needle, thread, buttons, and cologne. Washington reported that Berry's wife attended to the visitors as well; while they slept, she pressed their garments, added buttons, and made repairs. Guess were so impressed with the hotel's service that they returned time and time again and brought friends with them. The hotel was also a popular spot on Sundays for men who traveled considerable distances to spend the day there. By the time Berry retired—sometime before 1910—some sources say that he had fifty-five rooms and operated one of the finest hotels in the country.

Beyond the restaurant and hotel business, Berry was active in the Republican Party in southeastern Ohio and in summer 1889 sought a clerkship in the state government. During the early decades of the twentieth century, he served on the Board of Trustees for Wilberforce University in Ohio. Active in the Baptist church, he helped to finance and build Mount Zion Baptist Church in

Athens. For nearly fifty years he was a delegate and speaker at the Ohio Baptist Convention. He was also an advocate of temperance.

Berry credited his mother and his wife for his success. In his business efforts, he catered to the needs of his clients—an attribute that brought him recognition. Berry died in Athens on March 12, 1931. By then he had accumulated an estate worth $55,000.

*See also*: Food Service Industry

**Sources**

Levstik, Frank R. "Edwin C. Berry." *Dictionary of American Negro Biography*. Ed. Rayford W. Logan and Michael R. Winston. New York: W. W. Norton, 1982.

Walker, Juliet E. K. *The History of Black Business in America: Capitalism, Race, Entrepreneurship*. New York: Macmillan Library Reference USA, 1998.

Washington, Booker T. *The Negro in Business*. Boston: Hertel, Jenkins and Co., 1907.

Work, Monroe N. *Negro Yearbook and Annual Encyclopedia of the Negro*. Tuskegee, AL: Negro Year Book Co., 1913.

*Frederick D. Smith*

# Jesse Binga (1865–1950), Banker, Real Estate Broker

Jesse Binga was born in Detroit, Michigan, on April 10, 1865, the son of Robert Binga Jr. and Adelphia Powers, the youngest of ten children. (Reflecting the paucity of original source material, his parents' names are variously given.) He established himself in Chicago in 1893. His business success during the few years was so great that he was able to open the first private bank owned by an African American in the North in 1908. In January 1921, he established the Binga State Bank, a chartered bank that he continued to run almost as his own private bank. In so doing, he became one of the contemporary stars among black entrepreneurs. The bank prospered during the boom years of the 1920s but failed in 1930. Though the failure was due in part to the economic downturn, Binga was convicted of embezzlement in 1933. He began his ten-year prison sentence in 1935 but was released in 1938. He never recovered his affluence and spent the remaining twelve years of his life working as a janitor.

Binga's education ended after two years of high school; he took up his father's profession of barbering. From his mother, for whom he collected rents, he had an initiation in real estate. In 1885 he set out on eight years of wandering that took him to Missouri, Minnesota, Montana, Washington State, California, and Utah. He supported himself primarily by barbering but was also involved in land dealing. It is uncertain whether his efforts meant that he brought to Chicago capital to start his business activities or merely freedom from outstanding debt.

Reports of his early activities in Chicago are varied: He ran a fruit stand; he peddled coal oil in the streets; he worked as a shoe shine boy. All emphasize his humble beginnings. Binga himself claimed he had only $10 in pocket when he opened a real estate office at 331 South State Street in 1886 or 1898, the start of a very successful business career.

The growing numbers of blacks in Chicago contributed to a real estate boom in the black community, and early purchases placed Binga in a very favorable position to profit when black migration numbers took a spectacular upward turn around 1915. Segregation limited the availability of housing while ensuring a high rate of return on rental property. Binga became proficient in "block busting," that is, buying property in a block, renting to blacks, and buying up the remaining property at distress rates from fleeing whites. Thus his reputation had a dual aspect: He was admired for making housing available and becoming rich in the process, while he was also perceived as a hard-dealing, rapacious landlord as well as an imperious and mean person.

Binga was responsible for making State Street a center of the black South Side by moving tenants into a seven-story building in 1905, a move that accelerated white flight, and the street became a center of his real estate activity and other business. He is credited with extending the area of black occupation from South State Street toward the lake. His first bank, a private one, was established on State Street in 1908, and his riches and prominence grew. His business success made him a special target of white hostility, especially when he moved into a home in a previously all-white neighborhood. The home was bombed five times between 1917 and 1921.

Binga married Eudora Johnson in 1912. The marriage seems to have produced two children. There is an as yet unverified claim that there was a second marriage. In any case, Eudora Johnson was the sister of John "Mushmouth" Johnson, a notable numbers king, and in 1906 had inherited a fortune said to be $200,000 from her father. It is claimed that Binga entered this marriage for monetary reasons since the bride was no longer young and allegedly far from attractive. On the other hand, the marriage brought him social prestige, as there was little prejudice against the source of his wife's family's wealth. In fact, Binga brushed aside complaints in 1921 that one of his bank vice presidents, Charles Jackson, was both brother of noted numbers king Dan Jackson and a prominent operator himself. Both Eudora and Jesse Binga became active philanthropists. As socialites, they held annual twilight Christmas parties that were notable social events.

Binga was a founder of the Associated Business Club, an affiliate of the **National Negro Business League**. By the mid-1920s, in his real estate operations Binga owned some 1,200 leaseholds, and his bank had a capital and surplus of $235,000, with $1,153,000 in deposits. In October 1924, the bank moved to a new building, purportedly the first real bank building built by an African American.

In addition to his bank holdings, Binga was the largest real estate holder on South State Street below 12th Street. State Street began to deteriorate as the business center of the black community shifted southward, however, and the construction in 1929 of a major seven-story building and ballroom, the Binga Arcade, did not arrest the downturn. As the real estate market declined with the onset of the Great Depression, an overreliance on real estate mortgages proved very harmful to the fiscal health of the bank. The failure of the Binga State Bank in 1930 wiped out Binga's personal fortune of $400,000, as well as the savings of many depositors. The bank ended up with an uncovered deficit of $500,000.

Investigation of the bank failure by the banking examiner led to criminal charges. There is little doubt that some of the bank's activities were illegal as well as imprudent. For example, $267,612 in loans to Binga and his ventures has been approved on his sole responsibility, and the bank's largest block of securities, shares in the Binga Safe Deposit Company, were worthless. Binga's own insistence on remaining bank president, over the wishes of the board of directors, hindered efforts to save the enterprise.

Accused of embezzlement, Binga escaped conviction in his first trial in 1932 but was convicted of embezzling $22,000 in 1933. Appeals meant that he did not begin serving a ten-year prison sentence until 1935.

Binga still had enough support in the community for the organization of a petition drive to secure his freedom. Many people viewed him a victim of white racism, overlooking his illegal activities. Freed in 1938, when he was seventy-three, he could not reestablish himself and spent the remainder of his life in near poverty, earning $15 a week as custodian of St. Anselm's Catholic Church. Soon evicted from his home, he found shelter in the home of his nephew. His death there on June 13, 1950, is attributed to a fall on the stairs. He was buried in Oakwood Cemetery.

*See also*: Black Banks: Their Beginning; Real Estate Industry

**Sources**

Cantey, Inez V. "Jesse Binga, the Story of a Life." *Crisis* 34 (December 1927): 329, 350–352.

Harris, Abram J. *The Negro as Capitalist: A Study of Banking and Business among American Negroes.* 1936. New York: Negro Universities Press, 1969.

Ingham, John N. "Jesse Binga." *American National Biography.* Ed. John A. Garraty and Mark C. Carnes. New York: Oxford University Press, 1999.

Ingham, John N., and Lynne B. Feldman. *African-American Business Leaders: A Biographical Dictionary.* Westport, CT: Greenwood Press, 1994.

Osthaus, Carl R. "Jesse Binga." *Dictionary of American Negro Biography.* Ed. Rayford W. Logan and Michael R. Winston. New York: W. W. Norton, 1982.

———. "The Rise and Fall of Jesse Binga." *Journal of Negro History* 58 (January 1973): 39–60.

Smith, Jessie Carney, ed. "Jesse Binga." *Notable Black American Men.* Vol. 2. Detroit: Gale Research, 1999.

*Robert L. Johns*

# Black Banks: Their Beginning

In Reconstruction America some attempts were made to elevate former slaves into middle-class citizen. One way to achieve this was to help them develop concepts of industry and thrift by providing an economic institution that would facilitate this goal. The establishment of a savings institution for black soldiers was followed by one for black citizens. The venture worked well for the solders but not for the ex-slaves. The Freedman's Savings Bank and Trust Company, also known as the Freedman's Bank, was founded to encourage freedmen to save and to promote economic enterprise. It grew phenomenally but later failed; its demise left a legacy of suspicion and distrust among the very people that it has been established to serve. After that, private banks were established, but for the most part, the operation of these early financial institutions was short-lived.

The first known black banks in the United States were established during the Civil War. As soldiers often mishandled their money, Union officials established an allotment system to allow deductions from the soldiers' pay to be sent to relatives or to white banks. This worked well in some instances, but few states made this provision. Black soldiers' distrusted white officials as well as white banks and wanted more than an allotment system to help them to save money. Thus, on August 27, 1864, General Rufus Saxton announced in Beaufort, South Carolina, the establishment of the Beaufort Military Savings Bank, later known as the South Carolina Freedman's Savings Bank. In fall 1864 General Benjamin Butler established a bank in Norfolk, and in mid-1865 General Nathaniel Banks established the Free Labor Bank in New Orleans. The latter bank served black soldiers as well as freedmen from the plantations that the government had seized. The immediate success of these experimental military banks led blacks and their sympathizers to expand the focus of the black financial institutions and make it possible for all newly freed slaves to save the money that they made.

On January 27, 1865, while the Civil War was still in progress, twenty-two businessmen, philanthropists, and humanitarians from New York met to consider founding a savings institution for black soldiers. Abolitionist, teacher, and minister John W. Alford summoned the meeting; he had seen firsthand the difficulties that black soldiers had in handling the money they received as pay and bounty. He also knew about the experimental banks and their success.

The men sent Alford and Reverend George Whipple of the American Missionary Association to Washington, D.C. to seek congressional approval for a national rather than a state or local institution. Senator Charles Sumner presented a bill before the U.S. Senate on March 2, 1865, to establish additional banks for the emancipated slaves. This would help in the economic adjustment of the freedmen. On March 3, 1865, President Abraham Lincoln signed a law establishing the Freedman's Savings Bank and Trust Company. Section V of the Act of Incorporation provided for deposits "by or on behalf of persons" previously enslaved in the United States or their descendants. Two-thirds of the funds were to be invested in stocks, bonds, treasury notes, or other U.S. securities. The nonprofit concern was a simple mutual savings bank for blacks. The fifty trustees on the board were almost all antislavery sympathizers or abolitionists; they were leading businessmen, politicians, philanthropists, bankers, railroad presidents, lawyers, and so on, including people like Levi Coffin, a supporter of the Underground Railroad. All served without salary and without giving any security of trust. By 1867 several blacks were elected to the board, and by 1873 other blacks were added, among them prominent figures such as physician Alexander T. Augusta, businessman William H. A. Wormley, and politician and lawyer John Mercer Langston.

The bank, headquartered in New York, opened on April 4; later, the headquarters were moved to Washington, D.C. Soon after the bank's founding, branches were opened in Norfolk (June 1865), Washington (July 11, 1865), and Richmond (late June 1865). Educator William J. Wilson was named cashier at the Washington branch, becoming the first of twenty-one or more blacks that would hold that title. Later branches were opened in Louisville, New Orleans, Nashville, Memphis, and Vicksburg. So rapid was the spread that, by 1872, thirty-four branches had been set up; with the exception of offices in New York City and Philadelphia, they were all in the South. The banks were deliberately set up in cities where large concentrations of blacks lived. Jacksonville, then a small town, was the exception, but black soldiers in that area soon received bounty and back pay and needed access to a bank. Branches of the Freedman's banks were established in sixteen states and in the District of Columbia as follows:

| | | |
|---|---|---|
| Alexandria, Louisiana | Little Rock, Arkansas | Norfolk, Virginia |
| Atlanta, Georgia | Louisville, Kentucky | Philadelphia, |
| Augusta, Georgia | Lynchburg, Virginia | Pennsylvania |
| Baltimore, Maryland | Macon, Georgia | Raleigh, North Carolina |
| Beaufort, South Carolina | Memphis, Tennessee | Richmond, Virginia |
| Charleston, South | Mobile, Alabama | Savannah, Georgia |
| Carolina | Montgomery, Alabama | Shreveport, Louisiana |
| Chattanooga, Tennessee | Natchez, Mississippi | St. Louis, Missouri |
| Columbus, Mississippi | New Bern, North | Tallahassee, Florida |
| Columbia, Tennessee | Carolina | Vicksburg, Mississippi |
| Huntsville, Alabama | New Orleans, Louisiana | Washington, D.C. |
| Jacksonville, Florida | New York, New York | Wilmington, |
| Lexington, Kentucky | Philadelphia, Pennsylvania | North Carolina |

The charter was amended in 1870 to allow for one-half of the funds to be invested at the discretion of the trustees. Further, that investment was restricted to those bonds and notes that were secured by real estate mortgage. The amendment jeopardized the banks' security by allowing injudicious speculation. During the short period of its existence, the bank was in deep financial trouble. The reasons for the bank's impending failure were evident in its policies and practices. At first the staff was almost all white; then gradually blacks were hired, but they came as tellers, clerks, and lower-level supervisors. The control, however, was mainly by white men. Regardless of their race, some, though not all, of the staff were incompetent, and book-keeping practices were faulty. Improper loans were also made as result of political pressure. Such pressure led to bad loans by white banks being unloaded on the Freedman's Bank.

In 1873 the collapse of the value of railroad securities led to the collapse of a major New York bank, which set off a panic. While many failures occurred during the crisis, the failure of the Freedman's Bank was attributed to the lapses of black managers rather than those of the general financial situation.

Noted black orator and statesman **Frederick Douglass**, well unaware of the bank's difficulties or those of other financial institutions, was named president of the bank in March 1874. The trustees expected him to lift it from its difficulties and to restore its image in the black community and the community's faith in it. Blacks were given more power when they were added to the branches as members of boards of trustees and advisory councils. Most board members who attended meetings of the bank—now based in Washington—were black, some of whom took responsibility for the bank and tried to save it. Some sources suggest that white trustees deserted the "sinking ship." When Douglass realized that the bank was at risk, he used some of his funds to try to save it. He tried to assure the branches, whose depositors were alarmed over the bank's crisis, that there was no reason for their uneasiness. He was unsuccessful in his appeal to the Senate Finance Committee for more money for the bank. Congress placed the institution in liquidation as a means of saving it, but by now the public and officials had lost complete confidence in its ability to function.

When the bank officially closed on July 2, 1874—owing $2,993,790 on 61,144 accounts—some blamed Douglass, but many other black leaders, blameless or not, were held responsible as well. The public never censured those who actually benefited from the bank. Much of the $57 million that individual blacks as well as black organizations deposited in the bank during its existence was lost. The collapse of the bank dealt a serious setback to the economic development of the black community and led to a serious lost of faith in savings banks. According to William S. McFeely, the bank could have been rescued. He wrote, "A government flexible enough to support the financing of a vast railroad system," as the federal government did, "could have found a way to supply the capital needed to match the amount owed depositors." Since it did not, it allowed the bank that it founded to encourage savings and economic enterprise to leave a sad legacy—a loss of faith in savings institutions on the part of blacks.

## PRIVATE BANKS FOUNDED

The black banking business did not end with the closing of the Freedman's Bank. By 1888, several private black banks were established. The first of these was the True Reformers' Bank of Richmond, chartered on March 2, 1888, and opened for business on April 3, 1889. In 1910, the bank failed and

## Savings Bank of the Grand Fountain, United Order of True Reformers, of Virginia

*Charter*

1. Be it enacted by the General Assembly of Virginia, That W. W. Browne, Allen J. Harris, W. P. Burrell, R. F. Robinson, Eliza Allen, E. Monroe, M. A. Berry, C. S. Lucas, H. L. Minnus, P. S. Lindsay and S. W. Sutton, together with such other persons as they may hereafter associate with them be, and they are hereby, constituted a body politic and corporate by the name and style of the Savings Bank of the Grand Fountain, United Order of True Reformers, of Virginia, and by that name and style are hereby invested with all the rights and privileges conferred on banks of discount and deposit of this State by charter 59 of the Code of Virginia, 1873, and not inconsistent with the provisions of this act.

2. The capital stock of the said corporation shall not be less than ten thousand dollars, in shares of five dollars each, which may be increased from time to time to a sum of not exceeding one hundred thousand dollars; provided said bank shall not transact any business under this act until twenty per cent of the minimum shall have been paid up. The said bank shall be located in the city of Richmond, State of Virginia; the officers of said bank shall consist of a President, Vice-President, Cashier and Assistant Cashier (if necessary), and such other clerks and messengers as may be necessary to conduct the business of the same.

3. The Board of Directors elected by the Grand Fountain, United Order of True Reformers, shall constitute the Board of Directors of said Bank; they shall continue in office until the first meeting of the members; at such first meeting, and at every annual meeting thereafter, directors shall be elected, who may be removed by the Grand Fountain, United Order of True Reformers, in general meeting; but unless so removed, shall continue in office until their successors shall be duly elected and qualified. The day for the first meeting of the members shall be prescribed by the by-laws; provided that number shall not be less than five; by-laws may also provide for calling meetings of the members, and any meetings may adjourn from time to time.

Advertisement showing the resources and liabilities of the Alabama Penny Savings Bank in Birmingham, October 30, 1911. *Source: Monroe N. Work, Negro Year Book and Annual Encyclopedia of the Negro, 1912. Tuskegee, AL: Tuskegee Institute, 1912, p. 6.*

4. The Board of Directors shall elect one of their body President and Vice-President, and may fill any vacancy occurring in the Board unless it be by removal, in which case the members may fill the same in general meeting. The said Board shall appoint to hold office during its pleasure, the officers and agents of said Bank, prescribe their compensation, and take from them bonds with such security as it may deem fit.

5. The said Bank may acquire such real estate as may be requisite for the convenient transaction of its business, and such as may be bona fide mortgaged to it by way of security, or conveyed to it for satisfaction of debts contracted in the course of its dealing or purchased at sale upon judgment against persons indebted to it.

6. Said Bank may receive on deposit and grant certificates therefore, and may levy, sell and negotiate coin, bank notes, foreign and domestic bills of exchange and negotiable notes in and out of this State. It may loan money on personal and real security, and receive interest in advance; may guarantee the payment of notes, bonds, bills of exchange, or other evidence of debt, and may receive for safekeeping gold and silver plate, diamonds, jewelry and other valuables, and charge reasonable compensation therefor. The money received on deposit by said Bank, and other funds of the same, may be invested in or loaned on real security, or be used in purchasing or discounting bonds, bills, notes or other paper.

7. The object of this corporation is to provide a depository for the Grand and Subordinate Fountains of the United Order of True Reformers, a benevolent institution incorporated for such purposes by the Circuit Court of the State of Virginia.

8. All acts and parts of acts inconsistent with this act are hereby repealed.

9. This act shall be in force from its passage.

*Notes*: This bank, sometimes referred to as the nation's first privately owned black bank, received its charter on March 2, 1888, but opened for business on April 3, 1889. The Capitol Savings Bank of Washington, D.C. opened on October 17, 1888, and thus was the nation's first black-owned bank in operation.

*Source*: J. H. Harmon Jr., Arnett G. Lindsay, and Carter G. Woodson, *The Negro as Businessman* (Washington, DC: Association for the Study of Negro Life and History, Inc., 1919. Reprint, College Park, MD: McGrath, 1929), 58–60.

**Table 2.** Banks Established by Region, 1900–1975

| Area | Total Number of Banks in 1975 | *Period Established* | | | |
|---|---|---|---|---|---|
| | | 1900–1939 | 1940–1959 | 1960–1969 | 1970–1975 |
| United States | 45 | 8 | 2 | 11 | 24 |
| South | 19 | 8 | 1 | 2 | 8 |
| North | 21 | — | 1 | 6 | 14 |
| Northeast | 4 | — | — | 2 | 2 |
| North Central | 17 | — | 1 | 4 | 12 |
| West | 5 | — | — | 3 | 2 |

*Notes*: "—" Represents zero. Figures exclude black-owned banks that may have been established at an earlier time but were no longer in existence in 1975.

*Sources*: U.S. Department of Commerce, Bureau of the Census, "Black-Owned Banks by Period Established and Region: 1900–1939 to 1970–1975," *The Social and Economic Status of the Black Population in the United States: A Historical View, 1790–1978* (Washington, DC: GPO), 79; "Black Banks: An Overview," *Black Enterprise* 7 (June 1977): 92–95; 185.

**Table 3.** Black Banks in the United States by State, 1912

| State | Name of Bank | City |
|-------|-------------|------|
| **Alabama** | Alabama Penny Savings Loan Co. | Birmingham |
| | Alabama Savings Bank | Selma |
| | Anniston Penny Savings Bank | Anniston |
| | Montgomery Penny Savings Bank | Montgomery |
| | People's Investment and Savings Bank | Birmingham |
| | Prudent Savings Bank | Birmingham |
| | Safety Banking and Realty Company | Mobile |
| | Tuskegee Institute Savings Department | Tuskegee Institute |
| **Arkansas** | Penny Savings Bank | Edmondson |
| **Florida** | Afro-American Insurance Company | Jacksonville |
| | Capital Trust and Investment Company | Jacksonville |
| | National Mercantile Realty and Improvement Company | Jacksonville |
| | Progress Savings Bank | Key West |
| **Georgia** | Atlanta State Savings Bank | Atlanta |
| | Wage Earners Loan and Investment Company | Savannah |
| **Illinois** | Enterprise Savings Bank | Springfield |
| | Jesse Binga Bank | Chicago |
| **Kentucky** | People's Savings Bank and Trust Company | Hopkinsville |
| **Maryland** | Baltimore Penny Savings Bank | Baltimore |
| | Houston Savings Bank | Salisbury |
| **Massachusetts** | Eureka Co-operative Bank | Boston |
| **Mississippi** | American Trust and Savings Bank | Jackson |
| | Bank of Mound Bayou | Mound Bayou |
| | Bluff City Savings Bank | Natchez |
| | Delta Penny Savings Bank | Indianola |
| | Delta Savings Bank | Greenville |
| | Lincoln Savings Bank | Vicksburg |
| | Penny Savings Bank | Columbus |
| | People's Home Savings Bank | Shaw |
| | People's Penny Savings Bank | Yazoo City |
| | Southern Bank | Jackson |
| | Union Savings Bank | Vicksburg |
| **North Carolina** | Dime Bank | Kingston |
| | Forsythe Savings and Trust Company | Winston-Salem |
| | Holloway, Borden, Hicks & Company, Bankers | Kinston |
| | Isaac Smith Trust Company | Newbern |
| | Mechanics' and Farmers' Bank | Durham |
| | Mutual Aid and Banking Company | Newbern |

(*continued*)

Table 3. (continued)

| State | Name of Bank | City |
| --- | --- | --- |
| **Oklahoma** | Boley Bank and Trust Company | Boley |
| | Farmers' and Merchants' Bank | Boley |
| | People's Bank and Trust Company | Muskogee |
| **Pennsylvania** | People's Savings Bank | Philadelphia |
| **Tennessee** | Fraternal Savings Bank and Trust Company | Memphis |
| | One Cent Savings Bank | Nashville |
| | People's Savings Bank and Trust Company | Nashville |
| | Solvent Savings Bank and Trust Company | Memphis |
| **Texas** | Farmers' & Citizens' Savings Bank | Palestine |
| | Farmers' Improvement Bank | Waco |
| | Orgen Savings Bank of Dallas | Houston |
| | Penny Savings Bank of Dallas | Dallas |
| | Provident Bank and Trust Company | Fort Worth |
| | Farmers' and Mechanics' Bank | Tyler |
| **Virginia** | Brickhouse Savings Bank | Hare Valley Exmore, R.D. |
| | Brown Savings Bank | Norfolk |
| | Crown Savings Bank | Newport News |
| | Sons & Daughters of Peace Penny, Nickel & Dime Savings Bank | Newport News |
| | American Home & Missionary Banking Association | Courtland |
| | Mechanics Savings Bank | Richmond |
| | Nickel Savings Bank | Richmond |
| | Peoples' Dime Savings Bank Trust Company | Staunton |
| | Southern One Cent Savings Bank | Waynesboro |
| | St. Luke's Savings Bank | Richmond |
| | Star of Zion Banking and Loan Association | Salem |
| | Sussex-Surrey Savings Bank | Courtland |

*Source*: Published in Monroe N. Work, *Negro Year Book and Annual Encyclopedia of the Negro, 1912* (Tuskegee, AL: Tuskegee Institute, 1912).

was closed. In 1888 as well, the Capital Savings Bank of Washington, D.C. was founded. It opened for business on October 17 but failed about 1904. Again in the 1880s, a short-lived private black bank opened—the Mutual Bank and Trust Company of Chattanooga. It closed in 1893. On October 15, 1890, the Alabama Penny Savings Bank opened in Birmingham. Black banks experienced the ebb and flow of economic development and by 1918 there were seventy-two black banks. (For a snapshot of the post–Civil War banking industry, see Tables 2 through 9.) Although most were in the Southern states, Illinois, Indiana, Maryland, Ohio, Pennsylvania, West

**Table 4.** Banking Institutions: Characteristics, 1939, 1940

| | Deposits | | Capital | | Surplus and Undivided Profits | |
|---|---|---|---|---|---|---|
| | Dec. 30, 1939 | Dec. 31, 1940 | Dec. 30, 1939 | Dec. 31, 1940 | Dec. 30, 1939 | Dec. 31, 1940 |
| Citizens and Southern Bank and Trust Company Philadelphia, PA | $585,000 | $687,607 | $125,000 | $125,000 | $5,000 | $16,572[1] |
| Citizens Savings Bank and Trust Company Nashville, TN | 207,000 | 237,655 | 60,000 | 60,000 | 6,000 | 5,831 |
| Citizens Trust Company Atlanta, GA | 558,000 | 631,180 | 72,500 | 72,250 | 12,500 | 14,820 |
| Consolidated Bank and Trust Company Richmond, VA | 867,000 | 941,922 | 80,000 | 80,000 | 64,000 | 67,606 |
| Crown Savings Bank Newport News, VA | 467,000 | 606,202 | 36,750 | 36,250 | 14,250 | 21,114[1] |
| Danville Savings Bank and Trust Company Danville, VA | 229,300 | 289,964 | 34,700 | 34,600 | 23,000 | 30,517 |
| Farmers State Bank Boley, OK | 40,000 | 91,384 | 15,000 | 15,000 | 5,000 | 4,825 |
| Fraternal Bank and Trust Company Fort Worth, TX | 377,580 | 411,285 | 15,420 | 15,420 | 3,000 | 2,978[2] |
| Industrial Bank of Washington Washington, DC | 817,000 | 1,104,296 | 50,000 | 50,000 | 42,000 | 54,091 |
| Mechanics and Farmers Bank Durham, NC | 1,016,000 | 1,063,257 | 214,000 | 210,000 | 36,000 | 41,664 |
| Tuskegee Institute Savings Bank Tuskegee, AL | 169,000 | 149,787 | 25,000 | 25,000 | 25,000[2] | 14,067 |
| Victory Savings Bank Columbia, SC | 35,000 | 54,095 | 14,612 | 14,612 | 3,388 | 3,236 |

[1]Reserve and undivided profits together.
[2]Surplus only.

*Source:* Florence Murray, ed., *The Negro Handbook, 1942* (New York: Wendell Malliet, 1942), 13.

**Table 5.** Banking Institutions: Characteristics, 1947

| Bank and President | Total Deposits | Capital | Total Assets | Value of Bank Premises Owned |
|---|---|---|---|---|
| Citizens Trust Company<br>Atlanta, GA<br>Lorimer D. Milton | $3,793,718 | $100,000 | $4,009,666 | $53,778 |
| Citizens Savings Bank and Trust Company<br>Nashville, TN<br>Henry A. Boyd | 1,436,314 | 80,000 | 1,554,815 | 8,420 |
| Citizens & Southern Bank and<br>Trust Company<br>Philadelphia, PA<br>Emanuel C. Wright | 2,812,136 | 125,000 | 2,978,502 | 39,500 |
| Industrial Bank of Washington<br>Washington, DC<br>Jesse H. Mitchell | 5,365,110 | 100,000 | 5,670,385 | 50,000 |
| Danville Savings Bank and Trust Company<br>Danville, VA<br>Irvin C. Taylor | 1,096,389 | 50,000 | 1,294,453 | 50,000 |
| Mechanics and Farmers Bank<br>Durham, NC<br>C. C. Spaulding | 5,048,732 | 339,559 | 5,408,303 | 14,460 |
| Farmers State Bank<br>Boley, OK<br>Forest Anderson | 157,408 | 15,000 | 179,279 | 5,000 |
| Consolidated Bank and Trust Company<br>Richmond, VA<br>Emmett C. Burke | 3,478,404 | 80,000 | 3,706,562 | 50,000 |
| Crown Savings Bank<br>Newport News, VA<br>W. P. Dickerson | 2,374,219 | 50,000 | 2,514,036 | 22,800 |
| Fraternal Bank and Trust Company<br>Fort Worth, TX<br>W. C. McDonald | 1,024,041 | 15,720 | 1,068,277 | 4,572 |
| Victory Savings Bank<br>Columbia, SC<br>E. A. Adams | 901,948 | 15,000 | 930,943 | — |
| Tri-State Bank[1]<br>Memphis, TN<br>Dr. J. E. Walker | 1,083,419 | 200,000 | 1,322,217 | — |
| Douglass State Bank[1]<br>Kansas City, KS<br>H. W. Ewing | 302,545 | 125,000 | 458,561 | 58,831 |
| Carver Savings Bank[1]<br>Savannah, GA<br>L. B. Toomer | 119,775 | 100,000 | 239,594 | 2,000 |

[1]Data supplied by the Department of Commerce.
*Note*: From bank statements and U.S. Department of Commerce.

*Source*: Florence Murray, ed., *The Negro Handbook, 1949* (New York: Macmillan, 1949), 200.

**Table 6.** Banks in the United States, 1950

Fourteen banks owned and operated by blacks in 1950 had combined resources of approximately 35,000,000. At the end of the year they were serving approximately 110,000 depositors. At their 1950 meeting, the National Bankers Association stressed the problems of rising operating costs and gave special consideration to the limited sources available to blacks in business and the assistance which might be forthcoming from black banking institutions.

*Source*: Jessie P. Guzman, ed., *Negro Year Book: A Review of Events Affecting Negro Life, 1941–1946* (Tuskegee, AL: Department of Records and Research, Tuskegee Institute, 1947), 135.

**Table 7.** Building and Loan Association, 1899

| State | Number of Institutions |
| --- | --- |
| Philadelphia, PA | 3 |
| Wilmington, NC | 2 |
| Anderson, SC | 1 |
| Augusta, GA | 1 |
| Hampton, VA | 1 |
| Ocala, FL | 1 |
| Little Rock, AR | 1 |
| Portsmouth, VA | 1 |
| Sacramento, CA | 1 |
| Washington, DC | 1 |
| **Total** | **13** |

*Notes*: In 1899 a number of brokers and money-lending institutions were established, especially in cities like Washington, DC, where a large black salaried class lived. This group included building and loan associations.

*Source*: W.E.B. Du Bois, ed., *The Negro in Business* (Atlanta, GA: Atlanta University Press, 1899), 13. Arranged by the editors.

Virginia, and the District of Columbia had black banks as well. The banking industry was by this time plagued with larceny and ineptness, yet black banks began with limited capital, poor loan practices, and some misappropriation of funds—practices that almost ensure that they would be short-lived.

*See also*: Black Business Development and the Federal Government

**Sources**

Franklin, John Hope. *From Slavery to Freedom*. 6th ed. New York: Knopf, 1988.

McFeely, William S. *Frederick Douglass*. New York: Norton, 1991.

*Negro Year Book and Annual Encyclopedia of the Negro*. Tuskegee, AL: Negro Year Book Co., 1913.

*Negro Year Book, 1918–1919. An Annual Encyclopedia of the Negro*. Tuskegee, AL: Negro Year Book Publishing Co., 1919.

Table 8. Private Equity Firms, 2003–2004

| This Year | Last Year | Company | Location | Chief Executive | Year Started | Staff | Capital under Management* | Number of Funds | Total Number of Portfolio Companies |
|---|---|---|---|---|---|---|---|---|---|
| 1 | 1 | Fairview Capital Partners Inc | Farmington, CT | Laurence C. Morse/JoAnn H. Price | 1994 | 16 | 1600 | 9 | 148 |
| 2 | 4 | Pharos Capital Group LLC | Dallas, TX | Dale LeFebvre | 1998 | 14 | 350 | 3 | 29 |
| 3 | 5 | SYNCOM | Silver Spring, MD | Herbert P. Wilkins Sr. | 1977 | 8 | 250 | 4 | 25 |
| 4 | 3 | Smith Whiley & Co. | Hartford, CT | Gwendolyn Smith Iloani | 1994 | 12 | 222 | 3 | 25 |
| 5 | 6 | Quetzal/JP Morgan Partners | New York, NY | Reginald J. Hollinger/Lauren M. Tyler | 2000 | 4 | 170 | 1 | 2 |
| 6 | 7 | Porvender Capital Group LLC | New York, NY | Frederick O. Terrell | 1997 | 5 | 145 | 2 | 3 |
| 7 | 8 | Opportunity Capital Partners | Fremont, CA | J. Peter Thompson | 1993 | 8 | 135 | 4 | 20 |
| 8 | 9 | ICV Capital Partners | New York, NY | Willie Woods | 1999 | 10 | 130 | 1 | 6 |
| 9 | 10 | Black Enterprise Greenwich Street Corporate Growth Management LLC | New York, NY | Ed A. Williams | 1998 | 8 | 91 | 1 | 8 |
| 10 | — | United Enterprise Fund LP | New York, NY | John O. Utendahl/Jeffery Keys/Daniel Dean | 2000 | 5 | 41 | 1 | 6 |

*In millions of dollars, to the nearest thousand, as of December 31, 2004. Prepared by B. E. Research. Reviewed by the certified public accounting firm Edwards & Co.

Source: Black Enterprise 35 (June 2005): 194. Published by permission.

**Table 9.** Top Investment Banks

| This Year | Last Year | Company | Location | Chief Executive | Year Started | Staff | Total Managed Issues* |
|---|---|---|---|---|---|---|---|
| 1 | 1 | The Williams Capital Group LP | New York, NY | Christopher J. Williams | 1994 | 58 | 122.315 |
| 2 | 2 | Blaylock & Partners **LP** | New York, NY | Ronald E. Blaylock | 1993 | 70 | 109.329 |
| 3 | 3 | Loop Capital Markets LLC | Chicago, IL | James Reynolds Jr. | 1997 | 80 | 87.753 |
| 4 | 5 | Utendahl Capital Partners LP | New York, NY | John Oscar Utendahl | 1992 | 29 | 69.299 |
| 5 | 4 | Siebert Branford Shank & Co LLC | Oakland, CA | Suzanne Shank | 1996 | 45 | 50.957 |
| 6 | 6 | MR Beal & Co. | New York, NY | Bernard B. Beal | 1988 | 35 | 45.325 |
| 7 | 7 | Jackson Securities LLC | Atlanta, GA | Reuben R. McDaniel III | 1987 | 30 | 36.425 |
| 8 | 9 | SBK-Brooks Investment Corp. | Cleveland, OH | Eric L. Small | 1993 | 20 | 14.500 |
| 9 | 10 | Rice Financial Products Co.** | New York, NY | J. Donald Rice Jr. | 1987 | 26 | 12.388 |
| 10 | — | Powell Capital Markets Inc. | Roseland, NJ | Arthur F. Powell | 1990 | 5 | 2.982 |

*In millions of dollars, to the nearest thousand, as of December 31, 2004. This is for all issues including municipal debt and equity transactions for the year ending December 31, 2004.

**Rice Financial Products Co. not measured by Thomson Financial.

*Note*: Reviewed by the certified public accounting firm Edwards & Co.

*Source*: Thomson Financial. Published in *Black Enterprise* 35 (June 2005): 194. Published by permission.

Osthaus, Carl R. *Freedmen, Philanthropy, and Fraud: A History of the Freedman's Savings Bank.* Urbana: University of Illinois Press, 1976.

*Jessie Carney Smith*

# Black Business Development and the Federal Government

Following the Civil War there was an emergence of black aspirations in business ownership. While the dreams of these Americans were strong, so was the government's desire to suppress and stifle these businesses. In fact, black business development in the twentieth century was greatly influenced by the federal government's hostile recall of the 1875 Civil Rights Act. For this reason, the beginning of black businesses following the Civil War was hindered greatly by rulings of the U.S. federal government as well as actions of individual state governments. While American history is well served to keep the trends and updates of business development in the twentieth century at the forefront of scholarship and historic documentation, the history of black business development is not a model of American democracy. Despite this, black business development persevered and can be viewed as a significant national business model impacting many spheres of American society. It is pertinent to examine the struggles of black businesses in order to explain trends in today's business world.

According to John W. Handy in *Encyclopedia of African American Business History*, the outcry of angry white southerners following the Civil War led to the 1896 U.S. Supreme Court ruling in *Plessy v. Ferguson*. This decision upheld legal segregation in states citing the doctrine that minorities were "separate but equal." In addition to this, several southern states excluded blacks from their state constitutions. Amid this turmoil, minority business development efforts were abandoned by the federal government. Instead, these businesses were forced to generate out of the struggles and hostility of the labor market at that time. While they did not have support of the mainstream business market, blacks became their own business owners and customers. This self-reliance established black business owners as entrepreneurs in the business world.

Throughout American history this self-reliance continued to be the basic structure for building these black businesses. Businesses begin as a family project, which usually extends to friends and members of the community, in which the minority entrepreneur has some association. The community-building approach then becomes twofold. People from the community are given opportunities to join the workforce, therefore they create better lifestyles for themselves and allow them to give back to the community. Strategically, changing the number of unemployed to employed is a winning approach for keeping the socioeconomic cycle of the economy well nurtured. According to Catherine Fitch and Samuel Myers in "Testing the Survivalist Entrepreneurship Model," business types most common for minority owners include barbers, beauticians, manicurists, proprietors, managers, restaurants, and officials of retail stores.

In order for black businesses to survive, it was essential for black business owners to pursue political and legal forces to help support their establishments. This change was brought about by the civil rights movement of the mid-1960s. The movement's greatest impact on black business was the inclusion of a new federal government mandate in the civil rights legislation. This legislation not only included minorities but also included them by supporting their small businesses. This is particularly important because at this time in U.S. history, the only type of black businesses left were those small businesses. The civil rights movement helped to reclaim the federal government support toward addressing civil disadvantages of minorities as effective participants in national business enterprises. These legal and political forces were not only the driving forces, but also were the only sources powerful enough to secure support for the equalization of the labor market.

Relying on budgetary and political support can either develop or destroy small business programs. While the federal government may have implemented these business models during the early twentieth century, the standards and funding are reviewed and, in most cases, programs have been cut, with every new presidential administration. Although various presidential administrations have attacked these programs, the number of SBA loans continues to rise as time passes. The *Statistical Abstract of the United States* reports that in 1990 the amount of loans given totaled $2.367 billion, and in 2003 the amount of loans given totaled $20.180 billion, which reveals a 28 percent increase within thirteen years (Table 10). Asian Americans received the highest amount of loans between 1990 and 2003, followed by Hispanic Americans, African Americans, and Native Americans respectively. Congress is constantly amending laws in an attempt to salvage as many of these minority programs as possible.

To this end, the U.S. Senate gave entrepreneurs hope that the future of fourteen programs, either cut back or terminated by the Bush administration's 2006 budget, have been supplemented by an additional $78 million for Small Business Administration (SBA) programs. This business program is vital for African American entrepreneurs who want to thrive and survive in corporate America; its legacy yields profitable outcomes for society at large. Having a diverse economy model helps to maximize balance and promotion of financial and work equity in mainstream America.

However, these programs do not come without their fair share of problems. Common drawbacks of such programs are availability of funding, business failures, and limitations in market choice. The funding is driven by the votes of legal administrative bodies, which is inflexible; however, the remaining two challenges have visible solutions. For example, some businesses cease to operate due to mergers and acquisition of larger industries, but this does not have to be the case. Technology may unlock the vault to victory over business failures and market choice limitations.

One of the largest challenges facing black business development is that technology has created an entirely different setup and workforce, along with new needs within the workforce. Major investments are being directed toward this current development, and it has opened up a new market that will truly affect opportunity for new applicants to explore nontraditional areas of entrepreneurship. Minority-owned firms and businesses need to capitalize on the increasing field of technology in order to stay afloat and expand the life of their role in the Small Business Administration.

The proliferation of information being published, by both scholarly statisticians and economists, coupled with government civil responsibilities to developing a diverse workforce, shows that the minority and small business programs seem to be a profound solution to giving back to society. The workforce is one of the most critical areas of all society, especially as America is labeled a "super" nation; the economy is one of the indicators that help a country to retain such a status. It would behoove the government to try and support the labor market to reflect the philosophy of our country,

Table 10. Small Business Administration Loans to Small Businesses, 1990–2003

| Minority Group | Number of Loans | | | | | Amount (millions of dollars) | | | | |
|---|---|---|---|---|---|---|---|---|---|---|
| | 1990 | 1995 | 2000 | 2002 | 2003 | 1990 | 1995 | 2000 | 2002 | 2003 |
| Total Minority Loans | 2,367 | 10,877 | 11,999 | 14,300 | 20,180 | 576 | 1,838 | 3,661 | 4,250 | 4,213 |
| Percent of all loans | 12.0 | 18.1 | 24.8 | 25.0 | 28.0 | (n.a.) | (n.a.) | (n.a.) | (n.a.) | (n.a.) |
| African American | 513 | 2,770 | 2,120 | 2,146 | 3,769 | 96 | 293 | 393 | 422 | 399 |
| Asian American | 1,075 | 3,767 | 5,838 | 7,249 | 9,505 | 317 | 945 | 2,397 | 2,810 | 2,755 |
| Hispanic American | 694 | 3,940 | 3,500 | 4,270 | 6,112 | 149 | 539 | 768 | 891 | 941 |
| Native American | 85 | 400 | 541 | 635 | 794 | 14 | 61 | 102 | 127 | 118 |

*Source*: U.S. Small Business Administration, Management Information Summary, unpublished data. Published in U.S. Department of Commerce, *Statistical Abstract of the United States: 2004–2005*, 124th ed. (Washington, DC: GPO, October 2004), 497.

which is growing in leaps and bounds in a more culturally populated society. Having business development models in place is the tool that is needed to add value and quality to the country's existence.

Alan Hughes in *Black Enterprise* suggests excellent Web sites for further exploration, including the Small Business Administration Web site, located at http://www.sba.gov/regions/states.html and the Federal Business Opportunities bureau, located at http://www.fedbizopps.gov. These two Web sites lead to portals of online information specifically about business development and federal government regulation.

In many resources used to compile information on business development in the twentieth century, minority businesses are viewed as one condensed concept, most often pertaining to specific ethnic groups, such as African Americans. However, there is very little literature to support and track the development of more specific minority business owners, including gender-based and the activities of women. If small businesses want to hold a key status in the economy and society, the activity of women business owners needs to be made more visible, whether it is minority women or majority women. According to the 1997 report from the U.S. Census Bureau 51 percent of stock interest, claims, and rights of business firms were held by women. Such success stories should bode well for the long-term survival of minority business models and programs.

*See also*: Retail Industry; Women and Business

**Sources**

Fitch, Catherine A., and Samuel L. Myers Jr. "Testing the Survivalist Entrepreneurship Model." *Social Science Quarterly* 81 (December 2000): 985.

Handy, J. W. "Business Development Twentieth Century." *Encyclopedia of African American Business History*. Ed. Juliet E. K. Walker. Westport, CT: Greenwood Press, 1999.

Hughes, Alan. "In Business with the U.S." *Black Enterprise* 33 (October 2002): 60.

Jones, Joyce. "Amendment Seeks $78M in SBA Loans." *Black Enterprise* 35 (June 2005): 48.

Knight, Kenneth E., and Terry Dorsey. "Capital Problems in Minority Business Development: A Critical Analysis." *American Economic Review* 66 (May 1976): 328.

Palmer, Glenn A., and Juanita Johnson-Bailey. "The Career Development of African Americans in Training and Organizational Development." *Human Resource Planning* 28 (March 2005): 11.

Rhodes, Colbert, and John S. Butler. "Understanding Self-Perceptions of Business Performance: An Examination of Black American Entrepreneurs." *Journal of Developmental Entrepreneurship* 9 (April 2004): 55.

U.S. Census Bureau. "Quick Facts." 1997. http://quickfacts.census.gov/qfd/meta/long_87078.htm.

———. *Statistical Abstract of the United States: 2004–2005*. 124th ed. Washington, DC: GPO, 2004.

Walker, Juliet E. K. "Business Development in the Twentieth Century." *Encyclopedia of African American Business History*. Ed. Juliet E. K. Walker. Westport, CT: Greenwood Press, 1999.

*Thura Mack*

# Black Business Development in Missouri

Missouri lives up to its "Show Me" state motto, when one considers the historical and contemporary legacy of African American business. From newspapers to millionaires to the first black automobile dealership to billion-dollar companies, African Americans in Missouri have a long and impressive history.

During the nineteenth century, African Americans used their ingenuity, business acumen, and entrepreneurship skills to carve out a slice of freedom in a world of slavery. Yet they did not forget about their enslaved brothers and sisters. They accumulated wealth not only for themselves but for the benefit of their families and community. In Missouri, Emily Fisher, Elizabeth Keckley, John Berry Meachum, Sam Shepherd, Alphia Minor Smith, and Hiram Young are just a few of those pioneers of enterprise.

In 1827, Sam Shepherd, a skilled craftsman, built the first log courthouse in Independence, Missouri. This building, now a museum, stands as a reminder of African American contributions to business and commerce on the western frontier. Emily Fisher was the first owner of a hotel in Independence. She also marketed a healing salve. Fisher's salve and fine boarding establishment were well known among frontier travelers. Hiram Young was originally enslaved and worked hard to purchase his freedom as well as the freedom of his wife and children. Young manufactured ox yokes used to outfit pioneers for the Santa Fe Trail. While he was never educated, Young was an astute businessman, and he employed black and white workers. Unfortunately, the Civil War disrupted Young's prosperous business, and he never recovered. Alphia Minor Smith moved to Missouri in the 1860s from Leavenworth, Kansas. Smith became the owner of Kansas City's first African American dressmaking shop. Furthermore, she passed her expertise on to her family members. Throughout the twentieth century, her grandson Julius Jones owned and operated a Kansas City barbershop and pool hall.

In St. Louis, Cyprian Clamorgan, a son of West Indian fur trader Jacques Clamorgan and a slave mother, was a part of the emerging black middle class with significant landholdings and business enterprises. Yet African Americans who earned their freedom like John Berry Meachum left a more visible imprint on the community. Meachum, born a slave in Virginia, was skilled in carpentry, cabinet, and barrel making. He earned money to buy his freedom by 1815. Meachum then opened his own business, married, then purchased his wife's freedom as well. In his barrel-making company, Meachum hired slaves with the expressed intent of having them purchase their freedom. More than twenty slaves were freed this way. In the 1850s when laws became more stringent on the African Americans, Meachum built a steamboat and outfitted it as a schoolhouse. His floating school fell under federal jurisdiction and circumvented Missouri laws that prevented African American education. One of his teachers, Elizabeth Keckley, became the "modiste" or personal dressmaker to First Lady Mary Todd Lincoln.

By the turn of the century, black businesses that embodied the self-help impulse included the V. J. Williams training school for maids, cooks, and housemen in Kansas City and the Hardwick Brothers Grocery in Springfield. In 1909, the brothers Watkins, Theron B., and John established the Watkins Brothers funeral home in Kansas City. The business is still family owned and operated today. Watkins was also a co-owner with Reuben S. Street of the Street Hotel. The Street Hotel included the Rose Room, noted for fine dining, and the Blue Room. The Blue Room was considered to be "Kansas City's favorite cocktail bar," featuring a colorful bartender named Kingfish. After laboring over four decades, by 1950, the Reuben S. Street business enterprises were valued at over $300,000. Besides Kansas City's Street Hotel, the Lincoln and Cadillac Hotels in Kansas City and the Booker T. Hotel in Jefferson City provided accommodations for African Americans in the age of Jim Crow.

African American businesses in the early twentieth century benefited from the unlikely foe of segregation. Jim Crow laws in housing contributed to self-contained neighborhoods where African American businesses and professionals catered to the economic needs of their communities. For example, Missouri's first black city of Kinloch, a St. Louis suburb, thrived under segregation and by the 1950s had over eighty black-owned businesses. However, it was the 18th and Vine district in Kansas City and the Ville in St. Louis that became famous.

The Ville originally, Elleardsville, was bordered by Taylor Avenue, St. Louis Avenue, Sarah Street, and Dr. Martin Luther King Drive. The area was originally owned by Charles M. Elleard, a horticulturalist. Elleard operated a conservatory and greenhouse that employed black workers. As the area grew, it was called Elleardsville. By the turn of the century, most residents referred to their neighborhood as the Ville. In Kansas City, African Americans had migrated there to build the Hannibal Bridge in the late 1860s, and other workers found employment in the meatpacking plants. Immigrant migration to other parts of the city allowed blacks to move south and east of downtown. The African American neighborhood encompassed 12th as a northern border, with 28th the southernmost point. Charlotte was the western boundary, and Brooklyn was the eastern boundary. The 18th and Vine district was the hub of economic activity and immortalized in the song "Piney Brown Blues" by music legend Big Joe Turner.

In both cities, the business districts had a plethora of services including taxis, drugstores, barbershops, hair salons, detective agencies, law offices, real estate companies, loan offices, shoe stores, clothing stores, medical and dental offices, insurance agencies, and grocery stores, but three cultural innovations in particular aided business and commerce: baseball, jazz, and barbecue. In St. Louis, Tom "Honest John" Turpin and his brother Charles owned the **Booker T. Washington** Theatre. From around 1912 until the 1930s, entertainers like Ethel Waters and Bessie Smith performed there. Their father's Rosebud Café had previously been the center of ragtime music in the 1890s. Homer "Jap" Eblon built and operated one of the most elaborate theatres in Kansas City. The Eblon Theatre located across the street from the Robert's automobile dealership featured a twelve-by-eighteen-foot silver screen draped with velour curtains. The Eblon was noted for its beautiful frontage on Vine Street including brick work fashioned by skilled African American masons. The theater was also outfitted with the lasted technology including the RCA talkies for "talking and singing pictures." In Kansas City, musicians like Count Basie, Julia Lee, Bennie Moten, Charlie Parker, Big Joe Turner, and Mary Lou Williams help to create the Kansas City style of jazz. This flowering of music also fueled the clubs and nightlife in the historic district. During the Great Depression, bands knew they could always come to Kansas City to get work.

In 1920, Andrew "Rube" Foster established the National Negro League. His visionary business venture led to the Kansas City Monarchs and the St. Louis Giants, later the St. Louis Stars. The Negro League teams were integral to the business and social life in the African American community. For example, Elnora's Café in Kansas City was open in the late hours to accommodate baseball players and jazz musicians. And it was not unusual for ministers to end church services early when the teams were in town.

Besides sports and music, innovations in cuisine were also important in Missouri business history. In 1907, entrepreneur Henry Perry opened the first barbecue restaurant in Kansas City and perhaps the nation. His business was the forerunner of the nationally recognized Arthur Bryant's. Located at 18th and Brooklyn, the establishment received international acclaim from a Calvin Twillin editorial in the *New Yorker*. It is not unusual for celebrities, sports figures, and even American presidents to visit Arthur Bryant's. In 1946, George W. Gates established Gate's old Kentuck BBQ renowned for its sauce. Later the name was changed to Gates BBQ and is equally famous for its quintessential greeting, "Hi, may I help you?"

## MISSOURI'S BLACK WOMEN MILLIONAIRES

During the first half of the twentieth century, Missouri boasted two African American female millionaires. In Kansas City, Sarah Rector had inherited her money as a teenager when her land allotments, as a part of the Creek Indian nation, struck oil in Oklahoma. In 1916, the Rector family relocated to Kansas City, where Sarah was known for her lavish lifestyle. Her mansion remains on 12th and Euclid Avenue. Rector was considered to be a "gracious hostess" entertaining such notables as Duke Ellington, Count Basie, Joe Louis, and Jack Johnson. Rector used her wealth to underwrite her husband's business activities. Kenneth Campbell operated a Hupmobile agency on 19th and Vine. Unfortunately, when her money dissipated, so did the marriage in the late 1920s.

**Annie Turnbo Malone** was a hair-care entrepreneur and philanthropist. Malone established the Poro Beauty College in 1917 in the heart of the St. Louis Ville. Unlike Rector who spent most of her fortune on cars, clothes, and jewelry, Malone was an ardent philanthropist. Her gift of $25,000 to Howard University was the largest gift at that time to an African American college from an African American donor. Malone employed over 200 workers who trained beauticians in the Poro method of hair care and cosmetics. They also instructed salespeople how to market her products. Malone's operations were global, with outlets in the Caribbean, Africa, and the Philippines. She also established a finance company that offered mortgages and business loans. In the 1930s, Malone moved her business to Chicago.

Next to Malone, the most important business leader of the period was Homer B. Roberts. A World War I veteran, Roberts opened the first automobile dealership in Kansas City's 18th and Vine district. Roberts, like Malone, was an innovator in advertising and property ownership. He made local headlines when he paid $70,000 for his two-story office building with seventy-foot frontage. Roberts Company Motor Mart boasted it was the "the only negro [sic] automobile sales room in America." Like Malone, Roberts moved to Chicago and continued his business endeavors with Kenneth Campbell, former husband of millionaire Sarah Rector.

While the civil rights era brought legal equality, desegregation and urban renewal signaled the decline and end of many African American businesses. Since the 1930s, the Stuart Parker Memorial Funeral home and the Warren Funeral Chapel had occupied the home of ragtime legend John William "Blind" Boone at 10 North Fourth Street in Columbia, Missouri. According to the City of Columbia, the Warren Funeral Chapel, with offices in Fulton and Mexico, is the only African American business to have survived the urban renewal in the city. However, the black power movements of the 1960s did encourage black economic development. In 1968, the Kansas City founded the Black Economic Union, a community development corporation. And across the state line, the Black Chamber of Commerce of Greater St. Louis was established in 2001.

African American newspapers have continued to thrive throughout the twentieth century. In 1919, Chester A. Franklin founded the *Kansas City Call*. The newspaper is still published today under the helm of Donna Stewart in its original location in the historic 18th and Vine district. In 2005, the *St. Louis Argus* celebrated its ninety-third birthday, making it the oldest surviving African American business in St. Louis. St. Louis is also home to one of America's wealthiest black-owned businesses. World Wide Technology, Inc., founded in 1990 by **David L. Steward**, is a leading systems integrator providing technology and supply chain solutions. It is the largest African American–owned business in the United States and only the second company to exceed $1 billion in revenues in a year. The company had 650 employees in 2003 and a total of $1.4 billion in revenue in 2004. In June 2000, the company ranked number 1 on the *Black Enterprise* 100, the annual listing of the largest African American–owned firms. Steward's book *Doing Business by the Good Book* (2004) is symbolic of Missouri's African American business history. He argues that serving others can be profitable, successful, and community affirming. John Berry Meachum, the slave who left a visible imprint on the community, would agree.

*See also*: Real Estate Industry; Retail Industry; Women and Business

**Sources**

Durst, Dennis L. "The Reverend John Berry Meachum (1789–1854) of St. Louis: Prophet and Entrepreneurial Educator in Historiographical Perspective." *North Star: A Journal of African American Religious History* 7 (Spring 2004): 1–24.

Gillis, Delia C. *Kansas City*. Chicago: Arcadia Publishing, 2005.

Kremer, Gary R., and Antonio F. Holland. *Missouri's Black Heritage*. Columbia: University of Missouri Press, 2003.

Reese, DeAnna J. "Domestic Drudges to Dazzling Divas: The Origins of African American Beauty Culture in St. Louis, Missouri, 1900–1930." *Women in Missouri History in Search of Power and Influence*. Ed. LeeAnn Whites, Mary C. Neth, and Gary R. Kremer. Columbia: University of Missouri Press, 2004.

Wright, John A., Sr. *Kinloch: Missouri's First Black City*. Chicago: Arcadia Publishing, 2000.

*Delia C. Gillis*

# Black Businesses in Large Cities: A History

One constant phenomenon in the black experience is the ability of African Americans to establish themselves in the business community of America. The African men and women transported to America beginning in the fifteenth century had been engaged in various business enterprises of their own. Once in America, they were relegated to a life of slave labor, which built economic wealth in mainstream America. Some slaves used their ingenuity and creativity to establish their own businesses, even though they seldom kept all of the monies earned and faced overwhelming racism, discrimination, and violence in the process. Slaves sometimes managed to save enough money to purchase the freedom of their family members. Free blacks in northern American cities not only engaged in self-employment, largely service-oriented enterprises, but also property ownership and real estate development as well. Sustained business ownership for blacks in America, however, was difficult at best and sometimes injurious because at the core of black business activity was the lack of capital to sustain themselves, and legislation was enacted to reinforce racism, segregation, and economic affliction. While several black-owned personal service enterprises were founded during the Reconstruction era, they were short-lived.

The post–Reconstruction years, namely, 1880 through the dawn of the twentieth century, introduced a new direction among black leadership and entrepreneurs and new ways for blacks to do business in America. **Booker T. Washington**'s theory of self-help and black uplift and W.E.B. Du Bois's theory of black cooperative business ventures were instrumental in the new direction for black enterprises (Table 11). For example, African Americans founded and patronized black-owned banks. They founded insurance companies and purchased insurance from black insurers. Black journalists founded the black press, a phenomenal, informative tool that heightened prospective levels of business in the African American community. As a result, black entrepreneurs armed with courage and determination forged ahead, adopting and revising strategic marketing practices in search of results that would improve and sustain the economic quality of their lives in America.

From the post–Reconstruction era through the mid-twentieth century, most African Americans founded their own business enterprises to serve black rather than white consumers. However, Supreme Court and executive rulings of the 1950s that rejected segregation, discrimination, and racism greatly impacted the direction of

REAL ESTATE AND BUSINESS

# MOUND BAYOU, MISSISSIPPI

## The most noted Negro Town in the United States.

FOUNDED IN 1887 BY ISAIAH T. MONTGOMERY.

Surrounded by a Negro farming community in which colored men own and control thirty thousand acres of land.

The Bank of Mound Bayou, John W. Frances, Pres., Chas. Banks, Cashier, is one of the largest and most successful in the South.

Good schools, Carnegie library, a newspaper, telephone and electric lights, all advantages of a modern country town.

The Mound Bayou Oil Mill, erected at a cost of nearly $100,000, has just been completed.

Mound Bayou is situated in the Yazoo Delta.

The richest strip of land in the United States.

It is surrounded by a large Negro population and is capable of unlimited expansion.

Here is a chance for a man with brains and vision.

For further information address:

CHARLES BANKS, or
ISAIAH T. MONTGOMERY.

Advertisement describing the surroundings and giving some of the business and living attractions of the Yazoo Delta town of Mound Bayou, Mississippi, an all-black town founded in 1887. *Source*: Monroe N. Work, *Negro Year Book and Annual Encyclopedia of the Negro, 1912*. Tuskegee, AL: Tuskegee Institute, 1912, p. 6.

their business ventures. On one hand, black-owned businesses welcomed the opportunity for new marketing avenues opened by the rulings. On the other hand, exclusivity in black sales and marketing amounted to irreparable self-inflicted wounds and those who survived used innovative approaches to maintain their market share and adopt new strategies appealing to both black and white consumers. Two events in the 1960s profoundly changed the economic climate for African Americans in this country: manifestation of the civil rights era and manifestation of the black power movement. As African Americans became members of corporate America and higher-level

**Table 11.** Businessmen of Seattle, Washington, 1899

| Kinds of Business | Years in Business | Capital Invested |
|---|---|---|
| Real estate | 5 | $10,000 |
| Stock broker | 3 | 2,500 |
| Hotel | 2 | 1,500 |
| Club house | 2 | 700 |
| Barber | 6 | 3,000 |
| Saloon | 2 | 1,000 |
| Barber | 3 | 500 |
| Restaurant | 4 | 900 |
| Restaurant | 9 | 1,000 |
| Newspaper | 6 | 2,000 |

*Source*: W.E.B. Du Bois, ed., *The Negro in Business* (Atlanta, GA: Atlanta University Press, 1899), 37.

federal government employees, they gained more disposable income and acquired new personal associates. This phenomenon opened the doors for more opportunities for more African Americans to participate in mainstream American economic activities.

Though the recession of the 1980s negatively affected the national economy and legislative initiatives adversely affected African Americans, some black businesspeople, again, strategically changed the direction of their business enterprises. At this point, African American businesspeople began to merge their businesses, expand, acquire new ones, joint ventures, syndicate their products, and form conglomerates on large scales. The last decade of the twentieth century proved to be important years for black businesses in the economic sense, largely due to some White House initiatives but mainly due to a shift in concentration to strategic political positioning by black business owners (Tables 12 through 14). Many black enterprises have become megamillion-dollar establishments in America despite lingering political, economic, and racial issues, and despite the capitalistic society in which Africans still participate very lightly by comparison, thus limiting maximum productivity and profitability.

This essay discusses black businesses in large cities as early as 1880 throughout the new millennium. Particularly, it points out the benefits of segregation to African American enterprises up to the mid-twentieth century. It

**Table 12.** Top Ten Employment Leaders

| Company | Location | Employees | Sales* | Employee to Sales Ratio |
|---|---|---|---|---|
| MV Transportation Inc. | Fairfield, CA | 7,981 | $271.863 | 1:34 |
| Manna Inc. | Louisville, KY | 6,250 | 185.000 | 1:30 |
| Barden Cos. Inc. | Detroit, MI | 4,055 | 372.000 | 1:92 |
| The Bartech Group Inc. | Livonia, MI | 3,400 | 195.000 | 1:57 |
| V & J Holding Cos. Inc. | Milwaukee, WI | 3,200 | 90.000 | 1:28 |
| Thompson Hospitality | Herndon, VA | 2,650 | 165.600 | 1:62 |
| H. J. Russell & Co. | Atlanta, GA | 1,907 | 304.241 | 1:160 |
| RS Information Systems Inc. | McLean, VA | 1,800 | 321.000 | 1:178 |
| Radio One Inc. | Lanham, MD | 1,750 | 363.982 | 1:208 |
| The Gourmet Cos. | Atlanta, GA | 1,700 | 167.000 | 1:98 |

*In millions of dollars as of December 31, 2004. Prepared by B. E. Research. Reviewed by the certified public accounting firm Edwards & Co.

*Source*: *Black Enterprise* 35 (June 2005): 108. Published by permission.

**Table 13.** Top Ten Growth Leaders

| Company | Location | 2004 Sales* | 2003 Sales* | Percentage Increase |
|---|---|---|---|---|
| Bridgewater Interiors LLC | Detroit, MI | $645.309 | $167.407 | 285.47 |
| Peebles Atlantic Development Corp. | Coral Gables, FL | 202.925 | 82.000 | 147.47 |
| TAG Holdings, LLC | Troy, MI | 103.00 | 57.000 | 80.70 |
| CAMAC International Inc. | Houston, TX | 987.00 | 573.347 | 72.15 |
| Southeast Fuels Inc. | Greensboro, NC | 55.884 | 34.238 | 63.22 |
| Industrial Inventory Solutions (IIS) | Cleveland, OH | 37.800 | 24.000 | 57.50 |
| Telecommunication Systems Inc. | Annapolis, MD | 142.685 | 92.100 | 54.92 |
| Workplace Integrators | Bingham Farms, MI | 81.000 | 55.000 | 47.27 |
| Q3 Industries | Columbus, OH | 47.000 | 32.000 | 46.88 |
| Logistics & Environmental Support Services (LESCO) | Huntsville, AL | 73.900 | 52.000 | 42.12 |

*In millions of dollars as of December 31, 2004. Prepared by B. E. Research. Reviewed by the certified public accounting firm Edwards & Co.

Source: *Black Enterprise* 35 (June 2005): 108. Published by permission.

describes the economic changes to black businesses brought on by the integration movement of the 1950s and strategic approaches used by those enterprises to stay in business. It continues in discussion by focusing on the ability of black-owned businesses to thrive amid constant changes in the economy, marketing styles, politics, and capitalism. Several businesses were selected for discussion to note that large black businesses do exist and to demonstrate examples of various principles African Americans use to be successful concerns in America. Many of the principles include cutbacks, downsizing, restructuring, micromanaging, acquisitions, expansion, syndication, technology, joint ventures, and conglomerates.

Prior to 1888, there were no black-owned and -operated banks in the United States. By 1912, sixty-four banks had been founded in large cities, and forty-seven of those were still operational. The first black-owned bank with no fraternal affiliation was the Capital Savings Bank of Washington, D.C., which opened in 1888. The Grand Fountain of the United Order of True Reformers Bank of Richmond, Virginia, was founded by W. W. Brown and chartered by the Virginia legislature in 1888. Contrary to the credentials held by most banks established during the time, True Reformers had no fraternal affiliation. The Grand Fountain collected insurance premiums and

**Table 14.** Top Twenty Industrial/Service Companies

| This Year | Last Year | Company | Location | Chief Executive | Year Started | Staff | Type of Business | Sales* |
|---|---|---|---|---|---|---|---|---|
| 1 | 1 | World Wide Technology, Inc. | St. Louis, MO | David Steward | 1990 | 620 | IT Systems integrator, supply chain services of IT products | 1,400.000 |
| 2 | 2 | CAMAC International, Inc. | Houston, TX | Kase Lawal | 1980 | 1300 | Crude oil and gas exploration, production, and trading | 987.000 |
| 3 | 22 | Bridgewater Interiors LLC | Detroit, MI | Ronald E. Hall | 1998 | 1100 | Car seat and overhead systems manufacturer | 645.309 |
| 4 | 3 | Act-1 Group | Torrance, CA | Janice Bryant Howroyd | 1978 | 300 | Staffing and professional services | 622.729 |
| 5 | 4 | Johnson Publishing Co. | Chicago, IL | Linda Johnson Rice/ John H. Johnson | 1942 | 1699 | Publishing, TV production, cosmetics | 498.224 |
| 6 | 5 | Philadelphia Coca-Cola Bottling Co. | Philadelphia, PA | J. Bruce Llewellyn | 1985 | 1900 | Bottling and distribution soft drinks | 450.000 |
| 7 | 10 | Converge | Peabody, MA | Dala LeFebvre/ Frank Cavallaro | 2002 | 283 | Distributor of semiconductors and computer products | 390.000 |
| 8 | 6 | Barden Cos. Inc. | Detroit, MI | Don H. Barden | 1981 | 4055 | Casino gaming, real estate development, and international trade | 372.000 |
| 8 | 7 | Bing Group | Detroit, MI | Dave Bing | 1980 | 1414 | Steel processing, steel stamping, full seat assembly, mirror assembly | 372.000 |
| 10 | 8 | Radio One Inc.** | Lanham, MD | Alfred C. Liggins III | 1980 | 1750 | Radio broadcasting and other media businesses | 363.982 |
| 11 | 9 | Rush Communications of NYC Inc. | New York, NY | Russell Simmons | 1991 | 180 | Entertainment, fashion, and apparel licensing | 360.000 |

| | | Company | Location | CEO | Year | Employees | Business | Revenue* |
|---|---|---|---|---|---|---|---|---|
| 12 | 15 | RS Information Systems Inc. | McLean, VA | Rodney P. Hunt | 1992 | 1800 | Telecommunications, information technology, and system integration | 321.000 |
| 13 | 12 | H. J. Russell & Co. | Atlanta, GA | Michael B. Russell | 1952 | 1907 | Construction, real estate development, property management | 304.241 |
| 14 | — | Harpo Inc. | Chicago, IL | Oprah Winfrey | 1986 | 284 | Television and film production, publishing, and new media | 275.000 |
| 15 | 16 | MV Transportation Inc. | Fairfield, CA | Jon Monson | 1975 | 7981 | Public transit, paratransit, school bus services | 271.863 |
| 16 | 14 | Global Automotive Alliance | Detroit, MI | William F. Pickard | 1999 | 700 | Parts manufacturer for auto industry, warehousing and distribution provider | 262.300 |
| 17 | 24 | SET Enterprises Inc. | Warren, MI | Sid E. Taylor | 1989 | 450 | Metal processing for automotive industry | 212.000 |
| 18 | 42 | Peebles Atlantic Development Corp. | Coral Gables, FL | R. Donahue Peebles | 1994 | 274 | Real estate development and property management | 202.925 |
| 19 | 17 | Bartech Group Inc. | Livonia, MI | Jon E. Barfield | 1977 | 3400 | Professional staffing and outsourcing services and solutions | 195.000 |
| 20 | 20 | Manna Inc. | Louisville, KY | Ulysses Bridgeman Jr. | 1988 | 6250 | Wendy's Old-Fashioned Hamburgers franchisee | 185.000 |

*In millions of dollars, to the nearest thousand, as of December 31, 2004. Prepared by B. E. Research. Reviewed by the certified public accounting firm Edwards & Co.

**Radio One Inc. is publicly traded. Majority ownership of voting class stock is held by African Americans.

*Source: Black Enterprise* 35 (June 2005): 113. Published by permission.

used the bank as its depository. True Reformers' net worth in 1907 was $16,933,048. In 1903, **Maggie Lena Mitchell Walker** became the first black woman to own and operate a bank when she opened St. Luke Penny Savings Bank in Richmond. Her initial deposits totaled $9,000 and increased to over $375,000 by 1919. This bank afforded opportunities to blacks for education and housing. **Jesse Binga** in Chicago founded Binga State Bank in 1908. In 1922, **Anthony Overton** organized the Douglass National Bank in Chicago. When the banks merged and the new establishment became the Binga-Douglass National Bank, this meld represented the largest black bank organized before 1932. The names of several other black-owned banks established at the turn of the century deserve an honorable mention, but only six of the sixty-four established survived World War II, and only four of those remained operational until 1996. They include First Tuskegee Bank; Consolidated Bank and Trust, Maggie Walker, 1903; Mechanics and Farmers Bank, 1908; and Standard Life Insurance Company and Citizens Trust, Herman Perry, 1921.

Samuel W. Rutherford established the National Benefit Life Insurance Company in 1898. Also in 1898, the largest black-owned life insurance company in the country, North Carolina Mutual Insurance Life Insurance Company (formerly named North Carolina Mutual and Provident Insurance Company) was formed and continues to operate. While the initial formation failed in 1899, three black businessmen purchased the interests of the founders. By 1918, the insurance company earned over $16 million of in-force insurance. In the late 1990s, North Carolina Mutual's in-force premiums totaled over $8 billion. Today, the company ranks number 1 on the *Black Enterprise* Top 100s list of black-owned insurance companies. In 1905, a former slave named **Alonzo Franklin Herndon** founded the Atlanta Life Insurance Company and sold premiums almost exclusively to the city's black middle class. According to Charles Christian, Herndon was said to have been the wealthiest black businessman in the country at that time. Besides investing in the banking industry, in 1924 Anthony Overton founded Victory Life Insurance Company in New York. It represented the first black-owned insurance company in that city. Overton also established the Great Northern Realty Company in Chicago in 1911. In 1915 (the same year of Booker T. Washington's death), the black businessmen of the Atlanta Mutual Insurance Association founded the Booster's Club. The Washington–Du Bois theory had promoted the policy of blacks buying, selling, and trading with one another as the avenue to economic progression. Juliet E. K. Walker cites that in support of the theory, the purpose of the association was "to encourage Negroes to trade with one another; to buy groceries, take out insurance, buy medicine, and employ Negro professional men."

While many black-owned newspapers were established prior to the turn of the century, the oldest continuously published newspaper in the United States is the *Los Angeles Eagle*, founded in 1879. The *Philadelphia Tribune*, founded by Christopher J. Perry in 1884, and the *Baltimore Afro-American*, founded in 1892 by John Murphy, also continue to publish newspapers.

These publications were invaluable sources of information to the black community. The 1920s were deemed the "Golden Years." By 1920, thousands of African Americans had migrated to large cities and established themselves as independent businesspeople that sold goods and services almost exclusively to blacks consumers. **Annie Turnbo Malone** in 1902 in Chicago, **Madam C. J. Walker** in St. Louis in 1905, and Anthony Overton and **Sarah Spencer Washington** in 1913 and 1920 began the black hair-care and beauty industry for African Americans. While the stock market crash of 1929 devastated the black business community, especially banks, black enterprises resumed their growth during World War II and began to recover by the end of the 1940s, but with lower profits and fewer establishments. Manning Marable reports nearly 70 percent of all black businesses comprised restaurants, groceries, funeral parlors, shoe repair, laundries, barbershops and beauty parlors. Several black entrepreneurs, however, found niches in the publishing, health and beauty aids, music, and manufacturing industries, as they concern African Americans by mid-twentieth century.

**John H. Johnson**, for example, established Johnson Publishing Company in 1942, in Chicago with an initial personal investment of $500. He released the first issue of *Ebony* magazine in 1945, which depicted the goals and successes of the black middle class on the rise. The magazine was created also to parallel *Life*, a mainstream America magazine. *Ebony* was the first black magazine to attract advertising from white companies and is recognized as the most successful and most widely circulated black-oriented magazine in the world. The astounding success of *Ebony* prompted Johnson to expand his productions to include cosmetics, hair-care products, *Jet* magazine, and television production, all of which still produce today. Fashion Fair Cosmetics was founded in 1973 and is the world's leading company for cosmetics and skin care for women of color. Fashion Fair is sold in over 2,500 stores across the United States, Canada, Africa, England, France, Switzerland, the Bahamas, Bermuda, and the Virgin Islands. Johnson Productions Company, the holding company for the Johnson enterprises, was the first black-owned business to trade publicly on the American Stock Exchange (ASE) in 1973. In 1997, Johnson Publishing Company moved to reconstruct many of its major businesses. Some publications established in the 1980s, for example, were suspended. A catalog venture with *Spiegel* mail order catalog was discontinued. The hair-care division installed new management, and Johnson Publishing increased its ownership stake of Ebony *South Africa* from 51 percent to 85 percent, eliminating white investors. Gross sales for Johnson Publishing Company exceeded $490,000 in 2003.

The 1950s ushered in the rock and roll era in black America. Black vocal artists were forced to sign and record at white Production companies because the capitalists owned the companies. Seeing the niche for a market that appealed to black artists, **Berry Gordy Jr.** founded the Motown Record Corporation in Detroit, Michigan, in 1959. Gordy's multimillion-dollar business recorded several gold records for artists such as: The Supremes, The Four Tops, The Temptations, Martha and the Vandellas, and Mary Wells.

By 1973, Gordy had moved Motown Industries to Los Angeles and ranked number 1 on *Black Enterprise*'s Top 100s list with sales of $40 million. The company remained number 1 for the next ten years.

**Henry Green Parks Jr.** established Park Sausage Company in 1958, which was also one of the top 100 African American enterprises in 1973. It was also the first black-owned enterprise publicly traded on the National Association of Securities Dealers Automated Quotation exchange (NASDAQ) the same year.

The Supreme Court ruling of 1954 denouncing segregation set the stage for the Civil Rights Act of 1964 and the civil rights movement that culminated in 1968. In 1957, President Dwight D. Eisenhower signed into law the Civil Rights Act of 1957, which outlawed disfranchisement against blacks. Up to this point, the Fifteenth Amendment to the U.S. Constitution in 1870 that granted blacks the right to vote had been the most recent civil rights legislation. Between 1957 and 1970 several laws were signed into effect that opposed segregation, discrimination against blacks, and that were supposed to aid African Americans in founding successful business enterprises. Paradoxically, the same laws indirectly caused the demise of many black businesses heretofore established that exclusively served the black consumer market. Black-owned enterprises still marketed their goods and services mainly to black consumers through most of the 1960s even though integration in America had redistributed the black consumer market to various areas of the country. African American consumers who were no longer confined by law to neighborhood shopping, entertainment, and employment, were also no longer loyal, exclusive consumers to black enterprises. Blacks employed by corporate America and the federal government explored new economic and political avenues. They were able to participate more fully in mainstream retail purchases and remove African American dollars from that community. Some African Americans used the opportunities to propel themselves to new levels, such as business ownership and acquisition. Conglomerate building, leveraged buyouts, joint ventures and expansions and mergers became the "post–civil rights era phenomenon" in the black-owned business industry.

**Pierre Ellis Sutton** pioneered black conglomerate building in 1972 when he purchased Inner City Broadcasting, based in New York. From that premise, Sutton added cable television, video productions, and record production companies. He is the owner of the Apollo Theatre in New York. According to Walker, Earl G. Graves [EGG], Limited is the "trendsetter in conglomerate building." EGG, Limited is the holding company for **Earl G. Graves**'s several entities, including Earl Graves Publishing, namely *Black Enterprise* magazine based in New York; Earl Graves Marketing and Research; and EGG Broadcasting, Dallas and Fort Worth, Texas. Graves also owns the Pepsi-Cola of Washington, D.C. franchise, which he purchased in 1990 for $60 million in a joint venture with **Earvin "Magic" Johnson Jr.**

**James Bruce Llewellyn**, a multimillion-dollar black businessman, completed a leveraged buyout in 1969 of a white corporation when he purchased Fedco Foods, a white-owned grocery chain of ten stores in the South Bronx, for $3 million. To complete the deal, Llewellyn made a loan of $2.5 million with Prudential Insurance Company against the purchase price of $3 million. In 1984, he sold the chain, which had grown to twenty-seven stores and sales of $85 million, for $20 million. In addition, Llewellyn purchased a 36 percent interest in the Philadelphia Coca-Cola Bottling Company in a joint venture with entertainer Bill Cosby and basketball star Julius "Dr. J" Erving in 1983. In 1988, the trio purchased 100 percent interest in the company for $75 million. In 2004, the bottler and soft drinks distributor ranked number 4 on the *Black Enterprise*'s Top 100s list with annual sales of $447,000. In a joint venture in 1985, Llewellyn purchased Buffalo television station WKBW, Buffalo for $65 million. Just two years later, Camille Cosby, Julius Erving, and the Jackson family joined Llewellyn in the $125 million purchase of the New York Times Cable Company. After a $25 million down payment, they financed the remaining $100 million. Jackie Robinson was the first black American to play in a major professional sports league. In 1974, Robinson's intellectual and financial abilities founded Freedom National Bank, the first black in Harlem.

One of the most ingenious and successful business moves in African American history was the $985 million leveraged buyout of TLC Beatrice International by **Reginald F. Lewis** in 1987. Ten years later, the New York–based concern radically restructured the TLC assets. TLC sold its French food distribution business, which grossed $1.9 billion for $573 million. Despite the sale, TLC remained the largest black-owned business with annual sales of $1.4 billion. Having trimmed lots of excess, TLC remains significantly lean. It maintains a snack food company in Ireland, ice cream manufacturing companies in Spain and the Canary Islands, and bottlers in Europe and Thailand. Also in the 1980s many African American celebrities in the sports and entertainment industries set the stage for profound changes in black business ownership and development, which reigned throughout the turn of the century. Business decisions by black celebrities regarding their products affected the deposits to purses of mainstream America. Some African Americans no longer just accepted salaries for their performances but negotiated joint profits in exchange and even syndication rights to their own television shows. For example, multimillion-dollar entertainer and philanthropist Bill Cosby purchased syndication rights to his television shows, which include *Fat Albert* and the *Cosby Show*. In exchange for a salary, he joined in on the $333 million profits from the shows, plus syndication receipts. The *Cosby Show* went into syndication in 1988 for $500 million. **Oprah Winfrey**, syndicated television host of her own show, is highly recognized as one of America's wealthiest women. She pioneered the most successful television talk show in Chicago in the 1980s. HARPO Productions, also based in Chicago, is Winfrey's holding company for her television show, movie productions, and property ownership.

Three other industries in large cities penetrated by African Americans include architecture, real estate development, and the automobile industry. Roberta Washington owns the New York–based Roberta Washington

Architects PC, which she founded in 1983. Washington has worked on numerous projects around the country, and for the postindependence government of Mozambique. One major U.S. project is the Jazz and Negro Baseball Hall of Fame in Kansas City, Missouri. Washington also designed a new eight-story, 128-unit condominium unit in Harlem. Her firm also contributed to a new subway station in Brooklyn. Roberta Washington Architects PC is the largest African American, female-owned architecture concern in the United States. In an effort to change the complexion of the commercial property industry, nine black-owned brokerage and design firms formed the first conglomeration of commercial brokerages called Concordis Real Estate LLC. The brokerage firm is based in Chicago and was formed in response to a huge Hewlett-Packard Company real estate contract, which stipulated substantial minority broker participation. Concordis brokerage has since landed some contracts by its own merit. A few examples include large companies such as Sears-Roebuck & Company, Bank One Corporation, and the City of Houston. In 1987, R. Donahue Peebles founded the Peebles Atlantic Development Corporation in Miami, Florida. The chief product of the company is real estate development and property ownership. He is the owner of a Marriott hotel in Washington, D.C. and several other commercial properties. In south Florida, Peebles is in the process of adding a twenty-story high-rise with 112 units to be sold at a minimum of $2 million each. One of Peebles's most significant property acquisitions is the Royal Palm Crowne Plaza Resort in Miami Beach. His real estate, financial, and political background stem from his Washington, D.C. hometown experiences. Peebles successfully acquired the 417-unit resort. Peebles Atlantic Development Corporation ranks number 42 on the *Black Enterprise*'s Top 100s list for 2003.

Diversification, acquisition, and micromanagement are the marks for success in the automobile dealership industry. Since most African Americans had few, if any, avenues to secure sufficient capital to purchase dealerships, breaking into the automobile industry was a tough ordeal. Some were successful in acquiring dealerships during the 1970s, however, the several recessions in the country contributed to the demise of many black-owned dealerships before the dawn of the new millennium. Those dealerships that survived did so because of positive, strategic business practices. Reginald T. Hubbard, the chief executive officer (CEO) of the Charlotte-based Hubbard Automotive LLC in 1986, which he founded for example, takes a hands-on approach to manage the several dealerships he owns. Cashing in on the age of technology, Hubbard generates computerized accounting reports through an integrated accounting system to all of his dealership management teams on a weekly basis. He then meets with the general manager of each to resolve strategically low sales issues. Hubbard also uses forward-thinking vision and is one of the first dealerships to establish business development center departments at each of his dealerships. Rather than use traditional advertising, Hubbard's crews use a customer interactive approach searching for potential customers who will visit the dealership and contemplate purchasing its products. The crews also use an automated system to alert existing customers of service and warranty dates, as well as send birthday and holiday greetings. They get leads from the Internet, retrieving inquiries from the manufacturers of those in search of new automobiles. Hubbard Automotive LLC reported gross sales in excess of $152 million for 2003.

When major league baseball power hitter **Henry "Hank" Aaron** retired from playing baseball in 1976, he transferred his intellectual skills from the ballfield to the business arena. Aaron used the valuable contacts he had made while playing baseball to launch his first food franchise in Milwaukee. He sold his seven Arby's fast-food stores by 1994 and moved on to ownership of luxury automobile dealerships.

Along with the National Association of Minority Automobile Dealers (NAMAD), Hank Aaron participated in a campaign for automobile manufacturers to create opportunities for blacks to become automobile dealers. The relationships he built while campaigning helped to land his first luxury automobile dealership. Hank Aaron BMW was acquired in 1999. Aaron's name is also a big advantage to his business. His hands-on approach, including daily dealership visits, creates an owner-customer relationship and encourages potential customers to buy. Aaron's holding company for his several dealerships grossed over $76 million in sales in 2003.

**Ellenae Fairhurst** owns one other African American luxury automobile dealership located in Huntsville, Alabama. She was awarded a Lexus dealership in 1988 after completing the Chrysler Corporation training program. Fairhurst's dealership reported gross sales of $28 million in 2001, at which time she built a $7.3 million multiplex for all three of her dealerships. Over the years she has maintained a lean staff and micromanaged expenses and purchases. Fairhurst is the first African American woman to open a Lexus dealership.

*See also*: Black Banks: Their Beginning; Real Estate Industry; Retail Industry; Women and Business

**Sources**

Adams, Barbara L., and Viceola Stokes. "Performance Measures and Profitability Factors of Successful African-American Entrepreneurs: An Exploratory Study." *Journal of American Academy of Business* 22 (March 2003): 418–424.

"Auto Industry Leader Mel Farr Makes Big Investment in Urban Market." *Jet* 95.8 (January 1999): 38.

Bell, Derrick. *Faces at the Bottom of the Well: The Permanence of Racism.* New York: Basic Books, 1992.

Brown, Ann, Carmen Brown, Terri Guess, et al. "Expanding the Horizon; 25 Influential Black Women In Business." *Network Journal* 11 (April 2004): 30.

Christian, Charles. *Black Saga: The African American Experience.* Boston: Houghton Mifflin Company, 1995.

Coles, Flournoy A., Jr. *Black Economic Development.* Chicago: Nelson Hall, 1975.

Dingle, Derek T. "Dawn of the Black Millennium." *Black Enterprise* 28 (June 1998): 93–106.

———. "100s 31st Annual Report on Black Business; Reinvention through Innovation." *Black Enterprise* 32 (June 2002): 94.

———. "Only the Strong Survive: B.E. 100s 32nd Annual Report on Black Business." *Black Enterprise* 34 (June 2004): 101–103.

Edmond, Alfred, Jr. "Milestones of the B.E. 100s: 25 Years of Black Economic Empowerment." *Black Enterprise* 27 (June 1997): 86–90, 95–96, 102.

Farley, Reynolds, and Walker R. Allen. *The Color Line and the Quality of Life in America*. New York: Russell Sage Foundation, 1987.

Fuller, Lorraine. "Are We Seeing Things?" *Journal of Black Studies* 32 (September 2001): 120–131.

Gite, Lloyd. "The Road to Recovery." *Black Enterprise* 32 (June 2002): 159–164.

———. "Switching Lanes." *Black Enterprise* 31 (June 2001): 147–150, 154.

Hughes, Alan. "Only the Strong Survive: The Prince of South Beach." *Black Enterprise* 34 (June 2004): 128–140.

Marable, Manning. *How Capitalism Underdeveloped Black America*. Boston: South End Press, 1983.

Scott, Matthew S. "The Top 50 Black Powerbrokers." *Black Enterprise* 20 (August 1990): 126.

Spruell, Sakina. "Only the Strong Survive: The Tough Get Going." *Black Enterprise* 34 (June 2004): 111–116.

Starkman, Dean. "Blacks Attempt to Raise Profile in Real Estate." *Wall Street Journal*, October 22, 2003.

Sykes, Tanisha A. "Only the Strong Survive: Power Hitter." *Black Enterprise* 34 (June 2004): 161–169.

Walker, Juliet E. K. *The History of Black Business in America: Capitalism, Race, Entrepreneurship*. New York: Macmillan Library Reference, 1998.

"Years of Achievement." *Black Enterprise* 32 (June 2002): 91.

*Shelhea Owens*

# Black Corporate Directors Conference

The Black Corporate Directors Conference was founded in 2001 and sponsored annually by John W. Rogers Jr., chair and chief executive officer of the Chicago-based firm Ariel Capital, and Charles A. Tribbett III, managing director of the global executive recruitment and management assessment firm Russell Reynolds Associates. Tribbett noted the purpose of the conference in *Ebony* magazine, saying that it aimed "to bring together African-American directors to discuss issues relating to diversity and to network with one another." The third conference, held in Chicago in 2004, brought together eighty-five people who sit on boards of major corporations, community leaders, and academicians.

Blacks continue to be underrepresented on boards in corporate America. *Ebony* cited the results of its own work as well as a *Fortune* magazine study that shows a total of 185 blacks in such positions in 2004. Beginning in 1963, the report shows no black corporate directors. In 1964, 2 blacks held such posts: Samuel R. Pierce Jr., who was named to the board of U.S. Industries, and Asa

T. Spaulding, who was added to the board of W. T. Grant Company. Both appointments were made on the same day in June 1964. On January 4, 1971, **Leon Howard Sullivan** became the first black director of a major automobile company when he was elected to the board of General Motors. On March 18 of that year, **John H. Johnson**, founder and publisher of *Ebony* magazine, became the first black director of a major entertainment corporation when he was named to the Twentieth Century Fox board.

Other black firsts on corporate boards included Jerome Heartwell "Brud" Holland, later president of Hampton University, who in 1972 was the first black to serve on the board of the New York Stock Exchange. Mary K. Bush was the first black woman elected to the board of Texaco Inc., in 1997. In 1979, Dolores Duncan Wharton was the first black and first woman on the board of Gannett Company. In 1982 Sybil Collins Mobley became the first black woman member of the board of Sears, Roebuck and Company. In 1997 Julius W. "Dr. J." Irving became the first black board member of Proffits, Inc.

The number of appointees to boards increased since 1964, showing 80 in 1987, 146 by 1994, 179 by 1997, and 185 by 2004. Participants in the 2004 conference of Black Corporate Directors represented a wide spectrum of corporations, among them Verizon, McDonald's, Target, Exelon Corporation, and Delta. While some directors oppose being the sole black in the boardroom, others charged that black members should forget their race and hold fast to their position as a board member. They should "push for a shared American market." Small group sessions of new-generation black men and women corporate board members shared ideas and concepts on successful board membership. They wanted to use their positions to make a difference for all Americans.

**Sources**

Holloway, Lynette. "Behind the Boardroom Door." *Ebony* 60 (January 2005): 118–122.

Smith, Jessie Carney, ed. *Black Firsts*. 2nd ed. Rev. and expanded. Detroit: Visible Ink Press, 2003.

*Jessie Carney Smith*

# Black Fund Managers

In the world of high finance, mutual funds are combinations of stocks, bonds, and other financial instruments developed by investment companies that manage portfolios of securities for individuals or institutional investors. During the era of segregation, blacks of means could not, did not, or were not allowed to participate in the larger financial institutions and related industries; their response was to organize and develop financial services and entities within their own communities.

In 1924 the **National Negro Business League** established the National Negro Finance Corporation (NNFC) to provide working capital for individuals and partnerships involved in business enterprises. Another purpose of the corporation was to create and develop a market for listing, exchanging, buying, and selling "Negro securities." Its success was limited, impacted like the rest of the American economy by the 1929 stock market crash and the Great Depression of the 1930s, but the NNFC served as a precursor to future financial organization, activity, and development by black business professionals.

While African Americans became professional fund managers for a variety of investment firms in the postsegregation era, it was not until the 1980s that the first black-owned and -operated mutual fund companies operating in the mainstream American economy were established.

John W. Rogers Jr. is credited with starting the first African American institutional money management firm, Ariel Capital Management, in 1983, which was also the first black company to start a mutual fund. He was followed a few months later by Eddie Brown, who established Brown Capital Management. The Kenwood Group, owned and operated by Barbara Bowles, is recognized as being the first African American female-owned firm to launch a mutual fund, the Kenwood Growth and Income Fund.

These pioneers have been joined by others in recent years, yet the Reverend Jesse Jackson has stated that the ten largest American mutual funds invest over $2.85 trillion, which is 500 times the assets of the largest African American–managed mutual funds. The Wall Street Project of the Rainbow/PUSH coalition, which began in 1998, seeks to address this disparity and increase diversity in the investment process through encouraging charities, pension funds, and mutual funds to place 5 percent of their funds with African American and other minority asset managers.

African Americans as a group are also becoming investors in larger numbers. In addition to efforts led by Jackson, other entities, such as the Black Wealth Initiative developed by *Black Enterprise* magazine, the Black Wealth Network, the Coalition of Black Investors, the NAACP's (National Association for the Advancement of Colored People) economic reciprocity campaigns, and the National Urban League are stressing the importance of African American investments in and with black fund managers, specifically those who own and operate independent investment firms.

In recent years, the perception that persons must have a substantial amount of disposable (excess) income to become active in financial investing has been altered. Small investors have been encouraged and are now appreciated as an important sector of the investment community. During the 1980s, when mutual fund ownership increased significantly, 16 percent of American households with annual incomes below $25,000 owned mutual funds and 55 percent among households with incomes above $75,000.

The 2000 Ariel-Schwab study on African American investment patterns indicated that 64 percent of African Americans surveyed were active investors in the stock market. Black fund managers, along with the rest of the investment industry, have profited from the increasing numbers of new investors in money market mutual funds and other financial instruments. A report from the Milken Institute indicated that minority-owned investment businesses are a driving force behind the growth of financial investing by African Americans and other ethnic communities.

Despite the negative impact of such events as the terrorist attacks on America of September 11, 2001, the downturn in the stock market that followed, and the collapse of high-profile corporations such as Enron and WorldCom, African American mutual fund companies managed to ride out the "bear market" and in some cases outperformed other investment firms as a result of careful planning and sound financial strategies (Table 15).

Mark D. Lay, chairman and chief investment strategist for his company, MDL Capital Management, pursued a balanced approach involving stocks, bonds, and other financial instruments to preserve capital for investment clients during this period. Eric McKissack, portfolio manager and vice chairman of Ariel, indicated that their company would continue established investing patterns to ensure long-term value for their customers.

Prominent African American money managers such as Harold Doley (Doley Securities, Inc.), Eugene Profit (Profit Investment Management), and Steven Sanders (MDL Capital Management) have been involved in the Money Show, considered the world's leading producer of investment trade shows, cruises, and other events. They, as well as Rogers, Brown, Bowles, Lay, and others, have used platforms of this type as well as conferences of African American associations and organizations, traditional advertising, and Internet Web sites to promote minority participation in the investment markets.

Alphonse "Buddy" Fletcher Jr., chairman and chief executive officer of Fletcher Asset Management, announced in 2004 the establishment of a $50 million gift to individuals and institutions working to improve race relations and to honor the fiftieth anniversary of the *Brown v. Board of Education* Court decision. This leading Wall Street money manager had previously given $4.5 million to endow a professorship at Harvard, his alma mater, in honor of his father, Alphonse Sr. (African American scholar Cornel West has held this position).

Black fund managers, such as the persons mentioned above and others, are demonstrating that economic empowerment through financial investment can provide immediate and long-term benefits for individuals, families, companies, educational institutions, and the community at large. Their collective vision is to bridge the "wealth divide" and build true multigenerational assets and net worth for African Americans and others who become actively involved in the investment industry.

C. Kim Goodwin, senior portfolio manager, American Century Growth Fund, summarized the importance of investment for African Americans in this way: "We can't pass on our jobs [to our descendants], but we can pass on our wealth."

**Table 15.** Top Asset Managers

| This Year | Last Year | Company | Location | Chief Executive | Year Started | Staff | Assets under Management* |
|---|---|---|---|---|---|---|---|
| 1 | 1 | Ariel Capital Management LLC | Chicago, IL | John W. Rogers Jr. | 1983 | 88 | 21,433.00 |
| 2 | 2 | EARNEST Partners LLC** | Atlanta, GA | Paul E. Viera | 1998 | 35 | 13,934.000 |
| 3 | 3 | Rhumbline Advisers | Boston, MA | JD Nelson | 1990 | 15 | 10,307.000 |
| 4 | 4 | Brown Capital Management LLC | Baltimore, MD | Eddie C. Brown | 1983 | 24 | 5,278.000 |
| 5 | 6 | Advent Capital Management LLC | New York, NY | Tracy V. Maitland | 1995 | 40 | 3,848.000 |
| 6 | 5 | MDL Capital Management Inc.** | Pittsburgh, PA | Mark D. Lay | 1992 | 32 | 2,821.000 |
| 7 | 10 | Holland Capital Management LP | Chicago, IL | Louis A. Holland | 1991 | 24 | 2,628.000 |
| 8 | 7 | NCM Capital Management Group Inc. | Durham, NC | Maceo K. Sloan | 1986 | 25 | 2,145.000 |
| 9 | 9 | Edgar Lomax Co. | Springfield, VA | Randall K. Eley | 1986 | 12 | 1,962.000 |
| 10 | 8 | Smith Graham & Co. Investment Advisors LP | Houston, TX | Gerald B. Smith | 1990 | 25 | 1,958.000 |
| 11 | 12 | Swarthmore Group Inc. | West Chester, PA | Paula R. Mandle | 1992 | 18 | 1,877.000 |
| 12 | 11 | Utendahl Capital Management LP | New York, NY | Penny Zuckerwise | 1992 | 15 | 1,770.000 |
| 13 | 14 | Goode Investment Management Inc. | Cleveland, OH | Bruce T. Goode | 1999 | 4 | 1,282.000 |
| 14 | 13 | Hughes Capital Management Inc. | Alexandria, VA | Frankie D. Hughes | 1993 | 6 | 1,193.000 |
| 15 | 15 | Pugh Capital Management Inc. | Seattle, WA | Mary Pugh | 1991 | 8 | 894.000 |

*In millions of dollars, to the nearest thousand, as of December 31, 2004. Prepared by B. E. Research. Reviewed by the certified public accounting firm Edwards & Co.

**Includes subsidiaries and entities in which the firm has common control.

*Source:* Securities and Exchange Commission. Published in *Black Enterprise* 35 (June 2005): 192. Published by permission.

**Sources**

Austin, Kamau. "Black Wealth Network and Atlantic City Money Show to Feature Minority Money Managers Panel." *Einfonews*, July 5, 2004. http://www.einfonews.com/blogs/kamausblog.htm.

Bigelow, Barbara Carlisle, ed. *Contemporary Black Biography*. Vol. 5. Detroit: Gale Research, 1994.

Black Wealth Network. "African American Mutual Funds." http://www.bwonline.com.

Dingle, Derek T. "The Path to Future Financial Empowerment." *Black Enterprise* 31 (August 2000): 101–103.

Fairley, Juliette. *Money Talks: Black Finance Experts Talk to You About Money*. New York: Wiley, 1998.

Goodwin, C. Kim. "C. Kim Goodwin, Senior Portfolio Manager, American Century Growth Fund, on Investing and Taking Risk to Build Wealth." *Black Enterprise* 31 (August 2000): 106.

Greenwald, Douglas, ed. *The McGraw-Hill Encyclopedia of Economics*. New York: McGraw-Hill, 1994.

Halsey, Nicole. "Wrestling with the Bear: Black Fund Managers Are Adjusting Their Strategies for the Long Haul." *Black Enterprise* 33 (October 2002): 46.

Korn, Donald Jay. "Staying Ahead of the Pack (African American Mutual Fund Companies)." *Black Enterprise* 31 (April 2001): 28.

Nichols, James Lawrence, and William H. Crogman. *The New Progress of a Race*. Naperville, IL: J. L. Nichols, 1925.

Rimer, Sara. "$50 Million Gift Aims to Further Legacy of Brown Case." *New York Times*, May 18, 2004.

Sheimo, Michael, ed. *International Encyclopedia of the Stock Market*. Chicago: Fitzroy Dearborn Publishers, 1999.

Stein, George. "Jackson Calls for Minority Asset Managers." *Seattle Times*, January 13, 2004.

*Fletcher F. Moon*

# Black Press: Newspapers in Major Cities

Whatever African Americans wanted to know or have validated about them they looked to the black press. They wanted information as well as affirmation. Beginning with the first publication of a black newspaper in 1827, the editors Samuel E. Cornish and John B. Russwurm of the *Freedom's Journal* boldly emphasized their editorial purpose in the newspaper's first edition: "We wish to plead our own cause. Too long have others spoken for us. Too long has the public been deceived by misrepresentations of the things which concern us dearly" (*Freedom's Journal*). The black press continued to espouse a similar philosophy for decades after this publication. Advocacy became the major objective for black newspapers.

The publishers and editors of black newspapers were primarily motivated to deliver information that centered African Americans in the dialogue of what it meant to be an American and black. Prior to the first publication of any black newspaper, African Americans were usually referred to in the white or mainstream press in a derogatory manner. Following the U.S. government's recognition of blacks as citizens through the Thirteenth Amendment, the mainstream press continued to espouse racial prejudice against blacks. Mainstream papers supported stereotyped images of blacks and ignored the political, economic, and cultural goals of African Americans. Therefore, the mission of publishers and editors of black newspapers was to vindicate the race, respond to the misrepresentation of blacks in the mainstream press, and tell the story of the black experience from their perspective. Black publishers highlighted everything from the living conditions of blacks to their concerns, their problems, and most important, their achievements.

## HISTORICAL TIMELINE

The development of the black press can be divided into several phases. Newspapers that were published in the North before the Civil War dominated the first phase. The second phase of the black press followed the Civil War until the turn of the century. This second phase was prompted by the growing numbers of newspapers in the southern region of the United States, during a time when literacy among African Americans increased. Finally, scholars have marked the last two decades of the nineteenth century as the beginning of the third phase of the black press. The period does overlap with the second phase but was characterized according to its reaction and adjustment to the oppressive and violent conditions that African Americans experienced. During the latter phase, the antebellum and Reconstruction eras, newspapers shifted from campaigning for freedom to developing a proactive approach to assist the black community.

The campaign of the late-nineteenth- and early-twentieth-century press was to educate and uplift the black community. The late-nineteenth-century press was one of the major social institutions that equipped African Americans to handle the political, social, and economic hardships they faced during the post-Reconstruction years.

Since blacks were often overlooked or discounted by the mainstream press, the black press occupied the role of informant to the black community, catalyst for political and social change, and cultivator of community cohesion during a period of growing prejudice and discrimination against African Americans. This growing press also attempted to create a sense of solidarity among African Americans. The press also promoted black entrepreneurship through its advertisements. The black press covered the full range of human experiences. From births, marriages, and deaths to college graduation and higher achievements in academia, the black press gave voice to its readers. The main goal was to reflect a perspective that centered on their concerns and those of the black community.

## NEWSPAPERS AND PUBLISHERS IN FIVE MAJOR CITIES

### *Afro-American* (1892–Present)

On August 13, 1892, the first edition of the *Afro-American* was published. The early edition of the newspaper was edited by Reverend William Alexander, a pastor of the Sharon Baptist Church in Baltimore, Maryland. Alexander and his associates William H. Daly, George W. Reid, and V. E. Toney, all skilled workers and small business owners, were disappointed and frustrated with the conditions that blacks were subjected to live under in the 1890s. They decided to use the press as a venue to protest against horrible conditions and to publicize community concerns, as well as the church and business activities in the community. The *Afro-American* was taken over by Reverend Alexander's friend and business partner William Daly. Daly joined the newspaper with the Northwestern Family Supply Company in 1895. Unfortunately, the company filed bankruptcy, and John H. Murphy Sr., who had been a foreman and manager of the *Afro-American*'s printing department, found himself out of a job. Courageously, Murphy set out to chart a new path through the acquisition of the *Afro-American* newspaper. When the newspaper's printing machinery came up for auction in 1897, Murphy borrowed $200 from his wife, Martha Howard Murphy, to purchase it. On March 27, 1897, the *Afro-American* was published with John H. Murphy's name on its masthead as its owner and business manager. On January 1, 1900, Murphy and longtime friend George F. Bragg merged their two papers to form the *Afro-American Ledger*. The title *Afro-American Ledger* would remain until Bragg's departure in 1915. Thus the newspaper's masthead would read the Afro-American thereafter. The *Afro-American* is also the first African American newspaper to participate in book publishing. Through the Afro-American Company, Murphy released Harvey E. Johnson's *The White Man's Failure in Government* in 1900. The company would later publish *This Is Our War* in 1945.

It is not surprising that the success of the *Afro-American* newspaper continued under the leadership of Carl James Greenbury Murphy, son of John Murphy. Carl Murphy's presence and immediate success at the *Afro-American* won him his family's faith and support. Following the death of their father, John Murphy Sr., in 1922, Carl Murphy was elected by his family as president and chief editor of the *Afro-American* newspaper. Carl Murphy's forty-nine-year tenure as editor and head of the *Afro-American* Company began in 1918 and ended 1967. During his term, Murphy contributed to the paper in many ways. He diligently and passionately covered a range of issues at both the national and international levels. He used the editorial page to challenge local, national, and international injustices ranging from lynching, race and gender discrimination, poor housing, and poor schools to full citizenship for all Americans. He launched an editorial attack against the U.S. government for its military occupation of Haiti. Murphy sent *Afro-American* reporters abroad to report on the experiences of black soldiers during World War II. Following the war, he wrote in support of the decolonization of Africa. Murphy frequently communicated with prominent leaders and the many organizations they represented. These included Thurgood Marshall, National Association for the Advancement of Colored People (NAACP) legal counsel and later U.S. Supreme Court justice; Walter White, another NAACP leader; Urban League executives Eugene K. Jones and Lester Granger; Mary McLeod Bethune of the National Council of Negro Women; and scholars such as W.E.B. Du Bois.

Carl Murphy, reminiscent of his father, had a vision for the newspaper. He wanted to broaden the circulation of the *Afro-American* beyond Baltimore's black community. Under his leadership the newspaper continued its growth by establishing bureaus in Washington, D.C., Philadelphia, New York, Newark, and Richmond. There were even some subscribers in Africa. The superior guidance of Murphy won the *Afro-American* the title of the most successful black publication in the mid-Atlantic region. The major differences between the national edition of the *Afro-American* in Baltimore and the other city editions was that local news in various other cities was covered along with national news coverage.

The front page incorporated local news, but the editorial page remained essentially untouched. Murphy was very interested in providing readers with an understanding of the connection between their local experiences with national occurrences such as civil rights cases that were being filed in the courts, school integration, equal pay, and equal employment. He would often outline during meetings how each of the major stories would impact the other. Therefore, managing editors and city editors were asked to keep those issues in mind when deciding on the layout of the paper.

Like his father, Carl Murphy believed in equal rights for both men and women. Murphy encouraged all five of his daughters to learn the business, particularly since they were to inherit the business in the future. They were also encouraged to pursue academic careers in journalism and work for the *Afro-American*. Two of Murphy's daughters, Frances L. Murphy II and Elizabeth Murphy Moss, became chief officers of the Afro-American Company after his death. Frances became chair of the board and chief executive officer in 1971 until 1974, and Elizabeth became vice president and treasurer of the company. Elizabeth had served as the first black female war correspondent for the *Afro-American* during World War II.

Today the Afro-American Company publishes both the Baltimore and Washington, D.C. *Afro-American* news. The company claims a readership of more than 120,000 people, mainly in Maryland and the District of Columbia area. The newspaper is currently controlled by the fourth-generation Murphy family including Frances M. Draper, a granddaughter of the late Carl Murphy. She is also assisted by her cousin John J. Oliver Jr. and a host of family members who hold key management positions.

### *Chicago Defender* (1905–Present)

**Robert Sengstacke Abbott** along with John H. Murphy and many others have been credited with putting the black press on solid footing both as a successful economic enterprise and as a preserver of African American life and culture. Following in the tradition of his predecessors Russwurm and Cornish, Abbott founded the *Chicago Defender* in 1905.

Abbott was born on St. Simon Island, Georgia, on November 24, 1870. He spent his early years attending school in Savannah, Georgia, and would later learn the printing trade while attending school at the Hampton Institute in Virginia. Abbott continued his education in Chicago, where he earned a bachelor of law degree from Kent College of Law in 1899. Unfortunately Abbott failed to be admitted to the bar in Illinois, in Gary, Indiana, and in Topeka, Kansas. He finally returned to Chicago, where he established the *Defender*.

Abbott's success in the newspaper business made him one of the most popular African American news publishers and journalists of his time. Under his leadership the *Chicago Defender* became one of the most widely circulated black newspapers of the twentieth century. When Abbott first produced the newspaper, he was the publisher, editor, reporter, treasurer, and circulation and business managers. He began circulating the four-page paper throughout his Chicago neighborhood. Abbott delivered as many as 300 newspapers door to door for the first few years of its history. By 1910, the *Defender*'s circulation began to surge, and Abbott hired his first full-time employee, J. Hockley Smiley. Smiley's reporting style garnered reader interest, which prompted greater circulation of the newspaper. Moreover, southern blacks were subjected to oppressive conditions such as lynching, voter disenfranchisement, poor working conditions, and an economic depression that captured Abbott's attention. He used his newspaper's influence to start the "northern campaign," which encouraged many southerners to move away from their southern homeland and travel north. Many African Americans had already begun to leave the South in search of better conditions in the North. Abbott's southern ties made him aware of the situation, and he decided to use that information to his advantage. He and the *Chicago Defender* have been credited with helping to increase the number of black migrants to Chicago. In fact, between 1915 and 1917, more than 100,000 blacks migrated to Chicago from southern cities, almost tripling Chicago's black population. Furthermore, the *Chicago Defender*'s circulation had grown to reach more than 230,000 readers during those years. Abbott not only used this media to advocate for racial equality; he also used it to raise readers' awareness of racial problems in the North and the South.

By 1939 Abbott's health began to slowly decline; the newspaper's popularity also decreased. In an effort to save the newspaper, Abbott appointed his nephew, John Sengstacke, son of his brother Alexander, as the news editor and publisher. In February 1940, Abbott died, leaving Sengstacke in control of the newspaper. Under Sengstacke's leadership, the *Chicago Defender* would remain as one of the leading black newspapers, but the circulation numbers would slowly decline through the years. Sengstacke's tenure lasted over several decades, and by his death in 1997, the newspaper's circulation had dwindled to 20,000. To his credit, Sengstacke Enterprises was established, with several newspapers under its umbrella. They included Detroit's *Chronicle*, *Pittsburgh Courier*, and the Memphis *Tri-State Defender*.

Today Sengstacke Enterprises, now Real Times, Incorporated, is headed by John Sengstacke's son Robert, his daughter Myiti, and his nephew Tom Picou. The *Defender* and five other weekly newspapers that are controlled by Sengstacke Enterprises are under reconstruction. The new generation of leaders has made marketing toward a younger readership and community outreach programming an integral part of their campaign to return the *Chicago Defender* and its sister papers to their former glory.

### Pittsburgh Courier (1910–Present)

Robert Lee Vann, a Pittsburgh attorney and journalist, founded the *Pittsburgh Courier* in 1910. Vann, like Abbott, migrated to the North from the South. Vann was born in Ahoskie, North Carolina, and attended school at the Waters Normal Institute in Winston Salem, North Carolina. He would later attend Virginia Union University in Richmond Virginia. Also like Abbott, Vann headed north to attend law school. He earned a law degree from the University of Pittsburgh in 1909. Vann successfully passed the Pennsylvania bar examination and immediately started his law practice. Vann was very eager to establish a reputable business, so while waiting for the law practice to become profitable, he became interested in the newspaper business. His initial induction into the newspaper business was not as financially fulfilling as he had hoped. However, by 1914, the once mediocre paper had proved its staying power.

Vann focused on attracting readers to his newspaper not by using flashy headlines or radical news coverage but rather by focusing the news on church concerns, local society news, entertainment, and sports. His goal was not to ostracize any particular segment of the community through the *Courier*'s news coverage. During the period of the Great Migration many African Americans selected Pittsburgh as their new home, which created overcrowded conditions, health and living concerns, unfair employment conditions, and poorly equipped schools. As a way to address the tense situation, Vann decided to alter the course of the *Courier* to focus mainly on these social issues. Vann encouraged African Americans who were in a position to serve in the areas of health, business, and education to work within the black community. He also believed in formal education as a means to racial uplift in the black community. Through the paper's editorials, Vann encouraged African Americans to save their money in preparation for the return of white soldiers from the world war. Vann believed that their eventual return to the civilian workforce would render African

Americans jobless. Vann also editorialized about negative images of African Americans in mainstream media. He countered the negative coverage in the mainstream press by emphasizing African American achievement through his news coverage. Another strategy Vann used to attract readers was including a column in the *Courier* titled "News from Back Home." Its primary focus was to provide the new migrants from the South with news information from their former southern regions. He also sent reporters into the South to cover the violent and oppressive conditions blacks experienced in areas like Georgia, Alabama, Kentucky, and Oklahoma. The results of these types of news articles helped to increase the *Courier's* circulation and profits. Finally, Vann also heavily criticized the local police agency for its frequent raids in the black community.

By 1936, the *Courier's* circulation had reached a total of 174,000. Under Vann's leadership the *Pittsburgh Courier* gained a reputation for presenting the community with information with tact, diplomacy, and absolute accuracy. The *Courier* therefore became one of the leading black newspapers with regard to its editorials, its features, and its overall news coverage.

In 1966, John H. Sengstacke purchased the newspaper and renamed it the *New Pittsburgh Courier*. It then became part of Sengstacke's newspaper chain, the largest black newspaper enterprises in the country. Today the *New Pittsburgh Courier* remains under the leadership of the Sengstacke family and continues to serve the African American community. It publishes local editions twice weekly and serves primarily southwestern Pennsylvania.

### Norfolk Journal and Guide (1910–Present)

Originally known as the *Gideon Safe Guide* and the *Lodge Journal and Guide*, the four-page weekly would become a leading southern black newspaper in the twentieth century. The newspaper evolved from the fraternal order of the Supreme Lodge Knights of Gideon in 1900. The weekly was purchased by P. B. Young Sr. in 1910 and became the *Norfolk Journal and Guide*. With a circulation of 500, Young purchased the newspaper and became its editor and chief until his retirement in 1946. The early *Journal and Guide* occupied a less radical position than some of its contemporaries like the *Chicago Defender* and the *Pittsburgh Courier*. Part of the reason for its moderate stance was due to its geographic southern location. Southern black newspapers were faced with the harsh realities of the Jim Crow South that did not allow black newspapers to speak critically of the economic, political, educational, and social injustices experienced by southern blacks. Therefore the *Journal and Guide* relied less on sensationalism and more on factual journalism. Consequently, some of the major benefits to the newspaper were its gains made from advertising revenue from local and national white-owned businesses. The *Journal and Guide* appealed to these businesses because of its more conservative news coverage. The *Journal and Guide* gained advertisements from major national businesses including Goodrich, Pillsbury, and Ford as well as from local white-owned businesses.

Some of the major causes that the *Journal and Guide* crusaded for or against during the 1920s included lynching, voter rights, better water and sewage, crime reduction, improved housing, and education. Contrary to other black newspapers, the *Journal and Guide* did not advocate for African American migration to the North during the Great Migration period of the 1910s and 1920s. Young opposed the mass movement because it resulted in the loss of the large southern black labor force. He also believed that blacks could experience economic progress in the South if they supported racial solidarity and cooperation between blacks and whites. During the early period of the newspaper, Young founded and was elected the first president of the Norfolk chapter of the NAACP.

In the 1930s Young was joined by two of his sons—P. B. Young Jr. and Thomas White Young—who worked as staff and management assistants for the newspaper. Also many well-known journalists including T. Thomas Fortune served as contributors to the *Journal and Guide*. During its third decade in press the *Journal and Guide* became directly involved in the news coverage and legal funding of the Scottsboro defense case. The Scottsboro case involved nine African American boys convicted of the rape of white women in Alabama. The case gained national attention when it made its way to the Supreme Court in 1931. The *Journal and Guide*, along with a few other black newspapers, began immediate in-depth, on-the-scene coverage of the trial. The *Journal and Guide* also spearheaded a funding campaign for the nine boys' legal defense.

By the 1940s the *Journal and Guide*'s humble beginnings had grown from a small circulation of 500 to a thirty-two-page weekly with a circulation of over 80,000. The newspaper thus became the fourth leading black newspaper, led by the *Courier, Afro-American*, and the *Defender*. Young began to publish multiple editions of the newspaper, including a national edition, and local editions in Richmond, Portsmouth, and Hampton-Phoebus, Virginia. The paper even reached subscribers in Washington, D.C. and Maryland. The 1940s was also the last decade that the paper was under the direct leadership of P. B. Young Sr. During his final tenure as the *Journal and Guide*'s editor and publisher, Young focused the newspaper's coverage on integration in the defense industries and the War Department.

In 1946, Young Sr. retired from the newspaper, leaving his sons to manage. Subsequently, in 1962 Young Sr. died. Tragically his youngest son Thomas White Young died in a plane crash in 1967. The *Journal and Guide* was then sold to outside buyers. Bishop L. E. Willis, a Norfolk businessman, bought the newspaper in 1972 and sold it to J. Hugo Madison in November 1973. Madison, a successful attorney in Norfolk, owned the paper for one year before he sold it to Reverend Milton Reid in April 1974. In 1987, the *Norfolk Journal and Guide*'s masthead had Brenda Andrews as the publisher, editor, and owner. In 1992 its name was changed to the *New Journal and Guide*. Today the *New Journal and Guide* continues in the tradition and mission of the black press as an advocate for the African American community. The newspaper's major coverage includes events that give voice and meaning to the black experience in America. Although its circulation numbers have dwindled to 25,000 weekly readers, its mission and news quality are nonetheless felt by its faithful readers and supporters of the black press.

### Kansas City Call (1919–Present)

In April 1919, Chester A. Franklin founded the *Kansas City Call* and remained its owner, publisher, and editor until his death in 1955. His vision for the newspaper included a desire to build a strong business that would provide leadership in the local Kansas City, Missouri, community. He would eventually add to the success of the black press by making the *Call* one of the six largest African American weekly newspapers in the United States as well as the largest black business in the Midwest.

The *Call*, like many other black newspapers, began as a four-page weekly. In its initial stage the *Call's* circulation reached 2,000 people for five cents a copy. During his first few years of operation, Franklin relied on the help of his most vocal supporter, his mother Clara Bell Franklin. Clara Franklin served as his records keeper, delivery person, and countless other non-discriminate titles. The *Call's* popularity quickly grew among its midwestern readers. Part of the newspaper's appeal to the local African American community can be attributed to its stance against lynching, police brutality, segregation, and discrimination in housing, the workforce, and education. The *Call* also supported a policy of high standard news reporting free of sensationalist columns. The newspaper's editor Franklin wanted to record and highlight the achievements of the African American community rather than focusing on crime and negative stereotypes that were already highlighted in the mainstream press. The majority of the news that was reported in the *Call* was local newsworthy events that happened in Kansas City, including church news, sports and entertainment, and society news.

Franklin's thirty-six-year tenure as the chief editor and publisher of the *Call* ended in 1955. His wife, Ada Crogman Franklin, became the new owner and publisher of the *Call*. Lucille Bluford was appointed the new chief editor of the *Call*. She eventually became the owner and publisher of the newspaper, and her tenure with the newspaper spanned seventy-one years until her death in 2003.

The history of the black press in the United States is a remarkable achievement. Beginning in 1827 with the founding of the first African American newspaper, *Freedom's Journal*, African American publishers, editors, and journalists have been able to achieve on three fronts. First, as a business enterprise the African American press serves as one of the leading black institutions of the nineteenth and twentieth centuries. Second, it perhaps has contributed more to preserving the legacy of black business enterprises, activities, and black entrepreneurship than any other scholarly work. Third, the black press has been and continues as a leading force in helping to eradicate racial, economic, employment, and educational inequities both in their local communities and on the national scene. The African American press has focused on every major and minor event that provides insight into the black experience. This has been its mission since its inception in the nineteenth century and continues into the twenty-first century.

*See also*: Black Businesses in Large Cities: A History; Women and Business

**Sources**

*Afro-American*. http://www.afro.com.

Black Archives of Mid-America, Franklin Collection. "The History of the Kansas City Call." http://www.blackarchives.org.

Farrar, Hayward. *The Baltimore Afro-American, 1892–1950*. Westport, CT: Greenwood Press, 1998.

*Freedom's Journal*, March 16, 1827.

Muhammad, Baiyina W. "What Is Africa to Us?: The Baltimore *Afro American's* Coverage of the African Diaspora, 1915–1941." Ph.D. diss., Morgan State University, 2004.

*New Journal and Guide*. http://www.njournalg.com.

*New Pittsburgh Courier*. http://www.newpittsburghcourier.com.

Simmons, Charles A. *The African American Press with Special References to Four Newspapers, 1827–1965*. Jefferson, NC: McFarland Press, 1998.

Suggs, Henry Lewis, ed. *The Black Press in the Middle West, 1865–1985*. Westport, CT: Greenwood Press, 1996.

———. *The Black Press in the South, 1865–1979*. Westport, CT: Greenwood Press, 1983.

Wolseley, Roland E. *The Black Press U.S.A.* 2nd ed. Ames: Iowa State University Press, 1990.

*Baiyina W. Muhammad*

# Black Retail Action Group

The Black Retail Action Group (BRAG) was founded in 1970 to encourage and stimulate black participation in retail and wholesale industries. It runs intern programs for college students and educational programs for persons already working in the industry. BRAG grew out of the National Negro Retail Advisory Group (NNRAG). Brag takes a pragmatic approach to professional development with its internship, career counseling, and scholarship programs. In addition, BRAG president Gail Monroe-Perry accentuates basic principles of organizational reinforcement: punctuality, ownership, consistency, reliability, and conflict resolution.

It can be said that Abraham & Straus executives were right on time and punctual when they stepped to the plate and swung away at discrimination in America, becoming the first major retailer to sign on for President John F. Kennedy's Plans for Progress commission on opportunities for African Americans in 1968. Technical assistance to businesses owned by minorities and scholarships for minority interns in the retail industry emerged as BRAG was partially founded by Abraham & Straus executives in 1968 despite the fact that the official charter appeared in 1970. Founding member and president from 2003 and 2004, Gloria Hartley was largely responsible for expanding the group's influence through marketing, public relations, fund-raising, and networking. With a Bachelor of Science degree in psychology and a Master of Science degree in education from Fordham University, Hartley parlayed her life skills to establish a professorship at international acclaimed Fashion Institute of Technology in Manhattan and has successfully run an international marketing consulting firm as a sharp entrepreneur as well.

BRAG executives develop professionally through educational activities such as executive roundtables and leadership cultivation through direct pipelines to corporate leaders. Significant opportunities for undergraduates include the Executive Excellence Program (EEP), the Consumer Distribution Committee (CDC) Internship and Corporate Internships. The EEP provides store management and merchandize planning skills. The CDC internships provide academic credit and pay. The program is supported by partnerships with such established companies as Saks Fifth Avenue, Lord & Taylor, Bloomingdales, Tommy Hilfiger, Coach, Foot Locker, and Macy's. Focus courses such as Corporate Politics and Business Ethics, Presentation Skills, Security and Loss Prevention, Retail Mathematics, Customer Service, and Merchandising and Product Development expose interns to a wide range of industry issues.

Although an impressive surge of urban clothing lines in the 2000s such as Sean John, FUBU, Roc-a Wear, Maurice Malone, and Echo testify to the growing presence of blacks in urban clothing lines, BRAG's research concluded that many blacks still lack full understanding of behind-the-scenes activities. BRAG's culminating gala and dinner/dance is the group's primary fund-raiser for endowing scholarships and for linking promising high school and college students with the who's who of fashion and retail. Scholarship recipients and gala attendees are treated to valuable lessons from BRAG Business Achievement Award honorees who offer priceless guidance and resources to help the process of transformation in the industry to ensure that eventually blacks have more influence behind the scenes. The 2003 recipient Jeffrey Tweedy, executive vice president of Sean John, launched into action by funding two scholarships. Quoted in "Something to Brag About," Lloyd Boston, 2002 ceremony emcee and BRAG mentor, perhaps stated it best when he noted that "we have to own our own trends before they leave our community." Such comments certainly did not fall on the deaf ears of youth participants—Boston also began his ten-year ascension to Tommy Hilfiger vice-president as an unpaid intern.

Relying on BRAG for the inside track to opportunities and knowledge within the retail and wholesale industry has proven to be a sound human investment, for the return is limitless. In 2004, the *Network Journal*, a monthly publication dedicated to empowering and educating black business and small business owners, awarded former president Hartley with the 25 Influential Black Women in Business Award for BRAG expansion programs. Scholarships for fifteen students, the most in their history, were secured through programs for the Fashion Industries High School and the Fashion Institute of Technology Travel Abroad Scholarship. Clearly Hartley's leadership and BRAG's overall success provide something to brag about, not shallow rhetoric mired by theoretical jargon with no practical base.

*See also*: Fashion Industry; Women and Business

**Sources**

Black Retail Action Group. http://www.bragusa.org.

"BRAG Fetes Industry Achievers." *WWD*, November 3, 2003, 7. web5.infotrac.galegroup.com/itw/infomark/961/275/67058023w5/purl=rclGBFM.

Federated Department Stores, Inc. http://www.federated-fds.com/pressroom.

Smart-Young, Taiia. "Something to BRAG About: These Designers are Breaking Down Racial Barriers in the Retail Industry." *Black Enterprise* (November 2002).

"Tweedy Honored by BRAG." *Daily News Record*, November 3, 2003, 8. web5.infotrac.galegroup.com/itw/infomark/961/275/67058023w5/purl=rclGBFM.

*Uzoma O. Miller*

# Blacks in Agriculture

Agriculture has always been an essential function of human societies; in Africa, the varied climates and regions (desert, savannah, rain forests, mountains, river valleys, etc.) necessitated differing approaches to land cultivation, while also sparking the development of trade and merchant activity. Groups and individuals began to barter the crops they harvested (beyond the amount needed for themselves) in their immediate locations and traveled beyond their local surroundings to buy and sell other products of their labor.

The institution of chattel slavery took the merchandising process to a horrible extreme, with human beings, as well as agricultural and other natural resources, becoming products for purchase. In the case of Africans, this dehumanizing process led to their forced removal into other countries and regions of their home continent, Europe, Asia, and eventually, the Americas and the "New World."

The date 1619 is often cited as the beginning of African enslavement in what would become the United States, when twenty blacks arrived in Jamestown, Virginia, a colony of Great Britain. Blacks were brought to work as forced labor in what was primarily an agrarian society, benefiting white settlers and colonists who had begun the displacement of the Native American (Indian) tribes. For the most part, the Indians resisted servitude through warfare and/or relocation to areas away from the whites.

The captured Africans were disengaged from their societies culturally and geographically and forced to endure the horrors of the "Middle Passage" in slave ships bound for the Americas; untold numbers of lives were lost in the brutal and savage journeys due to disease, murder, suicide, and other atrocities. The (un)fortunate ones who somehow managed to endure the voyages became a perverse example of "the survival of the fittest" and were sold at market as human livestock shortly after arrival.

The majority of enslaved Africans were put to work in agricultural settings, primarily in the southern region of the colonies/states, where they provided unpaid labor producing large quantities of food and cash crops, including cotton, tobacco, and sugar. As a result, the landowners/slave owners profited immensely and, by extension, the American economy in both domestic and international markets.

Beyond the meager amounts of food and clothing allowed for their subsistence, and the bare minimum in shelter, "field Negroes" (as they were called) in the "slave quarters" in most cases had little of value or substance and "no rights which a white man was bound to respect." On the other hand, the "masters" enjoyed the fruits of slave labor in large farming and plantation settings, in cities and rural environments throughout the South.

While the Civil War and the Emancipation Proclamation supposedly brought an end to slavery as a way of life, the former slaves, for the most part, were still "tied to the land" and the landowners. The promise of "40 acres and a mule" never materialized; as a result, relationships changed into a system that came to be known as tenant farming or "sharecropping."

Blacks continued to work as farmers, in many instances on the same land they worked as slaves, but their labor was provided in the faith and hope that over time they could earn enough money/equity to own some part of the land after working it and "sharing its crops" and other products with whites. This became another exploitative relationship, where white landowners benefited without giving up control of the land and its resources. Despite the obstacles, a number of blacks persevered to become owners of small family farms and homesteads. Large families were not uncommon, as children (and sons in particular) provided additional assistance to their parents as agricultural workers.

James Clingman cites Robert D. Bullard, a leading expert on agriculture, who found that in 1910 black farmers owned over 16 million acres of farmland, and ten years later, there were 925,000 black farmers. Other sources indicate that the total amount of black-owned farmland may have been as high as 19 million acres at one point.

## AGRICULTURE AND BLACK EDUCATION: FROM RECONSTRUCTION TO SEGREGATION

The overwhelming majority of Africans in America had been denied access to education, in fact and/or by law prior to the Civil War and emancipation. After the war ended in 1865, the reconstruction of the South involved a brief period where blacks were allowed to vote in significant numbers. Their impact on the southern political system resulted in the election of African American legislators and public officials on the federal, state, and local levels, who pushed for the rights of blacks to receive education and other rights of citizenship until 1876, when reactionary elements used violence and the electoral, judicial, and legislative systems to disfranchise black officeholders and voters and effectively end their short season of political power and influence.

A number of entities, including the Freedmen's Bureau, the American Missionary Association, and other religious organizations, became involved in efforts to establish schools for the education of blacks, with the majority of these institutions located in the South and border states. Even as these early schools were being established, education for blacks varied greatly, especially in rural areas where "book learning" took a backseat to required and necessary labor during planting and harvesting seasons.

The debate over education for blacks after slavery reflected the realities of American society at that time. On the one hand, many felt that education for blacks should be designed to develop practical skills and trades that were necessary to ensure immediate survival, while others favored the development of schools that stressed the liberal arts and classical approach to intellectual development. The most negative groups and individuals did not want them to receive any education and actively sought to harass, disrupt, and even destroy persons, groups, organizations, and facilities that promoted educational development.

The earliest institutions for the higher education of blacks also reflected these realities and stressed one of two approaches: The first was the classical/liberal arts approach (for example, Fisk University in Tennessee and Howard University in the District of Columbia); others emphasized "normal" education focusing on agricultural and industrial skill development and applications, with Tuskegee Institute in Alabama as the best-known example. Some institutions, such as Lincoln University in Pennsylvania and Hampton Institute in Virginia, sought to achieve a balance between liberal and industrial education.

Two African American leaders, **Booker T. Washington** (graduate of Hampton and first teacher/principal/president of Tuskegee) and W.E.B. Du Bois (graduate of Fisk and first black Ph.D. from Harvard), became symbols of these two different philosophies. Washington's famous Atlanta Exposition address in 1895 and the publication of Du Bois's literary masterpiece *The Souls of Black Folk* in 1903, among other works, became key documentation of their philosophical differences on the subject of black education.

Prior to the emergence of the majority of higher education institution for blacks and leaders such as Washington and Du Bois, the U.S. Congress had begun the process of addressing the need for agricultural and industrial education alongside the liberal arts and classical educational model with the Morrill Act of 1862, which led to the development of state land-grant institutions.

The recently established black colleges and institutions were excluded, for the most part, in the Morrill Act, although there were isolated instances where private and public institutions for blacks were allotted limited funding (for example, Alcorn State University in Mississippi, Claflin University in South Carolina, Hampton Institute in Virginia, and Kentucky State College). The majority of funds were clearly designated for white state-supported institutions.

The success of the agricultural/industrial education philosophy, particularly at Hampton and Tuskegee, led to the Second Morrill Act in 1890. As neither of these institutions was state supported, they were denied land-grant status (Tuskegee would later receive a special designation alongside the other 1890 schools); however, these institutions became the model for the public black colleges that would achieve this distinction. Many schools actually came into existence or were assured survival as a direct result of the Morrill Acts, and some would incorporate the letter combinations "A&I," "A&M," "A,M,&N," or "A&T" into their names to clarify their focus on agricultural education, along with industrial, mechanical, "normal" and/or technical training (i.e., Tennessee A&I, Florida A&M, Arkansas A,M,&N, North Carolina A&T).

Tuskegee Institute's outstanding scientist George Washington Carver, who came to the college as head of the division of agriculture in 1886, was a pioneer and innovator in developing agricultural research in the black land-grant college setting. His many other personal achievements, discoveries, and inventions, which had national and international implications in agriculture, business, and other fields of activity, brought worldwide recognition to the man and the college.

Carver became director of the first agricultural research station on a black campus, created conferences and institutes for black farmers and workers, and practically applied agricultural research by traveling directly to farm settings to provide assistance, conduct research and studies, and share his findings to benefit farmers directly in their immediate environment. His discoveries and applications were credited with saving the southern agricultural system, and his products helped to create whole new industries.

The "Tuskegee system" was replicated in the black land-grant colleges in Alabama, Delaware, Florida, Georgia, Kentucky, Louisiana, Maryland, Mississippi, Missouri, North Carolina, Oklahoma, South Carolina, Tennessee, Virginia, and West Virginia. Overall, the model was successful, as it was perceived as useful, practical, and less threatening to the southern power structure and social order, which had evolved into the flawed doctrine of "separate but equal." Segregation of the races, especially in the southern states, had been made legal as a result of the U.S. Supreme Court's ruling in the 1896 *Plessy v. Ferguson* case.

## AGRICULTURE IN THE TWENTIETH AND TWENTY-FIRST CENTURIES

Other factors such as the industrial revolution, which moved America away from being an agrarian society, continuing social and economic hardships faced by blacks in the South, and the possibilities of better living and working conditions in the North led to the migration of larger numbers away from the agricultural setting. In the first half of the twentieth century, the Great Depression of the 1930s, extended drought and other adverse weather conditions, and the demand for industrial workers during the two world wars became incentives for many blacks to abandon farming lifestyles and occupations. The increasing mechanization and industrialization of agricultural processes, involving huge tracts of farmland as opposed to small family farms, combined over time with the influx of immigrant workers from Mexico and other countries, further impacted the decline of blacks as farmers and/or agricultural laborers (Tables 16 through 19).

Persons who chose to remain faced not only the dangers and humiliations of segregation in the South but the challenges of maintaining families, livestock, and farmland in the midst of numerous uncertainties such as weather and other natural conditions, quality of harvested crops, and efforts to disfranchise them from farmland and other property regardless of status, whether landowners or tenant farmers.

Assistance to farmers from U.S. Department of Agriculture extension service programs was formally established in 1923, with the development of relationships with state agricultural agencies and land-grant colleges. In the era of segregation, black agents, supervisors, and other extension workers comprised a small percentage of the total number of persons employed in this capacity, worked almost exclusively in black land-grant colleges and rural communities, and were paid considerably less than whites performing similar work. In addition, overall funding for extension services to the black rural farm population and the number of blacks hired to implement service programs were not equitable, considering their percentage of the total U.S. rural farm population.

The civil rights movement of the 1960s brought an end to legal segregation and reestablished voting rights for blacks in the South and elsewhere, leading to increased access to public accommodations, education, and elective offices. Even with these landmark changes, challenges remained for blacks in farming and agriculture in the "New South" as well as in other parts of the nation. One notable example of progress with connections to agriculture was Michael Espy, who, when elected from Mississippi in 1986, was the first African American from his state to serve in Congress since the Reconstruction period a century earlier. Espy made history again when he was appointed as the first African American secretary of agriculture in 1993, during the Clinton administration.

Agricultural research has continued to thrive as an important component of the 1890 land-grant institutions, with ongoing support from the federal government, foundations, and/or national/multinational corporations. Collaborations, partnerships, and other initiatives have been established and maintained with universities, governments, and other organizations in the United States, emerging African nations, and other developing countries in various parts of the world to address immediate and long-term agricultural needs.

Black agricultural scientists, engineers, and researchers continue to conduct their work from the black land-grant colleges and universities, as well

**Table 16.** Average Hourly, Daily, and Weekly Cash Wages, Average Hours and Days Worked during Week for Hired Farmworkers, by Race and Sex, United States and Major Regions, May 1945*

| Area, Race, and Sex | Cash Wages Earned May 20–26, 1945 (on reporting farm) | | | Time Worked May 20–26, 1945 (on reporting farm) | | |
| | Hourly | Daily | Weekly | Hours per day | Days per week | Hours per week |
| | Dollars | Dollars | Dollars | Number | Number | Number |
| **United States** | | | | | | |
| White | .41 | 4.00 | 19.80 | 9.8 | 4.9 | 48 |
| Nonwhite | .28 | 2.70 | 10.60 | 9.7 | 3.9 | 38 |
| Male | .38 | 3.70 | 18.20 | 9.8 | 4.9 | 48 |
| Female | .33 | 3.00 | 10.20 | 9.1 | 3.4 | 31 |
| **Northeast** | | | | | | |
| White | .38 | 3.60 | 21.60 | 9.7 | 5.9 | 57 |
| Nonwhite | .65 | 5.70 | 27.70 | 8.7 | 4.9 | 42 |
| Male | .39 | 3.80 | 22.20 | 9.7 | 5.9 | 57 |
| Female | .59 | 4.90 | 22.30 | 8.3 | 4.6 | 38 |
| **North Central** | | | | | | |
| White | .30 | 3.20 | 18.10 | 10.7 | 5.6 | 60 |
| Nonwhite | .27 | 2.90 | 12.00 | 10.5 | 4.2 | 44 |
| Male | .30 | 2.80 | 18.40 | 10.8 | 5.6 | 61 |
| Female | .28 | 2.40 | 10.30 | 8.4 | 4.4 | 36 |
| **South** | | | | | | |
| White | .66 | 2.80 | 11.10 | 9.6 | 3.9 | 38 |
| Nonwhite | .23 | 2.30 | 8.60 | 9.7 | 3.8 | 37 |
| Male | .27 | 2.70 | 11.10 | 9.7 | 4.2 | 40 |
| Female | .21 | 2.00 | 5.80 | 9.4 | 2.9 | 28 |
| **West** | | | | | | |
| White | .30 | 6.10 | 33.70 | 9.2 | 5.5 | 51 |
| Nonwhite | .70 | 6.60 | 35.70 | 9.3 | 5.4 | 51 |
| Male | .66 | 6.10 | 34.00 | 9.3 | 5.5 | 51 |
| Female | .72 | 6.20 | 32.40 | 8.7 | 5.2 | 45 |

*Excludes approximately 87,000 custom workers since the hire of machinery, equipment, or workstock was included in their reported cash wages.

*Note:* Estimates based on data from enumerative sample survey of the Bureau of Agricultural Economics.

*Source:* Published in Jessie P. Guzman, ed., *Negro Year Book: A Review of Events Affecting Negro Life, 1941–1946* (Tuskegee, AL: Department of Records and Research, Tuskegee Institute, 1947), 162.

**Table 17.** Farm Operators, by Race, for the United States, by Regions, 1940 and 1930

| Race | Number of Operators | | Increase 1930 to 1940 | |
|---|---|---|---|---|
| | 1940 | 1930 | Number | Percent |
| **United States** | | | | |
| Classes | 6,096,799 | 6,288,648 | −191,849 | −3.1 |
| Negro | 681,790 | 882,850 | −201,060 | −22.8 |
| White | 5,377,728 | 5,372,578 | 5,150 | 0.1 |
| **The North** | | | | |
| Classes | 2,579,959 | 2,561,785 | 18,174 | 0.7 |
| Negro | 8,898 | 11,104 | −2,206 | −19.9 |
| White | 2,567,257 | 2,545,829 | 21,428 | 0.8 |
| **The South** | | | | |
| Classes | 3,007,170 | 3,223,816 | −216,646 | −6.7 |
| Negro | 672,214 | 870,936 | −198,722 | −22.8 |
| White | 2,326,904 | 2,342,129 | −15,225 | −0.7 |
| **The West** | | | | |
| Classes | 509,670 | 503,047 | 6,623 | 1.3 |
| Negro | 678 | 810 | −132 | −16.3 |
| White | 483,567 | 484,620 | −1,053 | −0.2 |

A minus sign (−) denotes decrease.

*Source*: U.S. Bureau of the Census. Published in Jessie P. Guzman, ed., *Negro Year Book: A Review of Events Affecting Negro Life, 1941–1946* (Tuskegee, AL: Department of Records and Research, Tuskegee Institute, 1947), 154.

as other institutions, and participate in the development of the next generation of scientists and scholars in the field. Their activities remain vitally important, as agriculture remains essential to the survival and progress of humanity in all parts of the world.

The decline in the number of black and white farmers continued throughout the twentieth century, even as agriculture became the domain of large corporate interests. Black farmers, who continue to persevere despite their reduced numbers (from nearly 1 million in 1920 to around 18,000 by 1999; 1 percent of U.S. farmers) and decades of land loss, as recently as 2002 were still documented as owning 7.8 million acres of farmland. They have organized into associations such as the **National Black Farmers Association** and the Black Farmers and Agriculturalists Association and brought a class-action lawsuit involving approximately 22,000 black farmers against the U.S. Department of Agriculture in 1997 for discrimination in farm lending practices and unfair foreclosures of farms owned by African Americans.

The case was settled in 1999, with the government paying 12,597 farmers more than $629 million in claims and forgiving at least $17.2 million in outstanding loans, according to U.S. Department of Agriculture (USDA) statistics. However, nearly 9,000 lost in efforts to file claims that were

**Table 18.** Farms of Negro Operators by Tenure—Number, Acreage, and Specified Values, for the United States, 1900–1940

| Tenure | 1940 | 1930 | 1920 | 1910 | 1900 |
|---|---|---|---|---|---|
| | | | *Number of Farms* | | |
| Total | 681,790 | 882,850 | 925,708 | 893,370 | 746,715 |
| Owners | 174,010 | 181,016 | 218,612 | 218,972 | — |
| Managers | 413 | 923 | 2,026 | 1,434 | — |
| Tenants | 507,367 | 700,911 | 705,070 | 672,964 | — |
| | | | *Lands in Farms (acres)* | | |
| Total | 30,785,095 | 37,597,132 | 41,432,182 | — | 38,233,920 |
| Owners | 10,314,283 | 11,198,893 | — | — | — |
| Managers | 153,601 | 249,072 | — | — | — |
| Tenants | 20,317,211 | 26,149,167 | — | — | — |
| | | | *Value of Land and Buildings (dollars)* | | |
| Total | 836,067,623 | 1,402,945,799 | 2,257,645,325 | — | 396,145,262 |
| Owners | 251,328,726 | 334,451,396 | — | — | — |
| Managers | 8,208,132 | 14,844,767 | — | — | — |
| Tenants | 576,530,765 | 1,053,649,636 | — | — | — |
| | | | *Value of Buildings (dollars)* | | |
| Total | 224,388,138 | 340,409,360 | — | — | 71,902,265 |
| Owners | 81,129,400 | 105,741,696 | — | — | — |
| Managers | 1,998,971 | 4,023,544 | — | — | — |
| Tenants | 141,259,767 | 230,644,120 | — | — | — |
| | | | *Value of Implements and Machinery (dollars)* | | |
| Total | 40,193,537 | 60,327,856 | — | — | 18,859,757 |
| Owners | 15,671,208 | 19,784,411 | — | — | — |
| Managers | 539,663 | 623,050 | — | — | — |
| Tenants | 23,982,666 | 39,920,395 | — | — | — |

*Notes:* Data for 1940 and 1930 relate to April 1; for 1920 to January 1; for 1910 to April 15; and for earlier years to June 1; — = not available.

*Source: General Report on Agriculture*, vol. 3, 1940, chap. 3. Published in Jessie P. Guzman, ed., *Negro Year Book: A Review of Events Affecting Negro Life, 1941–1946* (Tuskegee, AL: Department of Records and Research, Tuskegee Institute, 1947), 154.

challenged by the USDA, and many say that they still face the same kind of discrimination that led to the lawsuit.

According to Gary Grant of Tillery, North Carolina, head of the Black Farmers and Agriculturalists Association, the average age of black farmers is sixty years old. The next generation is turning away from farming as an occupation, due in part to witnessing the hardships and challenges faced by their parents and elders, as well as the many other educational and career options now available to young black people.

Leaders and advocates for black farmers indicate that if current trends are not reversed, agriculture, which was blacks' first occupation in America, will become virtually nonexistent as a career choice and lifestyle. The National Black Farmers Association, Black Farmers and Agriculturalists

**Table 19.** Trends in the Number of Farms in the United States by Color and Tenure of Operators, 1910–1940 (Decennial Censuses)

| | Number of Farms | | | | Percent 1910, 1930, and 1940 Are of 1920 | | | |
|---|---|---|---|---|---|---|---|---|
| | 1940 | 1930 | 1920 | 1910 | 1940 | 1930 | 1920 | 1910 |
| **Number of Farms (total)** | 6,097 | 6,289 | 6,448 | 6,362 | 94.5 | 97.5 | 100 | 98.6 |
| By color of operators | | | | | | | | |
| White operators | 5,378 | 5,373 | 5,498 | 5,441 | 97.8 | 97.7 | 100 | 98.9 |
| Nonwhite operators | 719 | 916 | 950 | 921 | 75.7 | 96.4 | 100 | 98.9 |
| By tenure of operators | | | | | | | | |
| Full owners | 3,084 | 2,912 | 3,367 | 3,355 | 91.6 | 86.5 | 100 | 99.6 |
| Part owners | 615 | 657 | 559 | 594 | 110.1 | 117.6 | 100 | 106.3 |
| Managers | 36 | 56 | 68 | 58 | 53.1 | 81.6 | 100 | 84.9 |
| All tenants | 2,361 | 2,664 | 2,455 | 2,355 | 96.2 | 108.5 | 100 | 95.9 |
| Proportion of tenancy (percent) | 38.7 | 42.4 | 38.1 | 37.0 | 101.6 | 111.2 | 100 | 97.1 |
| Croppers (southern states) | 541 | 776 | 561 | * | 96.5 | 138.2 | 100 | * |

*Not available for 1910 census.

Source: Published in Jessie P. Guzman, ed., *Negro Year Book: A Review of Events Affecting Negro Life, 1941–1946* (Tuskegee, AL: Department of Records and Research, Tuskegee Institute, 1947), 163.

Association, and other organizations are seeking to influence and collaborate with 1890 land-grant colleges, black churches and religious organizations, other institutions, and individuals to educate African Americans and others about the plight of the black farmer and the continuing significance of agriculture.

Black people spend billions of dollars on food every year but presently own only nineteen supermarkets in the entire United States, according to reports and commentaries. Without black farmers and landownership, others would completely control the supply of food. These realities underscore the ongoing need for, and importance of, continued African American involvement in all phases of agriculture in the twenty-first century.

**Sources**

Burrell, Thomas. "History of African American Landownership." Black Farmers and Agriculturalists Association, Inc. http://www.bfaa.net.

Clingman, James. "Economic Empowerment: Black Farmers Still Fighting." http://www.coax.net/people/lwf/ee_black.htm.

Gilbert, Jess, Spencer D. Wood, and Gwen Sharp. "Who Owns the Land? Agricultural Land Ownership by Race/Ethnicity." *Rural America* 17 (Winter 2002): 55–62.

McGee, Leo, and Robert Boone, eds. *The Black Rural Landowner—Endangered Species: Social, Political, and Economic Implications*. Westport, CT: Greenwood Press, 1979.

National Black Farmers Association. http://www.blackfarmers.org.

Neyland, Leedell W. *Historically Black Land-Grant Institutions and the Development of Agriculture and Home Economics, 1890–1990*. Tallahassee: Florida A&M University Foundation, 1990.

Parker, Suzi. "The Vanishing Black Farmer." *Christian Science Monitor*, July 13, 2000.

Schapsmeier, Edward L., and Frederick H. Schapsmeier. *Encyclopedia of American Agricultural History*. Westport, CT: Greenwood Press, 1975.

Smith, Jessie Carney, and Carrell P. Horton, eds. *Historical Statistics of Black America*. Detroit: Gale Research, 1995.

*Fletcher F. Moon*

# Booker T. Washington Business Association

Founded in Detroit in 1930 at the beginning of the Great Depression, the Booker T. Washington Trade Association, as it was known then, aimed to support and create more black businesses and at the same time create more employment opportunities for blacks. It was named for the noted black educator and founder of the **National Negro Business League, Booker T. Washington**. It was one of several strong local organizations established in cities with large black populations and extensive black business enterprises. Its founder, the Reverend William H. Peck, was pastor of Bethel A.M.E. Church and an activist as well; he witnessed a need to help blacks establish businesses at a time when many were coming to Detroit in flight from poverty and racism that they experienced in the South. The founding members were local black professionals.

From the start the association held weekly meetings and missed only one due to a temporary city ordinance forbidding meetings from occurring during serious race riots. The sessions were luncheon meetings held each Wednesday and provided a time for members to raise questions regarding the improvement and development of business enterprises. Prominent local black entrepreneurs were invited as speakers. Until World War II, the association published a monthly trade journal and also mounted business exhibits; the monthly trade journal was resumed later on. The association has always been a strong supporter of the National Negro Business League and has attended its various conferences.

Established initially as the Booker T. Washington Trade Association, in time the organization changed its name by replacing "Trade" with "Businessmen's." As women became involved, members changed the name again to become the Booker T. Washington Business Association (BTWBA) to make its name gender neutral but retained its vision. The noon luncheon, first held in 1932, continues to attract women. When its seventieth luncheon was held in 2004, only women attended. Ethnic groups, such as the Hispanic Chamber of Commerce and Arab American and Asian American organizations, are encouraged to work with the association and may send representatives to board meetings. In 1987, BTWBA elected Betty Pulliam of the Payne-Pulliam School of Trade and Commerce, Inc. as president (for the years 1987–1989), making her the first woman to head the organization. Since then, Margo Williams became a vice president and, along with other women, helped to revitalize the organization. She began networking and soon received business from major companies who sought her work as head of a media relations and training firm. She spearheaded a successful drive to invite Michigan's 34 black millionaires to a dinner. Working with *Black Enterprise* magazine, the annual affair now attracts 500 people, an increase over the 100 who first attended.

Located at 2885 East Grand Boulevard, the BTWBA has now become the African American Chamber of Commerce in Detroit. Its goals, according to its Web page, focus on "business development and growth, business and financing opportunities, technical assistance and referral services, entrepreneur training for area youth, economic stability in the African American Community, [and] reciprocal business/trade practices." There are 360 corporate and individual members. Its members or supporters include Detroit automobile dealer **Melvin Farr**, manufacturer Dave Bing, former National Basketball Association star and entrepreneur **Earvin "Magic" Johnson Jr.**, and Michigan's former Secretary of State Richard Austin. Corporate members include churches, banks, casinos, International Business Machines (IBM), and the Henry Ford Health Corporation.

BTWBA's efforts continue to be analogous to a "black chamber of commerce"; it supports the work of small and large businesses owned by blacks. It is the preeminent organization in the city for black entrepreneurs and offers programs, luncheons, seminars, training sessions, and conferences for aspiring black entrepreneurs. While recent leaders prefer not to dwell on race, they do focus on the bright future of black businesses "in a town that has just elected its third black mayor," wrote Alan Fisk. The mayors—Coleman A. Young, Dennis W. Archer, and Kwame M. Kilpatrick—all have been BTWBA members.

**Sources**

BTWBA. http://www.btwba.org/web/html.

Fisk, Alan. "Association Trades in Business Success." *Detroit News*, February 26, 2003. http://www.detnews.com/2003/detroit/0303/05/s06-p4271.htm.

Oak, Vishnu V. *The Negro's Adventure in General Business.* Yellow Springs, OH: Antioch Press, 1949.

*Jessie Carney Smith*

## Booker T. Washington Trade Association. *See* Booker T. Washington Business Association

## Ruth Jean Bowen (1925– ), Businesswoman, Entertainment Agent, Booking Company Executive

Ruth Jean Bowen is the first African American woman to own her own talent agency. Her first company was founded in 1959. By the late 1960s, the Queen Booking Corporation, a talent clearinghouse located in New York City, was the largest black-owned booking agency in the world. For nearly fifty years, Bowen has been responsible for overseeing and managing the careers of some of the world's greatest performers including Aretha Franklin, Ray Charles, Marvin Gaye, and Sammy Davis Jr. She booked her clients in national as well as international venues. Using her astute management techniques, she has succeeded in a male-dominated industry and has survived against fierce competitors.

Born September 13, 1925, Ruth Jean Baskerville completed her elementary and part of her secondary education in Danville, Virginia. She graduated from Girls High School in Brooklyn after the family moved to New York. She studied business administration at New York University for two years. In 1944, at the age of nineteen, she married singer Billy "Butterball" Bowen, who was an original member of the Ink Spots. She met this saxophonist who later became a member of the famed singing group at the Savoy Ballroom. The Ink Spots had vocal styles and musical arrangements that reached both black and white audiences. Traveling with the group she learned valuable practical information about the entertainment business.

She became even more knowledgeable about the industry by managing her husband's business affairs. Being on the road with the group, she faced the same racial discrimination in lodging and restaurants that blacks encountered during the 1940s, 1950s, and 1960s.

Having a spouse as a successful entertainer for over thirty years allowed Bowen to socialize with musicians, singers, and newspaper writers. She was introduced to rhythm and blues singer Dinah Washington in 1945, and a year later Washington became Bowen's first client. At Washington's encouragement, she became her press secretary and later assumed responsibility for the singer's personal affairs. Before Bowen became her manager, unscrupulous managers and booking agents had exploited Washington, as had been many singers of the 1940s and 1950s. As publicist and business manager for this gifted vocalist, Bowen significantly impacted the singer's career by bringing an organized approach to the business side of her career. In 1959, the team of Bowen and Washington formed a publicity company with a small investment of $500; Washington named their business Queen Artists. Bowen booked the engagements and Washington provided the contacts. Before getting her booking license from the state of New York, Bowen studied the management style of Joe Glasser, who was the agent for Louis Armstrong, Billie Holiday, and Dinah Washington. Bowen observed Glaser's attention to the details of every contract and took note of the time he took reading and answering all correspondences relating to his client. When Glaser refused to book Washington for European engagements, Bowen assumed responsibility for this aspect of Washington's career as well. Some of Bowen's other early clients included saxophonist Earl Bostic, songwriter and vibe player Johnny Lytle, guitarist Kenny Burrell, and the Basin Street East nightclub.

Ten years after the agency was formed, it was renamed the Queen Booking Agency (QBC) in 1969. In 1959 the agency began with a staff of four that booked acts in Washington, D.C., Harlem, and Chicago. As the company grew, Bowen hired and trained agents who were required to follow her exacting example of putting the needs of the client first. Because they were competing with established agencies like Rockwell-O'Keefe and William Morris, her agents had to place their talent in the best venues, get top dollar for their services, and take care of lodging, security, and other services associated with each performer's individual needs.

For almost fifty years, Bowen has represented some of America's most talented artists. Her clientele included individual performers, groups, gospel choirs, and comedians. During the zenith of her career, she managed over 100 performers. Some of her clients include Lola Falana, the Dells, Al Green, Patti LaBelle, Smokey Robinson, Stevie Wonder, Redd Roxx, Richard Pryor, the O'Jays, Gladys Knight and the Pips, the Delfonics, the Stylistics, Shirley Caesar, the Staples Singers, the Isley Brothers, Kool & the Gang, the ChiLites, the O'Jays, Teddy Pendergrass, Ike and Tina Turner, the Four Tops, Dee Dee Warwick, Reverend James Cleveland, Andrae Crouch, Slappy White, Clara Ward, The Mighty Clouds of Joy, Stu Gilliam, and Willie Tyler.

Bowen learned business theory at New York University. She learned the practical side of the entertainment industry traveling with her spouse and managing Dinah Washington's career. She is a shrewd businesswoman who has not only survived but has excelled in an arena dominated by men. During the 1950s and 1960s she was a member of the Rinky Dinks, a club formed by the wives of New York musicians that raised funds for charitable organizations. She has been a member of Operation PUSH and presently works for the Parkinson's Foundation. Bowen is currently chief executive officer of the Bowen Agency, Ltd. In a 1993 article, the *Chicago Defender* featured her in its "Black Legends" column.

The legendary Ruth Bowen is a superagent. She used her formal and informal training along with her special talents to work on behalf of her clients. She made unknown artists household names and improved the careers of performers whose careers were stifled by poor managers.

*See also*: Women and Business

**Sources**

"Africa and the Diaspora Timeline." http://home.acceleration.net/clark/papervu/timeline.htm.

*Daily News*. http://www.nydailynews.com/front/story/101907p-92151c.html.

Goodson, Martia Graham. "Ruth Jean Bowen." *Notable Black American Women*. Book II. Ed. Jessie Carney Smith. Detroit: Gale Research, 1996.

Hine, Darlene Clark, ed. *Facts on File Encyclopedia of Black Women in America; Business and Professions*. New York: Facts on File, 1997.

Locke, Tara Y. "Black Legends: Ruth Bowen Founded a Booking Corporation." *Chicago Defender*, March 31, 1993.

Original Ink Spots—Newspaper articles from January 1, 1943. *Cleveland Call and Post*, July 9, 1949. http://inkspots.ca/ispress2.htm#49

Smith, Jessie Carney. *Black Firsts: 4,000 Groundbreaking and Pioneering Historical Events*. 2nd ed. Rev. and expanded. Detroit: Visible Ink Press, 2004.

Washington, Dinah. http://www2.worldbook.com/features/aamusic/html/washington2.htm.

*Gloria Hamilton*

# Richard Henry Boyd (1843–1922), Entrepreneur, Banker, Educator, Preacher, Publisher, Civil Rights and Political Activist, Author

Richard Henry Boyd may have been born a slave, but by the time of his death in 1922, he was one of black America's most leading business personalities. An adherent of **Booker T. Washington**'s economic self-sufficiency philosophy and founder of the National Baptist Publishing Board, one of his greatest entrepreneurial endeavors was his role as a founder of the One-Cent Savings Bank and Trust Company, now known as Citizens Savings Bank and Trust Company (the nation's oldest continuous African American–owned and –operated banking institution). A founder and owner of one of the city's first black newspapers, the Nashville *Globe*, and a principal in the Union Transportation Company, Boyd also served as vice president of the **National Negro Business League**. During the early 1890s, he cautioned his fellow citizens of African descent that the dominant members of society were engaged in retracting the advances made in the African American civil rights struggle. The combination of his religious prominence, business ventures, and his reputation as a "race man" catapulted Boyd into a national leadership position among African Americans of the late nineteenth and early twentieth centuries.

Born to a slave mother, Indiana Ann Dixon (1820–1915), on March 15, 1843, in Noxubee County, Mississippi, Boyd was originally given the name of Dick Gray. As a slave lad, the young Gray played with white children until age ten. After age ten, Gray labored as a slave, serving as a mule boy, hauling cotton to the weighing wagons, ginning cotton, and bailing it for hauling to the market. After the death of his mistress, one of her family members purchased Gray and took him to Texas, where he remained until the outbreak of the Civil War. During the war, Gray accompanied his master and served as his body servant in the army of the Confederate States of America. After the battle of Chattanooga, he returned to Texas and worked on and managed the Gray plantation. Gray, as all other American slaves, received his freedom in December 1865 with the ratification of the Thirteenth Amendment to the U.S. Constitution. However, slaves in Texas did not receive notification of the amendment's ratification until June 19, 1866. After the death of the surviving head of the Gray family, Dick became a cowboy. In 1868, he married Laura Thomas, who died within a year of the marriage. The following year, he joined the Baptist church, changed his name to Richard Henry Boyd, and became a Baptist minister.

In 1871, Boyd married Harriett Albertine Moore, and they became the parents of six children, three boys and three girls (Henry Allen, J. Garfield Blaine, Theophilus Bartholomew, Lula, Mattie, and Annie). With the assistance from his wife, he attended Bishop College in Marshall, Texas. However, because of the growth of his family and the paucity of financial resources, he withdrew from Bishop to support his family. Refusing to acquiesce from his work as a Baptist minister, the Reverend Boyd used his time and talents organizing African Americans and churches of the Baptist faith across the state of Texas.

Boyd, with the assistance from a southern white minister, organized the Texas Negro Convention. In 1875, he organized the Lincoln District Baptist Association. Serving as a district missionary between 1870 and 1874, the Reverend Boyd became educational secretary of the Texas Negro Baptist Convention. In 1879, he was elected moderator of the Central Baptist Association. As educational secretary for the Texas Negro Convention, Boyd abhorred the paternalistic authority that white Baptist officials from the North exhibited with respect to vested African American Baptist officials. He and others resented the white American Baptist Publication Society's (ABPS) endeavor to control the writing and distribution of African

American Sunday School literature as well as the ABPS refusal to publish and distribute religious materials written by African American sermonizers. Tired of the paternalistic domination of the northern APBS, Boyd conceived of the idea of African Americans supplying their own congregations with religious periodicals.

In the mid-1890s, Boyd moved to Nashville, Tennessee, where he became an influential leader among those in the African American community. A contemporary of attorney **James Carroll Napier**, the Reverend Preston Taylor, and others who adhered to the philosophy espoused by Booker T. Washington, which emphasized the acquisition of property and economic independence, he developed into the quintessential "race man."

## BECOMES ENTREPRENEUR

The Reverend Boyd and others organized the National Baptist Publishing Board (NBPB) that provided African Americans churches with religious literature, church pews, and other appurtenances for church services. He established or supported the National Negro Doll Company, the first business enterprise to market black dolls to African American consumers; the One-Cent Savings Bank and Trust Company; the Globe Publishing Company, which published the Nashville *Globe*; the *National Baptist Union Review*, an African American denominational newspaper; and the Home Mission Board of the National Baptist Convention, which distributed religious literature and supported missionary efforts. A man for all seasons, Boyd cautioned Tennesseans of African ancestry that whites were intent on castigating their civil rights. When Nashville implemented the state's legislatively mandated "Jim Crow" streetcar law, the Reverend Boyd and others called for African Americans to boycott the city's public transportation company. They followed the instituted tradition of political and economic protest of the pre-1890s against racial injustice and oppression that demanded racial equality. In keeping with the Washingtonian philosophy, they established the Union Transportation Company.

Chartered in 1896 by the Reverend Richard Henry Boyd and a group of African American businessmen, the National Baptist Publishing Board became operational by 1898. Incorporated according to the laws of Tennessee on August 15, 1898, the National Baptist Publishing Board occupied three buildings on Market Street (now Second Avenue) in downtown Nashville. According to Bobby Lovett in *The African American History of Nashville*, Boyd strongly felt that African Americans must "furnish his Sunday School with religious knowledge, his choirs with music, and his firesides and parlors with wholesome literature, written and manufactured by his own energy." Said the Reverend Boyd, "The literature that is best for the Caucasian of today is not always best for our children, under the present 'Jim Crow' crisis. Whatever is taught in the Sunday schools of this generation will be the doctrine of the church in the next generation." By the end of the first decade of the twentieth century, the NBPB employed over 100 African

Americans and became a successful symbol of "race enterprise." Initially printing Sunday school lessons penned by whites, by 1910 the African American–owned and –operated board employed African Americans to write short sermons and moral discourses, which were distributed to thousands of African American churches throughout America.

Additionally, the NBPB published song sheets and religious hymnals that became the standard for African American churches. The gospel community knew Thomas Dorsey, the "father of gospel music," because many of his songs were published through the NBPB before he moved to commercial presses. Bringing pride to an oppressed people, the board also published numerous books. Between 1899 and 1901, the board published twenty-four book titles, including Boyd's *Pastor's Guide and Parliamentary Rules* (1900). Between 1902 and 1905, the NBPB continued publishing hymnals and books by African American authors, including but not limited to the third edition of the *National Baptist Hymnal* (1903). Rendering a useful service to the general African American populace and authors as well, many of the books represented an indispensable collection of early-twentieth-century African American Baptist history. Continuing to advocate race pride among African Americans, Boyd established the National Doll Company at NBPB Nashville headquarters.

Management of the National Doll Company was under the leadership of Henry A. Boyd, while his father handled the company's monetary affairs. Established with the purpose of instilling race pride in African American children, Boyd purchased the black dolls from a manufacturer in Europe and advertised them in the Nashville *Globe*. According to Bobby Lovett in *A Black Man's Dream*, one *Globe* advertisement read: "These dolls are not made of that disgraceful and humiliating type that we have grown accustomed to seeing Negro dolls made of. They represent the intelligent and refined Negro of the day, rather than the type of toy that is usually given to the children and, as a rule, used as a scarecrow."

In 1908, the National Baptist Convention endorsed the Negro dolls. Boyd, a strong proponent of the "buy black" campaign that was directed by the country's African American leaders, faced insurmountable criticism from some inside the convention because of the National Doll Company being operated in the publishing board's facilities. Viewed as a private venture of the Boyds, opponents wanted an operational separation of the publishing board's affairs from those of the doll company. While the National Baptist Doll Company failed to be a profitable business undertaking, it nonetheless illustrated Boyd's sensitivity to the unrelenting demoralizing and psychological effects of African American oppression within the U.S. borders.

Seven years after arriving in Nashville and becoming one of the city's principal African American leaders, Boyd and several other prominent African American leaders discussed the reestablishment of a banking institution for their community. On November 5, 1903, the executive committee members of the Negro Business League met in James C. Napier's offices and seriously contemplated the opening of an African American bank. Agreeing upon the concept, the attendees scheduled another meeting a week later. At that conclave, the One-Cent Savings Bank and Trust Company was organized and capitalized with $1,600. Elected officers included the Reverend Preston Taylor as chair of the board of directors, the Reverend Robert H. Boyd as president, and attorney James C. Napier as cashier (manager). The new banking establishment opened two months later on January 16, 1904, in the Napier Court Building on 411 North Cherry Street (now Fourth Avenue, North).

With Napier's assistance, the Reverend Boyd supervised the direction of the new banking institution with parsimony and competent management. In 1908, according to the Nashville *Globe* and cited in *A Black Man's Dream*, Boyd emboldened stockholders to reinvest their annual 6 percent dividends in the banking enterprise and stated: "It should be clearly understood by the stockholders that this institution was born out of real necessity." Said President Boyd, "It was not organized as a loan company and investment company, an industrial insurance company, nor a pawn shop, and the idea of 'getting rich quick' was never in the minds of the officers of this institution." After the 1874 collapse of the Federal Savings Bank and Trust Company (founded by the U.S. Congress in 1865, there were thirty-three branches, including one in Chattanooga, Nashville, Columbia, and Memphis, Tennessee), Boyd worked arduously to restore the African American community's confidence and to encourage pride in the aptitude and capability of blacks to own and operate their own commercial institutions. The incisive banker and those who followed him became members of the National Bankers' Association, which was organized at the 1905 National Negro Business League convention.

The One-Cent Savings Bank and Trust Company weathered America's recurring economic depressions of 1914, 1921, and 1929. Growing slowly and remaining fiscally sound under the conventional economic strategies of its board members, the bank's name was changed to Citizens Savings Bank and Trust Company in 1920. Two years later, the bank's functionaries relocated the financial institution from the Napier Court Building to the Colored Young Men's Christian Association Building. Surviving for more than 100 years, Citizens Savings Bank and Trust Company is the nation's oldest continuous African American–owned and –operated banking institution. A year after entering the banking business, R. H. Boyd and other African American community leaders found themselves embroiled in civil rights issues emanating from the U.S. Supreme Court's 1896 *Plessy v. Ferguson* decision, which enunciated the "separate but equal" doctrine.

When the Tennessee General Assembly convened in January 1905, Davidson County Representative Charles P. Fahey introduced Bill No. 87 "to separate white and colored passengers on streetcars." Tennessee's "streetcar law" passed the legislative body on March 30. Effective on July 5, the law required streetcar operators to designate by conspicuous signs which part of the car was for "white" or "colored" passengers. African American leaders who were angered by the law's passage met at NBPB's headquarters on the same day the law went into effect and organized a boycott against Nashville's public transportation system. An adherent of economic self-determination, the Reverend Boyd said in *A Black Man's Dream*: "[T]hese discriminations are only blessings in disguise. They stimulate and encourage, rather than cower and humiliate the true, ambitious, self-determined Negro." As vice president of the Negro Business League, he hosted another meeting on July 31. A month later, they established the Union Transportation Company. Chartered by fourteen men on August 29, 1905, they elected the Reverend Preston Taylor as president and Boyd as treasurer. Numerous community rallies were held to raise $16,000 in needed capital to finance the company's public transportation venture. Boyd went to work putting the company into business. He traveled to Tarrytown, New York, and purchased nine steam cars from the Mobile Machine Company. The Union Transportation Company began serving its African American clientele on September 29. Charging five cents, the lines operated three routes. However, because of Nashville's hilly terrain, the steam-driven cars prove to be less than effective. Boyd traded the steam cars for fourteen electric cars that became operational in July 1906. He installed generators in the facilities of the NBPB, where the batteries were charged at the end of the business day. Three months before Boyd purchased the electric cars, the Nashville City Council passed a "privilege tax" of $42 per car on private streetcars, which was a contributing cause to the African American–owned transportation company's failure. During a May 1907 meeting, Boyd, Taylor, and others officers decided to sell the electric cars and pay off the company's indebtedness of $735. Selling the cars to the Jamestown Exposition, the Union Transportation Company, Nashville's only African American–owned public transit corporation, ceased operation. Notwithstanding the business defeat, the struggle against racial discrimination and inequity continued, and the Reverend R. H. Boyd continued to be a combatant in the African American battle against systematic racial segregation.

## FINANCES THE NASHVILLE *GLOBE*

The Reverend Richard Henry Boyd was not only an author, banker, publishing house executive, and civil rights activist; he was also a newspaperman. The 1905 Nashville streetcar boycott provided Boyd and the NBPB an opportunity to enter the newspaper business. The same year he financed the Nashville *Globe*, which was printed at the NBPB's facilities. Boyd's son Henry Allen Boyd and Joseph O. Battle served as the newspaper's editors, and his son J. Blaine Boyd and Frank Battle also participated in the newspaper business. Boyd stated that the *Globe*'s mission was to enlighten African Americans about the boycott against segregated streetcars. To divest the newspaper's enterprise from the NBPB's operations, the founders of the Nashville *Globe* chartered the Globe Publishing Company. Managed by Dock A. Hart, the Globe Publishing Company paid the NBPB for printing the *Globe*.

In 1909, when the Tennessee General Assembly approved a normal school in each of the state's grand divisions and one for the state's 472,987 African Americans, editors of the Nashville newspaper used its pages to wage a successful campaign for the state normal college (now Tennessee State University) to be located in the Davidson County. After Battle's 1910 death, H. A. Boyd served as the *Globe*'s editor. During its first decade of existence, the *Globe*'s readership reached approximately one-fifth of Nashville's total population. Between 1910 and 1930, it had the largest circulation of any African American newspaper in the state. Mirroring with specificity the values and ideologies of the Boyds and the leadership of the African American Baptist Church and the African American community in general, the *Globe* served as the community's griot, chronicler of events, and promoted the Association for the Study of Negro Life and History's Negro History Week. It became the African American community's political voice, publicized social and cultural development, and served as an important organ advancing African American businesses. The newspaper published reports about the fiscal viability of both the One-Cent Savings Bank and Trust Company and the People's Bank. Through its leaders, the *Globe* endorsed the "buy black" campaign, and its editorial page critized those who oppressed African Americans, opposed the nation's system of racial apartheid, promoted morality, and praised all who made constructive contributions to the African American race. It also encouraged African American political participation and emboldened city functionaries and African American businessmen to improve living conditions within the community. As Nashville's most successful African American newspaper, it served as the community's voice and conscience for more than a half a century. It ceased operation in 1960, less than a year after the death of Henry Allen Boyd.

While pursuing business developments, Nashville's African American leaders created an active chapter of the YMCA. They perceived this as an opportunity to holistically address the needs of individuals. After all, it was the YMCA's mission to develop "body, mind, and spirit." The Boyds, both Richard and Henry, Preston Taylor, James C. Napier, and others felt this was particularly important when the dominant society rebuffed African Americans and considered them nonconstructive participants in and contributors to the social order. Although an earlier YMCA movement died, with assistance from William N. Sanders and the Rosenwald Fund, African American leaders in Nashville revitalized the "Y" movement. In 1917, the Boyds, Taylor, and others purchased the Duncan Hotel facility to use as the site for the Colored YMCA. Considered a "mission" of the white YMCA, which also held the facility's $70,000 mortgage, the prominent leaders of the African American community sought an independent charter from the Y's national headquarters. Disillusioned by the display of white paternalism, the Boyds, Taylor, Napier, and William Beckam again stepped forward and raised the necessary funds to take over the Duncan's mortgage. Each man, with the exception of Napier, contributed $1,000 to the Colored YMCA. Attorney Napier contributed $500 to the cause.

With judicious management, the NBPB became the largest publishing enterprise operated by African Americans in the United States. However, the 1915 dispute over the relationship of the NBPB to the National Baptist Convention split black Baptist churches across the nation and caused a chasm within the convention. This chasm became the basis for the convention to split into two different denominational conventions, the National Baptist Convention and the National Baptist Convention, U.S.A., Incorporated. Notwithstanding, the NBPB remained in Nashville, and the Reverend R. H. Boyd presided over its operations until his 1922 death, when he was succeeded by his son, Henry Allen Boyd (1976–1959). H. A. Boyd expanded the company's business during leadership of thirty-seven years. After H. A. Boyd's death on May 28, 1959, his nephew and R. H. Boyd's grandson, Theophilus Bartholomew Boyd Jr., headed the company. During his twenty-year leadership, he acquired and developed the NBPB's $1 million modern printing plant in west Nashville on Centennial Boulevard. On April 1, 1979, T. B. Boyd died, and the mantle of leadership fell upon his son, Theophilus Bartholomew Boyd III, who became the fourth generation of Boyds to head the NBPB's operations. In 1978, he was elected to the board of directors of Citizens Savings Bank and Trust Company, of which he became chairman in 1982.

The Reverend Richard Henry Boyd's work was ceaseless. He assisted in the work of the American Missionary Convention, the American Foreign Mission Convention, and the Education Convention. He traveled to various parts of the world, including the World's Baptist Alliance Meeting in London. Boyd wrote numerous denominational books, including *Plantation Melody Songs* (1910) and *The Story of the Negro Publishing Board* (1915). In addition to his denominational writings, in 1909 he also penned *The Separate or "Jim Crow" Car Laws, or Legislative Enactments of Fourteen Southern States. The Separate or "Jim Crow" Car Laws*, which encapsulated the National Baptist Convention's expostulation against racial bigotry and intolerance, served as a constructive compilation of Jim Crow laws in various states. Boyd earnestly entreated African Americans to employ the booklet to demand enforcement of the U.S. Supreme Court's, infamous as it may have been, ruling in the "separate but equal" case of *Plessy v. Ferguson*. A leader of the 1905 streetcar boycott staged by Nashville's African American community, he served as purchasing agent for the Union Transportation Company. In the forefront of establishing the One-Cent Savings Bank and Trust Company, the Nashville *Globe* newspaper, the National Baptist Church Supply company, the National Doll Company, and the Baptist Sunday School Congress, Boyd was a member of numerous fraternal, civic, and professional organizations.

Preceded in death by his son, J. Blain (April 6, 1922), the Reverend Richard Henry Boyd died at home on August 22, 1922. He was survived by his wife Hattie M. Boyd and children Mattie B. Johnson, Annie L. Hall, Lula B. Sanders, Henry Allen Boyd, and Theophilus Bartholomew Boyd. The remains of the Reverend Richard Henry Boyd, entrepreneur, banker, educator, preacher, publisher, political and civil rights activist, and author were left uninterred until the National Baptist Convention of America met in Nashville from September 6 through 11, 1922. On September 9, 1922, convention delegates met at Greenwood Cemetery for the interment of Boyd's remains.

*See also*: Black Banks: Their Beginning; Black Press: Newspapers in Major Cities

**Sources**

Harvey, Paul. "'The Holy Spirit Come to Us...': Richard H. Boyd and Black Religious Activism in Nashville." *Tennessee History: The Land, the People, and the Culture.* Ed. Carroll Van West. Knoxville: University of Tennessee Press, 1998.

Lovett, Bobby L. *The African American History of Nashville, Tennessee, 1780–1930. Elites and Dilemmas.* Fayetteville: University of Arkansas Press, 1999.

———. *A Black Man's Dream, the First One Hundred Years: The Story of R. H. Boyd.* Nashville, TN: Mega Corporation, 1993.

McDougald, Lois. "Richard Henry Boyd (1855–1922)." *Profiles of African Americans in Tennessee.* Ed. Bobby L. Lovett and Linda T. Wynn. Nashville, TN: Local Conference on African American Culture and History, 1996.

Scribner, Christopher MacGregor. "Nashville Globe." *Tennessee Encyclopedia of History and Culture.* Ed. Carroll Van West. Nashville, TN: Rutledge Hill Press, 1998.

Wynn, Linda T. "Nashville's Streetcar Boycott, 1905–1907." *Profiles of African Americans in Tennessee.* Ed. Bobby L. Lovett and Linda T. Wynn. Nashville, TN: Local Conference on African American Culture and History, 1996.

*Linda T. Wynn*

# Sarah Breedlove. *See* Madame C. J. Walker

# Sheila Bridges (1964– ), Interior Designer, Entrepreneur

Sheila Bridges is one of the most talented and successful interior designers in America. Her trademark, urban chic style has brought her wide acclaim and a clientele that would be the envy of any professional designer. Bridges is also a savvy entrepreneur. Since she founded the business in 1994, Sheila Bridges Designs, Inc. has grown into an over $1.5 million company. Bridges's experience in business is one of the cornerstones of her accomplishments, and she continues to do her own marketing and managing. Her work has been showcased in publications across the country, and she was named America's best designer by *Time* magazine and CNN in 2001. She currently hosts her own television show, *Sheila Bridges Designer Living*, on the cable TV network Fine Living. The paperback version of her book *Furnishing Forward*, originally published in 2002, was rereleased in the spring of 2005.

Bridges was born on July 7, 1964, in Philadelphia, Pennsylvania. The daughter of a dentist and a schoolteacher, Bridges went on to Brown

University, Providence, Rhode Island, to study sociology. She graduated in 1986, completing her senior thesis on race and gender in advertising. With a career in advertising in mind, she set her sights on New York City. Upon her arrival in New York, initially Bridges found it difficult getting the type of work she sought. Originally she had hoped to become the accounts executive for the advertising firm Ogilvie & Martha. However, that was not to be, and Bridges turned to the fashion industry, taking a job at Bloomingdale's and training to become a retail buyer. She later landed a job with Georgia Armani, but the world of fashion retail failed to hold Bridges's attention. She enrolled at the Parsons School of Design in New York City, continuing to work in the day and taking classes at night. During this transitional phase, Bridges secured a job at the prestigious architecture firm Shelton, Mindel and Associates. The firm undertook both commercial and residential projects, exposing Bridges to a whole host of creative and vocational possibilities. And thus it was there that she discovered her passion—interior design.

After graduating from college in 1993 with a degree in interior design, she did a stint in Florence, Italy, where she studied decorative art at Polimoda design school, further refining her sense of style and composition. Subsequently, Bridges decided to establish her own interior design business. The decision to launch her own company, Sheila Bridges Designs, Inc. the self-assured designer attributes to the lack of African Americans in the industry. Bridges's objective was to fill the apparent void and provide African Americans with the resources and services to create living environments that were stylish, yet also a reflection of their own cultural experience and tastes. Consequently, out of her own basement, in 1994, Bridges began to ply her trade as an interior designer. She continued to work for the architecture company but used her breaks, lunch times, and weekends to solicit clients and market her talents.

Ironically, it was Bridges's own home that became the showcase for her dazzling designs. Bridges moved into her landmark historic apartment in Harlem, New York, in 1993. With a spacious canvas before her, she fashioned a masterpiece that became a testament to her creativity and style. Prior to her arrival, Bridges's apartment served as the set for **Spike Lee**'s movie *Jungle Fever*, but it was as a classic display of interior decorating that the apartment would find its fame. Again Bridges's astute understanding of business came into play. She submitted pictures of her apartment to design magazines to promote her up-and-coming company, and people began to pay attention to the young and talented Bridges.

Nevertheless, success did not come easily for Bridges; the New York world of interior design is not for the faint of heart, and Bridges's one-woman show had to battle against staunch competition from well-connected, established companies. Her big break came when she heard that former Uptown Records president Andre Harrell was looking for a new apartment. The determined Bridges called Harrell for four months before he agreed to let her assist him. Bridges ended up selecting and providing the interior design for the apartment. Fashioned in the style of the 1920s Harlem Renaissance, Bridges's talents were so artistically and authentically applied that the finished product was featured in *House & Garden*. Yet that was just the beginning of an ever-increasing list of celebrity clients.

Publicity for Bridges's growing talents continued to grow, as she was interviewed or featured in all the leading design publications and appeared on newsstands across the country. Recognized in *House Beautiful* magazine's list of "America's Most Brilliant Decorators," and proclaimed best interior designer in America by *Time* magazine and CNN in 2001, Bridges went from strength to strength, building her professional portfolio and receiving critical acclaim from a myriad of critics and clients.

Indeed, it is her ability to capture the imagination of such a diverse audience that sets Bridges apart form other interior designers. Despite the original impetus for founding Sheila Bridges Designs, Inc., she is reluctant to be pigeonholed as an exclusively African American designer. Bridges has the rare and uncanny ability to envision and bring to life the decorative desires of any client. She is able to inspire trust in her clients, allowing them to share in the creative process, while ensuring they feel comfortable with the decisions that are made. Her celebrity clientele include former President Bill Clinton, hip-hop entrepreneur and rapper **Sean "Diddy" Combs**, computer software elites Eileen and Peter Norton, former MTV host Bill Bellamy, and acclaimed author Tom Clancy. Bridges embraces the cultural significance of design, but her calling card is the timeless style she encapsulates in the homes and workspaces she decorates.

Although Bridges describes herself as a high-end designer, her work is not colored by the pretentious and gregarious taste that limitless finances can often bring. Bridges is equally at home in designer furniture stores or flea markets. Her creative modus operandi is to craft comfortable homes that are a timeless fusion of antique pieces with modern style that fit the client's requirements and budget. Moreover, it is Bridges's goal to branch out and bring her designs to a wider audience, particularly the twenty-five- to forty-five-year-old homemaker—a feat she is accomplishing with her characteristic aplomb and hence the release of her book in 2002, *Furnishing Forwards: A Practical Guide to Furnishing for a Lifetime*. The book provides useful tips to those who enjoy interior design and want to create wonderful homes but who cannot necessarily afford to hire a professional. Bridges gained further exposure with the launch of her network TV show *Sheila Bridges Designer Living*, which is now in its fourth season. Bridges also appears frequently on NBC's *Today Show*. In 1999 Bridges opened her own antique furniture store in Hudson, New York; however, the store subsequently closed.

Ultimately, Bridges aspires to brand her style and products and make them available nationwide. She is particularly interested in producing and marketing furniture, bedding, rugs, and her own line of paint. Her zeal for quality design has already put her among the elite interior decorators in the country, yet according to Bridges, the greatest design ventures evolve over time, so maybe the best is yet to come.

*See also*: Women and Business

**Sources**

Arango, Jorge. "Eminent Domains." *Essence* 31 (June 2000): 134–138.

Bridges, Sheila. "Places of the Heart." *Victoria* 16 (October 2002): 42.

Brown, Carolyn M. "Timeless Designs for Modern Tastes." *Black Enterprise* 28 (July 1998): 30.

Coleman, David. "Harlem Renaissance." *Elle Decore Style*, May 2005. http://www.elledecor.com.

*Contemporary Black Biography*. Vol. 36. Detroit: Gale Group, 2002.

Galts, Chad. "Designing Women." *Brown Alumni Magazine* 99 (1999). http://www.brownalumnimagazine.com.

Kelly, Marsha. "I Love This Job!" *Essence* 35 (December 2004): 126.

Luscombe, Belinda. "Nest Maker." *Time* 158 (September 2001): 60.

McGrady, Catherine. "Sheila Bridges Designs." *USA Weekend*, June 10, 2001. http://www.usaweekend.com.

Philadelphia, Desa. "People to Watch: Sheila Bridges." *Time* 156 (October 2000): 32.

Whitcomb, Claire. "Design Shrine." *Detroit News*, May 18, 2002. http://www.dedtnews.com.

———. "Sheila Bridges's Study in Serenity." *Victoria* 13 (May 1999): 64.

*Gabriella R. Beckles*

# Andrew Felton Brimmer (1926– ), Economist, Government Official, Educator

Andrew Brimmer, the son of sharecroppers, is an economist whose interest includes monetary policy, international finance, economic development in the African American community, and education. He moved from the cotton fields in Louisiana to become the first African American governor of the Federal Reserve System and from the segregated schools of Louisiana to visiting professor at Harvard University.

Brimmer was born in Newellton, Louisiana, on September 13, 1926, to Andrew Brimmer Sr. (a sharecropper and warehouseman) and Vella Davis Brimmer. He spent part of his young life picking cotton, and he attended segregated elementary and high schools. However, this did not preclude his parents from holding him to high standards and values. They encouraged him to have self-confidence and constantly urged him to "do something worthwhile." After graduation from high school, he moved to Bremerton, Washington, lived with an older sister, and worked as an electrician's helper in a navy yard. He was drafted into the army in 1945; upon the completion of his military service, in 1946, he entered the University of Washington, where he earned a B.A. degree and was awarded a John Hay Whitney Fellowship in economics (1951). Brimmer's interest in foreign economics led to his winning a Fulbright Fellowship to India, where he engaged in postgraduate work at the Delhi School of Economics and the University of Bombay. As a result of this period of study, he published several articles on

Indian economy. Of this experience in India, Brimmer has indicated that India afforded him new opportunities and served as a major influence in his maturing into his professional interest, economics. In 1952, he enrolled in Harvard University, became a teaching fellow, and completed the Ph.D. in 1957.

While enrolled at Harvard University, he worked as a research assistant at the Center for International Studies Massachusetts Institute of Technology, and from 1955 to 1958, he worked as an economist at the Federal Reserve Bank in New York City. During this time, he served as a member of the Federal Reserve Central Banking mission to Khartoum, Sudan, and aided in establishing a central bank (1956). As a result of his travels, he published an article in the *South African Journal of Economics* (March 1960) titled "Banking and Financing in the Sudan." Following the completion of his Ph.D., he taught economics at Michigan State University (1958–1961) and at the Wharton School of Finance and Commerce, University of Pennsylvania (1961–1966). In 1963, he took a leave from teaching and began working as a part of President John F. Kennedy's administration in the U.S. Commerce Department in Washington, D.C. He became more knowledgeable and experienced in U.S. foreign investment policies and practices. Brimmer was also a proponent of tax increase as a way of curbing inflation. In 1966, he was appointed deputy assistant secretary for economic affairs in the U.S. Department of Commerce. In this capacity, he was the chief economist and in charge of the voluntary program.

President Lyndon B. Johnson swore Brimmer in as a member of the Board of Governors of the Federal Reserve System, the first African American governor of the Federal Reserve System (1966–1974), in 1966. He later (1974) became the Thomas Henry Carroll Visiting Professor at Harvard Business School, a post he held for two years. Brimmer left Harvard and formed his own company, Brimmer & Company, Incorporated (1976), an economic and financial consulting firm based in Washington, D.C. He returned to the Federal Reserve as governor of the Federal Reserve in 1997 and moved on to become the first African American to become vice chairman of the Federal Reserve System.

From 1995 to 1998, he chaired the District of Columbia Financial Responsibility and Management Assistance Authority; one of the tasks of this group was to initiate a comprehensive study of the University of the District of Columbia and its challenges. Brimmer has served as a member of the Board of Governors and vice chairman of Commodity Exchange, Inc.; Board of Directors of Bank America; Board of Trustees (chairman) of Tuskegee University; Advisory Board, North American Economics and Finance Association; trustee of the Black Student Fund, Board of Directors of Gannett Company; a Harvard trustee (twice elected); and cochair of the Interracial Counsel for Business Opportunity. His involvement and business expertise have been appreciated through such awards and recognitions as Government Man of the Year by the National Business League (1963); Arthur S. Fleming Award and Russwurm Award (1966); and Horatio Alger Award of the National Urban League (1974). He was renamed president of the Association for the Study of Afro-American Life and History (1989), and he became the chairman of the Joint Center for Political and Economic Studies in Washington, D.C.

In addition to the posts Brimmer has held, he has been productive as a scholar. His publications include *Trends, Prospects, and Strategies for Black Economic Progress* (1985); *International Banking and Domestic Economic Policies: Perspectives in Debt and Development* (1986); "Central Banking and Systematic Risks in Capital Markets" in *Journal of Economic Perspectives* (1989); "Economic Cost of Discrimination against Black Americans" in *Economic Perspectives on Affirmative Action*, edited by Margaret C. Simms (1995); and *The World Banking System: Outlook in a Context of Crisis* (*The Joseph I. Lubin Memorial Lectures*). He contributed a column to *Black Enterprise* magazine titled "Economic Perspectives." His scholarship was instrumental in his being elected to the Washington Academy of Science in 1991.

**Sources**

"Andrew F. Brimmer." *Contemporary Black Biography.* Vol. 48. Thomson Gale, 2005. Reproduced in *Biography Resource Center.* Farmington Hills, MI: Thomson Gale, 2005. http://galenet.galegroup.com/servlet/BioRC Document Number: K1606002957.

"Andrew F. Brimmer." *Notable Black American Men.* Gale Research, 1999.

Reproduced in *Biography Resource Center.* Farmington Hills, MI: Thomson Gale, 2005. http://galenet.galegroup.com/servlet/BioRC Document Number: K1622000043.

"Andrew F. Brimmer, Dr." *Who's Who among African Americans.* 18th ed. Gale, 2005. Reproduced in *Biography Resource Center.* Farmington Hills, MI: Thomson Gale, 2005. http://galenet.galegroup.com/servlet/BioRC Document Number: K1645522574.

*Helen R. Houston*

# Brotherhood of Sleeping Car Porters

The Brotherhood of Sleeping Car Porters was established on August 25, 1925, in the hall of the Imperial Lodge of Elks at 160 West 129th Street in New York City. During that first meeting, 500 porters chose A. Philip Randolph to lead the fledging union and adopted their rallying cry, "Fight or Be Slaves." The event was the culmination of a long and multifaceted relationship between the Pullman Company and the black railroad porters. On one hand, the Pullman corporation provided jobs, salaries, and intangible benefits to blacks after the Civil War. On the other hand, the company had deliberately exploited its porters for decades. Though treated badly by the company, the black community held railroad porters in high esteem.

In 1937, twelve years after the first Brotherhood meeting in New York, the Pullman Company and the porters' union signed an agreement. It was the first labor contract between a large American corporation and a union of black personnel. The agreement provided union representation, a reduction in the number of hours worked, a pay hike, and job security. The historical prelude, the intervening years, and the subsequent outcomes encompass a compelling story. The story of the Pullman porters is symbolic of and parallel to the struggle for equal rights of African Americans after the Civil War.

George Pullman's first sleeping cars, which were a vast improvement over earlier versions, went into service in September 1859. However, Pullman's business acumen made him realize that providing great service to his customers was the means to increased profits. Fortuitously for Pullman, the end of the Civil War resulted in a large potential workforce of unemployed former slaves. The newly freed men needed jobs, and Pullman needed staff members who were used to working long hours and accustomed to taking orders.

Nowadays, few people less than fifty years old remember overnight travel on a railroad train. An integral ingredient to that type of travel was the Pullman porter. The porter helped people on and off the trains and helped them with baggage. Overnight passengers, who could afford it, purchased berths in which they could sleep at night. To ensure the comfort of the Pullman travelers, the porter made up the berths, served refreshments, polished shoes while riders slept, mopped floors, cleaned cuspidors, and responded to any other needs throughout the day and night.

The job of Pullman porter represents the dichotomy many African Americans experience in the workplace. The attendants were well paid in comparison to more menial jobs. They earned good tips, which during pre-income tax days sometimes enabled them to double their salary. Although the porters were exploited, they also had the opportunity to observe the comportment, plush belongings, and speech of their affluent clientele. Using the circumstances to their advantage, the railcar attendants studied and learned from their exposure to the prosperous travelers. After witnessing this unfamiliar, enviable lifestyle, porters realized that education was an important step to social and financial success. The porters decided that they wanted to give their children the opportunity to obtain a good quality, formal education. Because of the opportunity to travel, their sophistication, their exposure to important people, and even because of their uniform, family members and the broader African American population admired them.

During an era when jobs for black workers were scarce, black American men were pleased to obtain employment on the trains, but the job had serious drawbacks. For example, porters, the lowest rank on the train, earned the poorest wages. In addition, the company required them to spend unpaid time to prepare the sleeping cars for passengers and to pay for their uniforms, lodging, and food. Company policy allowed the porters only four hours of rest each night, when they could sleep on a couch in the men's restroom. Relying on tips to supplement their salaries, the attendants, while maintaining their ubiquitous smiles and decorum, were expected to act as servants and to endure all types of demeaning behavior from white travelers. For example, in the tradition of slavery, when slaves were called by the first name of the master, passengers called all of the porters "George" (after George Pullman) or "boy."

Under the guidance of Asa Philip Randolph (1889–1979), a union organizer and civil rights activist, the porters sought to improve wages, work conditions, human rights, and treatment. Although Randolph never worked for the railroad, his reputation as champion for the rights of workers earned him a leadership role in the organization of the Brotherhood of Sleeping Car Porters.

Randolph was born on April 15, 1889, in Crescent City, Florida. As a boy, he experienced the growing trend against equal rights for African Americans, following the passage of Jim Crow laws by southern state governments. However, he had a positive role model in his father, who encouraged learning and who required that his sons walk, rather than use segregated public transportation. As a young man, Randolph became infuriated by **Booker T. Washington**'s moderate approach to racism but inspired by W.E.B. Du Bois's early, assertive philosophy. While a college student, he developed an interest in socialism, which viewed unions as a tool for obtaining better working conditions. Randolph and a friend, Chandler Owen, used the sidewalks of Harlem and the press to communicate their rebellious and militant ideas. In 1917, they launched a magazine, *The Messenger*, which urged African Americans to form labor unions. Using *The Messenger* as their "soapbox," the friends vehemently denounced capitalism, writing, "Capitalism is a system under which a small class of private individuals makes profits out of the labor of the masses by virtue of their ownership of the machinery and sources of production and exchange," wrote Daniel Davis in *Mr. Black Labor*. Linking capitalism to racism, the journalists urged worker revolution and industrial democracy. Randolph and Owens made an abortive attempt to organize a union of black elevator operators, but inevitably such rhetoric and activity attracted the attention of sympathizers, as well as U.S. government officials who branded Randolph as "the most dangerous Negro in America." In June 1925, Pullman porter Ashley Totten approached Randolph and solicited him to help Pullman porters form a union. Totten reasoned that Randolph understood the porter's problems and was a persuasive speaker. In addition, since Randolph was not a railroad employee, he could not be fired for his involvement in organizing the workers.

By using facts along with his powerful, fiery, oratory, Randolph convinced gatherings of porters that they were powerless as individuals but potentially influential as a group. As a result, he won support for a union from porters across the nation. To help spread the message across the nation, Randolph enlisted the assistance of former porters, including Ashley Totten, Milton

Webster, E. J. Bradley, C. L. Dellums, and Morris "Dad" Moore, whose contributions were indispensable to the success of the Brotherhood.

The Pullman Company did not take the union's threats lightly. They planted informants to report on the involvement of porters in union activities, resulting in dismissal of those workers, including Ashley Totten, the man who had recruited Randolph. Hundreds of union supporters were fired, requiring many of the members to keep their membership in the Brotherhood secret. Randolph was a prime target of character assassination and fabricated lies, which suggested that he was planning to run off with the porters' money. To diminish the efforts of Randolph and the Brotherhood, the Pullman Company asked several employees to start a competing union, the Pullman Porters Protective Association. However, a large majority of porters voted for the Brotherhood to represent them.

## BROTHERHOOD BECOMES RECOGNIZED UNION

Despite years of constant and consistent effort to achieve better working conditions, Randolph was unsuccessful. It took twelve years for the Brotherhood to obtain concessions from the Pullman Company when, in 1935, the National Mediation Board certified the Brotherhood as the legally recognized representative of the porters and maids. Monthly pay for porters increased from the average 1925 salary of $67.50 to a minimum of $89.50, and the work hours were reduced from 400 hours a month to 240 hours. Though the gains were modest, the concessions inspired the entire race. In addition, in 1935, the American Federation of Labor (AFL) granted an international charter to the union, under the name of International Brotherhood of Sleeping Car Porters and Maids.

While the Brotherhood presented a predominantly male public image, there was a significant female presence in the background. A. Phillip Randolph's wife, Lucille Campbell Greene Randolph (1883–1963), contributed to the financing of her husband's union work and *The Messenger* with proceeds from her **Madame Walker** beauty salon. Knowing that success of the union required support from the porters' spouses, Randolph organized the women into separate Women's Economic Councils, which offered political, financial, and moral support to their husbands and to the cause. Following the signing of the contact with the Pullman Company, the wives believed that they too had won respectability and the status of "ladies." In September 1938, delegates from the Women's Economic Councils held a convention in Chicago and established the International Ladies Auxiliary Order to the Brotherhood of Sleeping Car Porters. Through these organizations, the women contributed significantly to the union's efforts. Typical of the era, the Brotherhood gave low priority to the working conditions of the black Pullman maids, even though their lives were more difficult. In addition, despite the fact that they attended union meetings and paid union dues, the maids did not receive the equal respect and treatment from the Brotherhood. They, unfortunately, were the victims of the sexism as well as the racism of the times.

The success of the Brotherhood made other African Americans realize that they were entitled to freedom and equal rights. The organizational struggles of the Brotherhood became a breeding ground for activist ideas, protest tactics, and the development of a core of leaders who would make significant contributions to the subsequent civil rights movement. Involvement and support of the members of the Brotherhood of Sleeping Car Porters led to other activities and accomplishments, including the integration of blacks in the broader labor movement, the March on Washington of 1941, the Fair Employment Practices Committee, and the 1963 March on Washington. In addition, Randolph's radical and revolutionary positions in the early 1900s foreshadowed the views of black militants in the 1960s and 1970s. However, perhaps the most significant legacy of the Brotherhood of Sleeping Car Porters was the individual and collective commitment to providing an education for their children, thus producing the beginning of the African American professional class. Numerous successful African Americans have a family connection to Pullman porters or other railroad workers. The list includes noteworthy individuals such as, Malcolm X, Thurgood Marshall, Robert Dellums, Roy Wilkins, **Vernon Eulion Jordan**, William Kennard, Ellen Story Martin, Leroy Richie Jr., Tom Bradley, Wellington E. Webb, Willie Brown, Matthew Henson, Claude McKay, Gordon Parks, and Benjamin Mays.

**Sources**

"Brotherhood of Sleeping Car Porters." *The Reader's Companion to American History.* Ed. Eric Foner and John A. Garraty. Boston: Houghton Mifflin, 1991. http://www.answers.com/topic/brotherhood-of-sleeping-car-porters.

Chateauvert, Melinda. *Marching Together: Women of the Brotherhood of Sleeping Car Porters.* Urbana: University of Illinois Press, 1998.

Davis, Daniel S. *Mr. Black Labor: The Story of A. Philip Randolph, Father of the Civil Rights Movement.* New York: Dutton, 1972.

Reef, Catherine A. *Philip Randolph: Union Leader and Civil Rights Crusader.* Berkeley Heights, NJ: Enslow Publishers, 2001.

Santino, Jack. *Miles of Smiles, Years of Struggles: Stories of Black Pullman Porters.* Urbana: University of Illinois Press, 1989.

Tye, Larry. *Rising from the Rails.* New York: Henry Holt and Co., 2004.

Wright, Sarah. *A. Philip Randolph: Integration in the Workplace.* Englewood Cliffs, NJ: Silver Burdett Press, 1990.

*Cheryl Jones Hamberg*

# Todd C. Brown (1949– ), Food Marketing and Banking Executive

Todd C. Brown is an outstanding corporate marketing executive who made his reputation with Kraft Foods of North America. He held several positions over a twenty-year span, which finally culminated with an executive vice presidency of the company and president of Kraft's E-Commerce Division. Brown's fields of expertise cover executive and operations management, new business and product development, sales leadership, branding, and customer relationship management. In 2003, Brown made a career transition to the community banking business and became vice chairman of ShoreBank Corporation, chairman of the board of directors of ShoreBank in Chicago, and chairman of the board of directors of ShoreBank Cleveland.

Brown has had three successful careers—one in higher education, another in marketing, and one in community banking. A native of Rahway, New Jersey, Brown was born on June 12, 1949. He graduated from Colgate University in 1971 with a baccalaureate degree in sociology and completed a master's degree in higher education administration from Columbia University in 1974. Brown began his early career serving in various positions in the New Jersey education system, which led to jobs in higher education, including the assistant dean of students at Colgate University and director of student services at The Wharton Graduate School at the University of Pennsylvania.

Brown completed his Master of Business Administration degree (M.B.A.) at the Wharton Graduate School in 1980 and made the transition to the business sector that same year, when he became the assistant product manager for the Meals Division with General Foods. General Foods was later purchased by Kraft Foods, a subsidiary of the Philip Morris Companies, Inc. Both companies are a part of the Altria Group, which enjoys Fortune 500 status. Brown left Kraft from 1982 to 1985 to become vice president of marketing for SSA, Inc., a direct marketing firm.

When Brown returned to Kraft, he continued to achieve increasing levels of executive managerial responsibilities. In 1998, Brown was promoted from executive president of Kraft Foods and general manager of the Beverage and Desserts Division to executive vice president of Kraft Food Services Division. In that position, he supervised the manufacturing and distribution of Kraft Food Services to hotels, restaurants, hospitals, schools, and other markets.

Brown was employed with Kraft Foods for twenty-three years, while being promoted to high-profile positions, including two executive vice president appointments. At the time of his retirement in June 2003, Brown was the executive vice president of Kraft Foods North America, as well as the president of its E-Commerce Division, making him one of a few African Americans executives to attain such prominence in the **food service industry**. According to Brown, the e-commerce Web site was the "internet market leader in consumer package goods." Under his leadership, the Web site integrated Internet marketing with the launch of *Kraft Food & Family Magazine*, a free innovative publication, distributed in print and electronic versions. The print version is sometimes distributed in Sunday newspapers, but individual customers can also subscribe to it via the Kraft Web site. The online edition (http://www.kraftfoods.com/kf/FoodandFamily) encourages customers to sign up for free recipes and menus.

Demonstrating a lifelong commitment to mentoring, Brown has used his leadership skills and knowledge to help others, especially young people. He has actively participated with Operation Opportunity, a General Foods–

sponsored program focused on encouraging high school students to seek summer employment. Among his many accomplishments at the food mega-corporation was the implementation of Kraft's African American Council, a development effort and network charged with recruiting, retaining, and advancing African American executives employed by Kraft Foods.

In August 2003, Brown launched a new career in the banking business, when he accepted executive positions with ShoreBank Corporation, a $1.4 billion asset financial institution, specializing in community and environmental banking. ShoreBank supports community growth and revitalization by implementing and promoting financial and informational services. Brown supervises the company's marketing campaign and branding initiatives. His job includes building ShoreBank's customer base, attracting new deposits, broadening the company's loan portfolio, and expanding its branches. Brown will also endeavor to open new services to financially stressed communities.

He currently sits on the boards of ADVO, Inc., JohnsonDiversey, and Colgate University. He is a member of the Executive Leadership Council, an organization of African American executives who promote a business leadership mentoring for African Americans on a national level. Within that organization, he leads the Corporate Board Development program, which endeavors to place more African Americans in corporate boardrooms across the United States. Brown also serves on the board of the Jesse Owen Foundation in Chicago, which targets youth development, and he is a member of the Community Action Council in Danbury, Connecticut. In October 2004, the *Chicago Tribune* reported that Brown had been elected to the Metropolitan Planning Council's board of governors. Brown married his wife Sheyrl in 1973, and they have one daughter, Heather.

*See also*: E-Commerce and the African American Community

**Sources**

*Introducing Todd C. Brown*. Chicago: ShoreBank, 2003.

Jackson, Ben. "Kraft Veteran at Shore Bank Likes Development Recipe." *American Banker*, November 6, 2003.

"Krafts General Foods Names New V.P. of Pollio Division." *New York Voice*, June 29, 1994.

"People: A Look at Local Promotions and Career Moves." *Chicago Tribune*, October 4, 2004.

"Speaking of People." *Ebony* 50 (August 1995): 10.

# Dorothy E. Brunson (1938– ), Radio and Television Executive

Dorothy Edwards Brunson has accumulated impressive credentials in radio and television communications. A pioneer and visionary in the field, she is the first African American woman owner of a radio station, and the first black female to own a full-power television station.

Brunson was born in Glensville, Georgia, March 13, 1938, but grew up in Harlem, New York. Her childhood dream was to be wealthy and to accomplish something noteworthy in her life. Brunson's inspiration developed from her love of reading about the black experience. One heroine in particular, Mary McLeod Bethune, influenced her belief that economics is a greater factor in oppression than color or ethnic differences. Brunson assumed that since her literary heroes were successful she would be, too. She is the founder and president of Brunson Communications Incorporated, owner of broadcast and cable operations and other enterprises that include Citimedia, a company that secures national advertisers for radio.

An innovative leader in the field of broadcast media management, Brunson began college at Tennessee State University, but left disillusioned after a year and a half. Returning to New York, she studied accounting and finance at Pace College and Empire State College, receiving her bachelor's degree from Empire in the late 1960s. While attending college, Brunson worked in a variety of jobs gaining valuable experience that would later benefit her career. At the W. T. Grant retail chain she attained bookkeeping skills. Experience with newspaper layouts, advertising, and promotions came from a position with an advertising agency. In 1964, Brunson joined Sonderling Broadcasting as an assistant comptroller at WWRL-AM, Long Island, New York. She began immediately to build on her existing skills in accounting and advertising by taking courses, reading books, and working overtime in order to make the transition from employee to entrepreneur. Brunson organized the changeover in station format from foreign language to black programming. After only three months as the assistant comptroller, she was promoted to comptroller. Brunson credits her success to hard work, being goal oriented, persistent, and eager to learn.

Brunson left her position at Sonderling in 1969 to join Howard Sanders in launching the first black-owned advertising agency on Madison Avenue. Her partnership with the agency was short lived. Brunson invested her buy-out funds into a retail dress shop catering to plus sizes for women. Unfortunately, the business folded, as it was unable to compete with large discount merchandisers. In 1973, at the request of Inner City Broadcasting Corporation, Brunson pulled together a group of investors, most of them personal friends, who contributed $5,000 to $10,000 each to help the financially troubled company. Brunson was offered the job of general manager for Inner City's radio station in New York, WLIB-AM. She accepted the challenge, despite her reservations concerning the company's financial future. Brunson's experience at Inner City marked the beginning of a period of station revitalization that distinguished her career from that point forward. She cut staff, redesigned jobs, and restructured programming to a more community-oriented focus. Brunson is credited with creating a winning programming formula consisting of marketing and management techniques that focused on the station as the voice of the community. She pioneered the urban contemporary format, a strategic mix of pop music coupled with black rhythm and blues. She instituted the call-in and talk show formats that had been rarely used in black radio. As senior executive, she restructured the indebtedness of the station to enable the purchase of WLIB-FM, its sister station. With increased advertising revenues, the business expanded to a total of seven radio stations with a value approximating $50 million.

As an entrepreneur Brunson was always on the lookout for new challenges. In 1979, she left Inner City to pursue her own quest in broadcast communications. With $3 million in loans, she acquired the failing WEBB-radio in Baltimore. Although this purchase made her the first black woman in the country to own a radio station, there were many obstacles to overcome. The station had a long list of Federal Communications Commission violations and unpaid taxes. Brunson faced mounting community opposition from both blacks and whites, who were opposed to having additional radio station towers. Reluctantly she settled for lower wattage at another location where the towers could be constructed. Her primary purpose was to build the station as the mouthpiece of the black community. Her success in expanding the business was in part enabled because she had won the confidence of her investors who saw her potential to raise ratings and profits. By 1986, she had transformed WEBB into a twenty-four-hour station that was one of the best in the community. Brunson acquired two additional radio stations, WIGO-AM in Atlanta and WBMS-AM in Wilmington, North Carolina.

In 1990, seeking to expand through acquisitions, she sold her three radio stations to venture into the television industry. Her communications media company, Brunson Communications, successfully sought to acquire the independent Baltimore-based WGTW-TV broadcasting to Philadelphia and Delaware valley audiences. The frequency had not been in operation for nine years, and it was another four years before the legal battle for the FCC site license was won. At a time when only about 2 percent of minorities owned television and radio stations, Brunson ventured into ownership of a full-power TV station. She revamped the programming with new shows to target wider audiences, particularly minorities in New Jersey and Delaware. Brunson's goal was to give a voice to the black community with alternative news, current events, health issues, and shows that portrayed blacks in a positive light. This type of programming geared specifically for the black community marks the kind of revitalization and outreach that Brunson has provided during her forty years in the media business.

Lecturer and speaker Brunson is a board member of the Association of Local Television Stations and a charter member of the Association of Black Owned Television Stations. The latter organization works to boost minority ownership by acting as role models for black would-be station owners thus helping to ensure their success. Brunson is the recipient of many accolades and honorary awards for her pioneer spirit, leadership, and visionary entrepreneurship in radio and television.

### Sources

Frost, Randall. "Dorothy Edwards Brunson." *Notable Black American Women*. Book III. Ed. Jessie Carney Smith. Detroit: Gale Group, 2003.

Mueller, Michael. "Dorothy Brunson: Broadcasting Executive." *Contemporary Black Biography*. Vol. 1. Ed. Michael L. LaBlanc. Detroit: Gale Research, 1992.

Paris-Chitanvis, Jacqueline. "Dorothy Brunson: The Making of an Entrepreneur." *Women Making History: Conversations With Fifteen New Yorkers.* Ed. Maxine Gold. New York: Ed. Maxine Gold. New York City Commission on the Status of Women, 1985. (ERIC microfiche ED 266 707)

Simpson, Peggy. "[Women Who Have Changed the World] The Revolutionary of Radio." *Working Woman* 11 (August 1986): 45–46.

Smikle, Ken. "[Three Powerful Women] Dorothy Brunson." *Black Enterprise* 17 (April 1987): 45–46.

*Janette Prescod*

# Thomas J. Burrell (1939– ), Marketing and Communications Mogul

Thomas J. Burrell's 1960s meteoric ascension through corporate Chicago ranks in the advertising field ultimately led to the independent establishment of Burrell Communications Group, a full-service marketing and communications firm that has revolutionized multicultural penetration. By 1980, Burrell was the largest African American agency in the country; by 1998 it had surpassed $168 million in billings; and in 2005 it was quickly approaching the $200 million billings plateau. Burrell's legacy in target marketing of the emotional appeal of such noted corporations as Procter & Gamble, Coca-Cola, and McDonald's is firmly cemented and has garnered him substantial recognition, the least of which is his illustrious induction into the American Advertising Federation's (AFF) Hall of Fame in March 2005.

As a forward-thinking visionary, Burrell, a Chicago native, graduated with a B.A. degree in English from Roosevelt University in 1962 but while still a student received his entry as a mailroom clerk with Wade Advertising in 1961. Taking advantage of the wealth of information available to him, Burrell parlayed this opportunity into management interaction, wherein he was promoted to copywriter in 1961. This experience afforded him lateral movement to Leo Burnett in 1964 before advancing to copy supervisor at London's Foote, Cone and Belding (1967–1968). He returned to Chicago and landed the position of creative supervisor for Needham Harper and Steers (1968–1971). With the requisite knowledge, demonstrated skills base, and necessary confidence to actualize one's entrepreneurial spirit, Burrell opened Burrell McBain Advertising with business colleague Emmett McBain in 1971. With the phrase "Black people are not dark-skinned white people," Burrell immediately set out to debunk stereotypical marketing ploys to an African American demographic by offering strategies instead that focused on black buying power, intelligence, and multilayered dimensions that encompass the diasporic experience.

The essence of Burrell's genius can be appreciated as one considers how his firm convinced McDonald's and Coca-Cola in the early 1970s that appealing more realistically to black consumers could be achieved without marginalizing the white demographic at the same time. Furthermore, the strength in such a formula has resonated to the tunes of billions in advertisement spots through the 1980s, 1990s, and 2000s where, in many instances, youth-driven black culture has proved more influential on the white population as a whole. Accordingly, his proven advertising model focuses on appealing to positive realism instead of preemptive and trite methodologies and has bolstered his impressive client lists to include Lexus, Bacardi, Toyota, General Mills, Verizon, Marriott International, and Nielsen Media Research. By keeping step with current socioeconomic realities, Burrell has demonstrated the necessity of staying ahead of the times from a research perspective, in that the pulse of the nation ultimately sets the very trends co-opted by advertisers attempting to capitalize on such innovations.

In a 2000 article published in *Advertising Age*, Burrell identified the increasing need for niche marketing because data indicate that nonwhites in America will be the majority demographic by the middle of the century. With this in mind, he points to what he terms the "psychographic" approach to marketing, whereby an attempt is made to understand how individuals' self-images are conceptualized and manifested. How to personally address these visions is the desired marketing objective. Burrell further points out that older marketing formulas must constantly evolve by embracing substantive youth movements. The thrust of this argument is based on the central role that urban youth, particularly the African American sector, plays in impacting global popular culture. He notes that this demographic in reality sets trends of extreme proportions, to the degree that influence spreads through race, gender, and age demarcations in ways that become second nature, impulsive, and routine.

Burrell's insightful analyses concerning advertisers' need to address the appealing qualities of the lay public have proven to be accurate. One need only consider ads such as McDonald's 2004 "I'm Loving It," which uses a jingle by Justin Timberlake, a white male singer with obvious African American rhythm and blues sensibilities, with an ethnically diverse cast of young actors and actresses to sale hamburgers and fries. Burrell's influence can also been seen from an impressive list of protégés who have graduated from what has affectionately come to be known as the Burrell School. One such person of the hundreds is Steve Conner, architect of the award-winning Budweiser commercial "Whassup!" By accentuating an urban vernacular phrase throughout the 2000s, the ad proved to be a virtual cross-appeal hit. Feeling that his primary work was now secure enough to leave in the hands of his able students, Burrell implemented a strategic succession plan where Conner, Fay H. Ferguson, and McGhee Williams became Burrell's new managing partners in 2004.

As many organizations and/or businesses falter after the primary leader stops working with it from a hands-on perspective, the businesses that continue to prosper and flourish are the ones whose vision and organizational scope prepared for such a time from inception. Such is the case with Burrell Communications because Burrell left it in able hands to carry on his mission. Conner, Ferguson, and Williams have proven committed to expanding their leader's vision by further broadening its reach throughout the black diaspora. Additionally, they have exemplified an ability to engage the broader advertising world in research proprietorship where one could capitalize on such data as consumer reports on spending by African American mothers. Despite Burrell's passing of the baton, he still remains active by serving on the board of directors, the Chicago Urban League; the board of visitors, the **John H. Johnson** School of Communications, Howard University; the corporate advisory board, the Thurgood Marshall Scholarship Fund; the American Advertising Federation Foundation Standing Committee on Diversity and AAF Board Taskforce on Diversity and Multicultural Advertising, cochair; and director at large, the Ad Council, Inc.

In 1985–1986, Burrell was recognized with the Albert Lasker Award for Lifetime Achievement in Advertising by the Chicago business community. In 1988, he was featured in the article "Going Once, Going Twice . . . Sold!" for his renaissance appreciation and collection of African American art in *Black Enterprise*. The next year he was profiled on the PBS show "Bridgebuilders." The University of Missouri's School of Journalism awarded him the Missouri Honor Medal for Distinguished Service in Journalism in 1990. In 1995, Burrell was named by *Advertising Age* as "One of 50 Who Made a Difference" and in 1999 included him on its list of the "Top 100 Advertising People" of the century. In 2003, the famed Chicago DuSable Museum honored Burrell with the History Maker Award, and in 2004, he was a recipient of McDonald's National Lifetime Achievement Award. Such accolades are most fitting for one whose marketing zeal has so substantially impacted how blacks and other minorities in America are viewed: as people first, then as consumers, buyers with faces.

*See also*: Advertising and Marketing

**Sources**

AdAge.com. http://www.adage.com/century/people078.html.

American Advertising Federation. http://www.advertisinghalloffame.org/members/member_bio_text.php?memid=832.

Burrell, Thomas J. "Make It Personal: Urban Leadership, Reaching the Consumer Who Doesn't Fit Neatly into a Demographic Group Is the Critical Challenge for Marketers." *Advertising Age* 23 (February 14, 2000): S18–S20.

Chandler, Dahna M. "Burrell CEO Steps Down: Succession Plan Will Help Maintain the Vision of This Advertising Firm." *Black Enterprise* 35 (August 2004): 23–25.

Davis, Tonya Bolden, and Kevin D. Thompson. "Going Once, Going Twice . . . Sold!" *Black Enterprise* 19 (December 1988): 73–76.

Howard University. John H. Johnson School of Communications. http://www.howard.edu/schoolcommunications/Development/Thomas-Burrell.htm.

McDonald's. http://www.mcdonalds.com/usa/news/2004/conpr_09172004.html.

Northwestern University's Kellogg School of Management. http://www.kellogg.northwestern.edu/BMAConference/tburrell.htm.

"Thomas J. Burrell to Be Inducted into Advertising Hall of Fame." *Jet* 107 (February 7, 2005): 52.

*Who's Who among African-Americans*. 18th ed. Detroit: Thomson Gale, 2005.

*Uzoma O. Miller*

# Roland W. Burris (1937– ), Accountant, Banker, Lawyer, State Official

Roland Burris began his career in 1963 as a comptroller and national bank examiner in the Office of the Comptroller of Currency in the U.S. Treasury Department. This gave him the honor of being the first African American to examine banks in the United States. He later held two high-ranking positions, Illinois's first African American comptroller and its first African American attorney general.

Roland Wallace Burris was born on August 3, 1937, in Centralia, a small coal mining town in Illinois, located in the south central part of the state. His father Earl ran a small grocery store to supplement his income as a laborer for the Illinois Central Gulf Railroad. His family lived there for four generations. It was a racial incident in Centralia at a local swimming pool—and the words of his father, who said, "[I]f we as a race of people are ever going to get anywhere in this society we need lawyers and elected officials who are responsible and responsive" (*Chicago Citizen*, February 5, 1995)—that sparked Burris to become a lawyer, then a statewide elected official. Burris earned his bachelor's degree in political science from Southern Illinois University, Carbondale, in 1959. He then studied for a year at the University of Hamburg in West Germany. Burris described his time there as an interesting experience. In a February 1995 interview with the *Chicago Citizen*, Burris said that "at first they thought I was African, and when they found out that I was 'Negro' American, they were dumbfounded. And when I spoke their language, they were even more intrigued." He said that during his second day there he was waiting at the train station to pick up his clothes trunk, and a little German boy became very fascinated with him and even went as far as to grab his hand and rub it to see if his color would rub off. Burris says he was treated very well in Germany, and the families there were constantly trying to explain how good the Germans were. After studying in Germany, Burris entered the Howard University School of Law, earning his J.D. degree in 1963.

Burris entered the workforce, serving as vice president of Continental Illinois National Bank, from 1964 to 1973, making significant contacts in both the corporate and African American communities. He began his government career in 1973, when he was appointed to the governor's cabinet as director of the Illinois Department of General Services. In 1968, Burris ran for a seat in the Illinois state legislature but finished last place among five other candidates. Then in 1976 he ran for comptroller on the ticket with Dan Walker, who ran for reelection to the gubernatorial seat but lost. Burris's break came in 1978 when he became the first African American to be elected to state office in the history of Illinois, where he began the first of three consecutive terms as state comptroller. As comptroller, Burris raised the bar of fiscal management and reform, cutting waste and reducing the time it took the state to pay bills from as much as five weeks to as little as twenty-four hours. During his years as comptroller, he served as national executive director for Reverend Jesse Jackson's Operation PUSH (People United to Serve Humanity). Burris said that he was hired by businessmen to help Jackson organize PUSH when it was just getting off the ground. He took care of the funds and the administration of the organization. In 1984, Burris decided to run for one of Illinois's seats in the U.S. Senate. He came in second in the Democratic primary to Paul Simon, who would eventually make a bid for the White House.

## ELECTED STATE ATTORNEY GENERAL

On November 6, 1990, Burris was elected attorney general of the State of Illinois. At that time, the only African American ranking higher in state office was Douglas Wilder, the governor of Virginia. He served as Illinois attorney general from 1991 to 1995. As attorney general, Burris was more than just an enforcer of state laws; he was an advocate for law and order. His initiative added grand jury powers to the office of attorney general to help other law enforcement agencies go after drug dealers doing business across county lines. He created the Women's Advocacy Division to help protect women who are victims of stalking and domestic violence. He established a Child Advocacy Division to focus on the prevention of child abuse. And he also created the Civil Rights Division to ensure the protection of Illinois residents' civil rights. In 1993, he announced his bid for governor of Illinois and seemed to have an excellent chance of winning, given his extensive public service background. However, Burris lost the Democratic primary by less than 100,000 votes. He then rejoined the Jones, Ware and Grenard Law Firm but soon pursued political office again. He ran a second time for mayor of Chicago against the popular incumbent Richard Daley and was defeated. He once again entered the governor's race in 1997 and again in 2001. Despite numerous attempts, and his twenty-six years of involvement in politics, Burris failed to win the necessary political support from the more homogeneous white "downstate" region of Illinois. In a March 21, 2002, interview with the *Chicago Defender*, Burris said that his third bid for governor would be his "last political outing." He said that "he did his best but wonders if there isn't a 'concrete ceiling' when it comes to Blacks getting elected governor."

Burris is currently a counsel with the Chicago law firm of Burris, Wright, Slaughter and Tom, LLC, and since leaving politics in 2002 continues to be a strong force in the Illinois community. In January 2003, Burris's name was suggested by the Laborers' International Union of North America as a candidate to oversee the administration of Chicago's Local 1001 as part of a voluntary reform agreement. The Laborers' Local 1001 represents nearly 3,000 municipal government employees. Also in 2003, Burris and his wife Berlean were made Advocate Trinity Hospital's honorary chairs of the Campaign for Advocate Health Care in Chicago. Advocate fosters community involvement in health care.

Through the years, he has belonged to numerous professional organizations and associations, including the American Bar Association, Alpha Phi Alpha Fraternity, Inc., the National Association for the Advancement of Colored People (NAACP), Boy Scouts of America, Chicago Cook County Bar Association, American Institute of Banking, Financial Accounting Foundation (trustee, 1992–1995), Howard University School of Law Board of Directors, Chicago Urban League, Southern Illinois University Alumni Association, and the National Association of Attorneys General, for which he served as chairman of the Civil Rights Committee. Burris has been active politically throughout his life and has served as leader of the Illinois delegations to several National Democratic Conventions and also served as vice chair of the National Democratic Committee in 1992. He has received numerous awards and accolades, including being inducted into the African American Hall of Fame and receiving the Distinguished Service Award from the Anti-Defamation League of B'nai B'rith and the Howard University Alumni of the Year award.

Burris has been married to Berlean Miller Burris for over forty years. She is a career educator with a doctorate from Northwestern University in social policy and higher education administration. They have two children, Rolanda Sue Burris and Roland Wallace Burris II.

**Sources**

"Advocate Health Care's Mission Tour Comes to Trinity Hospital." *Chicago Citizen*, June 12, 2003.

Alex-Assensoh, Yvette. "Roland Burris." *Notable Black American Men.* Ed. Jessie Carney Smith. Detroit: Gale Research, 1999.

Bayliss, Deborah A. "Roland Burris: An African-American History Maker." *Chicago Citizen*, February 5, 1995.

Brennan, Carol. "Roland Burris." *Contemporary Black Biography.* Vol. 25. Ed. David G. Oblender. Detroit: Gale Research, 2000.

Business/City Editors. "Appointment of Former Attorney General Roland Burris Urged for Role as Overseer in Union Administration." Chicago: Business Wire. http://www/thelaborers.net/LOCALS/LU1001/appointment_of_burris.htm.

Stausberg, Chinta. "Burris to Leave Politics." *Chicago Defender*, March 21, 2002.

*Sheila A. Stuckey*

# John Edward Bush (1856?–1916), Politician, Organization Founder

From slavery to founder of a national fraternal order, the Honorable John Edward Bush worked his way off the streets all the way to the U.S. Land Office. With honesty, tenacity, and drive to overcome his beginnings, he surmounted many of the barriers that hindered African Americans in the post–Civil War era. He never gave up, never backed down, and always displayed strength of character, becoming the proud founder of the Mosaic Templars of America in order to morally, socially, intellectually, and financially elevate African Americans.

John Bush was born a slave in Moscow, Tennessee, in 1856, and after the Emancipation Proclamation, he and his mother traveled to Little Rock, Arkansas, to avoid the federal troops' invasion of Tennessee. Soon after the move, his mother died, leaving the seven-year-old an orphan, and much of his childhood was spent seeking shelter from whomever would accept small labors in return for a place to sleep and food. His status as an orphan placed Bush in a suspicious light by most townspeople.

A catalyst for his future success was his place of refuge in a schoolhouse, where he was befriended by the teacher. He taught himself because he could not afford to regularly attend public school and later became a school-teacher. Bush was later dismissed from this post because he supposedly married outside his station in 1879, when he wed Cora Winfrey and later raised three children. He lived in several cities and worked as a principal, but his heart always remained in teaching.

While pursuing various interests, Bush was an active political figure for the Republican Party, appointed as a railroad postal clerk, serving as county clerk of Rosalie County, Arkansas, in 1884, and appointed twice as the U.S. Land Office receiver under Presidents William McKinley, Theodore Roosevelt, and William H. Taft. During Taft's administration, Bush survived the Republican Black Broom, a purge of all African Americans from federal offices. In addition to heading the Republican Party in Arkansas, he was also the last minority to attend a National Republican Convention as a "Big Four" state delegate. As a politician, Bush was known for his bitter honesty with all and as an activist against segregation.

In 1891, Bush directed a large-scale protest of the Jim Crow laws at Little Rock's First Baptist Church and another on the steps of the State House. He continued his protest against segregation in 1903, this time regarding the Gantt streetcar law, which segregated passengers of the same car. In addition, African Americans across Arkansas boycotted the streetcar system, cutting minority traffic by 90 percent in Little Rock. The actions led by Bush directly impacted the racial unity of the state, with African Americans escaping the violent outcomes that normally befell protestors of their race.

In 1882, Bush and Chester W. Keatts founded the National Order of the Mosaic Templars of America, which cites as its purpose to unite all persons of Negro descent from all professions and give its members moral and material aid through lectures, funding, and encouragement. By the 1920s, the order was considered one of the largest centers of African American capital, power, and influence in the United States.

Bush's biggest accomplishments were his illustrious political career—including surviving an assassination attempt—and his contributions to the progress of his race, creating the Mosaic Templars Society as a tool to empower women and African Americans during the Reconstruction era. His political influence was widespread and empowered African Americans all across the South.

## Sources

Bush, A. E., and P. L. Dorman. *History of the Mosaic Templars of America—Its Founders and Officials.* Little Rock, AR: Central Printing Company, 1924.

Dillard, Tom. "John Edward Bush." *Dictionary of American Negro Biography*. Ed. Rayford W. Logan and Michael R. Winston. New York: W. W. Norton, 1982.

Hamilton, G. P. *1911 Biography of Hon. J. E. Bush, Little Rock, Arkansas. Beacon Lights of the Race*. Memphis, TN: E. H. Clark and Brother, 1911.

Mosaic Templars Building Preservation Society. http://www.mosaictemplarspreser vation.org/default.asp.

Richardson, Clement, ed. "1919 Biography of John E. Bush, Little Rock, Arkansas." *The National Cyclopedia of the Colored Race*. Vol. 1. Montgomery, AL: National Publishing Company, 1919.

Sarto, Constance. "Saving the Mosaic Templars of America Headquarters Building in Little Rock: An Update." *Newsletter of the Historic Resources Committee*. http://www.aia.org/nwsltr_hrc.cfm?pagename=hrc_a_mosaic.

*Thura Mack*

# Business Ownership in Select Academic Institutions

Business ownership in academic institutions is a crucial means for educating business students, increasing faculty and staff wealth, and building capital and endowment funds for the institutions. The African American and urban markets in the United States are a trillion-dollar market that has traditionally been underserved by the African American community. Hampton University in Hampton, Virginia, Howard University in Washington, D.C., Tuskegee University in Tuskegee, Alabama, and Clark Atlanta University in Atlanta are among a group of Historically Black Colleges and Universities (HBCUs) that have business ownership ventures to benefit the universities and educate future entrepreneurs and businessmen.

Hampton University has several types of business ventures. The most traditional business is the real estate of the university that is used for other than academic programs. For example, located around the campus and the city of Hampton are numerous houses and buildings owned by the university that are not used for classroom or dormitory space. Faculty and staff rent most of the homes located near campus. In the Phoebus section of Hampton, the university owns a building used as a business incubation center.

In 1990 Hampton University constructed Hampton Harbors, a shopping center and apartment complex on campus that generates over $1 million a year for scholarship programs. When Hampton Harbors was in the planning stage, faculty and staff were offered the opportunity to invest in the project in a profit-sharing agreement. In the university Student Center, spaces are rented in the food court area to businesses such as Chic-Fil-A and Subways. Gourmet Services, a private catering service founded by African American Nathaniel Goldston III, services Hampton University's student cafeteria and caters most university affairs.

Hampton University's president William R. Harvey is an astute businessman who routinely advises students to invest in real estate. Harvey is sole owner of the Pepsi-Cola Bottling Company of Houghton, Michigan. He serves on the board of many corporations and organizations such as Fannie Mae, Trigon Blue Cross Insurance, Signet Bank, National Merit Scholarship Corporation, and the Harvard Cooperative Society. Harvey has been appointed by five U.S. presidents to serve on various national boards such as the President's National Advisory Council on Elementary and Secondary Education, the Defense Advisory Committee on Women in the Service, and the Fund for the Improvement of Postsecondary Education.

One recent venture of Hampton University is investment in the Town Center project in Virginia Beach, Virginia. Hampton University is lending developer Armada/Hoffler $18 million of its endowment fund to finance a hotel in Town Center. This hotel is expected to be revenue generating and to serve as a teaching facility for Hampton University's hotels and resorts management program that has opened in the Hampton University Virginia Beach campus located in the Town Center.

In 2005 Hampton University purchased the last piece of land that originally belonged to its founder Samuel Chapman Armstrong. This land is one of the last undeveloped parcels on Hampton Creek, situated cross the water from Hampton University.

Historically black colleges and universities are building hotels and conference centers to fill the void in African American ownership of this type of facility. In 1994, Tuskegee University opened a 108-room hotel and conference center. The W. K. Kellogg Foundation largely funds this facility. It has a 300-seat amphitheater, a 500-seat ballroom, a teleconference studio, a computer laboratory, executive boardroom, and 17,000 square feet of meeting space. It has hosted student conferences, professional meetings, regional conferences, family reunions, and other civic meetings.

In 1996, Clark Atlanta purchased **Paschal**'s Hotel and Restaurant in Atlanta and renovated it to provide graduate student and guest housing. This restaurant and hotel was widely known as a meeting place for leaders of the civil rights movement of the 1960s, often referred to as "the kitchen of the civil rights movement." Even though Clark Atlanta replaced the historic Paschal's structure with student residence halls, the Paschal's tradition is carried on by surviving brother **James Paschal** at two new locations—one near the Hartsfield Airport and the other on Northside Drive in Downtown Atlanta.

Howard University attempted a conference center venture with the opening of Howard University Hotel in the early 1980s. For this facility, Howard purchased the Harambee House Hotel from the Federal Economic Development Administration. The first few years of the Howard Hotel were profitable, but in 1995 Howard closed the hotel because it was not profitable. Gwynette Lacy, chair of the School of Management at Howard, believes that among the reasons the hotel failed were lack of support from the African American community and competition from other hotels that were built in Washington, D.C. during the same time period. In place of the Harambee Hotel, Howard often uses its Blackburn Center, which has meeting room space.

Often, business ownership ventures in academic institutions serve to improve the neighborhoods in which they are located. In 1997, the Clinton administration awarded $6.5 million to seventeen HBCUs to help them revitalize distressed communities near their campuses. Business ownership in academic institutions trains future entrepreneurs, builds up neighborhoods near campuses by job creation, new building development, and new homeownership, and enriches the scholarship and endowment programs of the institutions. It is vital to educating business leaders and to keeping the institutions financially viable.

*See also*: Centers for Entrepreneurship in Academic Institutions

**Sources**

"Clinton Administration Awards $6.5 Million in Grants to 17 Historically Black Colleges and Universities." *Columbus Times*, October 14, 1997.

Foston, Nikitta A. "Hampton University: Educating for Life in the New Century; Virginia Institution Celebrates 135th Anniversary." *Ebony* 58 (September 2003): 62.

Harvey, William R. Announcement to faculty of Hampton University. November 2004.

Howard University. Office of the Secretary. "Commencement 2004 Honorees." http://www.howard.edu/commencement/2004/honorees.htm.

"Preparing Future Business Leaders Today." *Black Enterprise* 27 (February 1997): 92–100.

Roach, Ronald. "The Promise and the Peril: Filling the Black Hotel and Conference Center Ownership Void; Tuskegee Has High Hopes; Clark Atlanta Moves Slowly; Howard Throws in the Towel!" *Black Issues in Higher Education* 14 (March 10, 1997): 26–29.

Skog, Jason. "Hampton U. Joins Town Center." *Virginian Pilot*, January 17, 2003.

*Elizabeth Sandidge Evans*

# C

## Cardozo Sisters, Hair Salon Owners and Stylists

In 1929, Elizabeth Cardozo Barker (1900–1981), with less than $50 in start-up money, began a beauty shop in her Washington, D.C. apartment, where it was not unusual for her to have customers until midnight. Four years later, Barker asked her older sister, Margaret Cardozo Holmes (1898–1991), to join her in the business venture. In 1937, they moved the business out of Barker's apartment to a location where Barker and Holmes named the shop Cardozo Sisters Hair Stylists and ran one of the best-equipped and most popular hair salons in Washington. Emmeta Cardozo Hurley and Catherine Cardozo Lewis joined their siblings by the mid–1940s, and from 1948 to 1965, Lewis was the salon's general manager. The thriving business expanded to five storefronts, consumed a city block on Georgia Avenue near the campus of Howard University, had twenty-five employees, coifed as many as 200 clients daily (approximately two dozen of whom had their hair styled by a Cardozo sister for forty-two years), and grossed more than $325,000 yearly by the time the salon was sold in 1971. As the Cardozo sisters' influence increased in the hairdressing industry over the years, they used their clout to demand that the industry meet the needs of African American clients and end discriminatory practices.

The Cardozo sisters were not the only prominent members of their family. Their paternal great-grandfather was Isaac Nunez Cardozo, who was a Sephardic Jew, veteran of the Revolutionary War, a weigher in the Charleston customs house, and vice president of the Reformed Society of Israelites. Isaac Cardozo later married a woman in Pennsylvania, and as a result of that union, he was the great-great-grandfather of Supreme Court Justice Benjamin Nathan Cardozo. However, prior to his marriage, Isaac Cardozo had a relationship with Lydia Williams, who was a free woman of African American and Native American ancestry as well as the Cardozo sisters' paternal great-grandmother. The couple had one daughter and two sons, one of whom was the Cardozo sisters' grandfather, Francis Lewis Cardozo Sr., a Congregational minister, educator, South Carolina's secretary of state

(1868–1872), and South Carolina's state treasurer (1872–1876). Cardozo High School in Washington is named in his honor. His son and the Cardozo sisters' father was Frances Lewis Cardozo Jr., a school principal in Washington and the husband of Blanche (née Warrick) Cardozo, a schoolteacher. In addition to their aforementioned daughters, Francis and Blanche Cardozo were the parents of William Warrick Cardozo, who was a pediatrician, a pioneering sickle cell anemia researcher, and an associate professor of pediatrics, and Frances Cardozo Payne, who taught school. Francis Cardozo hoped that his daughters would become schoolteachers; however, Payne was the only Cardozo daughter who became an educator. The six Cardozo siblings' first cousin was Eslanda Goode Robeson, the daughter of Francis Cardozo Jr.'s sister, Eslanda Cardozo Goode; Eslanda Robeson was a chemist, anthropologist, activist, and the wife of Paul Robeson, the renown entertainer and activist.

The Cardozo siblings' mother Blanche was the great-granddaughter of a woman who was reputed to have been an Ethiopian princess before she became an American slave. Blanche Cardozo's maternal grandfather was Henry Jones, who ran a catering business with a primarily white clientele; and her mother, Emma Jones, married William H. Warrick Jr. Warrick, a master barber, owned a chain of barber shops in Philadelphia, and his wife was a hairdresser and wigmaker, who owned salons in Philadelphia and Atlantic City. Blanche and her sister Meta worked as hairdressers in their mother's shops, and Blanche eventually became Emma Warrick's business partner. The Cardozo children's Aunt Meta did not become a partner in the hairstyling business. Instead, Meta Vaux Warrick Fuller pursued her passion in art and became a famous sculptress whose works predated, included, and extended well beyond the Harlem Renaissance in a career that spanned seven decades. Her husband, Solomon Carter Fuller, was a neurologist and psychiatrist.

Margaret Holmes, the eldest of Blanche and Francis Cardozo's six children, was born on July 5, 1898, in Washington; and Elizabeth Barker was born in 1900. Holmes, Barker, and their other siblings summered in Atlantic City with their mother, and the older girls helped in the hair salon. By the time Holmes was nine, she was drying the customers' long hair with a palm leaf fan, and when she was ten, she was setting the clients' hair as well as helping Emma Warrick, a prizewinning wig-stylist, weave hair for wigs. At least two of the girls (Holmes and Barker) were taught by their grandmother how to make hair products. The patrons at the shop on Atlantic Avenue at the shore resort as well as the clients at the Broad Street salon in Philadelphia were white.

During the summer when Holmes was eleven years old, her mother became ill, and her siblings returned to Washington while Holmes remained in Atlantic City to care for Blanche Cardozo; Holmes was kept out of school from September 1910 to February 1911. Prior to Blanche Cardozo's death in 1911, she told Holmes to return to Washington in order to help Barker and their paternal grandmother with the younger children. Meta Fuller was especially fond of Holmes, who, like her mother and aunt, had artistic talent. Holmes rejected Fuller's offer to adopt her and train her as artist because her family needed her. In 1915, Francis Cardozo Jr. enrolled Holmes, Barker, and Hurley in St. Francis DeSales Convent School, located in Rock Castle, Virginia. Holmes also attended Armstrong High School in Washington, which had an impressive art department. The younger girls, Payne and Lewis, attended school in Pennsylvania. In 1927, Hurley, who was considered the beautiful, Spanish-looking sister, traveled to Paris, where she was trained as a hairdresser. However, from 1930 to 1936, she lived in New York, passed for white, and was a showgirl with the Ziegfeld Follies. Hurley was ambivalent about her actions; she enjoyed the glamour, yet feared her identity would be revealed. After the Ziegfeld Follies, Hurley owned a beauty shop in Harlem and later owned a hair salon in Detroit. During the period in between the two salons, Hurley worked at an aeronautics plant, and during World War II, she joined the Women's Army Corps (WACS). After Hurley worked with her sisters for a brief time in the Georgia Avenue salon, she opened a branch in the Anacostia section of the District of Columbia.

When Barker opened the salon in her apartment in 1929, she was separated from her first husband, Julian Nicholas. Although Barker worked long hours, working at home was a successful arrangement because it allowed her to support her two young sons and herself as well as look after the boys. Barker was continuing the hairdressing tradition established by her grandmother with one major difference: Barker's clientele was African American. When Holmes joined her sister in the business in 1933, she left Philadelphia, where she was employed as a milliner, and began learning about all types of hair. She married Eugene Clay Holmes, who later became a professor and chair of the Philosophy Department at Howard University.

Barker moved into a larger apartment to have more space for the salon. Barker and Holmes were determined that their hairdressing business would become even more successful. They experimented on their own hair and developed some of the shop's products. When their customers wanted marcel waves, Barker passed for white (or "scouted" as she and her sisters, who were all fair enough to pass for white, called it) and studied with Emile, a leading hairdresser on Connecticut Avenue. Barker and Holmes, in their passing mode, would go to white salons as clients in order to learn new hair techniques and procedures as well as business operations. Other Jim Crow restrictions kept African American hairdressers from attending white trade shows, so Barker and Holmes scouted and attended the shows where they learned new techniques and gained information. Although their white supplier knew that the Cardozo sisters were African American, he did not block their attendance at the shows because they purchased his products. By the 1950s, Cardozo Hair Stylists had such status that the sisters insisted that all of their salon's operators be invited to the shows. The Cardozo sisters continued to be forces to be reckoned with in the hairdressing industry. They aided some manufacturers in the development of hair-care products. Holmes, who was one of the salon's fastest stylists, specialized in product testing, trained the shop's operators in the application of a variety of hair relaxers, and wrote an article about hair relaxation that remains unpublished. In 1963, Barker was appointed to the D.C. Cosmetology Board, and from 1967 to 1970, she was president of the board. During Barker's tenure on the board, the members voted to require salons and barbershops to serve all patrons regardless of their race and to install an integrated curriculum in cosmetology schools so that all licensed graduates would be able to work with all hair types. Barker was also a member of the Small Business Development Center's Board of Directors. Holmes was a member of the Business and Professional Women's Club in Washington.

Barker and Holmes were considerate of their customers. The owners used a permanent scheduling system where clients were able to book the dates, hours, and hairstylists for as far into the future as they wished and receive a written confirmation, which the Cardozos viewed as a contract. Two-thirds of their clientele had standing appointments, and many of them kept their appointments for years. At ten o'clock each morning, four clerks handled phone calls from women asking about cancellations. A section of the shop was devoted to taking care of the customers' wigs. The salon had a luxurious decor with air conditioning, and employees wore white uniforms. As long as the Cardozo sisters owned the business, they did not become complacent with their success; instead, they sought new styles and trends. Clients of the salon appreciated the talents, professionalism, and amenities of Cardozo Sisters Hair Stylists and continued to patronize the establishment after its location was not as fashionable as it was in the 1930s and after many people avoided the area following the assassination of Martin Luther King Jr. in 1968 and the subsequent riots.

Barker and Holmes were also considerate of their employees. The salon had its own training program and workshops. Cardozo Sisters Hair Stylists closed one day every three months in order for the operators to attend demonstrations by top hairstylists. As early as the 1930s, the Cardozo sisters allowed their employees scheduling flexibility in order to balance the demands of work and home. The salon included a large kitchen and family room for the employees.

From 1949 to 1965, Barker and Holmes' youngest sister, Catherine Lewis, was their general manager. She was married to Harry Lewis, who taught history at Howard University for forty-five years, and she helped him with his research. When she resigned as the salon's general manager, Camilia Bradford Fauntroy, a longtime employee and sister-in-law of Congressman Walter E. Fauntroy, became the new general manager. In 1971, the Cardozo sisters sold the salon to her. Barker and Holmes then served as consultants to Fauntroy.

Barker and Holmes, with their husbands, moved to Cape Cod, Massachusetts, in the 1970s. In 1981, ten years after the sale of the salon, Barker died at the age of eighty at Cape Cod Community Hospital in Hyannis Port. In addition to her four sisters, her survivors included two sons, Julian

Nicholas and Frank Nicholas; three grandchildren; and one great-grand-child. Barker was preceded in death by her second husband, Beltran Barker, who died in 1979. Holmes's husband Eugene died in 1979 or 1980. Two years after Elizabeth Barker's death, Margaret Holmes left Massachusetts and resided in Columbia, Maryland. In 1991, twenty years after the salon was sold, Holmes died at the age of ninety-two. Her survivors included two sisters: Catherine Lewis and Frances Payne. A perusal of Barker's and Holmes's obituaries indicates that Emmeta Hurley died in the interim between the deaths of her two oldest sisters.

Cardozo Sisters Hair Stylists is a prototype that continues to be emulated by subsequent generations of salon owners. Indeed, the talents, efficiency, professionalism, and consideration for clients as well as employees displayed by Elizabeth Cardozo Barker, Margaret Cardozo Holmes, Emmeta Cardozo Hurley, and Catherine Cardozo Lewis serve as a model worthy of emulation by all entrepreneurs.

*See also*: Minority Businesses in Major Cities; Women and Business

**Sources**

"Elizabeth Cardozo Barker Dies; Owned Beauty Shop." *Washington Post*, November 28, 1981.

Hill, Ruth Edmonds. "Margaret Cardozo Holmes." *Notable Black American Women*. Book I. Ed. Jessie Carney Smith. Detroit: Gale Research, 1992.

Hobson, Lillian. "From One-Room Emporium to Empire in Namesake Neighborhood." *Washington Post*, June 9, 1967.

Medea, Andra. "Cardozo Sisters." *Facts on File Encyclopedia of Black Women in America: Business and Professions*. Ed. Darlene Clark Hine. New York: Facts on File, 1997.

Miller, Margo. "The Legendary Sisters Cardozo." *Boston Globe*, March 16, 1980.

Trescott, Jacqueline. "From Bobs to Afros, 50 Years of Beautifying Black Women." *Washington Post*, October 25, 1977.

*Linda M. Carter*

# Albert Irvin Cassell (1895–1969), Architect, Educator, Planner, Entrepreneur

A prominent architect in the mid-twentieth century, Albert Irvin Cassell was best known for planning and designing buildings at Howard University in Washington, D.C. and for designing other buildings in the Washington area. He was architect for a number of other institutions and designed Masonic temples, hospitals, commercial and residential buildings, and structures at academic institutions. Late in life he joined a group of black architects to form Cassell, Gray, & Sulton architectural firm. Cassell had a wide range of interests that included providing employment, economic opportunities, and housing for blacks in the Washington, D.C. area during a portion of the Great Depression years, or 1932–1935, and into World War II.

Born on June 25, 1895, in Towson, Maryland, Alvin Irvin Cassell was the third child of Albert Truman Cassell and Charlotte Cassell. The family soon relocated to Baltimore, where young Cassell attended segregated public schools. When he was fourteen Ralph Victor Cook, a teacher at Douglas High School, began to teach Cassell the art of drafting. When he graduated from the school in 1914, he had completed a four-year carpentry program. The next year Cassell entered the architecture program at Cornell University, where he studied for two years before enlisting in the U.S. Army. His military service came during World War I and took him to France but not in combat. He became a second lieutenant in the 351st Heavy Field Artillery Regiment and was honorably discharged in 1919. Students whose studies at Cornell had been interrupted by war were honored by receiving "war degrees"; Cassell was one such student and received a B.A. degree from Cornell in 1919 without having to return to the campus.

Immediately after receiving his degree, Cassell began his career as an architect and worked with William Augustus Hazel to design five trade buildings at Tuskegee Institute (now University) in Alabama. The next year he was chief draftsman for Howard J. Wiegner, an architect in Bethlehem, Pennsylvania. Then he joined Hazel at Howard in late 1920, and the two were architects for the design of the Home Economics Building. After Hazel left the school in 1922, Cassell was named university architect and head of the Architecture Department; his tenure lasted until 1938, when Howard's president fired him after a long feud between the two, each accusing the other of various improprieties. The case was resolved in 1941, in Cassell's favor, and he and the university negotiated a small settlement. Cassell's departure from Howard, however, was not until he had created a "Twenty Year Plan" for Howard, transformed the physical appearance of the school, and created a visual order that had been lacking. He worked as surveyor and land manager, acquiring properties that were adjacent to the campus and bringing them into the campus fold of hilly terrain. Cassell's buildings at Howard included the gymnasium, field house, armory, College of Medicine, and three women's residence halls. The Chemistry Building and Frederick Douglass Memorial Hall—a classroom building—were completed in 1935 and became two of the most durable contributions to the university's setting. His crowning glory, however, was Founders Library, completed in 1939, in which he used the Georgian Revival style and gave the university an enduring architectural and educational symbol.

During and following his Howard years, Cassell engaged in various architectural projects that took him beyond the campus. He worked alone and/or partnered with other architects and engineers between 1924 and 1969, engaging in property appraisals, land planning, site planning, and architectural practice to create sizable private ventures. His buildings included a women's residence center at Virginia Union University in Richmond (1923) and men's residence buildings at Morgan State College in Baltimore. In Washington, D.C., he was architect for the Masonic Temple (1930); the Margaret Murray Washington Vocational School Addition

(1938); and the James Creek Alley Housing Development (1940–1941). Both in the District of Columbia and in Maryland he built civic structures.

Either independently or with the black architectural firm Cassell, Gray & Sulton, his buildings included the Washington Diocese of the Roman Catholic Church, municipal buildings for the District of Columbia, alterations to the Pentagon (1964), and U.S. Army installation at National (now Reagan) Airport.

His interest in providing blacks an opportunity to work was seen in 1932–1935—in the midst of the Great Depression—when he purchased with his own funds a 380-acre site on the Chesapeake Bay, in Calvert County, Maryland, to become a summer resort for blacks and to include a motel, shopping center, a marina, a beach, and other amenities. He built roads and several houses there, but the "Calverton" development was never realized. In the view of some, racial and political problems interfered. In 1942 he began the Mayfair Mansions (or Mayfair Gardens), Mayfair Extension Housing Developments, and Mayfair Extension commercial facilities in northeast Washington. Although the buildings were delayed due to the war and other reasons, they were finally completed. Cassell managed the Mayfair apartments and received a hefty income. Later he lost majority ownership of Mayfair Garden.

Cassell took great interest in public housing projects for blacks. He designed and supervised construction of three federally funded housing projects for blacks: the George Washington Carver Public Housing project in Arlington, Virginia (1942); Soller's Point, built for black war workers and their families in Dundalk, Maryland (1942); and James Creek dwellings in Washington's southwest section.

Notwithstanding the setbacks that he faced in his career, Cassell secured a place in history by the timeless design and integrity of his buildings and for his success in helping to meet the housing needs of blacks in Washington, D.C. and elsewhere.

**Sources**

"Albert I. Cassell and The Founders Library: A Brief History." http://www/howard.edu/library/Cassell/Founders.htm.

Lebovich, William. "Albert Irvin Cassell." *African American Architects: A Biographical Dictionary 1865–1945*. Ed. Dreck Spurlock Wilson. New York: Routledge, 2004.

Logan, Rayford W., and Michael R. Winston. "Albert Irvin Cassell." *Dictionary of American Negro Biography*. Ed. Rayford W. Logan and Michael R. Winston. New York: W. W. Norton, 1982.

*Jessie Carney Smith*

# Catering Industry

The catering business for black Americans predates the Civil War. Such businesses, however, were generally found outside the South, where slavery still existed and where blacks were forbidden to operate their own businesses. Some of these businesses grew out of the skills of black entrepreneurs, such as emancipated slave Emanuel, and fine cooks, such as Duchess Quamino. In the mid-eighteenth century, Emanuel established the first oyster and ale house in Providence. When he died in 1769, he was said to have a sizable estate. He was also the forerunner of many black saloon keepers, restaurant owners, and caterers who established businesses in the next century. Quamino (c. 1739–1804) was an accomplished pastry chef. Originally named Charity, she was an eighteenth-century chef who was so talented that she became known as "Rhode Island's Pastry Queen." Since slavery existed outside the South as well, laws governing the lives of slaves directed her life. When she was brought to Rhode Island as a slave child, she was already a talented pastry cook. As she worked for one of Newport's most prominent families—the Channings—her talents flourished. Her skill and enterprising ability led her to sell enough pastries to buy her freedom and that of her family. There is no doubt that Quamino had a fine reputation as pastry cook, for she was sought out for her skill, especially for her specialty—plum cakes.

The black catering business began during early-nineteenth-century America and for the most part was centered in northern cities such as Boston, New York, and Philadelphia. In Philadelphia, and perhaps elsewhere, catering took first place among several parallel enterprises for blacks, such as barbering, cabinetmaking, and upholstering. Many of the professions or businesses that involved blacks were considered an outgrowth of domestic service. The heyday for black caterers there appears to be between 1845 and 1883. Although these early caterers lacked formal education, they were very persuasive, charming, and polite and were masterful politicians. According to Juliet Walker in *The History of Black Business in America*, Robert Bogle became known as "the originator of catering"; he also professionalized the industry by dressing his staff in uniforms and ensuring that they had impeccable manners that equaled those of English butlers. He is credited with making Philadelphia the center of the catering industry. Willard Gatewood writes in *Aristocrats of Color* that Bogle "set in motion catering as it is known today." He was among Philadelphia's old families. At first he was a hotel waiter and later owned a coffee shop. He used his skills and polished manners to develop a prosperous catering business and acquired substantial wealth. Bogle contracted with the city's black and white elite and served elaborate banquets as well as formal dinners in fine homes. After he died in 1837, his name and reputation seem to have moved into obscurity, but his descendants were recognized among the city's black aristocracy.

Interestingly, *William Dorsey's Philadelphia and Ours* fails to recognize Bogle; instead, much credit is given to Thomas Dorsey (1810–1875), once a fugitive slave, and his son William Henry Dorsey (1837–1923). Among the black caterers who figured prominently in Philadelphia's history during the eighteenth century were Henry Minton (d. 1883), Levi Cromwell, and Andrew F. Stevens. There was also Henry Jones (d. 1875), a native Virginian who became wealthy after operating a catering business for thirty years;

he served Philadelphia's elite as well as wealthy whites in New York and New Jersey. Other prosperous caterers included Jeremiah Bowser, James Le Count, and James Prosser. John McKee, of Alexandria, Virginia, moved to Philadelphia in 1821, worked in Prosser's catering business, married Prosser's daughter, and later directed the business, becoming wealthy as well. He invested in real estate and land development, and by 1902, when he died, he was a millionaire. Like Prosser's and McKee's prosperous counterparts, their descendants figured prominently in Philadelphia's life for some time to come.

Haitian refugee Peter Augustine and his family of caterers, the Baptistes, ran a successful restaurant and catering business there, dating back to 1816 and continuing at least into the first of the twentieth century. When the black catering business in Philadelphia began to decline, it appears that fads in food and fashion were the chief causes. The increasing interest in French foods took hold, contributing perhaps to the continued success of Augustine and his family, the Baptistes, and to the Dutrieuille family that included Peter Dutrieuille (1838–1916) and his son Albert E. (1877–1944).

Caterer John S. Trower, born in Northhampton County, Virginia, in 1849, moved to Baltimore and worked as an oyster opener. He saved a part of his meager earnings and then in 1870 settled in the Germantown section of Philadelphia. In 1870 as well, Trower opened his first business, a restaurant, located near a local railroad station. His business was an immediate success, which prompted him to expand it into a catering enterprise. He needed more space for his lucrative business, and he knew that Germantown was ready for a first-class caterer's establishment. With the encouragement of wealthy citizens of the area, Trower purchased and refitted the Germantown Savings Fund building located within two blocks of his restaurant. The first floor of the facility held his office, a dining room, delivery department, and ice cream plant. On the second floor were a reception room, dining hall that seated 150 guests, and the baking department. A store room and laundry were on the third floor, and china closets and storage rooms were in the basement. Trower employed five black clerks as well as twenty people in the culinary, baking, and delivery services departments. Now with first-class quarters, he was in a position to take on more customers. In 1889, he won a contract to provide food for Cramp's Shipyard, a sizable corporation on the Delaware River and one of the world's largest shipbuilders. As many of the world's renowned war vessels entered the area, they called upon Trower for service. Unlike the early black caterers, Trower did not need to depend entirely on rich whites for business; instead, his prized contract made him a relatively rich man. On occasions, however, he catered for John Wanamaker, when Wanamaker was postmaster general. He also catered a reception for Wanamaker that was said to be the most elaborate ever given in Washington, D.C., where it was held. Trower extended his business beyond the shipyard to the entire state of Pennsylvania. He also extended his business into the South and West, shipping out orders to those areas.

In Washington, D.C., wealthy caterer James Wormley (1819–1884), who had founded his business before the Civil War began, expanded his enterprise when he opened a restaurant at 314 I Street, North. Soon his clients included Washington's Radical Republicans as well as Senator Charles Sumner, with whom he had a close association. He expanded his business more in 1871 when he established the Wormley Hotel, located at the corner of H and 15th streets. It was ideally located near Lafayette Square, the White House, and other federal buildings. His clients included well-known national politicians and foreign dignitaries. It was a pacesetter for post–Civil War luxury hotels, containing five stories, an elevator, telephone in each room and apartment, elegant dining facilities, a bar, and a barbershop. After Sumner's death, Wormley bought his furnishings for the hotel and used them to set up a "Sumner Parlor." Wormley acquired an estate worth $100,000. After his death, his son James managed the catering and hotel business until 1893, when it was sold.

Boston had its successful black caterers; in 1865, the leading catering enterprise there was headed by a black, Joseph Lee, who was at least a self-proclaimed descendant from the prominent Lees of Virginia. He served Boston's "first families." He also invented a bread-making machine.

New York's black catering business appears to have started with women. They had gained a fine reputation in service as cooks, and they used this experience to begin their own enterprises. Among the most notable women caterers who prospered between 1780 and 1820 was Cornelia Gomez. She catered for prominent, old families of the day, including the Rhinelanders, Goelets, Robinsons, and Gerrys. In *The Negro in Business*, **Booker T. Washington** recognized these names as still prominent in New York society by the turn of the century. Gomez's successor was "Aunt" Katie Ferguson, who continued the business until 1820, when a white male owner took charge.

Other blacks in New York who had successful catering businesses included Peter Van Dyke and Boston Crummell. Crummell was also an oysterman and the father of colonizationist, educator, and religious leader Alexander Crummell (1819–1898). There was also Thomas Downing, who operated Downing Oyster House in New York's business district and had a clientele of leading merchants, bankers, and foreign travelers. His son, George L. Downing, increased the family business when he relocated to Newport, Rhode Island, opened a catering business, purchased the Sea Girt Hotel, and accommodated the wealthy. George L. Downing also became a caterer on Capitol Hill in Washington, D.C. in 1866, serving in that capacity for thirteen years. He associated with white abolitionists on the "Hill," including Charles Sumner. He would return to Rhode Island and work in the area of equal rights. The Downings were prominent caterers in New York and Rhode Island for nearly a century. Other caterers who prospered in New York were David Roselle, a successful businessman of early years; W. H. Smith and his wife, who served the Wall Street district; William A. Heyliger, who served the same district and catered evening affairs; William E. Gross, who found ways to flatter his patronage; George Moore; and Jacob and Charles Day.

Westchester County, one of the wealthiest settlements in New York State, was the site of Francis J. Moultrie's business. From his birthplace in

Charleston, South Carolina, he came north shortly after the Civil War and worked in various catering houses in New York. Then he and his wife operated a small catering business from their home in Yonkers and in 1878 rented a downtown store to accommodate the growing business. He also operated with ten delivery wagons. He served Yonkers, Westchester County, and New York City as well. His business led him to a small fortune.

In time, the catering industry flourished in urban areas of the South. Walker found that Philadelphia was known for its elite black caterers, while southern blacks were more successful in the fine hotels and restaurants that they operated. Still they were not without their fine caterers. Among those who prospered were Jack Mccrae, a free black in Petersburg, and John Brewer, who at one time partnered with Mccrae. Jehu Jones prospered in South Carolina as owner of the Jones Inn, later known as Jones Hotel., which he purchased in 1816. He, too, served wealthy and well-known white clients, including South Carolina's governor. Among his staff were six slaves whom he owned.

## CATERING INDUSTRY DECLINES

As black catering enterprises declined in some areas, it flourished in others, for example, in Chicago, where Charles H. Smiley (1851–?) had a prosperous business. He was born poor in St. Catherine's, Canada, and was compelled to support himself early in life. He, too, had little formal education. The family relocated to Philadelphia when he was fifteen, and he remained there until 1881. He moved to Chicago in search of better employment. There he worked as a janitor and in his spare time as a waiter at dinners and parties. Soon he established an acquaintance with wealthy whites but gave up his janitorial work to serve as a waiter full-time. He catered weddings, where he provided the cake as well as appropriate floral decorations, ribbons, pillows, and other items and even supplied the waiters. He was known for providing employment for more blacks in Chicago than any other employer up to then. He maintained a fleet of delivery wagons and sixteen horses that he used to take his services out to various functions. By then his services included male and female security guards. As black businesses emerged and prospered in Chicago at that time, his was one of the few with white clientele.

Athens, Ohio, was the site of **Edwin C. Berry**'s restaurant established before he opened his hotel in 1893. Edwin Berry (1854–1931) was born in Oberlin, Ohio, moved to Athens, and from 1868 to 1872 apprenticed himself as a cook in a local restaurant. It was that position that influenced him to become a caterer and to open his own restaurant. In 1892 he opened Berry Hotel and became a highly successful hotel proprietor as well. The hotel became noted for its fine meals and precision service.

U.S. Census reports, cited in Smith and Horton's *Historical Statistics of Black America: Agriculture to Labor and Employment*, document the number of black caterers in select cities having twenty or more black merchants in

1899. There were six black caterers in New York City, five each in Baltimore and Philadelphia, and two in Washington, D.C. Other census reports cited show catering as a business profession among blacks in 1863, 1865, and 1919. Accounts of black catering cited elsewhere show that many black caterers in Philadelphia, once the leading city for such enterprises, had closed their businesses by the late nineteenth century. Among the factors that caused the black catering businesses to close was a demand for French food, or "haute cuisine," that the new white clients preferred. No longer was the old "meat and potatoes" menu of earlier times attractive to clients. Services were reduced to small functions, including dinner parties and social events for middle-class whites, although some caterers prepared services daily for special events. The black catering industry no longer enjoyed the income of antebellum caterers. The decreased number of caterers was seen in membership in the Public Waiters Association, founded in 1869; the next year there were nearly 500 black workers in the business, while there were only 33 members in 1905, when the association folded.

Another cause of the decline was clients' demand for alcoholic beverages. Black businesses increasingly became unable to afford the bond required by law and the license needed to serve liquor. Even so, the business had to be permanently located, and scarcely any black businesses fit this requirement. Black caterers began to rely on all-black trade—not because of racial preference but owing to the reasons just cited. Those who wished to continue catering did so, when they could, through service in hotels.

*See also*: Food Service Industry

**Sources**

Brod, Joanna. "Duchess Quamino." In *Notable Black American Women*. Book III. Ed. Jessie Carney Smith. Detroit: Gale Research, 2003.

Gatewood, Willard B. *Aristocrats of Color: The Black Elite, 1880–1920*. Bloomington: Indiana University Press, 1990.

Lane, Roger. *William Dorsey's Philadelphia and Ours*. New York: Oxford University Press, 1991.

Smith, Jessie Carney, and Carrell Peterson Horton, eds. *Historical Statistics of Black America: Agriculture to Labor and Employment*. Detroit: Gale Research, 1995.

Walker, Juliet E. K. *The History of Black Business in America: Capitalism, Race, Entrepreneurship*. New York: Macmillan Library Reference USA, 1998.

Washington, Booker T. *The Negro in Business*. Boston: Hertel, Jenkins and Co., 1907.

*Jessie Carney Smith*

# Centers for Entrepreneurship in Academic Institutions

African American business thrives on the spirit of entrepreneurship. According to recent reports from the U.S. Commerce Department's Bureau of the Census, minority-owned small businesses are growing at a rate of

30 percent, compared to 7 percent overall for new U.S. businesses. However, the failure rate in African American new business ventures is higher than average. Entrepreneurship programs at academic institutions strive for innovative means to pass along successful business practices and conduct case research with the goal of improving black business success rates. Although the visionary qualities of entrepreneurs cannot be taught in school, centers for entrepreneurship in academic institutions attempt to teach strategic concepts of business to students who possess an innate entrepreneurial talent. Entrepreneurship programs also support the colleges' and universities' traditional business and marketing curricula and give students a chance to meet and be mentored by successful businessmen and -women. Several Historically Black Colleges and Universities (HBCUs) have started entrepreneurship programs to support the aspirations of their students and to tap into the trillion-dollar African American and urban market.

In 1970, University of Washington professor Karl Vesper began collecting data on centers for entrepreneurship and found that there were only 16 in the country. Today, there are over 400 such programs, but African Americans fall behind other groups in the number of new businesses launched. Some of the reasons for this are lack of capital funding and an inability to secure Small Business Administration loans. Some African American businessmen like Robert Wallace, president of Bith Group, point to a lack of motivation among African Americans to risk starting a new business. The failure rate for all new business ventures is 70 percent, and many people including African Americans are reluctant to take the risk. African American businesses have become smarter, but an uncertain economy and elimination of set-aside and affirmative action programs have made it more difficult for African American business in recent years. Centers for entrepreneurship at HBCUs are attempting to fill the void in training and support for new African American businesses.

Howard University is establishing the Institute for Entrepreneurship, Leadership, and Innovation (ELI) after being awarded a $3.1 million grant by the Ewing Marion Kauffman Foundation in 2003. The ELI will enhance existing programs and create new ones. Howard plans to work in four areas—academic programs, a research center, business and community development programs, and a center for entrepreneurial thought. As of 2006, the Institute for Entrepreneurship, Leadership, and Innovation remains in the planning stage. When operational, the research areas will study the development of black entrepreneurship and African American/urban demographics. Research programs will host symposia, provide fellowships for faculty and students, publish a journal, and establish a clearinghouse of data about African American entrepreneurs and market opportunities.

Babson College in Massachusetts has a strong entrepreneurship program that dates back to 1919 when the college was founded. Babson, which is not an HBCU, has partnered with four HBCUs to create entrepreneurship programs. Babson's Arthur M. Blank Center for Entrepreneurship, named for the cofounder of the Home Depot, is the nucleus of the school's entrepreneurship program. Babson has joined Clark Atlanta, Spelman, North Carolina Agricultural and Technical State University, and Southern University to create curricula focusing on African American business and minority-owned new business ventures. The partnership between Babson and the HBCUs was financed by a grant from the Kauffman Foundation to fill the need for current research on African American new business ventures. Studies show that African American men with graduate degrees are twice as likely to start businesses as white men with the same level of education, but few case studies exist on African American businesses.

Another collaboration between Babson, several HBCUs, and Ford Motor Company aims to train African American students in the skills needed to succeed in new or expanding businesses. Babson faculty participates in exchange programs with faculty from the participating HBCUs—Morehouse, Clark Atlanta, Jackson State, North Carolina A&T, Grambling State, and Southern University. Through this program, students meet and study successful entrepreneurs and enhance networking skills.

Florida Agricultural and Mechanical University (FAMU) started an "industry cluster" in 1968 as part of the Johnson administration "Plans for Progress" initiative. The goal of this initiative was to increase minority representation in business, industry, and technology. FAMU has one of the largest business cluster groups in any HBCU. The cluster concept benefits the industrial community as well as FAMU. Industry recruits the brightest and the best from the university, and the students are trained in the skills required by the industry. Companies like Ford Motor, Sears, 3M, and others participate in the FAMU Industry cluster, which is touted as possibly the best program of its type in an HBCU. The federal government benefits by having an educated and diverse workforce.

Clark Atlanta's Center for Entrepreneurship was established in 1992 and emphasizes participatory learning for students. Students undertake a residency program with successful entrepreneurs, write business plans, and do case studies and data collection. In 1999, civic leader **Herman Jerome Russell** Sr., chairman of H. J. Russell & Company, donated $1 million to Clark Atlanta's Center for Entrepreneurship.

Russell also donated $1 million to Tuskegee University, Morehouse, and Georgia State University's J. Mack Robinson College of Business. With this donation, Georgia State's J. Mack Robinson College has established the Herman J. Russell, Sr. International Center for Entrepreneurship. The three areas of importance for the center are degree programs, worldwide knowledge creation, and participation in the community. The center provides scholarships and has won awards for its faculty and doctoral students. Engagement with the community is ensured through participation with the Society of Entrepreneurs. Access to successful innovators gives students a chance to learn business skills from experienced businessmen. Members of the Society meet with students and provide sites for student internships.

Tuskegee University will fund the Herman J. Russell Scholarship fund with the gift. This fund will ensure that students in business, hospitality management, and engineering and construction science are able to complete their degree requirements. Morehouse College will create a lecture series, provide curriculum emphasis in entrepreneurship, and contribute to building construction for the facility to house the entrepreneurship program.

Other HBCUs with entrepreneurship programs include Langston University, Spelman College, North Carolina Agricultural and Technical University, and Tennessee State. At North Carolina A&T, the Office of Technology Transfer and Commercialization works with the Nussbaum Center for Entrepreneurship to provide a small business incubator for new business in the service and light manufacturing arenas. In 2003 A&T also established a Center for Entrepreneurship and E-Business, a joint program of the School of Business and Economics, the School of Technology, and the School of Agriculture and Environmental Sciences. This ensures an interdisciplinary program in a collaborative learning environment. Students work with local entrepreneurs and bankers, write business plans, and make formal presentations. The center also partners with the East Market Street Development Corporation to revitalize the corridor next to the campus. Those who complete the program are given a Certificate in Entrepreneurship. At Tennessee State University, business students can minor in entrepreneurship. Also, through the business department, Tennessee State participates in several venues such as the Nashville Business Incubation Center, the Small Business Development Center, and the Women's Institute for Successful Entrepreneurship, which focuses on female business owners.

With the development of Centers for Entrepreneurship, historically black colleges and universities nurture future entrepreneurs and advance the economic status of the community by providing leadership and opportunities for job growth. Through the study of successful models, entrepreneurship programs provide successful business leaders destined to return to the community to mentor younger businessmen and -women.

*See also*: Business Ownership in Select Academic Institutions

**Sources**

"Babson College, HBCU Consortium to Develop Entrepreneurship Curriculum." *Black Issues in Higher Education* 20 (June 19, 2003): 15.

Florida A&M University. Florida A&M University Industry Cluster. http://www.famu.edu/cluster/clusterinfo.htm.

"Ford Launches First Ever Academic Program for Black Entrepreneurship." *Atlanta Inquirer*, July 10, 2004. http://www.proquest.com.

"The Founder of One of the Country's Largest Black-Owned Businesses Has Given $4-Million to Promote Entrepreneurship at Four Southern Colleges." *Chronicle of Higher Education* 46 (November 26, 1999): A41.

Herbert J. Russell Sr. International Center for Entrepreneurship. http://www.robinson.gsu.edu/rec/aboutcenter.htm.

Howard University Institute for Entrepreneurship, Leadership, and Innovation. Howard University School of Business. http://www.bschool.howard.edu/dean/ELI.htm.

McEwen, Thaddeus. "Entrepreneurship Program Affects Economic Development." *North Carolina A&T State University's School of Business & Economics*. Newsletter, n.d.

Office of Technology Transfer and Commercialization. North Carolina A&T State University. http://dor.ncat.edu/under/ottc/contact.htm.

Phillip, Mary-Christine. "Entrepreneurship Education: More Business Schools Are Focusing on Present-day Opportunities." *Black Issues in Higher Education* 12 (September 7, 1995): 8.

Williams, Stephen M. "Giving Students a Taste of the Executive Life." *Black Enterprise* 19 (1989): 181. http://www.proquest.com.

*Elizabeth Sandidge Evans*

# Chambers of Commerce and Boards of Trade of the 1920s and 1930s

As the 1920s and 1930s ushered in a new age of African American business with the founding of private African American banks, insurance companies, and other businesses, members of the new African American business community organized chambers of commerce and boards of trade to promote economic advancement, civic projects, and black trade with black businesses. Between 1910 and 1930, the African American population grew by 21 percent, with the urban population showing an increase of over 90 percent. This increase in population and urban concentration contributed to the rise of African American business. The chambers of commerce and boards of trade served as vital links to the corresponding white organizations, ensuring communication among businessmen.

In the aftermath of the Civil War a segregated society grew up in which two groups of African American businessmen emerged—the older traditional group employed primarily in service industries for white society and a newer group serving the African American market. The spokesmen for African American business were **Booker T. Washington** and W.E.B. Du Bois. Both men urged African Americans to seek economic self-sufficiency through business ownership. Washington contended that African Americans were responsible to address racial inequality themselves by making it clear that African American labor and capital were essential for the commerce of the nation. Du Bois was more assertive, urging political action as well as entrepreneurship to advance the status of African Americans.

In 1900, Washington organized the **National Negro Business League** (NNBL). Following that, chapters were founded in other cities. In 1902, for example, a group of Nashville businessmen organized the Nashville chapter of the NNBL, dedicated to arousing business interest among African Americans, promoting existing businesses, and developing new business. Eventually, conflicts arose in the group with the not-so-wealthy members accusing the wealthy members of being elitist. Charles Moore, an organizer for the NNBL, had to be called in to mediate in 1909. The Nashville chapter eventually disbanded, but Nashville's African American businessmen founded a new group in 1912, the Nashville Negro Board of Trade. Claiming to be the first group of its kind in the country, the Nashville Negro

Board of Trade paralleled the white chamber of commerce and board of trade.

## THE NASHVILLE NEGRO BOARD OF TRADE

The Nashville Negro Board of Trade was essentially a conservative organization that accepted racial segregation but worked to lobby for improved services for African Americans such as public parks, a public library, a new high school building for the black community, and city-sponsored nurses in the black public schools. The group also pooled money for disaster relief and poverty assistance funds.

There was internal strife in the Negro Board of Trade. Robert H. Boyd had been president of the Negro Board of Trade for a brief time and had adopted an accommodationist posture toward the white city leaders. In 1912, the Negro Board of Trade accepted the city's decision to locate the Negro Carnegie Library in a working-class neighborhood. This decision offended Nashville's elite blacks, and a call was put forth to remove the leadership of the Negro Board of Trade. In 1913, **James Carroll Napier** was elected president, but the Negro Board of Trade was never able to force a relocation of the proposed Negro Carnegie Library.

The Negro Board of Trade was instrumental in a change of leadership at Fisk University. After the death in 1900 of Erastus Milo Cravath, Fisk's longtime American Missionary Association–oriented president, the climate of leadership changed. The next two presidents, George Augustus Gates and Fayette Avery McKenzie, were men who worked independently of the black population of Nashville. They treated the students and black administrators with paternalism. McKenzie was especially detrimental to relations with the school. He was aloof, showed no interest in getting involved with the students or getting to know the black community, and fired many of the black staff to replace them with whites. He was autocratic, suppressing the student newspaper, refusing to allow establishment of a chapter of the National Association for the Advancement of Colored People (NAACP), and refusing to listen to recommendations made from the alumni society, the local black press, and even his own trustees. By 1924, many people were calling for a new president.

The entire climate in Nashville by 1924 was racially charged. Many incidents of murder, beating, and lynching of blacks occurred. Young black soldiers returning from World War I were appalled by the lack of civil liberties facing them at home. Many of these soldiers were students at Fisk. Fisk students requested the right to have student organizations like fraternities, sororities, and other clubs that existed in similar institutions. They requested a more informal dress code and an examination schedule that would allow them to go home for the holidays.

When McKenzie refused to consider these requests, Fisk students working with the Nashville Negro Chamber of Commerce and the Negro Board of Trade were eventually able to remove McKenzie as Fisk president. In 1926

Thomas Elsa Jones became the new president. Jones, a white Quaker, established a more relaxed atmosphere at Fisk.

## ATLANTA NEGRO CHAMBER OF COMMERCE

The Atlanta Negro Chamber of Commerce was one of the earliest black chambers of commerce. The Atlanta Chamber of Commerce—the segregated group—assisted in the formation of the Negro Chamber of Commerce. In Atlanta, as well as other cities, the Negro chambers of commerce promoted cooperation and goodwill through campaigns, contests, special weeks, and charitable works.

According to a 1939 issue of the *Journal of Negro Education*, there were more than fifty Negro chambers of commerce listed at that time. There were chambers in Atlanta, Memphis, Shreveport, Norfolk and Newport News, Virginia, San Antonio, Chicago, New York, and other cities. These early organizations created a forum where small businessmen and church and school leaders met to advance the economic and political status of the black community.

Other important chambers of commerce are the Houston Chamber, which had ties to the Houston College for Negroes and the National Negro Business League. Cities such as Birmingham, Miami, Jacksonville, Boston, Cleveland, Durham, Washington, D.C., Chicago, and others boasted Negro Chambers of Commerce. These organizations served as places of progress and commerce that advanced peaceful political challenges to unfair practices against black communities. For example, in Memphis, the Negro Chamber of Commerce was instrumental in settling an incident that involved an advertising billboard that offended the black community. At a time when race relations in Memphis were already strained by the 1866 Memphis race riot during which forty-six African Americans were killed, the White Rose Laundry erected a sign depicting a Negro Mammy bending over a wash tub with her undergarments showing. The local black community was insulted by this, and the Negro Chamber of Commerce wrote a letter to the owners of the laundry requesting removal of the sign. After several months of negotiations, the sign was removed.

Lobbying for social change and working behind the scenes to improve the business climate for African Americans, chambers of commerce and boards of trade made an incomparable contribution to the development of African American business.

Both historically and currently, African American chambers of commerce have specialized in goodwill campaigns, public relations, and gala events such as the Dallas and Chicago annual elections of a "bronze mayor." There is a strong education and research component to African American chambers of commerce. These organizations often provided forums, conferences, publications, and human resource development. Today's black chambers of commerce continue to serve as goodwill and networking organizations to bring together members of the business community and promote the cities or regions they represent. Chambers of commerce are essential networking organizations where educational leaders, church leaders, and entrepreneurs meet to foster economic growth for the community.

*See also*: National Black Chamber of Commerce

**Sources**

Blayton, J. B. "Are Negroes Now in Business, Business Men?" *Journal of Negro History* 18 (January 1933): 56–65.

Ingham, John N., and Lynne B. Feldman. *African-American Business Leaders: A Biographical Dictionary*. Westport, CT: Greenwood Press, 1994.

Lamon, Lester C. "The Black Community in Nashville and the Fisk University Student Strike of 1924–1925." *Journal of Southern History* 40 (May 1974): 225.

Lovett, Bobby E. *The African-American History of Nashville, Tennessee, 1780–1930*. Fayetteville: University of Arkansas Press, 1999.

Pierce, Joseph A. *Negro Business and Business Education: Their Present and Prospective Development*. New York: Harper and Brothers Publishers, 1947.

Suggs, Henry Lewis. "P. B. Young of the *Norfolk Journal* and Guide: A Booker T. Washington Militant, 1904–1928." *Journal of Negro History* 64 (Autumn 1979): 365.

Walker, Juliet E. K., ed. *Encyclopedia of African American Business History*. Westport, CT: Greenwood Press, 1999.

———. *The History of Black Business in America: Capitalism, Race, and Entrepreneurship*. New York: Macmillan Library Reference USA, 1998.

*Elizabeth Sandidge Evans*

# Debra Martin Chase (1956– ), Film Producer, Production Company Owner

Debra Martin Chase seems more of a savvy businesswoman than a corporate lawyer, which is evident in the establishment of her own production company, Martin Chase Productions. Although she is relatively new to the film industry, she has done in fifteen short years what many producers take lifetimes to accomplish. Her films have garnered award nominations as well as critical acclaim. Chase's primary motive is not the accolades but the difference her films can make in the lives of people, especially women. Her quick wit and background in law have provided her with an edge in her field.

Born in Great Lakes, Illinois, Chase spent most of her childhood on both the East and West Coasts but mainly in Pasadena, California. Her father was a film fanatic, which rubbed off on Chase. Weekends were often spent watching movies in the local theater, which became the centerpiece for dinner conversation. Chase graduated from Mount Holyoke College with high honors and from Harvard Law School.

After practicing corporate law for several Fortune 500 companies for five years, she was dissatisfied with her career path. Leaving law, Chase went back to her childhood love of movies. She spent a year and a half in New York learning about the film industry and the chain of command on a movie project. After discovering that the studio executive and the producer were the people responsible for coming up with movie ideas, Chase's goal was set.

Her path up the film industry ladder has been dotted with chance meetings with important Hollywood names. Soon after joining Columbia Pictures staff in the legal department in 1990, Chase met Frank Price, Columbia's chairman, at a luncheon. A few months later, she was working as Price's executive assistant. During this time, she learned everything she could about producing movies by attending meetings with Price, reading scripts, and asking every question she wanted.

A year later, Chase was Columbia's director of creative affairs, but she spent only six months in that capacity before another chance meeting changed her path—this one with Denzel Washington. The next week, she was running his production company, Mundy Lane Entertainment. With Washington, Chase produced *Courage under Fire* (1996) and *The Preacher's Wife* (1996) and was well on her way to becoming a filmmaking presence. While filming *The Preacher's Wife*, Chase met her next influential Hollywood contact—Whitney Houston. In 1995, the duo created their company, BrownHouse Productions, and in January 2000, Chase started her own production company, Martin Chase Productions. The Disney-based company has a first-look deal for any potential projects.

Most great producers have a niche they work from—an overarching theme that runs through their films—and Chase is no different. The majority of her projects support her personal philosophy of "female wish-fulfillment and empowerment"; however, she is steadily seeking projects to expand her role as a producer. Her beginnings in the female wish-fulfillment genre stem from Chase's belief that all individuals want to be the best they can be, to be loved, to have fun and enjoy life.

Chase's belief that women constantly struggle with society's changing role for them manifests itself in the positive images she produces onscreen, which are centered on a heroine who works to take charge and gain control of her life to achieve happiness and fulfillment. To Chase, everyone is chasing a dream of becoming more than who they are, but oftentimes children do not understand that people have to work to gain success. She wants to showcase the drive and work needed in the quest to become more. One of Chase's most successful films, *The Princess Diaries* (2001), exemplifying wish-fulfillment and empowerment, set her apart as a major Hollywood talent and grossed more than $153.7 million worldwide in the box office.

Perhaps part of her ambition to empower young girls derives from the hard work Chase has put in to be recognized in a white male-dominated field. For African American women, filmmaking is a difficult field to break into because other filmmakers believe they can exclude those who are new, young, and different. She has worked hard to get her share of the glory from the already established filmmakers in the business. For African Americans to get recognition in the entertainment business, especially in mainstream movies, Chase believes that a power base needs to be built on success. However, African American film professionals have a harder time realizing success because of the limited number of minorities in the business.

While her career path has diverged from her original destination, Chase has made the most of her law education. She got her foot in the door at Columbia Pictures as a lawyer and now uses her jurisprudence skills when making deals—often "rolling up her sleeves" and talking all the parties involved through the contract process. Chase's unique perspective and her dynamic rise to the top were a direct product of her drive—she has not wasted time observing and waiting for a breakthrough. She has confidence, but she also has the perfect balance of skills to succeed in the world of filmmaking.

Her professional talent, sophistication, and maturity stem from a backbone of clean, fresh integrity. Her work ethic speaks volumes to her peers, so she is often considered for new projects, expanding her credibility as a profitable producer. Chase is hands-on with her projects; she realizes who is needed to make them a success and has a savvy, almost preternatural sense of what will be a box-office hit.

One of the most significant of her career building blocks is her innate strength for identifying productive partnerships. In her collaborations, Chase has made impeccable business contacts and decisions. While sometimes being at the right place at the right time, she always takes the initiative to make what she wants happen. Her natural knack for the best business practices, coupled with a formal expertise in law, set Chase apart from others in her field.

For Chase, life exists outside the realm of Hollywood. She maintains a mantra of balance by playing as hard as she works. She reserves dinners for family and friends, tries to exercise five days a week, and reads frequently. Also, Chase stays involved in politics; she served on the national and New York finance committees for Michael Dukakis in the 1988 presidential race and raised funds for Democratic candidate John Kerry in the 2004 election. She also was a founding member of the Contemporary Friends of the Studio Museum in Harlem, New York, and serves on the board of trustees for Columbia College of Chicago.

*See also*: Women and Business

**Sources**

Alexander, George. *Why We Make Movies: Black Filmmakers Talk about the Magic of Cinema*. New York: Harlem Moon, 2003.

Chase, Debra Martin. Interview by Travis Cox. "Interview: Debra Martin Chase Discusses Her Career as a Hollywood Film Producer." *Tavis Smiley Show*, National Public Radio, March 26, 2004.

Collier, Aldore. "Making It real: Blacks in Los Angeles." *Ebony* 57 (May 2002): 150–162.

"Debra Martin Chase" (filmography). http://www.imdb.com/name/nm0153744.

Dingle, Derek T., et al. "The Producers: Whether Creating Groundbreaking Movies, Developing Original TV Programs, or Making Soulful Music, These 50 Power

Brokers Call the Shots in America's Most Dynamic Industries." *Black Enterprise* 33 (December 2002): 76–83.

Dunkley, Cathy. "10 Producers to Watch Dealmakers." *Variety* 380 (May 7–13, 2001). http://www.variety.com/article/VR1117798553?categoryid=1043&cs=1&query=dunkley+and+cathy+and+debra+and+chase&display=dunkley+cathy+a1.

Hines, Crystal Nix. "Hollywood Hit Maker." *Essence* 33 (April 2003): 138–142.

Longino, Bob. "Black Film Directors Land Mainstream Jobs." *Atlanta Journal-Constitution*, May 25, 2003.

Stanley, Carol. "Wonder Twins." *Hollywood Reporter*, December 18, 1999.

Struass, Bob. "The Hype Chasing a Big Dream." *Los Angeles Daily News*, August 16, 2001.

*Thura Mack*

## Leah Chase (1923– ), Executive Chef, Restaurant Co-owner

When Leah Lange Chase married, she gained more than a husband; she also gained a restaurant. Chase transformed Dooky Chase's, a small eatery created by her father-in-law and mother-in-law, into a culinary landmark in New Orleans, and in the process, Chase became known as the "Queen of Creole Cuisine." For more than fifty years, Chase has been the restaurant's executive chef and has fed a diverse range of people. During the 1950s and 1960s, Dooky Chase's served as a meeting place for civil rights leaders such as James Farmer, Martin Luther King Jr., and Thurgood Marshall as well as other civil rights workers. Other well-known individuals who dined at the restaurant include James Baldwin, Cab Calloway, Count Basie, Duke Ellington, Lena Horne, the Jackson Five, John F. Kennedy, and Sarah Vaughn.

Chase's culinary influence extends beyond her restaurant. She is the author of two cookbooks: *The Dooky Chase Cookbook* (1990; 2nd printing, 2000) and *And Still I Cook* (2003). In addition to hosting her own television show, *Creole Cooking with Leah Chase*, that premiered in 2000 and aired nationally on PBS, Discovery Channel Digital, and the Home & Leisure Channel, Chase has appeared on a number of other cooking shows including *In Julia's Kitchen with Master Chefs*, where Chase prepared fried chicken, biscuits, and sweet potato pie on a pecan crust with Julia Child.

In 1996, she was a visiting culinary professor at Nicholls State University. Chase, a community leader, is also recognized for her work with numerous nonprofit organizations in New Orleans. She has prepared meals for people at homeless shelters and public housing residents. When Hurricane Betsy hit New Orleans in 1965, Chase and an assistant cooked up all the food in the freezers at Dooky Chase's and gave the meals to the city's police officers, who distributed the food to people whose homes had lost electricity. Chase is also a patron of the arts, and her restaurant showcases the works of African

American artists. In 1995, Chase, speaking on behalf of the American Arts Alliance, the American Association of Museums, the Association of Art Museum Directors, and the New Orleans Museum of Art, addressed a subcommittee of the U.S. House of Representatives' Appropriations Committee and urged Congress members not to cut the National Endowment for the Arts budget.

Chase was born on January 6, 1923, in Louisiana (according to some sources, she was born in Madisonville, while other sources assert that Chase was born in New Orleans). She is the eldest of eleven children born to Charles R. Lange, who was employed at Jenke Shipyard, and his wife, Hortensia Raymond Lange. The Langes were Catholic Creoles. Chase, her eight sisters, and two brothers were raised in Madisonville, which was a rural area between Lake Pontchartrain and the Tchefuncte River. The Lange family was poor, yet the family ate well because Chase's father maintained a large garden. Although Hortensia Lange substituted an oilcloth for a tablecloth and used a wash bench for seating when she fed her family during the years of the Great Depression, she demanded that her offspring display good table manners. She also taught Chase and her siblings to be courteous and to pronounce words correctly. Charles Lange taught his progeny the alphabet and how to count before they were enrolled in school. When he sent the Lange children to the store, he insisted that they count the change owed them because that way, the elder Lange elaborated, they would never let anyone cheat them. When Lange sold vegetables from his garden, he only sold the best ones and would give the buyers something extra (a few cayenne peppers, for example). Lange's family knew that his motto was "Give the best of whatever it is you have to give." Chase and her siblings observed their parents' strong work ethic. Whether sewing, preparing food, maintaining the garden, or cleaning tools, standards had to be met. If not, the task had to be repeated. The husband and wife valued education and made their children do their homework after dinner. When the principal at the nearby white school threw books on a trash pile, Chase's father retrieved the texts before the pile was set on fire and used a wheelbarrow to take the books home to his children. Chase's mother sold "bricks" to as many individuals as she could, from the insurance agent to the mayor, in order to raise money for the new school the church planned on building; when the school opened, Hortensia Lange was the first president of the PTA.

Chase started school a year earlier than most of her peers; she attended St. Francis Xavier Catholic School, the parochial school for African American children. In 1937, Chase enrolled in St. Mary's Academy in New Orleans; while matriculating at the high school, she lived with her aunt. After graduating from St. Mary's, Chase's first job in New Orleans was at a laundry. Approximately one week later, she quit the job in order to work as a waitress at the Colonial Restaurant. When the owner closed the restaurant and opened the Coffee Pot, Chase and two other teenaged girls were in charge of the eatery that only served breakfast and lunch. Chase also held several other jobs during this period; for example, she served as a manager of several boxers from 1943 to 1944.

She met Edgar "Dooky" Chase II in 1945 and married him three months later in 1946. Her husband was a trumpet player, composer, and leader of the Dooky Chase Orchestra. His orchestra played throughout the Southeast and was hailed as the pride of New Orleans. He was the son of Edgar "Dooky" Chase Sr. and his wife Emily; they had opened a street-corner stand in 1941 where Edgar Chase Sr. sold lottery tickets and his wife's sandwiches. By the time their son married, the Chases no longer sold lottery tickets, and the eatery was extended to the adjacent building. When the elder Chase became ill, his son disbanded his orchestra in order to work at the restaurant. Between 1946 and 1953, Edgar Jr. and Leah Chase became the parents of four children: Emily, Stella, Edgar Chase III, and Leah. Chase did not work at Dooky Chase's while her children were small. Instead, she started sewing for other people and became quite successful at it. In addition, Chase was very active at her offspring's school, Corpus Christi Elementary, where she was the president of the PTA, head of fund-raising, and Girl Scout leader.

After Chase's youngest child was in school, Chase thought she would be the restaurant's hostess until she realized that no one in the kitchen knew how to prepare the meals she wanted to serve. In the beginning, Chase prepared dishes such as meatballs and spaghetti. When she cooked lobster thermidor, the customers did not like it, so Chase stuffed the lobster heads with shrimp dressing and boiled the tails; Dooky Chase's patrons liked it. When Chase changed the entire menu to Creole dishes, she was successful. Looking back at her arrival at the restaurant, Chase admitted that she had to "wing it"; she learned as she went along. After cooking all day and into the evening, she washed the walls and ceiling as well as took care of whatever else needed to be done. Indeed, Chase had to call upon the values and work ethic her parents taught her as well as the skills she learned while working at the Colonial Restaurant and the Coffee Pot.

During her early years at Dooky Chase's, she had to be very persuasive. Emily Chase was more upset with her daughter-in-law's proposed changes in the restaurant's decor than in the kitchen. Although the older lady would not let Chase redecorate the upstairs room that was used for private parties, she relented and allowed Chase to redecorate the downstairs dining room. Chase even found time to sew new satin draperies for Dooky Chase's. She had to convince her husband, who has been in charge of the restaurant's finances since his father's death in 1957, that a variety of expenses were justified because they were needed to increase profits. The restaurant underwent its first extensive remodeling in 1984.

Today, Dooky Chase's has evolved from an eatery where customers walked in, were handed eating utensils, and sat in chrome chairs at tables with plastic tablecloths into an elegant restaurant with three beautifully appointed rooms: the gold room, the main dining room, and the Victorian room. The most memorable aspect of the restaurant's decor is the artwork.

Each room contains items from Chase's collection of African American art; among the works on display are paintings by Elizabeth Catlett and Jacob Lawrence. Indeed, the artwork is second only to the cuisine that includes such dishes as crab bisque, eggplant with crab and shrimp, gumbo, jambalaya, and veal grillades. Chase has ignored the suggestions that she move the landmark restaurant from its 2301 Orleans Avenue location to a more upscale neighborhood. She is proud that Dooky Chase's has been part of the same community for more than fifty years; the community supported Dooky Chase's in its earliest days and continues to support it today.

To date, Chase has received more than thirty honors and awards. Among them are the Coalition of 100 Black Women's Candace Award (Chase was selected as one of ten outstanding African American women), 1984; Freedom Foundation Award, 1985; Women in the Forefront Award, 1986; Anti-Defamation League's Torch of Liberty Award, 1989; NAACP's (National Association for the Advancement of Colored People) Human Understanding Award, 1990; National Conference of Christians and Jews' Weiss Award, 1992; University of New Orleans' Entrepreneurship Award, 1996; National Council of Negro Women's Outstanding Woman Award, 1997; *New Orleans Times-Picayune* Loving Cup, 1997; House of Blues Foundation's Spirit of the Dream Award, 1998; Top Ladies of Distinction Community Service Award, 1998; Amistad Patronage of the Arts Award, 1999; Urban League's Golden Gala Award: Community Service, 1999; Holy Cross College's Humanitarian Award, 2000; Nicholls State University, Chef John Folse Culinary Institute's Lafcadio Hearn Award, 2000; Third Inductee in Chef John Folse Culinary Institute's Hall of Honor, Nicholls State University, 2000; American Federation of Chefs, Louisiana Chapter's Ella Brennan *Savoire Faire* Award for Excellence, 2000; Southern Foodways Alliance Lifetime Achievement Award, 2000; Penn College of Technology's Distinguished Hospitality Student Award (scholarship given in Chase's name), 2001; Honorary Doctorate of Education, Madonna College, Lavonia, MI, 2001; and New Orleans Museum of Art's Honorary Trustee for Life. In addition, Chase is one of seventy-five women featured in photographer's Brian Lanker's exhibit *I Dream a World: Portraits of Black Women Who Changed America*, which premiered at the Corcoran Gallery in Washington, D.C. in 1989 and appeared in book format that same year. A revised edition of *I Dream a World* was published to commemorate the tenth anniversary celebration in 1999.

Chase is a member of a variety of organizations including the Girl Scout Council of Greater New Orleans; Greater New Orleans Art Council; International Women's Forum; New Orleans Arts Council; New Orleans Chapter of Links, Inc.; New Orleans NAACP; Southern Food Alliance; and Urban League of Greater New Orleans. Chase has been appointed or elected to the Loyola University's Community Advisory Council, Nicholls State University's Advisory Council, and University of New Orleans's Community Advisory Council.

Chase and her restaurant have gained national and international prominence. The restaurant has even been immortalized in song. Ray Charles, whose favorite meal at Dooky Chase's was red beans, rice, and fried chicken, sings in "Early in the Morning Blues," "I went to Dooky Chase/To get me something to eat/The waitress looked at me and said/Ray you sure look beat/Now it's early in the morning/And I ain't got nothing but the blues." Decades after that song was written, many people continue to sing the praises of Leah Chase, master chef, restaurant co-owner, community leader, and patron of the arts.

*See also*: Food Service Industry

**Sources**

Allen, Carol. *Leah Chase: Listen, I Say Like This*. Gretna, LA: Pelican Publishing Co., 2002.

Jenkins, Nancy Harmon. "A Lover of Food Who Nurtured a New Orleans Institution." *New York Times*, June 27, 1990.

*Linda M. Carter*

# Kenneth Irvine Chenault (1951– ), Corporate Executive, Lawyer

As chief operating officer of the American Express Company, a worldwide travel, financial service, and network service provider, Kenneth I. Chenault is one of the most prominent leaders in American business. When Chenault joined American Express, it was on the brink of collapse, feeling pressure from other large credit card companies. Under his leadership, American Express fought back through a painful restructuring process. Known for his powerful communication and people skills, Chenault motivates and inspires as he leads the American Express Company to financial successes.

Chenault was born on June 2, 1951, in Mineola, New York, to Hortenius and Anne N. (Quick) Chenault. His father graduated from Morehouse College in Atlanta and was first in his 1939 class at Howard University's Dental School in Washington, D.C. During World War II, Hortenius served in the U.S. Army. Racial discrimination kept him out of the Allied Dental Corps until he joined the corps as an international member, after befriending officers from other Allied nations and learning French. Anne Quick's family owned a small shipping business in South Carolina. One of her ancestors was Thomas E. Miller, a representative in the U.S. Congress and a founder of South Carolina State College (now University). His mother graduated at the top of her class at Howard University's School of Dental Hygiene. Meeting her husband at Howard University, the Chenaults set up their own dental practice in New York and prospered together.

Chenault, second son and third of four children, grew up with his two brothers and a sister in Hempstead, Long Island, New York. Instilled with a love of poetry and art from his mother, Chenault's lack of success in his early school work worried his parents. His grades did not reflect his abilities.

He loved history and was an avid reader, especially biographies of great leaders. A late bloomer, he was nurtured by his teachers during his twelve years at the Waldorf School of Garden City on Long Island. The more innovative, upscale, private day school brought out the best in him. He was class president all four years of his high school years and graduated an honor student and captain of the basketball, soccer, and track teams.

Chenault won a sports scholarship to Springfield College in Springfield, Massachusetts. He spent a year there but transferred to Bowdoin College in Brunswick, Maine, at the suggestion of the head of his high school. One of 23 African American students, in a student body of 950, in a then small white all-male liberal arts college, Chenault graduated magna cum laude, with honors in history, in 1973. Chenault holds a juris doctor degree from Harvard Law School, where he was moot court champion. He was certified by the Massachusetts Bar Association in 1981.

Upon completing law school, Chenault worked two years in the New York City corporate law firm of Rogers & Wells. Intrigued by the theory and practice of business, he gave up the practice of law. From 1979 to 1981, he worked for the Boston management consulting firm of Bain & Co. His Harvard Law School classmate W. Mitt Romney, son of the former governor of Michigan, encouraged him to join Bain & Co. At Bain, Chenault was involved in the research and design of business strategies for some of the country's largest corporations. He acquired an extensive knowledge of all aspects of the corporate world while making contact with important business executives.

In 1981, on the recommendation of an executive search firm, Chenault was hired as the director of strategic planning for the American Express Company. The company is a leader in charge and credit cards, travelers checks, financial planning, investment products, insurance, and international banking. Within two years he was promoted to senior vice president of the Merchandise Services department. After more than tripling revenues to $500 million, Chenault was made department head. In 1986, he became executive vice president and general manager the Card Member Services department. Chenault introduced card application by telephone and the year-end account summaries for Gold and Platinum members. By 1988, American Express's market share of the card business was at an all-time high of 26.2 percent. He was named president of the Consumer Card Group in 1989. Disappointing business decisions resulted in the decline of American Express's market share of charge cards to 22.3 percent, as rival Visa's share rose to 43.9 percent in 1991. He promoted offering the company's revolving credit products to the general public and courted mass merchandisers to honor the company's credit cards. Chenault was promoted to president of American Express Travel Related Services in the United States, the company's largest unit, in 1993. He was responsible for the Consumer Card Group, Consumer Financial Services, Travel Services Group, and Establishment Services.

On January 24, 1995, Chenault was named vice chairman of the American Express Company. The promotion made him the highest-ranking

African American executive in America. As vice chairman, he also joined the Office of the Chief Executive, the company's senior-most management group. He added the responsibilities for worldwide brand management and advertising while continuing to oversee the Travel Related Services unit. His responsibilities included formulating policy and business strategy companywide and overseeing the consumer charge card and consumer lending businesses globally. In 1997, Chenault was named president and chief operating officer (CEO) of American Express. He oversaw the creation of the Membership Rewards, the Blue card, and continued to compete with Visa and MasterCard for customers.

In 1999, chief executive officer Harvey Golub announced that Chenault would succeed him as the company's CEO in 2001, upon Golub's retirement. The announcement assured an easy transition and enabled Chenault to increase his responsibilities. Early on, in 1997, Golub had selected Chenault as the primary internal candidate to lead the corporation. He had praised him for spearheading a number of initiatives at the company over his career, such as his efforts to segment American Express's charge card business, expand the credit card and other consumer lending businesses, increase merchant coverage, and reengineer other key business programs.

In January 2001, Chenault assumed the mantle of chief executive officer. Prepared to reverse the company's economic decline, Chenault's first year faced an overwhelming challenge. On September 11, 2001, American Express lost eleven employees and had many injured in the shocking terrorist attacks. The victims were in the World Trade Center directly across the street from the American Express Co. headquarters. The 3,200 employees in the headquarters building had to set up temporary offices in New York, Connecticut, and New Jersey, where Chenault relocated. September 11 had a devastating impact on the travel and entertainment business, which accounted for about half of the company's charge card revenue. The company's customer service helped more than 500,000 stranded cardholders get home. The company was able to move back into its headquarters in the World Financial Center in May 2002. Chenault had begun cost cutting before September 11 but was forced to cut deeper, slashing budgets and laying off some 13,400 employees, 15 percent of the workforce.

In 2002, American Express expanded its promotions and reward programs for the holders of its consumer cards. He expanded the company's corporate card base by attracting small- and medium-sized business customers. By 2003 and in 2004, American Express posted record earnings of $3 billion and $3.4 billion, respectively. In 2004, American Express held 22 percent of U.S. credit card charges, Visa has 43 percent, and MasterCard holds 30 percent. While the company has a smaller market share, its customers spend more money. Chenault wants American Express to sign up unconventional merchants and accept payments for insurance, college tuition, health care, and mortgages. He has plans for the use of radio frequency identification technology to facilitate purchases with the wave of a small key fob across a reader. Such proactive and forward approaches under Chenault's leadership position the American Express Company to continue its prosperous ascent.

Chenault has served on the boards of IBM, the Quaker Oats Company, the American Council for Drug Education, Junior Achievement of New York, Mount Sinai New York University Medical Center and Health Center, National Collegiate Athletics Association, and the Arthur Ashe Institute for Urban Health. He is a member of the Dean's Advisory Board for Harvard Law School and a member of the Council of Foreign Relations in New York City and the American Bar Association. He holds honorary degrees from Adelphi University (1995), Bowdoin College (1996), Howard University (1998), Iona College (1996), Morgan State University (1990), South Carolina State University (1997), Stony Brook University (1996), the University of Notre Dame (1998), and Xavier University (1997).

Committed to serve the community, Chenault cosponsored fund-raisers for the political campaigns of Virginia governor L. Douglas Wilder and Atlanta mayor **Maynard Holbrook Jackson Jr**. He chaired the fiftieth anniversary gala for the National Association for the Advancement of Colored People (NAACP) Legal Defense Fund. He has received the Robie Award for Achievement in Industry from the Jackie Robinson Foundation, the Anti-Defamation League of B'nai B'rith Torch of Liberty Award, the Ron Brown Award for Corporate Leadership, and the Morehouse College Candle in the Dark Award. He was named Corporate Patron of the Arts by the Studio Museum of Harlem. *Black Enterprise* magazine named Chenault its 1999 *BE* Corporate Executive of the Year, and in 2001, *Fortune* magazine named him one of the Fifty Most Powerful African American Executives in America.

Chenault, a Congregationalist, and his wife Kathryn (Cassell), an attorney, live in New Rochelle, New York, with their two sons, Kenneth Jr. and Kevin Addison. They have a summer home in Sag Harbor, New York. Kathryn, a political science major at Tufts University, went to New York University Law School. She has worked at the law firm of Donovan Leisure Newton & Irvine and the National Programs Division of the United Negro College Fund. The couple met at a party while he was attending law school, and they married on August 20, 1977. Though much of his time is spent with business clients, Chenault likes to spend time with his family, attend basketball games, play tennis, golf, swim, and ski.

**Sources**

Branch, Shelly, and Alfred Edmond Jr. "Kenneth I. Chenault." *Black Enterprise* 23 (February 1993): 88.

Creswell, Julie. "Ken Chenault Reshuffles His Cards." *Fortune* 151 (April 18, 2005): 180–186.

"Kenneth I. Chenault Appointed President and COO at American Express Company." *Jet* 91 (March 17, 1997): 8–9.

Pierce, Ponchetta. "Blazing New Paths in Corporate American: American Express President Set to Become First Black to Lead a Fortune 500 Company." *Ebony* 52 (July 1997): 58–62, 135–136.

Schwartz, Nelson D. "What's in the Card for Amex? New CEO Ken Chenault Has No Shortage for American Express. No. 1 on the List: Staying on Top." *Fortune* 143 (January 22, 2001): 58–70.

Shook, Carrie. "Leader, Not Boss." *Forbes* 160 (December 1, 1997): 52–54.

Smith, Eric L. "Someone's Knocking at the Door: Kenneth Chenault's Appointment as President and COO of American Express Threatens to Shatter One of the Final Barriers to Corporate America's Top Spot." *Black Enterprise* 27 (May 1997): 97–99.

*Kathleen E. Bethel*

# Robert Reed Church Sr. (1839–1912), Businessman, Philanthropist, Community Activist, Political Leader

Recognized as the South's first African American millionaire, Robert Reed Church Sr. was a noted Memphis businessman, philanthropist, community activist, and political leader. During the 1860s, he successfully invested in several business ventures that netted him financial wealth. A contributor to many civic and philanthropic causes, when the city of Memphis was reduced to a Taxing District, Church was the first citizen to purchase a $1,000 bond to help restore the city's charter. Church established the city's first park for African Americans, which included an auditorium that became a center for cultural, civic, and recreational activities. Later, in 1906, he founded the Solvent Savings Bank and Trust Company. Today he is remembered as one of Memphis's most distinguished citizens and entrepreneurs.

Church was born on June 18, 1839, in Holly Springs, Mississippi, to Emmeline, a slave seamstress, and Charles B. Church, a white steamboat captain. Church's mother died when he was twelve years of age. After the death of his mother, Church lived with his father until he reached young adulthood. He worked for his father as a cabin boy and steward before an ill-fated accident caused him to leave the life of a river steamboat. In 1855, when the luxury steamer *Bulletin No. 2* burned and sank, Robert and his father were among the few who lived.

After surviving the fateful river disaster, Church's life took another turn for the worse, when federal forces captured him during America's war against itself, while he was serving as a steward on the steamer *Victona*. Later he settled in Memphis, Tennessee, where he became one of the nation's most successful African American businessmen. Church used the experience and edification he obtained on the river to enter the world of entrepreneurial enterprises.

Although real estate was Church's main interest, he engaged in other business pursuits, including hotel, restaurant, saloon, and bank undertakings. In May 1866, one year after the close of America's Civil War, when whites attacked black Memphians, illustrating southern intolerance in the face of defeat and indicating unwillingness to share civil or social rights with the newly freed American blacks, Church was among the more than seventy people wounded. Shot and left for dead, he recovered and rebuffed the idea of leaving the "Bluff City" in spite of the carnage left in the city's black community. When Memphis experienced the dreadful yellow fever outbreak of 1878, Church again demonstrated his allegiance to the city and chose to remain, as others sought safer places of residency. He invested in local real estate, and when Memphis was reduced to a Taxing District, Church was the first citizen to purchase a $1,000 bond to restore the city's charter.

He established his hotel in downtown Memphis, on the southwest corner of South Second and Gayoso streets. Promoted as the only first-class "colored" hotel in Memphis, it had large airy rooms and a dining facility, and he furnished it with the best equipment of the day. The knowledge he gained as a steamboat steward equipped him to meet the individual needs of his clientele in a lavish style.

In 1882, Church unsuccessfully ran for the Board of Public Works, on both the People's Ticket and as an independent candidate. Although his political aspirations never came to fruition, his business acumen continued to produce positive results as his investments grew. Recognized as the South's first African American millionaire and philanthropic in disposition, Church contributed to many civic causes, including the purchase of land for the establishment of a park for the city's African American populace.

Because of the era's zeitgeist, the City of Memphis did not provide public parks and recreational facilities for African Americans. In addition to not providing park and recreational facilities, black performing arts groups had no place to perform their productions. In 1899, Church purchased over six acres of land on Beale Street near Fourth and Turley and constructed Church Park and Auditorium. The only undertaking of its kind in the United States, Church Park and Auditorium contained a playground, with all of the recreational accoutrements to entertain children, and an auditorium with the latest equipment and a seating capacity for more than 2,000 people. One of the largest stages in the South, its fire-proof drop curtain was a copy of an oil painting of the burning steamer *Bulletin No. 2*, which hung in the parlor of the Church residence. Beneath the auditorium was a large banquet hall and bar, with a soda fountain located near the entrance to provide refreshments for visitors. The recreational and cultural facility also contained a large bandstand where evening band concerts were held during the summer months. Later known as the "Father of the Blues," W. C. Handy functioned as orchestra leader at the park and auditorium. Internationally renowned musicians such as Duke Ellington, Louis Armstrong, and Cab Calloway, among others, all performed at Church's facility.

Serving Memphis's African American community, Church Park and Auditorium was built, owned, and operated by Church. As the community's cultural, recreational, and civic center, Church Park and Auditorium hosted some of the period's most popular theatrical groups, as well as some of the country's most noted leaders, black and white. On November 19, 1902,

President Theodore Roosevelt spoke to approximately 10,000 people at the auditorium. Roosevelt's appearance gave an outward indication of Church's political influence. Two years earlier, he served as a Memphis delegate to the Republican National Convention. On a tour through Tennessee, the "Wizard of Tuskegee," **Booker T. Washington**, and party also visited the site. Additionally, other noteworthy visitors included James Shlliday, Herbert J. Seligmann, James Weldon Johnson, and Walter White, all officials of the National Association for the Advancement of Colored People (NAACP). Established and organized by Robert Reed Church Jr. in 1916 to register and train African American voters, and to pay poll taxes, the Lincoln Republican League held its meetings in the auditorium, as did the state's first branch of the NAACP (founded by Church Jr. in 1917. Two years later, he was elected to the organization's national board). In addition, before the Church of God In Christ, founded by the Bishop C. H. Mason, built Mason Temple, the denomination held its convocations in Church's Park and Auditorium. With Church's success in the cultural, recreational, and civic enterprise, he continued to make inroads into America's capitalistic society.

Five years after establishing Church Park and Auditorium, Church embarked upon another business adventure when he established the first African American–owned bank in Memphis since the 1874 collapse of the Freedmen's Savings and Trust Company Bank. Following the lead of Nashville's African American business leaders and Booker T. Washington's **National Negro Business League**, he established the Solvent Savings Bank and Trust Company. Described by some as Memphis's most important African American business institution, Church founded the bank in 1906. Located on Beale Street across from the park and auditorium, shares in the banking enterprise could be purchased for $10 a share. Depositors could open an account with a minimum of $1. One year after its opening, Solvent Savings Bank and Trust Company withstood the economic hysteria of 1907, which closed the doors of older and larger banking institutions. To solidify the depositors' confidence and to forego a run on the bank's reserves, Church placed piles of money in the bank's windows with a notice declaring that there was adequate capital to pay off its depositors. One year after withstanding the financial panic of 1907, Church and his bank came to the aid of the Beale Street Baptist Church, which faced foreclosure. The bank paid off the church's notes and saved it from being sold. After fifteen years in business, the bank boasted that it was the largest bank in the world owned and operated by African Americans, with deposits over a million dollars. Church and his son Robert Jr. served as successive presidents. In the early 1920s, Solvent Savings Bank and Trust Company faced financial crisis.

After the failure of several borrowers in the early 1920s and to remain afloat, Solvent merged with the Fraternal Savings Bank and Trust Company in 1927. Robert R. Church Jr., who succeeded to the presidency of the bank following his father's death in 1912, deposited $50,000 to halt the panic, although no longer president. However, a year later, bank examiners found a deficit of $500,000, and the bank's president, Alfred F. Ward, was incarcerated. The failure of the bank preceded the stock market crash by one year.

Church married twice, and two children were born to each marriage. His first marriage to Louise Ayers Church ended in divorce, but their union produced a son, Thomas Ayers Church, who became an attorney, editor of his own journal, and the author of several books. Church's daughter Mary Church Terrell became the first president of the National Association of Colored Women (1896) and was an activist and one of the twentieth century's most prominent African American leaders. In 1885, he married Anna S. Wright, and they became the parents of Robert Reed Church Jr., who was known as the most powerful African American in the Republican Party, and Annette Elaine Church. A staunch Republican like her brother, she was one of three female charter members of the Memphis branch of the NAACP.

As asserted in "Robert R. Church Scholarship Fund," Church Sr. was a "self-made man in the broadest sense of the term." He had "no opportunity of the schools; he had no nucleus of wealth left to him by ancestor ... but he made his way to success over every possible obstacle." His contributions to the City of Memphis were felt in all of its sectors until his death on August 29, 1912. Church's remains were interred at Memphis's Elmwood Cemetery in the Church Family Mausoleum.

*See also*: Black Banks: Their Beginning

**Sources**

Church, Annette E., and Roberta Church. *The Robert R. Churches of Memphis: A Father and Son Who Achieved in Spite of Race*. Ann Arbor, MI: Privately Published, 1974.

Lamon, Lester. *Black Tennesseans, 1791–1970*. Knoxville: University of Tennessee Press, 1981.

Miller, M. Sammye. "Last Will and Testament of Robert Reed Church, Senior (1839–1912)." *Journal of Negro History* 65 (Spring 1980): 156–157.

Mitchell, Reavis L. "Robert R. Church, Sr. (1839–1912)." *Profiles of African Americans in Tennessee*. Ed. Bobby L. Lovett and Linda T. Wynn. Nashville, TN: Local Conference on African American Culture and History, 1996.

"Robert R. Church Scholarship Fund." Scholarship Funds. Community Foundation of Greater Memphis, Memphis: 2004.

Walter, Ronald A. "Robert R. Church, Sr. 1839–1912." *Tennessee Encyclopedia of History and Culture*. Ed. Carroll Van West. Nashville, TN: Rutledge Hill Press, 1998.

*Linda T. Wynn*

# Citizens' League for Fair Play

During the Great Depression of the early 1930s, the nation was experiencing severe hardships in the economy and significant depreciation of the American dollar. As a historic minority and systematically alienated group,

African Americans felt the heaviest brunt of this most futile condition. In 1934, in Harlem, New York, one of the leading per capita habitations of African and African-descended people outside the continent of Africa itself, the Citizens' League for Fair Play (CLFP) was formed as a nonpartisan and nondenomination coalition of social organizations, fraternal brotherhoods, and political groups. Though only in formal existence for less than a year, CLFP accumulated good mileage through mass picketing of white-owned business establishments that prevented blacks from working in nonmenial capacities. Hence, such 125th Street establishments as Blumstein's, Woolworth's, W. C. Grant Company, and Beck's Shoe Store all felt the sting of CLFP picketing in the pocketbooks and subsequently at least began hiring black women as clerks in response to their demands.

As a cross-based coalition, CLFP was composed of bipolar ideological points of view representing a moderate integrationist approach in the vein of the National Association for the Advancement of Colored People (NAACP) and the Urban League, on one end, and the Black Nationalist model espoused by **Marcus Garvey**'s potent United Negro Improvement Association (UNIA), on the other. Internal strife significantly impacted divisiveness that splintered the group, but the exemplified collective spirit of unity is a shining example of the power inherent in a cohesive front. Moreover, events that followed CLFP's demise underline the social tensions that made its formation a miracle to begin with. For example, many of its previously mentioned establishments admitted to hiring overtly only light-skinned black women, which reinforced class tensions among many in the black community. This class wedge was a sticky topic because the ideologically diverse leadership segment—consisting of Reverend John Johnson, pastor, St. Martin's Protestant Episcopal Church; Fred Moore, *New York Age* publisher; Ira Kemp, president, African Patriot League; and Arthur Reid, Marcus Garvey supporter from Barbados—ultimately had different views as to the policies and courses of action that should be taken by the coalition.

The rallying call and immediate impetus igniting CLFP's formation rang from Effa Manley, pioneering co-owner, with her husband Abe, of the Newark Eagles of the Negro Leagues' professional baseball fame. The initial meeting was with other progressive women, but from the agreed-upon findings, Manley decided to solicit broad support from black ministers in the cause of tearing down discriminatory employment walls plaguing 125th Street. The dire conditions of black unemployment were addressed through participation from eighteen black churches with assistance from organizations that included the Democratic Club, the Cosmopolitan Social and Tennis Club, the Premier Literary Circle, the Unity Democratic Club, the Young West Indian Congress, and the New York UNIA chapter in CLFP's massive formation. Manley's 1934 call for organized boycotting of Harlem stores who refused hiring black salesclerks resulted in the six-week picketing that grabbed the attention of profit-driven merchants whose business bottom line was impacted substantially from the slogan "**Don't Buy Where You Can't Work.**" Within one year, 300 blacks were hired in 125th street stores.

Another point that warrants attention is that despite the divisiveness that would splinter CLFP, it was the united picketing that produced tangible outcomes. Furthermore, the Negro Industrial Clerical Alliance (NICA), under the leadership of Sufi Abdul Hamid, and the Harlem Labor Union Incorporated (HLUI), led by Ira Kemp and Arthur Reid, would prove to have vibrant lifelines after a New York state court ruled that picketing on the grounds of race was illegal, all but bringing CLFP to a screeching halt. Hamid never was formally a member of CLFP leadership cadre, but his organization worked side-by-side with CLFP initiatives during the picketing campaigns and is historically aligned with the ensuing events. Feeling that picketing was the most effective strategy, his NICA resumed the practice and demanded further jobs for blacks by Blumstein's. In addition, HLUI started when Kemp and Reid grew fed up and became disillusioned with CLFP's lack of commitment to addressing the class issue within the platform of equality for all blacks.

The salient feature of a slavery-induced psychosis by African descendants cannot be ignored when analyzing how CLFP was plagued ideologically. Consider the life of Effa Manley herself. As a fair-skinned woman, evidence from oral interviews with her indicate that she actually was Caucasian but grew up in a household with black step siblings, as her mother of German, Asian, and Indian descent married a black man. Accordingly, she consciously led the life as a black woman. By *black* in this context we are referring to her politics and where her interests lay. This reality is evidenced from her devotion to CLFP causes in 1934 and her business affiliation with the Negro Leagues where she promoted Anti-Lynching Day at Ruppert Stadium in 1939. Still, she was identified by mainstream white society as white, or as a light skin, or "redbone" black woman at worst. So the Black Nationalists' appeals and criticisms launched on what they perceived to be conciliatory rhetoric from the likes of Blumstein was not simply hot air. In fact, as one reads an interview conducted in 1935, Blumstein was forthright in stating that his store naturally picked "the most attractive" personalities of the selection pool of black females.

As revisionist history can prove to be quite futile, the broader context of mass movements can be most appreciated from focusing on the right things. Thus, the fact remains that CLFP's existence, though relatively brief, was focused in its operation, and its greatest legacy lay in its ability to act in an effort of solidarity. The areas where it splintered should not be ignored because the differences were indeed real. However, students of history should not glorify and/or disproportionately revel in the obvious ideological tensions. Conversely, a more beneficial approach is to look at the possibilities afforded when artificial barriers are superceded. Moreover, institutionalized racism, sexism, and classism as social forces should not be marginalized either. Instead, when acknowledging the utility of umoja (the operational quality behind actualizing the sustenance of maintaining unity in the family, nation, race, and community), CLFP shines brightly.

*See also*: Retail Industry

## Sources

Crawford, Aimee. "The First Lady of Black Baseball, Manley Was an Innovator in the Negro Leagues." http://mlb.com/NASApp/mlb/mlb/history/mlb_negro_leagues_story.jsp?story=effa_manley.

Greengerg, Cheryl Lynn. *"Or Does It Explode?:" Black Harlem in the Great Depression.* New York: Oxford University Press, 1991.

Lowery, Charles D., John F. Marszalek, and Thomas Adams Upchurch, eds. *The Greenwood Encyclopedia of African-American Civil Rights: From Emancipation to the 21st Century.* Vol. 1. Westport, CT: Greenwood Press, 2003.

*Uzoma O. Miller*

# Alexander G. Clark (1826–1891), Entrepreneur, Civil Rights Worker, Church Leader

Alexander G. Clark rose from modest beginnings to become a man of wealth. He balanced his career by mixing interests in real estate, politics, the military, religion, the newspaper media, and law. He fought for a number of causes, such as suffrage for black men and women, school integration, and civil rights of blacks in general.

Born in Washington County, Pennsylvania, on February 25, 1826, Clark was the son of John Clark, a former slave of an Irish master, and Rebecca Darnes Clark, a full-blooded African. He began his education in Washington County but was moved to Cincinnati in 1939 to live with an uncle. He attended school for one year and at the same time learned his uncle's barber business. At age fifteen, he left to go south as a bartender on the steamer *George Washington*. In May 1842 Clark went to Muscatine, Iowa, where he opened a barbershop. Continuing his business ventures, he supplied wood to steamboats and used his profits to purchase real estate; this proved to be a wise choice, for he became a wealthy man. In 1848, Clark married Catherine Guffin and had five children.

Clark had a variety of interests. He began his public career in 1849, when he cofounded the local African Methodist Episcopal Church and served as trustee, steward, and superintendent of the Sunday school. His church activities took him to the Methodist Ecumenical Conference held in London in 1881.

He had an interest in the military as well and enlisted in the First Iowa Colored Volunteer Infantry in 1863, where, until the end of the war, he served primarily as a recruiter throughout the West. A physical disability prevented him from becoming physically active and accepting an appointment as sergeant-major.

Clark spent much of his life working with Masonic circles and held several high offices with the Grand Lodge of Missouri; he had jurisdiction over six states. In 1884, he organized the Hiram Grand Lodge of Iowa, then merged it with another grand lodge to form the United Grand Lodge of Iowa and served as its president.

A man with a vision, he became active in politics and was chairperson and spokesperson for the first Convention of Colored Men held in Iowa in 1868. He called for political equality of black men of Iowa. In 1869 year he became one of the vice presidents of the Republican State Convention of Iowa. In 1872, he was delegate-at-large from Iowa to the 1872 Republican National Convention in Philadelphia and later alternate delegate from his state to the Cincinnati convention. A great orator who had been favorably compared to his long-standing friend **Frederick Douglass**, Clark was often called the "Colored Orator of the West."

Clark supported a number of causes, including women's suffrage and civil rights. He successfully sued the local school board when his daughter was denied entrance to the Muscatine public schools. The state supreme court heard the case and ruled in his favor.

He entered law school when he was in his fifties and graduated from the University of Iowa Law School in 1884, then opened a law office in Chicago. He became one of the three owners of the newspaper the *Conservator* and used the paper to speak out against the ill treatment of blacks.

President Benjamin Harrison appointed him minister and consul-general to Liberia on August 8, 1890. He died there on May 31, 1891, but was returned to Muscatine for a state funeral.

Although little else is known about Clark as an entrepreneur, his wealth enabled him to live well and to engage in a variety of activities that benefited his race.

**Sources**

Davis, Aldeen L. "Alexander G. Clark." *Dictionary of American Negro Biography*. Ed. Rayford W. Logan and Michael R. Winston. New York: W. W. Norton, 1982.

Simmons, William J. *Men of Mark: Eminent, Progressive, and Rising*. Cleveland, OH: Geo. M. Rewell, 1887.

*Jessie Carney Smith*

# Coalition of Black Trade Unionists

The Coalition of Black Trade Unionists (CBTU) was established in 1972. It was a response to the failure of the ALF–CIO (American Federation of Labor–Congress of Industrial Organization) leadership to champion actively the interests of black and minority workers. Spearheading the efforts of CBTU in Chicago, Illinois, for its initial steering and planning committee on September 23–24 were William Lacy, international secretary-treasurer, American Federation of State, County and Municipal Employees (AFSCME); Nelson Edwards, vice president, United Auto Workers (UAW); William Simmons, president, Washington Teachers Union (WTU), Local # 6; Charles Hayes, international vice president, United Food & Commercial Workers Union (UFCWU); and Cleveland Robinson, president, Distributive Workers of America (DWA), District 65.

From its inception, CBTU has aimed to erect bridges with other labor organizations and/or civic groups whose objectives are organizing black and minority workers in trade unions and working toward fair wages and economic rewards, as well as increasing political awareness and participation. Among the slogans and objectives sought after by the organization are "Living Wages," "Job Safety," "Support for Public Schools," "Coalition Building," "Environmental Justice," "Voice at Work," "Union Contracts," "Comprehensive Health," "Town Hall Meetings," "Pay Equity," and "The Right to Organize Is a Civil Right Which No Worker Should Be Denied." From the inception too has been advocacy for the rights of women and the international labor connection. CBTU estimates that approximately 40 percent of the first 1,200 delegates were women and since that time have proven necessary elements, without whom their success could not have been attained. Moreover, they have served in high-ranking leadership positions including five on the initial executive committee in 1972. On the international front, in 1974 CBTU was the first American labor organization to pass strong resolutions calling for an economic boycott and change in U.S. policy toward South Africa.

Though not defined as a civil rights organization, CBTU has always fostered tendencies and a familiarity with this movement. In 1990 civil rights approaches to organizing the African American community were openly called upon by Richard Trumka, president of the United Mine Workers (UMW) and CBTU member who championed minorities in the labor movement in the United States to adopt approaches used in the civil rights movement of the 1960s to rally the African American community behind labor's struggles. Of further note from this appeal made in Buffalo, New York, was that for the first time CBTU received recognition from the very entity it had to distance itself from in the first place, the AFL–CIO. This acknowledgment grew not from a sudden benevolence toward the cause of minority rights but instead from CBTU's proven commitment to advancing the universal plight of workers and their inherent right to have decent wages.

CBTU's commitment to protecting business interests of minorities is apparent from its consistent youth development, consumer protection, and political literacy campaigns. Youth represent tomorrow's workforce, thus initiatives to decrease the nearly 50 percent black unemployment rate of persons under the age of eighteen and scholarship programs are sponsored. The inner cities, where black youth are disproportionately schooled, are target areas for programs designed to give students skill-based and living wage competency on workplace safety and labor law. CBTU also is a staunch advocate for programs that limit inflation rates on food, clothing, housing, and medical care and programs that will help minorities. Lastly, CBTU correlates the dynamics mentioned above with the degree to which political education and advocacy are instilled in its members. Therefore, CBTU has constantly devised and implemented workshops, projects, and drives to enhance involvement by union members in voter registration, education, and turnout.

The organization has remained consistent, however, and has been vocal in attacking what it perceives as contradictory practices by former allies in struggle. CBTU president William Lucy criticized Robert Mugabe, current president of Zimbabwe and former freedom fighter for Zimbabwe's independence from British colonialism in 1980, for failing to allow a Malawian labor organizer in 2003 entrance into Harare International Airport. Lucy was quick to note that he felt Mugabe continuously attacked the rights of workers who wished to assemble and abused his privileges to disrupt working-class interests. According to Mthulisi Mathuthu, Mugabe's government was accused of turning its back on principles that defined their independence. Although not a black separatist or civil rights organization, CBTU has maintained a proven track record of protecting economic, political, and social justice for trade workers and is composed of members who represent seventy-seven unions throughout the world and forty-two chapters in the United States.

**Sources**

Coalition of Black Trade Unionists: Organizing to Empower Working People. http://www.cbtu.org.

Dinkins, David, Richard Trumka, and Kenneth Young. "N.Y. Mayor, Mine Workers President and Kirkland's Assistant Salute CBTU Convention." *Labor Today* 29 (Spring–Summer 1990): 5.

Glynn, Matt. "Trade Unionists Aim to Help Recruit Minorities for New York Construction Jobs." *Buffalo News*, February 21, 2002.

Mathuthu, Mthulisi. "Unionist Denied Entry." *Asia Africa Intelligence Wire*, January 10, 2003.

Williams, Fred O. "Mentoring Program for Students Expanding." *Buffalo News*, January 31, 2005.

Williamson, Willie. "CBTU President Sets Framework for Action." *Labor Today* 25 (July 1986): 4.

———. "CBTU Spurs Fight against Reaganism." *Labor Today* 24 (July 1985): 7.

*Uzoma O. Miller*

# Daniel C. Cochran (1946– ), Financial Executive

Daniel Cochran is a senior vice president and the chief operating officer for Merrill Lynch, making him one of the first African Americans to hold a position of importance on Wall Street, a place traditionally difficult for African Americans to enter and advance. In fact, in 2002, Cochran was named one of the top fifty African Americans in the financial industry.

Cochran was born on November 14, 1946, in Chicago, Illinois. Cochrane earned a Bachelor of Arts degree at Amherst College in 1968. He received a Master of Public and International Affairs from Princeton in 1974. Cochrane speaks three languages in addition to English: Farsi (Persian), Spanish, and French. His knowledge of other languages was useful in 1969 when he joined the U.S. Department of State as a foreign services officer and was stationed in Iran. In 1974, Cochrane joined Exxon Corporation as assistant treasurer and finance manager for Exxon's U.S. operation. He stayed with Exxon until 1989, when he joined Merrill Lynch as first vice president and deputy treasurer for finance. Cochrane has held several positions at Merrill Lynch. In 1995, he moved to Hong Kong and served as chief administrative officer for Merrill Lynch's Asia Pacific Region. Cochran returned to New York in 1999 and assumed the position of senior vice president of Merrill Lynch's Corporate and Institutional Client Group. In addition to his financial responsibilities, Cochrane serves as trustee of Merrill Lynch's Winthrop H. Smith Memorial Foundation. He is senior adviser to Merrill Lynch's Rainbow Employee Network and a member of Merrill Lynch's Employee Advisory Council. Cochrane maintains connections with Amherst College and serves as a member of Amherst's Trustee Nominating Committee.

Cochran remains a groundbreaking African American in the Wall Street world. His dedication and hard work have opened doors that have previously been difficult to open. Cochrane, like many other powerful businessmen, is not content to just help himself. He is also active with charitable programs within Merrill Lynch and maintains ties with his alma mater.

**Sources**

Black Achievers Industry. "National Salute to Black Achievers in Industry." http://www.black-achivers.org/bailist.htm.

BlackEnterprise.com. "The Top 50 African Americans on Wall Street." *About Us*, September 18, 2004. http://www.blackenterprise.com/AboutUsOpen.asp?Source=AboutBe/1002.pr.html.

"Daniel Chester Cochran." *Who's Who among African Americans*. 18th ed. Detroit: Thomson Gale, 2005.

Dow Jones Newswire. "Merrill Lynch Appoints Ausaf Abbas Asia Chief Admin Officer." January 27, 1999. http://global.factiva.com/en/arch/display.asp.

Merrill Lynch. Foundation Trustees Global Philanthropy. 2002. http://www.ml.com/philanthropy/winsmith/mission.html.

Multicultural Advantage. "Black Enterprise Names the Most Influential Leaders of the Financial Industry." http://www.multiculturaladvantage.com/contentmgmt/anmviewer.asp?a=268.

"People." *Securities Week*, October 23, 1989. http://global.factiva.com/en/arch/display.asp.

Scott, M. S., A. Hughes, et al. "B.E. Wall Street All Stars." *Black Enterprise* 33 (October 2002): 88–101. http://search.epnet.com/login.aspx?direct=true&db=aph&an=7387251.

*Anne K. Driscoll*

# Marie Therese Coincoin (1742–c. 1816), Creole Matriarch, Entrepreneur

Marie Therese Coincoin rose from slavery to become a wealthy landowner in the late eighteenth and early nineteenth centuries, founding a lineage of "free people of color," who occupied an intermediate position between the mass of slaves and the dominant whites. She serves as a reminder of the multilayered dynamics associated with slavery in pre–Civil War Louisiana. In spite of her birth into slavery on the plantation of one of Louisiana's founding fathers, four decades of servitude as a domestic servant, and the responsibility of nurturing fourteen biological children, Coincoin would emerge as a major shaper of Creole history in Louisiana and as one of the richest free blacks in North America. Determined to free her children and extended family members from bondage, she used the wealth and land acquired from her common-law union with a Frenchman to found and develop Melrose Plantation, which cultivated tobacco, corn, indigo, and cotton and raised cattle on thousands of acres with many slaves.

Coincoin was born in 1742, the second-born daughter of two enslaved Africans on the plantation of Louis Juchereau de St. Dennis, the first commandant of Fort St. Jean Baptiste des Natchitoches, the oldest Royal French Colony in the state. While her rise in status was connected to her being a privileged house servant of a leading colonial family in Louisiana, the buildings on her plantation reveal clear traces of her African heritage. Coincoin would become a leading landholder and slave owner herself, whose wealth measured favorably with that of the shrewdest and wealthiest white male landowners of her era. This black woman's rise to wealth is exceptional in light of the constraints on both blacks and women during this time period.

By the age of twenty-five Coincoin had born four children with a black man, but she then entered a relationship with a newly arrived Frenchman, Claude Thomas Pierre Metoyer, that produced ten additional children. The two lived together for nineteen years. Documented records and oral legend conflict as to certain specifics regarding such matters as her year of manumission, whether she or Nicolas Augustine Metoyer, her oldest son, founded the Melrose Plantation, and what arrangements were made between her and Metoyer regarding the lives of their offspring. But what is undisputed is the outcome. Coincoin would purchase the freedom of all fourteen of her children and that of countless grandchildren as well. The rights of her four all-black children were secured without any assistance from Metoyer, and many slaves were purchased to clear land, to cultivate indigo, tobacco, corn, and cotton, and to raise cattle on Melrose Plantation.

There is no question of the extent to which African carryovers are manifest at Melrose. Of the eight colonial buildings erected, more than a third have overt African names: Yucca (c. 1796), the African House (c. 1800), and Ghana, which is generally believed to be nearly as old as the original foundations. As for Coincoin, her name is derived from the Ewe linguistic group of Central/West Africa and translates to "second-born daughter," the phonetic equivalent of "Ko Kwe." Oral tradition points to her parent's place of origin as the Congo.

In contrast to these memories of Africa, the Creole class that emerged from the African-Franco unions was one where color consciousness was pervasive—so pervasive in fact that the first generations were taught to distance themselves from their African roots and embrace only their French side. Discrimination may also be evident in the treatment of Coincoin's first four children. Documents suggest that in order to have Metoyer agree to manumit his own children, Coincoin had to agree to forgo the annuities he otherwise would have granted her.

Coincoin appears to have demonstrated the qualities of a shrewd businesswoman, as she was methodical, systematic, purposeful, and earnest in her dealings. From donations in 1786, grants in 1794, and purchases made in 1807, she was able to secure her financial base, become a landed lady, and found her family's fortunes. For ten years she employed Spanish manager José Mare to manage her properties on the west bank of the Old River Branch of the Red River. Mare managed Coincoin's crops and cattle and assisted in directing the operations on the plantation, while she continued to acquire land.

Coincoin's career underlines how local conditions affected slavery. It would have been well nigh impossible elsewhere than in Louisiana. It also illustrates a persistent tendency for light-skinned and relatively wealthy blacks to attempt to distance themselves from dark-skinned blacks. This three-way social division could develop in Louisiana with its "free people of color," but adamant white insistence on a sharp twofold distinction did not allow this idea to take deep root elsewhere.

Coincoin's endeavors measured within strictly business terms are remarkable; she acquired upward of 13,000 acres of land covering a nearly thirty-mile radius, making her family the wealthiest free black family in antebellum America.

**Sources**

Association for the Preservation of Historic Natchitoches (APHN). http://www .natchitoches.net/melrose.htm.

Ingersoll, Thomas N. "Free Blacks in a Slave Community: New Orleans, 1778– 1812." *William and Mary Quarterly*, 3rd ser., 48 (April 1991): 173–200.

Mills, Gary B. *The Forgotten People*. Baton Rouge: Louisiana State University Press, 1977.

Ringle, Ken. "Up Through Slavery." *Washington Post*, May 12, 2002.

Spivey, Christine. "Early Success of the Metoyer *Gens de Coleur Libre*." http:// www.loyno.edu/history/journal/1995-6/spivey.htm.

*Uzoma O. Miller*

# Virgis William Colbert (1939– ), Corporate Executive, Philanthropist

Virgis William Colbert serves as executive vice president of operations at the Miller Brewing Company. In 2002 he was ranked twenty-sixth on *Fortune* magazine's list of "The 50 Most Powerful Black Executives." He was born on October 13, 1939, in Jackson, Mississippi, but grew up in Toledo,

Ohio. He is the youngest of the eight children of Quillie, a factory worker, and his wife Eddie May. Colbert lives in Milwaukee with his wife Angela, an attorney, formerly employed with the Milwaukee law firm of Quarles & Brady. They have two daughters and one son.

After high school, Colbert attended the University of Toledo but dropped out in 1967 after one year. He settled into an assembly-line job at the Chrysler machining plant in Toledo. Although his hard work was rewarded with promotions to supervisory positions, he realized that his chances of entering upper management would be stymied if he did not further his education. While working at Chrysler, he attended classes at Central Michigan University, where he obtained a bachelor's degree in industrial management in 1974. He was promoted to general superintendent of plant operations in 1977.

Colbert's successful twelve-year career at Chrysler ended in 1979 when he was hired by the Miller Brewing Company as an assistant to the plant manager in Reidsville, North Carolina. The interpersonal and leadership skills he had developed at Chrysler proved beneficial in the brewing industry. Colbert's expectations regarding management opportunities were realized as he rapidly advanced to positions with increasing responsibilities. His future at Miller seemed assured. In 1990, he became chief of plant operations overseeing brewing combinations, container manufacturing, and product distribution. In 1993, he rose to vice president of operations and was elected to Miller's Board of Directors and Executive Committee. He moved into a senior vice president position in 1995, in charge of worldwide operations, and in 1997 was promoted to executive vice president with responsibility for brewing, quality assurance, purchasing, operations planning, and improvement and information systems.

With customers from all ethnic backgrounds, there is no doubt that Miller values diversity. Colbert is the company's only African American vice president. His responsibility includes working with about 400 minority vendors. Early in his career, he declined offers to move from plant services to public relations because he preferred the labor and staff operations side of the business. With responsibility for production, packaging, and shipping operations, he oversees a staff of 8,000 workers and a multibillion-dollar budget. His colleagues view his management style as team oriented. He considers his staff not just an assembly line but a production team. He leads by example.

Colbert strongly believes that those who have benefited from the positive outcomes of the civil rights struggle owe a debt to the community and have a responsibility to repay what they owe. The obligation to repay—nicknamed the "black tax"—is not merely a token gift but generous personal donations of time, money, and expertise. Colbert is particularly concerned about providing black youth with positive role models and visible connections through community service commitments. Along with education, role models present opportunities for youth to follow in the footsteps of successful executives. To this end, Colbert has blazed a trail of civic involvement working with several organizations within the community.

Colbert plays a major role in developing Miller's corporate social responsibility philosophy. The company has spearheaded a number of partnership initiatives that help people achieve economic success and contribute to the community's sustainability and future economic development. The Milwaukee Tutorial Program partners Miller employees with third-graders twice a week for tutoring. He is an avid supporter of the Thurgood Marshall Scholarship Fund that was created by Miller and the Office for the Advancement of Public Black Colleges to provide financial assistance to students attending Historically Black Colleges and Universities (HBCUs). He was also involved with the National Urban League's Black Executive Exchange Program and the **Opportunities Industrialization Centers of America**, an organization that provides technical skills to persons wanting to enter the workforce. Many programs have benefited from Miller's scholarship fund mainly because of Colbert's commitment of time and resources.

His excellence in leadership has been honored on numerous occasions. In 1996, Colbert was presented with the Distinguished Leadership Award from **100 Black Men of America**, Inc. for his commitment and outstanding leadership in the nation's black community. In 2001, he was named *Beverage Industry*'s Executive of the Year for his leadership at Miller and his commitment to many civic and community organizations. This was the first time in the award's twenty-seven-year history that it was presented to an executive in the brewing industry. He was also named to the list of best chief executive officers (CEOs) in America by *Institutional Investor* magazine. In 2004, the Thurgood Marshall Scholarship Fund honored him with a community leadership award. In 2005 Fisk University awarded him an honorary degree for his genius in counseling corporate and community efforts.

Colbert attributes his success in part to the strong work ethic he inherited from his father who died when Colbert was thirteen years old. Like his father, Colbert is a disciplined, determined, hard worker. He especially values education as the key to empowerment. In his public speaking engagements he talks about his drive to achieve, attributing his phenomenal success to going above and beyond the expected and being always on the lookout for new opportunities. His strategy for dealing with racism in the workplace is to focus on achieving results through stated goals and objectives rather than obsessing about the color barrier. He asserts that strong leadership, excellent interpersonal and organizational skills, a broad-based understanding of the business, and knowing when to take risks are absolutely essential to success.

Colbert devotes significant time to serving on the boards of various educational organizations and corporations. He was elected chairman of the Board of Trustees at Fisk University in 1999. He is a director at Delphi Corporation, the Manitowoc Company, Stanley Works, and the Weyco Group. In 2004, Colbert and his wife purchased a majority share in the Production Stamping Corporation of Milwaukee. They view this as a great opportunity to grow a minority business. Mrs. Colbert will assume control of daily operations. With his responsibilities at Miller, his leadership in this new business, community endeavors, and his passion for golf, Colbert will continue to juggle a demanding schedule of engagements.

**Sources**

Colbert, Virgis. "Securing the African-American Future: A Challenge for Today and Tomorrow" (address, September 21, 1993). *Vital Speeches of the Day* 60 (December 15, 1993): 141–143.

Doherty, C. "The Man from Miller." *Black Enterprise* 22 (June 1992): 370–373.

Holley, Paul. "Paying Back His Community: Miller Brewing Executive Follows in the Footsteps of Those Who Opened Doors for Him." *Business Journal-Milwaukee* 13 (July 6, 1996): 8.

Johnson-Elie, Tannette. "Couple Buys Majority Stake in Milwaukee Metal Stamping Factory." *Milwaukee Journal Sentinel*, November 18, 2004.

Theodore, Sarah. "Leading by Example." *Beverage Industry* 92 (November 2001): 22–26.

"Virgis Colbert: Corporate Executive with a Mission." *Ebony* 46 (September 1991): 31–33.

Williams, Marilyn, and Allison M. Marion. "Virgis William Colbert." *Contemporary Black Biography: Profiles from the International Black Community*. Vol. 17. Ed. Shirelle Phelps. Detroit: Gale Research, 1998.

*Janette Prescod*

# Donald Alvin Coleman (1952– ), Advertising Executive

Donald A. Coleman is chairman and chief executive officer (CEO) of GlobalHue, the first and largest minority-owned marketing communications agency focusing on multicultural audiences. Expanding to include branch offices in San Antonio, Dallas, New York, and Miami, Coleman's firm provides African American, Hispanic, Asian, and urban marketing expertise.

Coleman was born on January 11, 1952, in Toledo, Ohio, and is the son of Dorothy Bowers Coleman and Augustus Coleman. He received a B.A. degree in journalism in 1974 from the University of Michigan and an M.B.A. in 1976 from Hofstra University. Teaming as a linebacker for the University of Michigan, the New Orleans Saints, and the New York Jets, Coleman was permanently sidelined with knee injuries and in 1977 turned his professional attention to advertising. He married Jo Moore Coleman in 1976 and has a child, Kelli.

Beginning his career with Campbell-Ewald Advertising in Warren, Michigan, and holding several positions including vice president from 1977 to 1985, Coleman advanced to senior vice president of Burrell Advertising in Chicago from 1985 to 1987. In 1988, he founded Don Coleman & Associates, Southfield, Michigan, and served as president and CEO until the establishment of GlobalHue in 2002.

In 1999, Coleman became chief executive officer of the multicultural New America Strategies Group. This group, now known as GlobalHue, was formed in 2002 and includes the former Don Coleman Advertising and Montemayor y Asociados (a Hispanic agency), Innovasia Advertising (an Asian agency), New Perspectives Media, New Day Entertainment, and GlobalHue Publishing. It is the first and largest minority-owned national advertising and marketing communications agency dedicated to the multicultural consumer. In timely and effective response to the changing dynamics of the brand marketing and advertising industry and with increased spending in the multicultural and urban communities, and under Coleman's leadership, GlobalHue rethinks and reshapes its strategic planning to meet current representative client expectations. As reflected in the agency name, GlobalHue is no longer focusing on the African American client alone but has seriously expanded to include the existing and rapidly emerging multicultural and urban markets.

Due to the increasing competition from mainstream advertising and marketing agencies and urban boutiques, GlobalHue has also expanded to more effectively focus its expertise through its astute approach to the identification of and service to client and consumer needs and demands. GlobalHue is quite well known for its innovation in creating unique campaigns that reflect the essence of its clients' products, to which all client and consumer cultural groups can relate, that are adept at focusing on specific cultural groups, and that show cutting-edge expertise in diversity marketing. Facile at seamless business, financial, and creative functions, GlobalHue, with its consistently productive long-term vision, expands its services by utilizing a combination of magazine print ads, posters, radio and television spots, and Internet banners to reach its target diversity consumers and to gain market share. It continues to search for more innovative nontraditional brand messaging, including product placement in motion pictures and film, and continues to delve into cobranding opportunities as it competitively and effectively increases its distribution points.

A privately owned company headquartered in Southfield, Michigan, GlobalHue ended the fiscal year in December 2003 with estimated sales at $49 million, a one-year sales growth estimated at 6.7 percent, 160 employees, and a one-year employee growth of 5.9 percent. With branch offices in New York, Dallas, Miami, San Antonio, and Los Angeles, GlobalHue's clients include American Airlines, Hilton Hotels, DaimlerChrysler Corporation, KMart, Johnson & Johnson, Miller Brewing Company, Solomon Smith Barney, Blue Cross/Blue Shield of California, Mary Kay Cosmetics, Verizon Wireless, the U.S. Navy, and Microsoft.

GlobalHue's mission is to provide efficient and effective multicultural marketing expertise while reflecting the diverse consumer marketplace including different ethnic groups, the urban, young adult, gay, and transgender markets. Its range of expertise includes advertising, community relations, direct and urban marketing, celebrity entertainment, event marketing, research, media buying, and consulting—a multiplicity of services beneath one roof.

With a keen instinct regarding America's changing demographics and market growth attributed to population increases as well as rising income levels, Coleman sees that GlobalHue consistently and strategically remakes itself to identify trends and meet the demands of the true emerging multi-cultural market.

Coleman has been involved in numerous activities outside his work arena. His professional memberships over his career have included the American Association of Advertising Agencies, National Football League Players Association, the National Association for the Advancement of Colored People (NAACP), the National Association of Market Developers, the advisory committee of the Reggie McKenzie Foundation, the Adcraft Club of Detroit, and the University of Michigan Athletic Department Board in Control. Coleman also serves on the board of the Children's Center of Michigan and the Ad Council's Board of Directors and is chairman of the American Advertising Federation (AAF) Foundation and a member of its Multicultural Task Force.

Coleman recently won the prestigious Founders Award from St. John's Jesuit High School, where he has been a Board Council member since 1992. He helped found the Toledo 2020 program that incorporates an endowment of over $1.5 million in tuition assistance for bright minority students. Coleman was also honored in May 2004 by Junior Achievement's 12th Annual Southeastern Michigan Business Hall of Fame selection as a leader achieving enduring career success and exemplifying community commitment.

For his work with GlobalHue, Coleman has been recognized as a leader in his field of expertise. His firm has received top rankings on *Black Enterprise*'s list of Top Advertising Agencies as number 3 in 1999, number 2 in 2000, and number 1 in 2002, 2003, and 2004.

Coleman's cutting-edge status springs from a fresh multicultural perspective, unique client partnerships, excellence in creativity and strategic planning, internal talent growth, synergy, and teamwork. His keen insight into multicultural business perspectives has proven to consistently assure the development of highly effective strategic marketing plans and creative execution.

*See also*: Advertising Agencies; Advertising and Marketing

**Sources**

*Black Enterprise.* http://www.blackenterprise.com/BE100sAdItem.asp.

"Chrysler Group Retains GlobalHue as Its Multicultural Agency." *Hispanic Business.* http://www.hispanicbusiness.com/news/news_print.asp.

Coleman, Donald A. "Generate Insight for Strategic Plans." *Advertising Age* 69 (February 16, 1998): S12.

———. "Playing to Win in a Brand New Arena." Multicultural Marketing Resources, Inc. http://www.multicultural.com/experts/art_multicultural.html.

"Donald A. Coleman, Chairman and CEO, GlobalHue." Marketing Opportunities in Business & Entertainment. http://www.mobe.com/next/bio/dcoleman.html.

Hayes, Cassandra. "30 Years of the BE 100s." *Black Enterprise* 32 (June 2002): 199–207.

Hayes, Cassandra, and Jules Allen. "A Creative Point of View: BE Advertising Agency of the Year." *Black Enterprise* 28 (June 1998): 164.

Hughes, Alan. "United Colors of GlobalHue." *Black Enterprise* 33 (June 2003): 186–190.

Irwin, Tanya. "GlobalHue Names a President." *Adweek Midwest Edition* 43 (September 2, 2002): 4+.

"Junior Achievement Honors Outstanding Business Leaders, May 20, in Dearborn." Hoover's. http://www.hoovers.com/free/co/news/detail.xhtml.

Miley, Michael. "Faster Than FedEx." http://cgw.pennet.com/Articles/Article_Display.cfm.

Multicultural Marketing Resources, Inc. Sponsor's Profile. http://www.multicultural.com/experts/multicultural.html.

*Target Market News.* Recent Headlines. http://www.targetmarketnews.com/recentnews.htm.

"Three Men Receive St. John's Highest Honors." St. John's Jesuit High School. http://www.sjjtitans.org/web/nhonorsalums.htm.

*Who's Who among African Americans.* 18th ed. Detroit: Thomson Gale, 2005.

*Linda Combs Hayden*

# Kenneth L. Coleman (1942– ), Technology Executive, Entrepreneur

Instead of retiring to his Hawaii home after twenty-five years as a successful executive in the technology industry, Kenneth L. Coleman has embarked on a new career as an innovator of a software product designed to improve information technology (IT) management for chief information officers (CIOs). The start-up company, ITM Software, is Coleman's brainchild. He is one of the founders, its chairman, and the chief executive officer (CEO). Even before he began ITM Software, Coleman was recognized by *Black Enterprise* as one of its top twenty-five blacks in the technology industry for 2001.

Coleman began his technology career in 1972, following completion of his education at Ohio State University (OSU) and four years in the U.S. Air Force. He was hired by the consumer information technology giant Hewlett Packard and worked there for ten years in many capacities including corporate staffing, personnel, and manager of northern European personnel. His next position was with Activision Inc., a company that develops, publishes, and distributes interactive entertainment and leisure products. During his years at Activision, he served as vice president of human resources and vice president of product development.

For the next fourteen years he worked for Silicon Graphics Inc., a technology organization that produces servers, supercomputers, visualization systems, workstations, storage solutions, and software. At the California-headquartered $2.3 billion company, he was promoted from senior vice president of administration and business development to executive vice president of Global Sales, Services, and Marketing. His responsibilities included overseeing sales, marketing, and services, and he was responsible for revenue and gross margins.

After he retired in August 2001 from his career as a senior technology manager, he began a new adventure that would become ITM Software. Even though the market for technology companies was weak in 2001, ITM Software was the result of an attempt to resolve a problem that had plagued Coleman when he was a manager of information and technology. According to ITM Software Company, the dilemma centered on the frustration of "communicating the value of IT . . . to executives across the company . . . and the inability to answer many of the basic business questions relating to IT in a timely manner." He was willing to start his company during the weak technology market. In a *Black Enterprise* article in November 2002, he expressed that during an economic downturn expectations are low, good people can be found, and rents are cheaper. In order to put his vision into action, he gathered around him experienced information technology experts. The other founders and members of the company's management team, board of directors, and advisory committee are VIPs (very important persons) of the technology and financial industries. Coleman went from being an executive at a large company of over 4,000 to an entrepreneur of a company with 30 employees. In his new position, he uses all his previous experiences and contacts, tapping available resources to raise funds for his start-up company. His effective explanation of his product and services along with his stellar record as a manager brought major investors on board despite the current climate of fear of losing money in yet another technology company with great promises and little delivery.

ITM Software is privately held. Its product is an integrated business suite that aids company CIOs and IT departments. ITM not only creates the software package but also provides services to its customer that only a company with the expertise of its staff can present. Significant in his approach to launching this new company is that he has sought advice as well as investors from the African American community. Coleman is described as a visionary, a pioneer, and a coalition builder with an active mind filled with ideas. Since its founding, the company has been described by *Business Wire* as an emerging leader in the enterprise software industry because of its skilled management team, its products, and its best practice expertise. ITM Software seeks customers from Fortune 2000 corporations, government agencies, and universities. It has gained a reputation for its customer service relations and its single focus to help chief information officers be more successful in their management of the information technology function. That is a direct reflection of the CEO's philosophy, which is to serve the customers' needs. His goal is to earn more than $10 million in revenues per year.

Based on the leadership of its CEO, one of the values of the company is its commitment to involvement in the community. Throughout his career he served on the board of directors of Acclaim Entertainment, MIPS Technologies, and United Online. He has served as a member of the Ohio State University Alumni Advisory Council and the Dean's Advisory Council for the business schools at Ohio State and Santa Clara universities. He has served as board member of the Bay Area Black United Fund, the University of Santa Clara Industrial Advisory Commission, the Children's Health Council, the University of California San Francisco, and City National Bank.

For his achievements, Coleman has received recognition and awards. From his alma mater, Ohio State University, he received the Distinguished Service Award during the 2003 commencement. He is the recipient of the National Alliance of Black School Educators Living Legend Award, the American Leadership Forum of Silicon Valley Exemplary Leader Award, and the One Hundred Black Men of Silicon Valley Lifetime Achievement Award and was inducted into the Junior Achievement Hall of Fame Honoring Business Leaders of Silicon Valley and Monterey Bay in 1998. He received the Award for Excellence in Community Service for San Jose, California, and the Marketing Opportunities in Business and Entertainment Award.

A popular speaker, Coleman has spoken at the Stanford Business School Conference on "People of Color in the Economy." He is a member of the OSU Fisher College of Business Dean's Advisory Council. Before he retired from SGI, he, along with the staff, helped design the college's computer/communications network. He provides advice to students in the OSU Advanced Center of the Arts and Design.

Coleman grew up in the small southern Illinois town of Centralia with only 10 percent of the population of 14,000 African Americans. He left Centralia to attend Ohio State University, where he earned both a B.S. degree in industrial management and an M.B.A. Coleman would one day manage at a company that employed as many people as there were African Americans in his hometown. He is a retired U.S. Air Force captain. He is married to Caretha Coleman; they have five children—Kennetha, Karen, Kimberly, Kristen, and Kenneth. He lives by the creed of the company motto: "We say what we do; we do what we say . . . we act together in harmony, which allows us to execute with excellence and deliver on our promises."

### Sources

Activision Investor Relations. Company Background. http://investor.activision.com/background.cfm.

Dean's Advisory Council. "Kenneth L. Coleman." http://fisher.osu.edu/About/Office-of-the-Dean/DAC/Coleman.

Donaldson, Sonya A. "Anatomy of a Startup." *Black Enterprise* 35 (November 2004): 112–123.

———. "Back to Business." *Black Enterprise* 33 (November 2002): 60.

"ITM Software Closes $6 Million Equity Financing Round." *Business Wire*, May 12, 2005. http://www.businesswire.com.

ITM Software Company. http://www.itm-software.com.

Junior Achievement of Silicon Valley & Monterey Bay, Inc. "Business Hall of Fame Laureates of 1998: Kenneth L. Coleman." http://www.jascc.org/hall/hfkcoleman.htm.

Maui Aloha Investment Fund. http://mauialohafund.com/about.asp.

*Standard & Poor's Register of Corporations, Directors and Executives.* New York: Standard and Poor's Corporation, 2003.

Stanford Graduate School of Business. "Kenneth L. Coleman and Mozelle W. Thompson to Keynote Stanford Business School Conference on People of Color in the New Economy." News Release, April 3, 2001. http://www.gsb.stanford.edu/news/bbsa.html.

*Who's Who among African Americans.* 18th ed. Detroit: Thomson Gale, 2005.

*Gloria Hamilton*

# Colored Merchants' Association

Black economic development of the early twentieth century included a black cooperative movement that involved department stores, shoe stores, grocery stores, and other retail establishments. The most notable among these cooperatives was the Colored Merchants' Association, or CMA, founded on August 10, 1928, in Montgomery, Alabama, under the efforts of A. C. Brown—a local grocer. Members of this early group of twelve black grocers who attended the founding meeting agreed to operate their businesses under the banner "C.M.A. Stores." Members would be a part of a voluntary chain, yet the proprietor's name would be written below the title "C.M.A. Stores." As the organization grew and spread to other states, it adopted the slogan: "Quality, Service, and Price." It also considered using a uniform color scheme in its member stores. The CMA differed from other cooperatives in its reliance on cooperative buying as well as intensive selling. Members were taught to move their merchandise rapidly to increase profit. The stores also did cooperative advertising, promoting their businesses weekly in local newspapers when they had special bargains that the organization's efforts made possible. Although the national effort was short-lived, it had successfully helped blacks solidify the economic gains that they had made up to and during this period.

During its founding meeting, the CMA elected H. C. Ball as president and David F. Lowery Jr. as secretary. Lowery had shared Brown's enthusiasm for such an organization. The organization moved swiftly to secure each store's financial resources. A uniform accounting system was installed in

View of a model Colored Merchants' Association (CMA) store bearing the name Horne's. *Source:* Thomas O. Fuller. *Pictorial History of the American Negro.* Memphis: Pictorial History, Inc., Publishers, 1933, p. 139.

Interior of a model Colored Merchants' Association (CMA) store. *Source*: Thomas O. Fuller. *Pictorial History of the American Negro*. Memphis: Pictorial History, Inc., Publishers, 1933, p. 140.

member stores. The group met each Tuesday night at a member store and identified their purchasing needs as a whole. The next day local wholesale grocers quoted prices for the combined order. President Ball was the buyer at first and served without salary; then a buying committee was established under Ball's chairmanship. Each member had a specific assignment, such as to obtain price of a commodity—meat, flour, sugar, rice, and so on. Members of the association agreed to sell their goods as rapidly as possible, hoping that the fast turnover would lead to larger profits and stabilize operating conditions. To do this, they pooled the money set aside for promotional activities, and each week advertised their specials in the local press—the *Montgomery Advertiser* and the *Montgomery Journal*. They reprinted the advertisements on fliers and distributed them to all black homes within each store's vicinity.

So successful was the CMA in Montgomery that the Negro Business League of Montgomery and its president invited the secretary of the **National Negro Business League** (NNBL) to visit the city and examine firsthand the work of the CMA stores. On November 1928, Albon L. Holsey, the national secretary, met with the association's entire membership and visited some of the member stores.

Holsey was immediately impressed with what he called the "Montgomery Plan" and presented it to the league's president, Robert R. Moton, who was also president of Tuskegee Institute in Alabama, with the recommendation that the league should spread the idea to other cities. Holsey became national CMA organizer and successfully encouraged grocers to join the chain of stores. In following the plan, Holsey knew that in areas where there were ten or more retail stores, the stores would be eligible to join CMA. He knew also CMA's three primary objectives: to bring retail grocers into a group that would study the then-modern methods of selling, to teach them the psychology of the black consumer, and to unite them with local jobbers and wholesalers. Around this same time the president of the local business league in Winston-Salem, North Carolina, called for help to stimulate local interest in the plan and the work of the NNBL in promoting the CMA. The plan had spread to Winston-Salem, making it the second city to organize CMA stores; the first such store opened in May 1929.

The Winston-Salem project was well thought out. It embraced the Montgomery Plan, required a connection with national advertisers, and called for a model grocery store patterned after one set up earlier in Louisville and arranged to handle a sizable stock. The local black college, Winston-Salem Teachers College, provided students and faculty from its Home Economics Department; they joined local high school students and helped to set up demonstrations in the "model store." After a local store was remodeled to become the model store, it was stocked with fresh goods, and young men from a local high school, who worked under the supervision of Atlanta University president John Hope Jr., inventoried the stock. Doors opened to the public on May 4.

The local campaign, spearheaded by the NNBL, had widespread interest. Housewives took a new interest in the black stores, storekeepers saw amazing financial results, and large numbers of citizens turned out to hear Moton and his campaign and a representative of the Domestic Commerce Division of the U.S. Department of Commerce. On May 6, heads of commercial departments at Hampton Institute in Virginia and Bluefield Institute in West Virginia—both black colleges—came with some of their students to inspect the model store. When the NNBL's campaign in Winston-Salem ended on May 6, CMA membership had reached twenty-four; by July there were thirty-five members. Nearly all of the stores reported immediate and accelerated growth and a rapid increase in profits for its affiliates. As the stores saw an increase in profit, they provided employment for blacks in the local community. Further, as the Winston-Salem plan was promoted, Albon Holsey noted in an article on "The C.M.A. Stores Face the Chains" that organizations such as the "Association of National Advertisers, the Associated Negro Press, the Commission on Race Relations, the National Association of Retail Grocers, and the National Urban League" supported the work of the NNBL. Clearly, the plan had great potential for the local and national community. Quoted in the same article, the *Norfolk Journal and Guide* said,

---

# ANNOUNCING
## THE C. M. A. STORES
### (Colored Merchants Association)

### An Organization of Progressive Local Grocers

Under our new organization plans, the member stores will be attractive and convenient. Co-operative buying will enable each store to maintain a uniform, standard service and to sell

#### QUALITY MERCHANDISE AT LOWEST PRICES

### Cash Specials for Saturday May 4th

| | | | |
|---|---|---|---|
| Lard (fine quality) per pound | 12½c | Sugar, 2 pounds for | 11c |
| Flour (excellent quality) 12 pounds for | 48c | Rice, 4 pounds for | 25c |
| Octagon Soap, 6 bars for | 25c | Tomatoes (No. 2 full pack) 2 cans for | 25c |
| California Yellow Cling Peaches (Large size—best quality) | 24c | Lowe Bros. Blue Ribbon Bread, loaf | 9c |

These and many other bargains will be offered at our opening sale Saturday, May 4th—BARGAIN TABLES IN EACH STORE

Visit ELLINGTON'S—the Demonstration Store
723 EAST SEVENTH STREET

Same Prices at Each Store—Orders Delivered — Telephone Orders Will Receive the Same Prompt and Courteous Attention.

### "There is a C. M. A. Store in Your Neighborhood"

W. T. CHRISTIAN
Ridge Ave. and 9th St.
PHONE 1345

F. A. CARRIGAN
4th and Linden Sts
Phone 1629-J

J. A. EVANS
700 Vargrave St.

JAMES A. ELLINGTON
725 East 7th St.
Phone 1223-W

DAN ANDERSON
1100 N. Trade St.

MARCUS GRAHAM
1001 Vargrave St.
Phone 9290

J. C. CHRISTIAN
2301 N. Cherry St.
Phone 9283

ROYAL PURYEAR
716 East 2nd St.
Phone 1359

CHARLES ROBINSON
Salem

SAMUEL FARMER
410 East 7th St.

AARON DAVIS
1629 East 11th St.
Phone 4029-J

HAIRSTON GROCERY CO.
1300 Cleveland Avenue
Phone 1547

T. H. HOOPER
700 Patterson Ave.

L. C. KERNS
1202 Shuttle St.
Phone 3410

SAM DISMUKE
1201 N. Main St.

E. D. CRAIG
Salem

CURTIS GRAHAM
Glenn Ave. and Gale St.

A. L. HANES
12 Park Avenue
Phone 9255

R. E. WALKER
2136 Waughtown
Phone 4315-J

F. S. SIMMONS
1230 Centerville
Phone 2493-W

JAMES CRAIG
Clements Road

W. E. WILSON
209 East 7th St.

## BAKERIES

LOWE BROTHERS, 936 N. Trade Street
PHONE 2456

DAVID STEVENS 314 East 4th Street

Advertisement for one of the Colored Merchants' Association stores located in Winston-Salem, North Carolina. *Source:* Albon L. Holsey. "The CMA Stores Face the Chains." *Opportunity* 7 (July 1929), p. 210.

"If it could be possible to carry the plan (Winston-Salem Campaign) to other cities in rapid succession, Negro business would undergo a real rehabilitation."

## CMA STORES SPREAD RAPIDLY

Through Holsey's efforts, stores were organized in most of the major American cities. Those in the South were Dallas, Tulsa, Atlanta, Jackson (Mississippi), Nashville, Louisville, Richmond, Hampton, and Norfolk. Those outside the South were in Omaha, Chicago, Detroit, Philadelphia, New York, Brooklyn, and elsewhere. Within three years the members paid cash for their goods and received larger discounts. They also sold mostly for cash, especially on heavy shopping days—Fridays and Saturdays. They aroused the interest of national advertisers, who realized the rapidly developing purchasing power of blacks.

Before the CMA moved into Harlem, there were more than 200,000 blacks living in some 300 city blocks in that area. Whites owned 98 percent of the grocery stores that served the residents. Edwin E. Hurd reported in the *Southern Workman* that blacks tended to patronize the white stores, and the few black grocers that were there failed to cooperate with each other in business ventures. Not only were they unacquainted with each other; they never consolidated interests, showed no unity of action, lacked general direction, and had no buying power. They knew nothing about good business procedures, such as bookkeeping and merchandizing. "The appearance of the stores was noted with anything but pride," he said.

Holsey moved on to New York and campaigned for the CMA. He distributed circulars to the grocers and encouraged them to attend a series of meetings where the purpose of CMA was explained. Training became essential to the success of CMA members; thus, they met two or three nights each week to study modern merchandizing methods under the tutelage of experts. The lecturers included an official of the Associated Grocery Manufacturers, a representative of the U.S. Department of Commerce, a bank cashier, and an editor of the *Progressive Grocer*. Some of the stores had an insufficient variety of fresh goods, sold at higher prices than white-owned stores, and gave customers poor service. Then the CMA said that its members should appeal to customers on the basis of quality, service, and price and that the idea of using racial pride as a factor for shopping at the CMA stores should be incidental. As soon as this plan became operational in the Harlem stores in October 1929, membership began to increase; in two years there were twenty-three member stores, two model stores, and several others that were transforming themselves into model stores. That the growth occurred during the stock market crash of 1929 was at most an interesting coincidence: One remodeled store saw its sales increase from $450 a week to $1,200 a week. Some sources claimed that CMA failed during the Great Depression; however, Vishnu Oak asserts that they were unaffected by this economic downfall.

The CMA established national headquarters in New York in October 1929 as well. Members were required to purchase one share of its stock and to pay a small, weekly fee for CMA services. It was through the headquarters that training, bookkeeping systems, printing, advertising, and other services were handled for members. The stores continued to operate under the CMA banner, yet they retained ownership of their business. So impressed with CMA's progress was its chief advocate, the National Negro Business League, that it devoted the program of its thirty-first annual meeting in Detroit in 1930 to the analysis of blacks' purchasing power.

In time, the effects of the Great Depression may have been felt. Added to that, various signs of internal dissension and disruption emerged. By 1933, three stores in Harlem were sold at public auction; they cited a lack of operating capital as the chief reason for the failure. The problems mounted. Some members withdrew from the CMA. Although prosperous, some members were in debt to wholesalers. In *The History of Black Business in America*, Juliet Walker found some of the wholesalers "racketeering in character." When some grocers were in debt to wholesalers, the wholesalers threatened them with foreclosure if they joined CMA. A lack of cooperation among members, failure to attend the training sessions, and a growing question concerning the professionalism of CMA management were cited as threats to the security of CMA. There were also claims that the CMA was, in fact, white owned and that Holsey, the organizer, was no more than a front man. Further erosion came when black consumers lost confidence with CMA and when some members undersold or intentionally oversold each other, especially the "specials." Some preferred to advertise or sell chain brands rather than CMA-labeled brands. Wholesalers also fought the CMA movement openly and vigorously. For black grocers, the very idea of "oneness of action" was lost completely in this venture, yet up until World War II blacks established many other cooperatives.

By 1936, many stores began to withdraw from CMA membership, thus causing little need to continue the New York warehouse; it was then liquidated. When CMA ceased operations, member stores owed the organization over $7,000 for the branded merchandise. While at first CMA stores increased by leaps and bounds, their closure came with similar rapidity. Yet what is important about CMA's work is its success in organizing a chain of stores nationwide, which had operated under similar purposes, filled similar needs in the black community, and when in their heyday, brought increased and substantial profits to stores that previously reaped little profits. CMA's plan of operation, especially as seen in the Winston-Salem project, reaped benefits as well. No doubt the idea of involving the community in business development, using scientific approaches to business development, catering to the needs of the community, and providing much-needed jobs in the black community, especially for its youth, weighed heavily on the minds of those who wanted to see success. But for those who wanted to steer business away from CMA-affiliated stores, the failure was welcomed.

The CMA was an experiment that stood the test of time. One of its primary interests—that of cooperation—continues as a practice observed in current business enterprises. The experiment was an example of "black self-help" put to practice.

*See also*: Advertising and Marketing; Consumer Cooperatives; Grocery Store Enterprises; Retail Industry

**Sources**

Harris, Abram L. *The Negro as Capitalist: A Study of Banking and Business among American Negroes*. 1936. New York: Negro Universities Press, 1969.

Holsey, Albon L. "The C.M.A. Stores Face the Chains." *Opportunity* 7 (July 1929): 210–213.

Hurd, Edwin E. "A New Co-operative Movement: Colored Merchants' Association." *Southern Workman* 60 (January 1931): 38–40.

Oak, Vishnu V. *The Negro's Adventure in General Business*. Vol. 2. Yellow Springs, OH: Printed for the author by Antioch Press, 1919.

Pierce, Joseph A. *Negro Business and Business Education: Their Present and Prospective Development*. New York: Harper and Brothers Publishers, 1947. Reprint, Westport, CT: Negro Universities Press, 1971.

"Survey of the Month." ("The Colored Merchants' Association") *Opportunity* 8 (June 1930): 187.

Walker, Juliet E. K. *The History of Black Business in America: Capitalism, Race, Entrepreneurship*. New York: Macmillan Library Reference USA, 1998.

*Jessie Carney Smith*

# Sean "Diddy" Combs (1969– ), Entrepreneur, Multimedia Executive, Popular Culture Mogul

Sean Jean Combs's success began as a trend-setting executive in the world of urban hip-hop music but has transcended race, class, and gender to penetrate the essential fabric of American popular culture through music, fashion, and ultimately persuasive attitude. The onetime college sophomore found his path from intense determination and the refusal to be refused. His hard work now beats to the tune of almost billionaire status at the preprime age of thirty-six years young and finds him in colleague company with the likes of Bill Gates, Donald Trump, and Hugh Hefner financially. Combs emerged in 1988 as an unpaid intern, only to have his own label by 1994. Throughout the next decade, no dialogue could properly be mentioned on music and culture in America without him in the conversation.

In her review of *Bad Boy: The Influence of Sean "Puffy" Combs on the Music Industry* published in *Black Issues*, Janine Gardner states, "A conglomerate all his own, 'Puffy' has made his presence known in just about every medium. From hip-hop to fashion, and even the restaurant business, Puff Daddy (P. Diddy) is worth his weight in gold." To have a full-length book written about you by a leading music journalist on your impact on one of the most lucrative industries in America at the young age of twenty-nine speaks volumes. Yet considering his accomplishments, Combs's accolades cannot be ignored. He is the chairman and chief executive officer (CEO) of Bad Boy Worldwide Entertainment Group, an annual $300 million global empire that is made up of Bad Boy Records, Combs Music Publishing, Janice Combs Management, Sean John Clothing, Justin's Restaurant Chain, and Daddy's House Studios. He has undergone several name changes during his career, becoming known as "Puffy," "Puff Daddy," and "P. Diddy"; since August 2005 he prefers to be known as simply "Diddy."

He was born Sean Jean Combs in Harlem, New York, on November 4, 1969, and attended Mount Vernon Montessori School and Mt. St. Michael Academy before attending Howard University in Washington, D.C. While at Howard, an eager and aggressive Combs landed an internship with Uptown Records that would lay the groundwork for the eventual independent entrepreneurial zeal that would sustain his career. Though only nineteen, his immediate contributions and consistent quality produced a promotion to A & R director. Under his direction, a new subgenre termed *hip-hop soul* was branded in the early 1990s that would solidify his place on the landscape of hip-hop historiography. The sound, image, and routes to success for Mary J. Blige and Jodeci were crafted by Combs. His production and marketing teeth were cut at this stage due in large part to mentorship from Andre Harrell. As Uptown president and hip-hop pioneer with legendary Dr. Jeckyl & Mr. Hyde fame, Harrell would mold Combs's raw tenacity and attention to detail with the craftsmanship needed to have longevity in this most fickle business.

Ever full of ambition, Combs was not content with limitations on his creative and business judgments, so he founded Bad Boy Records in 1994. Combs's reputation for delivering quality goods would be further solidified with the judgment he rendered in signing Christopher Wallace, better known as Biggie Smalls and/or The Notorious B.I.G., whose debut CD *Ready to Die* achieved platinum success in 1994. Along with B.I.G.'s second album in 1997, *Life after Death*, Bad Boy's place in hip-hop legend was firmly implanted. In just three years, Combs's company was producing chart-smashing records and shaping a definitive sound in the case of B.I.G., who is widely regarded as one of the most prolific lyricists in the history of hip-hop. Though Combs's top-selling artist B.I.G. would succumb to an untimely murder in 1996, the legacy his work left will always be associated with the relationship he shared and careers catapulted with Combs. Bad Boy is much more than a production company, however, but many critics at the time of B.I.G.'s passing were openly skeptical of whether Bad Boy could sustain itself.

Referring to entrepreneurial embodiment by African American hip-hop record executives in the mid-1990s, David Sanjek includes Combs in his narrative. In *American Music*, Sanjek notes how Combs of Bad Boy Entertainment has a distribution agreement with a larger company but retains control over the content of his recordings in addition to significant shares of profit. This is where the effectiveness of Combs's business acumen is to be most appreciated. As the handler of his own business matters, he was successfully able to negotiate a 50–50 deal for distribution with Arista records in 1996, which was unprecedented at the time and fostered guaranteed support for his growing roster of artists including Faith Evans, Junior Mafia, 112, Carl Thomas, Black Rob, Craig Mack, New Edition, and his own solo projects. Consistent with Combs's mastery of business sophistication, he split with Arista in 2002—but not without 100 percent of his artist's catalogs, master recordings, and publishing rights. In 2003 he signed a distribution deal for his company with Universal that still gives him total control and ownership of company records.

In 1997 Combs established Justin's Fine Dining Restaurants in New York City, and in 1999, the second operation opened in Atlanta, Georgia. Estimated gross revenue from each restaurant was $8 million in 2004. In 1998, Sean John Clothing was established, which by 2002 was reaping annual gains of $175 million a year. Feeding the men's urban clothing market was a no-brain decision for Combs, but its success lay in the fact that he virtually defined the hip-hop urban world from a marketing standpoint through his production and cultural influence from previous years. One hand feeding the other is an ideal desired by all involved in the process of business making. However, few have been as successful as Combs in penetrating a culture and market as affectively.

**Sources**

BBO (Bad Boy). http://www.badboyonline.com/flashindex.htm.

"Business of Entertainment." *Black Enterprise* 33 (December 2002): 76–98.

Gardner, Janine. "Hip Hop with an R & B Twist." *Black Issues Book Review* 4 (January–February 2002): 47.

McKinney, Jeffrey. "The Hip-Hop Economy." *Black Enterprise* 33 (September 2002): 98–103.

Ogbar, Jeffrey O. G. "Slouching Toward Bork: The Culture Wars and Self-Criticism in Hip-Hop." *Journal of Black Studies* 30 (November 1999): 164–183.

Ro, Ronin. *Bad Boy: The Influence of Sean "Puffy" Combs on the Music Industry*. New York: Pocket Books, 2001.

Sanjek, David. "One Size Does Not Fit All: The Precarious Position of the African-American Entrepreneur in Post–World War II American Popular Music." *American Music* (Winter 1997): 535–562.

Sanneh, Kelefa. "Believe the Hype." *Transition*, no. 80 (1999): 120–148.

*Uzoma O. Miller*

# Conferences and Studies on the Negro in Business: The Early Years

The development of black business enterprises traditionally has been a primary concern among those who aimed to provide economic uplift to the black community in America. Atlanta University saw a need for a systematic and thorough investigation of problems affecting blacks in cities and initially planned to hold a conference in November 1895 to address such issues. It was to coincide with the Atlanta Exposition. Instead, the first conference was postponed until 1896. Efforts to enhance the social conditions of blacks were reported during the Third Annual Conference for the Study of the Negro Problems held at the university on May 25–26, 1898. Among the findings was a list of "Co-operative Business Enterprises" for blacks; reports of new business enterprises, such as the Coleman Manufacturing Company in Concord, North Carolina; and "Organized Benevolent Efforts" showing examples of economic provisions for blacks.

Resolutions passed at the Third Annual Conference prompted planners to develop the next conference around the theme "The Negro in Business." The resolutions committee included such prominent people as W.E.B. Du Bois as well as a publisher, minister, iron foundry manager, and grocer. On May 30, 1899, Atlanta University held its Fourth Annual Conference to further the discussion on issues affecting African Americans.

Noting the "disproportion in the distribution of Negroes in the various occupations," as seen in the report *The Negro in Business*, participants sought to remedy the situation by encouraging an increased number of blacks to enter into a variety of business ventures, thus avoiding a one-sided development in business life and increase competition in specific lines of industry. Second, the resolutions called for well-trained merchants who were well grounded in English and who held high school but preferably college education. Third, the resolutions called for businessmen to meet customer demands for courtesy and honesty. Fourth, black masses should "buy black"— that is, patronize black-operated businesses. Fifth, many of the 1,900 business leaders who attended the conference were recognized as having made a creditable record in businesses and were "pioneers of a great movement." The sixth resolution was the most encompassing and suggested ways to further develop black businesses, such as to agitate through schools, churches, and the press to encourage young blacks to enter businesses; to encourage young people to be thrifty and to save money; and to encourage every town, hamlet, and community where blacks lived to develop Negro Business Men's Leagues.

Among the papers presented were "The Meaning of Business" by John Hope, president of Atlanta Baptist College (now Morehouse College) in Atlanta, who noted the change in the status of blacks since the Civil War but that the black remained "the laborer, the day hand, the man who works for wages." He called for workers to take their wages, turn the wages into capital, and then increase it. Employment of blacks was a critical need and would have to come to "Negroes from Negro sources." Other papers addressed topics such as "The Need of Negro Merchants"; "The Negro Grocer"; "A Negro Cooperative Foundry," or the Southern Stove Hollow-ware and Foundry Company temporarily organized on February 15, 1897, and permanently organized and incorporated in Chattanooga on August 15, 1897; "Negro Business Ventures in Atlanta, Georgia"; and "The Negro Newspaper."

*The Negro Yearbook* for 1947 reports that between 1939 and 1946 various conferences on black business were held. Around 1940–1941 black as well as white business leaders gave considerable discussion to the general importance of the "Negro" market. These leaders concluded that the nation's largest minority market should be equipped with the means of increasing its purchasing power. As result, the nation as a whole would prosper economically. Among the many conferences held was a meeting in Savannah, Georgia, that attracted 200 business and professional women from Alabama, Georgia, and South Carolina. Although the group was not identified, the *Yearbook* notes the women's final recommendations: "Develop a Negro market by the creation and operation of agencies for that purpose; through cooperatives, government and private loans, and reinvestment earnings, bring about a continuous and progressive increase in available capital for business expansion." In 1950, the Virginia Trade Association met at Hampton Institute in Virginia and called for a "movement to speed economic security by opening more opportunities in business through ownership and employment."

Over thirty years after the Atlanta Conference, in 1941, the U.S. Department of Commerce began a series of conferences on black businesses, the first held on April 18–19, 1941. Emmer M. Lancaster, adviser on Negro Affairs in the department, called the conference together. Those in attendance included prominent business leaders, business educators, and laypeople who had an interest in black business. Among the successful business ventures reported was the Brown Belle Company, a bottling business in Knoxville and Chattanooga, Tennessee, that offered carbonated water and carbonated soft drinks.

Although a second conference was planned, the country's entrance into World War II delayed it for five years, until October 17–18, 1946. It was held in Washington, D.C. There was a report on the George W. Kerford Quarry Company, established in 1886; its location was unnamed. A third conference was convened on April 1–3, 1948, still under Lancaster's leadership. At each conference various government officers who had an interest in small black enterprises gave lectures and demonstrations. Entrepreneurs who had established unusual business ventures also gave accounts of their work. Some of the successful ventures cited at the third conference were reports of the Cameron Dairy Company (Canton, Mississippi, 1936); the Rose Meta House of Beauty, (Harlem, 1947) under the leadership of **Rose Morgan**; an engineering firm, A. A. Alexander, Inc. (Des Moines, Iowa, 1914), founded by **Archie Alphonso Alexander** and later became Alexander and Repass Company; Commons Coal and Ice Company (Birmingham, 1920); the G. W. Brown Drayman Corporation (Scranton, Pennsylvania, 1882); and Bell & Hudgins—A Mail Order Firm (New York City, 1942). It was at the third conference that a group of business teachers formed the National Business Education Association. All three conferences attracted large attendance.

Conferences on black businesses had also been the focus of the **National Negro Business League** (NNBL). NNBL was one of the early organizations founded to support blacks in business. A vital organization, it operated early on as a federation of chambers of commerce or state and local business leagues. According to Vishnu Oak in *The Negro's Adventure in General Business*, the U.S. Department of Commerce attracted much greater attendance at its conferences than the NNBL.

Studies of black business and business education continued and enhanced much of the work of the early Atlanta conferences. Notable among these studies was the Atlanta University/National Urban League study begun February 1, 1944, and extended to about February 1, 1946. A grant from the General Education Board funded the study. Those who were invited to Atlanta to participate in the original planning meeting included representatives of the National Negro Business League and the U.S. Department of Commerce. **Joseph Alphonso Pierce**, then professor of mathematics at Atlanta University, led the investigation and published the results under the title *Negro Business and Business Education: Their Present and Prospective Development* (1947).

Black-owned and -operated business enterprises studied were found in Atlanta, Baltimore, Cincinnati, Durham, Houston, Memphis, Nashville, New Orleans, Richmond, Savannah, St. Louis, and Washington, D.C. Of special importance also was the attention given to business education courses offered at the participating black colleges, including Atlanta University, Fisk University, Morehouse College, North Carolina College for Negroes (now North Carolina Central University), Spelman College, Tennessee Agricultural and Industrial State College (now Tennessee State University), and Wilberforce University.

Findings showed that black businesses captured a small percentage of their potential patronage; for example, 99 percent of black consumers who bought clothing and shoes did so at a white-owned business. While there were 293 black-owned grocery stores, only about 28 percent of black consumers traded at these stores. Other findings were reported. Among the problems responsible for the lack of black patronage at black-owned businesses as well as issues that affect business operations were: little attention given to sales promotion by the entrepreneurs; inadequate business training among black managers and their personnel; and poor and inadequate record-keeping practices in black enterprises.

The results provided the groundwork for Atlanta University to go forward with its plan to establish a graduate School of Business Administration, for the National Urban League (NUL) and its various branches to enlarge job opportunities for blacks, and for NUL to link with cooperating colleges and universities to improve services to local black communities. The business leaders would also be encouraged to venture out into new areas of growth and to satisfy needs of the new black consumer.

*See also*: Black Business Development and the Federal Government; Chambers of Commerce and Boards of Trade in the 1920s and 1930s

**Sources**

Du Bois, W.E.B., ed. *The Negro in Business*. Atlanta, GA: Atlanta University Press, 1899.

Guzman, Jessie Parkhurst, ed. *The Negro Year Book: A Review of Events Affecting Negro Life 1941–46.* 10th ed. Tuskegee, AL: Department of Records and Research, Tuskegee Institute, 1947.

Oak, Vishnu V. *The Negro's Adventure in General Business.* Yellow Springs, OH: Antioch Press, 1949.

Pierce, Joseph A. *Negro Business and Business Education: Their Present and Prospective Development.* New York: Harper Brothers Publishers, 1947. Reprint, Westport, CT: Negro Universities Press, 1971.

*Jessie Carney Smith*

## Conferences on African American Businesses

African Americans have been involved in business enterprises since their arrival in the areas that would eventually become the United States. Even in slavery, many were able to develop skills and trades that they would use for the benefit of their owners and over time managed to secure funds to purchase freedom for themselves and for others. Before the Civil War and the Emancipation Proclamation, the smaller number of free blacks (located primarily in the northern states) included persons who also turned their abilities into trades and businesses. In a few rare instances, African Americans even were documented as being slaveholders.

In 1830, the National Negro Convention Movement (NNCM) was founded by free blacks as a response to efforts of the American Colonization Society, which promoted efforts to relocate free and enslaved African Americans to Liberia in West Africa. The NNCM represented the first national organization of blacks that was not church based or religious in nature; opposed slavery, colonization, and other racial hostilities; and encouraged landownership and economic advancement.

The majority of NNCM members were African American businessmen from northern states who advocated the development of additional black businesses, commercial farming, international trade with African nations, and the establishment of a national black bank. The organization held eleven national conferences before the Civil War, sponsored state conventions, and was a forerunner of the major African American organizations that would appear in the twentieth century.

In 1898, W.E.B. Du Bois convened the Fourth Atlanta Conference and focused its agenda on "The Negro in Business." He urged that Negro businessmen's leagues be formed in every local community where there was a considerable black population, then organize on the state and national levels.

The **National Negro Business League** (NNBL) was founded in 1900 by **Booker T. Washington**, who used the opposite approach. The first meeting, held in Boston, included 300 blacks from thirty-four states in varying occupations, with the purpose of promoting the commercial, agricultural, educational, and industrial advancement of African Americans. One primary focus of the organization was to encourage more black people to go into business independently or in collaboration with others.

During the period Washington served as president of the NNBL, the organization grew quickly, with 320 chapters by 1905, 3,000 members by 1907, and estimates as high as 40,000 members in more than 600 state and local chapters by 1915. The annual national conferences included testimonies and case studies of successful black business owners and operators, who shared strategies and techniques for developing and expanding consumer markets for products and services.

Several other black business associations were direct descendants of the NNBL, or began as caucuses of the organization, including the National Negro Insurance Association, the National Negro Bankers Association, the National Negro Bar Association, and the National Negro Undertakers Association.

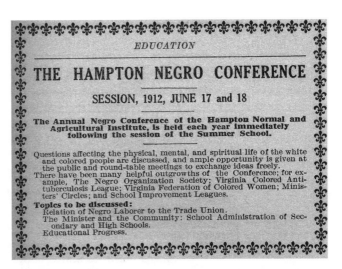

Hampton Normal and Agricultural Institute (now Hampton University) in Hampton, Virginia, advertises its annual Negro Conference for June 17–18, 1912. The Hampton conference was one of several held for African Americans during the late 1800s and into the first third of the twentieth century. *Source:* Monroe N. Work, *Negro Year Book and Annual Encyclopedia of the Negro, 1912.* Tuskegee, AL: Tuskegee Institute, 1912, p. 11.

Other major black organizations and institutions that developed in the early years of the twentieth century—such as the National Association for the Advancement of Colored People (NAACP; 1905), National Urban League (1910), **Marcus Garvey's UNIA** (Universal Negro Improvement Association) (1914; 1917 in United States), the Hampton Normal Agricultural Institute, and the **National Association of Negro Business and Professional Women's Clubs** (1934)—also stressed business and economic development during their annual conventions and conferences as one of many key factors in the progress of African Americans.

African American female entrepreneur **Madame C. J. Walker**, the first American woman to independently become a millionaire by developing the model for the modern ethnic hair/beauty industry, had a national network of salespersons promoting the products and services of her companies. It is documented that she and her daughter, **A'Lelia Walker**, traveled throughout the United States to meet with groups of their salespeople, but not necessarily in the format of a formal business conference or convention.

Despite success, wealth, and subsequent fame, Walker faced sexism as well as racism, being ignored at a meeting of the NNBL in 1912 until boldly interrupting the proceedings; the next year, Walker was a presenter at the convention. The national headquarters building for the Walker companies in Indianapolis, the first black-owned and -operated building of its kind in the country when erected in 1928, became an informal convention center for black professionals and entrepreneurs.

The theme of economic empowerment continued as one facet of the larger agenda of newer organizations that came to prominence in the middle years of the twentieth century. Examples of such organizations and their leaders were the **Brotherhood of Sleeping Car Porters** (Asa Philip Randolph), Congress of Racial Equality (James Forman and Roy Innis), the Southern Christian Leadership Conference (Martin Luther King Jr. and Ralph Abernathy), the Nation of Islam (Elijah Muhammad and Malcolm X), and People United to Save (later Serve) Humanity, which evolved into the Rainbow/PUSH coalition led by Jesse Jackson Sr.

Since these and other organizations were more oriented toward direct action in response to a variety of social and civil rights issues facing African Americans, business and economic development, while considered important, were not the primary focus of their conventions and conferences. One notable exception was Black Expo, which was developed in the early 1970s by PUSH in cooperation with a number of African American businessmen. The four-day event, first held in Chicago, highlighted black culture and black business and set the stage for a number of African American business conferences sponsored by established and emerging organizations.

*Black Enterprise* magazine, founded in 1971 by **Earl G. Graves**, became the first national monthly publication devoted specifically to African American businesses and businesspersons, economics, and personal finance issues. Its success spurred additional interest in business operations, blacks in corporate America, graduate business schools, investment, entrepreneurship, and business networking among African Americans. The magazine would eventually create and sponsor its own annual event, the Black Enterprise Entrepreneurs Conference, beginning in 1996.

Federal assistance for black business, one of many governmental responses to the civil rights movement, included the development of new and existing programs under agencies such as the Small Business Administration, the Office of Economic Opportunity, and the Office of Minority Business Enterprise, which was later renamed the Minority Business Development Agency (MBDA). The MBDA began support of the **Minority Enterprise Development Week** national conference in 1983 and as of 2005 described it as the largest federally supported activity held for the benefit of minority businesses.

The 1990s brought more organizations and conferences, convened by such diverse groups as the **National Black Chamber of Commerce**, African American Women in Business, Black Business Professionals and Entrepreneurs Conference, **National Black MBA Association**, and the Black Business Expo and Trade Show, among others. In recent years, author and speaker George Fraser has been cited as a leading authority on business networking and has convened the national PowerNetworking Conference on Professional Growth and Development in his hometown, Cleveland, Ohio.

Critics of these numerous events express the view that they generate more profits for sponsors and high-profile individuals than substantial and long-term benefit to the larger African American community, even as business and economic development still require the marketing of products and services, the exchange of ideas and information, along with actual financial transactions. While technology and the Internet have provided new approaches to communication and created entire new industries (email, interactive videoconferences, Web sites), the conference setting remains viable for in-person contact and the development of business relationships.

In the largest sense, whenever African American associations organize and convene conferences, black business and economic development is not only discussed but put into action through networking; mentoring; sharing of best practices, new ideas, and technology; and developing business relationships through actual transactions that take place in these settings.

### Sources

*Black Enterprise.* http://www.blackenterprise.com.

Elliott, Joan Curl. "Madame C. J. Walker." *Notable Black American Women.* Ed. Jessie Carney Smith. Detroit: Gale Research, 1992.

FraserNet/George Fraser. http://www.frasernet.com.

Hutchinson, Earl Ofari. "The Lucrative Business of Black Leadership." *Black World Today*, June 13, 2000.

Smith, Jessie Carney. "National Organizations." *The African American Almanac.* 9th ed. Ed. Jeffrey Lehman. Detroit: Thomson/Gale Group, 2003.

Walker, Juliet E. K., ed. *Encyclopedia of African American Business History.* Westport, CT: Greenwood Press, 1999.

———. "The Federal Government and Black Business." First Annual Conference, University of Texas Center for Black Business History, Entrepreneurship, and Technology, Austin, October 17, 2003.

Woodard, Michael D., and Hollis F. Price Jr. "Entrepreneurship." *The African American Almanac.* 9th ed. Ed. Jeffrey Lehman. Detroit: Thomson/Gale Group, 2003.

*Fletcher F. Moon*

# Ward Connerly (1939– ), Consultant, Political Activist

Ward Connerly is a California businessman who has become a leader in the effort to abolish affirmative action, that is, the consideration of racial or gender factors in such areas as admission to educational institutions, award of government contracts, and employment. His most publicized victory is the passage in 1996 of the highly controversial California Civil Rights Initiative (Proposition 209), which banned preferential treatment of women and minorities by the state of California. He is a political supporter and friend of then governor Pete Wilson, who appointed him to a twelve-year term on the University of California Board of Regents in March 1993. As a university regent Connerly's antiaffirmative action stance first received wide publicity in the discussion leading up to the board's decision in July 1995 to end the use of race as a factor in admission to the university. He continues to support similar efforts elsewhere. In fall 2003 he supported an initiative to bar the collection of racial data in California. This initiative did not pass.

Connerly was born in Leesville, Louisiana, on June 15, 1939. His family has a very mixed-race ancestry, and he was officially labeled "colored" by the state on his birth certificate—Louisiana also classified people as "white" and "Negro." His father disappeared from his life before he was two; by the time Connerly saw his father again, in 1998, the man's memory was gone, and he was soon to die. Connerly's mother died when he was four. The child was cared for by his extended family, headed by his grandmother Mary Smith Soniea, the child of a marriage between a Choctaw Indian and a white mother. Soniea herself had married a light-skinned Cajun. The children of this marriage were light-skinned enough to experience rejection by their dark-skinned fellow students at school. Some family members claim that Soniea was prejudiced against dark-skinned blacks; other members deny this bias. Persons opposed to Connerly's position on affirmative action point to this family background as part of their effort to "explain" his rejection of racial preferences as due to antiblack bigotry inculcated by his family. They see Connerly's marriage to a white woman as further proof of prejudice. Connerly rejects these ideas.

Since Connerly's grandmother feared that the boy's father would attempt to reclaim the child, Connerly was sent to live with his aunt Bertha and her husband James Louis on the West Coast. The Louises soon settled in Sacramento, California, where they were over time joined by other members of the family, including his grandmother. James Louis, a laborer, had a major influence on Connerly, inculcating the values of hard work, pride, and responsibility. When Connerly was eleven, his grandmother took him to live with her. She was a strict disciplinarian, and in addition to insisting on regular church attendance, she supervised his studies and insisted he read aloud to her everyday something from his studies or from the Bible.

It is alleged that some of the stories Connerly tells of his childhood poverty are exaggerated, but his life was far from affluent. He attended Sacramento State University, graduating in 1962. At the university, where he was a Young Democrat, he pledged an all-white fraternity, Delta Phi Omega, and was elected student body president. After graduation Connerly's political views shifted sharply to the Right.

Connerly entered state government, joining the Department of Housing and Community Development and serving as the department's liaison to the legislature. There he met state representative Pete Wilson, who recruited him for a staff position on the assembly's housing committee. A close friendship between the two endured as Wilson became in succession mayor of San Diego, a U.S. senator, and in 1991, governor of California.

Connerly became a very successful consultant in Sacramento, where he was an expert on compliance with state land-use laws. Some business came his way as a black because of the mandates of affirmative action, but his success owed much more to his skills in his work and his political connections. When Wilson became governor, he offered Connerly a variety of positions; since Connerly was absorbed by his work, he accepted the post of regent of the University of California with the idea that the job would not require much time.

## QUESTIONS RACE-BASED ADMISSIONS

In 1994 Connerly was led to consider the role of racial background in admissions to the university. His sense of justice was outraged by the disparity in such things as the high school grades of the freshmen admitted. In that year, on a scale where A is equal to 4, Asian American students averaged 3.75; whites, 3.69; Hispanic Americans, 3.50; and blacks, 3.24. His outrage opened a debate that led to the decision of the board of regents on July 21, 1995, to abolish racial preferences in admissions for women and minorities. The uproar over his stance led Connerly to commit much time and effort to his cause. Many blacks labeled him a traitor to his race, calling him such things as a "house slave" and a "puppet of the white man."

Connerly's race was a consideration when he was later asked to head the effort to pass Proposition 209, which extended antiaffirmative action to the state level, but his political skills were also rated highly. Far from a figurehead in the effort, he displayed considerable fund-raising abilities. When he took over in November 1995, the campaign was broke, but he was able to attract money and supporters to lead to a successful outcome. The proposition passed on November 5, 1996.

On Martin Luther King's birthday the following year, Connerly announced the creation of the American Civil Rights Institute to continue the battle against affirmative action. Since then he has been involved in such efforts in many areas of the United States. He remains constant in the antiaffirmative action stance he assumed in 1994, taking time from his work as consultant to further his cause.

**Sources**

ACRI (American Civil Rights Institute) People. http://www.acri.org/people.

Ayres, B. Drummond, Jr. "Fighting Affirmative Action, He Finds His Race an Issue." *New York Times*, April 18, 1996.

Bearak, Barry. "Questions of Race Run Deep for Foe of Preferences." *New York Times*, July 27, 1997.

Connerly, Ward. *Creating Equal: My Fight against Race Preferences*. San Francisco: Encounter Books, 2000.

Murphy, Dean E. "Affirmative Action Foe's Latest Effort Complicates California Recall Vote." *New York Times*, August 3, 2003.

Wallace, Amy. "He's Either Mr. Right or Mr. Wrong: What Drives Ward Connerly in His Crusade to End Affirmative Action? Faith in America, Loyalty to His Old Friend, the Governor, and the Certainty That His Life Story Holds a Lesson for Us All." *Los Angeles Times*, March 31, 1996.

*Robert L. Johns*

# Consumer Cooperatives

The modern consumer cooperative movement began in England in 1846. While there is no strict definition of a consumer cooperative, the general principles are that the cooperative is owned by the members and exists to provide services to the membership, usually in the form of consumer items such as food at a lower price than they would be available at privately owned retail stores. Principally, the cooperative removes the profit motive, as any profits are either redistributed to members or used to expand the cooperative's services or are applied to other community needs such as education. Consumer cooperatives cross into the realm of politics in that they were and are often organized as a response to perceived abuses by the business community or the economic inability of members to meet their needs as individuals. Consumer cooperatives are often seen as a rejection, at least in part, of capitalist principles. American farmers turned to cooperatives both as consumers and as producers in the 1870s. Today, there are millions of members in cooperatives across the United States; most are buying clubs or small supermarkets.

African Americans have formed consumer cooperatives on their own and also in concert with other nationalities since the late 1800s. The first examples are African American farmers in the Grange movement in the 1860s and 1870s. Other examples of African American farmers attempting to form cooperatives in the South and Southwest are cited in various sources, but there is little information on their long-term success. In part, the success of consumer cooperatives is based on their members' ability to support them. The dire economic straits and political oppression faced by African Americans in the South would have made maintaining cooperatives difficult, if not impossible. It is particularly important to note that any cooperative would require organization and the conscious promotion of the group's interest. Southern planters or large landowners were reported to have had a major influence in both the Grange movement and the Farmers' alliances during the late 1800s, reinforcing the belief that any truly independent economic initiatives would have been difficult for black farmers.

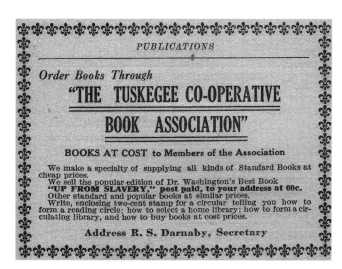

Advertisement for the Tuskegee Co-operative Book Association located at Tuskegee Institute, Alabama. This is an example of the cooperative movement in the African American community. Booker T. Washington's autobiography *Up from Slavery* is promoted here. *Source*: Monroe N. Work, *Negro Year Book and Annual Encyclopedia of the Negro, 1912*. Tuskegee, AL: Tuskegee Institute, 1912, p. 227.

**Table 20.** Names, Addresses, Organization Dates, and Principal Officers of Eleven Selected Cooperatives, 1945

| Name of Cooperative | Address of Cooperative | Date Organized | Principal Officer |
|---|---|---|---|
| College Co-operative Union | Fort Valley State College Fort Valley, GA | 1939 | R. H. Beasley Fort Valley, GA |
| Georgia State College Co-op Association | Georgia State College Savannah, GA | 1935 | J. H. Gadson Jr. Georgia State College, Savannah, GA |
| Altgeld Gardens Co-operative, Inc. | 1025 E. 130th Street Chicago, IL | 1944 | Wilmoth Bowen 13342 Corliss Avenue, Chicago, IL |
| United Transport Service Employees of America (CIO) | 3451 S. Michigan Avenue Chicago, IL | 1945 | Ernest Calloway 3451 S. Michigan Avenue, Chicago, IL |
| Gibraltar Consumer Co-operative, Inc. | 1720 Emerson Street Evanston, IL | 1940 | R. S. Simmons 1720 Emerson Street, Evanston, IL |
| Co-operative Commonwealth, Inc. | 2556 Monroe Street Gary, IN | 1941 | Leslie Joseph 2556 Monroe Street, Gary, IN |
| Northwestern Co-operative Buying Club | 1716 Madison Avenue Baltimore, MD | 1944 | Rev. C. Baker Pearle Payne Memorial, A.M.E. Church |
| Modern Co-operative Inc. | 479 W. 150th Street New York, NY | 1940 | W. A. Beckles 160 W. 133rd Street, New York, NY |
| Hood Theological Seminary Book Service | Livingstone College Salisbury, NC | — | Wilson Q. Welch Jr. Livingstone College, Salisbury, NC |
| Aberdeen Association, Inc. | Aberdeen Gardens Hampton, VA | 1937 | T. D. Lane 7 Russell Road, Hampton, VA |
| Red Circle Stores, Inc. | 900 James Street Richmond, VA | 1937 | E. E. Storrs 500 W. Clay Street, Richmond, VA |

*Source*: Joseph A. Pierce, *Negro Business and Business Education: Their Present and Prospective Development* (New York: Harper and Brothers Publishers, 1947), 167.

An essay by Bruce Baker in the journal of *Labor History* on the Hoover Scare of 1887 in South Carolina records white reaction to black farmers' organizing independent groups including a consumer cooperative. White leaders in the South saw any such organizing efforts by blacks as a direct threat to their power.

Consumer cooperatives in an urban setting and as part of a conscious campaign to resist racial oppression and improve the economic standing of African Americans began to evolve after World War I (Tables 20 through 22). It appears that both the increased nationalism in black communities as well as the existence of new urban communities spurred this development. The most comprehensive discussion of cooperatives during the period was led by W.E.B. Du Bois in the pages of the National Association for the Advancement of Colored People (NAACP) journal the *Crisis*. Du Bois and the NAACP encouraged the formation of cooperatives as early as 1917. With the economic crisis of the 1930s and the growing popularity of

**Table 21.** Outstanding Problems and Achievements of Seven Selected Cooperatives, 1945

| Name of Cooperative | Problems | Achievements |
| --- | --- | --- |
| Georgia State College Co-op Association, Savannah, GA | Creating and maintaining membership interest; securing component managers. | Financing through reinvestment of earnings. Grew from 54 members in 1935 with $32 capital to 600 members and $4K capital in 1943. Have recently organized a co-op housing project. |
| Altgeld Gardens, Chicago, IL | Leaders somewhat inexperienced in tasks of setting up an organization of this type. | Were assisted with organization problems by other co-op groups in the city and by central organizations. |
| Co-operative Commonwealth, Gary, IN | Educating ministers and the general public. | Number of people joining constantly. Good location. |
| Northwestern Co-operative Buying Club, Baltimore, MD | Small attendance at meetings; getting information about co-ops over to the people. | — |
| Modern Co-operative Inc., New York, NY | Small capital. | Survived four years of struggle against tremendous odds, yet has a fine, loyal nucleus of members. |
| Aberdeen Association, Inc., Hampton, VA | Employment of competent manager. | Community has developed a school co-op in the elementary school. Also a chicken-raising co-op. |
| Red Circles Stores, Inc., Richmond, VA | Government regulations and manpower shortage; capital investment per member needs to be more than doubled in order to finance the store operations adequately. | Opportunity for youth development. Won out in price war started by chain store competitor. Pioneer co-op in Richmond. Operates three branch stores, has 1,250 members—more than any predominantly Negro group. |

*Source*: Joseph A. Pierce, *Negro Business and Business Education: Their Present and Prospective Development* (New York: Harper and Brothers Publishers, 1947), 169.

socialist ideas, cooperatives gained support throughout the country and in African American circles as well.

Du Bois first brought up the idea of consumer cooperatives in the *Crisis* in 1917. James Peter Warbasse provided a more extensive discussion under the heading "The Theory of Cooperation" in the March 1918 issue of the NAACP journal. In 1923, at an "All Race" conference in New York sponsored by major African American groups including the NAACP, the African Blood Brotherhood, and others, Richard B. Moore of the African Blood Brotherhood called on African Americans to pursue Gandhi's methods and specifically to establish consumer cooperatives.

Robert Weems notes a growing interest in the idea of cooperatives during the 1930s and that the distribution of profits within the African American community held a special appeal. The **Brotherhood of Sleeping Car Porters**, led by A. Phillip Randolph, supported the formation of cooperatives in Harlem and other black communities. Ella Baker, then living in Harlem, was active in

**Table 22.** Services Provided, Annual Volume, Patronage Rebates, and Central Cooperative Affiliation of Eleven Selected Consumer Cooperatives, 1945

| Name of Cooperative | Services Provided | Annual Volume | Patronage Rebated (percent) | Co-op Affiliation |
|---|---|---|---|---|
| College Co-operative Union | Merchandise and service, school supplies, books, cold drinks, sandwiches, and sundries | $12,000 | 6 | Southeastern Co-operative League* |
| Georgia State College Co-operative Association | Bookstore, cafeteria, clothing and notions, confectionary and groceries | $25,000 | 10, 5, 4 | Southeastern Co-operative League |
| Atlgeld Gardens Co-operative, Inc. | Groceries and meats | $6,150 | None (too young) | Central States Co-operatives, Inc. |
| United Transport Service Employees of America (CIO) | Federal Credit Union and Co-op Study Club | Not indicated | — | Council for Co-operative Development; CUNA |
| Gibraltar Consumer Co-operative, Inc. | Groceries | $9,600 | None | Central States Co-operative, Inc. C.L., USA |
| Co-operative Commonwealth, Inc. | Not yet in operation; erecting a $50K building | — | — | Not indicated |
| Northwestern Co-operative Buying Club | Groceries | $9,260 | None | Consumers' Co-operative of Baltimore, MD |
| Modern Co-operative Inc. | Books and school supplies | $5,200 | None | Eastern Co-op League |
| Hood Theological Seminary Book Service | Books and school supplies | Not indicated | None | None |
| Aberdeen Association, Inc. | Retail groceries and meats | $34,000 | 5 | None |
| Red Circles Stores, Inc. | Groceries and meats | $100,000 | 3 (three years) | Potomac Co-operative Federation |

*The league was inactive during the period 1943 to 1946. Plans are being made for its reactivation in 1947.

*Source:* Joseph A. Pierce, *Negro Business and Business Education: Their Present and Prospective Development* (New York: Harper and Brothers Publishers, 1947), 168.

promoting these cooperatives. The Housewives' League of Detroit was founded by Fannie B. Peck in June 1930 with 50 members. It had grown to 10,000 members by 1935. Members pledged to buy from black-owned businesses and purchase products and services produced or delivered by blacks. Similar organizations existed in Chicago, Baltimore, Washington, Cleveland, and New York City and were considered powerful in their communities. In part, there was a growing sophistication among black consumers who began to see the call to patronize black-owned businesses as benefiting the business owners more than the community. If black business wanted the black community to patronize them, they should transform their businesses into cooperatives.

Writing in 1936, African American intellectual St. Clair Drake stated that the "plea to make the dollar do 'Double Duty' often falls on deaf ears"; a shift to cooperatives would have greater appeal because the dollar would do "triple duty." The purchase would support black enterprise, and the increased purchasing would lead to an end-of-the-year dividend to members of the cooperative community. Ultimately, advocates argued, a successful cooperative movement, if it genuinely spread, would give black communities real economic clout, and tied in with that would be political power.

An example of this movement was the Consumers' Cooperative Trading Company, organized in Gary, Indiana, in 1932 by Jacob L. Reddix, a local African American teacher. Reddix was responding to the problems African Americans faced in the depression; over half of the 20,000 African Americans in Gary were on public relief. He familiarized himself with the principles of organized cooperation and started the organization as a buying club with 15 families and $24. Reddix began teaching night classes at Roosevelt High School on cooperative economics. By 1935 there were 450 families in the cooperative, which included a grocery store with annual sales of $35,000, a **credit union**, and a cooperative ice cream and candy shop run by children. With the end of the depression, however, Reddix's cooperative ended during the early 1940s.

## DU BOIS'S VIEW OF COOPERATIVES

W.E.B. Du Bois saw consumer cooperatives as a key part of a larger cooperative state, a "nation with-in a nation" during the 1930s. It is important to note that Du Bois's emphasis on cooperatives and the nationalist concept of nation within a nation reflected both his socialist economic beliefs and his growing frustration with the resistance of whites to integration and racial justice. African Americans would only be able to rely on themselves, and economic, along with political, cooperation would be at the heart of this change. According to Joseph DeMarco, Du Bois believed that African Americans were exploited as consumers; they lacked their own capitalist class. Cooperatives formed in neighborhoods would, out of necessity, buy from white-owned wholesalers. Lower prices would lead more people to join the cooperatives, encourage people in the African American community to work together, and bring even lower prices. Ultimately, they would be able to place more pressure on wholesalers and even support emerging African American businesses with their buying power. African American cooperatives, then, contributed to the general sense of cooperation and community building.

There is also some evidence of a consumer cooperative movement in African American communities during the 1960s and 1970s, when the movement for cooperatives revived. During 1966–1967, two white sociologists, Gerald Schaflander and Henry Etzkowitz, took their students and worked with the African American community in the Bedford-Stuyvesant neighborhood of Brooklyn, New York, to build a neighborhood cooperative that emphasized interracial principles. The cooperative included medicines, food, and other goods and also reinvested profits back into the neighborhood. The reinvested profits were used to support social services such as child care, medical care, and education. By 1968, they operated a parking lot, gas station, general store, pharmacy, and child-care center. Founders saw themselves as rejecting both the "growing racialism of black nationalism and a testament against the unchecked immorality of American capitalism." The Bedford-Stuyvesant effort reflects the ideas that Du Bois, St. Clair Drake, and others promoted in the 1930s. An oral history of this effort is available at Duke University.

It is evident neither that cooperatives pose a serious challenge to traditional businesses nor that they relieve the economic stresses that African American communities face. It does appear that they represent significant examples of self-help, community organization, and an alternative vision of how people and communities may work together.

**Sources**

Baker, Bruce E. "The 'Hoover Scare' in South Carolina, 1887: An Attempt to Organize Black Farm Labor." *Labor History* 40 (August 1999): 261–282.

Bedford-Stuyvesant Community Cooperative Audio Tapes. http://scriptorium.lib.duke.edu/franklin/OralHistory.html.

DeMarco, Joseph. "The Rationale and Foundation of Du Bois's Theory of Economic Cooperation." *Phylon* 35.1 (March 1974): 5–15.

Drake, St. Clair. "Why Not Cooperate?" *Opportunity* 14 (August 1936): 233.

Hughes, C. Alvin. "The Negro Sanhedrin Movement." *Journal of Negro History* 69 (Winter 1984): 1–13.

Warbasse, James Peter. "The Theory of Cooperation." *Crisis* 15 (March 1918): 222.

Weems, Robert E., Jr. *Desegregating the Dollar: African American Consumerism in the Twentieth Century*. New York: New York University Press, 1998.

*John W. Wood III*

# Nathan G. Conyers (1932– ), Automotive Executive

Nathan G. Conyers would not have graced *Black Enterprise*'s list of Top 100 Black Businesses without his family. His road to winning *Time* magazine's

"Quality Dealer Award" began with a family dream and a coin toss and continues with innovative business practices as well as family and community involvement. In the last thirty years, Conyers has proven time and time again why he has endured in a field that has swallowed so many individuals. His business savvy and shrewd understanding of race relations have propelled his auto dealership, Conyers Riverside Ford, to be *Black Enterprise*'s 1995 "Dealership of the Year" and Conyers as the 1995 "Auto Dealer of the Year." Although the odds have consistently been in Conyers's favor, he is a firm believer of corporate social consciousness and always doing the right thing.

The Great Depression hit the "Black Bottom" neighborhood of East Detroit especially hard because of the downturn in the automotive industry, which affected the predominantly African American factory workers. In this environment, Conyers was born on July 3, 1932, to John Conyers Sr., a worker at a Chrysler factory and an international representative for the United Auto Workers, and Lucille Simpson Conyers. As John Sr. never progressed past elementary school, he set high aspirations for his four surviving children and stressed education and self-reliance during kitchen-table family conferences. At these family conferences, the Conyers began laying the foundation for owning their own business.

It took the discipline of the U.S. Army to instill the importance of education in Conyers. He graduated from Northwestern High School, where he was known as a "bright and likeable underachiever," in 1950 and later received his bachelor's and law degrees from Detroit's Wayne State University. He passed the Michigan bar in 1959 and spent the next year as a special assistant attorney for the state attorney general and as a closing attorney for the Veteran's Administration and the Small Business Administration. In 1960, Conyers joined the firm of Keith, Conyers, Anderson, Brown and Wahls, a historic practice specializing in civil rights.

The 1960s was a time of turmoil for the city of Detroit; the reversal of demographics in the inner city, police abuse, and social inequality gave rise to the Detroit Riots of 1967. The riots lasted five days, left 43 dead, 1,189 injured, and more than 4,000 incarcerated. The National Guard, 82nd Airborne, and police force fought to contain the fires, looting, and vandalism that spread from the 12th Street area of northeast Detroit to the east side. In the aftermath of this chaos, a partnership of business, political, and community leaders formed New Detroit, a coalition dedicated to putting the city back together after the carnage, devastation, and social unrest of the riots. New Detroit realized they needed to establish proactive race relations and extend business opportunities to the city's minorities to replace the flight of white businesses.

In this dynamic climate, the Conyers family finally got their chance to go into business for themselves in 1969 when an auto dealership became available. Henry Ford, Ford Motor Company chairman, stressed the need for more African American auto dealers, and the Ford Company financed the franchise purchased by John Jr. and Nathan for $400,000. Both brothers were doing well in their professions—John Jr. was a Democratic congressman for the First District, and Nathan was a senior partner in his law firm—but someone had to give up his job to run the dealership. The post fell to Nathan with a flip of a coin, and Conyers Ford (later Conyers Riverside Ford) was established in 1970. The company employed ninety-one people as of 1995, grossed $35.2 million in sales in 2002, and graced the *Black Enterprise* 100 largest African American owned businesses for thirty consecutive years.

During his thirty years as president of Conyers Riverside Ford, Conyers has been the model of adaptability. Perhaps his consistent and flexible approach to change is one of his best business practices for the dealership. When the community around Conyers Ford deteriorated in the early 1980s, he relocated to the downtown edge of the Detroit River. With this move, his clientele shifted as well, from predominantly African American to Caucasian, white-collar workers and commuters from the suburbs. However, Conyers quickly formulated a comfort-centered business plan to attract his new consumer market. He increased the number of white salespeople and managers and aggressively marketed his service component to the downtown officeworkers to bring them into the dealership.

Conyers always "courted" his customers, which was another key business tenant. He made his dealership's presence known with an enormous blimp visible to commuters to the city, offered workers limousine transportation from the dealership to a large office complex, and found financing for low-income African American car buyers. He specializes in government contracts, which accounted for almost 70 percent of the dealership's annual sales. In 1999, he broadened his dealerships by securing a deal to franchise a Jaguar dealership in Novi, Michigan, located thirty minutes from downtown Detroit. Conyers was only the second African American to own a Jaguar dealership in the United States. The success he has enjoyed has largely come from the support of his family.

Like many other minority-owned businesses, the Conyers dealerships have been kept in the family. All five of Conyers's children have helped the family business in some way, and as of 2002, three were actively working for the dealership. Steven, his oldest son, was the general manager of Riverside Ford and set to be the next president of the company; Peter is part of the Jaguar dealership; and Nancy, the most independent child, serves as the director of marketing, advertising, promotions, and community relations. Nancy stated in a 1995 *Black Enterprise* interview with Dan Holly that the pull of responsibility to the family company prevails in even the most reluctant children.

A Detroit native through and through, Conyers has never considered following his white counterparts to the suburbs, where everything costs less and people have more money to spend. The suburban flight is widely considered to be an effect of the high proportion of minorities in the city, around 88 percent in 2000, and Conyers does not want to contribute to what he considers "racist attitudes." The Conyers dealership has given back to the community at large with a tradition called "Community Awareness

Day," which has introduced the community to much-needed services such as homeless shelters, adoption agencies, job placement agencies, and an AIDS (acquired immunodeficiency syndrome) testing mobile unit.

Conyers has also continued to champion minorities in the business world and has used his dealerships as a jumping-off point for African Americans to open their own dealerships. As of 2002, thirty-six former employees, several of which are women, had opened their own businesses, which is something Conyers believes to be one of the greatest rewards of the company. He established and served as the first president of the National Association of Minority Automobile Dealers, which is committed to keeping minorities in the auto dealership business. His advice for any minority getting into entrepreneurship is location, capitalization, comprehension, and vision.

Through his illustrious career, Conyers has been lauded as the "Dean of America's Black-Owned Automobile Dealerships"; recognized for excellence in business and community service by the Howard University School of Business and Public Administration and by former President Jimmy Carter; and presented the keys to the cities of Atlanta, New York, Chicago, and Detroit. He is a board member of the Greater Detroit Chamber of Commerce, the Greater Detroit Area Hospital Council, and Blue Cross/Blue Shield of Michigan.

Although Conyers has been the golden child of the minority-owned auto dealers, he could not prevent the economic downturn at the turn of the twenty-first century. A decline in the sales of American-made cars claimed the Riverside Ford operation in 2003, and afterward, rival Bob Maxey bought it. The Jaguar dealership, however, remains strong; Conyers knows how to roll with the punches the economy can bring. His career began on complete chance and continues with a flexible, accommodating business plan to ensure the comfort of his customers. A relentless drive to expand and strong family ties have repaid Conyers with widespread success and the knowledge that minority business owners can and will succeed.

*See also*: Minority Businesses in Major Cities

**Sources**
"African-American Dealers—Ford Motor Dealers." *Ebony* 56 (March 2001): 54–57. http://www.findarticles.com.
Gite, Lloyd. "Marathon Men: Revisited." *Black Enterprise* 32 (June 2002): 92.
The History Makers: Business Makers. "Nathan Conyers." 2001. http://www.thehistory makers.com/biography/biography.asp?bioindex=215&category=businessMakers.
Holly, Dan. "Heads, We Win." *Black Enterprise* 25 (June 1995): 134.
"Outstanding Business Leader: Nathan G. Conyers." Northwood University. http://www.northwood.edu/pr/fl/index.asp?section=2000&subsection=2000&id=16.n.
Rohan, Rebecca. "Pumping the Brakes." *Black Enterprise* 33 (June 2003): 11.
Walker, Juliet E. K., ed. *Encyclopedia of African American Business History*. Westport, CT: Greenwood Press, 1999.
Walsh, Tom. "Ford Dealer Fights Blight." *Detroit Free Press*, November 30, 2003. http://66.54.33.107/money/business/walsh30e_20041130.htm.

*Thura Mack*

# Edith W. Cooper (1961– ), Investment Company Executive

Edith W. Cooper, at a young age of forty-one, became the managing director, Global Head of Futures, at Goldman Sachs & Co. Cooper oversees Goldman Sachs's global listed derivatives business. She works with and manages various teams to successfully implement highly sophisticated financial transactions for Goldman's clients worldwide.

Goldman Sachs announced on October 18, 2000, that it had invited 202 individuals to serve as managing directors, and 114 others would join their Partnership Pool when the firm's fiscal year began on November 25 that year. Chairman and chief executive officer Henry M. Paulson Jr. commented on the selections, saying, "These leaders represent the best of Goldman Sachs and their contribution will continue to drive the firm's worldwide growth." The selection placed Cooper among some of the most promising executives in the nation.

Cooper has a strong academic background that serves her well in the business world. She has a B.A. degree from Harvard University and an M.B.A. from Northwestern University.

In addition to Cooper's education, her experience in the business world played a big part in her current position and career success. Cooper had coheaded Goldman's commodities division in Europe and Asia. She has also worked at Morgan Stanley, Bankers Trust, and First Chicago Bank, where she gained a broad range of experience in marketing and executing over-the-counter derivatives transactions.

Cooper believes that in order to be successful on Wall Street one must create value for one's client, colleagues, and organization. It is apparent that Cooper's education and experience in the business world prepared her for her current position and career success.

In an article online in 2005, *Black Enterprise* (*BE*) announced what it called "the most influential black leaders of the financial industry," having published the selections in the October 2004 issue. Here the editors' picks for the top fifty black leaders on Wall Street represent an expansion from the twenty-five named in 1992 and 1996. Calling Wall Street the "capital of free-market America and the seat of global financial power," *Black Enterprise* saw Wall Street as a strong symbol of African American's struggle for full and equal access to the economic power that mainstream Americans consistently enjoy. Cooper shared *BE*'s top fifty list with such executives as **Franklin Delano Raines** (then with Fannie Mae), **Kenneth Irvine Chenault** of American Express, **E. Stanley O'Neal** with Merrill Lynch, John W. Rogers Jr. with Ariel Capital, **Carla Ann Harris** and Melissa James of Morgan Stanley Dean Witter, and **Vernon Eulion Jordan** with Lazard Féres.

Leaders such as Cooper continue to move forward, however, removing barriers to economic advancement and to leadership posts in the financial market. Both Goldman Sachs and *Black Enterprise* acknowledge her as a leader in the financial industry and one who can bear the intense pressure and high performance standards that accompany advancement.

*See also*: Women and Business

**Sources**

"Black Enterprise Names the Most Influential Black Leaders of the Financial Industry." http://www.multiculturaladvantage.com/contentmgt/anmviewer.asp?a=268.

"Goldman Sachs Announces New Managing Directors and New Members of the Partnership Pool." http://www.gs.com/our_firm/media_center/articles/press_release_2000_article_919110.html.

"The Top 50 African Americans on Wall Street." *Black Enterprise* 33 (October 2002): 96. http://www.blackenterprise.com.

*Nkechi Amadife*

# Corporation of Caterers
## Waiters' Beneficial Association

Before the Civil War, black caterers appeared to dominate the industry; they were elite themselves, and they served "the rich, well-born, and powerful," wrote Juliet Walker in *The History of Black Business in America*. Black caterers in New York realized that white caterers acknowledged and challenged their success. Thus, in 1869 twelve local caterers founded the Corporation of Caterers as well as the Public Waiters Association. Since the industry had become so successful for blacks, they wanted their success to continue. One sure way to accomplish this, they reasoned, was to set and maintain high professional standards. The large weddings, parties, banquets, balls, and social functions that they served placed a demand on them for good, high-quality service. Those who were irresponsible were not to jeopardize the industry by attempting to serve such functions. Thus, the corporation had a genuine interest in its members, their business ventures, and the black **catering industry** as a whole.

By now, some of the members had acquired costly possessions: They owned fine, imported china and silver; and they had other caterer's provisions, ranging in value from $1,000 to $4,000—a considerable sum at that time. The size of the organization increased, and by 1870, membership, now including other black employees in the industry, reached 500. The Corporation of Caterers reorganized in 1872 to become the Waiters' Beneficial Association, yet membership in the new organization was just over 100. Like other beneficial organizations, the members emphasized mutual-aid insurance benefits. The original purpose of the corporation had changed to focus on other important issues, such as sickness and provisions for burial.

Other organizations that aided black caterers were established. In 1866, for example, leading black caterers in Philadelphia—once the center of the catering industry—organized the Philadelphia Caterers' Association. Peter

Dutrieuille (1838–1916), who in 1873 established his own catering business, was credited with founding the new group. Its purpose was to keep intact the stronghold that blacks had on the catering industry. Yet as the end of the century neared and the industry's needs changed, so did the number of blacks working as caterers. Several blacks, however, entered the industry late in the century and enjoyed success. The Caterers Manufacturing and Supply Company, organized in 1894, served its membership by either renting or providing at wholesale prices items such as china, silver, tables, chairs, and linens. Their efforts were to assist blacks in the industry and help them to maintain their businesses.

The Public Waiters Association folded in 1905, when it had a membership of only thirty-three. The caterers who had supported the association were no longer in demand. Those who continued their businesses supported a declining patronage; the large affairs that they had served previously were no longer available to them. New licensing laws were passed to regulate the industry and put demands on black caterers that many were unable to meet.

The elite antebellum black caterers who had flourished before the Civil War as well as those who carried on the industry much later made important contributions to the history of black business development. They met high standards—those imposed by their clients as well as those that were set by themselves or their organization.

*See also*: Food Service Industry

**Sources**

Walker, Juliet E. K., ed. *Encyclopedia of African American Business History*. Westport, CT: Greenwood Press, 1999.

———. *The History of Black Business in America: Capitalism, Race, Entrepreneurship*. New York: Macmillan Library Reference USA, 1998.

*Jessie Carney Smith*

# Credit Unions

The history of cooperative credit programs is difficult to trace with accuracy. There were widespread cooperative movements in European towns and rural areas as early as the 1830s. Others followed; for example, in 1844, the Rochdale cooperative store opened in England. There were cooperative schemes in France in the 1830s and 1840s and in 1848 in Belgium. The first "true" credit union, or cooperative credit society, was created in Germany in 1850, and the movement continued to spread. Their founding was in response to crop failures and usury. Reformers in the 1840s and 1850s challenged the economic system and formed credit unions, or "people's banks," to provide skilled workers a place to borrow money for business purposes.

The movement spread to the United States in 1908; the next year, several citizens formed the first union in Manchester, New Hampshire. Among those who popularized and promoted the credit union movement was Edward A. Filene (1860–1937), a wealthy and outstanding department store owner in the Boston area whose name is still recognized in the field of business. Generally, philanthropic business leaders were the early pioneers in the movement. After U.S. officials studied the cooperative credit movement abroad, they returned and translated their findings into laws governing the operation, in one state after another. The organization of the Credit Union National Extension Bureau in 1921 and hiring of Roy Bergengren (1879–1955) as the first full-time chief executive in 1921 helped the movement to achieve great strides.

African Americans saw a need early on to devise ways to help themselves survive and improve their economic conditions. They began various forms of self-help as early as the mid-1700s—well before true credit unions were established—when they founded self-help or mutual-aid societies. One of the first such organizations was the Free Africa Society, founded by religious leaders Absalom Jones (1746–1818) and Richard Allen (1760–1831). Jones was the first black Episcopal priest and founder of St. Thomas, the first black Episcopal Church; Allen founded the African Methodist Episcopal (AME) Church, the first black-controlled religious denomination. Early secret societies in the black community consisted of two classes: the old-line organizations, such as the Masons, the Odd Fellows, and the Knights of Pythias; and the benevolent societies such as the National Order of Mosaic Templars, the True Reformers, the Grand Union Order of Galilean Fisherman, and the Independent Order of St. Luke. These societies often had large treasuries and generally invested their funds, purchased property, and later began to address the health and economic needs of their members. As well, they established a wide array of black business enterprises, such as insurance companies, churches, banks, and cooperatives. The credit union in the black community is an example of a black cooperative.

As the credit union movement spread across the United States, it also touched African Americans who used cooperative credit unions for the purpose of saving and borrowing money (Tables 23 and 24). By the end of 1944, the U.S. Department of Labor reported that there were ninety-one African American credit unions; they were organized under the Federal Credit Union Act. Seventy-four, or 81 percent of them, were active at the end of the year; the others were either inoperative or their charters had been cancelled. Considering all federal credit unions that had been established, whether white or black, 74 percent were active.

By 1944 as well, credit unions were found in churches, having been established with the encouragement of the Federal Council of Churches in America. George Edmund Haynes (1880–1960), a black social work pioneer, educator, advocate for urban black workers, and a founder of the National Urban League, took an active interest in the credit union movement in the Harlem section of New York City. Working on behalf of the Federal Council of Churches, his efforts resulted in the founding of six or more unions in larger churches. In Detroit, Bethel AME Church established

**Table 23.** Credit Unions, Assets of Black Associations Compared to Total, 1944

| Item | Reporting Negro Associations | Reporting Federal Associations |
|---|---|---|
| Total number of associations | 72 | 3,795 |
| Actual membership as percent Total membership | 34 | 33 |
| Average members per association | 174 | 343 |
| Total share capital | $642,711 | $133,586,147 |
| Average per association | $6,926 | $35,200 |
| Average per member | $51 | $102 |
| Total assets | $683,100 | $144,266,156 |
| Total loans outstanding | $230,756 | $34,403,467 |
| Percent current | 87 | 85 |
| Percent military loans | 2 | 5 |
| Percent delinquent, twenty mos. or more | 11 | 10 |
| Reserves for bad loans as percent of loans outstanding | 9 | 13 |
| Total loans since organization | $1,723,451 | $657,786,637 |
| Bad loans as percent of total | 0.09 | 0.13 |

*Source*: Jessie P. Guzman, ed., *Negro Year Book: A Review of Events Affecting Negro Life, 1941–1946* (Tuskegee, AL: Department of Records and Research, Tuskegee Institute, 1947), 187.

the Fannie B. Peck Credit Union and by 1941 claimed 3,000 members. The union also had made 390 loans to members for a total of $15,573.70; assets totaled $6,372.48. The involvement of churches in credit union development continues.

Although the date is unknown, in North Carolina, Simpson P. Dean organized the Light of Tyrrell Credit Union, located in Tyrrell County. The credit union financed several business and building projects, including a cooperative sawmill and the construction and remodeling of sixteen homes. The union also launched the Light of Tyrrell credit store and had as many as 300 members. As result of the union's financial projects, there were seventy-two black-owned farms in the county and savings accounts for some blacks included $2,500.

Black credit unions are closely tied to the beginnings of some black cooperatives. There were urban cooperatives such as the People's Consumers Cooperative Store in Chicago; and rural cooperatives, such as the Peoples Cooperative Store located at Tuskegee Institute in Alabama and the Ayden Cooperative Exchange in North Carolina. The Ayden project began in 1941 as Bright Leaf Credit Union. Credit unions were an important factor in stimulating interest and accumulating sufficient capital reserves for businesses to begin operations.

By September 1951, some 102 credit unions for blacks were chartered under state and federal laws. The unions operated in twenty-six states, with

**Table 24.** Federal Credit Unions, 1935–1940

| Year | Number of Active Unions | Total Number of Members in Unions | Total Loans Made to Members | Interest on Loans | Returned in Dividends | Loans to Members Outstanding | Savings (share balance) |
|---|---|---|---|---|---|---|---|
| 1935 | 5 | 467 | $4,360 | $52 | — | $2,460 | $3,160 |
| 1936 | 18 | 1,251 | 16,552 | 427 | 38 | 7,541 | 10,134 |
| 1937 | 28 | 2,295 | 32,626 | 1,114 | 240 | 16,258 | 20,649 |
| 1938 | 44 | 3,680 | 63,320 | 2,463 | 622 | 30,239 | 37,810 |
| 1939 | 48 | 5,047 | 125,804 | 4,891 | 1,554 | 62,013 | 67,117 |
| 1940 | 51 | 6,462 | 202,529 | 8,855 | 3,028 | 102,403 | 108,796 |

*Source:* Florence Murray, ed., *The Negro Handbook, 1944* (New York: Wendell Malliet, 1944), 162.

North Carolina leading the list and operating 30. The number varied in other states as follows: Louisiana, 19; Texas and Missouri, 5 each; Virginia, Oklahoma, New York, and Kansas, 4 each; Alabama, California, and Ohio, 3 each; West Virginia, Michigan, and Maryland, 2 each; and Arkansas, Florida, Georgia, Illinois, Kentucky, Massachusetts, Minnesota, Mississippi, New Jersey, Pennsylvania, South Carolina, and Tennessee, 1 each. Credit unions were not restricted to a particular occupational group; they were found among teachers, colleges and schools, farmers, insurance companies, organizations (such as the National Association for the Advancement of Colored People [NAACP]), and as noted earlier, churches.

Credit unions continued to develop and serve the needs of African Americans. As well, the communities have been encouraged to maintain self-help programs, such as those proposed by African American organizations that were founded during the civil rights movement of the 1960s. The Student Nonviolent Coordinating Committee (SNCC), which began to take hold around 1960, came to prominence in 1966 when Stokely Carmichael (1941–1998), later known as Kwame Ture, headed the organization. SNCC promoted the "Black Power" concept and, among other assertions, said that blacks should form their own economic institutions, such as credit unions. The increasing acknowledgment of self-worth encouraged African Americans to promote self-help programs.

In time, a number of organizations began initiatives to promote credit unions in the black community, among them the Federation of Southern Cooperatives, later known as the **Federation of Southern Cooperatives Land Assistance Fund** (FSCLAF). Founded in 1967, the FSCLAF has provided self-help economic opportunities for low-income communities across the South. The founders were representatives of community organizations and leaders who had been molded or influenced by the civil rights movement of the 1960s. Two of its primary objectives are to retain black-owned land and to use cooperatives to support land-based economic development. Since the FSCLAF was founded, its work in encouraging and developing low-income people in the community has been significant. The three major themes of the federation's mission over the past thirty-seven years are to develop cooperatives and credit unions to help people enhance their lives as well as their communities; to save, protect, and increase southern black family farmers' landholdings; and to develop, advocate, and support various public policy issues that benefit black and other family farmers as well as low-income rural communities.

The FSCLAF continues its organization of low-income grassroots members. There are over seventy cooperative member groups, themselves with a membership in excess of 20,000 families who work cooperatively across ten southern states. They are concentrated in Alabama, Georgia, Mississippi, and South Carolina.

Credit unions for African Americans were promoted further by the Mississippi Association of Cooperatives (MAC). Chartered in December 1972 as a nonprofit organization, according to *About Us*, MAC aimed to "administer, coordinate and supervise technical assistance, educational training and financial programs for member cooperatives in the Mississippi state." It serves members by helping them to help themselves. The organization is similar in purpose to the Federation of Southern Cooperative Land Assistance Fund. Among MAC's objectives are to organize and develop self-help community development strategies for rural residents through cooperatives and credit unions; to help increase economic viability of small farmers through marketing cooperatives; to facilitate preservation and retention of lands owned by black farmers; to advocate appropriate public policy changes; and to support training and educational programs for rural residents. Membership consists of several cooperatives, buying clubs, and credit unions located across the state.

## FAITH-BASED CREDIT UNIONS CONTINUE

As previously noted, some black credit unions were founded in churches, among them those encouraged by the Federal Council of Churches in America. Church involvement in the civil rights movement of the 1960s often came as testament to their concern for helping African Americans secure their rights in the community. Congregations began to unite around the needs of low-income residents—both black and white—who deserved financial institutions to support their needs. Many of the first credit unions established in communities throughout the United States were faith based. Such unions are faith based when their founding, governance, and membership are derived from a religious institution. Faith-based credit unions are characterized by smaller memberships and assets; they offer limited services; they focus chiefly on savings and loans; they have limited hours of service each week but include some after-church services; and most have all-volunteer leadership and staffs. The larger credit unions of this type serve many local churches, far-flung dioceses, multiple parishes, or churches spread over an entire region.

Churches maintain that these credit unions should remain at the forefront of efforts to serve the community in a holistic way. Nationwide, about one-third of the total credit union population is faith based. Such credit unions appear to address the best traditions of low-income people in communities who work to help others with similar needs. Some believe that it is through such direction that churches return to the real meaning of the community.

For African Americans, the real benefit of the federation's efforts began in 1992, after three years of research to determine whether or not church-based credit unions (CBCUs) were viable in economic development. Then the federation established the African-American Church Credit Union Program (CCUP). The federation asserts that it was the first organization to recognize the enormous potential of the African American CBCU. The federation was concerned about self-help in the black community and saw the CBCU as an untapped resource for black economic power; it would also serve as a model of self-help programs in African American communities nationwide. The federation's board of directors in 1997 voted to change the name from the Church Credit Union Program to the Faith-Based Credit Union Program (FBCUP)—the name by which the program is currently known. The FBCUP is open to faith-based credit unions regardless of their religious affiliation. Funds to support the program come from various foundations that support religious-affiliated credit unions. The federation organizes annual Faith-Based Credit Union conferences around the country and holds that such an event illustrates the increasing strength of the faith-based movement as well as the federation's role in the movement. The most recent conference—the sixth—was held in San Francisco on June 8–11, 2005.

The work of the National Credit Union Foundation (NCUF) in promoting credit unions for African Americans is worthy of mention. Joining the Consumer Federation of America (CFA) and the Credit Union National Association (CUNA) in an investigation, the organizations reported in "New Research Shows Growing Wealth Gap" that in the past ten years the wealth gap between the poor and other Americans has been larger than their income gap. Thus, the groups initiated an America Saves campaign to help increase the wealth of lower-income individuals and families. NCUF has been especially concerned with combating payday lending and other services that exploit low-income people rather than help them. Foundations and federal agencies that joined the NCUF/CFA efforts to provide quality and affordable financial services to low-income people include the Ford Foundation, the U.S. Department of Housing and Urban Development, and the U.S. Department of the Treasury. Credit union leaders in 2004 launched a new America Saves through Credit Unions programs. America Saves through Credit Unions benefited from the success of America Saves. NCUF and CFA formed a partnership to increase the savings rates among the targeted members and to help close the wealth gap. They also encouraged the credit unions to include America Saves messages in their promotional efforts.

Led by the NCUF, the credit unions launched several new initiatives that targeted lower-income households. Sixteen broad-based local Saves campaigns were begun while others were planned. Among those operating nationally are Black America Saves, Hispanic America Saves, Faith Saves, and America Saves through Home Ownership.

For low-income blacks and such members of other groups, the Freddie Mac program is a viable option. Since Freddie Mac is keenly focused on credit unions, efforts have been made to make them successful mortgage lenders. Increasingly, credit unions are challenged to enter what has become a new frontier for them—mortgage lending. In Winston-Salem, North Carolina, Allegacy Federal Credit Union has maintained a close relationship with Freddie Mac, drawing upon its vision, insight, and expertise in the area of mortgage loans. Although Allegacy began its mortgage business in 1988, it did so with employees who were inexperienced in mortgage lending. Now Allegacy sells its mortgage loans to Freddie Mac for cash on a flow basis.

The credit union movement in the African American community has progressed from the efforts of mutual-aid and secret societies, churches, and efforts of cooperatives both in rural and urban areas. For the most part, the aim has been to encourage self-help activities in the black community. Clearly current and intense efforts of such groups as the Faith-Based Credit Union Program and the Black America Saves program continue to foster economic development in the African American community and to reduce the wealth gap between the low-income groups and those of more desirable levels of wealth.

*See also*: Consumer Cooperatives; Faith-Based Entrepreneurship

**Sources**

Citizens Community Credit Union. http://googolplex.cuna.org/timeline.html?doc_id=461&sub_id=25018.

Guzman, Jessie P., ed. *Negro Yearbook: A Review of Events Affecting Negro Life, 1941–1946.* Tuskegee, AL: Department of Records and Research, Tuskegee Institute, 1947.

———. *Negro Yearbook: A Review of Events Affecting Negro Life, 1952.* New York: William H. Wise and Co., 1952.

"Mississippi Association of Cooperatives." *About Us.* http://www.mississippiassociation.coop/id19.html.

Moody, J. Carroll, and Gilbert C. Fite. *The Credit Union Movement: Origins and Development, 1850–1970.* Lincoln: University of Nebraska Press, 1971.

"New Research Shows Growing Wealth Gap between the Poor and the Rest of America." Consumer Federation of America. Press Release, February 17, 2004. http://www.consumerfed.org/releases2.cfm?filename=cfa_ncuf_cuna_lowincome.txt.

*Frederick D. Smith*

# D

## Calvin Darden (1950– ), Shipping Company Executive

Senior vice president of operations for United Parcel Service (UPS), Calvin Darden worked his way up through the ranks. Darden's philosophy of treating people the way he wants to be treated, building respect, and living a strong work ethic has led him to success with UPS. He is eighth on *Fortune* magazine's annual list of the "50 Most Powerful Black Executives in America." Darden fits *Fortune*'s criteria for the list of executives who put their power to active use.

Darden was born in Buffalo, New York, on February 5, 1950. He graduated from Canisius College, Buffalo, New York, in 1972 with a degree in business management. In an interview in *Canisius College Magazine*, he stated that he enjoyed the rigors of the Jesuit teaching style and felt it prepared him well for his career. While in college, he began working part-time for United Parcel Service, unloading trucks. After graduation, he started full-time work with UPS.

In January 1974, he was promoted to customer service supervisor. Next, he became manager at the Buffalo hub and later managed three packaging centers. In his positions, Darden increased distribution centers efficiency, improved service, and boosted employee morale. In 1993, Darden's next promotion was to vice president and regional manager of a nine-state region, with a base in California.

In 1995, Darden became the quality coordinator and moved to UPS headquarters in Atlanta. He focused on customer satisfaction, employee empowerment, process improvement, and effective methods of measurement. In 2000, he became head of all U.S. operations.

On November 12, 1998, Darden spoke before the Columbia, South Carolina Urban League. In this speech, he advocated the "Three E's": Education, Empowerment, and Entrepreneurism. Darden stressed the importance of hiring the most educated personnel and providing continuing education opportunities for them. He stated that involving people in the company and encouraging creativity in carrying out day-to-day operations lead to continued success of the individual. And successful people within a company move that company forward.

Darden has implemented new technology that allows UPS to deliver to central points. He is responsible for the pickup and delivery of 13.5 million packages a day, serving 8 million customers. In addition to his commitment to his work life, Darden is involved in several church and community organizations. He and his wife Patricia Gail Ellis, whom he married in 1971, have raised three children, Calvin Jr., Tami, and Lorielle.

Darden is on the National Urban League board and helps run the National Urban League Black Executive Exchange Program. A February 2003 article in *Business Ethics Newsline* features a speech in which he advocates diversity leadership. One supportive program is the UPS Community Internship Program (CIP). He calls it a "sort of 'outward bound' for diversity awareness."

In the Community Internship Program, fifty managers, the top performers in midlevel management positions, are chosen to participate. The fifty interns go into communities where problems such as poverty, homelessness, spousal abuse, drugs, and crime are rampant. The interns live in the community under Spartan conditions for a month. They work on projects seven days a week tutoring preschool Head Start children, orphans, or kids with AIDS (acquired immunodeficiency syndrome). They may also teach prisoners resume skills, visit nursing homes and mental health facilities, work in soup kitchens, and do minor home repairs.

Darden has been through the program along with more than 1,200 other UPS managers since the program started in 1968. Darden states in *Executive Speeches* for June–July 2003 that "the interns are often initially shocked by the challenging living conditions, but many report seeing the hopefulness of people trying to cope." Interns "return to work if not changed people, people with changed perspectives." He says that they are less rigid in looking at employee issues and tend to listen with more empathy, which leads to understanding and improving employee relations. Some may become more involved in their communities and organize volunteers both at work and in private life. Darden states that CIP "gets the student to teach him or herself through living the experience." He says, "It unlocks an attic in the mind of well-intentioned people that may only be accessible by taking the time to walk in someone else's shoes."

Darden focuses on economic opportunities for African Americans. In a speech to the Greater Baltimore Urban League, published in vol. 7 of *Executive Speeches* he talked about developing a shared vision for economic empowerment. In the speech, he advocated vision and commitment. He cited a study by the Milken Institute that concludes that "economic growth can't be sustained without the inclusion of minority businesses and an infusion of capital into those businesses."

UPS, Darden says, provides economic opportunities through its Supplier Diversity network. UPS partners with minority- and women-owned businesses. Another program Darden supports is a college education tuition incentive. The Metro College Program provides tuition-free education for part-time UPS employees through a cooperative effort of state and local governments and UPS. Darden stresses in *Executive Speeches* for 2003 that "partnerships between business and governments provide economic empowerment." Darden is placed number 8 on *Fortune* magazine's "50 Most Powerful Black Executives" list. He credits his success to being willing to start in an entry-level position, to work long hours, and to move when necessary.

Darden retired in March 2005, after a thirty-three-year career. He has directed U.S. operations for the past seven years and has been a member of the UPS Board of Directors since 2001.

Business Wire for February 9, 2005, quotes UPS chairman and chief executive officer Mike Eskew, who said, "Cal Darden has made outstanding contributions to this company and to this Board and will be greatly missed." He continued, "The legacy of his 33 years is one of leadership and operational excellence. It's also a legacy of friendship, commitment, integrity and high standards. He raised the bar for all of us."

**Sources**

Brennan, Carol. "Calvin Darden." *Contemporary Black Biography*. Vol. 38. Farmington Hills, MI: Gale, 2003.

Browka, Audrey R. (Alumni Profile.) *Canisius College Magazine* (Winter 2001): 26–27.

Business Wire. February 9, 2005. Lexisnexis.com/universe. http://www.canisius.edu/alumni/magazine/winter2001/default.asp.

"Delivering on Diversity Leadership: A Walk in the Other Guy's Shoes." February 25, 2003, Calvin Darden speech before the Southern Institute for Business and Professional Ethics. http://www.globalethics.org/newsline/members/issue.tmpl?articleid=0317016434579.

*Executive Speeches* 15 (December 2000–January 2001): 37.

——— 17 (June–July 2003): 20.

History Makers. "BusinessMakers: Calvin Darden." http://www.thehistorymakers.com/biography.asp?bioindex=74/&category=businessMakers.

*Who's Who among African Americans*. 18th ed. Detroit: Thomson Gale, 2005.

*Virginia D. Bailey*

# Edward Davis (1911–1999), Automobile Dealer

After owning a creative and successful used car business in Detroit, Edward "Ed" Davis became the first African American to own and operate a new car dealership for one of America's "Big Three" automakers. He overcame racial prejudice in many areas, from commercial lending practices to denial of an automobile franchise. His latest reward came near the end of his life, when he was inducted into the Automotive Hall of Fame.

One of ten children, Davis was born in Shreveport, Louisiana, on February 27, 1911. He was influenced early on by his father, Thomas H. Davis, who had a large-scale catering business and served oil-pipeline construction workers with Standard Oil Company. Young Davis knew that he wanted to own his own business and that entrepreneurship was a means to economic freedom. His mother, Hester Bryant Davis, died when he was ten years old. When he was a teenager, he envisioned that life would be better in Detroit, where racial conditions were better than they were in Louisiana. His father approved his move to Detroit, where he lived with an aunt and enrolled in Cass Technical High School. His plan was to become an account, but he reconsidered when a white teacher told him that practically no African Americans entered that profession at that time.

Davis sought work as an automobile repairman. At first he was hired in exchange for bus fare, or twenty cents a day for the ten-mile trip. The work gave him invaluable experience that would serve him well later on. This was in the middle of the Great Depression, when the few jobs that were available went to white men. He persuaded a gas station proprietor to allow him to wash cars for his customers. A Dodge assembly plant supervisor was so impressed with the way the energetic young man worked that he offered him a regular job. Davis worked in the foundry and later as a machine operator. He cashed his first paycheck at a check-cashing vendor and vowed that he would never pay for such a service again. The next week he opened a bank account and thereafter cashed checks at his bank; he also deposited from $2.00 to $3.00 each week.

He continued to work at Dodge and began to sell cars for a local Chrysler dealer. He left his job at Dodge in 1935 and worked full-time as a car salesman; he also continued to build his bank account. By 1936, Davis was making from $500 to $600 monthly. He enrolled in the night program at Wayne State University and studied business administration. Racial prejudice at the business was so difficult to endure that he used his savings of $2,900 and opened his own used-car business in 1938—Davis Motor Sales.

Despite the economic conditions that existed during the depression and the racial discrimination that he endured, Davis's business was successful from the start. He persuaded car dealers to allow him to have one car to put on his lot. Reluctantly, they agreed and gave him cars that they were unable to sell, and he sold them. Next, he purchased a vacant building and paid off the land contract that he had been given in about five years. His business continued to prosper, and soon he handled almost every make of car. The property was located near downtown Detroit, where his business remained until 1963.

In 1940, Davis became a franchised Studebaker dealer, added a service department, and retained his used-car business. Since no new cars were manufactured between 1942 until 1946 due to World War II, he concentrated on his used cars and on his service department. He also maintained Studebakers for the U.S. Army, which had a large depot near his place of business. So substantial was his business with the army that he received a draft deferment because his work was deemed essential to the war effort.

## AWARDED CHRYSLER-PLYMOUTH FRANCHISE

Studebaker closed its company in 1956, and Davis relied on his used-car and automobile service business as his means of support. He was also vice president of a Ford dealership. In 1963, he learned that Chrysler-Plymouth was searching for qualified businessmen; race was not an issue. Davis was approved and opened the dealership with his own money, not that of Chrysler-Plymouth. He relocated his business from the downtown facility to the west side of Detroit, on Dexter and Elmhurst, and opened Ed Davis Chrysler-Plymouth in late 1963, becoming the first African American to be awarded a new car franchise from one of America's top three automakers. The "Big Three," as they were called, were General Motors, Ford, and Chrysler.

Detroit underwent a change in 1967, when riots devastated much of the commercial property. His business was left intact. When the riots were quelled, however, white-owned businesses opened the way for African Americans to join their staffs, thus cutting into the pool of good staff for Davis. In fact, white companies raided Davis's business and took sales-persons, mechanics, and supervisors. A combination of problems that included vandalism, unavailability of staff, increasing insurance costs, and unionized sales led to the end of his business in February 1971.

Determined to use his expertise to benefit others, Davis started a training program for entrepreneurs and managers. In October 1971 he joined Detroit's mass-transit authority as manager of the Department of Street Railway (DSR) Systems. He led the system out of inefficiency and waste, strengthened its financial base, and improved employee morale. He retired and from 1974 to 1994 provided consultant services to minority automobile dealers and black business owners.

In 1979, Davis wrote his autobiography, *One Man's Way*. He was honored in 1993 when the National Association of Minority Automobile Dealers established a Pioneer Award and a scholarship in his name. He was honored again in 1999, when he was the first African American inductee into the Automobile Hall of Fame.

Davis married Mary Agnes Miller in the late 1930s. He died in Detroit on May 3, 1999. He is remembered as a leading citizen of Detroit, a successful automobile dealer, and one who shared his expertise in the field of business with others.

*See also*: Minority Businesses in Major Cities

**Sources**

Brennan, Carol. "Ed Davis." *Contemporary Black Biography*. Vol. 24. Ed. Shirelle Phelps. Detroit: Gale, 2001.

Davis, Ed. *One Man's Way*. Detroit: Ed Davis Associates, 1979.

"Ed Davis, First Black Auto Dealer, Honored in Detroit." *Jet* 95 (February 1, 1999): 46–48.

Obituaries. *New York Times*, May 5, 1999.

Seder, John, and Berkeley G. Burrell. *Getting It Together: Black Businessmen in America*. New York: Harcourt Brace Jovanovich, 1971.

*Frederick D. Smith*

# Erroll B. Davis Jr. (1944– ), Public Utility Official

Erroll B. Davis Jr. believes in competition in all he does, whether on the tennis court, the golf course, or in the boardroom. His competitive nature enabled him to climb the corporate ladder of a *Business Week* 1000 company and become the only African American to head a major public utility. Davis, a self-proclaimed workaholic, frequently finds the time to go into the field to check quality control, to write handwritten letters of commendation to employees, and to give motivational speeches to minority teens affected by drugs, abuse, and broken homes.

Born in Pittsburg to working-class parents, according to Lisa Jones in an article in *Ebony*, Davis was greatly inspired by his grandfather, remembered as "strong, giving and dignified." He received his bachelor of science in electrical engineering from Carnegie Mellon University and a master's of business administration from the University of Chicago. During junior high, Davis befriended his wife-to-be, Elaine, an academic adviser at the University of Wisconsin, Madison, and fourteen years later that friendship sparked into romance. The couple has two children, Christopher and Whitney.

Davis began his career with positions at Ford Motor Company and the Xerox Corporation as a financial executive; it was not until 1978 that he ventured into the utilities industry, when he moved to Madison, Wisconsin, and accepted a position as vice president of finance with Wisconsin Power and Light (WPL). Within ten years, he had moved from his first position to executive vice president to a member of the board of directors to president of WPL's gas, electric, and water utility, and finally, to the post of chief executive. Two years later, in 1990, he was appointed president and chief executive of WPL's parent company, WPL Holdings, Inc.

In 1998, WPL Holdings merged with IES Industries, Inc. and Interstate Power Company to form Alliant Energy Corporation, which provides utilities to more than half a million consumers in Wisconsin.

Davis is considered an innovator and has shifted Alliant's conservative policies to hard-hitting competition in order to gain an advantage in the industry. To his employees, he does not appear the ruthless executive normally associated with competitive managers—he is considered personable, thoughtful, and hands-on. The majority of Alliant's employees call him by his first name, are invited to brown-bag lunches to discuss the company, and receive handwritten notes of appreciation. He biannually accompanies front-line employees into the field to maintain quality control and monitor workers' concerns.

Bimonthly, Davis meets with his top twelve executives to discuss short- and long-term goals. He also puts the company before himself: In 2002, he and six other top executives skipped their annual bonuses for the next two years to cut costs. In light of the Enron and WorldCom scandals, Davis has taken a proactive step in Alliant's auditing procedures: Lead time for audits was reduced 66 percent, and he doubled the number of audits a year in order to create a more efficient system.

As an African American executive, Davis has strived to create career paths for minorities within Alliant, which has had problems retaining non-whites. He admits that diversity is a problem, but not more than at any other large company. Alliant has also implemented internship programs for minorities, and the minority managers heavily recruit African Americans. The issue of diversity has also touched Davis in his personal life—being in the public light, he does not drink or smoke and strives to be a role model.

While Davis does not consider himself an activist, because of his busy work schedule, he does reach out to the minority community in Madison. In addition to speaking to underprivileged teens, both Davis and his wife supported diversity at the University of Wisconsin by bestowing minority scholarships. Davis is a director of the Edison Electric Institute, Electric Power Research Institute, Wisconsin Manufacturers and Commerce Association, Association of Edison Illuminating Companies, Federal Reserve Bank of Chicago, American Society of Corporate Executives, BP p.l.c, PPG Industries, Inc., and Union Pacific Corporation. In addition, he is a lifetime member on the Carnegie Mellon University and the U.S. Olympic Committee Boards.

**Sources**

Electricity Advisory Board. "Errol B. Davis, Jr." http://www.eab.energy.gov/index.cfm?fuseaction=home.biographies#davis.

"Errol B. Davis." *World-Generation-Class of 2003.* http://www.world-gen.com/class03/davis.html.

"Erroll B. Davis, Jr." http://www.usocpressbox.org/usoc/pressbox.nsf/(staticreports)/Breaking+News/$File/ErrollDavis.pdf?Open.

Jones, Lisa C. "Winning the Power Game—Erroll B. Davis Jr., Head of WPL Holdings Inc." *Ebony* 50 (November 1994): 70. http://www.findarticles.com/p/articles/mi_m1077/is_n1_v50/ai_15885848.

*Who's Who among African Americans.* 18th ed. Detroit: Gale, 2005.

*Thura Mack*

# Thomas Day (1801–1861), Cabinet- and Furniture Maker, Woodworker, Woodcarver

A free black in North Carolina, Thomas Day operated one of North Carolina's largest furniture industries and was highly regarded through the

South as one of its finest cabinet- and furniture makers. He operated his furniture businesses between 1827 and 1859. A skilled craftsman, his services were in great demand. Among his primary clients in the state were the governor and distinguished families. He was as astute in his business dealings as he was in his craft and reportedly became one of the wealthiest free blacks in the area of Milton, North Carolina, where he operated his businesses.

While sources vary on the place and date of his birth and the facts of his early life, most agree that he was born in Halifax County, Virginia, near Petersburg, in 1801. Although his parents' names remain unknown, his mother was freed in North Carolina. His father was a cabinetmaker and may have had some influence on the craft that Thomas Day would practice later on. He may have practiced cabinetry in 1818 while living in Virginia, where he is said to have opened a shop. Some sources claim that the Day family moved to North Carolina in 1817. Whatever the case, his early experiences enabled him to read well and to write in elegant penmanship.

During the first quarter of the nineteenth century, cabinetmaking was a prosperous business in North Carolina. Many free blacks in the state were entrepreneurs, working as artisans and tanners. Although Milton—where Day now lived—was in the center of wealthy tobacco farming in the state, it was also the home for many cabinetmakers. Day may have been an apprentice in one of these shops and learned or enhanced the art of cabinetmaking at that time. By 1827, however, he opened a shop on Milton's Main Street, across from the local post office, having paid $550 cash for the facility. He ventured into a series of enterprises between 1827 and 1850. He was an investor, purchasing stock in a local agency of the state bank in 1834. In 1848 he purchased Union Tavern, sometimes known as the Yellow Tavern, which had a reputation as one of the state's largest and finest taverns. It became his workshop as well as his residence; later on he expanded the building by adding a two-story wing to the gabled brick building. Altogether he invested $5,800 in the facility—a considerable sum at that time. Day expanded his workforce by twelve. A slave owner, Day used his two slaves both in his furniture shop and on the farm that he owned and operated. He also apprenticed white bondservants and was said to have more apprentices in his shop than any other businesses in the state at that time. Since Day lived in a high-farm area, known for its tobacco crop, he extended his enterprise to include a 270-acre farm.

The distinctive furniture that Thomas Day crafted consisted of bedsteads, benches, French sofas, chairs, chests, footstools, and tables. Often the pieces were carved and/or included other minute details, giving further evidence of his skill. He also built coffins, stairways, and rooms with interior trim. The chief materials used were mahogany, walnut, and oak—all available in North Carolina's woods. Some of his mahogany was imported from the West Indies.

Day sold directly to his clients, who were prominent families, wealthy tobacco growers, and politicians; for example, North Carolina governor David S. Reed, who held office from 1851 to 1854, was a chief customer and placed sizable orders with him. His work with educational institutions included the

University of North Carolina at Chapel Hill, where he built shelving for the Philanthropic and Dialetic societies. His work with religious institutions included Milton Presbyterian Church, a church with a racially mixed congregation where he and his family regularly attended and where Day served as elder.

On January 7, 1830, Day married Aquilla Wilson, a free black Virginian who at that time, could not move to North Carolina due to the state's immigration law of 1827 that would not allow her in the state. Day's clients, who already valued his work and saw him as one whom whites could trust, came to his support and had North Carolina's General Assembly waive the law in this case, finally abolishing it on December 31 that year. They had three children—Mary Ann, Devreaux, and Thomas Jr., who were all educated in Wilbraham, Massachusetts, at Wilbraham & Monson Academy. Again, racial restrictions in North Carolina would not allow education for free blacks, causing the Days to educate their children elsewhere. After Day's business suffered from the economic crisis of 1857 and nearly closed, his son, Thomas Jr., bought him out and ran the shop until 1871. Thomas Sr. had died ten years earlier, sometime in 1861. Later Thomas Jr. moved to Asheville and married the head of Stevens School in Washington, D.C. He relocated to Seattle, operated furniture business, and later died a tragic death. Mary Ann Day married Luke Dorland, who founded Scotia Seminary, a school for blacks located in Salisbury, North Carolina. Devreaux Day became president of a company in South America and succumbed of an unidentified fever.

Thomas Day was a well-built man with a commanding appearance. He was unassuming and unaffected by his skill, wealth, and statue in the community. He was deeply religious and considered fairly well educated by standards of his time. Day's legend survives in the re-creation of his furniture by Craftique company as well as in the original pieces that are housed at the North Carolina State Museum of History in Raleigh, at historically black North Carolina Agricultural and Technical State University in Greensboro, the Greensboro Historical Museum, and in private homes in the South. In 1929, some of his masterpieces that were extant were in the hands of G. G. Donoho and included a small mahogany side table covered with a marble top, seven small mahogany chairs that may have accompanied the side table, and a writing table. There were claims that Day's furniture was scattered all over North Carolina but concentrated in Greensboro, Durham, Raleigh, Fayetteville, Charlotte, and Winston-Salem.

**Sources**

Barfield, Rodney. "Thomas Day." *Thomas Day, Cabinetmaker: An Exhibition of the North Carolina Museum of History*. Raleigh: North Carolina Museum of History, Department of Cultural Resources, 1975.

Day, Tom, and Mary E. Lyon. *Master of Mahogany: Tom Day, Free Black Cabinetmaker*. Glenview, IL: Scott, Foresman, 1995.

Franklin, John Hope. *The Free Negro in North Carolina 1790–1860*. Chapel Hill: University of North Carolina Press, 1943.

Kranz, Rachel. *African-American Business Leaders and Entrepreneurs (A to Z of African Americans)*. New York: Facts on File, 2004.

Logan, Rayford W., and Michael R. Winston, eds. *Dictionary of American Negro Biography*. New York: W. W. Norton, 1982.

*Jessie Carney Smith*

# Suzanne de Passe (1947– ), Music and Film Producer and Executive, Screenwriter, Talent Coordinator, Educator

Suzanne de Passe is best known for her part in Motown Productions Company, grassroots for the careers of such music icons as Diana Ross, Lionel Ritchie, Marvin Gaye, and Jackson Five. While de Passe's seminal starts revolve around music, the fifty-nine-year-old visionary has been involved in the film industry via production of prime-time music shows such as *Motown 25: Yesterday, Today, Forever*, which was a source for winning an Emmy in 1982, as well as the NAACP (National Association for the Advancement of Colored People) Image Awards. De Passe's interaction with film transcends the production arena into the conceptualization and writing process, hence the Academy Award nomination for her efforts in cowriting *Lady Sings the Blues* in 1972. Beyond this feat in film, her most notable success story lies within her creative development and business savvy needed to manifest the final project of the mini series *Lonesome Dove*, which was awarded a Peabody, a Golden Globe, and an Emmy. So great was de Passe's notoriety that she garnered attention from the academic world. As noted in *Harvard Business Review* online, Harvard University began a series of case studies based on her business leadership style in 1997, and ultimately in 2002 she was asked to become a part of the faculty as the AOL Time Warner Professor in the Department of Radio, Television and Film at one of America's most prestigious institutions of higher education, Howard University in Washington, D.C.

De Passe was born in Harlem, New York, in 1947 to her parents, a schoolteacher and account executive for Seagrams, who divorced when the young de Passe was three years old. Regardless of the challenges stereotypically attached to such family dynamics, she was nurtured by a solid family structure. She attended Lincoln School, one of New York's finest private schools, which provided a diverse makeup. De Passe admits to receiving the essential skills— "opinion, analysis"—to survive in any industry while studying at Lincoln. Her literary abilities led her to attend Manhattan Community College in 1966, where she studied English. De Passe surprisingly ended her collegiate career shortly thereafter, beginning her career as a music talent scout for the Cheetah Club—a local dance club on New York's night scene.

This opportunity afforded de Passe the tools needed to hone her visionary abilities: She was responsible for assessing acts based on their skills and appeal to the public as well as basic management of these acts. In conjunction with learning the skeleton of music management at this time, de Passe made use of the networks availed to her. Cindy Birdsong, of the Supremes, is credited with introducing de Passe to **Barry Gordy Jr.**—former Motown Productions owner. In time, she was given the opportunity to be Gordy's creative assistant in 1968. The early stages of her career with Gordy were trying at times; Gordy recalls that stage as being tear-filled for de Passe as she learned to aptly handle the pressures of the industry. De Passe herself admits to crying for the first decade of her work because she had to fight ageism even then; the youthful looking de Passe was constantly suspected to be a groupie and thus hassled by security and other stage managers when managing acts. With a budget increase from $12 million to $65 million in a nine-year span after taking over Motown's TV/Film sector in 1980, it can be said that de Passe triumphed over perceptions of backstage security and those who control the production of stories that promote the value of African American life. In spite of her intensely busy life, de Passe found time to start a family with actor Paul Le Mat in 1978. Unfortunately the union was later dissolved.

Her work has been a contribution not only to age issues; it has broadened racial and feminist trajectories for the entertainment industry, so much so that *Ms.*—a reliable source for informing the public of the advancement and support of women's development (personal, political, or business) in America—highlighted de Passe after her triumph in a primarily white male world with the production of *Lonesome Dove*.

While many Hollywood producers, primarily male, failed to see the potential of *Lonesome Dove*, an insightful de Passe made the connection and secured rights for the novel at the meager price of $50,000 before its Pulitzer Award–winning status. This action resulted in a profit for those involved. The visionary recalls how an unintended meeting with Gloria Steinem led to dinner with author Larry McMurty; the event led to de Passe reading the novel piecemeal. McMurty was surprised by her offer to make his book (one that even his agent could not sell to Hollywood) into a film. De Passe enthusiastically assured the author that her interests in a western, a film genre Hollywood deemed trite, were valid based on an endearing memory of her grandfather, who took her to a rodeo when she was four. She recalls in *Media Week*, "I had this little fringe skirt, two pearl handled pistols and a hat." While this action may be judged to be romantic and void of business sense considering Hollywood's treatment of westerns at the time, it testifies to de Passe's commitment to the creative process and her visionary gift, which allows her to see beyond the constraints.

It is arguable that de Passe has surpassed Hollywood's tendency to be profit focused alone. She has joined efforts that produced shows that families can watch with ease, for example, *Lonesome Dove* and its subsequent specials; *The Temptations*, a quasi-documentary based on the memoir from the late Otis Williams, which in 1998 garnered an Emmy nomination; and syndicated shows on WB—*Sister, Sister*, beginning in 1993, and *The Smart*

*Guy*, beginning in 1997. Her values also pronounce her commitment to the African American community. *The Temptations* telefilm "puts black men in front of the audience who are multidimensional," said de Passe in *Media Week*. Imbuing black males with human characteristics consisting of successes and failures amid cultural demonization of them is also a part of de Passe's legacy.

She is unafraid of controversy, which is evident when considering the production of *The Temptations*. Despite popular disagreement with her approval of using Philadelphia as the set instead of Detroit, owing to budget constraints, or the lawsuit from David Ruffin's family because the script depicted his death caused by addiction to drugs, de Passe proceeded with production. Even when the miniseries was threatened to never appear on the network, de Passe was wise enough to seek assistance from miniseries guru Hallmark Entertainment. Amid hostile rumors that before Hallmark's involvement de Passe's leadership was unstable, there are testimonies from sources such as Temptations' manager Shelly Berger, who claims de Passe's organization and guidance made the unforeseeable a reality.

Risk taking is a natural act for de Passe, who managed to convince Gordy to take interest in the Jackson Five in 1968. Gordy, in his mentorship, granted her space to make mistakes in the early years, and it has made a difference. This same energy spawned her move from Motown Productions in 1988; she eventually started her own company in 1992.

In 2004, de Passe was aptly given the **Madam C. J. Walker** award from *Ebony*'s annual Outstanding Women in Marketing and Communications committee, commemorating her contribution to the business world on behalf of African Americans, in particular African American women. Other recipients were L. Marilyn Crawford, president and chief executive officer of PRIMETIME ONMIMEDIA, and Susan Mboya, associate director of African-American Multicultural Business Development at Procter & Gamble. Her accolades continue with the American Film Institute's Producer of the Year Award in 1995. In the corresponding press release, more of de Passe's community involvement was listed: board membership at the American Film Institute as well as at the L.A. Opera. In 2003, she also received the Whitney M. Young Jr. award, which is the highest honor receivable from the Los Angeles Urban league. Her accomplishments are not only personal but communal as well. Other prestigious recognitions include her induction into the Black Filmmaker's Hall of Fame in 1990 and placement in the Legacy of Women in Film and Television in 1992. De Passe's legacy extends beyond awards. In an interview with Gail Mitchell of *Billboard*, de Passe articulated, "For so long I've been told, 'we want more minorities, but we can't find anybody.' I want to help." And she is. De Passe is the epitome of diversity via her roles as producer (movie/music/TV), writer, and educator; she also promotes the inclusion of minorities on America's silver screen while managing to do projects beyond the *Lonesome Dove* spin-off *Buffalo Girls*. Among her many other responsibilities as president of her own company and professor at Howard University, de Passe is said to be the current executive producer for the upcoming miniseries based on the Negro Baseball League, started in Kansas City. Like Walker, de Passe has been resilient and successful. Her career is marked with a commitment to promoting African American involvement in the entertainment industry not only as faces on the silver screen but as creators and producers as well.

*See also*: Women and Business

**Sources**

Alley, Robert S., and Irby B. Brown. "Suzanne de Passe." *Women Television Producers: Transformation of the Male Medium*. Ed. Robert S. Alley and Irby B. Brown. Rochester, NY: University of Rochester Press, 2001.

Button, Graham. "The Golden Dove." *Forbes* 143 (1989): 58.

Castro, Janice. "Hitsville Goes Hollywood; Motown Hopes to Bring Its Golden Touch to Films and Television." *Time* 133 (1989): 51.

"Ebony Honors Outstanding Women in Marketing and Communications." *Ebony* 59 (June 2004): 104.

Jarmon, Laura C. "Suzanne de Passe." *Powerful Black Women*. Ed. Jessie Carney Smith. Detroit: Visible Ink, 1996.

Johnson, Lisa. "Negro Baseball League to Be Subject of Mini." *FilmStew*, January 25, 2005. http://www.filmstew.com/Content/Article.asp?ContentID=10645&Pg=1.

Mitchell, Gail. "De Passe Speaks Out: CEO Keeps Her Finger on the Pulse and to the Ground." *Billboard* (June 2003): 21.

Reynonds, Rhonda. "25 Black Women Who Have Made a Difference in Business." *Black Enterprise* 25 (1994): 76.

Roberts, L. "Lady Sings the Blues." *Newsweek* 132 (1998): 48.

Sharkey, Betsy. "Ball of Confusion." *Media Week* 8 (1998): 32.

"Suzanne de Passe." Lexis Nexis Academic, 2005. http://web.lexis-nexis.com/universe.

"Suzanne de Passe, Production Executive: She Gave Lonesome Dove Its Wings." *People Weekly* (Spring 1991): 64.

*Althea Tait*

# "Diddy." *See* Sean "Diddy" Combs

# "P. Diddy." *See* Sean "Diddy" Combs

# Charles Diggs Jr. (1922–1998), Politician, Mortician

Charles Diggs was the first African American voted into Congress from Michigan. His influential career changed Congress from the inside out, as he founded the Congressional Black Caucus when minorities were a marginal presence on Capitol Hill: He was in the company of only two other African Americans, Adam Clayton Powell of New York and William Dawson of Chicago, at the time.

Diggs was born on December 2, 1922, into a prominent African American family. At a time in America's history when blacks were seeking equality and basic civil rights, Diggs's father, Charles Diggs Sr., operated his own mortuary business in an area that refused to bury African Americans. Diggs Sr. was also a member of the Michigan State Senate. Being his father's only son, in fact only child, Diggs Jr. followed in his father's footsteps and was highly successful as well.

He was educated at Miller High School in Detroit, which led him to attend the University of Michigan at Ann Arbor, where he completed two years of schooling (1940–1942). In 1942, he attended Fisk University for one year before serving his country in the U.S. Army from 1943 to 1945. He eventually completed a degree at Wayne College of Mortuary Science in 1946. Diggs's education was unceasing. After completing his degree in mortuary science, he studied law at the Detroit College of Law in 1950. In 1954 he began his federal governmental career when he was elected to Congress within the Democratic Party.

Considering that in 1944 as a military officer he had to use the backdoor to a restaurant in Alabama, Diggs was proactive in the war against racial injustice. He inaugurated his work in Congress by attending the Emmett Tills trial, which became a catalyst for the civil rights movement and those concerned with the racial issues at hand. Diggs eventually convinced President Dwight D. Eisenhower of the need for a congressional session focused on the issue of race relations in America at the time.

While Diggs's career is a legacy for African American people, in particular politicians and political reformers, it is not without controversy. Like many prominent African American political reformers—W.E.B. Du Bois and **Marcus Garvey**—Diggs found himself involved with legal proceedings. He was accused of inappropriate spending of over $60,000 and eventually convicted for his acts.

He gave a forty-page account of why certain employees of his were paid a greater amount so that they could pay for some of his personal expenses. He readily admitted that he had been in financial constraints, and some of his employees volunteered to help him. The result was a premeditated plan on Diggs's part, which he claimed had no mark on his conscience because he did not know he was committing a crime. He was so convinced of his stance that after two years of appeals he undauntingly planned to run for office after the controversy in 1978. Eventually he conceded to the charges and convictions, resigning from office in 1980 and turning himself over to serve his prison sentence.

Ironically, while censured by Congress in 1978 because of the aforementioned acts, Diggs was reelected by popular vote. The inconsistency between Congress and America's public remains. While many reported Diggs's early retirement as a disgrace and gave him a sentence of shame beyond the seven months served of his three-year term of imprisonment, there were others who continued to value his wisdom. Some time after his release from prison, Diggs was asked to return to Washington as a consultant to the Congressional Black Caucus.

In August 1998, Diggs died of a stroke. At his funeral, which over 600 guests attended, prominent spokespersons commented on Diggs's life. According to *Jet* magazine for September 1998, Andrew Young, civil rights advocate and politician, noted Diggs as one who "bore the cross not expected of a Congressman" by extending support and a voice to the Emmett Till case, to the racially charged city of Selma, and to the apartheid-torn South Africa when it was not a popular cause.

Diggs was so dedicated to ending injustice for African Americans that his cause became Pan-African; he offered his greatest support to these concerns as the first African American chair of the Foreign Affairs Subcommittee within the House of Representatives. Diggs is also known for his part in the Home Rule Act of 1973 for the district of Columbia that his former press secretary and sole Diggsean biographer Carolyn P. Dubose argues was his legacy. Home rule was initiated in 1973 while Diggs was House District Committee chairperson. The bill gave the district the right to govern itself within certain limits that caused Congress to be the immediate authority. Despite the bill affecting the district's budget, in particular, it gave residents the opportunity to elect the mayor and city council—an act that had not been done since 1874. Although Congress amended the bill post September 11, it retained congressional power over the district's spending amid spirited opposition from lobbyists and their unrepresented citizens. Some argue that despite the restrictions of the bill its primary originator, Diggs, used it as a lateral movement for more serious causes such as South Africa and the district itself. Others intimate that it was commonly known as the "Diggs Compromise." All of his political moves were not tinged with doubt. After the murder of Black Panther members in Chicago and that of two students at Mississippi's Jackson State, Diggs spearheaded investigations. He also convinced Eisenhower to visit two integrated schools in Little Rock, Arkansas, while on a goodwill tour.

His popularity reigned beyond America. Missouri representative William Lacy Clay recalls a visit to Sierra Leone, cited by Irvin Molotsky in the *New York Times*: "The plane was due to arrive at 8 o'clock at night. We were delayed until 1 A.M., but there were 10,000 people still there waiting at the airport to greet us." Because of his Pan-African efforts, he was delegated to the United Nations, which ended in late 1971 when Diggs made a statement with his resignation because America reportedly sold arms to South Africa and Portugal as well as the U.S. government, securing Rhodesian chrome.

Diggs's legacy extends itself beyond politics. After serving his sentence for a court conviction based on nineteen counts of fraud, he attended Howard University, earning a degree in political science. His life is marked by a continual interest in education. After a tumultuous career in politics, he became a scholar in the area he had practiced for twenty-six years. Never leaving his grassroots of protest against injustice, Diggs did not allow his setbacks to become permanent. He decided to open a funeral home in one of Maryland's areas that lacked a selection of funeral services run by African Americans who would serve African Americans, doubly following in his father's footsteps. After the state's funeral board refused to grant him a license in 1982, he appealed the ruling and won.

Even while serving his sentence at Maxwell Air Force Base Prison in Alabama, he edited the periodical *Hard Times*. Despite being caught between the poles of legacy and disgrace, Diggs stated to Edward Sargent of the *Washington Post*, "What has sustained me most is the support and understanding from the black community. It has offset what might have been a demoralizing experience."

## Sources

Booker, Simeon. "A News Media Report That Widow Darlene Diggs Was Preparing to Release the First 'Tell All Book.'" *Jet* 106 (September 27, 2004): 20.

"Charles Diggs, Former Michigan." CNN All Politics. August 25, 1998. http://www.cnn.com/ALLPOLITICS/1998/08/25/ap/diggs.obit.

"Diggs Will Run Again and Seek Former Post." *New York Times*, January 19, 1980.

Dubose, Carolyn P. *The Untold Story of Charles Diggs: The Public Figure, the Private Man.* Arlington, VA: Barton Publishing House, 1999.

Everett, Kay. "Blacks Also Made Great Contributions to Detroit." http://www.detnews.com/2001/detroit/0101/24/s09-179021.htm.

"Hundreds Pay Tribute to Late Rep. Charles Diggs' Civil Rights Record at Maryland Ceremony." *Jet* 94 (1998): 18.

King, Colbert I. "Democracy for the District, Too." *Washington Post*, September 29, 2001.

Molotsky, Irvin. "Charles Diggs, 75, Congressman Censured Over Kickbacks." *New York Times*, August 16, 1998.

Ragsdale, Bruce A., and Joel D. Treese. *Black Americans in Congress 1870–1989.* Washington, DC: U.S. Government Printing Office, 1990.

Sargent, Edward D. "Graduate Charles Diggs Looks to Future." *Washington Post*, May 14, 1983.

U.S. Office of the General Counsel of the District of Columbia. "District of Columbia Home Rule Act." http://www.abfa.com/ogc/hrtall.htm.

Washington, Adrienne T. "'Mr. Africa' Was Critical to Home Rule's Birth." *Washington Times*, September 1, 1998.

"When the House Is No Longer Home." *Newsweek* 99 (January 18, 1982): 21.

*Althea Tait*

# Don't Buy Where You Can't Work Movement (1929–1941)

The purchasing power of black America was seen early on as one of the benefits of employment; such power had an important affect on the American economy. There have been many efforts in history to address the economic potential of a race and to help the unemployed or underemployed or simply denied employment due to race. Thus, in 1929 former prizefighter Big Bill Tate joined A. C. O'Neal, editor of a Chicago newspaper, the *Whip*, and organized a boycott of white merchants in Chicago who failed to hire blacks. During the Great Depression of the 1930s, the movement, which had been successful in Chicago, spread quickly across the country to major cities and became a major form of black activism. It was variously called the "Don't Buy Where You Can't Work" movement, "Jobs for Negroes Movement," or "Don't Spend Your Money Where You Can't Work" or took on other titles in different cities. It became the forerunner of the black economic boycotts of the modern civil rights movement.

The "Don't Buy Where You Can't Work" movement spread, becoming known variously in other major cities: the Future Outlook League (Cleveland, Ohio), the New Negro Alliance (Washington, D.C., 1933), the Colored Clerks Circle (St. Louis, 1929), the movement led by Prophet Kiowa Costonie (Baltimore, 1933), the *Sentinel* efforts (Los Angeles, 1934), "Don't Buy Where You Can't Work" (led by the Atlanta *World*, 1934), and the **Citizens' League for Fair Play** (New York City). Important branches of the movement were seen also in Philadelphia (led by the Urban League), Pittsburgh, Boston, and Richmond. In time, smaller cities such as Evansville, Indiana, and Alliance, Ohio, had branches of the movement. By the time the movement subsided in World War II, some thirty-five cities had joined in the organized boycotts and picket lines to seek economic and social equality.

The "Don't Buy" movement was promoted by the "Double Duty Dollar" doctrine that was preached each week from the pulpits of many black churches in what was known as "Bronzeville," or the black section of Chicago. According to St. Clair Drake and Horace R. Cayton in *Black Metropolis*, black minister Gordon B. Hancock, whose column appeared in several black newspapers, is credited with popularizing the term. Other speakers and writers in Chicago began to use the term as well. Church newspapers also promoted the Double Duty Dollar campaign, just as they advertised various black businesses, from "chicken shacks" to corset shops. Church congregations and at times participants in mass meetings were told the virtues of shopping at black enterprises to make the dollar do double duty—that is, to help the business financially and to advance the race.

Various activities grew out of the "Don't Buy" campaign and the Double Duty Dollar concept. There were organized boycotts, trade pack agreements, and block-by-block picketing. The campaigns were more aggressive in northern cities than those in the South, where individual boycotts replaced large, organized protests. In Atlanta, for example, individual boycotts of a white grocery forced the store out of business and also resulted in black employment in some white stores.

According to Abram L. Harris in *The Negro as Capitalist*, no record of the number of jobs that resulted from the "Don't Buy" movement has been shown. "In Washington, D.C., the total number is reputed to be less than seventy-five," he wrote. On the other hand, movements in New York City and Baltimore were headed "to achieve national scope." Some white merchants in Maryland, however, sought a legal end to the pickets and boycotts and took the issue to court. According to the black newspaper the *Afro-American* for April 13, 1935, cited in *The Negro as Capitalist*, the Court of Appeals of Maryland gave a ruling that "enhanced the prestige of the movement" and supported its philosophy. Accordingly, the court sanctioned "the general purpose of colored persons to improve the condition of their race" by refusing to buy where they did not work. As well, their methods of protest that included advertising in newspapers and circulars were peaceful and not intended to coerce white merchants. Any damage to the merchant as a result of these peaceful efforts came "without remedy," the court ruled. White merchants in Harlem also sought to suppress black boycotts. They obtained a federal district court injunction on the grounds that the black boycotts were a "violation of restraint of trade." Although the Court of Appeals upheld the case, *New Negro Alliance v Sanitary Grocery Co.*, 303 U.S. 552, according to Juliet Walker's *The History of Black Business in America*, the Supreme Court reversed the decision and held that "boycotts were labor disputes protected under the Norris-LaGuardia Act" and refused to issue injunctions to stop nonviolent picketing.

## THE HARLEM MOVEMENT

In Harlem, the movement was launched around 1930 and coincided with an effort to win clerical posts for blacks in local white-owned businesses. There were at that time no laws barring racial discrimination in private industry; thus, blacks were not visible in the local industries. Sufi Abdul Hamid, of self-proclaimed Egyptian but actually an American-born black, had been active in the successful Chicago campaign. Through picketing, he and his followers landed 300 jobs for blacks in two months. Now he moved on to Harlem and continued his antiwhite slogans that he and his separatist followers used in Chicago and alienated blacks and whites. He also continued his street corner speeches. The work of Hamid and his Negro Industrial Clerical Alliance became so violent and disruptive that it played a role in the Harlem Riots of 1935.

Others in the Harlem movement worked through an established network of church-based programs, fraternal organizations, women's groups, and political and social organizations and were aided through charismatic minister Adam Clayton Powell Jr. Powell organized the Citywide Coordinating Committee; the organization was instrumental in locating "jobs for Negroes." Although they sought a coherent movement, Harlem was so diverse that the backgrounds and political beliefs and aspirations of some conflicted with the goals and needs of others. There were also black businessmen who feared that the removal of racial barriers in employment in white-owned establishments would result in an increase in black customers there, resulting in a loss of black customers in black businesses. Nearly ten years would pass before Harlem's activists would organize a campaign sufficient to win jobs on a widespread basis.

Meanwhile, in 1931, the Harlem Housewives League, founded a year earlier, had over 1,000 members, most of whom were politically active. Its able leaders included Lucille Randolph (wife of **Brotherhood of Sleeping Car Porters** leader A. Philip Randolph) as vice president and Bessye Bearden (journalist and activist) as publicity chairperson. They urged black women to shop for groceries only at those stores that were members of the **Colored Merchants' Association**. Still, internal differences in the National Association for the Advancement of Colored People (NAACP) and other organizations slowed progress of the movement. As well, not all black leaders supported the movement; others questioned the use of boycotts over pickets. Nevertheless, the movement moved ahead as the women urged the Atlantic and Pacific Tea Company (better known as A&P), Woolworth's, and stores of similar popularity with branches throughout Harlem to hire blacks. Their work, coupled with that of Powell, led to black employment in New York Edison Electric Company, Bell Telephone Company, the New York Bus Company, and in 1939, the New York World's Fair. Powell and the Coordinating Committee sought nonmenial jobs for blacks at the fair; when their request was denied, they picketed the fair's headquarters in the highly visible Empire State Building. After that, the fair's organizers promised to hire several hundred blacks as clerical and other workers. So well received were Powell's efforts that he was catapulted into a seat on the city council and in 1944 to a seat in the U.S. Congress. Similarly, in Chicago, William Dawson's ascendancy into the political arena and into the U.S. Congress grew out of his leadership in the "Don't Buy" campaign.

Harlem's efforts and the larger "Don't Buy" movement ended with World War II, when black organizations and the black community faced many other compelling issues. On the whole, however, it appears that the national "Don't Buy" movement led to jobs for no more than a few thousand blacks. Although many blacks remained jobless, the movement provided an opportunity for the black community to test its economic strength, its ability to organize for a common cause, and its ability to determine the full economic needs of the community and to initiate bold, new strategies to bring about economic uplift.

*See also*: Economic Boycotts and Protests

**Sources**

Drake, St. Clair, and Horace R. Cayton. *Black Metropolis: A Study of Negro Life in a Northern City*. New York: Harcourt, Brace, 1945.

Greenberg, Cheryl Lynn. *Or Does It Explode? Black Harlem in the Great Depression*. New York: Oxford University Press, 1991.

Harris, Abram L. *The Negro as Capitalist: A Study of Banking and Business among American Negroes*. 1936. New York: Negro Universities Press, 1969.

Lowery, Charles D., and John F. Marszalek, eds. *The Greenwood Encyclopedia of African Civil Rights*. Vol. 1. Westport, CT: Greenwood Press, 2003.

Oak, Vishnu V. *The Negro's Adventure in General Business.* Yellow Springs, OH: Antioch Press, 1949.

Walker, Juliet E. K. *The History of Black Business in America: Capitalism, Race, Entrepreneurship.* New York: Macmillan Library Reference USA, 1998.

*Jessie Carney Smith*

# Frederick Douglass's Business Enterprises

One of America's most precious gems is the legacy left by Frederick Douglass to the world upon his death in 1895. Frederick Augustus Washington Bailey was born around 1818 in Easton, Talbot County, Maryland, to Harriet Bailey, a slave. His father's identity remains unknown, but slaves' rumors suggest the slave master was he. Upon reaching New Bedford, Massachusetts, after his final escape from slavery to freedom, Frederick Bailey—then Johnson—finally changed his surname to Douglass. He is mainly known as a gifted, multitalented black American abolitionist and lecturer whose outspokenness, power of persuasion, and literary aptitude significantly impacted nineteenth-century history. Not as well known perhaps are the numerous business enterprises in which Douglass engaged. Thus, it is important to highlight and discuss Douglass's business ventures and his ability to maintain them. Douglass's entrepreneurial efforts officially began when he was twenty years old and hired himself out as a caulker. Between ages twenty and fifty-nine, Douglass's business ventures included lecturing, the black press, and banking.

When just a young child, Douglass heard his master state that because education would provide too much enlightenment, learning to read and write was forbidden for slaves. From that moment forth, learning the art of education became Douglass's foremost desire—next to freedom. Through curiosity, ingenuity, and self-help, he learned to read and write at an early age and ultimately mastered the art of education. At age sixteen, Douglass was taught the trade of caulking ships and became an expert at using caulking tools by the time he turned eighteen. In 1838, Douglas persuaded one master to sanction his plan to self-hire. The agreement was for Douglass to pay for his own tools, clothing, room, and board and give the master $3 a week. This agreement can be construed as Douglass's initial business enterprise, for he was solely in charge of his own finances. First of all, because of his expertise in the trade, he commanded "the highest wages paid to journeymen caulkers." Douglass earned an average of $7 per week; during the busy seasons, he earned as much as $9, of which he paid his master $3. Second, Douglass demonstrated his ability to artfully negotiate and successfully persuade—even as a slave. While working in Baltimore, Maryland, in 1837, Douglass met his future wife, Anna Murray. Supporting Douglass in achieving his goal of freedom, she assisted him in his 1838 escape from slavery and met him in New Bedford, Massachusetts. They were married and ultimately had five children. She also stayed at home and took in piecework sewing to support her family and her husband's business ventures.

Douglass's second business venture came about when he became an ordained minister and pastored the New Bedford African Methodist Episcopal Zion Church. Under the auspices of his leadership, he taught blacks in New Bedford to read and write and often made speeches to them. One can infer that Douglass was paid for his pastorship—no matter how little—and collected some monies for the speeches he made. By 1841, Douglass had been heard on the lecture circuit by white abolitionists and was invited to speak before the convention of the Massachusetts Abolitionist Society on Nantucket. From the time of his arrival in New Bedford up to this point, Douglass had read as many abolitionist newspapers as he possibly could and had digested the mission of the editors and the societies they represented. But the *Liberator*, which was edited and published by William Lloyd Garrison, a chief northern abolitionist, especially influenced him. His thoughts and impressions of slavery were completely in sync with those of the Massachusetts Abolitionist Society. Douglass accepted the invitation and delivered his speech at the convention before more than 2,000 antislavery activists. The eloquence and sentiment of his presentation captivated the audience, and the Massachusetts Anti-Slavery Society offered him a three-month lecture assignment as a result. Before long, Douglass contracted to lecture on behalf of the American Anti-Slavery Society promoting antislavery, thus launching his third business enterprise.

## EXPANDS LECTURE CIRCUIT AND BUSINESS VENTURES

Some people who heard Douglass speak began to doubt truth in his claim to be a slave because he was so well spoken. To rid the public of any doubt, Douglass revealed the full account of his years in slavery at an American Anti-Slavery Society meeting in New York on May 6, 1845. He was immediately thereafter persuaded to publish the account. Thus, Douglass launched his fourth venture as the author of *Narrative of the Life of Frederick Douglass, an American Slave, Written by Himself* in 1845. The book was published in Boston by the Anti-Slavery Office in mid-May and sold over 4,500 copies at twenty-five cents each in less than six months. Having exposed himself as a runaway slave, Douglass's safety in America was jeopardized, and the thought of being "returned to a doom worse than death drove him to seek refuge in England, a place where American young gentlemen go to increase their stock of knowledge, to seek pleasure, and to . . . refine themselves through contact with the aristocracy," he wrote in that work. With the help of friends, he sought refuge in England as he embarked upon a ship in August 1845. Douglass's place of asylum proved advantageous in every way. On the one hand, he became acquainted with educated, distinguished people as he lectured in England, Scotland, Ireland, and Whales; on the other hand, he launched his fifth business enterprise as an international lecturer. In the process, Philip Foner wrote in *Frederick*

*Douglass* that he was "supplied with annual income by several English friends sufficient to enable him to be free from worry and to devote his whole life and energies to the anti-slavery cause." The *Narrative* was translated and published in several languages. Realizing his plight and standing in agreement with his position on slavery, Douglass's English friends paid 125 pounds of silver for his freedom in December 1846.

Douglass's English friends wanted to erect a testimonial in his honor to thank him for enlightenment and to express solidarity for his mission; however, Douglass expressed his preference for the means to purchase a printing press and printing supplies so that he could start a newspaper in America to "advocate the interests of his enslaved and oppressed people, thereby dispelling the myth that black men are naturally inferior to white men and unable to live without enslavement and oppression," Foner wrote. At that time, there was not a single standing, regularly published newspaper edited by blacks. Granting his desire, Douglass's friends presented him with $2,500 to meet start-up needs for his sixth business enterprise. Douglass left England after delivering his "Farewell Address to the British People" in London on April 4 and arrived in New Bedford—manumission papers in hand—onboard the *Cambria* in 1847. While Douglass had imagined himself a successful editor of a black newspaper, several of his abolitionist friends who had heard of his plans expressed total opposition, including his mentor and idol William Lloyd Garrison. In his narrative, Douglass names the four specific reasons Garrisonians cited to denounce his plans: No such paper was needed; it would interfere with his usefulness as a lecturer; he could certainly speak better than he could write; and the paper could not succeed.

Trusting his own ability and determination to prove the intelligence of his people, Douglass launched his first newspaper, the *North Star*, in Rochester, New York, in 1847. The newspaper was a large sheet that cost $80 a week to publish. With the physical assistance of his children, who printed the type, folded, wrapped, and mailed the papers, Douglass circulated approximately 4,000 copies. Douglass subsequently changed the name of the paper to *Frederick Douglass' Paper* in 1851, so as not to confuse it with so many other newspapers with the word "star" in their titles. Douglass also changed his position on the interpretation of the U.S. Constitution, which made his stance completely opposite that of Garrisonians and the American Anti-Slavery Society. As a result, Garrison withdrew his endorsement of Douglass's newspaper. In June 1858, Douglass began publishing *Douglass' Monthly*, a supplement to the weekly paper. The monthly supplement became a separate publication in January 1859 and continued until 1863.

Having established himself as one of the most influential black leaders of the nineteenth century, Douglass was sought and urged to become the editor in chief of a large weekly newspaper in Washington, D.C., which would proclaim the progress of black people throughout the country and defend and enlighten newly emancipated slaves and enfranchised people. He accepted the position and moved his family to the Cedar Hills area of

Washington in 1870. The goals of the *New Era* were achievable until 1874 when it experienced extensive financial loss. Besides having invested over $10,000 into the project at the onset, Douglass ultimately purchased the newspaper in 1874 for an additional $10,000 and changed its name to the *New National Era*, hoping to keep current subscribers, draw new ones, and reclaim those lost. Contrary to his efforts, the paper continued to suffer financially, causing him to cease publication. That enterprise was but one of Douglass's dismal failures as a businessman set in an administrative position.

The next saga of failure occurred in his position as president of the Freedmen's Savings and Trust Company. After the Civil War, the Freedmen's Bureau chartered a bank in each of the former slave states to encourage the newly freed black population to invest and save money. Douglass was offered the position of president in 1874 of the Washington, D.C. branch. Unaware that the bank had already reached a state of insolvency, he accepted the prestigious position and promptly deposited $12,000 to demonstrate his confidence and support of the institution. In less than three months, Douglass discovered, to his dismay, the bank's irreparable state. After a meeting with Congress to report the situation, the bank was closed. Douglass and the depositors who had not previously withdrawn their funds lost their money.

While Douglass held several government positions after his last business venture, he continued to lecture and did so for the rest of his life. One speech he continued to deliver was "The Self-Made Man." He died in 1895.

*See also*: Black Banks: Their Beginning; Black Press: Newspapers in Major Cities

**Sources**

Andrews, William L. *African American Autobiographies: A Collection of Critical Essays*. Englewood Cliffs, NJ: Prentice Hall, 1993.

———. *Critical Essays on Frederick Douglass*. Boston: G. K. Hall, 1991.

———. *The Oxford Frederick Douglass Reader*. New York: Oxford University Press, 1996.

"The Black Press Stresses Importance of Succession Planning for Family Business." http//www.surfwax.com/history/files/Frederick_Douglass.

Boyd, Herbert. *Autobiography of a People: Three Centuries of African American History Told by Those Who Lived It*. New York: Anchor Books, 2001.

Douglass, Frederick. *The Frederick Douglass Papers*. Ed. John W. Blassingame et al. 5 vols. New Haven, CT: Yale University Press, 1979–1992.

———. *Narrative of the Life of Frederick Douglass, an American Slave, My Bondage and My Freedom, Life and Times of Frederick Douglass*. Comp. Library of America. New York: Penguin Books, 1994.

Foner, Philip. *Frederick Douglass*. New York: Citadel Press, 1964.

Leeman, Richard W., ed. *African-American Orators: A Bio-Critical Sourcebook*. Westport, CT: Greenwood Press, 1996.

Martin, Waldo E., Jr. *The Mind of Frederick Douglass*. Chapel Hill: University of North Carolina Press, 1984.

*Shelhea Owens*

# Dr. Dre (Andre Young) (1965– ), Record Producer, Rap Artist

Dr. Dre (born Andre Ranelle Young on February 18, 1965, in Compton, California) has earned the reputation as one of the top record producers of his generation. Raised by his mother, he is married and the father of two children. His rise to the "top of the charts" followed a route up the ladder of opportunity. Beginning as a disc jockey (DJ) for dance parties hosted by his mother and friends in the community, he learned the technical ropes of the trade by practice on the job. He began as a young preteen, experimenting with editing, overdubbing, scratching, mixing, sampling, and the other artful skills of merging cuts from various sources into dance tapes for use at parties. Name recognition is often a major factor in becoming well known, and here serendipity may have played a role. One of his early inspirations came when he heard a song by Grandmaster Flash honoring a personal idol, the well-known sports figure Dr. J. (professional basketball superstar Julius Erving). This may have led him to style his own name as Dr. Dre.

From this beginning, he began to form friendships and associations with a variety of young artists and producers in the community. By 1982, at age seventeen, he was ready to step forth and try his skills in the open market. Working as a DJ at Eve after Dark, a popular Los Angeles club, he joined with his fellow DJ at the club, Antoine Carraby (Yella), to form a new production team named the World Class Wreckin' Crew. The new team produced a popular single demo, "Surgery." The demo had a good response, selling 50,000 copies as a single and convincing him that his future lay in music. Graduating from Centennial High School in Compton in 1983, he eschewed the offer of a job at Northrop Aviation, joined with **O'Shea Ice Cube Jackson**, left World Class Wreckin' Crew in 1984, and continued to excel as a DJ and artist, performing live at a variety of venues (clubs, dance bars, skating rinks, etc.). The next major venture in his career was combining with Eazy-E (Eric Wright) in 1985 to form a new group called N.W.A. (Niggaz with Attitude), including Ice Cube, Yella, M. C. Ren (Lorenzo Patterson), and Arabian Prince. Dre produced their first project, *Boyz in the Hood*, featuring Eazy-E. The record was successful enough to finance their next project, the single "Dopeman," followed by the platinum album *Eazy Duz It*.

Along the way, a low point was reached with several gangsta rap recordings with severe lyrics, including "Fuck Tha Police," out of Ruthless Records, earning an FBI (Federal Bureau of Investigation) warning for the company in 1988, as well as much open controversy in the press. This notoriety affected the company, both negatively and positively. Nevertheless, Dr. Dre went on to other ventures (and it is a well-known fact that negative publicity often sells recordings). A milestone in his continuing career came with the production of his first solo single, "Deep Cover," in 1992. The record marked the introduction of his new G-funk sound, which soon served virtually as Dr. Dre's signature sound.

Using his creative ingenuity and flair for experimentation, integrated with his technical skills as a DJ he took a new look at old-style hip-hop and featured samples from the superstar George Clinton. He took the ball and ran with it on an oblique new tangent. The old style had an uptempo, party time, lilting flavor, whereas Dr. Dre's new G-funk features a mellower sound, with a rich and blended bass line and a strong keyboard drive that serves as an underpinning for the melodic line and a creative vehicle for the lyrics. As he used G-funk, its versatility grew, as did his own maturity and temperament. His lyrics increasingly spoke to the music and motives of the streets and his generation.

At this time also, Dr. Dre entered into a new collaboration with another local artist, Snoop Doggy Dogg. Dr. Dre's stepbrother, Warren G., had produced a few good tapes with Snoop Dogg that showcased his talent. When Dr. Dre began to work on his next album, *The Chronic*, released in 1992, he featured Snoop Dogg as well as himself on several cuts, notably "Nothin' But a G Thang," "Dre Day," and "Let Me Ride." These hits enabled *The Chronic* to become a multiplatinum bestseller. At this point and going forward, G-funk was a major influence on mainstream hip-hop and its musical essence.

Due to inner intrigues among his associates and friends, including the well-covered public controversies alluded to above surrounding gangsta rap itself, and other negative factors, Dr. Dre left N.W.A. and joined Suge Knight to form Death Row Records. The first venture for the label was Snoop Dogg's signature album *Doggystyle*, of 1993, which set a record for its debut at number 1 on the *Billboard* Charts.

In 1996, collaborating with Death Row artist Tupac Shakur, Dr. Dre produced the highly successful song "California Love." Its success established both Dr. Dre and his new company Death Row as a major force in hip-hop and an industry leader in both production and creativity. Unfortunately, however, the success took a tragic about-face, with the shooting death of Tupac in Las Vegas in 1996 and criminal charges against Suge Knight, alleging racketeering. Adding to the notoriety of Tupac's death was its mysterious nature—and the mystery remains unsolved. Media reports and rumors told of the shooting occurring with Suge Knight apparently present in the car with Tupac and contributing little to the subsequent inquiry into the crime.

Sensing dire prospects for the continuation of Death Row, Dr. Dre withdrew from the company and formed another enterprise, Aftermath Entertainment, including various major artists such as Eminem and 50 Cent. The company's first release, *Dr. Dre Presents . . . The Aftermath*, featured songs by the new Aftermath artists, including Dre, and the solo track "Been There, Done That," suggesting that Dr. Dre had moved on to another level of performance and lifestyle. Very soon more productions followed, including Eminem's next album *The Slim Shady* LP in 1999 and *The Marshall Mathers* LP in 2000; both were highly successful despite somewhat controversial lyrics. Eminem's next album, *The Eminem Show*, released in 2002, was largely guided through production by Eminem himself.

Dre's next release was a new solo album, *Dr. Dre 2001*, released in 1999. This album, like a few previously released, featured the voices of several collaborators, as well as Dre himself, notably Devin the Dude, Hittman, Snoop Dogg, and Eminem. The lyrics assert Dre's claim to represent an important and reemergent hip-hop force, with the typical constants of scratch and noise inputs, plus some impressive musical innovations such as the use of synthesized sound mixed with string melodies, and a vigorous, deep and rich bass line, possibly showing an attempt to redefine G-funk's versatility.

Dr. Dre exhibits some of these newer techniques as well in work produced for other artists, notably "Let Me Blow Ya Mind" for Eve and Gwen Stefani, "Break, Break Ya Neck" by Busta Rhymes, and "Family Affair" by Mary J. Blige. Recently also, Dr. Dre appeared in the movies *Set it Off* (1996), *The Wash* (2001), and *Training Day* (2001), with one of his songs ("Bad Intentions") included on the soundtrack for *The Wash*. He disclaimed ambitions, however, for an acting career. His continuing work in production resulted in other collaborations. In 2003, Dre and Eminem together produced "In Da Club," a major-label hit single for Queens rapper 50 Cent. "In Da Club" was included on the album *Get Rich or Die Tryin'*.

Given his past, and rumors to the contrary, it seems very likely that his career in music will continue to flourish. A new album release, *Detox*, is planned for 2006, and he may well include other artists recently signed to Aftermath Entertainment, including Eminem, Ice Cube, 50 Cent, Eve, The Game, Stat Quo, and Busta Rhymes, to this or other forthcoming projects.

What can we anticipate for future years? One expects that there will be a continuation of intrigue, innovation, production, and distribution turns and twists, collaborations, and rejections. Many creative sparks will fly. We foresee a star producer who will be strong and innovative in meeting his new challenges.

**Sources**

Answers.com. http://www.answers.com/topic/Dr-Dre.

Beckman, Janette, and B. Adler. *Rap: Portraits and Lyrics of a Generation of Black Rockers*. New York: St. Martin's Press, 1991.

*Contemporary Black Biography*. Vol 30. Detroit: Gale Group, 2002.

VH1.com. http://www.vh1.com/artists/az/dr_dre/bio.jhtml.

*Darius L. Thieme*

# Joe L. Dudley Sr. (1937– ), Entrepreneur, Business Executive and Founder, Humanitarian, Philanthropist

Through dedication, persistence, hard work, and a shrewd sense of entrepreneurship, Joe L. Dudley built his business, Dudley Products, Inc., from a modest beginning to a multimillion-dollar hair-care and cosmetics company. In doing so, Dudley Products gained respect worldwide and is well renowned in the beauty industry. He has shared his wealth with the North Carolina community where he lives by establishing scholarships and mentoring programs for black youth who want to enter the field of business.

Joe Louis Dudley Sr. was born on May 9, 1937, in the rural community of Aurora, North Carolina, a small town in the eastern part of the state. He is the fifth of eleven children born to Gilmer L. and Clara Yeates Dudley and grew up in a three-room farmhouse.

He suffered a speech impediment and was diagnosed as mentally retarded, resulting in his retention in the first grade. His mother, however, had faith in him and helped him to overcome the obstacles that he faced early on. Her faith also spurred him to become successful and a role model for many. By age forty, he was a millionaire.

A successful college career at North Carolina Agricultural and Technical State University (A&T) in Greensboro would also dispel the notion that Dudley was mentally retarded. There he majored in business administration but needed money to help underwrite his college expenses. He saw Fuller Products Company as a source of part-time employment.

Dudley began his climb to success in 1957 when he joined Fuller Products Company. **S. B. Fuller** incorporated his company in 1929, established a line of thirty products including cosmetics and household items, and employed a cadre of salespeople to peddle the products door to door on Chicago's predominantly black South Side. Fuller became successful as a master salesman, a motivational genius, and one of the city's most successful black entrepreneurs and was known as a giant in African American entrepreneurship. Among his employees were George Johnson, later owner of Johnson Products, and Joe L. Dudley. In 1957 Dudley invested $10.00 in a Fuller Products sales kit and began door-to-door sales. He spent summers in Brooklyn, where he began to master Fuller's sales techniques and continued to sell Fuller Products.

In 1960, he met Eunice Mosely, who worked as an agent for Fuller Products to earn money for her college tuition. They married in 1961 and began to work full-time with the company in 1962. He had completed his Bachelor of Science degree and moved to New York, where he continued to work as a salesman for five years. The Dudleys moved to Greensboro in September 1967 and opened a Fuller Products distributorship. Two years later, however, the company ran into financial difficulty, and the Dudleys began a company of their own—Dudley Products. The Dudleys manufactured beauty products at home, on the kitchen stove. Eunice Dudley and the Dudley's two children packaged the products at night, and the next day Dudley and his sales force would sell the items. Soon they bought the rights to Rosebud Products and the popular Rosebud Hair Pomade but renamed the latter product to become Dudley's Scalp Special. Lacking fancy containers to package the product, the Dudley's washed, sanitized, and reused jelly jars, mayonnaise jars, or previously used containers for hair-care products and filled them with Dudley's Scalp Special. Success came quickly, and by 1976 the company included a chain of beauty supply stores scattered throughout the Southeast, beauty shops, a manufacturing plant, and a beauty college. Dudley Products had hired over 400 employees.

While Dudley Products began to flourish, Fuller Products continued its downward spiral: Sales dropped from $10 million in 1962 to $1.5 million in 1976. S. B. Fuller sought Dudley's help and asked him to come to Chicago in 1976 to run the company. Dudley agreed, and for eight years he was president of both the Fuller and Dudley companies. His main charge from Fuller, however, was to rebuild Fuller Products. In the meantime, Dudley entered the Partnership with Professional Cosmetologists and had direct sales with cosmetologists and barbers. Fuller Products never fully recovered. Dudley decided to concentrate on his own company and returned to Greensboro in 1984 and continued to develop Dudley Products.

## OPENS NEW CORPORATE HEADQUARTERS

In 1986 Dudley opened a new corporate headquarters and manufacturing facility. Two years later he established Dudley Cosmetology University (DCU) located in nearby Kernersville and offered a General Cosmetology Program and Advanced Training courses for cosmetologists who were licensed. He followed with the erection of a DUC Cafeteria, Dudley Travel program, Dudley Inn, and the Yeates Center. After Fuller died in 1988, Dudley purchased the manufacturing and distribution rights to Fuller Products.

The spiral upward for Dudley Products continued. The firm launched Dudley Products Cosmetics in 1992, featuring a full line of makeup designed for women of color. There were over 1,000 certified wholesalers of these products by 1997. Manufacturing and corporate needs were served better when, in late September 1994, Dudley Products moved into a new state-of-the-art facility in Kernersville. The company made a significant expansion that year when Dudley entered a global hair-care market, jointly establishing training programs for Zimbabwe, South Africa, Brazil, and several Caribbean countries.

The collegiate Sales Manager Trainee Program, launched in 1995, gives promising college students a chance to learn business, leadership, and entrepreneurial skills. Dudley's Beauty School System continues to flourish, with four schools in North Carolina and others in Chicago, Miami, the District of Columbia, and Baltimore. The company's workforce has exceeded 450, and retail sales of hair-care products and personal cosmetics are sold strictly through salons and barbershops. Its Q-Nails system for nail care was added in 1997. The company has enjoyed national and international success. It has been listed in the top 50 in *Black Enterprise* magazine's Top 100 Black Owned Businesses.

Dudley has extended himself to the community by serving on the board of trustees of his alma mater North Carolina A&T State University and as a board member of Southern National Corporation's Branch Banking and Trust. His memberships include Direct Selling Association, of which Dudley

Products is the first African American–owned company to become a sustaining member of the board. As well, his company has been a member of the American Health and Beauty Aids Institute, a black-owned manufacturer of health and beauty aids. The creator of innovative programs for disadvantaged youth and young people, Dudley established the Dudley Fellows and Ladies, a mentoring program with students in Greensboro's historically black Dudley High School; Dudley's Creative Program for college students who are interested in developing business and leadership skills; and Dudley's Scholarship Program for outstanding high school seniors.

His awards include North Carolina A&T Alumni Excellence Award; Greensboro NAACP (National Association for the Advancement of Colored People) Economic Development Award; President George Bush's 467th Point of Light Award for Dudley Fellows and Ladies Program; Direct Selling Association's Vision for Tomorrow Award for the fellows and ladies programs; Maya Angelou Tribute to Achievement Award; and the J. C. Penny's Non-Merchandise Supplier Grand Award. Dudley was inducted into the National Black College Alumni Hall of Fame and the Horatio Alger Association of Distinguished Americans. He holds honorary degrees from A&T and Edward Waters College in Jacksonville, Florida. His achievements include the "I Am, I Can, I Will" speaking tour.

Much of the company's success is due to Dudley's entrepreneurial skills and to the devotion of the entire Dudley family to the business, including son Joe Jr., daughter Ursula Dudley Oglesby, and youngest daughter Genea. The Dudley offspring bring to the business degrees in law and graduate degrees in business.

Through his work, Dudley has become a visible and positive role model for young people and has demonstrated through his teaching and personal example that one may become a successful entrepreneur.

*See also*: Retail Industry

**Sources**

Dawson, Nancy L. "Joe L. Dudley." *Encyclopedia of African American Business History*. Ed. Juliet E. K. Walker. Westport, CT: Greenwood Press, 1999.

"Dudley Products, Inc. The Company—Its History." http://www.dudleyq.com/Corporate/dudleyproducts.html.

"Joe L. Dudley, Sr., Entrepreneur and Humanitarian." http://www.dudleyproducts.com/Corporate/joedudley.html.

*Who's Who among African Americans*. 18th ed. Detroit: Thomson Gale, 2005.

*Frederick D. Smith*

# E

## E-Commerce and the African American Community

Successful e-commerce activities in the African American community and in the digital economy as a whole will lead to higher income levels for the community. There will be success for both the entrepreneur and for those who create the products that are sold, such as art, books, jewelry, cosmetics, and clothing. Perhaps the development of e-commerce in the African American community has been impacted by a digital divide between the races and economic groups. A number of studies identify elements of that divide. These elements include lack of personal computers (PCs) and Internet access in homes of many black and low-income families and in the homes of low-income rural Americans, along with the absence of appropriate technology training. The digital divide has been impacted positively by a variety of efforts to bridge that gap, such as educational programs on e-commerce in academic institutions, partnering programs involving various groups, and computer access in readily available places. As the divide has narrowed, it has set in motion an opportunity for e-commerce in the African American community to grow.

### BRIDGING THE DIGITAL DIVIDE

When he gave his State of the Union address in January 2000, President Bill Clinton unveiled a new federal program called "ClickStart." The program subsidized computer purchases and connections to the Internet for America's poor families. It also helped African Americans as a whole to get online. The targeted families were required to work in community service projects for a certain number of hours each week. Some claimed that, even at that time, better models were available that placed computers and appropriate training in schools and the community.

African American entrepreneurs in the technology world, such as Darien Dash, help set the stage for e-commerce activities in the community by founding businesses that became successful. In 1994, Dash founded Digital Mafia Entertainment (DME), known as DME Interactive Holdings, and ran it from his bedroom. It was the first technology firm owned by an African American to be traded on Wall Street. Dash expanded in June 1999, when he purchased Pride Automotive Group—an automobile leasing firm. Later that year his company acquired Kathoderay, a multimedia consulting firm. So noticeable was DME's success that in 1999 the U.S. Department of Commerce cited it as the minority technology firm of the year. Since Dash and his company believed in partnering, in 1999 the company entered an agreement with Places of Color and made low-cost Internet service available. Continuing in this vein, in 2000 DME partnered with Hewlett-Packard to sell personal computers at a low cost, not to exceed $250; added to that, the deal provided free Internet access in New York and New Jersey. Thus, DME saw an opportunity and seized it: It filled its mission of expanding the hardware and software infrastructure onto America's minority communities that had been disenfranchised from technology. Dash recognized the buying power of African Americans and minority communities as a whole. His vision further underscored the need for e-commerce activities in these communities.

E-commerce in the African American community necessarily expects that African American households will have access to computers and to the Internet. For a time, however, any Americans, including minorities and older Americans, were slow to sign on to a medium that failed to appeal to them. And low-income rural Americans were isolated due to connectivity issues. The rapid change in technology, partnerships between industries, governments, and racial group, and concerted efforts to bridge the racial and low-income geographical gap brought about an increase in the numbers of Internet users. Increasingly, access is provided in school, academic, and public libraries, community centers, and churches, thus ensuring a wide range of users and narrowing the racial connectivity divide.

An important effort to reduce the digital divide was the establishment of Black Family Technology Awareness Week in 1999. According to the Black Family Network, the awareness goal was to eliminate the digital divide for black families, to excite these families about the importance of personal computers and Internet access at home, and to help them understand the importance of making technology a reality in their lives. The campaigns that followed saw increasing numbers of community- and faith-based organizations, public schools, and other concerned organizations offer programs for families to address the digital divide. The campaign in 2004, for example, targeted those black families who were not taking full advantage of today's technologies. The program's vision was threefold: to see that black families have home access to a personal computer and the Internet and appropriate training to maximize the use of these tools; to see that the families used these tools to enhance their education, job opportunities, health, communications, and quality of life; and to see that black family members connect electronically with mentors who will encourage and motivate them to manager their lives better on a day-to-day basis.

Further to address the problem, the United Negro College Fund (UNCF) in 2001 launched a successful Technology Enhancement Capital Campaign to raise $80 million in two years to be used to bridge the digital divide on its member campuses. UNCF sought gifts from top technology companies, foundations, and individuals to provide faculty members with laptops or PCs and to enable students in the member colleges to purchase a PC at a low cost. Deals were made with Dell and IBM to make equipment and software available. Faculty training followed.

Other approaches have been used to provide solutions to the digital divide and to promote e-commerce. Historically black North Carolina Agricultural and Technical State University, located in Greensboro, offers its students an opportunity to prepare for e-commerce. In 2003, the university established a Center for Entrepreneurship and E-Business. The interdisciplinary program is offered in a collaborative learning environment; it is a joint program with the School of Business and Economics, the School of Technology, and the School of Environmental Sciences.

## E-COMMERCE ACTIVITIES EMERGE

E-commerce activities that deal with African American businesses are easily seen when searching the Internet. There is, for example, on Black-Find.com's Web site a listing for the BlackFind Search Engine, which contains thousands of black Web sites and businesses. The alphabetically arranged topics include Arts & Culture, Business & Economy, Industry, Life Styles (beauty and health), Literature, and Shopping. BlackFind has been revised and aggressively updates, expands, and makes its presence known in the black community. Among BlackFind's goals are "to strategically, aggressively, and successfully build a community with our [black] people, for our people and by our people."

Using another approach to serving the community, Black Quest—The Griot is an educational and heritage CD-ROM game designed to preserve and reinforce African American culture and history. It introduces and reinforces the experiences, contributions, and achievements of the race. It is considered a useful source for social studies, African American studies, and general and African American history. The Web site predicts that Black Quest "can serve as an essential medium to bring about the strong cultural identity that is crucial to the positive growth and development in the individual, family and community." Among the black luminaries pictured on the site are aviator Bessie Coleman, folklorist and anthropologist Zora Neale Hurston, musician/composer Duke Ellington, and school integrationist Daisy Bates. Black Quest also advertises other companies, such as Onyx Art, Egypt-Online Travel & Tours, and Buy Black, Buy Black. The promotion of "buy black" called "Buy Black Products from Black (African) Owned

Stores" is reminiscent of the Double Duty Dollar campaign that emerged in Chicago in the 1930s, during the Great Depression. Later, the campaign became a part of the **Don't Buy Where You Can't Work movement** that lasted from 1929 to 1941. Now, however, the emphasis is on supporting black businesses rather than boycotting mainstream stores.

The list of on- and offline places that Black Quest advertises and that provide for Afrocentric shopping includes Abu Fine Art (paintings and masks), Afra~tique (African-influenced clothing for women), Afrocentric Klips (clip art with an Afrocentric flair), Ajani Bookstore, Alomo Imports and Exports—The Kente Store, Arkenya Designs, Drum & Spear Books (African-American books and gifts), Kwanzaa Club Afrocentric Online Shoppings, Black Creations Cultural Store (including Negro League baseball shirts and hats, gifts, and books), Sisterspace and Books (books by and about African American women), True Essence (natural perfumes and body oils), and The Village MarketPlace (www.littleafrica.com/littleafrica-mall .html, African American online shopping mall).

A popular source that gives access to e-businesses is The Griot, a separate Web site from the one previously mentioned. The Web page for The Griot advertises and recommends black businesses, such as B. Smiths Union Station in Washington, D.C., describing its feature foods. Other listings are not necessarily endorsed by The Griot. The Griot's National Online Black Business Directory guides the user to services, such as hair and beauty products, salons, barbershops, and home repair. It lists sources of foods, such as restaurants, caterers, bakeries, and grocery stores. Professional services and sources of health care are provided as well. The section on retail stores guides the user to bookstores, clothing stores, art stores, and more. Other sections include churches, the community, organizations, nightlife, education, and the media.

The online directory is searchable by topic and then by city; for example, a search for antiques/collectables in San Francisco and Oakland leads to Creations of Color, a recently added listing located at 10003 Burr Street in Oakland. Telephone and fax numbers, and email and Web addresses, are given. Further, the listing describes About Creations of Color: It features "unique Afrocentric Gifts with a flavor."

The directory listings for Los Angeles, using Advanced Business Search, lead to My Father's Business Enterprise, L.L.C. (entertainment), and Affordable Computer (technology and consulting in Huntington Beach). Whether or not some of the ventures are African American owned and operated is an open question; however, the listings do suggest that the businesses welcome African American customers.

Using the Advanced Business Search to locate businesses in Memphis, the user is guided to such businesses as Global Solutions; Orpheum Theatre; and several catering firms, such as The Brown Pig, Sanders Catering, and Beneva Mayweather & Emma Lincoln Caterers. A further click on each business venture will give details of the venture.

In addition to the online directory, The Griot.com presents its National Black Business and Organizations Directory. The printed consumer guide features nearly 5,000 black-owned and black-targeted barbershops and other businesses in select cities. Those listed are Atlanta, Charlotte, Chicago, Dallas, Des Moines, Houston, Los Angeles, Kansas City, Memphis, Miami, New Orleans, New York, Philadelphia, and Washington, D.C.

There are, of course, e-commerce ventures that are not advertised in the various online directories. Cheryl Onley displays her works at http://louisesdaughter.com. Onley's abstract figures in her *Women of Color in Color* collection have evolved into distinct personalities, and the collection has grown in size. The Web site provides a list of stores, galleries, and art/craft fairs where Onley's works are available.

Jennifer Bickerstaff offers her unique, handcrafted light switch covers at http://www.jeniturnonart.com. Each light switch cover is an individual piece of art. Many of the colorful works are inspired by African masks. Customers can also choose from a variety of themes, including Afrocentric, music, sports, Asian, and women.

The popular online shopping site eBay offers the public an opportunity to set up an eBay Store and to advertise and sell their wares. Such stores allow sellers to customize their pages, show their listings, and give details about their businesses. This has been called a cost-effective way of building an online business. As well, the seller reaches millions of buyers who shop on eBay daily. A popular African American eBay Store is Sophisticated Sorors that offers merchandise of black Greek and other black fraternal organizations. Items include jewelry, wearing apparel, backpacks, and carry-on luggage.

In June 2005, Vando Rogers partnered with Rod Putnam in Nashville, Tennessee, to form Imagination Development Corporation and to launch the first-known digital magazine published in a magazine format. Called *Nashville Digital Magazine*, the DVD is Mac or PC compatible, with exclusive content and Internet connectivity. It works with any DVD drive. The inaugural issue (June 1995) includes a lead story (questions and answers by Nashville's first African American vice mayor Howard Gentry), a performance by the Fisk University Choir, crafts, interviews with local athletes, hobbies, business advertisements, and tips on photography. Businesses may advertise their enterprises or products in the monthly magazine. In *Nashville Digital Magazine*'s news release for July 2005, Rogers called the new product "a totally new concept in sharing information." The company's other products include a series of interactive travel DVDs, including *Dive South Florida and the Florida Keys* (http://www.divefilms.com), as well as touchscreen kiosks that use cutting-edge technology.

Though not an online source thus far, Rick Kittles and his partner Gina Paige founded the Maryland-based African Ancestry in 2003. Buyers may purchase from the company DNA-based genealogy tests that are able to pinpoint the location in Africa where the client's ancestors originated.

To begin the trace, clients must swab the inside of their cheeks and ship the DNA sample to African Ancestry. The samples are sent to Sorensen Genomics, a certified and accredited laboratory based in Salt Lake City. There the samples are processed to determine their DNA genotyping and sequencing. The samples are returned to African Ancestry, where Kittles cross-references and matches the DNA sequence with his ancestry database.

Four to six weeks later, African Ancestry validates the present country or region with which the client shares a genetic link. In some cases the precise ethnic group or tribe is identified as well. Although some 85 percent of the matches are identical, in some cases the database yields only those lineages that are closely related.

According to Allison Gilbert in *Black Enterprise*, the company's "genetic African Lineage Database" is a repository of "molecular blueprints of African peoples" that Kittles created. According to Gilbert, Kittles's database uses a "MatriClan Test of maternal DNA inherited from the mother" as well as a "PatriClan Test of paternal DNA inherited from the father." Clearly, the database closes the digital divide between African Americans who search for their lineage and other groups who have electronic access to considerable data. The growing database is the world's most comprehensive tool available on African lineages. Its potential for serving searchers online is high. The firm self-published a book on its services, *African Ancestry Guide to West and Central Africa*.

The African American community is well positioned to support e-commerce ventures. In all likelihood, the success of such businesses that are already operational will encourage other e-entrepreneurs as well as e-consumers to take fuller advantage of the market.

*See also*: Centers for Entrepreneurship in Academic Institutions; Faith-Based Entrepreneurship; Retail Industry; Women and Business

**Sources**
Black Family Network. http://www.blackfamilynet.net.
BlackFind. http://blackfind.com.
"The Black Quest." http://www.blackquest.com.
"Buy Black Products from Black (African) Owned Stores." http://www.saxakali.com/urafrican/buy%20black.htm.
Chappell, Kevin. "United Negro College Fund: Crossing the Digital Divide." *Ebony* 56 (September 2001): 174–178.
"Darien Dash." *Contemporary Black Biography*. Vol. 29. Farmington Hills, MI: Gale Group, 2002.
Dash, Darien. "Bridging the Digital Divide." *Inc.com*. http://www.inc.com/articles/2001/06/22953.html.
"Falling Through the Net: Defining the Digital Divide." U.S. Department of Commerce. Summer 1999. http://www.ntia.doc.gov.
Gilbert, Allison. "Tracing Your Ancestry." *Black Enterprise* 36 (August 2005): 55.
The Griot: National Online Black Business Directory. http://www.thegriot.com/blackworld/index.asp.
Hamberg, Cheryl. Interview with author, July 19, 2005.

*Nashville Digital Magazine.* Vol. 1 (June 2005). http://www.nashvilledigitalmag.com.
*Nashville Digital Magazine.* News Release. July 2005.
Rogers, Vando. Interview with author, July 19, 2005.
Sophisticated-Sorors. http://stores.ebay.com.

*Jessie Carney Smith*

## Economic Boycotts and Protests

Economic boycotts and protests as a tactic used by American blacks during their mid-twentieth-century struggle to gain civil rights as guaranteed by the U.S. Constitution was not a new strategy. Employed as a method of protest since the first nonviolent power struggles, to boycott is simply the act of withholding support or involvement in some activity as a means of protest to influence or bring about a change in policy or action protested. As the most common and widely known tactic, many well-known economic or consumer protests throughout history have used the tactic of boycotting—most notably the Boston Tea Party of 1773. During the 1800s, abolitionists in the North employed boycotting in their refusal to buy products from slave states, not wanting to buttress the South's system of finance. Early African Americans themselves also used boycott and protest methods to demonstrate against America's unjust treatment. Having staged several streetcar "ride-ins," Sojourner Truth sued a streetcar driver who forced her off his streetcar and won. At the close of the nineteenth century, American farmers called for boycotts of banks and large corporations in the populist revolt of the 1890s, while American workers used the boycott strategy during the labor movement in the early 1900s.

From 1900 to 1906, African Americans in more than twenty-five southern cities organized boycotts of segregated streetcars. The leaders of these boycotts included clergymen, businessmen, newspaper editors, and others who championed **Booker T. Washington**'s philosophy of accommodation, conciliation, self-help, and uplift. These boycotts occurred during the era of degenerating race relations, pervasive racial violence, and urban white leaders' unrestrained efforts to codify racial segregation with city ordinances. A half-century later, African Americans in Montgomery again instituted the boycott and economic withdrawals against the public transportation system. Inspired by Mohandas K. Gandhi's philosophy of nonviolence and direct civil disobedience, this ideology or system of belief not only sustained the Montgomery Bus Boycott for more than a year, but it infused other phases of the modern movement for civil rights.

Gandhi, who acknowledged that his stratagem was derived from women suffragist struggles in India and England, helped popularize the boycott in his campaign for Indian independence from Britain. In 1920, he called on the people of India to boycott linen imported from Britain and instead to weave their own cloth by hand. Ten years later, Gandhi called for a boycott of British salt to further demonstrate Indian independence from Britain. Since then, the boycott has become an international symbol of resistance, hope, and power.

In 1932, Reinhold Niebuhr, an American theologian and social thinker, wrote the following words in an essay titled "Moralists and Politics" that appeared in D. B. Robertson's *Essays in Applied Christianity*:

> The Negro will never win his full rights in society merely by trusting the fairness and sense of justice of the white man.... If he is well advised he will use such forms of economic and political pressure as will be least likely to destroy the moral forces, never completely absent even in intergroup relations, but which will nevertheless exert coercion upon the white man's life.

This prophetic statement certainly foretold one of the strategies ultimately used to bring down the seemingly insurmountable wall of racial segregation. However, it took more than twenty years for American blacks to mount any planned large-scale economic attempt to effectively dismantle the nation's system of racial apartheid and "interfere with the economic process controlled by the dominant economic groups," as referenced by Niebuhr.

Historical accounts of the modern civil rights movement are replete with demands for economic justice and were an imperative aspect of the grassroots mobilizations. Also, there was an economic component to the campaigns for equal and just treatment of African Americans as consumers—at lunch counters, movie theaters, hotels, and amusement parks, which were the immediate pressure in boycotts of downtown business districts. Another element or prong that was just as pervasive was demand for employment opportunities long denied to the African American populace. This element is demonstrated in slogans such as "Don't buy where you cannot be a salesman." As asserted by Elizabeth Jacoway and David Colburn in their work titled *Southern Businessmen and Desegregation* concerning the role of southern businessmen during the African American crusade for civil rights: "[I]n the 1950s and 1960s, white businessmen across the South found themselves pushed by the federal government and civil rights forces as well as by their own economic interest—and values—into becoming reluctant advocates of a new departure in southern race relations."

For most Americans, the 1950s were years of increasing personal prosperity. The booming economy brought about the precipitous growth of suburbs, as people migrated from the cities to their outer environs. Even so, the culture and politics of the "Affluent Society" were shaped mostly by the world's anxiety over the Cold War. These dynamics created several of the most important factors that contributed to the rise of American black protest. Among them are the return of black soldiers from foreign service during World War II; the growth of an urban American black middle class; television and other forms of popular culture; the culture of Cold War itself, which made racial injustice an embarrassment to Americans trying to present their nation to the world as the paragon of democracy; and the political mobilization of northern blacks. These factors brought the nation's social and racial problems more sharply into focus.

## BLACK ORGANIZATIONS AND PROTEST

After decades of struggles, an open crusade began in the 1950s against calcified racial intolerance and discrimination, a struggle that proved to be one of a relatively extended duration and the twentieth century's most problematical. Although American whites played a role in the modern civil rights movement, pressure from American blacks themselves was the fundamental component in elevating the question of race to prominence. The four major civil rights organizations—the National Association for the Advancement of Colored People (NAACP, 1909), the Congress of Racial Equality (CORE, 1942), the Southern Christian Leadership Conference (SCLC, 1957), and the Student Nonviolent Coordinating Committee (SNCC, 1966)—all applied various boycott and protest methods to exert economic pressure on America's social and institutional forms of injustices perpetrated upon American blacks.

One year before the founding of CORE, A. Philip Randolph, the fearless labor leader and civil rights activist, threatened to organize a demonstration in Washington, D.C. unless President Franklin Roosevelt barred racial discrimination in defense industries. Supported by the Urban League and the NAACP, he acknowledged that the only way the executive branch of the U.S. government would take up the interests of American blacks were if thousands of black protesters marched to the White House. In response to Randolph's threatened protest to inundate the streets of the nation's capital with thousands of protesting American blacks, Roosevelt responded by creating the Fair Employment Practices Committee that forbade racial discrimination in the defense industry. For the first time, the threat of direct action moved the White House to act on its commitment to equal opportunity. In 1941, the same year that Randolph caused the White House to take affirmative actions toward ending racial discrimination in the defense industries, Adam Clayton Powell Jr., New York City's first black city council member and later a U.S. congressman, led a successful four-week bus boycott in Harlem. A proponent of the **"Don't Buy Where You Can't Work movement"** Powell's leadership caused the bus company to hire drivers and mechanics from the black community.

CORE pioneered the strategy of nonviolent direct action, especially the tactics of sit-ins and freedom rides. From its formation in 1942, CORE began protests against racial segregation in public accommodations by organizing sit-ins. The first planned civil rights sit-in in America took place at Chicago's Jack Spratt coffeehouse, which refused to serve American blacks. Casual and quiet, members of CORE sat down in mixed parties of three and four. When law enforcement officials arrived, they told the eatery's management it had no grounds for removing peaceful customers. Jack Spratt's manager relented, and within weeks, patrons of a darker hue frequented the coffeehouse. By augmenting the sit-in tactic with picket lines, CORE experienced some success in desegregating northern public facilities in the 1940s. Later in 1947, to test the U.S. Supreme Court's decision in the *Morgan v. Virginia* (328 U.S. 373 [1946]) case, which mandated interstate bus desegregation, CORE initiated its Journey of Reconciliation with a group of interracial men traveling throughout the upper South. The NAACP brought forth the *Morgan v. Virginia* case to the U.S. Supreme Court on behalf of Irene Morgan, who in 1944 refused to move further back on a Greyhound bus as she was on her way to Baltimore from Virginia. CORE gained national attention with its Journey of Reconciliation when Chapel Hill, North Carolina, law enforcement officials arrested four riders, and three, including Bayard Rustin, were forced to work on a chain gang. Using direct nonviolent methods such as sit-ins, wade-ins, and other forms of protest, CORE captured national attention. By the 1950s, with the rise of the Reverend Martin Luther King Jr. and the success of the Montgomery Bus Boycott, CORE-style nonviolence became a weapon in the arsenal of the American black movement for equality and justice.

Two years before the Montgomery movement captured the nation's attention and capitulated King into the eye of the modern civil rights storm, in Baton Rouge, Louisiana, the Reverend T. J. Jemison initiated the first bus boycott by American blacks in the country's southern region. In January 1953, legislative members of Baton Rouge's parish council increased the bus fare from ten to fifteen cents. The fare increase angered African American patrons who made up more than 80 percent of the system's ridership. As in other southern cities, while the front seats were reserved for whites, African Americans were forced to sit in the back of the bus and pay full fare. At the parish council meeting on February 11, Jemison, the pastor of the Mt. Zion Baptist Church, condemned the fare increase and petitioned the council to terminate the codified system of reserved seating on city buses. Two weeks later, the council voted to amend Baton Rouge's seating code when it passed Ordinance 222. The amended code, which became effective March 19, 1953, permitted American blacks to sit in the front seats of the buses if they did not occupy the same seat as or sit in front of a white passenger. While Ordinance 222 abolished reserved seating, it required American blacks to board the buses from back to front and white passengers from front to back. City bus drivers ignored Ordinance 222 for almost three months. In early June, they were ordered to comply with the ordinance. Because two drivers were suspended for noncompliance, on June 15, the city's bus drivers went on strike for four days. The day before the bus drivers ended their strike, the United Defense League met and organized Baton Rouge's Bus Boycott. Led by Jemison, the black community conducted a seven-day boycott, which ended when city officials reaffirmed the ordinance. Although short-lived, the Baton Rouge Bus Boycott served as a paradigm for similar protests throughout the South, including the 1955 Montgomery Bus Boycott, when King consulted with Jemison about the tactics used to coordinate Baton Rouge's Bus Boycott.

## ECONOMIC BOYCOTTS IN THE SOUTH

At the onset of the modern civil rights movement, Montgomery, Alabama, was one of the first cities to employ economic pressure as a method of protest. As early as 1952, the Women's Political Council (WPC), a group of American black professionals, protested against Jim Crow practices on the Montgomery city buses. In a 1954 meeting with the mayor, which produced few tangible gains, WPC president Jo Ann Robinson reiterated the council's requests in written form. Her correspondence also insinuated that a boycott of Montgomery's buses was in the planning stages. Because of Rosa Parks refusing to relinquish her seat on a Montgomery bus and being arrested, according to Bruce J. Dierenfield's *The Civil Rights Movement*, the bus company's records indicated that 99 percent of the usual 30,000 black riders walked, hitchhiked, pedaled bicycles, and used car pools to make their way about the city. Black Montgomery's yearlong boycott caused the bus company, downtown businessmen, and the city of Montgomery to lose approximately $1 million. In due course, the economic boycott and a favorable ruling in 1956 by the U.S. Supreme Court in the *Gayle v. Browder* case brought a major civil rights victory to black Montgomerians. Bus boycotts and their concomitant economic withdrawals continued throughout the South.

As in Montgomery, when black Nashville leaders and students began their formal sit-in movement, they, too, added an economic prong later that devastated downtown merchants and business owners. The Nashville sit-ins, which were the largest and best organized of the sit-ins across the South, originally began in November and December of 1959, as black leaders and students sought to "test" the exclusionary racial policy of the downtown eateries in the major department stores. Approximately one month after students began their full-scale movement in February 1960, Fisk University professor Vivian Henderson estimated that blacks in Nashville poured approximately $50 million annually into the coffers of white businesses. This was a significant sum considering that the merchants witnessed many of their white customers move to the suburbs, and they became increasingly more economically dependent on Nashville's black population. The Reverend Kelly Miller Smith and Henderson organized a boycott of downtown merchants just before Easter, which was one of the most important shopping holidays. Empowered with their stated motto "No Fashions for Easter," the black community's "economic withdrawal" deprived storeowners of incalculable amounts of business.

By the beginning of April 1960, Nashville department stores were virtually empty, as whites, too, stayed away. Others also joined in the "economic withdrawal," as a show of support for the student demonstrators. "No Fashions for Easter" achieved its stated goal. This action caused the downtown retail merchants to lose approximately 20 percent of their business. Downtown's empty streets and empty cash registers caused merchants to seriously consider dismantling Jim Crow customs in Nashville's retail district.

Relenting under the pressure of the economic boycott, six stores rendered service to African Americans on May 10, 1960, making Nashville the first major city in the South to desegregate its lunch counters. Between 1961 and 1963, protests shifted to movie theaters (by May 1961 theater owners capitulated), fair employment practices, downtown hotels, and every other deliverance of public accommodations. By the spring of 1963, Nashville faced daily demonstrations against segregation, unfair employment, and discrimination against Nashville blacks in general. In March, the Nashville Christian Leadership Conference announced a "full-scale-assault" on segregation practices in Nashville. In addition to using protest marches, leaders and students of the Nashville movement implemented the proven weapon of an Easter economic boycott against downtown merchants and department stores to protest against unfair employment practices. The paucity of dollars flowing into the cash registers of Nashville merchants and businessmen caused the walls of racial segregation in Nashville to fall. As in Nashville, other cities across the South began the desegregation of the eating establishments.

American blacks continued their struggle to gain civil rights throughout America. CORE, which forged the modern sit-in movement in the early 1940s and initiated freedom rides in 1947, was also instrumental in the freedom rides of the 1960s. Modeled after its Journey of Reconciliation, it also tested the enforcement of the Supreme Court's decision in the 1960 *Boynton v. Virginia* case that extended the mandated desegregation order to all interstate transportation facilities, including terminals. However, after sending an interracial group of thirteen freedom riders into the deep, who were greeted with violence on May 14, 1961, CORE officials decided to abort its protest against segregated interstate buses and facilities. Notwithstanding the threats of violence and possible death, three days later, SNCC students, led by Nashville student activist Diane Nash, picked up the protest and continued the freedom rides. On September 22, under pressure from the Kennedy administration, the Interstate Commerce Commission issued regulations prohibiting segregated bus and train terminals. The regulations became effective on November 1, 1961. However, many southern cities incessantly treated the ruling with contempt.

Steadfast in the beliefs for which they were fighting and refusing to abdicate the cause, American blacks continued to address the cancerous disease of racism, whether de jure or de facto, that manifested itself throughout the nation's society. While continuing to sit in, stand in, sleep in, wade in, and freedom ride, they attacked other vestiges of the disease by using boycotts and protests. SNCC turned its attention to the lack of voting rights among people in the American black community. Armed with their surgical instruments of protests and boycotts, they invaded the Deep South and proceeded to help remove the malignant tumor's metastatic growth.

## CIVIL RIGHTS LEGISLATION ENACTED

Within four years and after numerous campaigns, protests, and boycotts, including the 1963 March on Washington and the assassination of President

John F. Kennedy, on July 2, President Lyndon B. Johnson signed the 1964 Civil Rights Act, which was one of the nation's most important and most comprehensive pieces of civil rights legislation. White defiance to the voting rights of American blacks in the Deep South continued unabated after the passage of the Civil Rights Act of 1964. In less than a month after the act was codified, voting rights activists James Chaney, Andrew Goodman, and Michael Schwerner were murdered in Mississippi. Deaths and the threat of violence continued into the next year. Known as "Bloody Sunday," on March 7, 1965, more than 500 persons protested the denial of American blacks' voting rights when they marched from Selma to Montgomery. As they crossed the Pettus Bridge leading out of Selma, state troopers and local police swarmed the group with tear gas, clubs, and cattle prods, causing multiple injuries that required medical treatment. A little more than three weeks later, on March 25, King successfully led approximately 25,000 marching protesters from Selma to Montgomery. The same day, Klansmen murdered Viola Liuzzo, a white woman from Detroit, Michigan. To further protest the senseless murders, the malevolent maltreatment of American blacks, and the refusal to adhere to the newly enacted civil rights law, organizations, companies, and individuals throughout America boycotted Alabama's goods and services during the spring of 1965. Approved by the majority of the U.S. Congress (333 to 48 in the House of Representatives and 77 to 19 in the Senate), five months later, on August 6, Johnson signed the Voting Rights Act of 1965.

A year before Johnson signed the Voting Rights Act of 1965, CORE's Brooklyn, New York, chapter planed a "stall-in" protest tactic for the opening day of the 1964–1965 World's Fair. The purpose of the "stall-in," which called for stalling cars and blocking subways on all major routes leading to the fair, was to focus attention on a broad range of complex issues and forms of racial discrimination in employment and housing. While in some ways the "stall-in" never took place, its effect resonated across the nation and demonstrated the power of ordinary people to influence and alter business as usual by merely threatening to close down the city. Just as CORE sought to bring down the walls of racial discrimination in the North, the Reverend Martin Luther King Jr. and the SCLC also focused their attention on the problems of racial discrimination in that region of the country.

Three years before his death, King and the SCLC, in an effort to transfer the campaign of direct-action protest above the Mason-Dixon Line, targeted Chicago, Illinois, one of the most segregated of cities in the North. Discussion sessions between SCLC and local civil rights groups proved to be unsuccessful in engendering a coherent set of priorities for the campaign; housing emerged as the major issue. Civil rights leaders called for marches and demonstrations against de facto housing discrimination. While their protests brought into national view the pattern of housing discrimination in the region and the country, it would take three years and the death of King for federal legislation (Civil Rights Act of 1968, also known as the Housing

Act of 1968 or the Fair Housing Act of 1968) to prohibit discrimination as it related to the sale, rental, and financing of housing.

Black Americans also used protests to secure fair wages and better working conditions as vividly demonstrated by the sanitation workers' strike in Memphis, Tennessee. Black sanitation workers in the "Bluff City" earned far less than did their white counterparts. While the initial impetus for the protest marches and demonstrations rested on the foundation of economics or the lack thereof, they amplified other social ills and conditions, including overt racism, that manifested themselves in the American black community. Civil rights leaders in Memphis called upon King to assist the black sanitation workers in their struggle. He arrived in Memphis on March 28, 1968, to give his support to the scheduled protest march, which turned violent. Troubled that the nonviolent image would become bankrupt, he returned to the city within the week, intending to lead a peaceful protest and protect the solvency of the direct nonviolent tactic. However, on April 4, 1968, the proponent of nonviolence was violently stricken with a fatal shot from an assassin's gun. Despite King's assassination, the Reverend James Lawson continued the march against the injustices placed upon the black sanitation workers and the American black community. Although many prognosticated the end of the movement, American blacks, civil rights organizations, and others continued to wage battles against racial discrimination and institutionalized racism in America.

The systematic strategies employed by American blacks in their struggle for equality and justice proved useful to activists in other social movements throughout the 1960s and beyond. The antiwar movement, the women's movement, the gay rights movement, the movement for the rights of disabled Americans, and others all used such instruments of protest as sit-ins, marches, and boycotts.

Throughout the 1960s and into the twenty-first century, black Americans have boycotted and protested with their wallets where the vestiges of racism remained covert rather than overt. They targeted such corporations as Texaco, Denny's, Coca-Cola, and Cracker Barrel, to name only a few.

Economic boycotts and protests aided in fostering a transformation throughout society, both national and international. The American Revolution began with the Boston Tea Party. The nonviolent movement that brought down the British Empire included Gandhi's imposed sanctions against British textiles. The Baton Rouge and Montgomery Bus Boycotts launched America's modern movement for civil rights among American blacks. The United Farm Workers in the United States, led by César Chávez, were unionized through exacting national boycotts against lettuce and grapes, and the international boycott of South Africa contributed significantly to the demise of its apartheid system. America's organized and legalized set of doctrines, ideas, and principles of racial segregation and political and economic discrimination against its citizens of African descent were dismantled by the effectiveness of boycotts and protests.

American blacks effectively used the premise put forth by Reinhold Niebuhr in 1932 when they successfully put into action economic and political pressures that "exert[ed] coercion upon the white man's life" and, more important, adversely affected the profit and loss margins of his businesses. American blacks' use of boycotts and protests made the twin tactics a force for positive social change. They fostered social cohesiveness throughout the community regardless of age, creed, economic or social class, gender, race, or religion. American black activists and others with their use of boycotts and protests aided in making America and its citizens more aware of, conscious about, and sensitive to all subjugated and oppressed groups discriminated against historically.

## Sources

Carson, Clayborne. *Civil Rights Chronicle: The African American Struggle for Freedom.* Lincolnwood, IL: Legacy Publishing, 2003.

Crawford, Vicki L., Jacqueline Anne Rouse, and Barbara Woods. *Women in the Civil Rights Movement: Trailblazers and Torchbearers, 1941–1965.* Bloomington: Indiana University Press, 1993.

Dierenfield, Bruce J. *The Civil Rights Movement.* New York: Longman Publishers, 2004.

Jacoway, Elizabeth, and David R. Colburn, eds. *Southern Businessmen and Desegregation.* Baton Rouge: Louisiana State University Press, 1982.

Meier, August, and Elliott Rudwick. "The Boycott Movement against Jim Crow Streetcars in the South 1900–1906." *Journal of American History* 55 (March 1969): 756–775.

Morgan, Robin. *Sisterhood Is Global.* New York: Feminist Press, 1996.

Niebuhr, Reinhold. "Moralists and Politics." *Essays in Applied Christianity.* Ed. D. B. Robertson. New York: Meridian Books, 1959.

Price, Mary. "Baton Rouge Bus Boycott." http://www.lib.lsu.edu/special/exhibits/boycott/background.

Theoharis, Jeanne, and Komozi Woodard, eds. *Groundwork: Local Black Freedom Movements in America.* New York: New York University Press, 2005.

Wynn, Linda. *The "Economic Withdrawal" during the Nashville Sit-in Movement.* Nashville, TN: Local Conference on African American Culture and History, 2005.

———. "Nashville's Streetcar Boycott, (1905–1907)." *Profiles of African Americans in Tennessee.* Ed. Bobby L. Lovett and Linda T. Wynn. Nashville, TN: Local Conference on African American Culture and History, 1996.

*Linda T. Wynn*

# Kenneth "Babyface" Edmonds (1959– ) and Tracey Edmonds (1967– ), Recording Artists, Songwriters, Record Producers, Business Executives

Kenneth "Babyface" and Tracey Edmonds are one of the most widely recognized celebrity couples in the music industry today. As cofounders of Edmonds Entertainment Group, Incorporated, they brought together their business savvy and musical talent to head a group of music, television, and film production companies. Their promotion and production of rhythm and blues (R&B) artists, film, and cable television have made them a major force in the entertainment industry.

As an award-winning songwriter and president of two major record labels, Babyface (a nickname given to him by guitarist Bootsy Collins) has written for major artists and singing groups such as Mariah Carey, Michael Jackson, Madonna, Aretha Franklin, Mary J. Blige, Faith Evans, N' Sync, and Backstreet Boys. Edmonds was born on April 10, 1959, in Indianapolis, Indiana, to Barbara and Marvin Edmonds. He was the fifth of six children born to the couple. Marvin Edmonds died when Babyface was in the eighth grade, leaving the challenge of raising six children to Edmond's mother. As a child, Edmonds was deeply interested in music and learned to play guitar. During the 1970s, Edmonds played with a funk group called ManChild, and later he played with the Crowd Pleasers. In 1981, Edmonds met his future business partner **Antonio "L. A." Reid**. Edmonds joined Reid and performed with the group the Deele. The discovery of Edmonds and Reid by Dick Griffey of Solar Records launched a new and rewarding phase in their careers as musical performers as well as songwriters. This shift would later inspire the two to pursue music production and ownership of their own recording label.

Under Solar Records, Edmonds and Reid enjoyed celebrity writing for well-known R&B and popular music artists such as Bobby Brown and the music group After 7. In 1987, the writing duo began working outside of Solar Records, and in 1989 Edmonds and Reid cofounded the LaFace Record label based in Atlanta, Georgia. Their talent and success were recognized when they won the Songwriters of the Year Award in 1990 by Broadcast Music Incorporated. During this period, they produced music for numerous performers including Johnny Gill, TLC, and Toni Braxton.

Edmond's success was not limited to songwriting and producing; he also continued to enjoyed celebrity as a performer. His second album *Tender Lover* (1989) included the hit song "Whip Appeal." His music would bring another reward of sorts. While Edmonds had been married once in the early 1980s, his marriage was brief. The search for models for his video led Edmonds to meet his second wife, Tracey McQuarn. McQuarn and Edmonds began dating and in 1992 were married. The couple has two sons: Brandon, born in 1997, and Dylan, born in 2001.

Tracey McQuarn Edmonds was born on February 18, 1967, in Southern California to Jacqueline and George McQuarn. McQuarn was the first child born to the couple; they also had a second child, Michael. McQuarn's mother was a homemaker and her father a college basketball coach. At an early age McQuarn displayed intellectual promise. She completed high school at sixteen and attended Stanford University. She planned to become a psychiatrist. Her major included studies in neurobiology and psychology. She graduated from Stanford in 1987. However, instead of pursuing medical school, she obtained her real estate license and established a business with her mother. She and her mother sold houses in the Los Angeles Area. When Tracey married Babyface, she used her business savvy to pursue her interests in music.

As the wife of a successful songwriter and record producer, Tracey interacted with various aspiring artists. Encouraged by these interactions, in 1994 she founded Yab-Yum, a song publishing company. The name of the company is a Japanese phrase meaning "God of love." Recognizing her ability, Sony offered Tracey her own recording label.

While Tracey worked with Yab-Yum, her husband continued to write and to produce for other artists, as well as work on his own musical career. In 1995, Babyface produced and wrote music for the *Waiting to Exhale* soundtrack. He also wrote and produced the Boyz II Men hit single "End of the Road" for the 1993 film *Boomerang*. In the early 1990s, Babyface released remix album *A Closer Looker*, and in 1993 he released *For the Cool in You* and in 2001, *Face2Face*.

Babyface and Tracey Edmonds decided that rather than working apart, they would use their comparable strengths to establish an entertainment company that would involve music, film, and television. The company was Edmonds Entertainment Group, founded in 1997. The various entities of the corporation include: e2filmworks, edmondsmusic publishing, e2recrods, and Edmonds management. The decision was agreeable not only because of its potential financial rewards but because it would allow them to spend more time together.

As chief executive officer and president, Tracey Edmonds in 1997 guided Edmonds Entertainment through its successful premier with the production of the film and movie soundtrack *Soul Food*. The film won five NAACP (National Association for the Advancement of Colored People) Image Awards in 1997. The success of the movie led to a cable television series on Showtime, also produced by Edmonds Entertainment. *Soul Food* won the NAACP Image Award in 2004 for Best Dramatic Series. Since *Soul Food*, Edmonds Entertainment Group has continued to enjoy success in the film industry. In 1998, Edmonds produced the film *Hav Plenty*, released by Miramax, and in 1999 Edmonds produced the film *Light It Up*, released by Fox 2000. The Edmonds Group has also worked with independent film writers. In 2002, Edmonds produced the award-winning film *PUNKS*. *PUNKS* won Best American Independent Film at the Cleveland International Film Festival.

Edmonds Entertainment Group has also continued to work in television and other media. Edmonds Group produced the show *College Hill*, which premiered on Black Entertainment Television in January 2004. The company is also working on several other television projects. In 2002, Edmonds Entertainment produced the play *Love Makes Things Happen*. The musical comedy from David Talbert was met with strong critical approval and was nominated for multiple NAACP awards.

Recognized for their talent and success, the Edmondses have won numerous awards. In 2005, Tracey Edmonds won the National Organization for Women's Excellence in Media Award, and in 2000, she won the Turner Broadcasting System's Tower of Power Award. Babyface has won ten Grammy Awards. In 1998, he won the award for producer of the year for the third time.

He was nominated for his song "That's the Way Love Goes," the theme song for the Showtime series *Soul Food*. He has been the recipient of the Soul Train Music Award, the Broadcast Music Award (BMI), the NAACP Image Award, and the American Music Award. The influence of Babyface is evidenced by his creation and production of over 100 top R&B and popular songs in the past twenty years.

The Edmondses have played a significant role in the development of popular media for the past twenty years. Their efforts are remarkable not only because of the pleasure they bring to an American and even global audience but also because of the inspiring example they provide for those current and future entrepreneurs in the entertainment industry.

## Sources

Aldore, Collier. "Babyface in a New Place in His Life and Music: Singer and Wife Redefine Hollywood Power and Togetherness." *Ebony* 57 (December 2001): 74.

"Baby Face: On His New Album, Family Life and Fans." *Jet* 100 (September 2001): 58.

Edmonds Entertainment Group. http://www.edmondsent.com.

"Kenneth Edmonds." *Contemporary Black Biography*. Vol. 31. Ed. Ashyia Henderson. Gale Group, 2001. Reproduced in Biography Resource Center. Farmington Hills, MI: Thomson Gale, 2005. http://galenet.galegroup.com/servlet/BioRC Document Number: K16060001962.

"Kenneth 'Babyface' Edmonds." *Contemporary Musicians*. Vol. 12. Gale Research, 1994. Reproduced in Biography Resource Center. Farmington Hills, MI: Thomson Gale, 2005. http://galenet.galegroup.com/servlet/BioRC Document Number: K1608000870.

"Kenneth Edmonds." *Newsmakers*, no. 4. Gale Research, 1995. Reproduced in Biography Resource Center. Farmington Hills, MI: Thomson Gale, 2005. http://galenet.galegroup.com/servlet/BioRC Document Number: K1618001372.

"Tracey Edmonds." *Notable Black American Women*. Book III. Ed. Jessie Carney Smith. Detroit: Thomson Gale, 2002.

*Rebecca Dixon*

# Elleanor Eldridge (1785–1865?), Entrepreneur, Tradeswoman

Elleanor Eldridge worked in a variety of then-gender-based domestic and manufacturing activities and through shrewd practices made a profit from her work. In addition to those activities in which she was engaged to support herself, such as a domestic, nurse, rug-sewer, whitewasher, painter, and paper hanger, she also became a successful soap manufacturer. Later she acquired considerable real estate, wrote her memoirs, and made regional lecture tours to promote her book. An early, enterprising antebellum black woman, she became wealthy by standards of her day.

Eldridge wrote in her autobiography that she was the granddaughter of an African trader who, with his family, was kidnapped, sold into slavery, and brought to America. Her father and her two uncles became free when they volunteered for the American Revolution. When freed, they were promised

200 acres of land in Mohawk County in western New York, but the land was never granted. Robin Eldridge managed to save enough money to buy and build a house in Rhode Island. Finally settling in Warwick, Rhode Island, Robin Eldridge met and married Hannah Prophet, who was part Narragansett Indian. Thus, Elleanor was born free in Warwick on March 26, 1785. Only five of her seven siblings lived to maturity. Hannah Prophet died when Elleanor was ten years old. Elleanor Baker, a laundry customer and friend of Hannah's, persuaded Robin Eldridge to allow the child to move in with her. It was during her comfortable life with the woman that young Elleanor learned many skills that would serve her well when she joined the workforce and also entered her own profit-making businesses.

When only ten years old, Eldridge worked as a domestic and earned twenty-five cents a week. She developed skills in a number of areas, and by the time she was fourteen, she knew several useful trades that enabled her to hire herself out for local jobs, such as managing a dairy, wallpapering, and weaving. She was in charge of Captain Benjamin Greene's dairy farm in Warwick Neck, where she worked from age seventeen to twenty-four. While there she made "premium" quality cheeses. She had become a fine cloth-maker and knew well the art of spinning. She had also become a weaver, practicing plain, double, and ornamental techniques. Double weaving, considered a difficult process, was used when making items such as carpeting, coverlets, damask, and bed ticking. The enterprising young woman had impressive savings that she put to good use. Local residents knew her talent and spoke highly of the work of this free, unwed, black woman.

When Eldridge was nineteen, her father died. Then she went to Adams, Massachusetts, some 180 miles from Warwick, and helped her family to secure letters of administration for her father's estate. Once that business was done, she returned to Warwick Neck and to her work with Captain Greene. After Greene died in 1812, she returned to Adams and lived with her sister, Lettise.

Eldridge and her sister established a variety of business ventures, including weaving and soap-boiling. The frugal Elleanor had saved enough money to buy a lot and build a house. She rented the house to others for $40 a year. She returned to Providence three years later and hired herself out for various jobs, such as painting and whitewashing; she also did laundry and housework for families as well as hotels. By age forty-six she had purchased another lot for $100 and built a house in Providence for $1,700. Sometime later she made two additions to the house, lived in one section, and rented the other part for $150 a year. As she worked and saved, she also continued her interest in real estate. She borrowed $240 with an annual interest rate of 10 percent and made a verbal agreement to purchase another house for $2,000. She would pay $500 down and the balance in four years. Then she left to visit relatives in Adams. Before returning to Providence, she became ill from a bout with potentially fatal typhus, and her trip was delayed for several days. Local townspeople spotted her and spread the word in Providence that Eldridge was near death; some even said that she had died.

Meanwhile, a chain of events took place that nearly resulted in financial ruin for Eldridge. The property that she owned, valued at $4,000, had been illegally acquired to compensate for the $240 note that she owed on her latest transaction. In fact, the mortgage holder was overcompensated for the loan that he had made to Eldridge. The property was not advertised, and no efforts were made to notify her of the impending sale. All of Eldridge's efforts to retrieve her property failed. Confident that she would find the money that she needed, she entered into an agreement to repurchase the property that she had owned. She would pay more than the property's original value. Eldridge had the support of many friends, both white and black. They supported her lawsuit against the sheriff in Providence for allowing improper sale of her property. She dropped the lawsuit later on, after the buyer agreed to sell her the property. Both race and gender had been involved in the illegal activities. While she was free and well respected, legally she was denied the protection that whites would have received. It is possible, too, that popular support alone would have forced the return of her property without incident.

The account of Eldridge's life is given in her autobiography; there are described her business activities, including the rewards that she gained from her entrepreneurial activities. The record is that of an unusual free black woman who made her way and at the same time won the respect and support of white and blacks in Providence, Rhode Island. Her death date is uncertain but has been placed at 1862 or 1865.

*See also*: Women and Business

**Sources**

Greene, Frances. *Memoirs of Elleanor Eldridge*. Providence, RI: Albro, 1838, 1839.

Logan, Rayford W. "Elleanor Eldridge." *Dictionary of American Negro Biography*. Ed. Rayford W. Logan and Michael R. Winston. New York: W. W. Norton, 1982.

*Jessie Carney Smith*

# William Ellison (1790–1861), Artisan, Planter

William Ellison was born a slave, gained his freedom, and became one of the richest free blacks in the United States. He owed his wealth to his ability to exploit a new technology much in demand as planters expanded their production of cotton. About 1802, Ellison—then known by the single name of April—was apprenticed to a maker of cotton gins, learning how to make the machines and keep them in repair. After his apprenticeship, he lived and worked almost as a free black for some years, and 1816 he probably purchased his freedom from his father or his brother—the relationship is surmised but explains the favorable treatment he had enjoyed as a slave. After moving to Statesburg, South Carolina, to avoid competing against the man who trained him, Ellison built a fortune by exploiting his knowledge of cotton gins and by farming. He bought slaves as a labor force, and by the time of his death, he owned sixty-three slaves and 900 acres of land. His ambiguous status in the community is shown by his being allowed in 1824 by Holy Cross Episcopal Church to move his family from the balcony reserved for blacks, slave and free, to a bench at the back of the main floor. Its yearly rent was greater than that of the side pews in the church.

Ellison seems to have been born on a plantation near Winsboro, South Carolina, in 1790. He attained his freedom as April Ellison in 1816, subsequently changing his name to William in 1820 to efface his slave name. Ellison's mother, probably one of the seventeen slaves on the plantation, died still a slave in 1837, but he purchased and freed his wife and daughter by 1817, since the first of his three sons was born free in that year. A natural daughter born in 1815 remained technically a slave all her life, but her father made sure she lived as a free black and gave instructions for her manumission on his death. His other children, their spouses, and their children—sixteen persons in 1850—shared living space in two houses he owned in Statesburg. The free black society of Charleston supplied the marriage partners.

In the year Ellison petitioned for a change of name, he owned two slaves. Over the years there are other milestones of his rise. In 1821 he felt sure enough of his position in the community to sue a white man for debt. The following year he bought an acre of land in a prime commercial location and set up his workshop. By 1838 he owned two substantial homes on the other side of the road—one the childhood home of Civil War diarist Mary Chesnut.

In 1840 Ellison owned thirty-six slaves; the number had increased to sixty-three by 1860. Although some were used in the cotton gin workshop, most worked the nearly 900 acres of land he owned. Among the slaves is probably the ancestor of twentieth-century writer Ralph Ellison. There is no evidence that this workforce was treated better than slaves belonging to white owners. Indeed, the age and sex distribution of the group give probable cause to suspect that he was selling off female children for whom he had no use.

Ellison died on December 5, 1861, so he did not live to face the problems brought on by the Civil War and Emancipation. A store replaced the workshop, and the land was rented out, but a continuing decline in family fortunes led the family to gradually move away. The second wife of Ellison's son William was the last family member to reside in the family home at her death in 1920.

Ellison benefited from his white relatives' influence to secure technical training for him, which laid the foundation of his substantial financial success. Typically of his time and place, he invested his surplus capital in the plantation economy. It seems that, insofar as possible, he adopted the values of the white community around him—although there is simply not enough evidence for a definitive conclusion. In a society that was organized on the sharp distinction between free and slave, which was supposed to translate into white and black, he occupied the anomalous position of free black.

Making the most of his opportunities, he displayed great skill in becoming a large slave owner and a very affluent person.

*See also*: Blacks in Agriculture

**Sources**

Johnson, Michael P., and James L. Roark. *Black Masters: A Free Family of Color in the Old South*. New York: Norton, 1984.

————. *No Chariot Let Down: Charleston's Free People of Color on the Eve of the Civil War*. Chapel Hill: University of North Carolina Press, 1984.

Smith, Jessie Carney, ed. *Notable Black American Men*. Detroit: Gale Research, 1999.

*Robert L. Johns*

# Evern Cooper Epps (19?– ), Corporate Executive

Evern Cooper Epps began her career humbly at United Parcel Service (UPS) in 1974 as a part-time package handler. Epps was attending Emory University, earning her master's degree, and needed extra money to make ends meet. Through additional training, she was promoted and made it behind the wheels next as a delivery truck driver. Eager to learn as much as she could about UPS, Epps landed positions dealing with strategic planning, delivery information, training, and business development. A native of Detroit, Epps earned a bachelor's degree from Michigan State University in English and journalism before working as a high school English teacher. Early in life she was instilled with values of charity and generosity.

Over the next eighteen years she built her reputation as a devout and industrious employee. In 1992, her hard work paid off. She was promoted to associate director of the UPS Foundation. This background would have a strong impact on the roles she would elevate to as she made corporate history twice, becoming the first woman and the first African American to be named president of the UPS Foundation in 1998. She also maintains the post of vice president, UPS Corporate Relations, where she repeated both of those firsts. Epps refined her business skills through a master's degree in education at Harvard University to prepare her for running the charitable component of the multibillion-dollar corporation. Her formal and practical training have proved beneficial for UPS because Epps has successfully expanded worldwide philanthropic implementation. Global volunteering, literacy, and hunger relief all reflect her dynamic output.

The primary focus of the UPS Foundation is to have a positive impact on the lives of the underserved, underprivileged, and underrepresented; therefore, it is imperative that its director be an effective relationship builder. This is key because she must seek favorable alliances and partnerships with programs and organizations that share comparable principles with UPS. Epps is a communications broker between UPS and many of the nation's leading community and civic organizations and is the ambassador for UPS's model for corporate responsibility. At the two-day workshop in

Boston, Massachusetts, "Reshaping Corporations: Adding Value through Responsible Business Practices," held on January 25–27, 2004, Epps spoke about the growing need for corporations to be more responsible regarding the environment and society at large. The challenges created from these realities were presented in a way in which opportunities opened up, according to Epps. Furthermore, Epps is careful to keep in mind UPS founder Jim Casey's fundamental aspiration, making his company community based and community friendly. This is achieved by the implementation of such direct incentives as college assistance, employee stock, and benefits.

Relationship building by Epps is demonstrated by Vanderheyden Hall and the Women's Alliance. In 2002, in an effort to support family and workplace literacy, the UPS Foundation provided a $5,000 grant to Vanderheyden Hall in Wynantskill, New York, which takes care of the needs of children, young adults, and families with services that challenge and enable them to do for themselves. Commenting on UPS's support of such an endeavor, Epps emphasized that humanitarian, financial, and educational help in areas of enhancing social welfare needs were at the top of the Foundation's priority list. In 2005, Epps's applied formula was at work again at the Women's Alliance National Conference. Through an initiative and partnership called welfare-to-work, Epps indicated that providing job opportunities for women on public assistance was a positive and proactive move for the company. She went on to add that UPS had a long history of community-based outreach, even with those on public assistance. She pointed out, however, that it was considered then, just as now, as doing smart business instead of being called welfare.

Epps has stated that in all that she has done professionally she is most proud of the Volunteer Impact Initiative, which began in 1998 as a program to explore innovative ways for charities to recruit and retain volunteers. This gave Epps the opportunity to be directly involved with a cause that she spearheaded. She is boastful that the UPS Foundation is one of the first to focus on the volunteer aspect of philanthropic activities.

Epps's impressive contributions have earned her affiliation on numerous national and local professional organizations in Atlanta, Georgia, home of UPS corporate operations. Epps is a board member for the Metro Atlanta YMCA; Close Up Foundation; Zoo Atlanta; Project Grad; Point of Light Foundation; International Advisory Board for the Center for Corporate Citizenship at Boston College; and Andrew Young School of Policy Studies. She chairs the boards of Atlanta Partners for Education; Directors of the Northwest Georgia Girl Scout Council; and Women Looking Ahead, respectively. In addition, she formally served as the chair, Board of Corporate Advisors of the United Way of America. In 2005, the YWCA's Greater Atlanta Academy of Women Achievers as their Woman of Achievement chose Epps. She was inducted into this body in 1997. Epps is listed by Georgia as one of its "100 Most Powerful and Influential Women in Corporate America," and *Business to Business* named her in 2004 as one of its divas.

Epps has remained as humble as she began. She sees herself as simply a woman who took full advantage of every opportunity to arrive where she is today.

*See also*: Women and Business

**Sources**

America's Fund for Communities. http://www.americasfund.org/affc_overview03.html.

*Atlanta Woman* (May–June 2003): 19.

*Contemporary Black Biography*. Vol. 40. Detroit: Thomson Gale, 2004.

Girl Scout Council of Northwest Georgia. http://www.girlscoutsnwga.org/resources/index.asp?page=adult_recognition.

History Makers. http://www.thehistorymakers.com/biography/biographyasp?bioindex=740&category=businessMakers.

Saposnick, Kali. "Face to Face, the Spirit of Giving at UPS: Doing Well by Doing Good." *Leverage Points: For a New Workplace, New World.* http://www.pegasuscom.com/levpoints/lp45.html.

UPS. http://www.pressroom.ups.com/mediakits/otherexec/bios/0,2329,74,00.html.

Vanderheyden Hall. http://www.vanderheydenhall.org/highres/pressrelease.html.

Women's Alliance. http://www.thewomensalloiance.org/supporterquotes.html.

*Shannon L. Mathis*

# Eta Phi Beta Sorority, Inc.

To meet the growing demands of civic-minded and economic responsive black women, Eta Phi Beta emerged in 1942 as a national business and professional women's sorority founded by eleven Lewis Business College graduates in Detroit, Michigan. With the specific aim of establishing stronger links among Detroit's black professional businesswomen circles, the sorority immediately started partnerships with local high schools and retarded citizens' agencies centered on scholarship procurement and programming, respectively. The pioneers who acted on their progressive instincts and launched into action include Merry Green Hubbard, Ann Porter, Lena Reed, Earline Carter, Ivy Burt Banks, Dorthy Sylvers Brown, Ethal Madison, Mae Edwards Bolling Curry, Katherine Douglas, Mattie Rankin, and Atheline Shelton.

To carry out its work, Eta Phi Beta through the years has blossomed to promote and provide technical assistance in the encouragement of business standards' improvement and the recruitment of qualified and trained professional black women. Most of its members are recruited out of college and after demonstrating a propensity toward excellence in the harsh climate of business professionalism. By the awarding of scholarships and the implementation of career development opportunities, they have proven to be extremely efficient. The national outreach project of the organization has remained the mentally handicapped, and its primary civic contributions have gone to the United Negro College Fund, National Association for the Advancement of Colored

People (NAACP), the Urban League, March of Dimes, United Way Drive, YWCA, YMCA, Boys and Girls Scouts of America, and the National Council of Negro Women. Additionally, annual functions in support of sorority objectives include the Hobo Scholarship Dance, the Christmas Candlelight Vespers Service, Founders' Day Observance Luncheon, and the Queen Bee Contests.

The Queen Bee initiative for Eta Phi Beta members is very prestigious and revolves around one of the key components of business development. The national Queen is secured by the woman who raises the most capital for national scholarship campaigns. Accordingly, from 1992 to 1994 Louise Hoskins Broadnax of Chicago's Alpha Lambda chapter was the anointed Queen. The former director of Institutional Care of the Chicago Department of Public Health, Broadnax benefited from the residual "Queen" status by being elected to the top post of Grand Basileus in 2002, a post she currently still holds. Moreover, as the black woman has historically been the backbone of the black family, Eta Phi Beta business parameters have not been created devoid of the broader family connections necessary for sustaining a strong, healthy family tree. Thus the Shad Club, Bee Ettes, Senords, and the Eta Kids were established to enable the entire family to grow from annual convention activities.

The Shad Club is an auxiliary unit consisting of members' husbands, whereas the Bee Ettes are middle and high school aged females and the Senords the male counterparts. To complete the cycle are the Eta Kids who make up the under-twelve youth demographic. Not just for ceremonial purposes, contrastingly these auxiliary groups have miniconventions and workshop sessions built into their conferences. One such example of the organizations' commitment to support the utilization of resources and business success to improve inner-city communities was the 60th Anniversary Convention celebrated in Raleigh, North Carolina, on October 28–29, 2002, where Sara White, wife of Hall of Fame National Football League defensive lineman Reggie White, was honored for her outstanding contributions in enhancing living standards in underserved communities. Hence the group's motto "Not for ourselves but for others" is pragmatically reinforced.

For its contributions, Eta Phi Beta has been acknowledged for its continued work in developing business and professional relationships within respective northern, southern, eastern, western, southeastern, and mideastern regions, geographically representing thirty-two states and the Virgin Islands with 110 chapters. There should be no surprise in reading of their esteemed incorporation into Grace House of Louisiana Inc.'s 11th Annual Women of Substance Luncheon in New Orleans that honored and showed respect to empowered women on May 21, 2005. "Women Making a Difference" was the theme of a luncheon session sponsored by the sorority's omicron chapter. Moreover, founders of Eta Phi Beta Sorority, Inc. had the wisdom to channel their energies through charitable good, advancing education and business responsibility within the context of communities. More than sixty years later, the women who comprise membership continue to make a difference and impact positively on black communities generally and humanity at large.

*See also*: Women and Business

**Sources**

Eta Phi Beta, Alpha Gamma. http://www.angelfire.com/fl4/alphagamma.

Eta Phi Beta, Southern Region. http://www.etaphibetasouthern.org/history.htm.

National Report. "Julia H. Davis Re-elected Eta Phi Beta Prexy." *Jet* 90 (September 23, 1996): 22.

———. "National President of Eta Phi Beta Sorority, Inc. Re-elected." *Jet* 107 (April 11, 2005): 10.

Newsmakers. "Eta Phi Beta Sorority, Inc. Celebrates 25th Biennial National Convention in North Carolina." *Jet* 102 (October 28, 2002): 55.

Nolan, Nell. "Swiss Soiree and Lunchtime Laurels." *Times-Picayune*, May 21, 2005.

*Uzoma O. Miller*

# F

## Faith-Based Entrepreneurship

African American religious organizations, whether individual churches, mosques, synagogues, formal fellowships of congregations as in denominational systems, or groups developed independently as a result of individual charismatic religious leadership, have always contained an element of faith-based entrepreneurship. This concept can be defined in broad terms as the use of the financial resources of religious organizations and clergy to support and empower business and other economic initiatives inside and/or outside their immediate community.

Within the scope of this definition, the black minister must be considered the earliest example of a faith-based entrepreneur, and the black church or religious organization itself as an economic as well as a spiritual enterprise that has been developed through entrepreneurship involving various levels of risk and reward. Both free and slave preachers brought an African perspective to their new religion and in different ways adapted it to the social and economic realities of American bondage and servitude in the southern United States while retaining faith regarding eventual freedom.

While some believed the liberating work of God was found in the afterlife or for future generations, others used biblical examples to justify more radical and high-risk approaches to securing freedom. In several instances the leaders of major slave revolts were preachers, with Denmark Vesey in South Carolina (1822) and Nat Turner in Virginia (1831) being the most famous examples. In response, many southern states outlawed religious meetings of slaves or tried to maintain strict control over all gatherings.

These early leaders used whatever meager resources they could muster to establish their fellowships, many of which were formed and remained as secret organizations. If they were allowed to meet openly in a space approved by their masters and under their supervision, they had to become adept in the skillful use of coded language and other behaviors to inform and inspire their congregations, without offending their overseers and jeopardizing themselves and their fellow slaves in the process.

The slave preacher also had to exhibit entrepreneurial skills such as negotiation and diplomacy, to ensure that the master(s) would not perceive their gatherings as a threat to the existing order and allow them to continue to meet. The first order of business for the slave preacher and church, as in any enterprise, was survival.

While the free Negro church leaders in the North may not have had the immediate threat of physical survival as an issue, they had to negotiate through white-controlled systems to establish viable organizations. They became entrepreneurs out of necessity, starting their churches in many instances as a response to unfavorable treatment in congregations organized and managed by whites.

Another approach was the tradition of itinerant or "traveling preachers," which can be considered as another early form of faith-based entrepreneurship, where the minister came to the people and provided religious inspiration and services at whatever site was considered appropriate and available, indoors or outdoors, for varying amounts of time before moving on to other locations. These types of services, including "tent revivals," hearkened back to biblical descriptions of the travels of the children of Israel after their liberation from Egypt with their tabernacle, tents that served the purpose of a portable worship space until they could settle in the promised land and eventually build a permanent structure.

Even as the nation of Israel depended on God and each other during their travels, the traveling evangelists of early and modern America relied on the people's generosity to sustain them in the course of moving from location to location to fulfill their spiritual vocation. Ministers also had to have other skills and be able to take on other types of work, in order to survive when the contributions and resources of the congregations were inadequate.

For black clergy, this was even more so the case, given the extremely limited financial resources of most African American communities. However, the ongoing importance of spirituality among a majority of blacks in America enabled the development of both formal institutional structures by groups and creative spiritual entrepreneurship by individuals.

As faith-based entrepreneurs, black ministers always ran the risk of credibility with their congregations, especially in the case of traveling evangelists who had no direct or permanent ties and accountability to the communities they served. As a result, most meaningful group economic development and entrepreneurship took place when religious institutions and organizations were firmly established in one or more communities, with stable leadership, membership, and financial resources.

## ENTREPRENEURSHIP IN EARLY BLACK CHURCHES

From these humble beginnings, numerous black churches and other religious organizations became centers for support and development of African American communities in all parts of the country. The development of African American religious denominations can in one sense be considered faith-based entrepreneurship, as black ministers organized various collective structures as support mechanisms for individual churches and congregations.

While most denominations were based on similar approaches to doctrine, worship style, and other factors, in at least one instance an African American economic organization helped to develop a major African American church. The Free African Society, a mutual-aid organization founded in Philadelphia by Richard Allen and Absalom Jones in 1787, emphasized solidarity and community development among free blacks in the city and was an early African American voice for the abolition of slavery.

In 1794, the society provided the support to establish the Mother Bethel African Methodist Episcopal (AME) Church, the founding congregation of what became the nation's first independent African American denomination in 1816. Allen later became the presiding bishop of the AME churches and led the denomination in such entrepreneurial activities as forming the first black publishing house, along with organizing national antislavery "Negro Conventions" and linking churches as locations for passage of escaped slaves on the Underground Railroad.

After the Civil War and the end of slavery, many of the early black churches and religious organizations exhibited faith-based entrepreneurship by establishing educational institutions on their own or through collaborations with sympathetic white individuals, churches, and other organizations. A majority of historically black colleges and universities (HBCUs), public as well as private, can trace their beginnings to influential black ministers and church organizations, with many actually being founded in church buildings.

In some instances, black ministers were the first presidents of these institutions, while continuing their pastoral responsibilities in the church and communities where they served. In other cases where the support and influence of whites was significant, white ministers took on the leadership role of institutions for blacks, seeing their work as an extension of missionary outreach. Even when the leaders were nonministers, they had to work effectively with ministers and churches, as well as others, to ensure continued support in the community for the new schools.

**Booker T. Washington**, while not a minister himself, was a prime example of a faith-based entrepreneur who was successful in using the economic as well as the spiritual resources of churches, other religious organizations, and outside individuals and groups to develop Tuskegee Institute (now Tuskegee University) in Alabama. He was instrumental in the development of numerous black businesses and organizations, including the **National**

**Negro Business League** (NNBL), based on the philosophy of acquiring productive skills and trades in the industrial education model of Hampton Institute (now Hampton University), the HBCU he had attended in Virginia.

Washington was also a promoter of strong moral values based on Christian principles, which he felt would give blacks the respect needed to advance as individuals and as a group, despite the segregation of the races on various levels throughout American society by the end of the nineteenth century. His message was accepted by many blacks and acceptable to most whites and enabled him to exert great political and economic influence toward achieving many of his desired objectives.

Many other black leaders of the time, in the religious community as well as the larger African American community, disagreed with Washington's accommodation of segregation while agreeing that entrepreneurship and economic development were essential to black progress. W.E.B. Du Bois, Washington's most prominent critic, argued that educational and business development could not be separated from the fight for full equality, yet also realized that segregation caused blacks to develop and support their own institutions and enterprises.

## A MODEL OF FAITH-BASED ENTREPRENEURSHIP AND GENERATIONAL WEALTH

Other religious organizations and denominations followed the lead of the AME church in establishing publishing houses and other faith-based religious enterprises, such as the National Baptist Publishing Board (NBPB), founded in 1896 and headquartered in Nashville, Tennessee. The driving force behind the creation of the NBPB was minister, entrepreneur, and leader **Richard Henry Boyd** (1843–1922).

Boyd spent his formative years as a slave in Mississippi, Louisiana, and Texas with the name Dick Gray and continued working on the Gray plantation after the Civil War and Emancipation. His mother had become a Christian and Baptist around 1860, and in 1869, Dick Gray was baptized and changed his name to Richard Henry Boyd.

By the early 1870s Boyd had entered the ministry, married the former Harriett A. Moore, and begun raising a large family. He also attended Bishop College, one of several HBCUs founded by the American Baptist Home Mission Society, an organization of white northern Baptists. Boyd spent the early years of his ministry organizing black churches and religious associations in Texas and eventually partnered with white southern Baptists in order to launch the NBPB after relocating to Nashville.

The success of the NBPB came as a result of Boyd's entrepreneurial skills in dealing with religious associations of both races and navigating through the controversies of the turbulent religious and racial environment of his times. As a result, he became nationally recognized for his efforts but was also envied and criticized for turning the NBPB into a profit-making business beyond its religious purposes. To protect the company, Boyd and his supporters legally incorporated the NBPB as a separate entity from the Baptist denomination in 1898.

In 1902 Boyd, attorney **James Carroll Napier**, and others founded the Nashville chapter of the NNBL, and Boyd launched the National Baptist Church Supply Company the same year. The Nashville NNBL leadership group went on to establish the One-Cent Savings and Trust Bank in 1903, with Boyd as president. By 1920 the bank's name was changed to Citizens Savings and Trust Company Bank, and it continues to the present time as the oldest continually operating banking institution owned and operated by African Americans.

Boyd also launched additional business ventures such as the NBPB Sunday School Congress in 1904, a convention geared toward black Baptists of all ages who were users of company publications, other products, and services. During the same year the NBPB also developed the National Negro Doll Company, an initiative to provide positive images to black children. Boyd was also instrumental in the development of Nashville's first African American newspaper, the Nashville *Globe*, through his Globe Publishing Company; the National Baptist Church Supply Company; and the Union Transportation Company. The NBPB continued to flourish, and by 1905 it was the largest black publishing company in America.

When Boyd died in 1922, he was succeeded by his son, Henry Allen Boyd, who modernized operations and helped the company grow to new levels of success. Along with his work in building upon his father's achievements in ministry and entrepreneurship, Boyd was also highly influential in the founding of Tennessee State University, the only public HBCU in the state, in 1912.

By the centennial of the NBPB in 1996, leadership had passed to Theophilus Bartholomew (T. B.) Boyd III, the fourth generation of the Boyd family to head the company. His father, T. B. Boyd Jr., had been the first executive to pastor a church and run the company simultaneously, another example of the black minister as faith-based entrepreneur.

T. B. Boyd III also renamed the NBPB the R. H. Boyd Publishing Corporation in honor and recognition of his great-grandfather, its visionary and founder, in 2001. He is also a graduate of the university his family helped to establish and presently board chairman of Citizens Savings Bank, continuing the faith-based entrepreneurial legacy of his ancestors into the twenty-first century.

## CHARISMA AND CONTROVERSY

Many faith-based entrepreneurs developed a variety of business ventures after developing religious organizations based on their personal magnetism and charisma. Critics went so far as to say that followers and supporters of these charismatic individuals were part of a cult in worst-case scenarios, especially when the leaders operated outside of established religious traditions; at the very least, followers were considered part of a "cult of personality."

Persons such as James Francis Marion "Prophet" Jones, "Sweet Daddy" Grace, and M. J. "Father" Divine are notable examples of individuals who built considerable personal wealth after attracting numbers of followers during the mid-twentieth century. These persons also attempted various business enterprises as a means to gain credibility in the community and/or as vehicles for employment of some of their followers, with varying degrees of success. Divine, despite personal controversy, is credited with using his resources and influence to create systems to feed thousands during the Great Depression of the 1930s.

While these individuals became well known, their influence was not extended to the national level of persons like **Marcus Garvey** and Elijah Muhammad, whose respective organizations, the Universal Negro Improvement Association (UNIA) and the Nation of Islam (NOI), drew considerable attention for their entrepreneurial ventures as well as their messages of racial empowerment aligned with spiritual/religious principles. These men took Washington's philosophy of racial accommodation to segregation to the radical extreme of advocating separate development from whites and extending racial pride to the point of advocating black superiority and God as a black deity.

Garvey attempted several entrepreneurial ventures under the UNIA, which at its peak was the largest mass movement in African American history. Due in part to his Jamaican background and international travels, UNIA influence extended beyond the United States to Canada, the Caribbean, Central and South America, West Africa, and England.

From its U.S. base in Harlem, New York, the UNIA created the Negro Factories Corporation and the *Negro World* weekly newspaper in 1918, which employed thousands of African Americans. Offshoots from these operations included a doll factory, tailoring business, grocery stores, restaurants, a printing press, and other related companies. The most ambitious economic enterprise of Garvey and the UNIA was the Black Star Line steamship corporation, which launched its first ship in 1919.

Despite widespread excitement and tremendous support of the Garvey movement, internal and external pressures, criticism, sabotage, and investigation of Garvey led to the demise of this and other attempts to unify persons of African heritage with his "Back to Africa" spiritual, philosophical, social, political, and economic/entrepreneurial initiatives. Garvey's arrest, imprisonment on mail fraud charges, and deportation from the United States hastened the end of his movement, but his efforts inspired other African Americans to develop organizations and programs incorporating many of his ideas and concepts.

Elijah Muhammad brought the Nation of Islam to national prominence in the 1940s after becoming a disciple and successor of its founder, W. D. Fard, in Detroit, Michigan, during the 1930s. Along with some aspects of traditional Islam, Fard and Muhammad included and expanded upon aspects of Garvey's pro-African philosophy by incorporating doctrines indicating that blacks were the original and superior human race and that whites were evil oppressors who would eventually be destroyed by Allah.

The organization was targeted for police harassment because of its ideas, activities, and growing influence despite internal divisions when Muhammad became its leader in 1934 and labeled a subversive group by the Federal Bureau of Investigation (FBI). The NOI expanded from Detroit to Chicago, Milwaukee, and Washington, D.C. before Muhammad and other Muslims were arrested on charges of draft evasion and sedition for refusing to participate in World War II, with Muhammad serving a federal prison sentence from July 1943 to August 1946 for his activities.

The NOI survived despite these problems, and in 1947 Muhammad began moving the organization in the direction of business enterprise after his release from prison. The first ventures were a restaurant and bakery in Chicago, the new headquarters for the group. After Malcolm X became a minister of the NOI in 1954, his charisma and subsequent celebrity helped the organization to rapidly expand its membership and financial resources, which in turn helped the NOI to expand into landownership, farming, and other economic initiatives.

Despite the loyalty of Malcolm X to NOI doctrines of black pride and black separatism, his personal magnetism as NOI national representative began to overshadow Muhammad's leadership of the organization. By 1963, when Malcolm X violated orders from Muhammad regarding comment on the assassination of President John F. Kennedy and was suspended from his ministry for ninety days, it became obvious that he was now considered as more a liability than an asset to the organization.

Malcolm X also verified rumors of moral and financial irregularities in the affairs of Muhammad and the NOI, and the backlash led to his leaving the organization and subsequent assassination in 1965. After Muhammad's death in 1975, the NOI split into factions led by one of his sons, Wallace Muhammad, and Louis (X) Farrakhan, who replaced Malcolm as national representative and had remained loyal to Elijah Muhammad.

Farrakhan retained many of Muhammad's original doctrines, while Wallace Muhammad moved his followers toward more traditional Islamic practices. Over time, the Farrakhan-led NOI gained control of several properties and business concerns once connected with Elijah Muhammad, and Farrakhan has used his own charisma to rebuild the NOI to meet his objectives in another variation of faith-based entrepreneurship.

## MINISTERS, MINISTRIES, AND MEGACHURCHES

During the civil rights movement of the 1950s and 1960s, the human, financial, and spiritual resources of black churches were heavily utilized by all of the major civil rights organizations and were essential to its success. A majority of movement leaders, including Dr. Martin Luther King Jr., were ministers who balanced their involvement in civil rights activities with the spiritual and executive duties involved in pastoral responsibilities. The organizations they created, such as the Southern Christian Leadership Conference (SCLC), as well as their relationships with established groups like the National Association for the Advancement of Colored People (NAACP) and National Urban League, required an entrepreneurial approach to financing and fund-raising activities in support of movement objectives, along with collaboration and strategic planning.

One of the ironies of the postsegregation era was that with greater access to the American mainstream African Americans no longer had to use services and resources in their own communities out of necessity. As a result, many African American–owned and/or –operated businesses were forced to close, while others experienced great difficulty in maintaining their operations.

Especially in the larger urban areas, African American churches became part of the small group of institutions that remained viable, and their continued success was tied in varying degrees to their relevance to community needs. The challenges and problems in black communities (including the loss of industries and jobs; crime; alcohol and drug dependency/abuse; limited social, educational, and recreational services; and other issues) impacted churches as well and forced them to make choices in order to respond to these realities.

In urban, suburban, and rural settings, many African American churches took on the challenges of community issues and turned them into opportunities, in the tradition of previous generations. Progressive church leaders saw the connection between ministry to the physical, economic, and social needs of their communities and the traditional focus on spiritual needs and development.

Well-established African American congregations and denominations began to embrace entrepreneurship as a key component in their community development initiatives, using the resources of their membership base before branching out to embrace their neighborhoods and the community at large. They were joined in community development and entrepreneurship by organizations such as the Congress of National Black Churches (CNBC), based in Washington, D.C.; **Opportunities Industrialization Centers** (OIC), developed by Rev. **Leon Howard Sullivan** in Philadelphia; People United to Save/Serve Humanity (PUSH), based in Chicago and led by the Reverend Jesse Jackson; and the more recent phenomenon of African American megachurches.

The black megachurch itself can be considered as another variation of faith-based entrepreneurship. While many are usually independent congregations led by charismatic leaders attracting large memberships and considerable financial resources, in some cases megachurches are also connected to traditional church denominational structures or create new subsidiary congregations as a result of their expanding influence. Successful megachurches often employ dozens, and in some cases hundreds, of persons to carry out their various programs and directly impact their communities.

In recent years, the best-known minister in this category is Bishop **Thomas "T. D." Jakes**, who rose from humble beginnings and small churches in his native West Virginia to found and pastor the Potter's House church in Dallas, Texas, a multiracial, nondenominational ministry that grew to over 30,000 members. Along with his dynamic preaching style and personal charisma, Jakes wrote several bestselling books; provided ministry-related products and services using multiple media formats and outlets; convened regional and national conferences; traveled and broadcasted internationally; and created a variety of outreach programs to address the emotional, socio-economic, and physical needs of his parishioners and the larger community from a spiritual foundation.

Many megachurches and congregations from traditional church organizations developed separate nonprofit 503(c) (3) corporations to utilize the human and financial resources at their disposal in community development efforts. Focus points of these efforts included developing child-care facilities and schools; building new housing units; revitalizing existing residential and commercial real estate; partnering with corporate and civic organizations on business development and entrepreneurship; outreach to underserved communities through job/career, health, food distribution, mentorship, and counseling services; establishing financial services, institutions, and relationships designed to promote wealth creation, management, and economic stability for individuals, families, and the larger African American community; and global missions outreach.

Some of the many additional examples of faith-based entrepreneurship and entrepreneurial leadership included Abyssinian Baptist Church (former pastors Adam Clayton Powell Sr. and Jr.; succeeded by Calvin Butts), Greater Allen AME Cathedral of New York (Floyd Flake) and Christian Cultural Center (A. R. Bernard) in New York City; West Angeles Church of God in Christ (Bishop Charles Blake) and Crenshaw Christian Center (Frederick Price) in Los Angeles; New Birth Missionary Baptist Church (Bishop Eddie Long) and World Changers Church International (Creflo Dollar) in the metropolitan Atlanta area; Windsor Village United Methodist Church in Houston (Pastor Kirbyjon Caldwell); and Word of Faith International Christian Center in metropolitan Detroit (Bishop Keith Butler).

Flake in particular symbolized both tradition and innovation, as he continued to pastor while serving as a U.S. congressman from 1986 to 1997. Upon his return to full-time ministry, his congregation grew to megachurch status from its AME roots. In 2002 he became president of his alma mater, Wilberforce University in Ohio, the AME-affiliated HBCU founded in 1856, and utilized his leadership and entrepreneurial skills to the benefit of both institutions.

Payne Memorial AME Church in Baltimore, formerly pastored by Bishop Vashti Murphy McKenzie, proved that all churches active and successful in faith-based entrepreneurship were not led by men. The success of McKenzie in spiritual and economic/entrepreneurial objectives set the stage for her election as the first female AME bishop in 2000, and first female president of the AME Council of Bishops in 2004, with responsibility for the worldwide operation of the African Methodist Episcopal Church.

Jesse Jackson endured controversies related to political and personal activities and continued to champion entrepreneurship and economic development through PUSH and other initiatives. In 2001, his organization launched the One Thousand Churches Connected project to provide information, technology, resources, and training to pastors and congregations interested in economic literacy to achieve personal and community financial objectives.

African American clergy and congregations were also identified as active or potential participants in the faith-based initiatives of President George W. Bush and his administration during the first decade of the twenty-first century. These programs created controversy due to the political and constitutional implications of direct federal support to church-affiliated programs, services, and economic/entrepreneurial activities and called into question the nonprofit, tax-exempt status of religious organizations.

These religious leaders and followers, past and present, forged new directions for ministry and service to African Americans and others using faith-based entrepreneurship in its many variations. Their successes and failures in seeking to create and maintaining hope, progress, and group development in natural as well as spiritual concerns have come as they have embraced the multiple dimensions and responsibilities of leadership and empowerment, with the risks and rewards of "stepping out on faith."

## Sources

"Black Megachurches' Mega-Outreach." September 8, 2004. ReligionLink: Resources for Reporters. http://www.religionlink.org/tip_040908b.php.

Clingman, James. "The Business of the Black Church." http://www.blackmeninamerica.com/clingmanarchives.htm.

"Investiture of Bishop Vashti Murphy McKenzie Observed." *Nashville Pride*, December 10, 2004.

Laderman, Gary, and Luis Leon, eds. *Religion and American Cultures: An Encyclopedia of Traditions, Diversity, and Popular Expressions.* Santa Barbara, CA: ABC-CLIO, 2003.

Lehman, Jeffrey, ed. *African American Almanac.* 9th ed. Farmington Hills, MI: Gale Group, 2003.

Lovett, Bobby. *A Black Man's Dream: The First One Hundred Years: Richard Henry Boyd and the National Baptist Publishing Board.* Jacksonville, FL: Mega Corporation, 1993.

McRoberts, Omar M. "Black Churches, Community, and Development." *Shelterforce Online* (January–February 2001). http://www.nhi.org/online/issues/115/McRoberts.html.

Potter's House. http://www.thepottershouse.org.

Reese, T. David, and Christina A. Clamp. *Faith-Based Community Economic Development: Principles and Practices.* Boston: Federal Reserve Bank of Boston, 2001. http://www.bos.frb.org/commdev/index.htm.

Roof, Wade Clark, ed. *Contemporary American Religion.* New York: Macmillan Reference USA, 2000.

Smith, Jessie Carney, ed. *Notable Black American Men*. Detroit, MI: Gale Research, 1998.

*Fletcher F. Moon*

# James Conway Farley (1854–1910?), Photographer, Portraitist, Artist

James Conway Farley was born in Prince Edward County, Virginia, on August 10, 1854. His parents were slaves. He was the first prominent black photographer in the United States. In 1861, following the death of his father, Farley relocated with his mother to Richmond, Virginia, where they settled permanently.

Farley's mother was employed as a hotel storeroom keeper, and Farley assisted her in her work, which included candle making. During the evenings, an old cook from the hotel tutored him in the basics in reading and writing. He was fortunate to attend public schools for three years to conclude his brief education. Since he needed to work to supplement his mother's meager earnings, he entered apprenticeship training in candle making and baking. Farley was employed as a baker following his apprenticeship but soon became disillusioned with the long hours of labor in the bakery. Endeavoring to enter some other profession, he was hired to work in the chemical department of the C. R. Rees photography company in Richmond in 1872. Within a short time it became obvious that he had a keen interest and talent to perform this work. He attracted the attention of another photographer, G. W. Davis, who hired him to work as a photographer at the Davis Photograph Gallery.

In 1875, it was highly unusual for a black man like Farley to work in the field of photography or even to be given the independence and autonomy that he had at the Davis Gallery. He was allowed to set his own scenes and complete the chemical process of making the photographs. His freedom and authority angered four white operators in the darkroom at the Davis Gallery. They demanded Farley's dismissal but declined to give their reasons. Since Farley was black, it was assumed that his race was the primary cause of their grievance. They refused to continue working with him. Not wanting to cause a disturbance at the business or embarrassment to Davis the proprietor, Farley offered his resignation. Davis recognized that Farley's skill was a great asset to the business. To settle the problem, he retained Farley and dismissed the white operators. Farley became the most competent operator with the Davis Company, completing most of the work himself and more than had been done previously by other operators. During his thirty-five-year association with the company, he helped it to expand and prosper. After many failed attempts to place other white operators in charge, Farley was promoted to chief operator of the company's newly established gallery. The business at the gallery continue to thrive with a high volume of photographs being produced each day. By 1879, it was one of the most successful galleries in the southern United States.

In 1876, Farley married Rebecca P. Robinson of Amelia County, Virginia. To this union seven daughters were born. He was considered a fine gentleman and officiated as a deacon in the First Baptist Church. Farley continued to work at the Davis Gallery until 1895 when he became an independent operator with the opening of his own establishment. The Jefferson Fine Arts Gallery, located on Broad Street in Richmond, became a very profitable business for Farley. It attracted both black and white patrons, including prominent Virginia business leaders and society families.

Farley's work ranked nationally along with other photographers of the period. He became known through exhibitions at fairs across the country and was recognized as one of the most accomplished photographers in the South. He was awarded many prizes for his photographic talent. In 1884, he won a first prize for his exhibit at the Colored Industrial Fair in Richmond. His also exhibited at the World Industrial and Cotton Centennial Exposition in New Orleans in 1885, where he received complimentary reviews in the photographic journals of the time. Unfortunately only a few of his photographs have survived. Those remaining are held in the Valentine Museum on Clay Street in Richmond, Virginia. Farley's work represents the earliest entry of blacks into the field of photography and portraiture.

**Sources**

"J. C. Farley." *Evidences of Progress among the Colored People*. By Richings, G. F. Chicago: Afro-Am Press, 1969.

"James C. Farley, Esq." *Men of Mark: Eminent, Progressive and Rising*. By William J. Simmons. New York: Arno Press, 1968.

Spradling, Mary Mace, ed. *In Black and White. A Guide to Magazine Articles, Newspaper Articles, and Books concerning Black Individuals and Groups*. 3rd ed. Vol. 1. Detroit: Gale Research, 1980.

Willis-Thomas, Deborah. *Black Photographers, 1840–1940: An Illustrated Bio-Bibliography*. New York: Garland, 1985.

———. "Farley, James Conway." *Dictionary of American Negro Biography*. Ed. Rayford W. Logan and Michael R. Winston. New York: W. W. Norton, 1982.

*Janette Prescod*

# Melvin Farr (1944–  ), Automobile Dealer, Entrepreneur, Professional Football Player

Challenged by racism, the oil crisis of the 1970s, and declining sales in American automobiles, Mel Farr, former professional football player, persevered to become one of the most successful African American businessmen of the late twentieth century. Farr is the owner of Mel Farr Automotive Group—the largest African American–owned automobile dealership in the United States. The company includes a chain of dealerships composed of

Toyota, Ford, and Lincoln-Mercury cars located in five states. Farr is recognized for inspiring through his great example other businessmen in the automobile industry as well as others. According to Farr, his experiences as an athlete informed his success in the business world; as an athlete he learned the value of endurance and a positive mind-set.

Farr was born to Dorthea and Miller Farr on November 3, 1944, in Beaumont, Texas. His mother was a domestic worker, and his father was a truck driver who eventually succeeded in owning and running his own used car dealership. Melvin Farr was recognized at Herbert High School as a talented athlete and won a football scholarship to the University of California at Los Angeles (UCLA). In 1963, Farr entered UCLA and twice was named to the All-American team. During this period he married his first wife, Mae, and they had three children—two sons, Melvin Jr. and Michael, and a daughter, Monet. Farr left the university without his degree to pursue his career as a football player. In 1967, he was the first-round draft pick of the Detroit Lions.

Farr was a defensive back for the Detroit Lions from 1967 to 1973. He was named offensive MVP (Most Valuable Player) in 1967 and in 1968. He was also named to play in the National Football League (NFL) Pro-Bowl in 1968 and in 1971. Farr enjoyed success with the Detroit Lions but also continued to think about a future outside of football. During the off-seasons, he worked for Ford Motor Company. He was a part of one of their minority requirement programs and helped to encourage other African Americans to work for Ford.

After retiring from football in 1974, Farr turned his attention once again to the automobile industry. Farr saved money from his career in football and negotiated with Ford to buy his own dealership. Ford agreed to his offer to buy a dealership but wanted Farr to have a mentor and partner for his business. The mentor was John Cook, and shortly after, Cook-Farr Ford dealership was opened in a suburb of Detroit, Oak Park, Michigan. By 1978, Farr bought out his partner. The dealership was in financial trouble, however, and the oil crisis, couple with declining sales in American automobiles, threatened to overwhelm Farr's business. He recovered with loans and the help of Ford Motor Company.

During the late 1970s and the 1980s as Farr attempted to recover, he used advertisements to promote interests in his business. As a former football player, Farr was well recognized in Detroit, and he appeared in his own commercials, hoping to use his celebrity to his advantage. His television commercials were a success; in the advertisements, he appeared dressed as a superhero, proclaiming himself to be Mel Farr Superstar. Advisers to Farr credit the commercials in part for Farr's ability to recover. In the 1980s, Farr opened his second Ford automobile dealership and later established dealerships in New Jersey, Ohio, Maryland, and Texas. He also opened his own finance company: Triple M Financing Company; the financing company serves to assist low-income clients who may not have qualified for financing with Ford Company. Studying the trends in automobile popularity, Farr saw the increasing interest in Japanese cars and worked to profit from it. In 1989, he succeeded in opening Mel Farr Toyota in Bloomingfield, Michigan. As with Ford, Farr has worked to encourage Japanese automotive dealers to employ African Americans.

In 1992, Farr was named by *Black Enterprise* magazine Auto Dealer of the Year, and he has been frequently listed on *Black Enterprise*'s list of Top 100 Black Businesses in the United States. In 1997, Crain's Detroit Business ranked Mel Farr Automotive Group forty-sixth among all automotive dealers in the United States. In July 2004, Farr added to his list of accomplishments when he married for a second time. His wedding to Johnson Publishing Company chief executive officer and president **Linda Johnson Rice** in Chicago was attended by some of the most powerful American business executives.

Recent years have brought challenges to Farr, and by 2003, Farr sold all his dealerships except for a used car dealership in Detroit, Michigan. However, Farr is a foundational figure in twentieth-century African American business. His great courage, intellect, and patient endurance are examples for current and future African Americans in the financial world.

**Sources**

"Mel Farr." *Contemporary Black Biography*, Vol. 24. Ed. Shirelle Phelps. Gale Group, 2000. Reproduced in Biography Resource Center. Farmington Hills, MI: Thomson Gale, 2005. http://galegroup.com/servlet/BioRC Document number: K1606001534.

"A Wedding to Remember." *Ebony* 50 (July 2004): 9.

*Who's Who among African Americans*. 18th ed. Gale, 2005. Reproduced in Biography Resource Center. Farmington Hills, MI: Thomson Gale, 2005. http://galegroup.com/servlet/BioRC Document number: K1645527654.

*Rebecca Dixon*

# Fashion Industry

Evidence of blacks in the early fashion industry was seen among free blacks in the 1700s, when Stephen Jackson of Virginia learned the art of turning leather and fur into hats. It was seen also in 1852 when a free man named Cordovall was the leading mercer and tailor in New Orleans and created styles that were the vogue among white elites. Until the hostility of slavery drove such enterprising blacks from the South, there were highly respected tailors in business as well, among them Albert and Freeman Morris, and Fellow Bragg of New Berne, North Carolina. Prominent people of the area followed Bragg around wherever he worked, so that he might handle their business. Abolitionist and reformer Eliza Ann Gardner (1831–1922) supported herself by dressmaking in Boston and used her skills to benefit racial uplift. Other prominent women with dressmaking businesses included Sarah Eddy, daughter of African Methodist Episcopal bishop

Richard Allen; Grace Bustill Douglass, daughter of noted Philadelphian Cyrus Bustill; and Catherine Delany, wife of black nationalist Martin R. Delany. The black fashion industry also has its roots in the work of slave women in America, who worked on large plantations as seamstresses and embroiderers. Later some of them became widely known. Blacks had a long association with the industry's development; for example, between 1863 and 1913 blacks owned businesses in dressmaking, millinery, and tailoring. By 1929 there are also accounts of black proprietors of apparel stores, including accessories and clothing for men, women, and families. Since then there have been a number of successful fashion designers, but their full recognition would not come until after the 1970s.

A great black seamstress of record was slave woman Elizabeth Keckley (c. 1824–1907), who was hired out and earned enough in her sewing business in St. Louis to help support seventeen family members. Later she bought her freedom and in 1860 moved to Baltimore and on to Washington, D.C., where she built another sewing business. She hired as many as twenty young ladies and taught them dressmaking as well as charm and elegance. She was sought out for her fine work. Less than a year after starting her business, Keckley became dressmaker and fashion designer for Mary Todd Lincoln. The inaugural ball gown that she designed for Mary Todd Lincoln—her signature piece—hangs in the Smithsonian Institution with a copy in the Black Fashion Museum in Washington, D.C., where the works of blacks in the fashion industry are showcased. Her clients also included the wives of Stephen Douglas and Jefferson Davis.

According to N. H. Goodall, "[I]t was not until the mid-twentieth century that black women came into the spotlight as both models and designers." Goodall identified a number of black women dressmakers and designers who may not have reached Keckley's stature but made important contributions to the industry. These included Fanny Criss (c. 1866–1942), whose clients were wealthy white women in Richmond, Virginia. Criss moved to New York City around 1918 and continued her career. Many black women worked in their own communities and designed and created items for church functions, fashion shows, and other activities. As they became known, white women sought their talent and promoted their work among their friends. While living in the state of her birth, Ann Lowe (1899–1981), for example, created the inaugural ball gown for the wife of Alabama's governor. After that, the teenager was called to sew for white Alabama society, including debutantes and politicians. She moved to New York when she was sixteen and began formal study in a design school. Lowe opened a dressmaking shop on Madison Avenue and became couturier to the rich and famous, including the Astors, du Ponts, Rockefellers, Roosevelts, and Vanderbilts. She created over 1,000 gowns a year, all one-of-a-kind items, for New York's society. Her creations were sold in stores such as Henri Bendel, Neiman Marcus, and I. Magnin. It was not until 1953, when she designed the bridal gown, bridesmaid's dresses, and the mother-of-the-bride dress for Jacqueline Bouvier's wedding to then Senator John Fitzgerald

Kennedy that her work was widely recognized. The bridal gown, however, was her most famous design and consisted of over fifty yards of ivory silk and taffeta.

Dressmaker Lillian Rogers Parks (1898–1997) began her adventures in the White House in 1909, when her mother became a maid for President William Howard Taft. Lillian Parks continued in the White House and served during the administrations of Taft, Wilson, Harding, Coolidge, Hoover, Roosevelt, and Truman; was seamstress for their wives; and mended items in the White House as needed. She was trained in a Washington, D.C. community where dressmaking shops were set up in the homes of black women and later worked for a shop on Connecticut Avenue. Although Parks never owned a shop, she became known for making exquisite fashions and for her work in the White House, accounts of which were published in her book My Thirty Years at the White House (1961).

Milliner Mildred Blount's work was seen but not publicly acknowledged. Her clients included Joan Crawford, GloriaVanderbilt, other Hollywood stars, and society greats. Her creations were seen in the films Gone With the Wind (1939) and Easter Parade (1948) and elsewhere, and the August 1942 cover of Ladies' Home Journal featured her hats.

Other black fashion businesses emerged, as seen in 1963 when Jesse A. Terry opened a shop in Roanoke, Alabama. In time, Terry Manufacturing Company had as many as eighty people on payroll and grossed over $1 million a year. The company made a variety of items including dresses, coats, sweaters, jackets, uniforms, dashikis, and other African-style garments, and they were sold in dress shops and in stores of retail giants such as Sears, Roebuck. The family operation included Terry's wife and three sons. By late 1970, his own label accounted for over half of the clothing that the company manufactured.

From the early 1970s through the 1990s, black women designers became highly recognized. Such women include Tracy Reese (whose clients included Bergdorf Goodman and Ann Taylor), Therese Rogers, Beverly Olivace, Shirley Gibson, Barbara Bates, Yvonne O'Gara, Coreen Simpson, and Sandy Baker. Their crafts include hand-crafted jewelry, works in leathers and suedes, and other items and fabrics.

## YOUNG DESIGNER BECOMES SUCCESSFUL

One of the fashion industry's most successful young designers in the 1970s and 1980s was Willie Donnell Smith (1948–1987). He was also a freelance illustrator. Known as Willi Smith, he had emerged in the late 1960s along with a number of black designers. The Philadelphia native attended Philadelphia College of Art (1962–1965) and graduated from Parsons School of Design (1969). In 1965 he worked in New York City for Arnold Scaasi, then became a designer for Bobbie Brooks in 1969. For six years (1969–1975) he was employed with Digits, Inc., a sportswear company. By the end of the 1970s, he had covered the gamut of the sportswear industry. Meanwhile, in 1973 he founded his own business with his sister Toukie. Lacking in knowledge for operating a successful business, Smith soon closed his company and began a partnership with a company on Seventh Avenue and allowed the firm to use his name in return for the financial assistance that it gave. Since he had already built a solid reputation as a designer, the use of his name was beneficial for the new firm. Smith resented designing clothes out of costly fabrics and focused the designs on the very young. He was successful in his suit to regain rights to his name and began to freelace while seeking career options with other large sportswear firms.

In 1976 Smith met an old friend, Laurie Mallet, who sold shirts imported from India. The two traveled together to India, and he designed a collection in Bombay. He and Mallett then founded WilliWear Limited, with Mallet as president and Smith as vice president and designer. Although the company made about $30,000 the first year, Smith had designed a line of pants that was very popular and became his signature design—the WilliWear pant. The baggy fatigue had a high waist and became known as the Willi Smith look. Other designers copied his style. His next collection was highly successful and brought $200,000 to the company. WilliWear grossed over $5 million by 1982. He introduced WilliWear Men in 1978 and was successful again with a line that embraced formality as well as casualness. Most of his pieces were separates and allowed items from one season to be used with new designs in the next season. Smith designed his own textiles and oversaw their production in India.

As he matured, his designs became more tailored and traditional. By mid-1980 his designs were in 1,100 stores in the United States and others in London. In 1986, his thriving company grossed $45 million. Among his customers was Edwin A. Schlossberg, for whom he designed an outfit for Schlossberg's 1987 wedding with Caroline Kennedy.

After working for AMVETS and decorating windows in an Yves Saint Laurent boutique in Atlanta, designer Patrick Kelly (1954?–1990) entered the world of fashion during the 1970s. He ran an antique clothing boutique in that city until the end of the decade, when he moved to New York City and became a clothing designer. In 1979, he moved to Paris, where he designed costumes for Le Palace. In the early 1980s he sold original designs on the streets of Paris and at flea markets. In 1984, Kelly partnered with Bjorn Amelan and designed fashions for the boutique Victorie and for Benetton. He unveiled a ready-to-wear line in 1985. Two years later he signed with Warnaco, Inc. and expanded his line of fashions. He was the first American to showcase a couture collection in Paris. In 1988, Kelly became the first American elected to the Chambre Syndicate du Prête-à-Porter, a world-class fashion designers association based in Paris.

Other blacks in the fashion industry emerged during the 1970s, among them Jeffrey Banks, a major black fashion maker. Banks was design assistant to the president of Ralph Lauren/Polo in 1971–1973 and to the president of Calvin Klein/Calvin Klein Ltd., in 1973–1976. Next he designed for

Nik-Nik Clothing & Sportswear, and in 1978, when he was age twenty-five, he established his own business, Jeffrey Banks Ltd., in New York City. He established a second company, Jeffrey Banks International, and in 1980 began to design furs for men and boys for Alixandra. He has also designed for other companies, including Oxford Industries. His designs have been worn around the world.

Those who emerged during the 1980s and 1990s included Maurice Malone, known for his line of clothing that appealed to the urban, hip-hop male. Malone began his designs in his native Detroit, where he launched Hardware, a line of leather coats. His clothing included T-shirts and blue jeans, and he became more successful with each line that he produced. He relocated to New York City and later found a partner to finance another line, Label X. That line featured hip-hop styles and boxer shorts. Malone moved back and forth from Detroit to New York City and launched a line of jeans, opened a retail outlet—the Hip-Hop Shop—on Detroit's west side, and later designed a tailored suit. In 1999, he unveiled at the same show a men's line as well as his first women's line. Subsequent lines included Italian-made jeans called the Maurice Malone Platinum collection. His sales had moved from $2 million in 1997 to $8.5 million in 2000.

Byron Lars, of San Francisco, began sewing prom dresses for his high school friends, then studied fashion design at Brooks College in Long Beach and the Fashion Institute of Technology in New York City. He was an apprentice with Kevan Hall, a designer in Los Angeles. In 1990, now living in New York, he launched his own collection and peddled it from store to store. The next year he released a second collection, for which *Women's Wear Daily* named him Rookie of the Year. He had orders from high-end retailers such as Bloomingdale's, Neiman Marcus, and Henri Bendel. At first he funded his own business, but in 1995 he signed with San Siro Inc., allowing the firm to make his Byron Lars' Shirt Tales. The firm also sold his designs at outlet stores and discount markets, causing the high-end retailers who carried his line to protest. Lars won a court case in 1997 that barred Sans Siro from using his name, but by then he was no longer a top-selling designer. But he would rise again. In spring 1997, he created designs for the world-famous New York Fashion Café; through an arrangement with the Mattel company, he created a collection for the Barbie doll. He also created African American Barbies. Mars returned to his signature design—the shirt—and in 2001 launched a collection of feminine tailored shirts under his Beauty Mark label.

Born in Hampton, Virginia, Lawrence Dion Steele had an interest in fashion while he was a child and became fascinated with the work of Ralph Lauren's designs. After studying at the Art Institute of Chicago, Steele moved to Italy to explore Italian clothes, which he considered superior to all others. After a five-year apprenticeship with Franco Moschino, he opened his business in 1994. By 1996 his reputation had reached Japan, Germany, and Italy, and high-profile models volunteered to appear in his shows. In 1998, when he was only thirty-eight years old, Steele's design house offered four lines: White Label, Blue Label, Lawrence Steele Design, and LS_D Collection. Still in Italy, his work was slow to gain recognition in the United States; however, prominent actresses such as Julia Roberts and Meg Ryan gave exposure to his work here. In 2000, Jennifer Aniston wore one of his designs to the Oscars and another in her wedding to Brad Pitt. His fall 2000 line catered to those aged twenty to forty.

Contemporary black fashion designers include a number of lesser-known names as well as those of acclaim, such as **Russell Simmons** (known for his Phat Fashions), Kimora Lee Simons (known for her Baby Phat line), Karl Kani, and hip-hop mogul **Sean "Diddy" Combs**. Combs, for example, has a successful Sean John clothing line for men. By October 2005 his clothing line for women made its debut; it aims to reflect the diversity of the young lifestyle. Rapper Nellie's Nellie Apple Bottom Line also targets the young. There are also designers with lines such as Rocawear, Ecco, and Enyce/Lady/Enyce.

Black designers have had a profound effect on the fashion industry. Their works range from inaugural gowns for the wives of U.S. presidents to various items for the rich and famous, to classic designs for well-established white fashion houses, to costly and splashy evening wear, and to trendy items of the hip-hop generation. Although the list of these designers is extensive, relatively few have been known among the general public. Many have been highly successful entrepreneurs who accumulated sizable wealth.

*See also*: Retail Industry

**Sources**

Alexander, Lois K. *Blacks in the History of Fashion*. New York: Harlem Institute of Fashion, 1982.

Cooksey, Gloria, and Ashyia N. Henderson. "Lawrence Steele." *Contemporary Black Biography*. Vol. 28. Detroit: Gale Research, 2002.

Decker, Ed. "Willi Smith." *Contemporary Black Biography*. Vol. 8. Detroit: Gale Research, 1995.

Garrett, Marie. "Elizabeth Keckley." *Notable Black American Women*. Ed. Jessie Carney Smith. Detroit: Gale Research, 1992.

Goodall, N. H. "Fashion Industry." *Black Women in America: An Historical Encyclopedia*. Ed. Darlene Clark Hine. New York: Carlson, 1993.

Murphy, Karen L. "Patrick Kelly." *Contemporary Black Biography*. Vol. 3. Detroit: Gale Research, 2002.

Sanchez, Brenna. "Byron Lars." *Contemporary Black Biography*. Vol. 32. Detroit: Gale Research, 2002.

———. "Maurice Malone." *Contemporary Black Biography*. Vol. 32. Detroit: Gale Research, 2002.

Seder, John, and Berkeley G. Burrell. *Getting It Together: Black Businessmen in America*. New York: Harcourt Brace Jovanovich, 1971.

Smith, Jessie Carney, and Carrell Peterson Horton, eds. *Historical Statistics of Black America: Agriculture to Labor and Employment*. Detroit: Gale Research, 1995.

Wolf, Gillian. "Jeffrey Banks." *Contemporary Black Biography*. Vol. 17. Detroit: Gale Research, 1998.

*Jessie Carney Smith*

# Federal Records for African American Business History

African American business history records available at the U.S. National Archives and Records Administration (NARA) provide data relating a wide variety of enterprises from one- or two-person operations like barbershops and beauty salons to multinational corporations. NARA headquarters, which houses the permanently valuable noncurrent records of the federal government, is located in Washington, D.C., and NARA II is in College Park, Maryland. NARA also administers regional record centers and presidential libraries located throughout the United States. Numerous printed and online guides are available to help researchers navigate the voluminous NARA collections.

*Black History: A Guide to Civilian Records in the National Archives* includes many references to African American business history. Some of the records are obvious, such as the records of the Small Business Administration, but others are filed with federal records among which few would readily examine for business history. To find the archival materials described in this entry, the researcher should use the *Black History* guide. It is important to note that in the era before the passage of the civil rights laws of the 1960s and 1970s, probably the most common African American business records relate to the **black press**. The importance of the fourth estate, as evidenced in many files, is obvious. Sometimes files will include only one issue of a newspaper, some clippings, or some correspondence. Other times researchers will find information about African American newspaper publishers, reporters and staff, circulation numbers, and government surveillance and investigative reports. It is important to note that in order to aid researchers in finding the NARA records, this entry adheres to the language used in the files such as *Negro*, *Afro*, and *Afro-American*. When the United States was legally segregated, the federal records reflect the racial divisions. Consequently, African American history records are easier to find. Conversely, in the period after the 1960s, in records like those of government contract offices, the researcher needs to know the name of the business in order to locate records. This entry focuses on the period up to the civil rights movement of the 1960s and is designed to help guide researchers to the NARA records. It is limited in its treatment of federal files available for African American business history.

## BUREAU OF THE CENSUS AND THE DEPARTMENT OF COMMERCE

Decennial census records—beginning in 1790—are available on microfilm and online. Because the questions asked on the censuses changed, especially during the nineteenth century, the schedules provide varying amounts of business data. Some censuses only list individual occupations without further information about business ownership or place of employment. Even with scant information, however, business information can be ascertained. For example, in 1924, Harvard-trained historian Carter G. Woodson published a volume titled *Free Negro Owners of Slaves in the United States in 1830, Together with Absentee Ownership of Slaves in the United States in 1830*. Utilizing the statistics in this volume, Woodson and his researchers demonstrated that although some African Americans owned slaves because they purchased family members in states where they were not allowed to emancipate them, some blacks did indeed own plantations and used enslaved African American laborers to work their fields.

The U.S. Census Bureau regularly published reports drawn from information collected during censuses. Many of these publications include data about the businesses and occupations of African Americans. Sometime there were special censuses. For example, in 1929, there was a census of business distribution with information about wholesale and retail business establishments. Each section of the 1929 census is arranged alphabetically by state, the name of the industry, and the name of the individual companies. The schedules also provide the name of the owner, the location, the dates of its establishment, a description of the business, the type of business, the number of employees, expenses, stock on hand, sales of merchandise and products, and a list of net sales by commodities and indicate whether the business was "owned and operated by Negroes."

Administratively, the Census Bureau is under the Department of Commerce. During the presidency of Franklin Delano Roosevelt, the number of records in the Commerce Department relating to black businesses multiplied. The secretary of commerce correspondence for the period 1928 to 1950 includes letters and reports relating to the department's Negro Advisory Council and the Negro Affairs Section, headed by Charles E. Hall. Other correspondence pertains to problems unique to blacks such as black **chambers of commerce**; the appointment of Eugene Kinckle Jones, former executive secretary of the National Urban League, as an adviser to the department; blacks and the Texas Centennial Celebration; and the purchasing power of blacks. Other records relate to publications about black newspapers and periodicals, and other black businesses, especially **black banks**.

Emmer Martin Lancaster was appointed adviser for the Division of Negro Affairs in the Office of the Secretary of Commerce on May 25, 1940. The division had been established in 1933. Lancaster filled a vacancy created by the resignation of Eugene Kinckle Jones. The National Negro Business Advisory Council was formed to serve the Division of Negro Affairs. Lancaster's records include correspondence with insurance companies owned and operated by blacks, 1942 to 1953; correspondence with banks owned and operated by blacks, 1942 to 1953; correspondence with black lending institutions, 1942 to 1943; and correspondence and reports pertaining to "Conferences on the Negro in Business," 1940 to 1953. Lancaster's records indicate that he often traveled to visit African American business leaders in various U.S. cities and offered advice to students and faculty at a number of historically black colleges and universities (HBCUs).

The Division of Negro Affairs also had a small business and inquiry reference service. The division's voluminous correspondence included requests for information and publications; inquiries about conference activities; questions about the Committee on Negro Defense Contracts; questions from black trade associations and real estate brokers; and materials relating to post–World War II planning, housing, and emergency programs. The division also issued a series of annual reports primarily relating to African American banking institutions, but some periodic reports also relate to insurance companies, postwar planning for blacks in business, and a directory of black businesses in the United States. Although many of the materials in the files are routine letters with requests for information or publications, they still provide some details about the scope of African American business endeavors. Often the letterheads on the stationery provide useful information. Division correspondents include manufacturers, architects, real estate agents, journalists, hair-care producers, beauticians, attorneys, film producers, shop owners, funeral directors, builders, business students, and publishers.

The reports that are among the Lancaster papers provide a wealth of information. For example, a one-page September 1943 report, "Construction Costs and Architect-Engineers' Fees for Eight War Housing Projects Designed by Negroes," includes the project number and location, the estimated total construction cost, the name of the architect, and some related fees. Three projects were located in Tuskegee (Alabama), three in Ypsilanti, one each in Newport News and Fort Huachuca. The four architects or firms involved in the eight projects were Edward C. Miller, Hilyard R. Robinson, and Moses and Dutton.

The Bureau of Foreign and Domestic Commerce was created in the Department of Commerce and Labor in 1912 to promote the development of U.S. commerce and industry by compiling and distributing information on trade matters. Most of the records compose the central file, 1914 to 1956. The category labeled "Negro, 1927–50" provides information about arrangements for **conferences on African American businesses**, business education, and the services of the bureau to black businesses. These records include a small folder with documents relating to the Negro Affairs Division.

## OTHER BANKING AND INSURANCE RECORDS

Some files relating to African American insurance companies are also interspersed among the Records of the Temporary National Economic Committee for the period 1938 to 1941. Two of the companies included are the Afro-American Life Insurance Company and North Carolina Mutual. Other African American insurance companies must be accessed by name. Each file includes a questionnaire, exhibits, the annual statement for 1937, and some correspondence.

The Records of the Office of the Comptroller of the Currency include materials relating to the Freedman's Savings and Trust Company. The bank, chartered by the U.S. government on March 3, 1865, for the benefit of freed slaves, was controlled primarily by white officers who proved themselves to be both incompetent and criminal. From 1865 to 1870, thirty-three branch offices were established. When the bank officers made unwise investments and fraudulent deals, they knew the bank was failing. At that time, they asked abolitionist and statesmen **Frederick Douglass**—who was ignorant of the bank's financial condition—to become the head of the bank. The Comptroller of the Currency liquidated the bank in 1882, but records relating to it extend well into the twentieth century. The bank organization and liquidation files, arranged by bank charter number, include information about other banks, some of which were controlled by African Americans, such as the Douglass National Bank of Chicago. The Douglass, called "the first U.S. Bank directed by Negroes," also failed.

## NEW DEAL AGENCIES

The Reconstruction Finance Corporation (RFC) was created in 1932 to extend aid during the depression to agriculture, commerce, and industry by providing direct loans. Most of the records for the RFC are arranged by type of business or industry. It is necessary to know the name of a black-owned business in order to find materials. The card index relating to loans made to public works and public agencies includes two cards for the Florida Agriculture and Mechanical College for Negroes in Tallahassee, Florida, 1939 to 1942. The RFC project files, 1941 to 1947 for the Defense Homes Corporation, a subsidiary of RFC, include a folder for the Mayfair Corporation in Washington, D.C. A cover letter in the file provides some background on Mayfair: "Early in 1941, a group of colored people headed up by Elder L. S. **[Lightfoot Solomon] Michaux** and **Albert I. [Irvin] Cassell**, an architect, started planning a large scale housing project in recognition of the need in Washington, D.C., for habitable housing for colored families."

The records of the Works Progress Administration research and records library, 1933 to 1945, include a number of publications and studies about African Americans in some major cities and information about education, commerce, newspapers, skilled workers, housing, and religion.

## EXECUTIVE DEPARTMENTS

The records of the Office of the Secretary of Agriculture, especially for the period from 1917 to 1955, include letters relating to African American business such as the black press, black farmers and soldiers in the defense effort, black farmers organizations, and farm contracts for African Americans. There are also some records relating to **Marcus Garvey**. The records of the Department of Labor include much correspondence with the black press. One of Labor's offices, the Women's Bureau and the Bureau of Labor Statistics, contain some records relating to small or home-based businesses owned by black women. Although for the first half of the twentieth century the Women's Bureau records primarily focus on black women as domestic workers, laundresses, and service workers, the correspondence and reports also include information about black women as business owners or operators such as beauticians, boardinghouse proprietors, and labor organizers. To locate such records, see NARA Special List 40, *Selected Documents Pertaining to Black Workers among the Records of the Department of Labor and Its Component Bureaus, 1902–69*.

## POWER OF THE PRESS

Records relating to the African American press and its publishers, editors, and reporters appear in many record groups. The press correspondence with the government usually pertains to some sort of advocacy for black population. This is especially true of the records of the Departments of Labor, Justice, State, and Agriculture. The records generated by the U.S. government departments and agencies are usually investigative. These records occasionally provide information about newspapers' circulation and the nature of their readership. Investigative files sometimes give detailed information about black journalists. In the period after the Russian revolution through the 1960s, blacks who advocated equal rights for U.S. citizens regardless of color were often labeled as communists or socialists.

The Records of the U.S. Postal Service include case files relating to the denial of second-class mailing privileges to periodical and other publications under section 12 of the Espionage Act of June 15, 1917 (40 Stat. 217). The act provided that any publication advocating treason, insurrection, or forcible resistance to any law of the United States was nonmailable. The records relating to the Espionage Act of World War I, 1917 to 1921, include some files about black-owned periodicals and newspapers and about propaganda directed to African Americans. Included in this series are files relating to **Robert Sengstacke Abbott**'s paper the *Chicago Defender*; *Crisis*, the National Association for the Advancement of Colored People (NAACP) magazine edited by W.E.B. Du Bois; the *Messenger*, edited by labor unionist A. Philip Randolph; and the *Negro World*, an organ of Marcus Garvey's Universal Negro Improvement Association (UNIA). Other records in this series relate to "Negro propaganda," the *New York News*, and the *Veteran*. A few fliers, pamphlets, and books among the records also relate to the 1917 Espionage Act: "Justice for the Negro," "Why the Negro Should Vote the Socialist Ticket," "Chicago Race Riots," and *The Black Man's Burden*, by E. Morel.

The U.S. government's interest and surveillance of Marcus Garvey, the Black Star Line, the UNIA, and the organization's newspaper—the *Negro World*—produced voluminous files. The multivolume *Marcus Garvey and the Universal Negro Improvement Association Papers* provide copies of many of the NARA documents generated by Postal Service, the Customs Bureau, the Office of the Chief of Naval Operations, the Department of State, Department of Justice, the Federal Bureau of Investigation, the Bureau of Ordinance, the U.S. Shipping Board, the Bureau of Marine Inspection and Navigation, and the War Department General and Special Staffs.

Files relating to the Espionage Act of World War II, 1943 to 1945, pertain to the denial of mailing privileges for black publications including the National Negro Council letter *New Negro World*, the *Black Dispatch*, and the *Philadelphia Afro-American*.

## WORLD WAR II AGENCIES

Immediately after President Franklin Roosevelt's declaration of a state of national emergency on September 2, 1939, the military services began planning wartime censorship of international communications. The Office of Censorship was established by an executive order of December 19, 1941, to censor all communications between the United States and any foreign country. The administrative subject files of the Office of Censorship, 1941 to 1945, include some information about black-owned newspapers. Subject headings include "Restrict Information/Racial Problems"; "General Radio/ Racial Discrimination," which contains information about a Paul Robeson broadcast on NBC radio in June 1943; "General Press/Racial Discrimination"; "Troops and Troop Movement/Negro Troops"; "Race Riots"; and "General Press/Negro Press." Collectively, these files only include a few dozen documents and consist mostly of correspondence cautioning black newspapers about revealing the movements of black troops and correspondence with the publishers and the Negro Newspaper Publishers Association concerning the relationship between the black press, the Office of Censorship, and National Negro Newspaper Week. "General Press/Racial Discrimination" includes reports about the black press for January and March of 1943 with information about the *Pittsburgh Courier*, Ira F. Lewis, editor; the *Washington Afro-American*, Carl Murphy, editor; the *Chicago Defender*, Louis C. Harper, editor; and the *People's Voice*, Adam Clayton Powell Jr., editor. There are also two folders titled "Afro-American Censorship Review."

The Office of Government Reports (OGR) was created in 1939 to help coordinate the home front aspects of the defense and war effort and to provide a clearinghouse for government information. Among the weekly media reports, 1942 to 1943, there is information about editorial opinion in the black press and reports and special memorandums relating to topics such as "Is the Negro Press Pro-Axis?"; "Statement of Negro War Aims" by the National Newspaper Publishers Association; "Recommendations Made by the OWI Advisory Committee on the Negro Press"; "Northern Negro's Most Aggressive Politician, Adam Clayton Powell, Jr."; and several reports about A. Philip Randolph and the March on Washington Movement. In 1942 the OGR was consolidated with other agencies to form the Office of War Information.

## OFFICE OF WAR INFORMATION

The Office of War Information (OWI) was established in the Office for Emergency Management by Executive Order 9182 of June 1942 to coordinate the government's war information program. OWI formulated and carried out programs to disseminate information in the United States and abroad about the progress of the war and government policies, activities, and objectives. OWI was very interested in gaining the support of the African American press. The subject file of the Office of Facts and Figures, the Committee on War Information and the Censorship Policy Board, 1941 to 1942, includes several folders titled "Negro." The primary area of concern in these records is the low morale of black civilians and soldiers. To address this problem, OWI organized a March 20, 1942, conference with a number of black leaders, including those in business, who could provide "counsel and advice" for "securing unity of thought and action in this war for democracy." The folders include copies of letters to black leaders announcing that a black lawyer named Theodore M. Berry had recently become a staff officer in OWI's Liaison Bureau. Subjects covered in these files include the black press; the appointment of a black war correspondent, William Alexander, a black journalist who worked in OWI's Press Division; the "Negro Problem and Radio"; and other matters.

The general records of OWI's News Bureau, 1942 to 1943, include correspondence of Theodore Poston, chief of the Negro Press Section, interspersed throughout the correspondence of the Bureau. For example, in the folder titled "National" there are several dozen letters between Poston and the **National Negro Business League**, the National Association of Negroes in American Industry, the National Negro Congress, the National Negro Insurance Association, the National Negro Publishers Association, and the National Urban League. Most of this correspondence was written in 1943. There is also a folder for Charles Alston, a black artist who drew cartoons for the OWI that were used in the black press. There are a number of vouchers for payments to Alston and a copy of the contract between Alston and OWI.

The records of OWI's Negro Press Section include the general correspondence of Theodore Poston, chief of the section, 1942, and a number of press releases. Poston corresponded with the black press on news features, photographs, cartoons, launching of naval ships named after blacks, and other subjects. Poston collected a number of pictures of blacks in industry and government that depict blacks in shipbuilding and other war industries.

The Office of Price Administration (OPA) became an independent agency in 1942 and was charged with stabilizing wartime prices and rents. OPA had racial relations advisers including T. Arnold Hill and Frances Williams, who monitored and encouraged rationing and pricing. The office received complaints about disproportionately high prices in black neighborhood and inequitable administration of rationing. It investigated these complaints and also maintained contact with black organizations and businesses.

## COMMUNITY ACTION PROGRAMS

Records of Agencies for Economic Opportunity and Legal Services (formerly Office of Economic Opportunity [OEO]) include the files of the Community Action Program (CAP). CAP was based on the principle that poor persons were themselves to be involved in the development and operation of the programs intended to help them. Community action agencies could devise solutions to local problems derived from or causing poverty. There are narrative progress reports, 1966 to 1967, that demonstrate the many different types of programs funded by OEO. There are programs such as day-care centers, legal services, **credit unions**, dental and health clinics, job training and placement, small business development, Head Start, adult education, and neighborhood multiservice centers. Black communities developed many of the programs.

NARA audiovisual and cartographic records also document some aspects of African American business history.

*See also*: Black Business Development and the Federal Government

**Sources**

Ham, Debra Newman. "Government Documents." *The Harvard Guide to African American History*. Ed. Evelyn Brooks Higgenbotham. Cambridge, MA: Harvard University Press, 2001.

Hill, Robert, ed. *Marcus Garvey and the Universal Negro Improvement Association Papers*. Vols. 1–9. Berkeley: University of California Press, 1983–1995.

Newman, Debra L., comp. *Black History: A Guide to Civilian Records in the National Archives*. Washington, DC: National Archives Trust Fund Board, General Services Administration, 1984.

———. *Selected Documents Pertaining to Black Workers among the Records of the Department of Labor and Its Component Bureaus. 1902–69*. Special List 40. Washington, DC: National Archives, 1977.

"Special Issue on Federal Records for African American History." *Prologue, A Quarterly Publication of the National Archives and Records Administration* 29 (Summer 1997): 2.

*Debra Newman Ham*

# Federation of Southern Cooperatives Land Assistance Fund
## Emergency Land Fund
## Federation of Southern Cooperatives

The Federation of Southern Cooperatives, now known as the Federation of Southern Cooperatives Land Assistance (FSCLA) Fund, was founded in 1967 as a self-help organization for farm families or rural inhabitants. It has enhanced the African American community by assisting low-income groups and their communities in programs of land retention and development. Although the organization targets African Americans, it essentially aids other farm families in need. The three major themes of the federation are to help people to enhance the quality of their lives and their communities as a whole by forming **consumer cooperatives** and **credit unions** as a collective strategy to create economic self-sufficiency; to aid black family farmers in the South by saving, protecting, and expanding their landholdings; and to benefit black and other family farmers and residents in low-income rural communities by developing, advocating, and supporting public policies that relate to their interests.

Community organizations and leaders, who were molded or forged in the 1960s civil rights movement, developed the federation. They knew that alternative means to achieving progress would be required, just as they knew that changes in public policies would be needed to support and institutionalize changes. Thus, they continued to work at the local, state, and national arenas to bring about policy changes to aid black farmers and to enhance persistently poor rural communities in the South.

While, from the start, the federation was committed to save and enhance the land resources of small family farmers in poor areas across the South, its vision was significantly broadened when in 1984 the federation merged with the Emergency Land Fund (ELF), the pioneer organization in black land retention, to become the Federation of Southern Cooperatives Land Assistance Fund. A sister organization before the merger, the ELF's goal was to work on the crisis seen then in black landownership. The merger led to a stronger organization and enabled the new organization to expand the land protection services offered to black farmers; it also encouraged them to work within cooperatives to achieve their goals. Some farmers who were not members of cooperatives later organized cooperatives of their own.

Among the highly touted activities of the federation is the 1992 "Caravan to Washington" in support of black farmers. Always working at the cutting edges to support family farms and rural communities, the federation has joined other coalitions on projects of mutual interest. Beginning in the 1980s, the federation worked to outline the basics of a "minority farmer's rights bill" that would aid the nation's people of color. Then the federation sponsored the highly publicized Caravan of Black and Native American Farmers that went to the nation's capital in September 1992. Members of the caravan held public protests at state capitols, the U.S. Capitol, and the U.S. Department of Agriculture, calling attention to their struggle. By participating as plaintiffs in lawsuits, the federation helped to build a base for change. These efforts resulted in the passage of national farm legislation that incorporated portions of the federation's demands.

The major federal program that addresses the needs of black farmers is the program that serves those black colleges affected by the 1890 Land-Grant Act, or the 1890 Land Grant Colleges. Tribal colleges and community organizations benefit as well. There is also the Agriculture Credit Act of 1987 that targeted land sales to people of color farmers. The 1990 FACT Act, Section 2501, acknowledged the problems of minority farmers and authorized funds for an "Outreach, Education and Technical Assistance

Program for Socially Disadvantaged Farmers." The 1996 FACT Act extended many programs provided for in the 1990 act.

In 1997, the federation became involved in the secretary of agriculture's series of Listening Sessions on Civil Rights. Held in Albany, Georgia, Memphis, Tennessee, and Belzoni, Mississippi, hundreds of farmers were able to attend the sessions and give accounts of neglect and discrimination by the U.S. Department of Agriculture (USDA). After that, the USDA prepared a report that included actions that the government needed to enforce to assure that the farmers' civil rights were upheld.

The federation's membership consists of grassroots people who have been organized into cooperatives and credit unions. A number of organizations collaborate with the federation, such as the National Cooperative Business Association, FARM AID, Southern Rural Development Initiative, 1890 Land Grant Colleges and Universities, and the National Family Farm Coalition. The changes made in the lives of the farmers and in their communities have been quantitative as well as qualitative. The strong community-based movement that the federation stimulated is experienced in a time-tested struggle for property rights; black farmers have known the distaste of fighting exploitation; and they have become more knowledgeable in the tactics, tools, and techniques they need to make progress.

Although the number of black farmers and landowners in the South has declined in recent years, over seventy cooperative member groups are active in the federation. They have a membership of over 20,000 families in cooperatives across ten southern states. Most of them are in Alabama, Georgia, Mississippi, and South Carolina. The families individually own small acreage but collectively own millions of acres of farmland. They collectively purchase supplies and market their crops through thirty-five agricultural cooperatives. The cooperatives provide technical assistance to the members and access to nineteen community develop credit unions. FSCLA is headquartered in East Point, Georgia.

*See also*: Blacks in Agriculture

**Sources**

Federation of Southern Cooperatives Land Assistance Fund. "History." http://www.federationsoutherncoop.com/history.htm.

———. "Mission." http://www.federationsoutherncoop.com/mission.htm.

———. "Overview." http://www.federationsoutherncoop.com/overview.htm.

*Frederick D. Smith*

# Food Service Industry

Legal and social restrictions imposed on people of African descent in the United States have limited the economic opportunities available to African Americans. Racist social mores not only permitted African Americans to work in service fields but also created the expectation that African

Americans would work in service professions; thus, black businesses in food service have been somewhat more acceptable. Accomplishments in the food industry in the eighteenth and nineteenth centuries were centered in the **catering industry** and hotel restaurants. There were ventures in catering and food service in the late eighteenth century in Rhode Island with Emanuel Manna and Mary Baroons, in Philadelphia with Cyrus Bustill, and in New York with Samuel "Black Sam" Fraunces. While these ventures were somewhat profitable, the most notable early successes in the food service industry were in the nineteenth century.

In the nineteenth century, African American businesses in catering were not only able to survive, but they also made their owners quite wealthy. In New York and in Rhode Island, the Downing family ran a well-respected catering business. Thomas Downing and later his son George Downing had a catering business and also a restaurant. In the nineteenth-century South, there were fewer business opportunities for African Americans than in the North, and black people who owned food establishments were prohibited from selling alcohol. Despite the social and legal barriers, there were a few hotel and restaurant businesses owned by African Americans that were successful; one of the most noteworthy of these southern businesses was a hotel and restaurant established in 1816 by Jehu Jones. Jones ran a successful operation until his death in 1833. While the accomplishments of Jones and the Downings are notable, the most significant economic achievements in the food service industry in the nineteenth century occurred in Philadelphia.

In Philadelphia, African Americans had a dominant presence in the catering business. From the early 1800s to the 1870s, there were a number of prominent businessmen in food service; these prosperous men included Robert Bogle, Peter Augustine, Eugene Baptiste, Thomas Dorsey, Henry Minton, Henry Jones, and Peter and Albert Dutrieuille.

Robert Bogle was one of the earliest of the Philadelphia caterers. His business was located on Eighth Street. In 1816, Peter Augustine founded his catering business on 3rd Street above Spruce Street where he served wealthy white families. In 1818, Eugene Baptiste established his catering business on South 15th Street. One of Augustine's sons, Theodore, married Clara Baptiste, the daughter of Eugene Baptiste. Theodore worked as an apprentice and established Augustine and Baptiste Catering. The business served as a great model for businessman Peter Albert Dutrieuille. After marrying Amelia Baptiste, Dutrieuille worked in the Augustine and Baptiste firm. In 1873, he established his own catering business at 108 South Eighteenth Street. Dutrieuille also helped to found the Caterer's Manufacturing and Supply Company. The company supplied caterers with table, chairs, linens, flatware, and china. Peter Dutrieuille's son, Albert E. Dutrieuille, began helping his father run the business at an early age, and following his father's death, he ran the company. In 1917, the company's name was changed to Albert E. Dutrieuille Catering. Albert Dutrieuille continued to run the catering business until 1967 when he retired. He died in 1974.

During the nineteenth century, Thomas Dorsey, Henry Minton, and Henry Jones enjoyed great prosperity in Philadelphia. Dorsey was born enslaved in Maryland in 1810. Dorsey escaped and emerged in Philadelphia. By the 1860s, he had established his catering business at 1231 Locust Street. Minton and Jones were also known for catering to wealthy white families. Minton was born in Virginia and moved to Philadelphia in 1830. He established a catering business and dining room. Jones also moved from Virginia to Philadelphia and established a catering business that served families in Philadelphia, New Jersey, and New York. The independence and wealth enjoyed by African American caterers helped to encourage African Americans engaging in these businesses in the Northeast. By the 1870s, catering businesses owned by African Americans were in decline. At the turn of the twentieth century, most of these businesses in Philadelphia had lost their clientele. During a time in which food service profits were declining for African Americans, James Wormley was building a comfortable fortune with his hotel and restaurant.

While there were many African Americans in the food service industry in Washington, D.C., the success of Wormley in the hotel and food service business is an exceptional case. Wormley (1819–1884) was born free to Mary and Peter Leigh Wormley in Virginia. In 1814, Peter moved to Washington, D.C., where he worked as a coachman and later opened a livery located on Pennsylvania Avenue. Wormley's business was successful. Wormley married Anna Thomspon in 1841; Thompson ran a business next door to Wormley's establishment. Before the Civil War, Wormley opened a catering business on I Street. Wormley's establishment became renown in both the black and white communities in Washington. In the 1860s, Wormley expanded his business and opened a restaurant at 314 I Street, North. Wormley was invited to travel and to work in England and France. He opened Wormley's Hotel in 1871 after returning home from Europe. The hotel was located on the corner of H and 15th Street. The hotel enjoyed the same popularity as his catering and restaurant businesses. When Wormley died in 1884, he passed on his successful businesses to his son James T. Wormley. At his death, Wormley's establishments were worth over $100,000. The hotel, however, was eventually sold and torn down several years following his death.

One of the country's oldest continuously existing black businesses is C. H. James & Co., a food-processing company located in West Virginia that has survived more than 100 years and over four generations of African American ownership. It was founded by Charles Howell James (1862–1929). In 1883, James and his brothers were peddlers; they pooled their money and bought merchandise, including ginseng, medicinal herbs, barks, and novelty items. At first their clients were extremely poor farmers who had no money. They traded their goods to the farmers for the produce that the farmers had grown and then sold these items in Charleston for profit. Since they needed transportation, they bought a mule and wagon to move their goods about. After Charles James married Roxy Ann Clark in 1885, they had children, only one of whom would reach adulthood and assist his father with the business. Thus, Edward Lawrence James partnered with his father, and they built a warehouse in Charleston called C. H. James & Son, Wholesale Produce.

From Cincinnati, Richmond, and elsewhere, they imported fresh produce and distributed their goods in the fleet of ten trucks that they now owned. They also had a staff of thirty, and all sales agents were black. After Charles James retired from the business in 1926, his son carried on. The stock market crash of 1929 took its toll on the business; Edward James filed for bankruptcy in early 1929 but reestablished the business later on. The business processed poultry for a while but stopped when two suspicious fires destroyed their plant. Later he sold frozen foods and canned goods to hotels, restaurants, and others. James Produce was incorporated in 1961 and then handed down to son Charles Howell James II, the third member of the family to run the enterprise. Between 1961 and 1989, the company prospered and slowed, and by 1991 half of the company's business came from national contracts. It continues to operate under the leadership of Charles Howell James III, the fourth generation of the James family who carries on the family's legacy.

## ECONOMIC VENTURES IN THE TWENTIETH CENTURY

During the twentieth century, opportunities for economic ventures by African Americans outside of food service improved. Increasingly, African Americans in the catering business could not compete with the European chefs and restaurants. However, in the later half of the twentieth century, there have been a number of African Americans whose accomplishments are outstanding. Two popular trends in food service emerged in the second half of the twentieth century. One of the trends is soul food. African American–owned restaurants and retail food products by African Americans have been based on traditional black southern cooking. The other trend in recent years is the ownership of fast-food franchises by African Americans.

Many African American businesses experienced difficultly with the decline of segregation. However, there are examples of restaurants established by African Americans before and during the civil rights era that enjoyed remarkable success. Examples of restaurants that were successful are Dooky Chase's of New Orleans, Louisiana; **Paschal**'s of Atlanta, Georgia; Swetts of Nashville, Tennessee; and Sylvia's of Harlem, New York.

In 1941, Emily and Edgar "Dooky" Chase Sr. opened Dooky Chase Restaurant in New Orleans. Emily Chase was chef. Following Emily Chase, for fifty years her daughter-in-law, Leah Chase, was executive chief and became known as the "Queen of Creole Cuisine." The business grew from a small eatery to become a fine restaurant of national and international reputation. Leah Chase published her recipes in the *The Dooky Chase Cookbook* (1990) and in the more recent *And Still I Cook* (2003).

In 1946, brothers **Robert and James Paschal** opened a lunchroom on Hunter Street in Atlanta. They specialized in chicken sandwiches. In 1947, their success allowed them to expand their business into a restaurant. In 1951, they acquired land across from their Hunter Street restaurant and expanded their business. Eventually they constructed a hotel and in 1960 opened La Carousel, a night club. They also opened two restaurants at Atlanta's Hartsfield Airport. In 1996, the Paschals sold their restaurant and lounge to Clark Atlanta University. Robert Paschal died in 1997, and in 2000 James Paschal entered a business relationship with **Herman Jerome Russell** to begin a new restaurant. In 2002, the new Paschal's opened at Castleberry Hill, within walking distance of the original building. The building includes a loft and banquet rooms and seats some 200 patrons in the restaurant.

Walter and Susie Swett opened Swetts Restaurant in Nashville in 1954. The restaurant is located on the corner of 28th Avenue, North and Clifton Road. The restaurant offers traditional southern African American food. Like Swetts, Sylvia's offers traditional southern cooking but in the North.

Sylvia's restaurant is located at 328 Lenox Avenue in New York. It was established in 1962 in Harlem by Herbert and **Sylvia P. Woods**. When the restaurant opened, it seated only 35 people; currently, the restaurant can accommodate 450 people. The owners advertised that their restaurant offered its customers traditional African American food. In the 1990s, under the direction of Van Woods, their son, the family began selling Sylvia's Soulfood products in grocery stores nationwide. These products include sauces, spices, mixes, soups, and canned beans and vegetables. The family also opened a second restaurant in Atlanta, Georgia, in 1997. The restaurant is located at 241 Central Avenue. In additional to food products, Sylvia's offers hair-care products and has published *Sylvia's Soul Food Cookbook* in 1992 and, in 1999, *Sylvia's Family Soul Food Cookbook*. Just as Sylvia's profited from family and traditional African American recipes, other black-owned companies would rely on family and tradition in their businesses.

Among the most highly recognized restaurateurs is **Barbara "B" Smith**, who has built her career round industries such as modeling, acting, writing, television shows, marketing housewares, and operating restaurants in New York City and Washington, D.C. Born on August 24, 1949, in Everson, Pennsylvania, she learned the art of cooking from her mother, a part-time maid, as well as from her aunts and grandmother. In the early 1980s Smith worked as a hostess and then manager for Ark's America in New York and by 1986 owned a share of Ark Restaurants Corporation. Then she opened a restaurant of her own, in New York's theater district. She provided an elegant but casual setting. After she bought her New York location, in 1994 she opened restaurants in Washington, D.C.'s Union Station and in 1988 one in Sag Harbor on Long Island. The restaurants cater to the needs of each locale, and she supplements food offerings with book readings, cultural programs, and political gatherings. Her work is promoted in her books, B. *Smith's Entertaining and Cooking for Friends* (1995) and B. *Smith, Rituals and Celebrations* (1999).

**Henry Green Parks Jr.** is an example of an African American businessman who used traditional recipes to make his fortune in the sausage industry. Parks was born in 1916 in Atlanta, Georgia. In 1951, he founded Park's Sausage Company in Baltimore, Maryland. In 1969, Parks Sausage became the first African American company to be traded publicly. The company's memorable commercials involved a child's demanding voice, "More Park's sausages, Mom! Please!" However, during the late 1970s, Parks sold his interest in the company. Parks died in 1989 at the age of seventy-two. Recently, the company was returned to black ownership when it was purchased by former National Football League star Franco Harris. He bought the company in 1996; however, efforts to revitalize the company failed and by 1998 Harris had sold the firm.

During the late 1970s and early 1980s, **Wally "Famous Amos" Amos Jr.** was known for his star quality cookies. Amos was born in Tallahassee, Florida, in 1936. When his parents divorced, he was sent to live with his Aunt Della in New York. While staying with his aunt, Amos was introduced to her chocolate chip cookie recipe. Amos was employed by William Morris Talent Agency and later independently worked to promote aspiring performers. When he decided to use his Aunt Della's recipe and sell cookies, his celebrity connections proved advantageous. Not only did Amos receive financial support from his celebrity friends to start his company, but his cookies were associated with stars. This association, along with the quality of his product, made the cookies widely popular during the 1970s and 1980s. Amos was able to open stores in the Los Angeles area and sell his cookies in department stores. He was closely associated with the cookies, as he appeared on the box wearing a Panamanian hat and Hawaiian shirt. Amos's success was met with problems of management of his company. In the 1980s, Amos decided to sell his company, retaining only a small percentage of the company's stock. He left the company in 1989, and in 1992 he founded the Uncle Norman Noname Cookie Company. He offered five varieties of gourmet cookies.

Another recent example of African American success in the food retail industry is Glory Foods. Again, this company markets its products by claiming to offer the taste of traditional African American home-cooked food. In 1989, Bill Williams, Iris McCord, and Daniel A. Charna founded Glory Foods. The company is located in Columbus, Ohio. It sells at least seventeen products including cornbread mixes, greens, peas, sweet potatoes, okra, and beans. Some of the items are canned and others are fresh; for example, there now are fresh turnip and collard greens in packages. The company attempts to use black farmers, black truckers, and black advertisers as often as possible. Glory products are distributed nationwide to supermarkets. The company was listed in *Black Enterprise* in the 1990s as one of the fastest-growing African American businesses.

Vivian Gibson was involved in various business ventures before establishing Mill-Creek Company, Inc. in 1994. The company specializes in hot sauce and seasonings. Similar to other African American companies, Gibson's company uses family and tradition to market her product. On the labels of her products are stories of her family and home. Gibson's products are sold in groceries stories in the Missouri and Illinois areas. Some of her products include Vib's Caribbean Heat, Vib's Bar-B-Q Sauce, and Vib's Southern Heat.

Like Dooky Chase's, Swetts, and Silvia's, Mildred Council's restaurant in Chapel Hill is popular for its traditional African American food. Council's cookbook *Mama Dip's Kitchen* was published by the University of North Carolina in 1999. The book features recipes for meals offered in Council's restaurant, Mama Dip's Kitchen.

The marketing of soul food and traditional "home-cooked" food is one popular trend in African American food service in the later half of the twentieth century; another popular trend is the purchase and management of preexisting fast-food establishments. One highly successful example of this type of African American–owned business is V&J Foods. This company was established by Valerie Daniels-Carter in 1982. The company includes thirty-six Burger King Restaurants. The restaurants are located in metropolitan Milwaukee and Detroit areas. V&J Foods also owns Pizza Hut franchises. The company is listed in *Black Enterprise*'s list of top 100 Industrial Service Companies in 2004. Also included in the *Black Enterprise* top 100 is Manna Inc. African American–owned Manna Inc. is located in Louisville, Kentucky, and owns and operates Wendy's franchises.

Success in twentieth-century food service by African Americans is exemplified by the work of prominent businessmen such as **Reginald F. Lewis** and his work as owner of TLC Beatrice during the 1980s. Another example of a business savvy leader in the food industry is **Regynald G. Washington**. Washington's most recent position is with Walt Disney. He is the vice president and general manger of Disney Regional Entertainment in Burbank, California. **Herman Jerome Russell** is known for his work in construction, but he also has profited from the establishment of Concessions International Corporation.

African American celebrities have purchased restaurants as well as allowed a restaurant to be named for them. There is, for example, Michael Jordan's in Washington, D.C. In 1997, Gladys Knight teamed with gospel singer Ron Winans to open a soul food restaurant in Atlanta, known as Gladys & Ron's Chicken and Waffles. The business is named after Knight's favorite cuisine. Since then, the owners have opened sites in Liothonia, Georgia, and Largo, Maryland. It is said that the chicken and waffles combination started at Wells Restaurant in Harlem—the landmark jazz supper club and restaurant founded during the Harlem Renaissance. Wells was a late-night place where many celebrities came together in the late hours. It catered to those who were unable to decide whether they wanted breakfast, dinner, or both; hence, chicken and waffles were served together. Much later, Motown singers also visited Wells Restaurant during late hours and ordered the famous combination. **Sean "Diddy" Combs** owns Justin's in New York City and Atlanta; the restaurants are named for his young son. **Earvin "Magic" Johnson** is owner of two TGI Fridays—one in Atlanta and the other in East Point, Georgia.

The various examples of success by African Americans from the eighteenth century to the present attest to the resiliency and ambition of African Americans. These examples of African American success in the food industry are remarkable, considering the social and political barriers meant to deter their economic growth. Their achievements serve as examples for future entrepreneurs.

*See also*: Grocery Store Enterprises; Retail Industry

**Sources**

"B.E.'s 100s Industrial Service Companies." *Black Enterprise* 35 (June 2005): 113.

Chase, Leah. *The Dooky Chase Cookbook*. Gretna, LA: Pelican Publishing, 1990.

"Company History." V&J Foods. http://www.vjfoods.com.

Conrad, Sharron Wilkins. "Nineteenth-Century Philadelphia Caterer Thomas J. Dorsey." *American Visions* (August 2000). http://www.findarticles.com.

Council, Mildred. *Mama Dip's Kitchen*. Chapel Hill: University of North Carolina Press, 1999.

Du Bois, W.E.B. *The Philadelphia Negro*. 1899. Millwood, NY: Kraus-Thomson, 1973.

Gladys Knight & Ron Winan's. http://www/gladysandron.com.

Harris, Wendy. *Against All Odds: Ten Entrepreneurs Who Followed Their Hearts and Found Success*. New York: John Wiley, 2001.

Ingham, John N., and Lynne B. Feldman. *African-American Business Leaders: A Biographical Dictionary*. Westport, CT: Greenwood Press, 1994.

"James Wormley." *Dictionary of American Biography Base Set*. American Council of Learned Societies, 1928–1936. Reproduced in Biography Resource Center. Farmington Hills, MI: Thomson Gale, 2005. http://galenet.galegroup.com/servlet/BioRC.

Jones, Joyce. "Parks Sausage Is Sold: Michu Corp. Reportedly Pays $10 Million for Historic Company." *Black Enterprise* 26 (November 1995): 21.

Kranz, Rachel. *African-American Business Leaders and Enterprises (A to Z of African Americans)*. New York: Facts on File, 2004.

Martin, Harold H. *Atlanta and Environs: A Chronicle of Its People and Events*. Athens: University of Georgia Press, 1987.

Mason, Herman "Skip," ed. *Going Against the Wind*. Marietta, GA: Longstreet Press, 1992.

"Reginald F. Lewis." The Reginald L. Lewis Museum of Maryland African American History and Culture. http://www.africanamericanculture.org/museum.

"Regynald Washington." *Contemporary Black Biography*. Vol. 44. Gale Group, 2004. Reproduced in Biography Resource Center. Farmington Hills, MI: Thomson Gale, 2005. http://galenet.galegroup.com/serblet/BioRC.

Smith, Eric L. "The Immaculate Reception of Park Sausage." *Black Enterprise* 27 (September 1996): 58.

Stone, Sherry. "African-American Entrepreneurship Continues to Thrive in Philadelphia." *Philadelphia Tribune*, February 11, 1997.

Sylvia's—Queen of Soul Food. http://www.sylviassoulfood.com.

Walker, Juliet E. K. *The History of Black Business in America: Capitalism, Race, Entrepreneurship.* New York: Macmillan Library Reference USA, 1998.

———, ed. "Catering, Inns, Hotels." *Encyclopedia of African American Business History.* Westport, CT: Greenwood Press, 1999.

Watts, Christina, and Lloyd Gite. "Emerging Entrepreneurs." *Black Enterprise* 26 (November 1995): 100.

*Rebecca Dixon*

# Barney Launcelot Ford (1822?–1902), Conductor on the Underground Railroad, Real Estate Baron, Political Leader

An escaped slave, Barney Launcelot Ford gained fortune and respect as a proprietor of barbershops, restaurants, and hotels. Through the Underground Railroad, he helped hundreds of slaves reach safety. Politically, he fought for the right for African Americans to vote and for laws that prohibited discrimination.

Ford was born in Stafford County, Virginia, around 1822 and grew up on a plantation. Marian Talmadge and Iris Gilmore indicate that he lived a good life—for a slave—receiving adequate shelter, food, clothing—even shoes—and the privilege of enjoying childhood. His mother Phoebe longed for her son to become free and live to do good for other people. She knew that young Barney must learn to read and write, and she wanted him to learn every word in the dictionary she borrowed. But Barney could understand none of them. So in the evenings, she took him to a fellow slave who taught him to read words from a "spelling book."

Ford learned to read sentences from a hymnal his mother had found. He taught himself to write by copying one of William Lloyd Garrison's editorials from the *Liberator*, an abolitionist newspaper, using sycamore bark as his slate. Phoebe had him record on a piece of bark his place and date of birth: near Stafford Court House, Virginia, January 22, 1822.

Ford failed to understand why his mother insisted on his education, but he gradually became fascinated with words. He loved to quote Shakespeare, Scripture, and hymns. A quotation from Napoleon became his motto: "If it's possible, it can be done; if it's impossible, it *must* be done."

Aside from keeping his education secret, Phoebe imposed another restriction—that Ford not wander too close to the "Big House." Still, he often climbed his favorite tree to watch the happenings there. He came to admire the "Young Master" and determined that, one day, he would gallantly welcome friends into his own home and hear people call him "Mister." He would later learn that he and the young plantation owner shared the same father.

After the "Old Master's" death, the family moved to South Carolina, and Ford became a field hand. One day, the master's widow summoned Ford, thinking to make him a house servant. Phoebe quickly realized that she had noted Ford's too-strong resemblance to her own son. Friends found Phoebe frozen in the river one night soon thereafter, having attempted to find a way for Ford to escape. The day after his mother's funeral, Ford was sold.

While serving as a house slave, he spent time each day reading in the library. When his owner discovered Ford's interest, she allowed him to attend school with her sons for a few hours each day. Life brought other new experiences. Working his master's gold claim, he vowed to make his own fortune one day. As a steward on a cotton boat, he learned to cook and honed his listening skills. In 1847, Ford escaped to freedom through the Underground Railroad.

H. O. Wagoner allowed Ford to work at his Chicago livery stable and sleep in his hayloft while waiting for other slaves to arrive for the trip into Canada. Julia Lyoni, Wagoner's sister-in-law, brought food. Ford loved her voice. She asked what name he would choose when he became free, so he asked for a suggestion. She mentioned a locomotive named the *Launcelot Ford*. He liked the sound of Barney Ford, adopted the name to please Julia, and began to sign his name as Barney L. Ford. He stayed in Chicago to help Wagoner with the Underground Railroad. The peddler's wagon he repaired and painted bright yellow carried as many as five people at a time to freedom—beneath the clatter of pots and pans and collections of pins and needles.

Julia mentioned an opening in the barbershop at the hotel where she worked. Ford paid $2 for lessons and earned his first paying job. Now, he could ask Julia to marry him. At the barbershop, he listened quietly as his educated customers talked politics. Then he listened intently as their talk turned to finding gold. Along with thousands of other people in 1849, Ford set his heart on going to California.

Ford intended to make the journey alone and send for Julia after making his fortune, but she refused to let him go without her. They waited until 1851, when the price of tickets on Commodore Vanderbilt's steamship *Prometheus* came down to a price they could afford. Vanderbilt had opened a quicker route to the West, through Nicaragua. Arriving in Greytown, they planned to go on to California. But the outgoing steamer held room only for first-class passengers.

## BECOMES WEALTHY ENTREPRENEUR

Forced to stay longer than planned in a land noted for yellow fever and malaria, Ford developed a fever. Julia nursed him to health, but they both realized he no longer possessed the strength to mine for gold. They decided to open a lodge and restaurant in Greytown to take advantage of the travel trade. Their fine establishment, the United States Hotel, served excellent food. In a land where slavery did not exist, Ford finally found the respect he had been seeking. People called him "Mister." The Fords grew wealthy but not rich enough to rebuild when fire destroyed their hotel.

Ford signed on as a steward on the steamship *La Virgin*. For a while, he owned the California Hotel at Virgin Bay. Eventually he and Julia made their way back to Chicago, where his friend Wagoner sold him the livery stable. Ford returned to helping people escape through the Underground Railroad. Traffic grew lighter as the Civil War loomed nearer. Ford took over much of Wagoner's correspondence with antislavery leaders.

When news of the 1859 Pikes Peak gold rush spread, Ford set out for Colorado. Julia stayed behind this time to await their first child. Ford reached Denver and decided to go on to Mountain City where prospects seemed brighter. He set about looking for gold and seemed on his way to making his fortune. But each time he tried to establish a claim, someone stole it. In his final attempt at Breckenridge, white men drove him and his friends from their claim. A rumor started that the blacks had buried their gold there on what eventually became known as "Barney Ford Hill."

When prospects had looked promising, Ford had sent for Wagoner. In 1861, they opened a barbershop and lunch counter in Denver. Julia and son Louis Napoleon came West. More fires destroyed buildings, but Ford persisted, and in 1863, he opened a grand establishment called People's Restaurant. In 1865, the Fords welcomed daughter Sarah Elizabeth, called Sadie, into their home. Ford became engaged in politics, working toward the inclusion of the right for blacks to vote in Colorado's bid for statehood, but the vote for statehood failed to pass.

Angry and disappointed, Ford returned to Chicago. He sold the hotel and hired an attorney to manage his other real estate. But friends soon persuaded Ford to go to Washington, D.C. to lobby against Colorado's statehood until blacks could vote. Successful in this attempt, he returned to Denver in 1866, opened a new restaurant, helped the black schools there, and stayed active in politics. In 1868, the Ford family welcomed daughter Frances, called Frankie. Ford served as delegate to the Republican convention and as an unsuccessful candidate for the Territorial Legislature.

As Ford's influence and wealth grew, he opened a restaurant in Cheyenne, Wyoming. In Denver, he built a mansion for Julia. Together, "Mister" Barney Ford and his wife graciously welcomed influential people into their home. Ford became trustee of a bank and a member of the Republican Party Central Committee. He served on a federal grand jury in Colorado, the first black to serve in this capacity.

At the height of Ford's ventures, he bought Denver's Sargent Hotel and renamed it Ford's Hotel. In 1872, he opened his grandest establishment, the Inter-Ocean Hotel. When the depression hit in 1873, he sold out, moved to Cheyenne, and opened another hotel and restaurant named Inter-Ocean. During the rest of his life, he continued to buy and sell real estate but never again lived in luxury. Still active in politics, in 1885, he saw Colorado pass a law against discrimination in public places.

By the end of his life, Ford had returned to his first trade, owning two barbershops in Denver. He hired managers and could sit and visit with customers, who often stopped by to listen to him quote Shakespeare, the Bible, or the classics. Ford died of a stroke on December 14, 1902. His beloved Julia had preceded him in death three years earlier.

Ford occasionally got sidetracked in pursuing his own goals of status and fortune. But he fulfilled his mother's dream of using his freedom to do good for other people. His work affected individual lives and strengthened the rights of African Americans in his own time and into the future.

**Sources**

Forbes, Parkhill. *Mister Barney Ford: A Portrait in Bistre*. Denver, CO: Sage Books, 1963.

Raymond, Maria Elena. "Ford, Barney Launcelot." *American National Biography*. Vol. 8. Ed. John A. Garraty and Mark C. Carnes. New York: Oxford University Press, 1999.

Schubert, Frank N. "Ford, Barney Launcelot." *Dictionary of American Negro Biography*. Ed. Rayford W. Logan and Michael R. Winston. New York: W. W. Norton, 1982.

Talmadge, Marian, and Iris Gilmore. *Barney Ford, Black Baron*. New York: Dodd, Mead, 1973.

*Marie Garrett*

# James Forten (1766–1842), Shipbuilder, Abolitionist

James Forten was an eighteenth-century shipbuilder who was one of the most powerful voices for the abolition of slavery and the full citizenship of all African Americans. As a successful businessman in Philadelphia, Forten amassed a large fortune and was one of the most powerful voices for blacks in the North. He was an outspoken critic of the American Colonization Society that sought to resettle freed slaves in Liberia. Forten was convinced that there were no biological differences between whites and blacks and that a plan to deport people to another land was like casting them into the savage forests of Africa and a route to return to slavery. He believed that slaves should be freed and educated to take their place in American society. Forten's views were innovative for the time and were later adopted by well-known writers like William Lloyd Garrison and Theodore Dwight Weld. In 1834, Forten and other black reformers founded the American Moral Reform Society, dedicated to the well-being, education, and liberty for all Americans. Opposition to Forten's views was strong as racial violence and death threats were accompanied by an erosion of civil rights for blacks in the North. In 1838, the Pennsylvania legislature changed its constitution to revoke the right for blacks to vote. Forten strongly opposed the legislation and financed the publication of the pamphlet *Appeal of Forty Thousand Citizens* by abolitionist and journalist Robert Purvis to distribute throughout the state. Although the pamphlet did not change the mind of the legislature, it spurred other abolitionists on to continue the fight for racial equality.

Forten was born on September 2, 1766, in Philadelphia, Pennsylvania. His ancestors were colonists of long standing. Forten's great-grandfather came over to Pennsylvania as a slave. His grandfather obtained his freedom at a time when it was difficult for people of African descent. Forten's father, Thomas, was a freeborn journeyman sailmaker in the sail-loft of Robert Bridges. Thomas Forten was anxious to pass on his skills to James so that he might become an apprentice. However, Thomas Forten died suddenly when James was only seven. His mother Margaret supported James and his sister Abigail throughout their childhood years. James was educated at the Quaker "abolitionist" school led by Anthony Benezet until the age of nine. Poverty forced Forten to work full-time for a Philadelphia grocer to help support his family.

In 1781, Forten joined the colonial navy and was a "powder boy" on the privateer *Royal Lewis* under the command of Stephen Decatur. Forten was captured by the British Navy in the fall of 1781 and was imprisoned on the prison ship *Jersey* for seven months. Despite hardships and terrible conditions aboard the ship, Forten survived the ordeal and was released in a prisoner exchange in the spring of 1782. He returned to Philadelphia to be with his mother and sister.

As a result of his wartime experience, Forten was skilled at maintaining and repairing sails. Forten signed up to work on the *Commerce*, a commercial ship bound for England. When he arrived in London, Forten found work in the shipyards and sail-lofts along the Thames River. Forten returned to Philadelphia twelve months later at age nineteen to become an apprentice to Robert Bridges. Bridges made Forten the foreman of the sail-loft in 1786. When Bridges retired in 1798, Forten took control of the business.

## BECOMES SUCCESSFUL SHIPBUILDER

At age thirty-two, Forten was owner of one of the most successful sail-lofts in Philadelphia. Much of his success in business is attributed to the invention of a device to handle sails. He was well respected among many of the merchants in Philadelphia. As an employer, Forten was noted for having a diverse workforce of both blacks and whites. Although he worked hard to teach underprivileged blacks the skills of shipbuilding, he did not discriminate or treat his white employees unfairly. His reputation extended beyond the city in which he lived and worked. In his *Diary*, the New York dramatist and painter William Dunlap mentions Forten as a "rich sail maker, having many journeymen and apprentices under him." Other accounts pointed to his good character and considerable property. By 1832, Forten had amassed a fortune of approximately $100,000.

Forten was an outspoken leader of the black community in Philadelphia. In 1799, he joined some seventy other black freemen in Philadelphia and surrounding counties in petitioning the U.S. Congress to act in preventing the kidnapping of free blacks into slavery under the Fugitive Slave Law. Although the petition was unsuccessful, Forten was undaunted in his efforts to obtain freedom and equality for blacks.

In 1816, the American Colonization Society (ACS) was formed to promote the resettlement of blacks to establish a colony in Liberia. Leaders came to Forten to seek his support and enlist his help in influencing the blacks living in Philadelphia and Pennsylvania to emigrate to the colony. Although Forten initially gave an unqualified endorsement to the idea of a voluntary movement, he became alarmed at rumors that the ACS was advocating that free blacks be forced to migrate to Africa. For the next twenty-five years, Forten helped lead the opposition to the ACS.

In November 1819, Forten presided over a large meeting of Philadelphia blacks to condemn the ACS for its policies toward slavery and to encourage blacks to oppose the proposed colonization of Africa. Forten continued his verbal attacks on the ACS throughout the 1820s despite increased political and social support for the immigration to Liberia. In 1829, the Pennsylvania legislature passed a resolution endorsing the ACS and urged abolitionists to seek national support.

During the early 1830s Forten became a close personal friend of William Lloyd Garrison, the editor of the *Liberator*, an abolitionist newspaper. Forten provided financial support for the paper and his collection of materials on the American Colonization Society to fuel Garrison's attacks on African colonization. In 1832, Garrison published the pamphlet *Thoughts on African Colonization*, which denounced the ACS's plans for gradual repatriation of blacks to Africa; it was widely read by abolitionists throughout the North and gained a great deal of publicity for Forten's views. The following year, Garrison helped to form the American Anti-Slavery Society in Philadelphia and elected Forten as a vice president in the organization.

During the last years of his life, Forten embarked on a larger agenda than just slavery. He pursued a full-scale moral reform of society, regardless of race or gender, committed to principles of education, temperance, economy, and universal liberty. In 1835, he was elected president of the newly formed American Moral Reform Society. However, the organization was short-lived due to the philosophical issues of race and socioeconomic status. Forten also faced challenges of a more personal nature as hostility grew against blacks in the late 1830s. Forten's wealth and social status singled him out as the recipient of death threats and physical attacks on his family members. Mobs destroyed some of Forten's real estate in Philadelphia and forced him to seek the help of the local law enforcement for protection of his own home.

Forten's greatest disappointment came in 1838 when the Pennsylvania legislature voted to revise its constitution to revoke the right of blacks to vote. Forten helped finance the printing of the pamphlet *The Appeal of Forty Thousand*, a statement of protest from the 40,000 black "freemen" living in Pennsylvania at the time. Unfortunately, the statement fell on deaf ears, as whites ratified the constitution by a large majority.

Despite his ailing health, Forten continued to fight for the rights of blacks and against slavery. He attended rallies and conventions in support of the antislavery movement. He wrote newspaper editorials and was the elder statesman for blacks who were successful businessmen in the United States. When he died in Philadelphia on March 4, 1842, Forten's funeral was one of the largest seen in Philadelphia and was attended by many citizens of all races. Eulogies and tributes proclaimed his achievements in business and his dedication to the causes of morality and freedom.

Forten's legacy continued to live on for several years after his death. He was esteemed as a man who had gained the respect of many in Philadelphia through his hard work in the shipbuilding industry and as a philanthropist to many virtuous causes. His visionary outlook on the status and equality of blacks was adopted by several abolitionists and influential writers like William Lloyd Garrison and Thomas Dwight Weld. However, as years passed, Forten's accomplishments were forgotten in light of more well-known activists like **Booker T. Washington** and W.E.B. Du Bois.

**Sources**

Billington, Ray Allen. "James Forten: Forgotten Abolitionist." *Negro History Bulletin* 13 (November 1949): 31–36, 45.

Douty, Esther M. *Forten the Sailmaker: Pioneer Champion of Negro Rights.* Chicago: Rand McNally, 1968.

Dunlap, William. *Diary of William Dunlap.* New York: B. Bloom, 1969.

"Forten, James." *American National Biography.* Vol. 8. Ed. John A. Garraty and Mark C. Carnes. New York: Oxford University Press, 1999.

———. "'A Person of Good Character and Considerable Property': James Forten and the Issue of Race in Philadelphia's Antebellum Business Community." *Business History Review* 75 (2001): 261–296.

———. "'You Know I Am a Man of Business': James Forten and the Factor of Race in Philadelphia's Antebellum Business Community." *Business and Economic History* 26 (1997): 213–228.

Winch, Julie. *A Gentleman of Color: The Life of James Forten.* New York: Oxford University Press, 2002.

*Mark L. McCallon*

# Ann M. Fudge (1951– ), Corporate Executive

For more than two decades, Ann Marie Fudge has been one of the most powerful female corporate executives in America. Fudge began her impressive career at General Electric in Bridgeport, Connecticut, as a personnel executive in 1973. Four years later, she accepted a position as marketing assistant at General Mills in Minneapolis, Minnesota, where she was promoted three times: assistant product manager in 1978, product manager in 1980, and marketing director in 1983. With Fudge's third appointment, she became the first female as well as the first African American woman to hold that position at General Mills. During her tenure there, Fudge helped develop and introduce the popular brand Honey Nut Cheerios. Although she was on track to become a general manager at General Mills, in 1986 Fudge left the company, moved to White Plains, New York, and became the director of strategic planning at General Foods.

The move to the East Coast was prompted by a variety of reasons including Fudge's desire to be near her mother who was ill. Three years later, Fudge was promoted to vice president for marketing and development in General Foods' Dinners and Enhancers division, and in 1991, she became the general manager of the division that produced such products as Kool-Aid, Stove Top Stuffing Mix, Minute Rice, and Shake N' Bake. While the rest of General Foods realized a 1 percent sales and earnings increase in 1991, Fudge led her division to a double-digit revenue increase. In 1993, Fudge was promoted to executive vice president at General Foods. When the company merged with Kraft Foods in 1994, Fudge was named president of Maxwell Coffee, where she introduced a line of flavored coffees including Irish Cream and French Vanilla and, as a result, doubled the division's earnings. In 1997, she was promoted to president of the Coffee and Cereals division.

During the next two years, she spent time with her family, traveled to such places as Thailand, Bali, and Morocco, and in conjunction with Harvard Business School, developed a tutoring program for African American children. Fudge ended her sabbatical in 2003 when she accepted an offer from WPP Group, the London-based communications company. Fudge, who had built a highly successful career in marketing, took on a new challenge—advertising. WPP appointed Fudge chairwoman and chief executive of its multinational advertising division, Young & Rubicam Brands, located on New York's Madison Avenue, as well as the chairwoman and chief executive of Young & Rubicam's largest division, Y&R Advertising. Y&R companies include Burson-Marsteller (public relations/public affairs), Landor Associates (brand consulting and creative design), Sudler and Hennessey (health-care communications), and Wunderman (direct marketing and database marketing). Thus Fudge became one of a few women to reach the upper echelons of advertising, the first African American woman to head a large division of a global advertising agency, and one of a few African American female chief executives in the United States. Although Fudge stepped down as head of Y&R in 2005, she remains the chairwoman and chief executive of Young & Rubicam.

Fudge was born on April 23, 1951, in Washington, D.C., to Malcolm R. Brown, a U.S. Postal Service administrator; and Betty (née Lewis) Brown, a National Security Agency manager. While growing up in the northwest section of the nation's capital, Fudge attended Roman Catholic schools. She acknowledged the influence of her eighth-grade teacher, Sister Marcellina, who, despite Fudge's objections, informed her that a test score of 100 was only average, and she had to do extra work. Fudge realized she had been taught a valuable lesson—"to go the extra mile." Sister Marcellina also encouraged Fudge to go to a high school that would test her academic abilities more than the high school she planned to attend with her friends. As a result, Fudge enrolled in the Immaculata Preparatory School, an all-girls school. As early as her teen years, Fudge's opinions began influencing individuals in the work world; she was a Teen Board member at Hecht's department store and advised teenaged customers on current fashions and visited the New York offices of fashion magazines. Fudge, who worked at department stores during her summer breaks from school, thought that she would one day become a buyer. However, after Martin Luther King Jr. was assassinated in 1968, and people began rioting in Washington and other urban areas across America, Fudge became determined to succeed in areas where African Americans were previously denied opportunities.

After Fudge graduated from Immaculata Prep in 1969, she enrolled in Simmons College, in Boston, Massachusetts. Matriculating at Simmons was a reversal of plans for Fudge, who anticipated attending a coed college until she met a Simmons student and considered the benefits of attending a women's school. Three weeks after Fudge arrived at Simmons, she attended homecoming at Bowdoin College, a men's school in Maine, and met Richard E. Fudge. They began dating. At Simmons, she met Margaret Hennig, who, along with Anne Jardim, founded the Simmons Graduate School of Business in 1974, which was the first M.B.A. program designed specifically for women, and wrote *The Managerial Woman* (1977), which was the first book on women in business. Fudge credits Hennig with encouraging her to pursue a career in business. During her sophomore year, she married Richard Fudge, who is a consultant for businesses and nonprofit groups. The couple's first child, Richard Jr., was born during Fudge's undergraduate years, and their second child, Kevin, was born in 1973, the same year Fudge graduated with honors from Simmons. Two years later, she heeded Hennig's advice and enrolled in Harvard University's Graduate School of Business and earned an M.B.A. in 1977.

Fudge is a member of the board of directors of Allied Signal, Catalyst, Federal Reserve Bank of New York, General Electric, Liz Claiborne, Inc., and Marriott International. She is also a board member of the Advertising Council and the Advertising Educational Foundation. Fudge is a trustee of the Brookings Institute and a former vice president and president of the Executive Leadership Council, a nonprofit group of African American corporate managers and directors. She is a member of the Committee of 200, a professional group of women corporate leaders and entrepreneurs; and a member of the Council of Foreign Relations. Since 1997, Fudge has served on the board of governors of the Boys and Girls Club of America, and in 2000, that organization presented her with its President's Award.

While at Harvard, Fudge was the recipient of the Alfred P. Sloan COGME (Council for Opportunity in Graduate Management in Education) fellowship (1975–1976). His additional awards and honors include Young Women's Christian Association's Leadership Award, 1979; inclusion in *Black Enterprise*'s "21 Women of Power and Influence," 1991; National Coalition of 100 Black Women's Candace Award, 1991 and 1992; *Glamour* magazine's Woman of the Year Award, 1995; Advertising Women of New York's Advertising Woman of the Year, 1995; Harvard Business School's Alumni Achievement Award, 1998; and an honorary doctorate from Howard University, 1998. Other honors include *Fortune* magazine's "Fifty

Most Powerful Women in Business," 1998, 1999, and 2003; Executive Leadership Council's Achievement Award, 2000; Sara Lee Front-Runner Award, 2000; New York Women in Communications' Matrix Award for Advertising, 2004; *Time* magazine's "Twenty-five Global Business Influentials," 2004; and the University of Arizona's Eller College of Management Executive of the Year Award, 2005.

Although Fudge is successful and well known in the business world, she refuses to define success in terms of wealth or fame; instead, she views success as life's potential fully realized. Fudge has pioneered new paths in the corporate world for women and African Americans as she continues to implement her definition of a true leader as one who is focused on the personal as well as professional growth of others.

*See also*: Advertising and Marketing; Women and Business

**Sources**

"Ann Fudge." *Contemporary Black Biography*. Vol. 11. 1996. Reproduced in Biography Resource Center. Farmington Hills, MI: Thomson Gale, 2005. http://gale net.galegroup.com/servlet/BioRC.

"Ann M. Fudge." *Take a Lesson: Today's Black Achievers on How They Made It and What They Learned Along the Way*. By Caroline V. Clarke. New York: Wiley, 2001.

Dobrzynski, Judith H. "Way Beyond the Glass Ceiling: Billion-Dollar Command Now, a C.E.O.'s Post Next?" *New York Times*, May 11, 1995.

Elliott, Stuart. "The Media Business: Advertising: Marketer to Lead Division of Big Agency." *New York Times*, May 13, 2003.

Fudge, Ann M., and Julia Lawlor. "The Boss: Nuns, Bicycles and Berries." *New York Times*, January 12, 2000.

Naden, Corinne. "Ann M. Fudge." *Notable Black American Women*. Book III. Ed. Jessie Carney Smith. Detroit: Gale Research, 2003.

*Linda M. Carter*

# Samuel B. Fuller. *See* S. B. Fuller

# S. B. Fuller (1905–1988), Beauty Supply Company Founder

From humble Louisiana beginnings to the ownership of a national industrial and sales empire that made him one of the wealthiest African Americans of the 1950s, the life of S. B. Fuller is an example of the achievements made possible by confidence, discipline, and determination, as well as the tenuousness of these achievements when they are drawn into the politics of race.

Samuel B. Fuller, the first of seven children, was born in rural Ouatchie, Louisiana, on June 4, 1905, to William and Ethel Johnson Fuller. In 1920, the family moved to Memphis, Tennessee, seeking better educational opportunities for the children. Fuller's mother died soon after this move, and in 1922 his father moved to Chicago, leaving S. B. responsible for his siblings. In 1923 Fuller married Lorena Whitfield, also a recent migrant to Memphis. Seeking better opportunities in employment and education, in 1928 Fuller moved to Chicago, found work in a coal yard, and soon sent for his family, by then three of his own children and his siblings, to join him. Through the economic challenges of the Great Depression, Fuller, who had only six years of sporadic schooling, began to teach himself through reading books such as *The Art of Selling*. In the early 1930s he became an insurance salesman for Commonwealth Burial Association in Chicago and was soon supervising the sales staff. Through daily morning lectures to his staff he honed a philosophy of black self-help and economic development.

In 1935, acting on his own philosophy, Fuller established his own business. Using $25 to purchase soap from a company going out of business, Fuller's Quality Soap began business in a rented room. The following year the Fuller Products Company was incorporated, and during the next few years the business grew to include cosmetics, beauty and household items, as well as hosiery, dresses, and men's clothing. Many of these products were sold door to door by Fuller salespeople. Company-owned Fuller Products branches were eventually established in over thirty states, while individuals were also able to establish Fuller distributorships, which were individually owned but supplied by the Fuller Products Company.

The headquarters of Fuller Products Company remained in Chicago but moved to successively larger spaces as the company grew. In 1951, the company purchased a seven-story building at 2700 South Wabash Avenue that became the Fuller Building. Fuller had also purchased the building's occupant, Boyer International Laboratories, which produced hair dressings and Jeanne Nadal Cosmetics with a market that was primarily white and southern. To address concerns that the white agents would leave once they discovered the new owner was African American, Fuller brought the agents to Chicago for a meeting at which he presented his plans for the company and the role they could play in achieving the goals. He indicated that very few agents left the company.

In October 1951, when the fifteenth anniversary meeting was held in Chicago, there were 3,000 people working with Fuller Products Company. In 1955, the company began to hold annual company conventions, at which the top salespeople were recognized with prizes such as a Cadillac for the top salesperson. During this period Fuller purchased the *New York Age* and also gained a controlling interest in the *Pittsburgh Courier*, both newspapers with an African American readership. In a September 1956 "Businessmen in the News" profile, *Fortune* noted that Fuller Products Company's gross sales were $18 million.

As Fuller Products Company grew, the demand for Fuller as a speaker at churches, community organizations, and white and African American business organizations grew. The speaking style that he had first used with

Commonwealth Burial Association salespeople had been refined. The self-help ethos remained but was supported by the visible results of the Fuller Products Company. By 1963 Fuller controlled nine corporations, including farming and cattle interests, a department store in Chicago, and the Courier chain of newspapers. In the early 1960s as the civil rights movement gained momentum, Fuller continued to speak out regarding the failings of the African American community. In December 1963 in a speech delivered at the National Association of Manufacturers' Congress of American Industry he provided a characteristically blunt critique of the obstacles to African American achievement. Fuller suggested that civil rights legislation was not the answer to removing the obstacles to African American achievement and that race was not the primary problem. He suggested that African Americans needed to own their own businesses and to become producers of goods that were in demand in order to be taken seriously by capitalist America.

Fuller's message to the manufacturers was not particularly new for him, but the level of coverage of his remarks was. Coverage by the **black press** was primarily critical. Civil rights leaders such as Jackie Robinson and National Urban League leader Whitney Young when asked to respond did so with anger, characterizing Fuller as a race traitor or "Uncle Tom" who had contributed little to the African American community but had benefited greatly from its patronage. In these early responses, the suggestion of an **economic boycott** of Fuller Products was vaguely offered as a possible avenue to express displeasure with Fuller's remarks.

Fuller attempted to respond to criticism through a lieutenant, Beverly Carter, who was editor of the *New York Courier*, a Fuller-owned newspaper. Carter noted that the statements to which the leaders were responding had been excerpts of a speech that had included Fuller's suggestion that African Americans take aggressive steps through saving and investment to own the businesses in the communities in which they lived, a statement seemingly in line with the "buy black" ethos of the time. Carter noted that white publications that carried the initial coverage of Fuller's remarks (picked up by the black press) had omitted this fact that he considered critical to understanding Fuller's philosophy. In response to criticism of Fuller's contribution to the African American community, Carter noted the many men and women who had benefited from Fuller's mentorship in establishing successful businesses (for example, hair products manufacturer George Johnson).

Carter's efforts did not resonate as widely as his critics' suggestions of a black boycott. Fuller Products sales declined. Fuller's visibility was also believed to have led to a boycott led by White Citizen's councils upon discovery that Fuller was African American. The controversy came soon after Fuller had embarked on a major expansion, and he spent the next years struggling to salvage his company. In 1968, Fuller Products filed for Chapter XI bankruptcy protection, which provides for relief from creditors while the debtor develops a reorganization plan. In 1970 the reorganization plan was accepted.

Attempts to salvage his business led to legal problems for Fuller. On May 22, 1972, he pled guilty to one count of a six-count indictment for selling unregistered high-interest-paying promissory notes. He was placed on probation for five years and required to pay the buyers back during this period. He had faced a maximum sentence of thirty years in prison and $30,000 in fines if convicted on all six counts of the indictment. Fuller had received funds in exchange for promissory notes from several individuals. Buyers of the notes ranged from an individual providing $100 to a Chicago church that invested $100,000.

In her biography *S. B. Fuller: Pioneer of Black Economic Development*, his daughter Mary Fuller Casey indicates that while Fuller was surprised at the negative response precipitated by his remarks, he was not bitter, attributing the responses to a lack of understanding on the part of the boycotters. In 1975 publisher **John H. Johnson**, hair-care products producer George Johnson, and a group of business colleagues, many of whom had been mentored by Fuller, hosted a gala dinner as a tribute to Fuller on his seventieth birthday. At the dinner, attended by 2,000 guests, Fuller was presented with a $70,000 check and $50,000 worth of stock certificates to use in rebuilding his business, his primary goal as he emphasized to those in attendance.

Fuller died of kidney failure on October 24, 1988. He was survived by his second wife Lestine (he and Lorena Fuller divorced in 1945); daughters Ethel, Mary Casey, Jessie Spraggins, Luella Moore, and Geraldine Green; thirteen grandchildren; eighteen great-grandchildren; and two sisters, Helen Jones and Lottie Smith. Fuller Products Company continues operations in Chicago.

Fuller overcame limited schooling by educating himself and used his knowledge to identify and develop cosmetics and other products and to build a network for selling these products through a corps of salespeople. Fuller was instrumental in launching the business careers of many men and women. The setbacks experienced by Fuller Products Company in the 1960s are a testament to the challenging environment for even relatively large African American businesses of the period.

## Sources

"Aiming for $100-Million Sales." *Fortune* 56 (September 1957): 76.

Casey, Mary Fuller. *S. B. Fuller: Pioneer of Black Economic Development*. Jamestown, NC: BridgeMaster Press, 2003.

"Cosmetics Tycoon Fuller Put on Probation Five Years for Sale of Unregistered Notes." *Wall Street Journal*, May 22, 1972.

"Fuller Answers Jackie Robinson." *New York Amsterdam News*, December 21, 1963.

Hailey, Foster. "N.A.M. Hears Defense by Webb of Space Plans' Cost and Aims." *New York Times*, December 7, 1963.

"It's Not Racial Barriers That Keep Blacks from Prospering: American Blacks Must Pool Capital in Order to Help Themselves." *Issues & Views* 7 (Summer 1991): 8.

"N.A.M. Denounced by Rights Leader." *New York Times*, December 16, 1963.

Narvaez, Alfonso A. "S. B. Fuller, Door-to-Door Entrepreneur, Dies at 83." *New York Times*, October 28, 1988.

"A Negro Businessman Speaks His Mind." *U.S. News & World Report*, August 19, 1963.

"Negro Newspaper Endorses Johnson." *New York Times*, October 6, 1964.

Robinson, Jackie. "Leaders Rip S. B. Fuller's Race Criticism." *New York Amsterdam News*, December 14, 1963.

"A Tribute to a Black Business." *Ebony* 30 (September 1975): 58–61.

"S. B. Fuller Dies." *New York Amsterdam News*, November 5, 1988.

"S. B. Fuller: Master of Enterprise." *Issues & Views* (Winter 1989).

Wycliff, Don. "Civil Rights and Sacred Cows: Some Open Minds Win Vindication." *New York Times*, November 7, 1988.

*Kevin McGruder*

# I. Owen Funderburg (1924–2002), Banker

One of the nation's must astute bankers, I. (Ilon) Owen Funderburg spent his entire professional life in the banking industry. He strengthened the historic Citizens Trust Bank in Atlanta, moving it from near failure to become the nation's third-largest black bank. His success was an important achievement both for Atlanta and for the nation, where black economic achievement historically had been a central issue in black life.

Funderburg was born in Monticello, Georgia, in 1924. He graduated from Morehouse College in Atlanta in 1947 with a Bachelor of Arts degree. He enrolled in the University of Michigan for the year 1947–1948. In 1959 he completed a program in banking at Rutgers University Graduate School of Banking, becoming the first African American to complete the program. By then, Funderburg had already worked in the banking field, having worked as a teller in the black-owned Mechanics and Farmers' Bank in Durham, North Carolina, in 1948, just after he left the University of Michigan. Sometime later he left for the Gateway National Bank in St. Louis, Missouri, where he was executive vice president and chief executive officer (CEO) from 1966 to 1974. Sometime during this period he became the bank's president.

In 1971, Funderburg resisted the offer to move to Atlanta and head the historic Citizens Trust Bank but had a different view in 1974. He surprised the board of Citizens Trust in 1974 and, when the offer came, accepted the position of president and chief executive officer. He took charge of the organization on January 9, 1975.

Citizens Trust Company had been a prominent institution in Atlanta since August 16, 1921, when it opened its doors on "Sweet" Auburn Avenue—the center for African American businesses in the city. **Heman Edward Perry**, the founder of Standard Life Insurance Company and the multifaceted enterprise called the Service Company, was its founder. The bank reorganized on September 8, 1927, with new Articles of Incorporation and By-Laws. L. D. Milton and Clayton R. Young headed the institution. Citizens was the first black-owned bank to become a member of the Federal Deposit Insurance Corporation (FDIC) and in 1947 was the first black-owned bank to become a member of the Federal Reserve Bank. Milton and his management team helped sections of Atlanta to become one of the most affluent areas for blacks to live: The bank developed the Hunter Road project and the Mozel Park subdivision and financed the Morris Brown subdivision and the Hightower community.

Under Funderburg's leadership, which began during tough times for banking, the bank grew impressively. He began by issuing to Atlanta area banks and other financial institutions a series of preferred stock and capital notes totaling $3 million. Beginning 1976 Funderburg and board chairman **Herman Jerome Russell**, a prominent local black businessman, aggressively pursued deposits and new business for the bank. In 1982, with board authorization, Funderburg sold the bank's headquarters facility and then leased space in the facility. Although assets continued to grow, by 1984, with $65 million in size, the bank needed additional capital. Through its holding company, Citizens Bancshares Corporation, it was in a strategic position to raise the capital needed. It was also paying strong dividends; consequently, the bank issued an additional $1.5 million in new stock.

Recognizing Funderburg's effective management style, strong leadership, and the advances that the bank made during his administration, in 1985 *Black Enterprise* magazine named Citizens Trust "Bank of the Year." Its reach continued, and by 1985 Citizens Trust added in rapid succession three new branches in local supermarkets. The branches were placed at Old National Highway, Wesley Chapel Road, and Citi-Center on Cleveland Avenue. Such close contact with the public enabled potential customers to learn firsthand what neighborhood banking was all about. Before the year ended, the bank exceeded the $100 million mark—an impressive achievement when compared to early struggles and bank failures in 1974.

Atlanta's black ministers and other black leaders initiated a campaign in 1988 to shift money to the city's black financial institutions. The three-month "Minority Economic Independent Campaign" was not promoted as a boycott. Instead, organizers said in "The Color of Money" that "their withdrawals...from white institutions will become deposits...in black ones." Until this time, local white-owned banks and savings and loans institutions rarely made home loans in black or integrated neighborhoods. As well, their banking services were not immediately accessible to blacks. Two black banks who helped to plan the campaign promoted it under the name of the Community Task Force for Economic Justice. Officials from Citizens Trust Bank and Mutual Federal Savings and Loan supported the campaign, and their officials attended the planning meetings. These two institutions noted that they were not exploiting the situation. "Exploitation carries a negative connotation," said Funderburg in "The Color of Money." "What we're trying to do is to promote Citizens Trust Bank and to take advantage of the fact...that we have been an active player in the community for all of our existence." Citizens also had launched a new advertising campaign. Citing an unidentified newspaper, "The Color of Money" quoted Funderburg, who said, "We've been giving credit where credit's due. For 67 years. We've had the courage to serve in areas where no one else would." In addition, Citizens distributed photocopies of "The Color of Money" and posted a new sign at the bank promoting its new service called "a discrimination hotline." Between April and May, new accounts at Citizens increased 58 percent, while new deposits increased 134 percent. The overall success of the campaign is unclear; however, Citizens did see some growth in its business.

The bank continued its push to support quality commercial projects, to improve communications within the community, and to entice new entrepreneurs into the community to help revitalize the area. So rapid was its expansion, however, that the bank's net revenue dropped significantly; nevertheless, with over $100,000 in assets in 1990 the bank challenged New York City's Freedom National Bank and Chicago's Seaway National Bank as the largest African American–owned bank in the United States.

By 1991 Citizens underwent a changing of the guard. Under Funderburg's leadership, the bank had opened in-store branches, installed automatic teller machines, and moved the business into a new era by installing technology. Operations doubled from some $60 million to over $100 million. Funderburg, after a legendary seventeen-year tenure as president, could retire with the comfort of knowing that he had been an effective leader in one of Atlanta's black financial giants, Citizens Trust Bank.

Funderburg's involvement in professional organizations included the first elected chairman of the National Bankers Association (1971 and 1981), formerly known as the National Negro Bankers Association. The organization changed its name in 1948 to include all minority-banking groups. He was also director of the Georgia World Congress Center and was inducted into the Atlanta Business Hall of Fame.

Funderburg was married to Clara Comeaux and the father of Ilon Owen, Douglas, and Ilon Edward. He was also stepfather to three other children. When not at work, he spent time on his twenty-three-acre farm near Atlanta. There he bred quarter horses and cooked for his Morehouse College schoolmates. In January 2002, he died of cancer.

Citizens Trust Bank continues to operate in Atlanta and has acquired other financial institutions while continuing to increase its assets. Its history between 1971 and 1991 was significantly shaped by I. Owen Funderburg who, among other achievements, moved the bank and its operations into the era of technology. He has been called the "dean of minority banking in the country."

*See also*: Black Banks: Their Beginning

**Sources**

Brenan, Carol. "I. Owen Funderburg." *Contemporary Black Biography*. Vol. 38. Detroit: Thomson Gale, 2003.

Citizens Trust Bank. http://www.ctbatlantahb.com/site/about_history.html.

Dedman, Bill. "The Color of Money." *Atlanta Journal-Constitution*, June 26, 1988. http://powerreporting.com/color/28.html.

Hughes, Alan. "Former Citizens Trust Bank CEO Dies at 77." *Black Enterprise* 32 (May 2002): 24.

*Frederick D. Smith*

# G

Edward Gardner is the cofounder of Soft Sheen Products, a black hair-care company that transformed the industry and established itself as a national and international success. Gardner has proven himself to be as passionate about rejuvenating the African American community in Chicago as he was about revolutionizing black hair care. Understanding the indelible link between politics and economics, Gardner spearheaded the effort to get Harold Washington elected as the first African American mayor of Chicago. Gardner has also organized a number of other initiatives designed to develop and support the African American community. Such projects include the renovation of the historic Regal Theater and programs that combat crime and increase educational opportunities.

Gardner was born on February 15, 1925, in Chicago, Illinois. He graduated from Fenger High School in 1943 and was drafted into the U.S. Army. Gardner served in New Guinea, the Philippines, and Japan, reaching the rank of staff sergeant.

Upon his return, Gardner pursued his education under the opportunities afforded by the G.I. Bill. He received his B.A. degree from Chicago Teachers College and subsequently landed a job as an elementary school teacher in the Chicago school system. Gardner went on to obtain his master's degree from the University of Chicago, which was a rare accomplishment, given the restrictive admissions practices employed toward blacks at the time. Gardner later became assistant principal of Carver Elementary School, then of Beethoven Elementary School in Robert Taylor Homes, one of Chicago's roughest housing projects.

Despite a successful career as an educator that spanned twenty years, life as a civil servant was not enough to satisfy the ambitious Gardner. Consequently, he turned his hand to sales and during his evenings and weekends went door to door selling hair-care products to local black beauty parlors.

Gardner became tired of selling other people's merchandise and, much to the consternation of his friends, decided to quit his job and begin manufacturing his own products.

Gardner began concocting hair treatments in his basement. The experiments were not always a success, and there were quite literally a few hair-raising moments for Gardner's daughter Terri and the family dog, who were the unfortunate guinea pigs in the early years. With his wife Bettiann, the cofounder, serving as accountant, and his four children contributing to the family enterprise in various guises, Gardner plied their trade using his connections and relationships with the local salons to build up a consistent clientele. Maintaining intimate ties with salon owners was a strategy that the Gardners would remain true to throughout their business tenure.

During the 1960s, E. G. Gardner Beauty Products, which changed its name to Soft Sheen in 1962, was one of many small, black-owned hair-care businesses operating out of Chicago. There was a huge void in the market for black hair products that white companies simply were not filling. Soft Sheen's sales continued to grow steadily, and by 1979 the company had approximately 100 employees and sales worth about $500,000 a year.

A series of events in 1976 conspired to present Gardner—and Soft Sheen—with his big break. Changes in product packaging regulations, administered by the Federal Trade Commission, had a huge impact on the industry. Gardner and his son Gary were quick to respond and turned misfortune into opportunity. Soft Sheen released a line of products that avoided the labeling restrictions and increased its prominence in the market.

The real breakthrough, however, came with the rise in popularity of the Jheri curl, endorsed by celebrities such as Michael Jackson. The process of arriving at this new softer look was extremely arduous for hairstylists and customers, and Gardner realized there was money to be made if only the right product could be manufactured. The Gardners created a product that allowed the Jheri curl styling process to be completed in two hours, instead of the customary eight. Care Free Curl was an instant success.

The Jheri curl hairstyle simultaneously propelled the black hair-care industry at an unprecedented rate—over 30 percent annually. Soft Sheen rode the wave of expansion as the first black-owned company to capture that corner of the market. By 1982 Soft Sheen controlled approximately 55 percent of the black hair-care market, with a turnover of over $50 million. The following year the company appeared on the *Black Enterprise* 100 list of top African American–owned businesses. Soft Sheen recorded sales of $81 million in 1987.

The Gardner family business faced staunch competition from white-owned cosmetics companies. Thus, smaller black-owned businesses galvanized a unified attack in defense of their livelihood. Spurred on by what were deemed insidious remarks by Revlon representatives, Gardner and other members of the black business community, along with Reverend Jesse Jackson, launched the PUSH (People United to Serve Humanity) campaign, boycotting Revlon products. The boycott served as a catalyst for joining the American Health and Beauty Aids Institute (AHBAI). Gardner was an eminent member of the minority trade association and was at the forefront of its $3 million campaign, which urged black consumers to purchase black products.

Gardner also fended off the competition by expanding his business interests and diversifying his operations. Gardner and his son Gary, who was now president and chief operating officer, developed a business strategy that allowed them to establish a variety of companies in related business fields. The Gardners set up Brainstorm Communications, an advertising agency, headed by daughter Terri; Bottlewerks, a packaging firm, headed by son Guy; and *Shoptalk*, a trade magazine, headed by Bettiann. Daughter Tracey became vice president of science and technology.

Soft Sheen also enlisted superstars such as singers Anita Baker and Luther Vandross to endorse their products. The company sponsored a nationwide concert tour, becoming the first black-owned business to accomplish such a feat. Soft Sheen, however, had set its sights on an even larger market. Gary Gardner devised a plan for global distribution of Soft Sheen's products and subsequently moved into the Canadian, African, and West Indian hair-care market, leading *Black Enterprise* magazine to name them Company of the Year in 1989.

The activist spirit that Gardner displayed in his business affairs was mirrored in Gardner's commitment to the development of the Chicago community. Gardner provided financial backing for the VOTE campaign, which urged African Americans to let their voices be heard in the 1983 mayoral election. The campaign was a tremendous success, and Harold Washington, who had been a real longshot, became the first black mayor of Chicago.

Later that year a Soft Sheen employee was assaulted. This prompted Gardner to initiate the Black on Black Love Program, promoting love and respect among members of the black community. The program spearheaded the No Crime Day campaign, which condemned black-on-black crime. The program evolved into an umbrella organization that coordinates community action groups and programs aimed at providing recreational outlets and services that increase educational opportunities.

Gardner further demonstrated his dedication to the rejuvenation of the Windy city, investing $4 million into the renovation of the city's legendary Regal Theater (formerly the Avalon). The theater rivaled the Apollo Theater in New York in its prime, hosting illustrious performers such as Duke Ellington and Jackie Wilson. Gardner sought to recreate that quality cultural and artistic experience for blacks in a venue as magnificent and breathtaking as the acts that graced the stage.

Gardner gradually passed on the functional responsibilities of Soft Sheen to his children, yet he continued to indulge his passion for business. Gardner purchased shares in the National Basketball Association's Chicago Bulls and began to develop his own investment firm, Gardner Investment Partners. In

1998, after some corporate restructuring and irresolvable internal challenges, Soft Sheen was sold to the French cosmetics company L'Oreal—but not before Gardner negotiated a deal with L'Oreal that ensured Soft Sheen's headquarters remained in Chicago. Indeed, despite his many accomplishments, Gardner considers his greatest achievement the number of jobs (over 625 annually) his company has created in one of the most impoverished areas of his beloved city. In 1999, Gardner was honored with the "Black on Black Love" first annual Golden Pyramid Award for outstanding business leaders. The magnificent awards gala was fittingly held at Gardner's new Regal Theater, and proceeds from the event were donated to the organization, a testament to Gardner's dedication to uplifting black lives.

*See also*: Black Businesses in Large Cities; Economic Boycotts and Protests; Retail Industry

**Sources**

Clarke, Caroline V. "Management Dynasties." *Black Enterprise* 22 (June 1992): 305–310.

*Contemporary Black Biography*. Vol. 45. Detroit: Gale Group, 2004.

Dingle, Derek T. "Soft Sheen's Triangle of Trade." *Black Enterprise* 19 (February 1989): 222–226.

"Edward Gardner Receives Golden Pyramid Award." *Jet* 95 (May 24, 1999): 12–14.

Hocker, Cliff, and Sakina P. Spruell. "Bad Hair Days: African American Firms Losing Control of the Ethnic Hair Care Industry." *Black Enterprise* 31 (November 2000): 144–153.

Ingham, John N., and Lynne B. Feldman. "Edward G. Gardner." *African-American Business Leaders: A Biographical Dictionary*. Westport, CT: Greenwood Press, 1994.

"PUSH Salutes Business Leader Edward Gardner at Convention in Chicago." *Jet* 78 (August 20, 1990): 28–31.

"Soft Sheen Products Dedicates New Building, 'Miracle on 87th Street.'" *Jet* 62 (August 16, 1982): 36–38.

"Taking Black Business into the 21st Century." *Black Enterprise* 17 (June 1987): 111–122.

*Who's Who among African Americans*. 18th ed. Detroit: Gale Research, 2005.

*Gabriella R. Beckles*

# Marcus Garvey's UNIA Enterprise

Marcus Moriah Garvey was a proud, multitalented black man who was born in St. Ann's Bay, Jamaica, in 1887. His descendants, Maroon tribesmen, led slave revolts against their British slave masters over 200 years ago, which led to their freedom. His father was a very stubborn, well-educated man whose trade was stone masonry. Garvey believed black people should have their own country, govern themselves, and control their own money. It is no wonder then that Garvey embraced a Black Nationalist school of thought. He spent his entire life promoting black pride, unity, and self-reliance. His legacy, while otherwise controversial, says that Garvey, a uniquely talented man, possessed the power to capture millions of followers as no other leader in the world has done. Garvey's legacy is explored here through an examination of the founding and activities of the Universal Negro Improvement Association (UNIA), the umbrella organization for the numerous enterprises that he founded between 1914 and 1920, and the way in which he used his multitalents to bring about a mass movement of the black race.

Long before and after organizing the UNIA in Kingston, Jamaica, in 1914, Garvey demonstrated leadership skills, the ability to organize and influence, and courage to agitate for blacks in the society. Particular examples include leading a group of printers in Jamaica to strike; encouraging workers in Costa Rica to form unions and negotiate better working conditions; and using his own newspapers to circulate scathing editorials denouncing ill treatment of black people. He was promptly expelled from the country. Garvey's expulsion, witness of racial injustice for black people in South and Central America and in England, led him back to Jamaica in 1914, where he founded the UNIA to instill racial pride, unity, and self-sufficiency in blacks and to lay the groundwork for transporting his people back to their homeland where they would rule and provide for themselves. Garvey spent the next two years promoting the UNIA in Jamaica, but support for his enterprise was indifferent, so he moved to Harlem, New York, in 1916 to carry out his mission.

Not long after his arrival, Garvey began a lecture tour delivering invigorating speeches to the masses of poor, low-esteemed, ill-treated African Americans in the United States to uplift spirits and provide hope for the future. Sometimes Garvey simply preached his messages on street corners, then in churches nationwide, marketing black pride, self-worth, and the value of education to black people. After giving an igniting speech in 1917, Garvey established a branch of the UNIA in Harlem. Garvey, an outsider, met with a power struggle with elected officials of Harlem who ultimately took control of Garvey's organization. Not to be deterred, Garvey and his friends started a new branch, of which he named himself president, and called it the New UNIA. Nevertheless, Garvey started a newspaper in 1918 in Harlem called *Negro World* that proved to be a powerful instrument for communication with blacks all over the world. The journal cost ten cents per copy and was circulated to over 50,000 in the United States, Canada, the West Indies, Europe, and Africa. Garvey traveled more extensively to promote circulation of the newspaper, and before the end of the year, he claimed 30 chapters around the world. Eventually the UNIA boasted 700 branches in thirty-eight states in the United States and 200 branches in Central America and South America. Garvey held membership meetings in rented halls until 1919 when, paradoxically, **Madame C. J. Walker**, the wealthy African American cosmetics manufacturer who invented the straightening comb, helped to amass financial support for the purchase of an auditorium in Harlem, which Garvey named Liberty Hall.

## ESTABLISHES BLACK STAR STEAMSHIP LINE

In 1919, Garvey established the Black Star Steamship Line, which was a company solely owned and operated by blacks. Garvey invited black investors from all over the world to become stockholders. Advertisements for shares of stock that sold for $5 apiece appeared in black newspapers. Having internalized Garvey's compelling messages, blacks took pride in becoming owners of the new company. Before the end of the year, Garvey had garnered upward of half a million dollars. The next step was for Garvey to purchase the first ship, which he did at a cost of $169,000, and renamed it the *Frederick Douglass*. The UNIA ultimately purchased two additional vessels. Garvey had gigantic plans for the steamship line and founded the Negro Factories Corporation (NFC). The NFC was a conglomeration of factories that manufactured products for distribution to black enterprises established by the UNIA. The UNIA employed over 1,000 blacks all over the country, and several small businesses were started, including restaurants, grocery stores, laundry, and a printing plant as a result of loans and start-up assistance Garvey provided for the people. The life of the *Frederick Douglass* and each of the subsequent vessels, which cost a combined total of $95,000, was short-lived. As a matter of fact, the entire Black Star Line venture was disastrous, as it never turned a profit and ceased operation in 1923, showing a deficit of $500,000 after four years of operation.

In 1920, the UNIA held its first international convention at Liberty Hall in Harlem. Many thousands of blacks from over twenty-five countries attended. Following World War I, the climate in the United States from a black perspective was lukewarm. Poor blacks who migrated northward hoping to escape racial discrimination and hostility that prevented them from being employed in factories and other desirable places were dismayed upon their arrival in northern cities. Furthermore, housing in the cities amounted to ghettoes, as black people were the exclusive residents in many neighborhoods. On the other hand, more affluent blacks migrated to New York, particularly in 1920, to express their frustration and pain and to showcase their art and talents. The period is known as the Harlem Renaissance because for the next ten years blacks gained more renown for commendable measures than ever before. Garvey published many works of black artists in the *Negro World*, which commanded a circulation in excess of 200,000. So the timing of the UNIA international festival and convention was perfect for promoting blackness. Garvey raised over $2.5 million to fund the extravagant affair, which ultimately ended with a parade to Madison Square Gardens, a distance of 100 city blocks lined with 30,000 spectators. The marchers included several other auxiliaries created by the UNIA: the African Legion, the military unit; Black Cross nurses, symbols of nurture by black women; the women's auxiliary of the African Legion; the Universal African Motor Corps; and the juvenile and adult Black Flying Eagles. According to Anne Schraff in *Marcus Garvey*, Garvey boasted that "the demonstration was of such as never seen in Harlem." The convention lasted for one month.

The summer of 1921 marked the beginning of the end of Garvey's empire. While the UNIA held its second convention in August with as much pageantry as the first, many stockholders in the Black Star Line were disappointed and charged Garvey with mismanagement of funds. Garvey continued to solicit stockholders even though the steamship line was defunct and initial investors had never benefited from their $750,000 investment in the company. In January 1922, federal government agents arrested Garvey and charged him with mail fraud. Black intellectuals in general did not like Garvey and felt certain that there existed irregularities in the steamship company. They also questioned his relationship with the Ku Klux Klan. With the urging of the black intellectual community, Garvey was sent to trial. He was found guilty of one count of mail fraud in May 1923 and was sentenced to five years in prison. When Garvey met bail of $15,000 while awaiting an appeal, he formed yet another shipping company called the Black Cross Trading and Navigation Company and sold stock to black investors. Garvey purchased the *Gerald G. W. Goethas* with $100,000 and paid $60,000 for refitting the ship, only to meet with a fourth disaster—the ship sailed to Panama but never returned to New York.

In February, Garvey lost his appeal and was immediately taken to the Atlanta Federal Penitentiary. Ironically, his work assignment was in the library. Garvey continued to communicate with the UNIA and wrote letters himself to President Calvin Coolidge asking for a pardon. In the summer of 1926, over 100,000 black followers rallied for his release. In consideration of the attorney general's urging and many letters supporting Garvey from stockholders, the president commuted Garvey's sentence in November 1927. Garvey felt his work was incomplete in the United States and petitioned for citizenship. However, his request was denied, and he was immediately deported as an undesirable alien. Garvey continued his work and ultimately settled in London, where he died in 1940.

**Sources**

Adams, Russell L. *Great Negroes: Past and Present.* Chicago: Afro-American Publishing Co., 1984.

Altman, Susan. *Extraordinary African-Americans.* New York: Scholastic, 2001.

Branham, Charles R., and DuSable Museum of African American History. *Profiles of Great African Americans.* Lincolnwood, IL: Publications International, Ltd., 1998.

Franklin, John Hope, and Alfred A. Moss Jr. *Up From Slavery: A History of African Americans.* New York: McGraw-Hill, 1994.

Marcus Garvey and UNIA Papers Project. http://www.international.ucla.edu/africa/mgpp.

Quarles, Benjamin. *Negroes in the Making of America.* New York: Simon and Schuster, 1987.

Schraff, Anne. *Marcus Garvey: Controversial Champion of Black Pride.* Berkeley Heights, NJ: Enslow Publishers, 2004.

Smith, Jessie Carney, ed. *Notable Black American Men.* Detroit: Gale Research, 1999.

UNIA. http//www.unia.org.

*Shelhea Owens*

# A. G. Gaston (1892–1996), Entrepreneur

A self-made millionaire, A. G. Gaston rose from poverty and built an empire that was worth over $130 million. He had a passion for the welfare of African Americans and used the businesses that he founded, primarily in racially segregated Birmingham, Alabama, to enhance the black community and the lives of its inhabitants.

The grandson of slaves, Arthur George Gaston was born in his paternal grandparents' cabin in Demopolis, Alabama, on July 4, 1892. He was the son of Arthur George Gaston, a railroad worker, and Minnie Gardner Gaston, a cook. Young Gaston's father died while his son was an infant, leaving his mother to seek a living on her own. She left her son with Joe and Idella Gaston, young Gaston's paternal grandparents. After spending some time in Greensboro and later in Birmingham—away from her son—Minnie Gaston took her son with her to Birmingham in 1905, where they lived above the stable that her employer built near his residence.

Gaston attended school regularly when he lived in Demopolis, but Birmingham offered few opportunities for education of its black citizens; consequently, his education was interrupted. Later, with the assistance of Minnie Loveman, for whose family Minnie Gaston was employed, young Gaston enrolled in the Carrie Tuggle Institute, a local boarding school for blacks, and completed the tenth grade—the highest grade offered. Educator **Booker T. Washington** spoke regularly at Tuggle during Gaston's years there; he inspired the youngster to take advantage of opportunities whenever he could. Thus, Gaston wanted to attend Tuskegee but was unable to do so. Instead, from 1910 to 1913 he became an entrepreneur; he sold subscriptions to the *Birmingham Reporter*—a local black newspaper—and later worked in Mobile as a bellhop at the Battlehouse Hotel.

He joined the army and served with distinction in France. When Gaston returned home in 1919, he was unable to find work of his choice; instead, he drove a delivery truck for the OK Dry Cleaning company. The next year he worked in the mines and railroad car workshop for the Tennessee Coal & Iron Company. To supplement his income, he sold lunches that his mother had made to his coworkers and also loaned money to them for a return of twenty-five cents on the dollar.

In 1923 Gaston married his childhood friend, Creola Smith, and with his father-in-law, A. L. "Dad" Smith, founded Brother Gaston Burial Society, incorporated in 1932 as Booker T. Washington Insurance Company. He and Smith sold and collected small premiums door to door. The company grew and became the cornerstone for the empire that he would develop over the years. It also became the largest black-owned insurance company in Alabama. He also bought Mt. Zion Cemetery.

He opened Booker T. Washington Business College in 1939 and provided training for staffs of businesses and the federal government. His wife had died in 1938, and he married Minnie Gardner in 1943; they had one son, Arthur George Gaston Jr. Minnie Gaston directed the BTW Business College in New York City. Although his businesses were generally successful, the Brown Belle Bottling Company, maker of the Joe Louis Punch, was not. He said that it had been built on greed—purely as a profit-making venture. When the business closed, he absorbed the loss rather than pass it along to the stockholders, who were his friends.

Gaston ventured out again, this time into the motel business. In 1954 he opened the A. G. Gaston Motel, hosting blacks who traveled south and such black luminaries as Willie Mays and Joe Louis. It also became a landmark during the civil rights movement and headquarters for Martin Luther King and the Southern Christian Leadership Conference. He was already in his seventies when the civil rights movement came to Birmingham. As influential as he was, some criticized him for his conservative stance on how certain activities should proceed. In addition to opening his hotel to civil rights leaders, he was a powerful force behind the scenes, negotiating with Birmingham's white power elite and spending over $160,000 of his own funds to bail local protestors out of jail. In retaliation, both his hotel and his home were bombed.

There had been no black banks in Birmingham since 1915. Gaston saw a need to move into the financial market and opened the Citizens Federal Savings and Loan, which was chartered in 1957. He filled an important need among his race by making it possible for blacks to obtain loans for homes, churches, businesses, and other purposes.

## OPENS MILLION-DOLLAR BUILDING

Another addition to Gaston's enterprise came in 1962, when he opened the imposing $1.3 million A. G. Gaston Building to house his various business interests. He expanded further to build the A. G. Gaston Boys and Girls Clubs in 1966, using $50,000 he received from donations; there thousands of young people received athletic training and moral guidance. Other investments included the acquisition in 1975 of WAGG and WENN radio stations, which formed his Booker T. Washington Broadcasting Company. His construction business, the A. G. Gaston Construction Company, established in 1986, became Alabama's largest black-owned construction firm. So compassionate was Gaston for others that, in 1987, through a stock option program, he turned his Booker T. Washington Insurance Company over to his employees. In 1992 *Black Enterprise* magazine listed the company among its top 100 black businesses.

Gaston served his community well. He was a member of the board of trustees for Tuskegee University, Daniel Payne College, and the YMCA. Among his other contributions were membership on the Coordinating Council of the City of Birmingham, the Birmingham Chamber of Commerce, the Boys' Club of America, and the American Legion. A staunch supporter of black business, he was president of the Birmingham Negro Business League and president of the **National Negro Business League** that Booker T. Washington helped to found. His recognitions and honors were numerous. On October 24, 1984, Birmingham celebrated "A. G. Gaston Day." In 1992 *Black Enterprise* magazine named him Entrepreneur of the Century. He also received awards from the National Association of Colored Women's Clubs, the Birmingham Jaycees, the U.S. Commission on Civil Rights, and Alabama Education Association, and numerous churches, businesses, and fraternal organizations. He held honorary degrees from Tuskegee, Paul Quinn College, Daniel Payne College, Pepperdine University, the University of Alabama, and elsewhere.

Gaston's health began to fail by the mid-1980s; he lost a leg to diabetes and was confined to a wheelchair. A mild stroke that he suffered on January 22, 1992, failed to keep him from his office, where he returned two weeks later. He lived on until January 19, 1996, when a second stroke felled him at the Medical Center in East Birmingham. He was 103 years old.

During his lifetime Gaston was called the richest black man in the country. He lived a full life and was one of the nation's most successful black entrepreneurs.

**Sources**

Gaston, A. G. *Green Power: The Successful Way of A. G. Gaston.* Troy, AL: Troy State University Press, 1968.

Jenkins, Carol, and Elizabeth Gardner Hines. *Black Titan: A. G. Gaston and the Making of a Black American Millionaire.* New York: Random House, 2004.

*Jessie Carney Smith*

# Karen Patricia Gibbs (1952– ), Financial Journalist, Television Anchor

Karen Gibbs is a trailblazing business journalist and television anchor. Since June 2002, she has served as co-anchor of PBS and *Fortune* magazine's prime-time widely watched financial news television program *Wall Street Week with FORTUNE.* Gibbs brings an impressive portfolio of experiences to the program. As cohost of *Wall Street Week with FORTUNE,* Gibbs interviews executives of the nation's largest corporations, financial institutions, and government and comments on significant financial issues affecting the stock market and the corporate world. Gibbs's education and professional experience provide an ideal foundation for this high-profile position, and the business/financial insights and journalistic skills garnered in over twenty years of experience in her field aptly qualify her for the cohost role.

Gibbs's career in investments and finance began at the Chicago Board of Trade (CBOT), where she was the first woman to work on the floor. Before leaving the CBOT, Gibbs had become a member of its Office of Investigations and Audits. After leaving the CBOT in 1982, she worked briefly at Harris Trust and Savings Bank in Chicago as a government securities representative. She then joined Dean Witter Reynolds, Inc., serving there for nearly ten years in positions of increasing responsibilities—hedging trading strategist, senior futures analyst, and vice president. As a futures analyst, her perceptive financial analyses were considered critical to the decision makers in the investment/banking and financial services community as well as to decision making of individual investors. Gibbs left Dean Witter in 1992 to take a position as anchor at CNBC, specializing in credit and futures markets and hosting financial education programs. She held this position until 1997 when FOX News Channel (FNC) beckoned. Gibbs left CNBC to become senior business correspondent for FNC in April 1997. At FNC, Gibbs contributed to the weekday business news program *Your World with Neil Cavuto* and served as substitute anchor for that program. She was also a regular panelist on FNC's weekend program *Cavuto on Business*.

Gibbs knows her stuff. In "Co-Anchor Biography: Karen Gibbs." Gibbs notes that she "is one of the very few anchors who actually knows what it takes to put billions of dollars at risk in the markets." Besides being so knowledgeable, Gibbs is polished and articulate and has a definite "presence," invaluable assets in the world of television reporting.

Gibbs is the daughter of James and Bertha Gibbs. She was born in Boston on May 9, 1952. In 1976, Gibbs received an undergraduate degree in business administration from Roosevelt University's Walter E. Heller College of Business Administration and a Master's in Business Administration in finance and marketing from the University of Chicago's Graduate School of Business in 1978. Building on this valuable education, Gibbs has forged a solid and impressive career in her industry. Gibbs is a published author and widely sought speaker. She serves/has served as secretary to the board of directors of the Henry Booth House (1981–1985); board of directors, Chicago Lung Association (1984–1987); secretary to the Chicago chapter of the **National Black MBA Association** (1985–1986); member of National Association of Corporate Security Professionals; and member of University of Illinois College of Medical Advisory Board.

In her "Trading Places Has Its Advantages," Gibbs spoke of her personal ideals—"honesty, integrity, and teamwork." She commented on her goal to provide the public with straightforward, relevant, and useful financial information. To the public, her insightful interviews of corporate executives and her straightforward commentaries help to remove the mystery and confusion surrounding finances and investing. Today many are befuddled by fuzzy numbers in business reports, double talk from corporate executives, and perceived rampant corruption throughout the business world. Thus, Gibbs's philosophy of honesty and integrity and her straight talk in financial reporting have engendered trust. She has made her mark in financial journalism. No doubt many future journalists will look to her as a role model. She maintains her business in Fort Lee, New Jersey.

## Sources

"Co-Anchor Biography: Karen Gibbs." *Wall Street Week with Fortune*. http://www
.mpt.org/pressroom/productions/wswwf/wswwf_bios.doc.

Gibbs, Karen. "Trading Places Has Its Advantages." *Wall Street Week with Fortune*, June 20, 2002. http://www.pbs.org/wsw/opinion/karen0620.html.

*Who's Who among African Americans*. 18th ed. Detroit: Thomson Gale, 2005.

*Alicia Henry*

# John Trusty Gibson (1878–1937), Theater Owner, Producer, Directing Manager, Entrepreneur

John T. Gibson pioneered in developing African American theatrical entertainment in Philadelphia and the East from 1910 to 1929. He forged an important theatrical empire in Philadelphia. He owned three theaters in Philadelphia, including his most successful enterprise, the New Standard Theatre, and thus controlled all of the African American theatrical business in that city. Gibson was also the first African American businessman in Philadelphia to make a great investment in property. He became directing manager and producer of plays at his Standard and Dunbar (later renamed Gibson) theaters and signed on as eastern representative for the **Theater Owners Booking Association** (TOBA).

John T. Gibson. *Source*: Fisk University Franklin Library's Special Collections.

Born February 4, 1878, in Baltimore, Gibson, also called "Little Giant," was the son of George Henry and Elizabeth Johns Gibson. He attended the local public schools and for two years studied at Morgan College Preparatory School (now Morgan State University) in Baltimore, and in June 1928 he received an honorary (LL.D.) degree from the school. Gibson moved to Philadelphia in the 1890s, and to make a living, he peddled meat, upholstered chairs, and was involved in several minor and unsuccessful business enterprises before settling into what became a prosperous venture for him. He seized the opportunity to become a partner with local businessman Samuel Reading in a small theater in 1910, thus marking the beginning of the finest chain of theaters in the country owned and operated by blacks.

The North Pole Theatre was a modestly successful black-controlled business located on South Street. The aging structure had become unprofitable as a movie and vaudeville house. The partnership failed and was dissolved a little over a year later when Gibson bought out Reading for $800. The theater appealed to Gibson, however, who made it a moderately successful enterprise. The theater was poorly situated, both in terms of its street location and the physical facility—a bleak, barren structure with dressing rooms in an attic. Around the end of World War I, he sold the theater and purchased the New Standard Theatre.

A man of patience, Gibson developed his ideas methodically and around 1918 invested half a million dollars in the larger and then-modern Gibson New Standard Theatre. His building, illustrated in the *National Cyclopedia of the Colored Race*, was also located on South Street at Twelfth, the third greatest business street in Philadelphia and a better section of the city. In fact, this was an upper-middle-class section of town. It was ideally situated and easily accessible to the vehicles that brought his customers to the theater.

Lobby, entrance, and ticket seller's booth, John Trusty Gibson's New Standard Theater in Philadelphia. This was his most successful of the three theaters that he owned in Philadelphia between 1910 and 1929. *Source*: Clement Richardson, ed., *National Cyclopedia of the Colored Race*. Vol. 1. Montgomery, AL: National Publishing Co., 1919, p. 323.

The structure was majestic in appearance, throwing off a myriad of lights at night that could be seen from a distance. The interior, which included some marble, was decorated with gold, purple, and tints of rose. So successful was the New Standard that Gibson became a wealthy man.

An important and one of the highest-class theaters on the TOBA Circuit, the New Standard brought in notable black stars such as Bessie Smith, Butterbeans & Susie, the Whitman Sisters, the Nicholas Brothers, and Ethel Waters. In fact, some of these entertainers got their start at the Standard. In 1921, Milton Starr, president of TOBA, named Gibson his eastern representative for the association. Among the stock companies that at various times were in residence at the Standard was the Standard Stock Company, with Eddie Hunter as manager; in 1921 the company produced *The Insane Asylum*. Gibson also became a producer and for two successive seasons (1924 and 1925) presented an annual review, *The Chocolate Box Review*. Among those featured were his family members, Berthel Gibson and the Gibson Trio. Singer Bessie Smith enjoyed popularity at the Standard as well. Her shows *Happy Times* and *Gossiping Lisa* (1930 and 1931, respectively) had long runs there.

In 1919, the banking firm Brown & Stevens bought another famous black-controlled theater, the Dunbar Theatre (later renamed the Gibson Theatre). It featured both vaudeville and drama. The owners, black entrepreneurs E. C. Brown and A. F. Stevens, were theatrical entrepreneurs. When their financial interest in another business, the Quality Amusement Corporation, began to decline, they sold the Dunbar to Gibson in 1921 for $120,000. This venture would put Gibson in a highly visible and enviable position in Philadelphia; now he controlled all of the major African American theaters located in the city. The Standard had made him rich, and he hoped that the Dunbar would strengthen his financial base even more. As Gibson experienced with the North Pole, the Dunbar was in an unfavorable location, Broad and Lombard Streets. Attracting patrons was difficult; his black patrons at the Standard would not attend the Dunbar. He tried several venues to bring the theater's business around, such as the leading headliners of the TOBA, the well-known Whitman Sisters Company, and the Lafayette Players. He also signed on leading orchestras and celebrated musical shows, including *Shuffle Along* and *Liza*. He continued to lose money, however, and had to use profits from the Standard to support the Dunbar. One final but unsuccessful effort to save the Dunbar came in 1927, when he changed the name from Dunbar to Gibson Theatre. The stock market crash of 1929 dealt the final blow, and Gibson sold the theater for a loss. Facing almost financial ruin, he was also forced to sell the Standard around 1930. These sales ended Gibson's theatrical empire and ended an important black-controlled theater empire of the era, for the new owners were white. The Standard became the Burns & Russell Company, a resident musical stock company that had been active since 1922.

Beyond his business enterprise, Gibson participated in a number of community organizations and activities. He was a member of the Chamber of Commerce, the Board of Trade, the Broad Street Association, and Citizen's Republican Club; director of Douglass Hospital; trustee of Morgan College; and a member of Kappa Alpha Psi fraternity. He gave his business address as 4200 Spruce Street, Philadelphia.

Gibson married Ella Lewis of Chester County, Pennsylvania, on September 15, 1914. As they prospered in Philadelphia, the Gibsons lived in a beautiful estate at Meadowbrook, in northern Philadelphia. He named the countryside manor "Elmira," in honor of his wife Ella, and the home was called the showplace of the East. Gibson acquired other real estate, including an apartment house, a row of houses, and several tenement houses.

A small man, Gibson was only five feet three inches tall and weighed 110 pounds. He was a public spirited citizen and was also slightly arrogant, shrewd, humorous, ambitious, energetic, and sagacious. Many sought his counsel on business ventures. He had a keen interest in matters that involved the uplift of African American people and shared his fortune with others, such as his gift of $5,000 to Morgan College. He became known worldwide due to his successful career, his work with the TOBA and other companies, and the fine theaters that he owned and operated. He had joined E. C. Brown, Sherman H. Dudley, and **Harry H. Pace** as prominent leaders in the financial end of black show business in the 1920s.

The stock market crash left Gibson in poverty that he had not overcome by the time of his death on June 12, 1937, at home in West Philadelphia— by then his only asset. His success in black theatricals and his stature earned him the nickname "Little Giant."

## Sources

*National Cyclopedia of the Colored Race.* Vol. 1. Ed. Clement Richardson. Montgomery, AL: National Publishing Co., 1919.

Peterson, Bernard L., Jr. *The African American Theatre Directory, 1816–1960.* Westport, CT: Greenwood Press, 1977.

———. *Profiles of African American Stage Performers and Theatre People, 1816–1960.* Westport, CT: Greenwood Press, 2001.

Sampson, Henry T. *Blacks in Blackface: A Source Book on Early Black Musical Shows.* Metuchen, NJ: Scarecrow Press, 1980.

*Who's Who in Colored America, 1933–37.* 4th ed. Brooklyn, NY: Thomas Yenser, 1937.

*Jessie Carney Smith*

# Bruce S. Gordon (1946– ), Telecommunications Executive, Organization Leader

Bruce S. Gordon has been listed as one of the most powerful black executives in America. He started his career at Bell Atlantic Corporation and worked for the giant telephone corporation for thirty-five years. He rose to the position of chief executive officer (CEO) with the Bell industry as president of Retail Markets for Verizon Communications. His position carried the responsibility of Verizon's consumer and small business sales and marketing units, online and DSL sales and marketing, corporate advertising, and brand management. On June 26, 2005, the National Association for the Advancement of Colored People (NAACP) named Gordon as president and chief executive; he became the first business executive to head the organization.

Gordon was born in Camden, New Jersey, on February 15, 1946, to parents Walter and Violet Gordon. Gordon married Genie Alston on February 20, 1970. They are the parents of Taurin S. Gordon.

Gordon received a Bachelor of Arts degree from Gettysburg College in Gettysburg, Pennsylvania, in 1968. He attended the University of Illinois in 1981. He also attended the University of Pennsylvania, Wharton Executive Management School. He was selected as an Alfred P. Sloan fellow in 1987 at the Massachusetts Institute of Technology (MIT). He received the Masters of Science from the Sloan School of Management at MIT in Boston, Massachusetts, in 1988 as a Sloan fellow.

Gordon's illustrious career with Bell Atlantic began in 1968 as a college trainee at Bell of Pennsylvania in management in the consumer sales organization. Gordon continued to move up the corporate ladder at Bell industries, serving as office manager from 1970 to 1972. In 1972, he served as sales manager and also in marketing. In 1974, he served as personnel supervisor; in 1976, as market management supervisor; in 1978, as division staff manager; and in 1980, as division operations manager. In 1981, he was division manager of the phone center, and later in 1981 until 1983, he was a marketing manager II. In 1983 he was moved to vice president of marketing and in 1988 served as Bell Atlantic Network Services group retail president. In 1993, he served as president of Enterprise Business Group. After the merger of Bell Atlantic and GTE in July 2000, Gordon was moved to president of Retail Markets Group/Verizon Communications. Verizion Communications is one of the world's leaders in providing wireline and wireless communications, with more than 250,000 employees and revenue of $67 billion in 2004. Verizon's presence extends to over forty-four countries in the Americas, Europe, Asia, and the Pacific. Verizon is the third largest long-distance carrier for U.S. consumers and is the largest directory publisher in the world.

Gordon's selection to head the NAACP comes at a sensitive time: President George Bush declined invitations to speak at the NAACP's summer convention; and the Internal Revenue Service questioned the organization's tax-exempt status. Until now, activists, ministers, or political figures had headed the NAACP. Although Gordon was raised by activist parents, he chose another route to bring about change within the powerful Verizon industry with a networking program that he founded to help black executives advance in the company. The NAACP noted his approach to working for change and envisioned that, as a businessman, he could appeal to young blacks who set entrepreneurship as their main goal.

Along with his outstanding marketing and leadership skills, Gordon has shown a deep involvement in the community. Gordon serves on the board of trustees of Gettysburg College. He has served as a director of the Urban League. In 1985, he was a member of the board of directors of Inroads of Philadelphia. In 1985–1988, he chaired the United Negro College Fund Telethon and volunteered for the United Way. In 1994, Gordon was selected to the Southern Company board of directors. He is currently serving on that board, and in 1995, he was also selected to the board of directors of Bartech Personnel Services. He also served as a trustee of the Alvin Ailey Dance Company Foundation and the Lincoln Center. Gordon has also served as a member of the Bell Atlantic Executive Leaders Council, a networking organization for senior black executives in Fortune 500 companies. This group was founded in 1986 with 19 members and now has nearly 300 members. He held membership in Toastmasters International. Gordon was the founder and past president of Alliance of Black Managers.

In 2002, Gordon was appointed to serve on the board of directors of Tyco International Limited. Tyco is a diversified manufacturing and service company and is the world's largest manufacturer and servicer of electrical and electronic components. It is also the world's largest designer, manufacturer, installer, and servicer of undersea telecommunications systems. In addition to being the world's largest manufacturer, installer, and provider of fire protection and electronic security services, Tyco is also the world's largest manufacturer of specialty valves. Gordon's leadership skills in the consumer services market served as an asset for this appointment.

Gordon has received awards recognizing him for his leadership skills. In 1998, *Black Enterprise* magazine named him executive of the year. In July 2002, *Fortune* magazine named him one of the fifty most powerful black executives. Gordon was ranked number six of the fifty. Under his leadership, *Fortune* twice named Verizon on its list of 50 Best Companies for Minorities, in July 2001 and again in July 2002.

Gordon continued to give back by organizing a self-mentoring program called Developmental Roundtable for Upward Mobility (DRUM) at Verizon Communications. This organization is composed primarily of black males at Verizon Communications. The group has grown from 9 to over 100.

Gordon was also known in the industry for his accessibility. He believed in receiving firsthand feedback from all levels. Gordon believes that people make the difference. Gordon is also known for his support of upward mobility for minorities in the industry and his commitment to diversity. In a speech to the Multicultural Business Forum on February 27, 2003, Gordon emphasized "Diversity: Make Progress Every Day." He stated that Verizon's approach to diversity is one way it makes progress every day. Its approach is the same as any other initiative: set goals, create a plan, and hold people accountable for results. Under his leadership, Verizon has been recognized for its efforts in diversity.

Gordon has shown his commitment earlier by presenting his alma mater, Gettysburg College, with a $500,000 gift to support diversity among students. The Bruce Gordon Endowed Scholarship is a merit grant given to promising students who are members of groups historically underrepresented at Gettysburg College.

Gordon also credits the late Dr. Martin Luther King Jr. and the civil rights movement for opening the door of opportunity for him and others to advance. He seized the opportunities to expand his horizon and reached back to help others to advance and make a difference in this world.

On December 31, 2003, Gordon retired from Verizon Communications, ending thirty-five years of leadership in the communications industry. He leaves a legacy for others to follow in moving to the top by being sensitive to the needs of people, by being supportive of others trying to move up, and by showing care and concern for humanity. Gordon is a true role model for the youth of our communities. His examples of dedication and following a set plan will inspire future generations of young businesspeople looking for examples in climbing the corporate ladder.

## Sources

Barry, Ellen. "NAACP Picks Retired Verizon Executive as New Leader." *Nation*, June 26, 2005. http://www.latimes.com/news/nationworld/nation/la-na-naacp26 June,0,29575190.story?coll=la-home-headlines.

"Bell Atlantic Assigns Officials." *Wall Street Journal*, July 1, 1993.

"Bruce Gordon Becomes Director of Tyco." Press Release, January 13, 2003. http://www.eetimes.com.

"Bruce Gordon Retires from Verizon." News Wire, December 25, 2003.

"Bruce S. Gordon." Biography Resource Center. http://www.galenet, galegroup.com.

Daniels, Cora. "The Most Powerful Black Executives in America." *Fortune* 146 (2002): 60.

Elkin, Tobi. "Bruce S. Gordon." *Advertising Age* 72 (2001): 27.

Gordon, Bruce B. "Diversity: Make Progress Every Day." Speech delivered at the Multicultural Business Forum, February 27, 2003.

"Gordon, LeVan Work Together in Support of Diversity." April 2001. http://www.gettysburg.edu/administration/publications.

Hickman, Jonathan. "50 Best Companies for Minorities." *Fortune* 48 (2003): 103–120.

Jones, Joyce. "Former Black Enterprise Executive of the Year Retires." December 2003. http://www.blackenterprise.com.

"Most Powerful Black Executives." Fortune 500 Ranking: Full List. July 22, 2002. http://www.fortune.com.

Networking the Telecom Industry. http://www.lightreading.com.

Sabir, Nadirah. "Keeping the Lines of Communication Open." *Black Enterprise* 25 (June 1995): 54.

*Who's Who Among African Americans*. 18th ed. Detroit: Thomson Gale, 2005.

*Orella R. Brazile*

# Berry Gordy Jr. (1929– ), Record Producer, Entrepreneur

Berry Gordy combined business acumen and a keen appreciation of changes in the music business to make his firm, Motown, the largest black-owned business of its era, and in so doing, had a major impact on the course of popular music in the 1960s. Gordy founded Motown in 1959. It became a major player in the field during the 1960s, moving from rhythm and blues, which appealed to a mostly black audience, into the much more lucrative pop field, which attracted white audiences as well. Between 1968 and 1972 Gordy moved his base of operations from Detroit to Los Angeles and added moviemaking to his operations, with mixed success. Gordy was insolvent by late 1979, but quickly reestablished his finances. In 1988 Gordy sold Motown to the major music giant MCA. He retained control of his television and movie interests as well as his publishing company Jobete. Since Jobete controlled the rights for all Motown music, it was a very lucrative enterprise, and the industry was surprised when Gordy sold half of it to EMI Music Publishing for $132 million in 1997.

Berry Gordy was born in Detroit on November 28, 1929. He was named for his grandfather and father. The close-knit family had moved to Detroit in 1922. In spite of difficulties during the Great Depression, his father offered a role model as a businessman, and early on Gordy joined him on construction jobs on weekends. An early ambition of the young man was to become a professional boxer, and he eventually fought fifteen times before giving up this career in 1950 to pursue his alternative professional goal, becoming a songwriter. He was drafted and sent to Korea but not to combat, and soon after his return, he married for the first time. Songwriting was not bringing much income, and children were arriving, so Gordy took a factory job. In 1957, after about two years, he gave up this line of work to try full-time songwriting again, this time achieving some success. He also met William "Smokey" Robinson and began a collaboration that contributed greatly to Motown's success. Gordy founded his music publishing company Jobete, and in 1959 he founded Tamla Records, which had a hit recording, "Come to Me," sung by Mary Johnson. Then to issue a song written in collaboration with Smokey Robinson, Gordy founded Motown.

Gordy now began to work with Mary Wells, who became very popular, and he aimed at a breakthrough into a national audience. Showcasing Mary Wells, Gordy began to develop a recognizable sound built on large ensembles using elaborate arrangements. To take charge of sales he hired a white man to distribute his records. In turn Barney Ales used only white salesmen for sometime until Motown had the clout to insist that industry people treat all its representatives with respect. Wells continued to bring success to Motown until 1964, when she turned twenty-one and her contract ended. She broke with Motown but subsequently had little success.

Gordy's relations with both Ales and Wells bear on his reputation. His hiring of Ales was criticized by many in the black community, who saw any catering to a white audience as a sellout. The criticism became more outspoken when Gordy left Detroit for Los Angeles and peaked again when he sold Motown to a large music conglomerate. A number of performers such as Mary Wells felt they had been exploited and mistreated by Motown. This bitterness is a constant thread in the story of Motown, and much information about Barry and his companies is found in court records of litigation.

In spite of criticism and sometimes difficult relations with performers, Gordy built Motown into a major purveyor of pop music. Following Mary Wells, he introduced major new stars such as Marvin Gaye, Diana Ross and the Supremes, Stevie Wonder, and Martha Reeves and the Vandellas. Gordy was a persistent perfectionist, the label's success was tied to his attention to detail and quality control. New releases were developed in weekly staff meetings, noted for frank speaking. An emphasis on marketing was also evident in his schooling of the performers in the social graces. Not every effort was a success, and there continued to be defections from his labels, but Gordy also found major new talent like Gladys Knight and the Pips and the Jacksons, and some artists stayed with him. For example, Stevie Wonder received $23 million for renewing a contract with Motown in 1976. His overall success in the music business may well be summed up by the *Billboard* listings for the final week of 1968: Motown had five of the top ten hits in the United States.

Gordy began in 1968 to transfer his operations to Los Angeles, and in 1972 the official headquarters of Motown was moved to that city. It was Gordy's relation with Diana Ross, both personal and artistic, that led him to films. In 1972 *Lady Sings the Blues* was a triumph; subsequently, *Mahogany* (1976) and *The Wiz* (1978) were major flops. Gordy did not make a major impression for his efforts in film.

On the whole, Gordy was on a downward trajectory during the 1970s with successes becoming rarer. It has been suggested that his hands-on management style clashed with the needs of a large-scale organization. In late 1979 Gordy was insolvent, but a bank loan enabled him to ride out the crisis and reestablish his footing within a year. Diana Ross defected to RCA in 1981, but he still retained major artists such as Lionel Richie and the Commodores, as well as Stevie Wonder. The Jacksons did not leave until 1985. Gordy flirted with selling Motown to MCA in 1982, but the sale to MCA, for $68 million, eventually took place in 1988. Gordy retained control of Jobete, his music publishing company, a very lucrative asset, then valued at $100 million, and his television producing companies. His television efforts had mixed success, but he was a coproducer with **Suzanne de Passe** for the miniseries *Lonesome Dove* in 1989, which was a huge success and garnered several major awards including an Emmy. Gordy, however, soon ceded control of the television ventures to de Passe. He was now largely in semiretirement.

Gordy married several times and had numerous liaisons, most prominently with Diana Ross. Marriages and liaisons produced eight children.

Gordy had a major impact on American pop music. The 1983 television special celebrating the twenty-fifth anniversary of Motown featured Smokey Robinson and the Miracles, Martha Reeves, Mary Wells, Stevie Wonder, Marvin Gaye, the Four Tops, the Temptations, the Jackson 5, Michael Jackson solo, and Diana Ross. Although many of the stars had left Motown, and the luster was largely gone from the label by this time, this roster of stars reflects the impact that Motown had had in its heyday. Gordy's success was due to his effectiveness in building up Motown as a business entrpreneur combined with his acumen in music.

### Sources

Gordy, Berry. *To Be Loved.* New York: Time Warner, 1994.

*The New Grove Dictionary of American Music.* 4 vols. New York: Macmillan, 1986.

Posner, Gerald. *Motown: Music, Money, Sex, and Power.* New York: Random House, 2002.

Singleton, Raymonda Gordy. *Berry, Me, and Motown.* Chicago: Contemporary Books, 1990.

Smith, Jessie Carney, ed. *Notable Black American Men.* Detroit: Gale Research, 1999.

*Robert L. Johns*

# Earl G. Graves (1935– ), Entrepreneur, Publishing and Magazine Executive, Activist, Developer, Author

Widely recognized as one of the most influential black business individuals in the country, Earl G. Graves is a nationally known authority on **black business development**. He is also founder and publisher of *Black Enterprise* magazine, which is a business service publication serving the black professionals, executives, entrepreneurs, and policymakers in the public and private sectors. Often recognized by his mutton-chop sideburns, which he regards as one of his trademarks, Graves has indeed contributed immensely in the development of entrepreneurship and helped many African Americans to become players in business. Graves is also a major player in business. In addition to serving as the president and chief executive officer of Earl G. Graves, Ltd., which is the parent corporation of Earl G. Graves Publishing Co., the publisher of *Black Enterprise*, he has numerous business interests that include the majority ownership of a multimillion-dollar Pepsi-Cola Co. franchise. Currently he and his family are intensifying diversification of their business interests.

Graves was born on January 9, 1935, in New York City. His parents, Earl Godwin Graves and Winifred Sealy Graves, were the children of immigrants from Barbados. Graves and his siblings, Sandra, Joan, and Robert, grew up in the New York City borough of Brooklyn. His father Earl Godwin Graves was a great disciplinarian, role model, and mentor for the family. His father worked in the garment industry as a clerk and later as an assistant manager, as well as sold clothes on consignment out of the house. Growing up, Graves watched his father's sales capabilities. Oblivious to Graves, he absorbed his father's business acumen. At age seven, Graves sold Christmas cards door to door. He excelled in high school, where he was a track star, and used his athletic skill to assist with his tuition. While attending Morgan State University in Baltimore, on scholarship, Graves participated in the ROTC program, worked as a life guard, and established himself as an entrepreneur on campus. Some of his escapades include sale of flowers during Homecoming week and other events. In 1958, Graves earned his bachelor's degree in economics. Graves also completed the Airborne Ranger's school and was a captain with the Green Berets. Additionally, he was commissioned as a second lieutenant in the U.S. Army. In 1960 he married his wife, Barbara Kydd. They have three married sons who are successful professionals working in the family business.

In 1962, Graves worked as a narcotics agent with the U.S. Treasury Department. He also sold and developed real estate and was instantly successful. In 1966, he was hired as an administrative assistant on the staff of Senator Robert F. Kennedy. In that capacity, he planned and supervised events. The traumatic death of Kennedy in 1968 rendered Graves unemployed. After a period of grieving, restlessness, and reflections, Graves initiated Earl G. Graves Associates, a management consulting firm to advise corporations on urban affairs and economic development.

Graves's vision was to contribute to the economic development of black America. It was in line with this dream that he went to Fayette, Mississippi, to work on the mayoral campaign for Charles Evers, brother of slain National Association for the Advancement of Colored People (NAACP) leader Medgar Evers. That campaign was successful, and Evers was elected as the city's first black mayor in 1969. This exercise helped improve the town's black community. In his quest to further help the black community, Graves tapped into the Nixon administration's effort to bring black Americans into the country's economic development programs. Apparently, Graves understood that it was time to plan, develop, and produce a monthly periodical devoted to news, commentary, and articles for blacks interested in business. He had initially considered starting a newsletter to serve this purpose but was advised by some good friends from his Kennedy network to think bigger. He did and opted for publication of a magazine instead, with which he brought his vision to reality.

His vision made him accept a Ford Foundation grant to study black-owned business in Caribbean countries. He borrowed $150,000 from the Manhattan Capital Corporation of Chase Manhattan Bank to start his own company. In 1970, Graves presented the prospective leaders with a working draft of *Black Enterprise*. That same year, *Black Enterprise* was launched. It was the first publication ever devoted to African American entrepreneurs and corporate executives. The magazine is a resounding success to date. Graves created his magazine business to teach black entrepreneurs how to tap into the billions of dollars they generate. It offers readers practical advice on how to achieve career and financial success. In his 1997 book *How to Succeed in Business without Being White: Straight Talk on Making It in America*, Graves laid down tips to help both this generation and the next.

Before the August 1970 debut of *Black Enterprise*, Graves garnered advertising money. He adopted a sales strategy that he still uses to date. He emphasized "the green side of black"; in other words, he endeavored to convince potential clients that it was in their own best interest to tap into the buying power of the growing black middle class. This strategy obviously was successful because he received $500,000 in advertising commitments before the first issue of *Black Enterprise* was published. By the tenth issue of the publication, it showed a profit that has consistently increased.

Graves, a self-made man, believes that every businessperson has personal and professional obstacles to overcome regardless of race. However, racism poses a unique challenge. Graves deals with this unique challenge by regarding it as a nuisance. For Graves, racism is more of a nuisance than a major obstacle. He actually calls racism "the 30 percent nuisance factor," because in his sales presentations, both in the past and present, the problem of race generally takes up 30 percent of his time.

In their quest to diversify their interests, Graves and his family are now concerned with a personal finance and business book publishing house, an executive conferences division, and a $90 million private-equity fund that invests exclusively in minority-owned or -managed businesses. Graves intends to launch another fund, given the fact that the one launched in 1997 did excellently well.

His many awards, honors, and achievements include being named in 1972 as one of the ten most outstanding minority businessmen in the country by the president of the United States. He also received the National Award of Excellence in recognition of his achievements in minority business enterprise. In 1998, he received the Marietta Tree Award for Public Service from the Citizens Committee for New York City, Inc. In 2002 he was named by *Fortune* magazine as one of the fifty most powerful and influential African Americans in corporate America and also was appointed to serve on the then administration's Presidential Commission for the National Museum of African American History and Culture. He is a trustee of Howard University. His other recognitions include the Charles Evans Hughes Gold Medal Award from the National Conference for Community and Justice; the Ronald H. Brown Leadership Award from the U.S. Department of Commerce; the Merrick-Moore Spaulding National Achievement Award at the 100th Anniversary celebration of North Carolina Mutual Life Insurance Company; Boys Scout Awards; and being named New York City Entrepreneur of the Year by Ernst and Young. He was inducted into the National Sales Hall of Fame by the Association of Sales and Marketing Executives. He holds honorary doctorates from Dowling College (1980) and Bryant College (1983), among many other academic institutions.

Graves's foresight, vision, tenacity, and considerable concern for the development of the black American community propelled him to become one of the best entrepreneurs, businessmen, and corporate executives in the nation. His vision was to contribute to the economic development of black Americans, and he has brought it to fruition, even as he continues to contemplate and find more avenues to extend his vision to help blacks in America.

*See also*: Advertising and Marketing

**Sources**

"The Biography of Dr. Earl G. Graves." http://www.howard.edu/convocation/2003/convocationbio2.htm.

*Current Biography*. New York: H. W. Wilson Company, 1997.

"Earl G. Graves Inducted 2005." http://www.academyofachievement.org/honorees/earl_graves.htm.

Graves, G. Earl. *How to Succeed in Business without Being White: Straight Talk on Making It in America*. New York: HarperBusiness, 1997.

"How We Got Started. Earl Graves: Black Enterprise." http://www.fortune.com/fortune/smallbusiness/articles/0,15114,474727,00.html.

Whigham, Margorie. "20 Years of Black Enterprise: A Portrait of Earl G. Graves Ltd." *Black Enterprise* 21 (August 1990): 63–71.

*Who's Who among African Americans*. 18th ed. Detroit: Thomson Gale, 2005.

*Nkechi Amadife*

# Sylvester Green (c. 1940– ), Insurance Executive

Sylvester Green is the chairman and chief executive officer for e2Value, Inc., a Web-based property valuation company providing digital solutions for the insurance industry and one in which Green oversees management, raising capital, and customer development and marketing. The recently retired managing director and executive vice president of the Chubb & Son, Inc. Global Property and Casualty Company, Green culminated a thirty-six-year career by managing Chubb's U.S. and Canadian operations. Beginning his professional insurance career as a management trainee and starting his rise quickly up the corporate ladder as one of Chubb's youngest branch managers, Green early on exemplified highly effective business skills that were further mirrored in his coming to the fore as instrumental in his promotion of the company's ongoing total quality management program. Always interested in a better way of doing things and having engineered Chubb's outsourcing and management restructuring programs, Green now also serves as mentor to the two founders of e2Value and consistently stresses the cutting-edge importance of melding strong traditional and experienced insurance industry skills sets with the rapidly evolving e-business technology. Green now promotes the e-system designed for speed and accuracy as one that fills a niche and serves as a driving force for appraisal, underwriting, and risk analysis, as well as process consistency, personnel training, and outsourcing solutions for both the traditional and emerging demands in the insurance industry.

Born in the early 1940s, the fourth child out of five, Green was the first African American professional hire as a Chubb & Son, Inc. management trainee just after graduating from Mount Union College in 1964. Within five years, Green was promoted as a New Jersey branch manager and became known as an expert casualty underwriter and dealmaker. A year later he became the casualty insurance manager for the eastern region. In 1974, Green opened and managed a new office in Westchester County, New York; in 1977, became vice president; and in 1978, founded the National Insurance Industry Association.

In 1982, Green returned to New York City to manage Chubb's downtown office. Completing Harvard's Advance Management Program in 1988, Green became heavily involved in the company's total quality management program, received the Best Branch award for several consecutive years, and became senior vice president. In 1990, he became managing director and in 1997 oversaw Chubb's U.S. and Canadian Field Operations and was elected executive vice president, positions he held until his retirement from Chubb on August 1, 2000.

Green was instrumental in forming Chubb's Minority Development Council and is past president, chairman of the board, and a member of the Executive Leadership Council for INROADS, Inc. of New York City. INROADS is a national nonprofit corporate sponsorship program that provides African American, Latino, and Native American college students with corporate internships.

Green is currently chairman of the board of trustees for Mount Union College and has served as an advisory board member for Florida Agricultural and Mechanical University, Emory Business School, and Fairfield University. He is past board chairman for the United Way of Westchester, Westchester County Urban League, and the Urban Family Institute.

Among Green's many awards are the Mount Union Alumni Service Award, the M-Club Award of Excellence, the Frank C. Carr Community Service Award, and the Westchester Urban League Community Service Award. He is also a Heartshare Community Leader Honoree and has three children with his wife Kim.

Often referred to as an icon in the insurance business due to the breadth and depth of his career experiences and with reemphasis on his professional history of global focus, Green's actualized vision, foresight, and leadership firmly establish him as one of the highest-ranking African Americans in the insurance industry.

*See also*: E-Commerce and the African American Community

**Sources**

Beck, Linda. "Sylvester Green Is New Chairman of the Board of Trustees for Mount Union College." Mount Union College. http://www.muc.edu/article/articleview/1312/1/133.

Bowers, Barbara. "Linking for Success." *Best's Review* 101 (December 2000): 26+.

Clarke, Caroline V. *Take a Lesson: Today's Black Achievers on How They Made It and What They Learned Along the Way*. New York: Wiley, 2001.

Mack, Gracian. "At the Top of His Game." *Black Enterprise* 25 (March 1995): 84–87.

*Linda Combs Hayden*

# Grocery Store Enterprises

Black-owned and -operated grocery stores developed as a result of African American farmers' interest in receiving greater profits from their agricultural labors, especially when these profits did not have to be shared with whites in the tenant farming system known as sharecropping. They also were a response to the dependence on stores and markets owned and operated by whites as outlets for selling and buying food and other products. As early as the 1850s, J. Wilcox, a boat steward on the Ohio River, was also owner of a wholesale grocery in downtown Cincinnati, grossing up to $140,000 annually.

Fair treatment of blacks as agricultural producers and consumers was not assured in these settings, especially in the South during the era of segregation. As a result, consumer boycotts of white-owned businesses became a means to protest Jim Crow laws, while also underscoring the importance of African American spending power by "buying black" when possible.

A tragic example in this regard is the case of Willie Mae Williams, a successful grocer in Starksdale, Mississippi, until shot dead in her store by a white gunman in 1910. Despite the obstacles, by 1913, 6,339 blacks were identified as being owners/operators of grocery stores, second only to restaurants/eating establishments (7,511) in black business enterprises.

In the most basic form, the "produce market," black farmers would set up arrangements of fruits, vegetables, and other agricultural products on a portion of the land near the fields where the produce was grown. Other locations would include "stands" along well-traveled roads, mobile service from wagons, and over time the establishment of storefront locations in the black sections of towns and cities.

As more of these stores were developed to serve black families and communities in various parts of the country, efforts began to formally organize black merchants. Part of the vision of **Marcus Garvey's UNIA** [Universal Negro Improvement Association] **Enterprise** in the 1920s was the establishment and sponsorship of chains of black-owned groceries, restaurants, hotels, and laundries. Despite the support of millions of African Americans, these efforts failed when the Jamaican-born Garvey was convicted of mail fraud and deported from the United States.

The **National Negro Business League** (NNBL), which was organized by **Booker T. Washington** in 1900, provided the first successful model in this regard. After Washington's death in 1915, **James Carroll Napier** became president; in 1919 he was replaced by Robert R. Moton, who had also succeeded Washington as president of Tuskegee Institute in Alabama. Under Moton's leadership, the NNBL and Tuskegee provided strategic and financial support in the creation of a new organization, the **Colored Merchants' Association** (CMA), in 1928.

The CMA sought to address the needs of black grocers and other small merchants by organizing them into a "voluntary chain" to compete against white-owned grocery chains. Statistical data from 1929 documented that black-owned grocery stores generated the highest percentage (36.25 percent) of sales revenue, including restaurants, apparel/clothing, furniture/household, automotive, and other store categories.

In the early 1930s, grocery stores were considered the largest category of black-owned business enterprises. The CMA began in Montgomery, Alabama, and over time spread to other cities with sizable black populations, including Birmingham, Selma, Jackson, Dallas, Atlanta, New York, Brooklyn, Philadelphia, Richmond, Hampton, Winston-Salem, Nashville, Louisville, Detroit, Chicago, Tulsa, and Omaha. Each member city had a minimum of ten stores; members paid dues of $5 per week. Small grocery store owners could benefit from CMA volume purchases of goods, a uniform accounting system, cooperative advertising, and training in modern methods of merchandising. In 1932, the CMA opened a warehouse in New York's Harlem community, selling food products packaged with the CMA label. Despite a few years of success, the CMA went bankrupt by 1936, resulting from a combination of factors, including the American economy of the depression years, the problems of running a national business cooperative with great diversity in the membership and its business/financial resources and expertise, and pressure on small grocers from wholesalers and other larger interests affecting the ability to obtain and maintain inventories, secure credit, and pay incurred expenses/debts.

In 1947, **Joseph Alphonso Pierce** conducted the first systematic study of urban, black-owned businesses during the segregation period and documented a total of 491 grocery stores owned/operated by blacks. These enterprises, along with convenience stores and produce markets, continued as mostly small, independent, and in some cases, family-run businesses serving urban, suburban, and rural communities, with varying degrees of success.

After the civil rights movement of the 1960s succeeded in providing African Americans with increased access to public facilities and accommodations, businesses owned by whites were also driven to provide more equitable access and service to black customers. **Economic boycotts** of white businesses were again a potent weapon to initiate change, underscoring the "green power" of the black consumer market. An unfortunate by-product of the end of segregation was that with more options more black consumers began to patronize business and professional services that were owned by whites, to the detriment of black-owned businesses that had, in many instances, provided equal or better products and services. The numbers and strong economic base in black communities, unified out of necessity during segregation, were diluted into the mainstream. Most, if not all, black-owned grocery stores were already in competition with white-owned stores of varying sizes and could not survive as the country moved into the era of the supermarkets, which were developed and controlled by larger corporate interests.

One of the few successful black-owned supermarkets to emerge in recent years is Community Pride Food Stores in Richmond, Virginia, established in 1992. Under the leadership of Jonathan F. Johnson, the ten-outlet chain of grocery stores was ranked number 57 in the *Black Enterprise* Top 100 Industrial/Service listing for 2004, with sales revenues totaling $61.780 million.

According to commentator James Clingman, there were only nineteen black-owned supermarkets in the United States at the beginning of the twenty-first century, even though African Americans spend billions of dollars on food every year. Despite this reality, African American communities in the United States are far less likely to have quality grocery stores in their neighborhoods. Major grocery store chains tended to underestimate black spending power and overestimated the risks of locating in the central/inner city or other areas where there are large concentrations of African Americans.

The more recent success of Community Pride in Virginia, along with other supermarkets in Alabama, Illinois, Maryland, Michigan, Missouri, New Jersey, New York, Ohio, Tennessee, and Wisconsin, demonstrates that black-owned grocery stores can still thrive in African American communities. This underscores the potential for similar developments in other locations, given the proper combination of financial, leadership/management, and community support.

The major chains are starting to take notice; their renewed interest in African American and inner-city communities will have some positive impact, as access to this consumer base should also provide additional jobs and economic stability. However, the increased presence of major grocery store chains in African American communities will again create challenges and competition, impacting the viability of black-owned grocery stores.

*See also*: Blacks in Agriculture; Food Service Industry; Retail Industry; Roadside and Street Vending

**Sources**

Brown, Monique R. "Supermarket Blackout." *Black Enterprise* 90 (July 1999): 81–92.

Clingman, James. "Economic Empowerment: Black Farmers Still Fighting." http://www.coax.net/people/lwf/ee_black.htm.

Cohen, Lizabeth. *A Consumers' Republic: The Politics of Mass Consumption in Postwar America*. New York: Knopf, 2003.

Donohue, Ron M. "Abandonment and Revitalization of Central City Retailing: The Case of Grocery Stores." Ph.D. diss., University of Michigan, 1997.

Library of Congress. American Memory: Historical Collections for the National Digital Library. "The Colored Merchants Association." http://lcweb2.loc.gov/ammem/coolhtm/coolencf.html.

Smith, Jessie Carney, and Carrell P. Horton, eds. *Historical Statistics of Black America*. Detroit: Gale Research, 1995.

Walker, Juliet E. K., ed. *Encyclopedia of African American Business History*. Westport, CT: Greenwood Press, 1999.

Woodard, Michael D. *Black Entrepreneurs in America: Stories of Struggle and Success*. New Brunswick, NJ: Rutgers University Press, 1997.

*Fletcher F. Moon*

# H

## James Francis Haddon (1954– ), Investment Company Executive, Banker, Managing Director

James F. Haddon is the senior managing director and manager of Infrastructure Finance Group, Public Finance, at Citigroup (formerly Salomon Smith Barney). His current responsibilities include comanaging the department's infrastructure/transportation group and also serving on the division's planning committee. Haddon has worked over twenty years in the municipal bond industry, focusing on providing investment banking and financial advisory services to large city and state issuers.

Since 1999, Haddon has overseen the firm's infrastructure finance efforts. He coordinated the firm's new business efforts to gain lead underwriting assignments from state and local issuers, primarily in the firm's infrastructure/transportation group. He coordinates efforts to gain new lead underwriting assignments from large issuers. As the firm lead banker, Haddon is involved with state and local issuers electing to securitize its tobacco settlement revenue. His efforts contributed in making his firm rank as number one underwriter of tobacco settlement securitizations. During this period, Haddon also served as senior book running manager for sixteen issues totaling $10.75 billion in par.

Haddon also served as the account manager for the firm's financing activities for the city of New York, the largest borrower in the tax-exempt market. It is thought that he created the first-ever tax-exempt tobacco financing for the city of New York. Haddon's other municipal clients include the state of New York, the state of Iowa, the city of New Orleans, the city of Detroit, the city of Chicago, the District of Columbia, city of Houston, the state of California, the government of the Virgin Islands, and the government of Guam.

Haddon thrives on the intense competition for new business. He started bringing clients to his company when he was a junior vice president. He sees his current promotion to managing director as a recognition of his record as a producer for the firm and a leader in getting business. Haddon is so good in what he does that in October 1992 he was cited by *Black Enterprise* magazine, along with seven other municipal finance professionals, as one of "the 25 hottest blacks on Wall Street."

Prior to achieving this career level, Haddon was a member of the executive committee for the Municipal Securities Group of PaineWebber Inc. (now UBS Paine Webber). He also served as Mellon National Corporation real estate analyst from 1976 through 1978.

Haddon was born on August 12, 1954, in Columbia, South Carolina, the son of Ida Beatrice and Wallace James Haddon. He married Dr. Sezelle Antoinette Gereau on September 25, 1988. They have two children, Madeleine Louise and James Douglass.

In addition to his prior experience in the corporate world and the support of his family, his education also contributed to his success. Haddon received his B.A. degree from Wesleyan University, Connecticut, in 1976. He received his M.B.A. from Stanford University in 1980. Haddon is a member of numerous organizations, including board member of the National Association for Securities Professionals (1991) and Sponsors for Economic Opportunity Mentor Program.

Haddon's education, family support, perseverance, cooperate experience, hard work, and competency no doubt contributed to his success and sustained presence in the business world.

### Sources

"The Top 50 African Americans on Wall Street." *Black Enterprise* 32 (October 2002): 98. http://www.blackenterprise.com.

Clarke, Caroline. "25 Hottest Blacks on Wall Street" (Special section). *Black Enterprise* 23 (October 1992): 64.

King, Sharon. "Smith Barney Names Haddon Senior Managing Director." *The Bond Buyer.* http://web6.infotrac.galegroup.com.

*Who's Who among African Americans.* 18th ed. Detroit: Thomson Gale, 2005.

*Nkechi Amadife*

# Elliott Sawyer Hall (1938– ), Automobile Company Executive, Attorney

Elliott S. Hall was Ford Motor Company's vice president of governmental affairs in Washington, D.C., a position he held since 1987 and one held as Ford's first African American vice president. His brilliant career as a leading and enterprising African American in both the field of law and in the automotive industry is studded with firsts that consistently reflect his determination, intelligence, keen insight, and serious emphasis on both serving and recruiting minorities. His lifelong performance exemplifies a high level of excellence resulting in positive corporate growth and customer satisfaction, while his commitment to developing organizational talent and his adeptness at promoting entrepreneurial opportunities for minority-owned automotive industry supplier and dealer businesses place him at the forefront for diversifying his industry and effecting economic empowerment of minority communities with emphasis on appropriate and timely training programs and financial assistance.

Hall was born in 1938 in Detroit, the son of Ethel B. Hall and steelworker Odis Hall and the second youngest of eight children. Formerly wed to Evelyn Hall and having two sons, Lannis and Frederick, Hall is married to Shirley Robinson Hall and has a daughter Tiffany.

Educated at Wayne State University in Detroit with the B.A. and J.D. degrees, Hall defended civil rights cases in the mid-1960s. In 1972, he was elected head of the National Association for the Advancement of Colored People (NAACP; Detroit chapter) and was president of the local United Black Coalition. Serving as the first African American Corporation Council for Detroit in 1974–1975, Hall then entered private law practice from 1975 to 1983. From 1983 to 1985, he served the Wayne County Prosecutor's Office as the first African American chief assistant prosecutor and became a partner in the Detroit law firm Dykema, Gossett, Spencer, Goodnow and Trigg from 1985 until 1987, when he joined Ford Motor Company.

Hall has been honored with the Distinguished Alumnus Award from Wayne State University Law School and is past president of the Detroit Metropolitan Bar Association and Wolverine Bar Association. He was also a member of the board of the Washington Performing Arts Society, the National Symphony Orchestra, as well as the federal City Council, a private group of prominent Washingtonians.

Serving as board chairman of both the Joint Center for Political and Economic Studies in Washington, D.C. and the Music Hall Center for the Performing Arts in Detroit, Hall is also a board member of Georgetown University, Clark Atlanta University, and the Congressional Black Caucus Foundation.

Retiring after fifteen years with Ford Motor Company, also as vice president of Dealer Development, Hall further served the company as a consultant in continuing the development of minority-owned Ford dealerships. He practices law with Dykema Gossett PLLC with offices in Detroit and Washington, D.C., focusing on government policy and automotive industry related legislative issues as well as matters relating to municipalities.

From the first person in his family to attend college to civil rights activist to a distinctive pacesetter in his industry to distinguished and prominent attorney in Detroit, Michigan, to high-profile powerful Washingtonian, Hall's demand for equity and excellence, his productive imagination, and his deep sense of integrity have consistently served him well and have had a lasting positive impact on the legal and business world, as well as on the African American community.

## Sources

Dingle, Derek T., and Alan Hughes. "Navigating Rough Waters." *Black Enterprise* 32 (February 2002): 85–92.

Dykema Gossett PLLC. "Elliott S. Hall." http://www.dykema.com/bio/default.asp.

"Ford Motor Company Executives to Retire; Replacement Named." Collision Repair Industry Insight. http://www.collision-insight.com/news/20001015-ford.

Phelps, Shirelle, ed. *Contemporary Black Biography*. Vol. 24. Detroit: Gale Group, 2000.

*Who's Who among African Americans*. 18th ed. Detroit: Thomson Gale, 2005.

Linda Combs Hayden

# Marc R. Hannah (1956– ), Technology Industry Executive, Computer Graphics Expert

As principal scientist and vice president of Silicon Graphics Inc., the company that he helped to found, Marc Hannah has been highly successful as an engineer and special effects expert. Hannah is chief architect of the Personal IRSIS, Indigo, Indigo2, and Indy graphics subsystems. His three-dimensional graphics created effects for such films as *Terminator 2* (1991) and *Jurassic Park* (1993) that caught the eye and interest of a wide range of audiences.

Marc Regis Hannah was born in Chicago on October 13, 1956, the son of Hubert and Edith Hannah. He and his four siblings were raised under the banner of education. His father was an accountant and his mother a teacher; their chief concern was that their children excel in school. Hannah began to excel early. After graduating from high school in his hometown, he received a scholarship and a fellowship from AT&T's Bell Laboratories to support his studies at Illinois Institute of Technology, where he enrolled. He graduated in 1977 with a B.S. degree in electrical engineering. A second fellowship from Bell Laboratories financed his studies at Stanford University, where he earned a Master of Science degree in 1978. In 1985 Hannah received his Ph.D. degree from Stanford; both graduate degrees were also in electrical engineering.

Hannah spent some time working at Bell Laboratories, where he had developed an interest in 3-D. During his graduate studies at Stanford, he met Jim Clark, one of his professors who, ironically, had a research interest in that same area. Together they created a machine that improved on the way that 3-D images were manipulated. Clark invented the Geometry Engine, which was a computer chip that facilitated image manipulation. The chip replaced the previous 2-D flat image and enabled a computer user to rotate an image directly on screen in 3-D. In 1982, the two teamed up with five others and, with $33 million in venture capital and the computer chip, founded Silicon Graphics Inc. (SGI), located in Mountain View, California, in the middle of Silicon Valley. Clark was the brainchild of SGI.

When SGI was founded, Hannah's assignment was to recast and improve the Geometry Engine. So effective was Hannah in his work that the chip was the company's mainstay for the next six years. As result, SGI attracted a number of big clients and saw its revenue increase substantially. SGI developed high-powered workstations that were responsible for the flashy and computerized films that gained popularity in the early 1980s. These included *Mars Attacks!* (1996) and *Jurassic Park*. Other films using technology that Hannah helped to create include *The Abyss* (1989), *Field of Dreams* (1989), *The Hunt for Red October* (1990), and *Beauty and the Beast* (1991). Both Hannah and his company received a big boost when Industrial Light & Magic, a part of *Star Wars* producer George Lucas's empire, spent millions with SGI to purchase computers to create special effects for *Terminator 2*, starring Arnold Schwarzenegger. The helmets used in the opening of *Monday Night Football* were also among the company's designs, as were the graphics for two of Michael Jackson's videos, *Black or White* (1991) and *Remember the Time* (1992). Although his company's early products sold well, Hannah, the chief scientist for SGI, thought on a grand scale and began to develop less expensive computers than the $10,000- to $30,000-priced workstations that the company made at first. The lower-end workstations were still capable of producing powerful three-dimensional graphics, and his plan was to introduce an even lower-priced model, in the $5,000 range. Through lower prices, Hannah predicted that the market would be broadened.

At SGI, Hannah became known as a special effects whiz. The entertainment industry, a high profile for SGI, makes up about 15 percent of the business. Other designs by Hannah have been used, for example, to help build the Boeing 777 and applications for modeling biotechnology systems.

Hannah reduced his lengthy workweek at SGI and supervised construction of a 6,000-square-foot home in Silicon Valley that he helped to design. Further, he has served as a consultant for SGI as well as a few emerging companies. These include Omniverse Digital Solutions and Pulsent. Beyond SGI, Hannah became part owner of Rondeau Bay, a minority-owned construction company in Oakland, California, that struggled at first but later gained in revenue. Rondeau developed a method of sewer repair that was less expensive and less destructive to streets than traditional methods. Rondeau Bay would remind him that racism was still present, especially when he saw big city engineers doing everything they could to keep contracts from going to minority-owned companies.

He has received thirteen patents as well as numerous awards and honors. Hannah's recognitions include the Professional Achievement Award from Illinois Institute of Technology and the same award from the National Technical Association, both in 1987. He is a board member of Magic Edge and an investor in the company that supplies visual stimulation to amusement parks nationwide. Silicon Graphics provides the visual display system for Magic Edge, which provides the hardware. With its technology, Magic Edge may require use of a joystick to create a wide range of motions, including the motion of flying.

A quiet, shy person, Hannah continues to work in solitude as he seeks to develop exciting and affordable machines that will simplify life in the future.

**Sources**

"Computer Scientists of the African Diaspora." *Smart Computing.* http://www.math/ buffalo.edu/mad/computer-science/hannah_marc.html.

"Marc Hannah: Special Effects Wiz." *Ebony* 48 (February 1993): 55–58.

"Marc Regis Hannah." *Smart Computing Encyclopedia.* http://www.smartcompu ting.com/editorial/dictionary/detail.Asp?guid=A76EGB2FF6CB4B.

Partch, Marjorie. "Marc Hannah." *Contemporary Black Biography.* Vol. 10. Detroit: Gale Research, 1996.

Teitelbaum, Richard S. "Marc R. Hannah, 33." *Fortune* 122 (August 22, 1990): 105.

*Frederick D. Smith*

# Carla Ann Harris (1963– ), Investment Banker, Vocalist

Investment bankers may be notorious for all work and no play, but Carla Ann Harris is not only a managing director on Wall Street but also a noteworthy vocalist who released her first CD *Carla's First Christmas* in early 2000. Her ambition, professional drive, and quarterly "life checks" have ensured that she has not strayed from her professional goals.

Harris graduated with high honors from Bishop High School in Jacksonville, Florida. In 1984, she graduated magna cum laude from Harvard University with a bachelor's degree in economics and, in 1987, from Harvard Business School with an M.B.A. Shortly afterward she began her career at the Morgan Stanley Dean Witter firm. She married her hometown sweetheart, Victor Adrian Franklin, in August 2001.

After her sophomore year at Harvard, Harris became enamored with investment banking because of an internship on Wall Street provided by Sponsors for Educational Opportunity (SEO), a nonprofit mentoring organization. She had originally chosen law as her intended profession because she thought lawyers were the people who made the deals but later realized it is really the businesspeople who called the shots and gave advice.

During her ascent to the top of a Forbes 500 company (Morgan Stanley DW, Inc. ranked eighteenth in 2004), Harris has encountered more than a few stumbling blocks, but she did not let her color and gender stand in the way of her goals. In fact, Harris is only the second African American woman to become a managing director at Morgan Stanley. She began her work at Morgan Stanley in 1987 advising on mergers and acquisitions and later moved on to the true livelihood of investment banking—finance.

Before being appointed as the head of Morgan Stanley's Equity Private Placement Group, Harris was responsible for handling some of the firm's largest initial public offerings (IPOs)—UPS, Martha Stewart Living, Omnimedia, Donna Karan, Ariba, Redback, General Motor's sub-IPO Delphi Automotive, and the $3.2 billion common stock transaction for Immunex Corporation.

Harris worked her way to the top with hard work and raw intellect, oftentimes without a mentor, and she never thought she would encounter someone in a higher position who could not or would not teach her, either through insecurity or lack of experience. Instead of faltering, Harris adopted a "Never let them see me sweat" as her tactic. A close look at Harris's professional patterns reveals her firm belief in herself as exceptionally capable, and she works hard to quantify her professional success with tangible evidence.

Because of her lack of mentors, Harris has taken time out to mentor SEO and M.B.A. students, advising them to know their business, understand the corporate culture and unspoken rules of their company, and realize that perception must go hand in hand with reality. Harris's personal formula for success is to stay abreast of potential areas to grow, be flexible with one's strategy and the economy, know how to pitch marketable strengths, and stay focused on developing a career.

Harris may advise many up-and-coming businesspeople, but she still takes time out to reassess her own goals every year. It was her personal to-do list that prompted her to record and release her first album, *Carla's First Christmas*, which was released in 2000, the same year she launched one of Morgan Stanley's largest IPOs.

Harris has always wanted to sing professionally, and finally in 2000, she chose to cross "record a CD" off her to-do list instead of letting it roll over to the next year. The decision to record a CD was also prompted by a culmination of positive reviews from ten years of performances in clubs, off-off Broadway plays, fund-raisers, and as part of the St. Charles Gospelite Choir in Harlem. However, what really encouraged Harris to record her CD was her standing-room-only performance in August 1999 at *Notorious Magazine*'s "Notorious Nights." Her second album was released in September 2004. Since Harris has always believed in giving back, the proceeds of her album go to benefit two schools by funding the Carla Harris Scholarships at Harvard University and Bishop Kenney High School in Jacksonville, Florida.

Perhaps the single most driving factor in Harris's life is her faith. Constantly growing in her faith is at the top of Harris's "to-do list" year after year. A Roman Catholic, Harris recently discovered her deeper spirituality and how to tap into its power.

Harris's life obviously depicts a class act. Her "I dare you" mind-set is the roadmap she insists has kept her determined and successful, and her one-of-a-kind portfolio proves this strategy works. Her honors include *Fortune* magazine's "50 Most Powerful Black Executives in Corporate America," *Black Enterprise*'s "Top 50 African Americans on Wall Street," Bethune Award from the National Council of Negro Women, Ron Brown Trailblazer Award from St. John's University School of Law, Women of Distinction Award from the Girl Scouts of Greater Essex and Hudson Counties, and **Frederick Douglass** Award from the New York Urban League. Harris is a woman who goes after her goals and never takes "no" for an answer, which has taken her up the corporate ladder to her position as one of the few African American women on top of Wall Street.

*See also*: Women and Business

**Sources**

"Artist." *Nema-Amen.* http://www.budsinc.com/nema-amen/artist.htm.

Benson, Christopher. "Best Career Choices and Moves in a Tight Economy." *Ebony* 59 (January 2004): 62–65.

Booker, James E. "All About People." *New Voice of New York, Inc.* 43 (August 29, 2001): 3.

"Carla's First Christmas." *Nema-Amen.* http://www.nema-amen.com.

Clarke, Caroline V. "Winning on Wall Street: Carla Harris Uses Her Prowess to Make Billion-Dollar Deals and Uplift Youth" (interview). *Black Enterprise* 33 (February 2003): 104–109.

"15 at the Top in Corporate America." *Ebony* 59 (March 2004): 44–46, 48, 50.

Span-Baker, Felicia. "AACCCF: Carla Harris Equips Business Leaders with Economic Lessons." http://www.aacccforl.com/documents/harrispostarticle.doc.

———. "African American Chamber of Commerce Welcomes Keynote Speaker Carla Harris." http://www.orlando.org/clientuploads/temp/carlaharris_bio.pdf.

*Thura Mack*

# Lowell Hawthorne (c. 1960– ), Entrepreneur, Business Executive

Born of an entrepreneurial spirit along with ambition and perseverance, Lowell Hawthorne has turned a small family business with humble beginnings into a franchising mecca. Jamaican cuisine being served to the masses of Brooklyn, New York, with the help of family recipes more than a half-century old, is how it all started. The name Lowell Hawthorne is now synonymous with Golden Krust Caribbean Bakery and Grill.

Hawthorne, one of twelve children, was born to Ephrahim and Mavis Hawthorne of St. Andrew, Jamaica. Ephrahim and Mavis Hawthorne began their entrepreneurship in 1940. In 1949, they opened, owned, and operated Hawthorne & Sons Bakery. Hawthorne & Sons Bakery prepared great Jamaican cuisine with the help of old family recipes passed on to Ephrahim from his father Norman Hawthorne. Ephrahim, following in his own father's footsteps, passed on the family recipes and the ingredients for business and success to Lowell and his other children.

At the age of twenty-one, Hawthorne immigrated to New York, following other siblings having already made the migrant transition. Lauris, the eldest of the Hawthorne clan, was the first to leave their home in St. Andrew and become a U.S. citizen. She worked as a nurse aid and bought a home that became a haven for most of her siblings at one time or another as they made the trek from St. Andrew to New York. Hawthorne's journey to New York took place in 1981. His matriculation and desire for enrichment in the field of business administration led him to three educational institutions—Bronx Community College, Baruch College, and Lehman

College in New York. He earned an associate of science degree from Bronx Community College.

Although Hawthorne had some formal education and training, he had learned and understood early on how a successful business should be run as he worked and acquired experience in his parents' bakery in Jamaica. While attending college, Hawthorne worked for the New York City Police Department as junior accountant. He worked in this position for nearly eight years. According to an article in *Chain Store Age*, "By the end of the '80s, the wheels of entrepreneurship had long been turning in the head of Hawthorne." Starting his own business had been foremost on his mind; however, taking a risk such as this and leaving the comfort of income stability had to be evaluated thoroughly. Shortly after, Lowell took a leave of absence from his job and career with the Police Department.

As Hawthorne pondered the thought deeply, he turned to his brothers and sisters, Lauris, Lloyd, Velma, Milton, and Jacqueline, and pitched the idea of creating and perpetuating a New York–based family business of baking fresh Jamaican goods. Market research had been very instrumental in moving Hawthorne's ideas and desire of wanting a business from thought to action. According to Michelle Garcia of the *Washington Post*, "The Hawthornes' endeavor was well timed." The growing population of New York's Caribbean Islanders and especially Jamaicans had shown evidence of there definitely being a need and then ultimately a demand for the supply of Jamaican-style baked goods and products. After being presented with the plan and strategy to launch the business, Hawthorne's brothers and sisters were sold on the idea of working toward starting a family-owned bakery.

In 1989, Hawthorne and his family had a business plan, and they needed funding of $107,000 for start-up costs to set the plan in action. Trust and commitment are two values dear to Hawthorne's heart. He and his siblings applied for several business loans at banking institutions, and they did not get approval for any one of them. Staying true and committed, Hawthorne met with his brothers and sisters and soon-to-be business partners and made the suggestion that they fund the start-up costs themselves. He assured them that even though there would be some risk involved, they were calculated risks, which could prove to be successful if executed. They then, along with the help of their spouses, gathered all their resources and mortgaged their homes to open the Golden Krust Bakery located in New York City's world-famous Bronx community.

In the operations infancy, Hawthorne and family members "personally baked, sold and distributed all the products, which included bread, cake and meat patties," according to Linda Armstrong in the *Network Journal*. Some of the family members worked their regular full-time jobs each day and then went on to work shifts in the bakery. They were determined to making this a family business, and after a while they made an even greater commitment and worked solely for Golden Krust Bakery—leaving their other jobs and professions. Dedication coupled with support gave this family the edge that they needed to see that success in this venture was attainable. Even though this business was family driven, each member had more experience in certain areas than others. Hawthorne took on the position of chief executive, his brother Lloyd managed the operations that dealt with distribution, and his sister Lauris managed some of the baking operations.

After about two years, Golden Krust Bakery's growth in popularity and demand was quite apparent—now they operated two stores, and sales reached over $1 million. The "patty" is considered to be one of the bakery's most sought after and iconic delights. These patties, made with meats and/or vegetables that boast Jamaican spices and flavors baked into a flaky crust, are said to have a taste that is very close to home cooking. As the demand grew, so did the operation.

The year 1996 was the year of change for Golden Krust Bakery and the Hawthorne family. The production plant was relocated to the South Bronx, where a city block was purchased to accommodate the increase and expansion of goods and services at twenty-four locations. The bakery then became known as Golden Krust Bakery, Inc. The Golden Krust chain's accelerated rate of success opened the doors to a varied customer base and a number of contracts, some of which includes the New York School System, New York City Prison, supermarkets, and Pepsi. Along with its incorporation also came the licensure to sell franchises in over thirty-six states across the United States. There are more than eighty Golden Krust Bakery and Grill locations in New York, Philadelphia, New Jersey, Florida, Connecticut, Georgia, and California. Serving up more than just patties, a menu of combination meals, platters, and specialty dishes enables the company to cater to the mainstream's fast-food frame of mind. The operation has netted annual sales in amounts exceeding $16.5 million.

The communities in which Golden Krust establishments thrive are very important to Hawthorne—the president and chief executive officer. Golden Krust has given back to its communities in a number of ways. On December 4, 2004, Golden Krust released a children's book, the first in a series of free books, titled *Mr. Krust's Christmas*. The company supports two major scholarships both in the United States and in Jamaica.

Lowell, the Hawthorne family, and Golden Krust Bakery, Inc. have acquired many accolades since its inception in 1989. Golden Krust Bakery, Inc. has been ranked as one of *Black Enterprise* magazine's top 100 black-owned businesses. In 2001, Hawthorne was awarded the Ernst & Young Entrepreneur of the Year. Golden Krust Bakery, Inc. continues on its mission to spread the taste of the Caribbean across the United States, all the while increasing its business activity and economic success. Hawthorne's goal for the year 2010 is the addition of 165 Golden Krust Bakery and Grill locations.

*See also*: Food Service Industry; Retail Industry

**Sources**

Aikman, Beckly. "New York City–Based Restaurant Chain Aims to Make Caribbean Cuisine Mainstream." *Newsday*, November 22, 2004.

Armstrong, Linda. "All in the Family; Business Owned and Run by Families Are Insurance for Future Generations." *Network Journal* (August 31, 2003): 19.

Block, Valerie. "Eatery Chain Hopes Spice Is Right." *Crain's New York Business*, October 20, 1997, 26.

Donaldson, Sonya A. "30th Annual Report on Black Business: Going Against the Grain." *Black Enterprise* 32 (June 2002): 185–196.

Garcia, Michelle. "For N. Y. Caribbean Beef Patty Co., Business Is Cooking." *Washington Post*, February 15, 2005, A03. http://www.washingtonpost.com/wp-dyn/articles/A21778-February13.html.

"'Giant step' for Golden Krust in California." *Weekly Gleaner*, May 20–26, 2004, 11.

"Golden Krust Bakery Launches Children's book." *Weekly Gleaner*, December 2–8, 2004, 14.

"The Golden Touch of Lowell Hawthorne." *Gateway: A Bronx Community College Publication* (Winter 2004). http://www.bcc.cuny.edu/Alumni/Newsletter/Newsletter.pdf.

"Lowell Hawthorne." *Chain Store Age* (December 2000): 88.

Salaam, Yusef. "A Golden Fixture among Manhattan Eateries." *New York Amsterdam News*, August 14, 1997, 27.

Trager, Cara S. "Turning Mom-and-Pops into Miniature Empires." *Crain's New York Business*, May 24, 1999, 30.

*Dantrea Hampton*

# Darryl B. Hazel (c. 1950– ), Automobile Company Executive

Darryl B. Hazel stands out as a beacon to minorities that are constantly losing hope and demonstrating frustration and anxiety over the lack of progress being made in the corporate world in elevating minorities to executive positions. Hazel's appointment to the presidency of Lincoln Mercury by the Ford Motor Company appeared to energize persons trying to move up the corporate ladder. This appointment was extra special because Hazel was an insider and a lifer who had held many positions with Ford Motor Company at various levels.

Hazel joined Ford Motor Company as an analyst in Lincoln Mercury's New York District Sales office in 1972. Hazel also held the positions of marketing manager, business management manager, and field manager. He served in management positions in Washington, Philadelphia, Cleveland, and Boston.

Hazel received a bachelor's degree in economics from Wesleyan University. He later earned a master's degree in economics from Northwestern University.

Along with the managerial positions held by Hazel, he also held staff positions in North American Automotive Operations Management. He served as a marketing programs manager, strategy manager, education and training manager, and marketing research director.

Hazel started his work in production management in 1995 as a general sales manager for the Mercury Division. In 1997, he was appointed general marketing manager for the Ford Division. In February 1999, he was appointed executive director for North America for the Ford Motor Company Customer Services Division. In December 2001, Hazel was elected vice president of Ford Motor Company Customer Service Division. In August 2002, the Ford Motor Company named Hazel president of Lincoln Mercury Division.

To the automotive industry, Hazel was considered an insider when he was named president of Lincoln Mercury Company. Other executives and automotive dealers believed that he had paid his dues and that he knew the industry from the inside out. They believed his experiences would be beneficial in turning the Lincoln Mercury Company around. His thirty years in the automobile business and especially his fifteen years in the Lincoln Mercury Division of the Ford Motor Company were seen as a plus by others in the industry.

Hazel exhibits a commitment to the community and to diversity in the workplace. Hazel has been recognized for his efforts in diversity. In January 2003, at the 7th Annual On Wheels, Inc. Urban Wheel Awards, which celebrates diversity in the auto industry, he received the Edward Davis African American Executives of the Year Award. The On Wheels, Inc. is a multicultural media company. The award has been given annually since 1996 and recognizes African Americans for their contributions to the automobile industry. He was honored for his successful leadership, his policy of open and honest communications with employees, and his passion for diversity and mentoring through the Ford African American Network (FAAN) Resource Group.

The Ford Motor Company has listed Hazel as one of the key minority executives for 2003, but his involvement in the community has received recognition. He has volunteered in many capacities over the years. Hazel served as a board member of the Oakland Family Services. Oakland Family Services is a nonprofit organization that provides programs that strengthen families in southern Michigan. He contributed his time, inside and outside the corporate world, to make a difference for others.

Hazel's rise to the top of the automotive industry corporate ladder has been seen as an effort by the Ford Motor Company to promote diversity at the upper level of management. However, Hazel's accomplishments over his thirty-year career cannot be diminished by the appointment. In 2002, diversity was an issue among black automakers. Compared with other industries, the auto industry is in the middle when it comes to hiring, promoting, and retaining black executives. In 2002, only 5 of 130, or 3.8 percent of, corporate officers at General Motors, Ford Motor Company, and Chrysler Group were African Americans, although African Americans make up 14 percent of the auto industry workforce. Ford Motor Company, over the last two years, has earned national recognition for its commitment to diversity. The FAAN is one of the groups that promotes leadership development for minorities and women. Hazel serves as a mentor to this employee resource group.

Hazel has also been recognized for his sensitivity to the customers and dealerships of the Ford Motor Company. With years of experience in the Customer Service Division, he has firsthand knowledge of the complaints and solutions to correct customer problems. He has provided assistance to dealerships in helping to solve customer service problems.

Ford Motor Company has more black dealers than any other automobile company. Hazel supports the black dealers by his participation at the annual Ford Motor Minority Dealers Association (FMMDA) Conference and by supporting the opening and renovations of black-owned dealerships. He has also visited with successful dealerships. There are many testimonies to the care and concern exhibited by Hazel in reaching out to minorities in the auto industry and especially at Lincoln Mercury.

Hazel's appointment has made a great impact on the corporate world and especially in the automotive industry. His appointment came at a time when minorities were getting impatient with the slow progress being made in diversity at the executive levels of many corporations. Hazel came with the knowledge, experience, and leadership skills that are worthy to be emulated by any race, color, or creed.

**Sources**

Akinmusuru, Toyin. "Auto Show Ceremony Recognizes African Americans and Latinos." *South End.* http://www.southend.wagner.edu.

Connelly, Mary. "New L-M Chief Is Old Hand at Selling Cars." *Automotive News,* July 22, 2002.

"Darryl B. Hazel Named President of Lincoln Mercury Car Company." *Jet* 102 (September 16, 2002): 8.

"Ford's Minority Dealers Meet in San Francisco." *Jet* 103 (March 10, 2003): 25.

Garsten, Ed. "Lincoln Mercury Head Resigns." *Associated Press Wire,* July 19, 2002. http://www.ohio.com.

"Issues in the News." *Afro American Almanac,* March 5, 2002. http://www.toptags.com.

"Powerplay." *Black Enterprise* 33 (November 2002): 72.

Ramirez, Charles E. "Ford Motor Pioneers Diversity." *Detroit News,* June 9, 2003.

"7th Annual Urban Wheels Awards Celebrates Diversity in the Auto Industry." Press Release. http://www.noticieswire.com.

"Speaking of People." *Ebony* 58 (2002): 10.

Young, Joe M. "In the Belly of the Beast." A Personal View into the Management at Ford Motor Company. http://www.flatratetech.com.

*Orella R. Brazile*

# Ellenae Henry-Fairhurst (1943– ), Automobile Executive, Entrepreneur

In a relatively short period of time, Ellenae Henry-Fairhurst of Huntsville, Alabama, has risen to the forefront among this country's leading automobile executives. Referring to her adopted home and business ventures in a recent interview, summarized in *Notable Black American Women,* Henry-Fairhurst proudly proclaimed Huntsville to be "the best kept secret in the South." In the intervening years since that interview, her business ventures have grown by leaps and bounds. After opening the first black-owned Infinity dealership in North America, she has successfully undertaken the management of three dealerships in Huntsville under the rubric "Autoplex of Huntsville," selling and servicing Infinity, Lexus, and Dodge vehicles. Her "ace in the hole" apparently is her firm belief in the familiar business adage that the customer always comes first. This belief and her father's advocacy of cohesive team play as well as Chrysler's strong corporate emphasis on dealer development and training have brought much success to her managerial efforts. In terms of statistics, as reported in the June 2004 *Black Enterprise* annual survey of the auto industry, Fairhurst's Huntsville dealerships showed an aggregate of $62.9 million in yearly sales, rising to a ranking of forty-seventh among the *Black Enterprise* list of the top 100 auto dealers in the United States. (See Tables 25 and 26 for other top auto industry rankings.)

Henry-Fairhurst was born in Dayton, Ohio, on January 6, 1943, to Ellen Nora and Jack Hart. Her father was a successful football coach for thirty-six years at Dayton's Dunbar High School, and her mother taught study and learning techniques there for thirty-two years to students with learning disabilities for thirty-two years. Their educational values formed the basis of the management style their daughter was later to implement in her entrepreneurial and business career. A valedictorian at Dunbar High School, Fairhurst matriculated at Miami University of Ohio, earning her Master of Science degree in 1965. Her first step up the management ladder was taken in the late 1960s, when she served as a legal secretary at Motown Records. She soon saw the opportunity for advancement in the auto industry and "crossed the street" to the Ford Motor Company, working as a secretary and market analyst for eight years. Concurrent with her employment, she took

**Table 25.**   Top Ten Growth Leaders (Auto Dealers)

| Company | Location | 2004 Sales* | 2003 Sales* | Percentage Increase |
|---|---|---|---|---|
| Shack Findlay Honda | Hendersonville, NV | $110.000 | $73.540 | 49.58 |
| Prestige Automotive | Detroit, MI | 1066.579 | 766.507 | 39.15 |
| McKinney Dodge | McKinney, TX | 50.005 | 37.142 | 34.63 |
| Ultimate Pontiac Buick GMC Isuzu | Fredericksburg, VA | 40.600 | 30.200 | 34.44 |
| Walker Family Auto Group | Laurel, MS | 49.549 | 36.911 | 34.24 |
| Baranco Automotive Group | Lilburn, GA | 151.215 | 120.125 | 25.88 |
| Panhandle Automotive, Inc. | Crestview, FL | 140.000 | 111.881 | 25.13 |
| Nissan-Mitsubishi-Kia of Lake Charles | Lake Charles, LA | 42.581 | 34.048 | 25.06 |
| Forest Lake Ford | Forest Lake, MN | 29.944 | 24.094 | 24.28 |
| BMW of the Hudson Valley | Poughkeepsie, NY | 36.027 | 29.387 | 22.60 |

*In millions of dollars as of December 31, 2004. Prepared by B. E. Research. Reviewed by the certified public accounting firm Edwards & Co.

*Source: Black Enterprise* 35 ( June 2005): 136. Published by permission.

**Table 26.** Top Twenty Auto Dealers

| This Year | Last Year | Company | Location | Chief Executive | Year Started | Staff | Type of Business | Sales* |
|---|---|---|---|---|---|---|---|---|
| 1 | 1 | Prestige Automotive | Detroit, MI | Gregory Jackson | 1989 | 400 | Chevrolet, Pontiac, Ford, Saturn, Lincoln-Mercury, GMC Truck | 1066.597 |
| 2 | 2 | March/Hodge Automotive Group | Hartford, CT | Tony March/ Ernest M. Hodge | 1998 | 800 | GM, Toyota, Lexus, Honda, Infiniti, Volkswagen, Jaguar, Volvo | 558.383 |
| 3 | 3 | Martin Automotive Group | Bowling Green, KY | Cornelius A Martin | 1985 | 706 | Cadillac, Dodge, Jeep, Chrysler, Kia, Chevy, Ford, Hummer, Saab | 382.445 |
| 4 | 4 | S.Woods Enterprise Inc. | Tampa, FL | Sanford L Woods | 1989 | 354 | Dodge, Chrysler, Jeep, Toyota, Lexus, Honda, Hyundai | 343.556 |
| 5 | 5 | The Harrell Companies | Atlanta, GA | H. Steve Harrell | 1987 | 412 | Lexus, Nissan, Honda, Volvo, Kia, Hyundai | 287.791 |
| 6 | 7 | Boyland Auto Group | Orlando, FL | Dorian S. Boyland | 1987 | 380 | Dodge, Nissan, Ford, Honda, Mercedes-Benz | 241.630 |
| 7 | 6 | Family Automotive Group | San Juan Capistrano, CA | Raymond Dixon | 1993 | 320 | Ford, Toyota, Honda | 206.518 |
| 8 | 11 | Winston Pittman Enterprise | Louisville, KY | Winston R. Pittman Sr. | 1988 | 235 | Dodge, Chrysler, Jeep, Toyota, Lexus, Scion, Nissan | 167.578 |
| 9 | 9 | Legacy Automotive Group | McDonough, GA | Emanuel Jones | 1992 | 220 | Ford, Toyota, Scion, Mercury | 162.000 |
| 10 | 10 | 32 Ford Mercury Inc. | Batavia, OH | Clarence F. Warren | 1990 | 130 | Ford, Lincoln-Mercury | 161.388 |

(continued)

**Table 26.** (continued)

| This Year | Last Year | Company | Location | Chief Executive | Year Started | Staff | Type of Business | Sales* |
|---|---|---|---|---|---|---|---|---|
| 11 | 14 | Baranco Automotive Group | Lilburn, GA | Gregory T. Baranco | 1978 | 225 | Pontiac, GMC, Acura, Lincoln-Mercury, Buick, Mercedes-Benz | 151.215 |
| 12 | 12 | JMC Auto Group | Austin, TX | J. Michael Chargois | 1988 | 233 | Lincoln-Mercury | 146.814 |
| 13 | 18 | Panhandle Automotive Group | Crestview, FL | Leon Daggs Jr. | 1986 | 260 | Ford, Lincoln-Mercury, Dodge, Buick, Hyundai, Suzuki | 140.000 |
| 14 | 15 | Armstrong Holdings | Homestead, FL | William J. Armstrong | 1990 | 225 | Ford, Toyota | 128.000 |
| 15 | 13 | Hubbard Automotive LLC | Charlotte, NC | Reginald T. Hubbard | 1988 | 268 | Dodge, Chevrolet, Isuzu | 126.089 |
| 16 | 17 | Fitzpatrick Dealership Group | Modesto, CA | Ed Fitzpatrick | 1992 | 130 | Lexus, BMW, Infiniti | 125.000 |
| 17 | 19 | Southgate Automotive Group | Southgate, MI | Fred J Poe | 1994 | 130 | GM, Pontiac, GMC, Chevrolet, Mitsubishi | 112.000 |
| 18 | 39 | Shack Findlay Honda | Hendersonville, NC | William E. Shack Jr. | 1998 | 110 | Honda | 110.000 |
| 19 | 16 | Wade Ford Inc. | Smyrna, GA | Steven R. Ewing | 2002 | 100 | Ford | 103.425 |
| 20 | 32 | BMW/MINI of Sterling | Sterling, VA | Thomas A. Moorehead | 1999 | 87 | BMW, MINI Cooper | 100.855 |

*In millions of dollars, to the nearest thousand, as of December 31, 2004. Prepared by B. E. Research. Reviewed by the certified public accounting firm Edwards & Co.

Source: *Black Enterprise* 35 (June 2005): 141. Published by permission.

the opportunity to further her education, earning a master's degree in social and consumer psychology at the University of Detroit in 1986.

In her next venture, she saw the opportunity to "change ships" and accepted a position in the Chrysler Corporation's retail dealer development program. Upon graduating from that program in 1986, she was offered the opportunity to serve as president and general manager of the Cumberland Chrysler-Plymouth dealership in Fayetteville, North Carolina. Here her father's advocacy of strong team-building served her well and helped her develop her inner sensitivities, analytical strengths, and managerial skills. She is credited with assessing needs, helping her team set goals, and building a strong and mature organization.

In 1992, she sought her next challenge and contemplated a move to a larger location. After obtaining a good offer, and with the backing of the Chrysler Marketing Investment Division, she sold the Fayetteville business and moved to Huntsville, soon assuming 100 percent ownership of the Huntsville Dodge dealership. Her record at Huntsville bespeaks the continuous application of sound management skills: teamwork, setting high goals, and achieving positive results. Nine consecutive years of profitability earned her new franchise the Daimler/Chrysler Five Star award, signifying the company's highest commendation for successful management. In 1999, her team achieved several additional goals. They opened the first Infinity dealership in Huntsville, the first Nissan franchise owned by an African American woman; one of only thirteen in the country owned by African Americans. Perhaps the Nissan corporation saw this as a challenge as well. They pledged to increase the number of minority-owned dealerships in North America by 25 percent by the year 2002.

Henry-Fairhurst followed her Infinity initiative in 2000 with the opening of a new Lexus dealership: again a "double first"—for her and for African Americans. Her three dealerships were then combined in a new $7.3 million facility in 2001, as stated above. Her aggregate gross income for the combined dealerships rose to $59 million in 2001 and $62.9 million by 2004. Her own ranking grew to forty-seventh among the 100 top dealers in the country, as compiled in the June 2004 listing in *Black Enterprise*.

Henry-Fairhurst's professional association memberships include the National Automobile Dealers Association, National Association of Minority Automobile Dealers, and the board of directors of the Chrysler Minority Dealers Association. Her community organization affiliations include the board of directors of the Sickle Cell Foundation, the board of directors of the Huntsville Downtown Rescue Mission, and the board of directors of the Dayton Contemporary Dance Company.

*See also*: Women and Business

**Sources**

"Car Dealerships Expand as Local Economy Grows." *Huntsville Times*, December 3, 2002.

Thieme, Darius. "Ellenae Henry-Fairhurst." *Notable Black American Women*. Book III. Ed. Jessie Carney Smith. Detroit: Gale Research, 2003.

"Top 100 Auto Dealers Summary 2004." *Black Enterprise* 34 (June 2004): 149–158.
*Who's Who among African Americans.* 18th ed. Detroit: Thomson Gale, 2005.

*Darius L. Thieme*

## Alexis M. Herman (1947– ), Cabinet Official, Entrepreneur

After years of public service, Alexis Margaret Herman returned to the private sector in 2001 when she became chair and chief executive officer (CEO) of New Ventures, Inc. Herman, in her dual roles, advises corporations on workplace diversity. Prior to New Ventures, Herman was the twenty-third U.S. secretary of labor from 1997 to 2001; thus she was the first African American female and the fourth woman to hold the cabinet position. During Herman's tenure as head of the U.S. Department of Labor with its more than 17,000 employees and budget of $34.2 billion, she led the department's nine divisions: Bureau of Labor Statistics, Employment and Training Administration, Employment Standards Administration, International Labor Affairs Bureau, Mine Safety Health Administration, Occupational Safety and Health Administration, Pension and Welfare Benefits Administration, Veteran's Employment and Training Administration, and the Women's Bureau.

One of Herman's greatest accomplishments as labor secretary occurred a little more than three months after her May 1997 swearing-in ceremony; to the surprise of many, Herman, meeting with United Postal Service (UPS) officials and representatives from the striking International Brotherhood of Teamsters, negotiated a relatively quick end to the UPS strike. Another major accomplishment was her global efforts on behalf of children that resulted in projects that provided protection for children from abusive work conditions and that transformed 120,000 children in foreign countries from workers to students. Herman's previous public service employment includes positions as the director of the White House Office of the Public Liaison and an assistant to the president during the first four years of the Clinton administration from 1993 to 1997 as well as serving as the director of the Women's Bureau (WB) of the Department of Labor during the Carter administration. In 1977 when Herman was sworn in at the age of twenty-nine, she became the youngest person to serve as the WB's director as well as the highest-ranking African American woman at the Department of Labor. Herman's resume also includes the deputy directorship of the Clinton-Gore Presidential Transition Office, leadership roles with the Democratic National Committees and the Democratic National Convention Committee, years spent with her own marketing and management company, directorship of the Minority Women Employment Program, as well as her work with Recruitment and Training Programs, Catholic Social Services, and Interfaith.

Herman was born on July 16, 1947, in Mobile, Alabama. Her father, Alexander Herman, was a businessman, civil rights activist, and Alabama's first African American alderman. Herman's mother, Gloria Broadus Caponis, was an educator who, one year, was named Alabama's top schoolteacher. When Herman was five years old, members of the Ku Klux Klan forced the car she was riding in with her father off the road. Before her father got out of the car and locked the door, he told Herman to hide under the dashboard, gave her a pistol, and instructed her to pull the trigger if anyone opened the door. As Herman sat in the dark, she heard the men beat her father. That traumatic experience was not Herman's only encounter with the Klan. When she was in high school, her father took her to a Ku Klux Klan rally. Klan members reacted to their arrival by throwing things at them, but her father refused to leave and told his adversaries that he and his daughter had the right to be in the public place. He continued to teach his daughter to battle discrimination by taking Herman and her friends to segregated restaurants where they were denied service and to segregated ball games where they were escorted from the stands as garbage was thrown at them. Her father's exhortation to make people tell her no and then not accept it would serve Herman well in her career. Equally valuable was the example Herman's mother set. Caponis, a single mother, returned to school after Herman was born, graduated, and fulfilled her dream of becoming a schoolteacher; consequently, she showed her daughter that obstacles can be overcome. Herman graduated from the Heart of Mary High School, in Mobile, in 1965. She attended Edgewood College in Madison, Wisconsin, from 1965 to 1967, and Spring Hill College, in Mobile, in 1967. Herman then transferred to Xavier University, in New Orleans, where she received a bachelor's degree in sociology in 1969. Herman took graduate courses at the University of South Alabama, in Mobile, from 1970 to 1972.

After graduating from Xavier, Herman's first job was with Interfaith in Mobile, where she was employed as a community worker in 1969. She was employed as a social worker for Catholic Social Services, also in Mobile, from 1969 to 1972, and as an outreach worker for the Recruitment and Training Program (RTP) in Pascagoula, Mississippi, from 1971 to 1972. These three jobs enabled Herman to develop training programs for unskilled workers, young people, and new entrants to the workforce. Herman helped integrate a Pascagoula shipyard after she persuaded employers to provide apprenticeships to young African American men and women. In 1972, Atlanta's Southern Regional Council hired Herman for its Minority Women Employment Program (MWEP). Herman adapted a RTP that was designed to get construction jobs for African Americans into one that led to white-collar jobs for minority women. Herman coached the women enrolled in the program on interview skills and even allowed them to wear her clothes to interviews. In 1974, due to Herman's success in placing several hundred minority women in jobs in the private sector with such corporations as Coca-Cola and Delta Airlines, the MWEP became a national program with Herman as its director.

When Jimmy Carter was elected president of the United States in 1976, he selected economist Ray Marshall for the cabinet position of labor secretary. Marshall, who had recommended Herman for the MWEP job, then chose Herman to lead the Department of Labor's Women's Bureau. As director, Herman was a policymaker and program implementer who advised Secretary Marshall and President Carter on women's economic and social issues in the labor force. She also served as a White House representative to the Organization of Economic Cooperation and Development as well as cochair of a presidential task force to create a Women's Business Ownership Initiative for the federal government.

When Ronald Reagan became president in 1981, Herman left the federal government. She founded and became president of A. M. Herman and Associates. Although she was working in the private sector, she was still determined to help others succeed in the workplace and to eliminate as many labor market barriers as possible. Thus she advised state and local governments as well as corporations on these issues.

Herman returned to public service in 1989 when Ron Brown, who was then chairman of the Democratic National Committee (DNC), encouraged her to become the chief of staff for the DNC. In 1991, Herman was appointed deputy chair of the DNC and was also named the chief executive officer of the 1992 Democratic National Convention Committee. Herman's committee spearheaded the convention that was held in July at New York City's Madison Square Garden. In recognition of Herman's previous successes, she was named the deputy director of the Clinton-Gore Presidential Transition Office after Bill Clinton and Al Gore were elected president and vice president, respectively, in November 1992. From 1993 to 1997, Herman directed the Office of Public Liaison, which was the Clinton administration's link to various constituencies. When Ron Brown, who became the commerce secretary after Clinton was elected president, was killed in a plane crash on April 3, 1996, in Croatia, Herman arranged the public mourning for Brown.

After Clinton was reelected in November 1996, he nominated Herman as secretary of labor. However, labor unions and Republican members of Congress initially opposed her nomination; bipartisan questions were raised about Herman's activities as a businesswoman in the 1980s and her involvement in White House fund-raising efforts during her tenure as the director of the Office of the Public Liaison. Herman's confirmation process lasted 113 days as these issues were resolved in Herman's favor, and she was sworn in on May 9, 1997. At her swearing-in ceremony, the new secretary of labor announced that her five goals were to build workers' skills; transform welfare recipients into members of the workforce; monitor workers' pensions; improve workplace safety; and help individuals balance work and family. Herman recognized the irony in her attaining the top leadership position at the Department of Labor; remembering that her ancestors were enslaved in an America that was "built on slave labor," she acknowledged that for an African American woman "to have the responsibility of all labor ... [was] historic, special and humbling." During Herman's third year as labor secretary, she married Charles L. Franklin Jr. at the Bethlehem Chapel in the National Cathedral in Washington, on February 12, 2000. The honeymoon was delayed until March because Herman returned to work in order to prepare for a national labor convention.

Herman is chair of Coca-Cola's Human Resource Task Force and chair of the Toyota Diversity Advisory Board. She is a former chair of the National Commission on Working Women and is a founding member of the National Consumer Cooperative Bank. Herman has served on the board of directors for the Adams National Bank; Cummins, Inc.; District of Columbia Economic Development Finance Corporation; Energy Corporation; George Meany National Labor College; Leon H. Sullivan Foundation; MGM Mirage; National Council of Negro Women; National Democratic Institute; National Urban League; Presidential Life Insurance Company; and Xavier University.

Among Herman's many awards and honors are the Coalition of Labor Union Women's Award for Affirmative Action in the Workplace, District of Columbia's Outstanding Young Woman of the Year, Mexican-American Opportunity Foundation's Equal Opportunity Award, **National Association of Negro Business and Professional Women's Clubs'** Scroll of Distinction, National Black Women's Political Leadership Caucus' Woman of the Year Award, Negro Business and Professional Women's Clubs of Atlanta's First Woman Award, Non-Partisan Voters League's Award of Excellence, Outstanding Young Woman of America, Outstanding Young Person of Atlanta Award, and the Recruitment and Training Program's Dorothy I. Height Award. In 1979, *Ebony* selected Herman as one of 50 Future Leaders, and in 1980, *Ladies' Home Journal* named Herman as the Outstanding Young Woman of the Future. Among Herman's honorary doctorates are ones from Central State University and Lesley College.

During her impressive career in the private and public sectors, Herman has had to battle racial, gender, and age discrimination on a personal level. She surmounted such obstacles and thrived in each new position via her intellect, professionalism, dedication, diplomacy, and energy. Along the way, she made history in several influential positions because of her race, gender, and age. Today Herman is a recognized authority on workplace issues, and at New Ventures, Inc., she continues to generate employment opportunities for others.

*See also*: Women and Business

**Sources**

"Alexis M. Herman." *Contemporary Black Biography*. Vol. 15. Gale Research, 1997. Reproduced in Biography Resource Center. Farmington Hills, MI: Thomson Gale, 2005. http://galenet.galegroup.com/servlet/BioRC.

Edwards, Tamala M. "Labor of Love: Alexis Herman Works It! A Day in the Life of the Secretary of Labor." *Essence* (1998): 86.

Maxwell, Alison. "A Labor of Love: Alexis Herman Sees Her Job as a Dream." *USA Today*, August 28, 2000.

Randolph, Laura B. "A Black-and-White Alabama Homecoming—Secretary of Labor Alexis Herman—Interview." *Ebony* 53 (November 1997): 124–129.

Rudolph, Marva L. "Alexis M. Herman." *Notable Black American Women*. Book II. Ed. Jessie Carney Smith. Detroit: Gale Research, 1996.

*Linda M. Carter*

# Alonzo Franklin Herndon (1858–1927), Insurance Company Owner, Barber

Alonzo Herndon represents a rags-to-riches story as he went from being a former slave to a self-made successful entrepreneur. He began work at an early age doing various jobs. He was eventually led to Atlanta, Georgia, where he acquired barbering skills. Because he was requested often by wealthy white clients, he made enough money to open his own barbershop. At one time he had three such shops and wisely invested his funds into real estate. He later purchased an insurance company, Atlanta Life Insurance Company, and served as its first president. Atlanta Life was a profitable venture, providing jobs to many blacks in the Southeast. It remains viable today as the Atlanta Life Financial Group.

Born on June 26, 1858, into slavery in Walton County, Georgia, Herndon and his family were freed as the Civil War ended, when he was seven years old. Alonzo with his mother Sophenie, grandparents, and younger brother Thomas had only a few household items when they began life in freedom. Alonzo worked with his grandfather, who got a job pulling a cross-cut saw. When he was thirteen, he was hired as a farmhand in Social Circle by their former master, Frank Herndon, who was also his father. After he would finish his duties as farmhand, he peddled goods such as peanuts and candies. During this time, he only received a year of formal schooling.

In 1878, at the age of twenty, he left Social Circle and moved to Senoia, Georgia, and continued working as a farmhand. He also began learning the barbering trade, working part-time in this endeavor and earning $6 a month. His barbering skills greatly improved, which led to his ability to rent space in a barbershop. He saved enough to eventually open his own barbershop in Jonesboro, Georgia. He remained there for five years and produced a thriving business. In 1883, he settled in Atlanta, and when offered a position in the black-owned Dougherty Hutchins' shop, whose clientele were white and wealthy, he accepted. In six months, Herndon, because of his excellent and courteous service, was often requested by white patrons, and consequently, he was able to purchase half the business, becoming a partner. The shop was renamed Hutchins & Herndon.

In 1886, Herndon would again have a shop of his own, this time in downtown Atlanta. But by the next year, he would have rental space in the Markham House Hotel. His shop there grew to twelve chairs during his ten-year tenure until the hotel burned down in 1896.

In 1902, Herndon opened a grand-elegant barbershop that became known as an Atlanta attraction. Located around the corner of the famed Auburn Avenue at 66 Peachtree Street, this shop had marble floors, crystal chandeliers, twenty-five chairs, eighteen baths with tubs and showers, and solid mahogany front doors. His shop was widely recognized as the best barbershop in the South. By 1904, he owned three shops in Atlanta. Herndon steadily invested his profits from his barbershops into real estate and by 1900 was the largest black property owner in Atlanta. He also had real estate investments in Florida.

## ESTABLISHES INSURANCE COMPANY

In 1905, a new Georgia law required that industrial life insurance businesses deposit $5,000 with the state treasurer. Realizing that his company could not meet this requirement, Peter Bryant, a black pastor at Wheat Street Baptist Church and owner of Atlanta Benevolent & Protective Association, approached Herndon for capital to aid the failing company. Prior to the new law, blacks formed church relief societies that provided financial assistance for blacks including mortgages, loans, and life insurance. Herndon bought the company for $140, provided the $5,000 deposit from his private funds, and led its reorganization. In the early years of the company, Herndon continuously used his private funds to keep the company running. He bought other failing black insurance companies, which gave Atlanta Life a greater customer base. He hoped that this would also protect the reputation of black businesses in honoring the policies previously established. Initially renamed Atlanta Mutual Insurance Association, it was later renamed Atlanta Life Insurance Company in 1922. As Atlanta Life, the company was one of four black-owned companies to achieve legal reserve status. Herndon served as Atlanta Life's first president. Herndon headed the company for twenty-two years, opening several branch offices in Georgia, and expanded to six other southern states, providing jobs for hundreds of blacks. Atlanta Life was one of the largest black-owned businesses at that time. It was said that the insurance business was the most financially profitable business for blacks in the 1920s. Atlanta Life is still a profitable business in the twenty-first century.

In 1910, Herndon and his wife since 1893, Adrienne Elizabeth McNeil, a graduate and teacher at Atlanta University, completed construction of a mansion for their family, which included their son Norris. Adrienne, the main designer for the home, died three months later of Addison's disease. Herndon then married Jessie Gillespie in 1912 and continued to live in the mansion, now known as the Herndon Home, until his death on July 21, 1927. After his death, his son Norris became president of Atlanta Life and later established the Alonzo F. and Norris B. Herndon Foundation. Today, the Herndon Home is a museum documenting Hendon's life from slavery to entrepreneurship.

*See also*: Black Banks: Their Beginning; Retail Industry

**Sources**

"Alonzo Franklin Herndon." *Sweet Auburn Avenue: Triumph of the Spirit.* http://www.ga3d.net/sweetauburn/alherndon.htm.

"Alonzo Herndon: He Made His Opportunities." *Issues & Views* (Summer 1998). http://www.issues-views.com/index.php?article=1007.

Henderson, Alexa Benson. "Alonzo F. Herndon and Black Insurance in Atlanta, 1904–1915." *Atlanta Historical Bulletin* 21 (Spring 1977): 34–47.

———. "Alonzo Herndon (1858–1927)." *New Georgia Encyclopedia.* http://www.newgeorgiaencyclopedia.org.

Herndon Home. http://www.herndonhome.org.

"Herndon Home." National Park Service, *Atlanta: A National Register of Historic Places.* http://www.cr.nps.gov/nr/travel/atlanta/her.htm.

Merritt, Carole. *The Herndons: An Atlanta Family.* Athens: University of Georgia Press, 2002.

*La Loria Konata*

---

# Dennis Fowler Hightower (1941– ), Corporate Executive, Educator

Dennis Fowler Hightower is a retired corporate executive who has had distinguished careers in both the private and public sectors. He had more than thirty years of experience in global marketing, strategic planning, operations, and international general management. With an impressive resume, Hightower became the highest-ranking African American executive at the Walt Disney Company when he was named president of the Television and Telecommunications unit in 1995.

Hightower was born in Washington, D.C. on October 28, 1941, to Marvin William and Virginia H. (Fowler). He graduated from McKinley Tech High School at age sixteen. As the top U.S. Army ROTC cadet and a distinguished military graduate, he graduated from Howard University with a B.S. degree in 1962. Hightower rose to the rank of major by age twenty-seven, after serving on active duty as a regular army officer for eight years. He served in the airborne infantry and strategic and operational intelligence positions in the United States and abroad. He was a ranger and a senior parachutist. While on active duty, Hightower was awarded decorations for meritorious achievement and valor, including two bronze stars, three air medals, a Joint Service Commendation medal first class, a Purple Heart, and a Vietnam Honor Medal. He resigned his commission in 1970 after being selected to attend the U.S. Army Command and General Staff College.

Leaving the military, Hightower became a manager at the Xerox Corporation in Rochester, New York, from 1970 to 1972. Winning a two-year fellowship, he went to the nation's top business school, the Harvard University Graduate School of Business Administration, completing his M.B.A. in 1974. He was recruited to serve as a senior associate and engagement manager at McKinsey & Co., Inc., a leading international management consulting firm in Cleveland, from 1974 to 1978. He went to Monterrey, Mexico, to serve as the vice president and general manager with the General Electric Company from 1978 to 1981. He became president of corporate planning and a corporate officer of Mattel, Inc., in Hawthorne, California, from 1981 to 1984. For Russell Reynolds Associates, Inc., a leading international executive recruiter, he served as managing director and Los Angeles office manager from 1984 to 1987. Hightower believed that his constant movement reflected his risk-taking personality and goal of being the most complete manager that he could be.

Joining the Walt Disney Company in 1987, Hightower began as vice president of the Disney consumer products unit for Europe, working in Paris, France. As head of Consumer Products from 1987 to 1989, his responsibilities included book and magazine publishing, character merchandise licensing, children's records and music, computer software, film promotion and television sponsorship, as well as management of the sixteen Consumer Products subsidiaries, offices, and joint venture throughout Europe and the Middle East. Promoted to executive vice president of Consumer Products, Europe/Middle East from 1989 to 1992, Hightower also led Disney's entry into Eastern Europe, the former Soviet Union, the Middle East, and post-apartheid South Africa. He served as president of Consumer Products, Europe/Middle East/Africa, from 1992 to 1995.

Under his European tenure, sales for consumer products doubled from 6 percent to 12 percent of company revenues. He helped buy the company's publishing operations in Italy and purchased a textile facility in Portugal to supply Euro Disney stores. Disney's European publishing grew from 120 magazines and comics published in sixteen languages to 180 periodicals and comics in twenty-seven languages. Hightower elevated the quality and creativity of Disney products overseas while building retail sales from $650 million to $4.5 billion. With a territory spanning twenty-eight countries, Hightower traveled constantly.

Hightower was promoted to president of Walt Disney Television and Telecommunications on March 10, 1995. The company had recently lost several key senior executives, and Walt Disney chairman Michael Eisner wanted Hightower to head the unit that includes network television, television animation, the cable Disney Channel, syndication, pay TV, worldwide home video, and interactive media venture. Hightower was charged with expanding distribution of all Disney television entertainment, which involved managing the production of a broad array of quality programming, the creation of new interactive products, and the development of new distribution systems, particularly with the Americast joint venture with Disney's four telephone company partners.

Hightower retired from Disney on June 1, 1996. His decision to retire at age fifty-five was a surprise to many, but others suspected that Disney's need to restructure after its 1995 merger with Capital Cities/ABC prompted his departure. His lack of television experience was cited when he was placed in charge of the unit and at his retirement. His stated reason for early retirement was to devote more time to personal endeavors. He wanted to increase his involvement with Harvard University, Howard University, the European Institute of Business Administration (INSEAD), and the Camp Atwater Foundation of the National Urban League and to devote more time to education and youth development. Since 1989, he has been a guest lecturer at the Harvard Business School and at Howard University and INSEAD in France. For the year following his retirement, Hightower continued with the Walt Disney Company as an international business consultant.

From 1996 to 2000, Hightower was a professor of management and a senior lecturer at the Harvard University Graduate School of Business Administration. His teaching focused on issues of leadership, managing change, building emerging markets, and global management from the perspective of the general manager. From May 2000 to February 2001, Hightower was the chief executive officer of Europe Online Networks S.A., a privately held broadband interactive entertainment company based in Luxembourg.

Hightower has served on the board of directors for Accenture Ltd.; Brite-Smile, Inc.; Domino's, Inc. and its parent company, TISM, Inc.; the Gillette Company; Northwest Airlines Corporation; PanAmSat Corporation; Phillips-Van Heusen Corporation; and the TJX Companies Inc. He has been a member, officer, and recipient of awards from the boards of the Harvard Business School Alumni, the Harvard Business School Association of Southern California, and the Howard University Alumni Association. He has also served on the board of trustees for the Southern California Center for Non-Profit Management and the Casey Family Programs and as chairman of the Advisory Committee of the Andrew Young Center for International Affairs at Morehouse College. He has been a trustee of Howard University, his alma mater, since 1996.

Hightower received an alumni citation from the National Association of Equal Opportunity in Higher Education in 1985; the Alumni Achievement Award in Business from Howard University in 1986; the Alumni Achievement Award from Harvard Business School in 1992; and the U.S. Department of Commerce Pioneer Award in 1996. He was named one of the 25 Top Black Managers in America from *Black Enterprise* magazine in 1988.

Hightower married Denia Stukes on February 2, 1962. They have two children, Dennis Fowler Junior and Dawn Denise. Denia Hightower spends time between Washington, D.C. and Paris, maintaining the homes and holdings that she shares with her husband, also a Howard University graduate of the class of 1962. He enjoys collecting antique billiard equipment and eighteenth- and nineteenth-century oriental sculpture, photography, travel, scuba diving, and swimming. He is member of the Harvard Club in New York City, where he received their Edged Group Corporate Leadership Award in 1992. He also holds membership in Cercle Foch in Paris, France and the Jonathan Club and the California Club, both in Los Angeles, California. He is a limited partner in the Washington Baseball Club. Hightower is a guest lecturer at professional and marketing conferences throughout the world.

**Sources**

Branch, Shelly, and Alfred Edmond Jr. "America's Most Powerful Black Executives: Dennis F. Hightower." *Black Enterprise* 23 (February 1993): 109.

"Dennis F. Hightower." Accenture. http://www.accenture.com.

"Dennis F. Hightower." Washington Baseball Club. http://www.baseballindc.com.

"Dennis Hightower Retires as President of Walt Disney's TV and Telecommunications Unit." *Jet* 89 (May 6, 1996): 38.

Dunbar, Donnette. "The 'Lion King' of Television." *Black Enterprise* 25 (June 1995): 30.

King, Thomas R. "Hightower to Leave TV Post at Disney; Hopes to Do More at Harvard, Howard." *Wall Street Journal*, April 15, 1996.

Scott, Matthew S. "Wonderful World at Disney." *Black Enterprise* 26 (December 1995): 58–60, 64.

*Kathleen E. Bethel*

# Jesse Hill Jr. (1926– ), Insurance Company Executive, Actuary, Civil Rights Activist

Jesse Hill Jr., actuary and leader at Atlanta Life Insurance Company, was instrumental in many doors being opened to African Americans; he was often one of the first to enter the door. He was actively involved in the civil rights movement at a time when a large number of leaders feared association with the movement. In a letter of acknowledgment to Hill, cited in the papers of Martin Luther King Jr. online at Stanford University, King recognized his aid and support in collecting monies "to be used in our struggle for justice in the present situation in Montgomery." Not only was he instrumental in acquiring and supplying finances for the struggle, but he also provided moral and physical support and worked for voter registration to end school segregation in Atlanta, Georgia.

Hill was born on May 30, 1926, to Nancy Dennis Martin (a worker for the Pullman Company) and Jesse Hill Sr.; he grew up on the southeast side of St. Louis, Missouri, in a business world. His grandfather owned and operated Dennis Moving & Furniture Company, and he conducted business from a horse-drawn wagon. Operating on the premise that one man's trash is another man's treasure, he collected items that families no longer wanted and sold them in his small furniture shop. Additionally, he used the wagon to sell coal and wood in the winter and ice and watermelons in the summer. Thus, Hill grew up with an entrepreneurial model. Because of his grandfather's work, Hill had access to wagons that he too used; he hired young boys (ten to twelve years of age) to collect and recycle items using this equipment. He also sold black newspapers from various cities that he received through the mail; these included the *Pittsburgh Courier*, *Michigan Chronicle*, *Norfolk Journal*, and *Chicago Defender*. His ability to organize, to take initiative, and to capitalize on opportunities is reflected in his accomplishments. After high school, he entered Lincoln University in Jefferson City, Missouri, and graduated with honors with a B.S. degree in mathematics and physics in 1947. Because of his desire to combine math and business, he entered the actuarial science program at the University of Michigan Business School, and he completed the Master's of Business Administration in 1949.

Hill moved to Atlanta, Georgia, an area with numerous business opportunities for African Americans. Due to the location and the contacts he had made during his formal training and his work experience, he was hired as an actuarial assistant (only the second African American actuary in the country) at Atlanta Life Insurance Company (founded by a former slave). From an actuarial assistant, he worked his way through the ranks to vice president and chief actuary. By 1973, Hill was named the third president and chief executive officer (the first nonfamily member) of Atlanta Life Insurance Company. In this capacity, he expanded the company by acquiring the Chicago Metropolitan Life Assurance Company in 1990 and operated it as a separate entity; however, he was the chairman. With this acquisition, Atlanta Life became the largest minority insurance company in net worth and the second largest in assets. Under his leadership, Atlanta Life is credited with playing a role in breaking the bottleneck in home mortgage financing at fair interest rates for blacks in the city of Atlanta and the states of Alabama, Florida, Georgia, and Texas. He retired as chief executive officer in 1992 and as chairman of the Alonzo F. and Norris B. Herndon Foundation in Atlanta (the majority stockholder of the Atlanta Life Insurance Company and sponsor of the historic Herndon home). In 1979, he and his friends (**Herman Jerome Russell** of H. J. Russell & Company and Felker W. Ward, an attorney who owns an investment banking firm in the Atlanta area) founded Concessions International, a food and beverage management company that operates in seven major airports. These include Hartsfield-Jackson International in Atlanta, Georgia; Seattle-Tacoma International in Seattle, Washington; and Cyril E. King Airport–St. Thomas U.S. Virgin Islands.

As his business involvement and production grew, so did his community participation. In 1950, Hill became an influential force in the successful Atlanta voter registration drive and later became an enabling force in the student sit-in movement and the publication of the *Atlanta Inquiry*. This paper provided a public forum for those voices that could not be heard in other Atlanta papers. His political activism and involvement included chairing **Maynard Holbrook Jackson**'s successful campaign to be Atlanta's first African American mayor.

Hill's active participation in business and issues of racial equality led to a litany of African American firsts. These include the first African American member of the board of directors of Rich's Department Store, first African American president of the Atlanta Chamber of Commerce, and first African American on the Georgia Board of Regents (named by Governor Jimmy Carter). He served as chairman of the Atlanta Crime Commission and

National Alliance of Business. When Jimmy Carter became president, he named Hill chairman of the Minority Business Resource Center, a congressional committee commissioned to assure minority consideration in the awarding of government contracts for the rail system. He was asked to serve on numerous corporation boards, such as Sun Trust (Trust Company of Georgia), Delta Airlines, Knight Ridder, Incorporated, and the King Center (he served for fifteen years).

Hills's contributions have not gone without recognition. His awards include National Urban League EOE Award (1965); Most Distinguished Alumni Award, Lincoln University (1970); and the Abe Goldstein Award, Anti-Defamation League of B'nai B'rith (1973). Additionally, he has received honorary doctorates from Morris Brown College (1972), Chung-Ang University (1976), and the University of Michigan (1994).

Hill, who served two years in the Korean War, was decorated for his military valor. He married Juanita Azira Gonzales, a native of Cuba and a registered nurse. He is the father of two daughters—Nancy Cooke and Azira Kendall—and six grandchildren.

*See also*: Alonzo Franklin Herndon

**Sources**

"Jessie Hill, Jr." *African American Biographies: Profiles of 558 Current Men and Women*. By Walter L. Hawkins. Jefferson, NC: McFarland, 1992.

———. *Contemporary Black Biography*. Vol. 13. Gale Research, 1996. Reproduced in Biography Resources Center. Farmington Hills, MI: Thomson Gale, 2005. http://galenet.galegroup.com/servlet/BioRC Document Number: K1606000571.

———. *Notable Black American Men*. Gale Research, 1998. Reproduced in Biography Resource Center. Farmington Hills, MI: Thomson Gale, 2005. http://galenet.galegroup.com/servlet/BioRC Document Number: K1622000211.

"Martin Luther King, Jr. Letter to Jesse Hill, Jr." May 8, 1956. *The Papers of Martin Luther King Jr. Vol. 3: Birth of a New Age, December 1955–December 1956*. Ed. The Estate of Martin Luther King Jr. http://www/stanford.edu/group/King/publications/papers/vol3/560508.014-Letter_to_Jesse.

*Helen R. Houston*

# Casper A. Holstein (1877–1944), Policy Banker, Philanthropist

Casper Holstein was born in Christiansted, St. Croix, Virgin Islands, on December 6, 1877. He died in New York at the home of a friend on April 5, 1944, after a long illness. Although he died poor, during the 1920s he was one of New York City's most affluent African Americans. He was one of the most successful policy bankers in Harlem, with a reputed worth of $500,000 until white gangsters, initially under the leadership of Dutch Schultz, took over the operations of the banks in Harlem during the late 1920s and early 1930s, making black policy bankers salaried employees of the crime syndicate.

Holstein was educated in the public schools of Christiansted and worked in hotels and tourist resorts. He eventually made his way to New York with his mother in 1885. He attended high school in Brooklyn and joined the navy as a mess attendant, the only position open to blacks at the time. After leaving the navy, he found work as a porter in a Wall Street brokerage firm. At some point, probably between 1915 and 1920, he became involved in policy banking in Harlem.

To participate in policy gambling, a bettor selected three numbers and bet any amount from one cent up. The winning numbers were selected by use of an arbitrary rule applied to openly published numbers. This guaranteed a publicly verifiable randomly selected number, which typically paid off at 600:1 odds, giving a $6 return for a successful penny bet. In practice, the payoff was less since the winner was expected to tip his runner 10 percent. There are several versions of the origin of the game, including one that traces it directly to Holstein. Given a history of betting on lotteries in New York that extends back well into the nineteenth century, this is untrue. It could well be that Holstein's contribution to numbers was a rule for his operation, selecting a winning number from the totals of clearing house transactions, combined with a clear realization of how very small bets could add up to a great deal of money.

White gangsters, who controlled the wholesale distribution of the alcoholic beverages made illegal by Prohibition as well as segregated Harlem night clubs like the Cotton Club, initially considered the banks as small-time activities unworthy of their notice. In any case, there were numerous policy games in Harlem, and Holstein was only one of the most successful bankers. In 1931 he was only one of six persons considered big-time bankers—that list includes a woman, Stephanie St. Clair, who won considerable fame as the person to resist Dutch Schultz's takeover the most vigorously. Most of the other bankers found it prudent to give in without much public complaint.

Holstein was a very close-mouthed person who revealed little about his life. He neither drank nor smoked. While remaining noncommittal about his business dealings and the source of his affluence, he was prominently engaged in the community. He was, of course, known to be the owner of a Harlem club, the Turf, but he was also active in lodge activities. He was president of the (Negro) Elks in New York City and was instrumental in acquisition of the lodge building. In 1929 he ran unsuccessfully for the national presidency of the organization.

In other areas Holstein won recognition as a philanthropist and activist. He was a consistent contributor to West Indian causes. Not only was it a matter of help in school construction or hurricane relief, he had definite political views in mind. When the Virgin Islands passed to the United States in 1917, the navy ran the government until 1931. Finally a governor was appointed; he did not give satisfaction. In 1917 Holstein visited the islands and on his return founded the Virgin Islands Congressional Council. Claude McKay attributes to Holstein a consistent push for greater self-determination for the islands and sees his visit to the islands in 1935 as a major contribution to the governor's replacement in that year.

Such effort for improvement is the West Indies in consistent with Holstein's donations to such organizations as the Urban League. He contributed generously to the league's fund-raising and also to the literary prizes offered by the league's publication *Opportunity*. This munificence gained Holstein recognition and a seat at the awards banquets but not admission to the salons of Harlem Renaissance literary figures. In addition, he was noted for such endeavors as furthering education through donations to black colleges and scholarship help to students. Much of this activity passed little noticed since he did not publicize it by use of his name.

Holstein first attracted widespread notoriety in the press in September 1928 when he was kidnapped by white gangsters who demanded a $50,000 ransom. The events are murky. Holstein apparently resisted efforts at intimidation and seems not to have paid any ransom. He was released unharmed according to his own claims; the hoodlums apparently believed his assurances that he would fail to identify them. The police quickly rounded up several persons connected with the Dutch Schultz organization, headquartered in the Bronx. Holstein consistently claimed a complete inability to recognize any of the accused.

The exact course of Holstein's relations with the Schultz organization is a matter of speculation, but his prosperity as a Harlem policy banker was undermined along with that of all the others as the mob took over complete control as Prohibition came to an end and the profits from illegal alcohol ended as well. It is suggested by McKay that he ceased his operations entirely early on.

Holstein had to shut down his club in the mid-1930s after a series of apparently staged fights and shootings broke out on the premises. Finally, in 1937 Holstein was arrested on a numbers charge even though he claimed to be out of the business. In any case, he was convicted and spent about a year in prison. In addition to this misfortune, his real estate holdings fell apart. Again, specific details are lacking, but Holstein seems to have sought to shield his property by concealing his ownership, and his trust in his agents was ill placed.

When Holstein died on April 5, 1944, he was broke. He died at the home of a friend, and there is no mention of family in the obituary in the *New York Times*. As a policy banker during the 1920s, Holstein was only one among equals and probably not the most successful. He was unique, however, in his continued philanthropic endeavors. It must also be presumed that a substantial portion of the money he gained in Harlem was reinvested in the community through his real estate activities. Such investment possibilities disappeared as white mobs took over control of numbers in New York City.

**Sources**

Bell, Walter A. "Black Gangs of Harlem." http://www.crimelibrary.com/gangsters_outlaws/gang/harlem_gangs/index.html?sect=26.

Boris, Joseph J., ed. *Who's Who in Colored America*. Vol. 1. New York: Who's Who in Colored America Corp., 1927.

"Former 'Policy King' in Harlem Dies Broke." *New York Times*, April 9, 1944.

Ianni, Francis A. J. *Black Mafia: Ethnic Succession in Organized Crime*. New York: Simon and Schuster, 1974.

"Kidnapped Negro Freed by Captors; Five Seized in Plot." *New York Times*, September 24, 1928.

Lewis, David Levering. *When Harlem Was in Vogue*. New York: Oxford University Press, 1979.

McKay, Claude. *Harlem: Negro Metropolis*. New York: E. P. Dutton, 1940.

"Negro Back Home, Lauds Kidnapper." *New York Times*, September 25, 1928.

"Rich Negro Seized for $50,000 Ransom." *New York Times*, September 23, 1928.

Schatzberg, Rufus, and Robert J. Kelly. *African American Organized Crime: A Social History*. New Brunswick, NJ: Rutgers University Press, 1997.

*Robert L. Johns*

# Christine Moore Howell (1899–1972), Manufacturer, Cosmetologist, Author, State Official

From the 1920s through the 1940s, the standards of the beauty culture industry in the state of New Jersey were enhanced greatly due to the efforts of Christine Moore Howell. At first through the standards that she set for her own business—the beauty salon and the research laboratory that she founded and operated—and through her work as one of the first five state commissioners on the first New Jersey Board of Beauty Culture, Howell ensured that the training, operations, and products used were appropriate. She used an interracial approach to business operations, serving an interracial clientele.

Born in Princeton, New Jersey, on March 19, 1899, Howell was the daughter of entrepreneur William and Mary Adelaide Williams Moore, both natives of Hillsboro, North Carolina. She had one sister, Bessie, and two brothers—Arthur C. and Willie. At some point William Moore, who was known as "Sport," moved to Princeton, New Jersey, and became a successful owner of a secondhand store located in three buildings on Spring Street. Students from Princeton University sold their clothes to him to earn enough money to finance their trips to New York City. In his business Moore also sold furniture and antiques, while Adelaide Moore tended to the home and children. It was at this site that Christine Moore would operate a beauty shop business and laboratory for twenty-eight years.

Howell was the first African American to graduate from Princeton High School. In 1919 she received a diploma from De Laurenberg's in Princeton. For professional study in beauty culture, she attended Warren's Institute in Pittsburgh, Knock's School of Beauty Culture in Philadelphia, and Nestle's in New York City. Howell went abroad for further training and studied at

Sidonia Institute in Paris. While there she also made a shop-to-shop study of beauty salons. Returning to the United States, she had special laboratory training in New Brunswick, under the tutelage of chemist Louis Du Bois.

She opened two unique businesses that became highly successful— Christine's Beauty Salon, a skin care laboratory known as Christine Moore Corporation. Her modern laboratory, which she began to operate in 1936, adjoined her beauty salon, and she hired a capable chemist to manufacture the products that she needed. These included products for good grooming as well as those required for beauty culture work. She also conducted research in her laboratory and aided in producing hair preparation and cosmetics for blacks. Her line of cosmetics became known as Christine Cosmetics. Such products that were suitable for white clientele evolved and were sold mail order throughout the world. Altogether the laboratory manufactured eleven hair-care and beauty products.

Only highly trained, creative staff members who were skilled in the art of enhancing womanhood regardless of race were hired in her salon. Although she had some middle-class black customers, her shop had great appeal to those on the white and black social register, many of whom were limousine-driven customers. They included, for example, Mrs. Calvin Coolidge, who came from Northfield, Massachusetts; Mrs. Albert Einstein; Mrs. Samuel Shellebarger (whose husband was author of *The Prince of Foxes*); a black woman doctor; and the wife of a Princeton University professor. When she knew that Mrs. Coolidge was scheduled, she was deliberate and relentless in her efforts to maintain a quiet and pleasant atmosphere. In addition to Mrs. Coolidge, some customers drove long distances to visit her shop. Some came from as far away as Kentucky and visited during their semiannual pilgrimages.

For a while, black customers were few in number, due to the fact that Howell's shop did not straighten hair as many black women required. The shop specialized in permanent waves. In time, however, black customers grew in number as Howell began to master the permanent wave and offered more creativity in hair designs than she did when the shop first opened. Her laboratory developed a formula processing agent for black hair, removing the curly appearance characteristic of some types of black hair.

Her experience as a beauty culturist, researcher, and businesswoman inspired Howell to write *Beauty Culture and Care of the Hair*, published in 1936. A textbook, the work was used in public vocational schools as well as private beauty schools. Howell helped to improve standards for beauty culture throughout the state of New Jersey. Having become familiar with her reputation, in 1935 Governor Harold G. Hoffman appointed her to the first New Jersey Board of Beauty Culture Control. The board, which she had helped to establish, wielded great power in the beauty culture industry: It created rules and regulations for beauty shops and beauty culture training; issued licenses; and planned and monitored examinations that were given three times a week at the state department located in Newark. All beauty salons, whether white or black owned and operated, were subject to board examination.

The appointment came at a time when race relations in New Jersey were poor. The idea of appointing a black person to a new and powerful board aroused considerable protest among whites. As well, membership was extremely limited, with space for only five persons; people petitioned hard to gain one of the posts; and it was unthinkable to give one of those to a black. Quoted in *Ebony* magazine, Moore recalled: "The white people were enraged because I, a Negro, had gained the post. Ugly articles appeared in the *Trenton Times*." Howell dissuaded her friends from responding to the attacks. She wanted to handle the matter her way, and she was determined to meet her board responsibility to the best of her ability. This approach would allow her to "win the respect of those who felt that the color of my skin disqualified me," she added.

Howell's work on the Board of Beauty Culture Control became a matter of record. After her initial appointment as a commissioner, she was reappointed three years later and altogether served on the board for fourteen years, from 1935 through 1949. She was elected chair of the commission and served four terms, a position that paid $3,200 as well as expenses. While serving as a commissioner, Moore assisted New York and other states as they set up beauty culture departments.

The site of her business on Spring Street in Princeton, New Jersey, is shown as the Christine Moore Corporation in Princeton High School's online publication *PULSE*. It is also one of Princeton's historic landmarks. Moore operated her business from the 1920s to the 1940s.

In 1924 she married Edward Gaylord Howell, a native of New Haven, Connecticut, and a physician who devoted considerable time to the study and treatment of alcoholism. He had a medical practice in Princeton with a virtually all-white clientele. The Howells lived in New Brunswick, New Jersey, but at some point reportedly had a residence both in Princeton and in New Brunswick. Whatever the case, their residence was a mecca for interracial activity, whether social or civic. Christine Howell was a member of the New Brunswick Urban League, Princeton Group Arts, Inc., National Association for the Advancement of Colored People (NAACP), and the Links, Inc. She died on December 13, 1972, and was buried in the Princeton Cemetery of the historic Nassau Presbyterian Church, established in 1757. Her influence had been widely felt in the beauty culture industry in New Jersey and beyond. Through her work, including the book that she wrote, she helped raise the standards of the industry and demonstrated her skill and success as a black woman entrepreneur.

*See also*: Retail Industry; Women and Business

### Sources

"Beauty Salon for the Social Register." *Ebony* 4 (May 1949): 31–32.

"The History of the African American Community in Princeton, New Jersey." *PULSE*. http://athena.prs.k12.nj.us/groups/phs/pulse/business/business.html.

Moses, Sibyl E. *African American Women Writers in New Jersey, 1836–2000: A Biographical Dictionary and Bibliographic Guide*. New Brunswick, NJ: Rutgers University Press, 2003.

*Who's Who in Colored America*. 7th ed. Ed. G. James Fleming and Christian E. Burckel. Yonkers-on-Hudson, NY: Chistian E. Burckel and Associates, 1950.

*Jessie Carney Smith*

# Catherine "Cathy" Hughes (1947– ), Radio Personality, Broadcast Executive

Media maven Catherine "Cathy" Hughes is a unique personality in the U.S. broadcast arena. While her life story includes many challenges, she has been successful both personally and professionally through hard work, vision, and creativity. Not only is Hughes the first African American woman to have a publicly traded company on the New York Stock Exchange, but she also founded Radio One, a media company that is now the seventh largest radio broadcasting network in the nation and the largest African American–owned and –operated radio broadcast company in the United States. Throughout her career, Hughes has introduced new media formats that have become popular with urban listeners and set standards throughout the radio broadcast industry. She has championed black causes and focused her company's business on acquiring or managing struggling black-owned radio stations. In 2004, her company expanded its media interests by launching cable television channel TV One in partnership with Comcast. In 2005, Radio One acquired controlling interest in Reach Media, Inc., Tom Joyner's company formerly associated with ABC News. As a result of her accomplishments, Hughes has received numerous awards for her business acumen, community service, and philanthropic activities.

Catherine Elizabeth Woods Hughes was born on April 27, 1947, in Omaha, Nebraska, to William Alfred Woods and Helen Jones Woods and is the eldest of four children. Sources report that Hughes grew up modestly in an Omaha housing project. However, her father was an accountant and her mother, a nurse. The family set high standards. Her grandfather, Laurence C. Jones, founded the Piney Woods Country School in Mississippi in 1909. Piney Woods, located outside Jackson, Mississippi, is a private boarding school for African Americans in grades seven through twelve.

Hughes attended Duchesne Academy of the Sacred Heart, an elite Roman Catholic girls' school in Omaha. She dropped out of high school at sixteen to give birth to her only son (Alfred Liggings III, who later joined her in business). However, Hughes was married at seventeen and completed her studies, though the marriage ended in divorce when she was nineteen years of age. Never graduating from college, Hughes attended Creighton University and the University of Nebraska.

Prior to her move to Washington, D.C. in 1971, where she launched her career in radio, Hughes became a volunteer at black-owned KOWH radio station in Omaha. The experience impacted her significantly in that it allowed her to learn about the radio industry and to appreciate black radio ownership. From 1971 to 1973, Hughes was employed as a lecturer and assistant to the renowned broadcaster Tony Brown, dean of the School of Communication at Howard University. Because of her hard work, Brown appointed Hughes manager of WHUR-FM, the campus radio station, in 1973. During her tenure, Hughes made the station financially profitable and was appointed vice president and general manager in 1975, becoming the first African American general manager in the Washington, D.C. media market. It was during her tenure at WHUR-FM that she created a new format called the "Quiet Storm." Although Howard University refused to license it, the late-night romantic music and chatter format was popular and continues to dominate urban radio programming.

In 1978, Hughes moved to WYCB-AM in Washington, D.C., in search of more creative control and transformed the struggling station to an all-night gospel music station before leaving the position. In 1980, she purchased her first radio station, WOL-AM, in Washington, D.C. with new husband Dewey Hughes. The couple used personal savings and secured funding from investors and an African American venture capital firm but had to approach thirty-two banks before raising the required purchase price of $1 million. It is widely reported that this was one of the most difficult periods for Hughes. Her marriage dissolved shortly after the radio station was purchased, leaving her a single parent for the second time. In addition, financial problems forced Hughes to lose both her housing and car, and she and son lived in her radio station for eighteen months. Hughes implemented a twenty-four-hour talk show format at WOL-AM, but upon threats from the bank to cut funding, Hughes modified the format to include music. She met the challenges of little funding for personnel by starting her own talk show and playing records from her personal collection. However, it was through this venture that her current empire, Radio One, was born. She established her trademark of community service and being a champion of African American rights.

Hughes purchased her next radio station in 1987 and continued to add stations. She became the first broadcaster to own four stations in one market due to a Federal Communications Commission change that earlier had restricted local ownership to two stations. In 1999, Radio One purchased WKYS in Washington, D.C. for $40 million, becoming the largest transaction between two African Americans companies. Between 1998 and 1999, Radio One entered an aggressive acquisitions period and purchased eighteen stations within a twenty-month period. In 1999, the company was valued at $950 million and was traded publicly for the first time on the New York Stock Exchange.

Radio One is currently a network of sixty-nine radio stations, located in twenty-two urban markets around the country with 13 million listeners. It provides programming to XM Satellite Radio and operates a joint-venture cable TV channel with Comcast, TV One. The company has more than 1,700 employees with estimates of 1,500 being African American. Many are managers and women. The company has received many awards. In 2000, Radio One was named "Company of the Year" by *Black Enterprise*. In 2002, *Fortune* magazine named it one of the "Best 100 Best Companies to Work For." In 2003, Radio One was inducted into the U.S. Small Business Administration Hall of Fame. The company has also been inducted into Maryland's Business Hall of Fame.

Hughes has received many awards reflective of her business, community service, and philanthropic activities. Those awards include the District of Columbia Community Service Award (1995), Mayor's Business Award (1995–1999), Thomas A. Dorsey Leadership Award (1996), **National Black Chamber of Commerce** Business Person of the Year (1998), Prudential Media Black Woman on Wall Street (1998), Black History Hall of Fame Award (2000), National Action Network Keepers of the Dream Award (2000), National Association of Broadcasters Distinguished Service Award (2001), National Association of Black-Owned Broadcasters Life Time Achievement Award (2002), Broadcasters Foundation Golden Mike Award (2002), Ernest and Young Entrepreneur of the Year Award (2003), Associated Charities History Makers Award (2003), National Museum of Women in the Arts Enterprising Woman of Washington (2004), American Legacy Magazine, Strength and Courage Award (2005), and Doctor of Humane Letters, Howard University (2005).

With a $3 billion radio broadcasting network, TV cable holdings, and other media interests, Hughes is among the most powerful black business executives in the United States.

*See also*: Women and Business

**Sources**
About Radio One, the Urban Specialists. http://www.radio-one.com.
Clarke, Robyn D., and Derek T. Dingle. "The New Blood." *Black Enterprise* 29 (June 1999): 161–167.
*Contemporary Black Biography*. Vol. 27. Detroit: Gale Group, 2001.
*Current Biography Yearbook*. New York: H. W. Wilson, 2000.
Harvard Business School African-American Alumni Association. "Cathy Hughes." http://www.hbsaaa.org/conf2002/ES/confBioCathyHughes.htm.
Hawkins, Walter L. *African American Biographies*. Jefferson, NC: McFarland, 1992.
Johnson, Pamela K. "Cathy Hughes Changes Frequency." *Essence* 35 (September 2004): 130.
Jones, Charisse. "Owning the Airwaves." *Essence* 29 (October 1998): 112–119.
Jones, Joyce. "Keeping It in the Black." *Black Enterprise* 25 (May 1995): 22.
"Maryland's Top 100 Women." http://www.mddailyrecord.com/top100w/hughes.html.
National Museum of Women in the Arts. "NMWA Honors Catherine Hughes, Founder of Radio One Inc., as Enterprising Woman of Washington 2004." http://www.nmwa.org/news/news.asp?newsid=127.
Norment, Lynn. "Cathy Hughes: Ms. Radio." *Ebony* 55 (May 2000): 100–104.
Pyatt, Rudolph A., Jr. "Whatever the Race, Radio One Is a Winner." *Washington Post*, May 25, 2000.
Shepard, Alicia C. "Empire of the Air." *Washingtonian* (November 2001): 39–47.

Smith, Jessie Carney, ed. *Notable Black American Women*. Book III. Detroit: Gale Research, 2003.

Stark, Phyllis. "Radio One Owner/CEO Building an Empire: Cathy Hughes Paves the Way for Blacks, Women." *Billboard* 107 (January 14, 1995): 61.

*Who's Who among African Americans*. 18th ed. Detroit: Gale Group, 2005.

*Alma E. Dawson*

# I

## "Ice Cube." *See* O'Shea "Ice Cube" Jackson

## International Black Women's Congress

Founded in 1983 in Newark, New Jersey, as an international nonprofit organization for women of African ancestry, International Black Women's Congress (IBWC) responded to the complex milieu of needs of global African and African-derived women. Through the leadership of its founder/ global president, clinical sociologist, professor, consultant, and author LaFrancis Rodgers-Rose, IBWC established a broad yet focused agenda with political, social, and economic overtures, respectively. Primarily through networking and exchange of strategic planning professionalism, IBWC has evolved around the vision of establishing an international black women's bank and fund, purchasing homes throughout the United States, Caribbean, and Africa, and creating an international black women's research institute.

To achieve organizational objectives, IBWC has implemented initiatives through yearly conferences and seminars, resulting in ongoing international networking and educational tours as well as an operative Black Women's Speakers Bureau. By empowering themselves and subsequently spreading self-help and proactive tools for a better quality of life, IBWC has built strong relationships through stressing personal credibility. Addressed at the organization's homecoming 20th Anniversary Conference in Newark titled "Building Stronger Political, Social and Economic Relationships," on September 23–26, 2004, were economic sessions covering the role of personal transformation in debt management and investment resolution. The "Investing Success Seminar" encapsulates the group's efforts at empowering through tangible education-driven initiatives that simultaneously empower economically as well.

From its focused beginnings, IBWC has striven and actualized institutional development for issues that matter to women of color, the world over. With the charge "Save Our Lives" in Washington, D.C. in 1994, 500 black women convened to outline a research agenda for black women's health. Through a partial grant from the U.S. Department of Health and Human Services Agency for Health Care Policy and Research, IBWC was able to establish a base from which its institutional activities have been propelled in sustainable ways. At such activities as the 19th Annual Conference titled "African-American Women: Matters of the Heart," on September 26–28, 2003, cardiovascular disease took center stage. Additionally, at a Cleveland seminar titled "In Pursuit of Health, Heart and Happiness," on May 14, 2005, data indicated that of the nation's numbers waiting for kidney transplants annually, 35 percent were African American, despite this group's mere 12 percent of the total population.

Attention should be drawn here to the sustaining qualities inherent in economically viable nonprofits' ability to sustain themselves. In order to manage funds generated from public and private philanthropy properly, IBWC is community based and motivated by its ability to inform to the extent possible that human existence can be improved. Yet at the same time, it provides avenues of fund-raising that financially benefit the group at large, as well as individual members professionally. Through its Speakers Bureau, noted women such as Frances E. Ashe-Goins (deputy director and director of the division of policy and program development for the Office of Health and Human Services), Beatryce Nivens (renowned motivational speaker and author), and Lori S. Robinson (former *Emerge: Black America's Newsmagazine* editor and author of *I Will Survive: The African-American Guide to Healing from Sexual Assault and Abuse* [2003]) are afforded opportunities to professionally lecture and conduct workshops in areas of respective expertise.

Book tours on sexual assault and organ donation lectureships generate sources of revenue but are not profit driven. Instead, they provide necessary professional interaction toward the greater good of serving humanity in a holistic manner. Of note is Nivens's work on topics associated with success strategies for African Americans in professional achievement and career guides for black women. Nivens's business acumen has been highlighted in *Essence, Family Circle, New Woman, Black Collegian, Daily News, Mademoiselle, Glamour,* and *Black Enterprise.* Of further attempts to implement national and international community action programs that reclaim, empower, and transform the lives of women of African descent, IBWC has by no means offered words only on the global front. Consider the conference held at the University of Toronto on March 18, 2005, titled "Decolonizing Ourselves, Building Alliances: An Aboriginal/Black Dialogue," which engaged scholars and activists around the idea of decolonizing not only through educational mediums but through independent and economic freedom that allows ownership of mediums of communication as well.

*See also*: Women and Business

**Sources**

Armstrong, Kiley. "International Black Women's Congress to Meet to Establish Health." *New York Beacon*, August 5, 1994. HighBeam Research. http://www.highbeam.com/library/doc1.asp?docid=1P1:2271496&refid=ink_tptd_np&ske.

International Black Women's Congress. http://www.ibwc.info/html/conference_center.html.

National Black United Federation of Charities Member Organization Listings. http://www.cfcsiliconvalley.org/pages/NATIONAL_BLACK_UNITED_FEDERATION.htm.

Robinson, Lori S. *I Will Survive: The African-American Guide to Healing from Sexual Assault and Abuse*. New York: Seal Press, 2002.

Social Justice Cluster. http://www.socialjustice.utoronto.ca/decolonizing.html.

Speakers Platform Bureau. http://www.speaking.com/speakers/beatrycenivens.html.

United Network for Organ Sharing: Organ Donation and Transplantation. http://www.unos.org/helpSaveALife/promoteOrganDonation/findASpeaker.asp?display=s.

*Uzoma O. Miller*

---

# International Brotherhood of Sleeping Car Porters and Maids. *See* Brotherhood of Sleeping Car Porters

---

# J

## Maynard Holbrook Jackson Jr. (1938–2003), Politician, Attorney

In 1973 Jackson became the first black mayor of Atlanta, Georgia. During his tenure as mayor, Jackson empowered **minority businesses** with his set-aside program that guaranteed minority businesses contracts for government projects. The Hartsfield Airport was one such project that successfully used set-asides and was done on time and under budget. The success of this program influenced other local governments to implement similar programs.

Born on March 23, 1938, in Dallas, Texas, Jackson was the third of six children born to Maynard Jackson Sr. and Irene Dobbs Jackson. His family was considered part of the black aristocracy. His great-grandfather, Andrew Jackson, a former slave, founded the Wheat Street Baptist Church in Atlanta. Jackson Sr. was a Baptist minister who led the New Hope Baptist Church. He started a voter registration league for blacks and would later run for a seat on the Dallas school board. Although he lost by a wide margin, this may have influenced his son's interest in political life. Jackson's mother, Irene Dobbs, was from a political family as well. A Spelman College valedictorian (1929), she was the daughter of John Wesley Dobbs, who was a civic leader in Atlanta. J. W. Dobbs founded the Georgia Voters League and served as grand master of the Prince Hall Negro Masons of Georgia.

In 1945, when Jackson was seven, his family moved to Atlanta, where his father was pastor of Friendship Baptist Church. Jackson also considered becoming a Baptist minister but instead majored in political science and history at Morehouse College, entering at the age of fourteen as a Ford Foundation Early Admissions Scholar. He graduated in 1956 at the age of eighteen. He then pursued a law degree at Boston University Law School. However, he was unsuccessful after two separate attempts and dropped out. During the next few years, he worked as an encyclopedia salesman for P. F. Collier, Inc., earning $20,000 a year, and advanced to become assistant district sales manager. Prior to that, he worked as a claims examiner for the state of Ohio's Bureau of Unemployment Compensation in Cleveland.

After working as a claims examiner and encyclopedia salesman, Jackson returned to law school, this time at North Carolina Central University in Durham. His mother, Irene Dobbs, who had earned a Ph.D. in French in France, was head of the language department at North Carolina Central University. In 1964, Jackson earned his law degree, graduating cum laude. The following year, he moved back to Atlanta and married Burnella "Bunnie" Hayes Burke. During this time, he worked as an attorney for the National Labor Relations Board and the Emory Community Legal Services Center.

Jackson's first attempt at political office was in 1968 when he spontaneously entered the Democratic primary for U.S. Senate against incumbent Herman Talmadge. Although Jackson lost the race, it was a victory of sorts because he had succeeded in winning the majority of votes in Atlanta. The next year, he was elected vice mayor of Atlanta as he defeated thirteen-year veteran Milton Farris. Jackson was Atlanta's first black vice mayor. The success Jackson had in his race against Talmadge in getting the support of both the black and the white community was instrumental in Jackson becoming vice mayor and subsequently mayor. While vice mayor, Jackson was also president of the Board of Aldermen, which later changed to become the city council when Atlanta's charter changed. During this time, Jackson cofounded the first firm of black lawyers in Georgia—Jackson, Patterson & Parks.

## ELECTED MAYOR OF ATLANTA

In 1973, Jackson entered the race for mayor of Atlanta against incumbent Sam Massell and ten other candidates. Because Jackson only received 46.6 percent of the vote, with Massell receiving 19.8 percent, a runoff between the two took place. During the runoff campaign, Massell accused Jackson of being a reverse racist because Jackson ran on a platform of using affirmative action to reverse past discrimination against blacks in city jobs. The outburst by Massell negatively impacted his campaign. As a result, Jackson was elected mayor of Atlanta with almost 60 percent of the vote. In doing so, he became Atlanta's first black mayor and the first black mayor of a major southern city. In that same year, Los Angeles and Detroit also elected black mayors—Tom Bradley and Coleman Young, respectively.

One of Jackson's first priorities as mayor was to expand affirmative action to include minority hiring and promotion in the city's workforce and business set-asides. This stance infuriated white business leaders who saw this as "white exclusion." Jackson also took his stance to the private sector and pressured banks with large city deposits to hire minorities to executive positions. When one bank failed to comply, a half million dollars was moved from that bank to another bank in compliance with Jackson's mandate. Jackson eventually increased the number of blacks in city jobs from 38.1 percent to 55.6 percent, along with the number of black administrators from 7.1 percent to 32.6 percent, and city professionals from 15.2 percent to 42.2

percent. This included the hiring of a black police chief to replace the former white police chief who was demoted because of racial discrimination. Jackson also expanded the minority set-aside program of the Metropolitan Atlanta Rapid Transit Authority (MARTA) and established a city Minority Business Enterprise (MBE) program to award city contracts to black-owned firms. The MBE program increased the number of city contracts to minority firms to 19 percent by the end of Jackson's first term, to 34 percent by the end of his second term, while only being 1 percent in 1973.

In 1974, Jackson announced that Hartsfield Airport would be expanded to become an international hub. This announcement also included notice that minority firms would receive 25 percent of the contracts. White business leaders opposed this mandate, leading to a two-year conflict with Jackson over this policy. Jackson told the opposition that Atlanta would not build the airport unless they agreed to his mandate. He offered them 75 percent of the project—or else they would get nothing.

In 1976, a compromise was reached with a new mandate of only 20 to 25 percent of all contracts going to minority firms. Many thought the business set-asides would add millions to the cost and delay the project. Jackson was vindicated when the airport expansion was completed on time and under budget. His business set-aside program for minority firms made many blacks millionaires.

Jackson was elected to a second term in 1977. He also married his second wife, Valier Richardson, after divorcing his first wife in 1976. Because Atlanta's new city charter only permitted two consecutive terms, Andrew Young succeeded Jackson as mayor for two terms. During Young's two mayoral terms, Jackson partnered with Chapman & Cutler, a Chicago firm while also working as a bond lawyer. He returned to public office of mayor in 1989. During this terms, Jackson continued his affirmative action programs but realized that the city and the business leaders had to work together for the economic good of the city. Jackson took a more traditional, less-aggressive approach. He was involved in the planning process of bringing the 1996 Olympic Games to Atlanta. As he did earlier, Jackson made sure that minority firms received contracts for the Olympics. Of the $23.9 million in contracts to architects and engineers, $10.7 million was granted to minority businesses. Because of health reasons, Jackson did not seek a fourth term. He continued to work in the political realm, seeking in 2001 an unsuccessful bid for president of the Democratic National Committee (DNC) but heading an initiative for the DNC to increase voter participation among African Americans.

Jackson was also successful in private business. In 1987 he launched his own bond and security firm—Jackson Securities, Inc., rated by *Black Enterprise* as one of the top five black investment companies. Jackson proved influential in Jackson Securities landing several multimillion dollar contracts and becoming one of the largest black investment banks. In 1994 he partnered with his daughter Brooke Jackson Edmond and Daniel Halpern, a veteran in the food industry, to establish Jackmont Hospitality Inc., a food-services company. Jackmont Hospitality owns and operates T.G.I. Friday's restaurants in the airport in Atlanta and Greenbelt, Maryland; Washington, D.C.; and two in Philadelphia with revenue projected to be $27.5 million in 2004.

Jackson was also committed to public service beyond his political office. He cofounded the National Association of Securities Professionals (NASP), which serves as a resource for "minority professionals within the securities and investments industry" as well as the Atlanta Economic Development Corporation. He also established The Maynard Jackson Youth Foundation, which seeks to prepare tomorrow's leaders through mentoring. Jackson held several other organizational memberships: NAACP; Morehouse College Board of Trustees; Prince Hall Masons; **100 Black Men of America**; High Noon Legal Foundation; Georgia Voters League, Inc.; the National Conference of Christians and Jews; National Organization of Women; National Welfare Rights Organization; Urban League; National Gun Control Center; and a member of Alpha Phi Alpha Fraternity. He has served on numerous committees: Democratic National Committee—Executive Committee; White House Committee on Balanced Growth & Economic Development; and the White House Committee on the Windfall Profits Tax (vice chairman) to name a few.

Jackson has been honored as a recipient of The Jefferson Award for "The Greatest Public Service Performed by an American 35 Years or Under." He was also named by *Time* magazine (1975) as one of the 200 Young Leaders of America and by *Ebony* magazine (1976) as 100 Most Influential Black Americans. He has honorary degrees from Morehouse College, North Carolina Central University, and Delaware State College.

On June 23, 2003, Jackson had a heart attack at Reagan National Airport in Washington, D.C., and later died en route to the hospital. He was sixty-five years old. He is survived by his wife Valerie and their two children, Valerie Amanda and Alexandra; and three children from his first wife, Elizabeth, Brooke, and Maynard III. Shirley Franklin, current mayor of Atlanta and protégé of Jackson, spearheaded the renaming of the airport to "Hartsfield-Jackson International Airport" to honor his achievement in expanding the airport to become one of the busiest in the world.

**Sources**

Colburn, David R., and Jeffrey S. Adler, eds. *African-American Mayors: Race, Politics, and the American City.* Urbana: University of Illinois Press, 2001.

Dingle, Derek T. "The Ultimate Champion for Black Business." *Black Enterprise* 34 (September 2003): 72–78.

"Former Atlanta Mayor Maynard Jackson Dies." *Atlanta Journal Constitution,* June 23, 2003.

"Maynard Jackson." *Contemporary Black Biography.* Vol. 2. Detroit: Gale Research, 1996.

Rice, Bradley R. "Maynard Jackson (1938–2003)." *New Georgia Encyclopedia.* Athens: GA Humanities Council and the University of Georgia Press, 2004.

*La Loria Konata*

# O'Shea "Ice Cube" Jackson (1969– ), Rapper, Producer, Actor, Writer, Businessman

O'Shea Jackson is a California entertainment businessman who has become successful in several fields including rapping, writing, acting, and producing. His most acclaimed success in the business came when he launched his own movie production company, Cube Vision, in 2000. The production company is responsible for the success of such movies as *Friday* (1995) and two subsequent sequels, *Barbershop* (2000) and *Barbershop 2: Back in Business* (2004), and the 2005 release *Are We There Yet?* All of these films were incredibly successful, according to box-office standards.

Jackson was born on June 15, 1969, in Crenshaw South Central, Los Angeles. Unlike many of his contemporaries and people with whom he would later associate, O'Shea grew up in a middle-class two-parent household. His parents Doris and Hosea Jackson were employed at the University of California located in Los Angeles (UCLA). Hosea worked as a machinist at the university, while Doris worked as a hospital clerk. During his early years, Jackson attended Hawthorne Christian School in Los Angeles. He would later attend William Howard Taft High School in Woodland Hills, California.

On a dare to write a rhyme, when a friend challenged him in the middle of typing class, Jackson successfully met the challenge; he penned his first rap song in the ninth grade. In the mid-1980s, Jackson adopted the persona and hip-hop name "Ice Cube." The first song he wrote, "Boyz 'N the Hood," became famous a few short years later. Upon graduation from high school in 1987, Ice Cube left Los Angeles to attend Phoenix Institute of Technology in Arizona. Before totally committing himself to his music, Ice Cube wanted time off to study architectural drafting at the Institute. Within one year he completed a certificate and returned to Los Angeles to continue his newfound interest in music entertainment.

## ICE CUBE, HIP-HOP MUSIC, MOVIES, AND BUSINESS

At age sixteen, Ice Cube sold his first rap song, "Boyz 'N the Hood," to rapper Easy-E. He also began rapping with his partner Sir Jinx at parties hosted by hip-hop rap artist **Dr. Dre (Andre Young)**. Ice Cube's rhymes caught the ear of Dr. Dre and other rappers, quickly earning himself a spot in CIA, Dr. Dre's fledgling rap music production company. He returned to Los Angeles to start the first incarnation of N.W.A. (Niggaz with Attitude) with Dr. Dre, Easy-E, MC Ren, the Arabian Prince, and DJ Yella. Their first album, *Straight Outta Compton*, was released in 1989. It was a huge yet highly controversial hit, which put N.W.A. at the forefront of "gangster rap." With the release of songs like "Fuck the Police," N.W.A. would become historically significant as the first group to establish the new genre of hip-hop labeled "gansta rap." Initially the group's lyrics were commentary about police brutality and violence committed against blacks. Later the lyrics began to reflect more misogynistic and violent tones. Ice Cube remained with the group for another two years, and by 1990 he began a solo rap career in New York. He released five subsequent albums, all of which were successful and broadened his crossover appeal among white youth. Ice Cube has since recorded with other artists such as Mack 10, WC, and the West Side Connection.

Ice Cube made his acting debut in the hit 1991 movie *Boyz 'N the Hood*. His performance in the movie proved that he had star potential and catapulted his acting, producing, and directing career immediately. Ice Cube's success as an actor is clear, with films such as *The Glass Shield* (1995), *Higher Learning* (1995), the *Friday* films (*Friday*, 1995; *Next Friday*, 1999; *Friday after Next*, 2002), *Anaconda* (1997), *The Players Club* (1998), the acclaimed *Three Kings* (1999), *Ghosts of Mars* (2001), *Torque* (2004), *Barbershop* and *Barbershop 2* (2002–2004) among his credits. When asked if acting, writing, directing, and producing were an extension of music, Ice Cube said in an interview with Terry Gross that "it is just all about whether you got it or not; the camera don't lie." The former rapper says that he uses "the rhythm of timing" in his acting, the lesson he has derived from his music. "I think doing music, and videos, have kind of set me up to do what I am doing now."

In 2000, Ice Cube launched his own production company, Cube Vision. The company has since produced both *Barbershop* films as well as the box-office 2005 hit *Are We There Yet?* Besides Will Smith, Ice Cube has emerged as one of the most successful hip-hop music artists to have made the transition to acting. However, Ice Cube has exceeded Smith's success as musician and actor only through his work as director, writer, and producer. Off screen, Ice Cube is noted as quietly philosophical in how he deals with the fame that has been thrust upon him. "You know, it is part of what I have asked for. I take it as another extension of who I am. Not all of who I am but just a piece," he said in an interview with Monikka Stallworth.

One major challenge he faces in the film industry deals with perceptions of race and its impact on movie selections. Ice Cube finds disappointment with Hollywood film executives who only want to market to mainly black audiences for support of his films. Ice Cube intimated that the continued color barrier that exists in Hollywood comes from the people making the movies and not from the audience. In an interview with Tor Thorsen, he stated, "The studios target with blinders on. They're the ones who don't understand that if people want to see it. You don't have to target . . . they're not smart enough to see they [the audience] don't care about your color."

Ice Cube did not imagine that he would be in the position he has achieved today. His popularity among mainstream pop culture as a music artist, leading man, and entertainment executive is even more overwhelming for him. However, having been married since 1992 to wife Kim Jackson, and having four children, he believes having family has helped ground him. While he is unsure about his continued role in hip-hop music, Ice Cube would like to continue his role as actor, writer, producer, and director of films.

**Sources**

"Actor and Musician Ice Cube." Interview by Terry Gross. January 10, 2005. National Public Radio, Philadelphia, PA.

"The Africana QA: Ice Cube." Interview by Ronda Racha Penrice. January 15, 2004. http://archive.blackvoices.com.

"Barbershop: An Interview with Ice Cube." Interview by Monikka Stallworth. September 20, 2002. http://www.blackfilm.com.

"Cubevision." Interview by Tor Thorsen. December 2, 2002. http://www.donmega.com/cubevision.

*Baiyina W. Muhammad*

## Thomas "T. D." Jakes (1957– ), Evangelist, Entrepreneur, Author

Thomas Dexter "T. D." Jakes is a large-scale religious entrepreneur. In a comparatively short time, he has built up a megachurch with nearly 30,000 members and a nationwide television ministry. He holds meetings throughout the country and draws very large audiences to his conferences. In addition, he has produced award-winning gospel records and written and produced plays and movies, both of which have been very successful with predominantly fundamentalist Christian audiences. He is also the author of over two dozen books, including *Woman, Thou Art Loosed* (1993), which has sold more than 1.5 million copies. While his central ministry is supported by nonprofit organizations, his for-profit activities, like song and theater productions, and his writings contribute to his seven-figure income.

Jakes was born on June 9, 1957, in South Charleston, West Virginia. His mother, Odith, taught economics, and his father, Ernest Sr., had successfully built up a forty-two-person janitorial service. There were two older children. Early on he undertook such business responsibilities as running a paper route. His father suffered for many years from a severe kidney disease, and when his mother fell ill also, he dropped out of high school just short of graduation. He already felt the call to become a minister, preaching wherever he could in storefront Pentecostal churches. In 1980 he helped found a church in Montgomery, West Virginia, which began with ten members. Jakes married his wife Serita in 1981; the couple has five children.

Jakes became a full-time minister in 1982, the year his father died and he lost his job as the local Union Carbide plant closed. His initial affiliation as a minister was as a member of the Higher Ground Always Abounding Association, a Pentecostal oneness denomination. Oneness denominations do not espouse orthodox beliefs in the Trinity and baptize in Jesus's name only. His church is now nondenominational, and he downplays the exact nature of his theological beliefs and baptizes both "in Jesus's name" and in the orthodox "name of the Father, the Son, and the Holy Ghost," according to circumstances. This posture enrages those fundamentalist Christians who pride themselves on doctrinal purity but attracts large numbers of persons who are indifferent to the intricacies of Christian theology.

Jakes developed early on themes and techniques that quickly increased his outreach and spurred the growth of his church. For example, 1983 saw the first "Back to the Bible Conference," now simply the "Bible Conference." This conference began with eighty persons and grew over the years. He also showed his willingness to change his base of operations to reach larger audiences. When he moved to Charleston in 1990, his congregation tripled from 100 to 300.

In 1992, he discovered one of his major themes when he preached to a healing and inspiring sermon, "Woman, Thou Art Loosed," in Sunday school. This has proved to be extremely popular in his ministry. A book of the same title was published in 1993. Jakes's ministry has continually had a remarkable appeal to women. Conferences under the title "Woman, Thou Art Loosed" draw large audiences. In 1999 such a conference attracted 84,500 people to Atlanta's Georgia Dome; in addition, there was an overflow crowd of 20,000, breaking the previous record for attendance held by Billy Graham.

Various organizations organize Jakes's different activities. In 1992 he formed T. D. Jakes Enterprises, a for-profit organization, which handles his work as an author, a musician, and a playwright; his conferences are handled by the nonprofit Potter's House Ministry.

Jakes has been quick to exploit technology. In 1993 he began a weekly television show, which ran on both TBN (Trinity Broadcasting Network) and BET (Black Entertainment Television). He has since added a daily thirty-minute talk show to the weekly calendar. He is also on international television with a weekly program, and still keeping up with the latest technology, there are now live Webcasts of two Sunday services and a Wednesday evening one.

In 1996, continuing to expand his ministry, Jakes, his family, and fifty staff members moved their base from West Virginia to Dallas, Texas, where he purchased a former televangelist's church on twenty-eight acres of land for $3.2 million. Renamed the Potter's House, the church saw the congregation grow rapidly, and it now approaches 30,000. His congregation is unusually diverse, accommodating 13 percent Caucasian and 7 percent Hispanic. The congregation is 45 percent male, very high for a minority church.

To accommodate such numbers, there are four three-hour church services every Sunday. There are also a vast number of additional ministries, including a prison ministry said to reach more than 350,000 persons. Many of the efforts are addressed to persons in dire circumstances: the homeless, drug abusers, people with AIDS (acquired immunodeficiency syndrome), and women subject to domestic abuse. There is also a GED program. Jakes supports three major conferences, "The Pastor's Leadership Conference," "Manpower," an all-male ministry, and "Woman, Thou Art Loosed."

The foundation of these activities is Jakes's skill as a preacher. Both the *New York Times* and *Time* magazine have featured him. The *Times* named him in 1999 as one of the top five candidates to become the popular successor to Billy Graham. *Time* put him on the magazine cover in 2001, identifying him as "America's Best Preacher." He is also active as a columnist in three national religious magazines, including *Gospel Today*. He is also active as a columnist in three national religious magazines, including *Gospel Today*. His theater production company, Touchdown Concepts, launched another play, *Cover Girl*, in 2004. Two previous ones, *Woman, Thou Art Loosed* and *Behind Closed Doors* became in turn the number one gospel play. In 2004 a full-length movie version of *Woman, Thou Art Loosed*, with Jakes playing himself, appeared. The musical label Dexterity Sounds, a collaboration with EMI Gospel Music, has also been very successful with "The Storm Is Over" (2001), makings its debut at number one on *Billboard*'s Gospel chart.

Jakes has also published over twenty-five books. Three of his bestselling top five are books of religious advice: *Maximize the Moment: God's Action Plan for Your Life* (1999) and *The Great Investment: Faith, Family and Finance* (2000) join the runaway bestseller *Woman, Thou Art Loosed!* (1993). All except the last were published by a major mainstream publisher, Putnam. Jakes's first publication with Putnam was the novel *The Lady, Her Lover, and the Lord* in 1998 and was followed in 2002 by a second, *God's Leading Lady: Out of the Shadows and into the Light*. These works have shown Christian fiction to be very profitable for mainstream publishers and bookstores to the point that specialized Christian bookstores find their business adversely affected.

Jakes's activities have led to a very visible prosperity: a $1.7 million house, an expensive automobile, and fine wardrobe. But he is not a simply "believe and you will become wealthy" preacher; he emphasizes that God's will is not to make people happy but to teach them lessons. Adversity can be part of the plan. Still, he does appeal greatly to persons striving to become prosperous. Jakes has contributed to improvement at home and abroad ranging from improvements in urban conditions in Dallas to help in construction of a hospital in Belize and the provision of water wells in Kenya. The church is also very active in an outreach prison ministry in tandem with a federally sponsored program, The Texas Offenders Reenty Initiative program. A major instrument of this outreach to the urban community is the nonprofit Metroplex Economic Development Corporation founded in 1998, which among other activities sponsors a training program for budding entrepreneurs. A more traditional church-related activity is the foundation of a Christian college preparatory school, Clay Academy in 1998, which is in turn designed to be the centerpiece of a 1,000 single-family homes development. Jakes thus places himself in the tradition of religious teaching and social uplift characteristic of many black churches.

While there are doubters who label Jakes's preaching only a diluted version of pop psychology with the end goal of wealth and prosperity, detractors and admirers must agree that he is a master marketer. His message reverberates with many persons and helps them turn their lives around. The belief that individual moral reform is sufficient to create a better world is a weakness he shares with many evangelical believers. It is not yet clear how far he can go to find and hold a widening audience and whether his work will be more enduring than that of a long line of evangelical Christian reformers beginning with Charles Grandisson Finney in the nineteenth century.

## Sources

Dooley, Tara. "Women 'Shout to God'; 43,000 Flock to Reliant for a Revival." *Houston Chronicle*, July 18, 2003.

Freeman, Helaine R. "Making 'Loosed Women' of Them Bishop T. D. Jakes Brings His Gospel of New Life through Freedom from the Past to an Enthusiastic Crowd in Houston." *Arkansas Democrat-Gazette*, August 2, 2003.

Gruen, Dietrich, and Ralph G. Zerbonia. "Thomas 'T. D.' Jakes." *Contemporary Black Biography*. Vol. 43. Detroit: Gale Research, 2004.

Kehr, Dave. "Woman, Thou Art Loosed" (movie review). *New York Times*, October 1, 2004.

Niebur, Gustav, and Laurie Goodstein. "The Preachers: A Special Report; New Wave of Evangelists Vying for National Pulpit." *New York Times*, January 1, 1999.

The Potter's House. http://www.thepottershouse.org.

"T. D. Jakes." http://religiousmovements.lib.virginia.edu/nrms/jakes.html.

"T. D. Jakes' Musical Stage Play 'Cover Girls' Hits the Road for 2004." *Business Wire*, December 3, 2003.

Winner, Lauren F. "T. D. Jakes Feels Your Pain." *Christianity Today* 44 (February 7, 2000): 52–59.

*Robert L. Johns*

# Earvin "Magic" Johnson Jr. (1959– ), Basketball Player, Theater Chain Owner, AIDS Activist

Earvin "Magic" Johnson Jr., known for his basketball skills in the 1970s and 1980s, is now one of the top entrepreneurs in the country. After leaving basketball, Johnson has opened theaters in distressed areas of the city, signed agreements to sponsor franchises in Atlanta, Dallas, Miami, and Birmingham, Alabama, and as a developer has set his sights on acquiring residential and commercial property such as building coffee shops, restaurants, and movie theaters in urban areas of downtown Atlanta.

The sixth of ten children, Johnson was born in Lansing, Michigan, to Earvin Johnson Sr., an autoworker, and Christine Johnson, a cafeteria worker. Growing up in a large family was something Johnson enjoyed. Having the encouragement of his family and friends, the happiness on Johnson's face radiated when he smiled. A reporter gave him the name "Magic."

The six-feet-nine-inch Johnson led Michigan State University to a National Collegiate Athletic Association (NCAA) championship in 1977–1978.

In the 1979 NCAA championship game, Johnson was matched against Larry Bird, a longtime rival, in which Bird's team defeated Michigan. The two would meet again during the National Basketball Association (NBA) finals.

From Michigan State University, Johnson accepted an offer from the Los Angeles Lakers in 1980. There Johnson set numerous records. His rookie year in the sixth game of the 1980 finals, Johnson was named Most Valuable Player, a reporter described his performance as "the most extraordinary show in playoff history." Johnson scored forty-two points, fifteen rebounds, seven assists, three steals, and one blocked shot. Lakers veteran player Kareem Abdul-Jabbar was sidelined by an injury. Bird, a team player from the Boston Celtics, would win the Rookie of the Year Award.

With Pat Riley the coach, the Lakers would win their second championship in three years. Johnson's short-lived basketball career waned in the beginning. Many felt his salary contract was overwhelming for a rookie player. A squabble between Johnson and head coach Pat Westhead over a change in strategy resulted in the coach's firing. Many Lakers' fans were unhappy and several seasons booed Johnson. But rising to the occasion, the Lakers, under head coach Pat Riley, won the championship in 1982, and Johnson won the Most Valuable Player in the series.

Fame, fortune, and the lack of privacy that many top athletes and stars experience also embraced Johnson. Johnson traveled with body guards and lived in a guarded estate. According to *Contemporary Black Biography*, Johnson once commented that "the glitter is part of it, but so are the people with schemes, the thieves running scams; so are the people who want to get so close that it becomes scary. There is never a normal day."

During a routine physical examination for an insurance policy sought by the Los Angeles Lakers team, Johnson was found to have the human immunodeficiency virus (HIV), the virus that leads to AIDS (acquired immunodeficiency syndrome). This was a turning point in Johnson's life. He had married his longtime girlfriend Earleatha "Cookie" Kelly. Johnson continued to play basketball despite the diagnosis. Later, Johnson would become a spokesperson for the HIV virus.

Johnson participated in the 1992 NBA All-Star game and in the summer was selected for the Olympics team. The "Dream Team" at the Olympics won all eight of their games and received a medal in the event. Johnson would retire from basketball but would try to make a comeback; at the end of the 1995–1996 season, he would finally exit the game that he loved.

## BECOMES AN ENTREPRENEUR

Johnson's life after basketball would prove to be even more fruitful. Johnson started a development corporation. In 1990 Johnson purchased the Pepsi-Cola distribution plant in Forestville, Maryland. The Johnson Development Corporation in the ensuing years partnered with Loews Cineplex Entertainment to build movie complexes in Los Angeles, Houston, Atlanta,

Harlem, and Cleveland. Johnson met with Starbucks chief executive officer Howard Schultz to franchise the business in eight stores located in the inner city and urban locations.

Several years later, Johnson had business associations with Fatburger and opened a series of twenty-four-hour Magic Johnson Sports Clubs. Johnson tried his hand in film and television, as executive producer of the film *Brown Sugar* in 2002. Television shows *Who's Got Game* and *The Magic Hour* were shows that lasted only a few seasons.

In 2003, Johnson opened the eleventh Magic Johnson HP Inventor Center at the Black Child and Family Institute in Lansing, Michigan. Through the Magic Johnson Foundation the centers offer training and skill development and access to online services for Lansing area youths and adults. The center is founded by HP (Hewlett-Packard); the initiative has already established ten centers in Los Angeles, Washington, Atlanta, Harlem, Chicago, and Houston.

Introduced in 2004, Johnson and NASCAR have a program to invite more minorities into stock car racing as participants and audiences. "Magic," the program's name, will draw minorities to the sport from the grassroots, sparking interest for future generations.

Also introduced in 2004 is the MAGIC Cash card, a Bank of America project, which carries Visa's logo and Johnson's picture. The intent of the card is to offer a stored value Visa from start-up Celebrity Cards International, which will divert business from check-cashers and bring electronic payment services to customers.

In 2005, Johnson in partnership with Canyon Capital Realty (Canyon-Johnson Urban Fund II) has teamed up with two companies Daniel Realty Corporation and Selig Enterprises to build Plaza Midtown in downtown Atlanta. Units are expected to sell for $600,000. The complex will have 452 condo units and 70,000 square feet of retail space. The location of the 3.3-acre site is along Peachtree Place, near Technology Square.

Johnson's life after basketball has been a success, with several initiatives through the Johnson Development Corporation. Talk show host, motivational speaker, and all-around nice guy, Johnson has remained a central figure owing to his success in basketball and business. A pursuer of worthy causes, Johnson has brought jobs and businesses to minority communities. Despite retiring nearly twenty years ago from basketball, Johnson remains a headliner.

**Sources**

Canyon-Johnson Closes on New $600 Million Canyon-Johnson Urban Fund II; Successor to CJUF I Continues Tradition of Urban Development. *Business Wire*. http://www.findarticles.com/p/articles/mi_m0EIN/is_2005_March_23/ai_n13466340.

de Paula, Matthew. "Magic's a Downtown Hit. Now He's Got a Card." *US Banker* 114 (June 2004): 28.

Johnson, Earvin, Jr. *Contemporary Black Biography*. Vol. 39. Gale Group, 2003. Reproduced in Biography Resource Center. Farmington Hills, MI: Thomson Gale, 2003. http://galenet.galegroup.com/servlet/BioRCEarvin Johnson, Jr.

McMullen, Troy. "Magic's Atlanta Play." *Wallstreet Journal*, October 8, 2004.

Roach, Ronald. "Magic Johnson Foundation, HP Open Tech Center in Michigan." *Black Issues in Higher Education* 20 (2003): 9.

Spencer, Lee. "To Know List 5: Driving for Diversity." *Sporting News* 228 (May 13, 2004): 7.

*Marvella Rounds*

# Eunice Walker Johnson (c. 1920– ), Fashion Show Producer, Business Executive, Editor, Philanthropist

From her childhood love of making clothes for her dolls, Eunice Walker Johnson created a career in fashion. In addition to editing *Ebony* magazine's fashion column, she produces and directs its popular Ebony Fashion Fair each year. According to Wormley and colleagues, in "Uncovering History," one study of African American consumers identified five areas of impact of Ebony Fashion Fair and *Ebony* magazine: promoting a positive image for blacks and encouraging their potential; providing increased career opportunities in modeling, fashion designing, photography, and entertaining; generating millions of dollars for black charities and scholarships; highlighting blacks' interests beyond fashion in such areas as politics, business, entertainment, and social events; and changing white perceptions of blacks as consumers.

Johnson's investment in education, religion, and social causes seems rooted in family heritage. Her grandfather William H. McAlpine founded and served as president of Selma University in Alabama and the National Baptist Convention U.S.A. Her father, Nathaniel D. Walker, a firm believer in education, paid his way through school to become a physician. Her mother, Ethel McAlpine Walker, served as a high school principal and taught art and education at Selma University. Her two brothers became physicians and her sister a professor.

Johnson, in "Backstage," also attributes her love of fashion to her family's "history of beauty and excellence." Early in her Selma childhood, Johnson developed a love of crafting clothes for her doll collection. She wanted her dolls to be dressed well and built the best collection among her friends. By the time she was eight years old, she could make her own clothes, shirts for her father, and fur-collared coats. She entered and won many sewing contests, content to rip out seams until she got them right.

In college, Johnson studied social work while continuing her interest in fashion. She earned her B.A. degree from Alabama's Talladega College, with a major in sociology and minor in art. At Loyola University in Chicago, she worked toward a master's degree in social work. Further education included studies of great books at the University of Chicago and graduate courses in journalism at Northwestern University. She also studied at the Ray-Vogue School of Interior Design.

In 1941, Johnson married fellow Loyola student **John H. Johnson**. A son of sharecroppers, he founded the Johnson Publishing Company. Together, the Johnsons created *Negro Digest*, which later changed its name to *Black World*. In 1945, they began *Ebony*, a *Life*-like magazine targeted to the African American population. The Johnson Company also distributes *Jet*, *Black Stars*, and *Ebony, Jr.* magazines, publishes books, and owns Radio Station WJPC in Chicago. In 1973, the Johnsons formed Fashion Fair Cosmetics, which features skin care products designed specifically for the black complexion.

Johnson Publishing Company grew to become the largest black publishing company worldwide. While her husband filled the role of publisher and chairman, Johnson served as secretary-treasurer. She chose the name *Ebony* and edits its fashion column. The couple's daughter, **Linda Johnson Rice**, now serves as president and chief executive officer (CEO) of the company. Their son, John Jr., once a photographer for *Ebony* and *Jet*, died in 1981 at the age of twenty-five.

The idea for *Ebony*'s Fashion Fair originated in 1956 when Jessie Dent, wife of then Dillard University president Albert Dent, asked the publishing company to sponsor a fund-raiser for the Women's Auxiliary of New Orleans' Flint-Goodrich Hospital. Based on the success of the project, the Johnsons decided to take the event on the road to raise funds for other charities. Freda DeKnight, who edited the food and fashion section of *Ebony* at the time, organized the first national tour in 1958. Four models toured ten cities. At her husband's request to handle production of the show temporarily, Eunice Johnson began directing the Fashion Fair in 1961. Her eye for beauty, her knowledge of fashion, and her commitment to excellence soon captured national and then international recognition.

Johnson supervises the hiring and training of models and travels to Europe a couple of times each year "to buy clothes for five-foot-nine dolls," she said in "Backstage." She quickly caught the attention of designers by purchasing, rather than borrowing, her selections. The show, which includes everyday wear as well as high fashion, features the work of the world's top designers. Black designers like Steven Burrows, B. Michael, and Quinton de Alexander display their work alongside those of Givenchy, Oscar de La Renta, Christian LaCroix, and Pierre Cardin. Models from host cities often join well-known models on the runway. Each year the show builds around a theme, which Johnson selects.

Sponsoring organizations determine the cost of each ticket, which covers expenses, includes subscriptions to *Ebony* and *Jet*, and makes a contribution to a charity or scholarship. The Fashion Fair has raised millions of dollars for sponsors such as the United Negro College Fund (UNCF), the New York Urban League, and the National Association for the Advancement of Colored People (NAACP) as well as for local social and civic organizations.

Cities have hosted the fair in such diverse locations as high school gymnasiums and municipal auditoriums.

On two occasions, U.S. presidents have enlisted Johnson's service. Richard M. Nixon invited her to accompany his wife Patricia as a special ambassador to William R. Tolbert Jr.'s inauguration as president of Liberia. Gerald Ford selected her as the only African American in a blue-ribbon press corps of 200 that accompanied him to China, Japan, the Philippines, and Indonesia.

Johnson has made time to take part in a number of educational, cultural, and civic organizations. She has served on the board of directors of Selma University, Talladega College, and the Women's Division of the United Negro College Fund and on the advisory board of Harvard University School of Business. She has served on the board of trustees for the Coty American Fashion Critics Award and as a member of the National Foundation for the Fashion Industry. She sits on the Women's Board of both the Art Institute and the Lyric Opera of Chicago.

Johnson's dedication to education and the **fashion industry** have prompted numerous honors. In 1988, Chicago's Boys and Girls Club named her Chicagoan of the Year. In 1999, Turner Broadcasting System presented her its Trumpet Award for career excellence and contributions to the quality of African American life. In 2000, the Art Institute of Chicago honored her at its opening gala for its exhibit titled "To Conserve a Legacy: American Art from Historically Black Colleges and Universities." In 2001, the United Negro College Fund bestowed its **Frederick D. [Douglas] Patterson** Award for her support of education and the mission of the organization. In 2002, UNCF chose her for their Harold H. Hines Benefactor's Award. Several colleges have granted Johnson honorary degrees: Talladega, Selma, and Shaw. Talladega College renamed its social sciences and education department for her.

The child who loved to make clothes for her dolls not only became one of the world's best-dressed ladies but also came to produce and direct the world's largest traveling fashion show. In doing the work that she loves, she has influenced the international fashion industry, raised significant funds for charities, boosted the careers of numerous black women and men, and helped raise the self-esteem of a generation of black young people.

*See also*: Retail Industry; Women and Business

**Sources**
"Backstage." *Ebony* 43 (February 1988): 28.
"GM Salutes the 45th Ebony Fashion Fair Tour." *Ebony* 57 (October 2002): 35–40.
Smith, Jessie Carney. "Eunice Walker Johnson." *Notable Black American Women*. Detroit: Gale Research, 1992.
"UNCF Honors Ebony Fashion Fair Producer/Director." *Ebony* 56 (June 2001): 94–96.
Wormley, J. Carlyne, Barbara Heinzerling, and Virginia Gunn. "Uncovering History: An Examination of the Impact of the Ebony Fashion Fair and Ebony Magazine." *Consumer Interests Annual* 44 (1998): 148–150.

*Marie Garrett*

# John H. Johnson (1918–2005), Publisher, Entrepreneur, Philanthropist

John Harold Johnson, the grandson of slaves, was the founder, publisher, and chairman of Johnson Publishing Company, Inc. (JPC), which is the largest African American–owned and –operated publishing company. JPC is the corporate home of *Ebony*, the number one African American magazine with more than 12 million readers each month; *Jet*, the number one African American news weekly with more than 9 million readers; and JPC's Book Division, with Lerone Bennett Jr., prominent journalist, social historian, and *Ebony* executive editor emeritus, as the premier author. JPC also produces two spin-offs: Fashion Fair Cosmetics, the largest African American–owned cosmetics company, and Ebony Fashion Fair, the largest traveling fashion show. The Chicago-based JPC, located at 820 South Michigan Avenue, also has offices in Detroit, Los Angeles, New York, Washington, D.C., London, and Paris. For more than sixty years, JPC has been one of the most successful African American–owned businesses, and for decades, JPC has been one of the largest black-owned businesses. Johnson's vision of African American publications that promote black achievement, pride, and heritage broke through the American media's racial barriers as well as led to Madison's Avenue realization that African American consumers cannot be ignored. Johnson's implementation of his dream has earned him recognition as an African American publishing mogul, the preeminent African American businessman of the twentieth and early twenty-first centuries, and the first African American to be included on Forbes' list of the 400 wealthiest Americans.

Johnson was born in rural Arkansas City, Arkansas, on January 19, 1918, to Leroy Johnson, a worker in a sawmill and on a levee, and Gertrude Johnson, a domestic. Leroy Johnson was killed in a sawmill accident when his son was six years old. Gertrude Johnson, the daughter of former slaves, then married James Williams, who did not provide adequate financial support for his family. Thus, Johnson's mother cooked for a dredging company crew and for levee workers. With some help from her young son, she also washed and ironed the levee workers' clothes. Eventually, Johnson helped his mother prepare the meals for the workers. Johnson graduated from Arkansas City Colored School in June 1932. There was no public school for African Americans to attend in Johnson's hometown, and his family was unable to send him to boarding school in Pine Bluff or Little Rock. Johnson's mother decided that he would continue his education in Chicago, but the family was unable to save enough money for the move before she ordered Johnson to repeat the eighth grade. That was her method of keeping Johnson away from peer pressure and menial jobs.

The family moved to Chicago in July 1933, and in September, Johnson enrolled in Wendell Phillips High School, a predominantly African American school. After the school burned down, he attended another African

American school, DuSable High. During Johnson's secondary education years, he was not the only member of the student body who would later gain fame; Nat "King" Cole, Redd Foxx, and Harold Washington were among the future celebrities who were also enrolled in the high schools. Johnson, an honors student, participated in a variety of extracurricular activities at both schools including newspaper editor, year book manager, student council president, French club member, junior class president, and senior class president. Johnson was asked to speak at his 1936 graduation ceremony, and his topic was "Builders of a New World." He was awarded a $200 scholarship to the University of Chicago.

At a 1936 Urban League luncheon held in honor of high school students, Johnson met **Harry H. Pace**, who was president of Supreme Liberty Life (SLL) Insurance Company, which was the largest African American business in the North. Pace, who was one of the most prominent African American businessmen during the first half of the twentieth century, offered Johnson a part-time job at SLL in order to help him pay his college tuition. Johnson began working as an office boy at the insurance company on September 1, 1936, and he welcomed opportunities to learn about business from Pace and the other distinguished African American businessmen at SLL. Pace assigned Johnson the task of reading periodicals and selecting articles that would be of interest to the insurance company's African American clientele. Pace, after reviewing Johnson's choices, selected articles that were reprinted in *The Guardian*, SLL's monthly publication. In 1939, Johnson, who dropped out of college, was working full-time at the insurance company. He later attended Northwestern University.

In 1940 Johnson met **Eunice Walker**, a graduate of Alabama's Talladega College, who was completing her master's degree in social work at Loyola University in Chicago. Walker, a native of Selma, Alabama, was the granddaughter of Dr. William H. McAlpine, a founder of Selma University and its second president. Walker's father, Nathaniel D. Walker, was a prominent physician; and her mother, Ethel McAlpine Walker, was a high school principal and Selma University instructor. Johnson and Walker were married in Selma on June 21, 1941. They later adopted two children: Linda and John Harold Johnson Jr., who died of sickle cell anemia in 1981 when he was twenty-five years old.

As a result of Johnson's compilation of articles for *The Guardian*, he was inspired to create an African American version of *Reader's Digest*. Although loan officers at Chicago's First National Bank told Johnson that the institution would never lend money to African Americans and influential blacks discouraged him, Johnson remained determined to publish his magazine. Three people encouraged Johnson: his mother, who allowed Johnson to use her furniture as collateral for a $500 loan; his boss, who granted Johnson access to SLL's mailing list of 20,000 policyholders in order for Johnson to ask them to buy $2 subscriptions to *Negro Digest*; and his wife, who helped Johnson with editorial, circulation, and mailing chores. Johnson's subscription offer generated $6,000 from SLL policyholders. He ran his

Negro Digest Publishing Company in a corner of attorney Earl Dickerson's law library in the SLL Building. The first issue of *Negro Digest* appeared in November 1942. Johnson mailed 3,000 copies to prepaid subscribers and asked Chicago's largest distributor to sell the remaining 2,000 copies. Johnson was rebuffed; the distributor informed him that African American reading materials were excluded from the city's newsstands because they did not sell. Johnson's reaction was to have approximately thirty employees from SLL go to various Chicago newsstands and ask for *Negro Digest*. Thus, newsstand operators began requesting Johnson's magazine from the distributor; once *Negro Digest* appeared at local newsstands, Johnson gave the SLL employees money to buy the first issue. Johnson then developed a national strategy to promote sales of *Negro Digest*, and within eight months, the periodical's circulation reached 50,000 copies. In September 1943, Johnson quit his job at the insurance company. (Years later Johnson, who became SLL's largest stockholder, was elected the company's chairman and chief executive officer, and he sold the company in 1993.) A feature of *Negro Digest* was "If I Were a Negro," written by famous whites such as Pearl Buck, Marshall Field, Edward G. Robinson, and Orson Welles. When Johnson persuaded First Lady Eleanor Roosevelt to write the column for the October 1943 issue, circulation climbed to 150,000. Also in 1943, Johnson purchased his first building at 5619 South State Street, which became the new home for the Negro Digest Publishing Company.

## PUBLISHES *EBONY* MAGAZINE

The success of *Negro Digest* led to the creation of *Ebony* after Johnson noticed that many African Americans were purchasing *Life*, a pictorial magazine. Heeding his wife's suggestion, Johnson selected *Ebony* as the title for his new publication after his wife explained that ebony is a fine black African wood. The first issue appeared in November 1945, and *Ebony* was an instant success. When the initial run of 25,000 copies sold out in mere hours, Johnson had 25,000 additional copies printed. *Ebony* quickly amassed a readership of more than 400,000 and eclipsed *Negro Digest*. Although no advertisements were included in the beginning, ads from SLL as well as major white corporations such as Armour Foods, Chesterfield, Elgin Watch, Quaker Oats, and Zenith began appearing in 1946 after Johnson persuaded white advertising and corporate executives to give *Ebony* the same consideration extended to *Look* and *Life*. In 1949, Johnson renamed the Negro Digest Publishing Company the Johnson Publishing Company and moved the headquarters to 5125 Calumet. In 1951, Johnson began publishing *Jet*, which remains the most widely read African American newsweekly. Also in 1951, Johnson retired *Negro Digest* until 1961 when it was revamped as a literary quarterly. In May 1970, *Negro Digest*, with Hoyt Fuller as editor, became *Black World*. While *Ebony* and *Jet* document the civil rights struggles of the 1950s, 1960s, and beyond, *Black World* contributed to the Black Arts

Movement in the 1960s. The last issue of *Black World* appeared in April 1976. Over the decades, JPC has published at least five other magazines that were short-lived: *Hue, Tan Confessions, Ebony Jr., Ebony Man,* and *Ebony South Africa.*

In addition to *Ebony* and *Jet,* other JPC brands are its Book Division, Ebony Fashion Fair, and Fashion Fair Cosmetics. Although JPC printed its first book in 1945, additional books were not published until the Book Division was established in the early 1960s. Among its publications is Lerone Bennett Jr.'s classic *Before the Mayflower: A History of Black America* (1962; 7th rev. ed., 2003). JPC's success is not limited to magazines and books. Eunice Johnson is the creator, producer, and director of the annual Ebony Fashion Fair, which since 1958 has featured African Americans modeling the latest creations by American and European designers, with the proceeds going to various non-profit groups in approximately 200 cities. When Johnson and his wife noticed that the Fashion Fair models had to blend cosmetics to match their skin tones, they asked cosmetic companies to create products for African American women. After their attempts to persuade the cosmetic executives proved futile, the Johnsons went to a laboratory that created Fashion Fair Cosmetics in 1973. The makeup is currently sold in department stores throughout the United States and in foreign countries such as Africa, Canada, the Caribbean, England, and France.

JPC's influence also extends to the broadcasting industry. The company created television shows such as the *Ebony Music Awards* and *American Black Achievement Awards,* as well as the *Ebony/Jet Showcase,* which was a weekly variety show. Johnson invested in a Chicago cable franchise, and with his purchase of WGRT, he became the first African American to own a radio station in Chicago. Johnson renamed the station WJPC. Following that, he bought and sold several radio stations.

Johnson was a member of the board of various business corporations such as Arthur D. Little, Bell and Howell, Chrysler Corporation, Conrail, Continental Bank, Dillard Department Stores, Supreme Life Insurance Company, Twentieth Century Fox Film Corporation, VIAD Corporation, and Zenith Electronics Corporation.

Johnson was a consultant to America's top politicians. He accompanied Vice President Richard Nixon on trips to nine African countries in 1957 and to Russia and Poland in 1959. Johnson was appointed as special U.S. ambassador to the Independence Ceremonies of the Ivory Coast in 1961 by President John F. Kennedy; special U.S. ambassador to the Independence Ceremonies of Kenya in 1963, by President Lyndon Johnson; a member of the National Selective Service Commission in 1966, by President Johnson; and a member of the President's Commission for the Observance of the 25th Anniversary of the United Nations in 1970, by President Nixon.

Throughout the decades, Johnson received numerous accolades. In 2005, the John H. Johnson Cultural and Educational Museum, which is a replica of Johnson's childhood home, was dedicated in Arkansas City, Johnson's hometown. Arkansas City will also be the site of the John H. Johnson Cultural and Entrpreneurial Center, and the University of Arkansas at Pine Bluff will house an academic complex in Johnson's name. In 2003, Howard University named its journalism school the John H. Johnson School of Communications in honor of Johnson's $4 million contribution to the school earlier in the year.

Johnson received honorary doctorates from at least thirty-one institutions of higher learning including Carnegie-Mellon Institute, Harvard University, Howard University, Morehouse College, and Northwestern University. He was inducted into the Chicago Business Hall of Fame, 1983; Black Press Hall of Fame, 1987; Publishing Hall of Fame, 1987; Chicago Journalism Hall of Fame, 1990; Junior Achievement Hall of Fame, 1997; and the Arkansas Business Hall of Fame, 2001. In 1996, President Bill Clinton presented Johnson with the Presidential Medal of Freedom. Among Johnson's additional honors were the Black Journalists Lifetime Achievement Award, Chicagoan of the Year Award, Columbia Journalism Award, Founders Award from the National Conference of Christians and Jews, the Distinguished Service Award from Harvard University Graduate School of Business Administration, Robie Award from the Jackie Robinson Foundation, the National Association for the Advancement of Colored People's Spingarn Medal, National Press Foundation Award, and Wall Street Journal Dow Jones Entrepreneurial Excellence Award. In 1987, *Black Enterprise* named Johnson entrepreneur of the decade, and in 1997, the magazine cited Johnson as one of its five marathon men or "captains of the industry" in recognition of Johnson's inclusion on each *Black Enterprise* "100 list" during the magazine's first twenty-five years.

Today JPC remains a family corporation. Until his death on Monday, August 1, 2005, Johnson was the publisher and chairman. His daughter **Linda Johnson Rice** is the president and chief executive officer, and his wife Eunice is the secretary-treasurer and director of Ebony Fashion Fair.

*See also*: Fashion Industry; Advertising and Marketing; Retail Industry

**Sources**

Dingle, Derek T. "John H. Johnson: Johnson Publishing Company, Inc.: The Pioneer." *Black Enterprise Titans of the B.E. 100s: Black CEOs Who Redefined and Conquered American Business.* New York: John Wiley and Sons, 1999.

Ingham, John N., and Lynne B. Feldman. "John Harold Johnson." *African-American Business Leaders: A Biographical Dictionary.* Westport, CT: Greenwood Press, 1994.

"John H. Johnson." *Contemporary Black Biography.* Vol. 3. Gale Research, 1992. Reproduced in Biography Resource Center. Farmington Hills, MI: Thomson Gale, 2005. http://galenet.galegroup.com/servlet/BioRC.

Johnson, John H., with Lerone Bennett Jr. *Succeeding against the Odds: The Autobiography of a Great American Businessman.* New York: Warner Books, 1989.

Smith, Jessie Carney, ed. "John H. Johnson." *Notable Black American Men.* Detroit: Gale Research, 1999.

*Linda M. Carter*

## Magic Johnson. *See* Earvin "Magic" Johnson Jr.

## Robert L. Johnson (1946– ), Entrepreneur

Robert L. Johnson is an entrepreneur who amassed a great deal of money as the founder of BET (formerly Black Entertainment Television), which he sold in 2001 to Viacom for $2.33 billion and Viacom's assumption of $570 million in debt. His 63 percent holding of BET netted him $1.5 billion in Viacom stock, increasing his personal wealth to $1.63 billion. He thus became the first black billionaire, placing at number 172 on the "Forbes 400" list of the richest Americans. BET was the core of Johnson's financial ventures; many of his other entrepreneurial efforts, however, have met with less success. In the black community he has a mixed reputation: There is pride in his achievement in attaining great wealth mixed with disapproval for allegedly fostering a degrading image of blacks through the programming on BET, coupled with his failure to assume a highly visible "uplifting" leadership role.

Johnson was born on April 8, 1946, in Hickory, Mississippi, the ninth of ten children in a working-class family, which moved to Freeport, Illinois, by the early 1960s. He became the only one of the children to graduate from college, receiving his B.A. from the University of Illinois in 1968 and an M.A. in public administration from Princeton in 1972. In 1969 Johnson married Sheila Crump, daughter of a Chicago neurosurgeon. She is a talented musician and music educator. The couple adopted two children and divorced in 2002.

After his graduation from Princeton, Johnson worked for the Corporation for Public Television and the Washington branch of the Urban League and in 1973 became press secretary to Walter E. Fauntroy, then a nonvoting delegate to Congress from the District of Columbia. In 1976 he went to work for the National Cable Television Association, a lobbying organization, as vice president for government affairs. This last position gave Johnson a knowledge of the industry that served him well when he established Black Entertainment Television in late 1979.

Johnson borrowed $15,000 and secured two hours a week television time for free. A major infusion of capital came from Tele-Communications Incorporated, headed by John C. Malone, who was interested in access to the black urban audience and thus in Johnson's black cable channel. Malone's company invested $500,000, a sum that gave it in due time a 35 percent stake in the new company. That minority share was intact and controlled by another Malone company, Liberty Media, when BET was sold to Viacom in 2001; the sale brought Liberty Media $800 million in Viacom stock.

Beginning with two hours of programming late Friday nights, BET became a twenty-four-hour operation on October 1, 1984. It presented a mixed bag of programming at first, featuring movies and sports from black schools.

MTV, founded a year later than BET, quickly built a spectacular success on pop and rock videos. MTV, however, neglected black artists, whose studios usually failed to produce high-quality videotapes for them. Johnson grasped the opening and featured gospel, rhythm and blues, and soul. The newly emerging genre of rap also entered the mix. As rap skyrocketed to success, so did BET, which shed its former name Black Entertainment Television in favor of the letters at the same time as it actively portrayed itself as the black community's own channel. (The change was pragmatic, aimed to overcome buyer resistance from cable franchises with small numbers of black viewers.) In 1986 the company earned a small profit for the first time. The profits rose rapidly thereafter.

Increasingly, music videos became a staple of programming. As the popularity of hip-hop took off in the 1990s, BET became a major force in the music business. By 1996 over 60 percent of the airtime was filled by music videos, a percentage that continued to creep upward. While immensely popular, the channel was disparaged by some blacks for its alleged single-minded focus on sex in music. Many went on to complain that rap and hip-hop presented an unfavorable image of blacks in general and especially demeaned black women. Beginning in 1999, for example, such criticism surfaced in the comic strips in Aaron McGruder's "The Boondocks." Still BET presented news, public service programs, children's programs, and other features of interest to blacks even as it continued to rely on music and other types of programming with mass appeal for most of its programming and profits.

Critics also pointed out that BET paid its entertainers much less that comparable white entertainers received. For example, the hit *Comic View* was produced for about $18,500 per hour show. Established black comedians avoided appearing on the channel because of the pay scale. While charges were made against the content of BET, behind the scenes it became a cradle of black executives and producers in entertainment. In an industry still dominated by white men, of its current 290 employees, 96 percent are black and 52 percent women.

The rapid growth of the channel was supported by the growth of cable networking in urban areas, which made its programming increasingly available for its targeted audience. From 1990 to 1998 BET added around 4 million subscribers a year. In 1991 it was the first black-owned company traded on the New York Stock Exchange. Still it soon became clear to the market that the market for its entertainment was becoming saturated. In order to sustain growth at past levels, BET needed to move into new fields. Johnson, conceiving of BET as a brand identity, tried to expand into such areas as restaurants, credit cards, skin-care products, and movies, in addition to establishing such new cable networks such as BET on Jazz. Still BET's failure to convince investors that it had a viable and coherent diversification scheme caused its stock to perform below expectations, and Johnson took the company private in 1998.

## SELLS BET TO VIACOM

Then in January 2001 Viacom purchased BET for $2.9 billion. Johnson and his chief operating officer, **Debra Louise Lee**, continued in their positions with BET under a five-year contract. Johnson did not actively seek the sale, but when the opportunity arose, he found it too advantageous to refuse. The news dismayed some people: They felt that blacks were giving up the possibility of control of what was presented on television to unsympathetic and greedy white capitalists bent on exploiting the black community. The ownership controversy flared up again in March when Johnson fired Tavis Smiley, the popular host of *BET Tonight*. Johnson resisted a firestorm of criticism and refused to alter his decision.

After selling BET Johnson continued to explore other avenues in business, most notably in trying to develop a new airline. This effort fell through due to an unfavorable regulatory decision by the Federal Aviation Authority. In 2002 Johnson won much publicity when he became the first black to become a principal owner of a major sports team. The National Basketball Association awarded him the expansion franchise for Charlotte, North Carolina, after Johnson made full use of his negotiating skills, contacts, and financial worth in his pitch to the organization. The team began to play in the 2004–2005 season, and it will take all Johnson's skills, along with the continuation of favorable conditions in the market, to build up a profitable franchise.

Johnson deployed considerable skills in building up a major business, enriching himself in the process. He became for some an icon for black achievement, which in turn led him to be judged differently from the general run of entrepreneurs. Some people were incensed by BET's seemingly endless programming of gyrating pelvises and raunchy lyrics and called on him to abandon profit for uplift. Many of the same people who strongly disapproved of what he was doing were equally vocal in condemning him when he gave up ownership of BET to Viacom. What is certain is that Johnson is one of the most spectacular exemplars of the rags-to-riches story of the present day.

**Sources**

Hughes, Alan. "Slam Dunk! How Billionaire Bob Johnson Is Making History As the First African American to Aquire an NBA Basketball Franchise." *Black Enterprise* 33 (March 2003): 94–102.

Jones, Joyce. "BETting on Black." *Black Enterprise* 31 (January 2001): 58–61.

McAdams, Deborah D. "More Than a Music Channel." *Broadcasting & Cable* 130 (October 30, 2000): 46–50.

Pulley, Brett. *The Billion Dollar BET: Robert Johnson and the Inside Story of Black Entertainment Television.* New York: Wiley, 2004.

Sandomir, Richard. "Founder of TV Network Becomes First Black Owner in Major Sports." *New York Times*, December 19, 2002.

Whitford, David. "Taking BET Back from the Street." *Fortune* 138 (November 9, 1998): 167–170.

*Robert L. Johns*

# Caroline R. Jones (1942–2001), Advertising Executive

The president and creative director of the trailblazing company Mingo-Jones Advertising, Caroline R. Jones was one of the highest-ranking minority women in her field. She was a practicing advocate of diversity in advertising, as demonstrated when she left her first employer because of its indifference to diversity. She worked her way up the creative ranks in some of New York's major **advertising agencies**. She is said to have blended sophistication and soul in her advertising campaigns, and throughout her career, she was an inspiration to women and people of color whom she sought to persuade to enter the advertising industry.

Caroline Robinson Jones was born in Benton Harbor, Michigan, on February 15, 1942. She was the first of ten children born to Ernest and Mattie Robinson. As she grew up, she read widely. She was an entrepreneur early on; to earn money, she sold magazine subscriptions, greeting cards, potholders, and cosmetics. She also picked berries during summer months. Although very enterprising, suggesting an interest in business, Jones was determined to become an orthopedic surgeon. After graduating from high school in 1959, when she was just seventeen years old, she entered the University of Michigan as a premed student and with the support of a scholarship. She performed well in her courses but reconsidered her plan for medicine after fainting at the sight of a dead cat on a dissection table in an anatomy class. By the end of her second year, she changed to a dual degree program—science and English. Jones graduated in 1963 with a Bachelor of Arts degree. Realizing that employment opportunities were limited, she enhanced her career options by earning teaching credentials. While attending a career fair on campus, she met a representative from the J. Walter Thompson advertising firm in New York City, and her career in advertising would begin to take shape the next year.

In 1964, Jones moved to New York and joined Thompson in a beginning position as secretary. She volunteered for extra work in the firm and learned as much as she could about the business and advertising; her ambitions led to a promotion as secretary for a top creative director—J. Walter Thompson—who would become her mentor. Jones was also given a job as an interviewer in the consumer research department and eventually joined a copywriting team at the agency, becoming the first African American to hold the post. She realized also that assertiveness and aggressiveness would get her ahead. Jones forged ahead, studying successful advertising campaigns, examining their color, design, and word count; as a result, she knew the advertising business inside out. Her new knowledge would serve her well. Jones was promoted to supervisor of the Consumer Research Group. Now in the late 1960s, she knew that great black icons such as Martin Luther King and Muhammad Ali were popular, and she suggested a need to use more black images in advertising. As well, the slogan "Black is Beautiful" was widely recognized and accepted in the black community. But Thompson was unyielding, which prompted Jones to leave the company after a five-year stint.

In 1968 Jones cofounded Zebra Associates, a fully black-owned advertising agency; it was one of the first such firms to target African Americans. As vice president and cocreative director, she found it difficult to mix work and her new life as wife and mother and left two years later to become senior copywriter for Eckhardt Advertising. By now her experience in advertising had grown substantially, and she left that firm in 1973 to help found the Black Creative Group. A pioneer in black consumer marketing, she served as creative director from 1972 to 1975 and became vice president of the internationally known Batten, Barton, Durstine, Osborn (BBDO) Worldwide, New York. There she helped to create campaigns for Campbell's Soups and other well-known companies and was the first African American woman vice president at a major agency.

As yet disconcerted over the continued racial inequality in advertising, Jones wanted to make a drastic and immediate change in the way the industry operated. Thus, in 1977 she left and cofounded Mingo, Jones, Guilmenot, which later became Mingo-Jones Advertising. The agency is best known for the slogan it developed for Kentucky Fried Chicken (as it was known then): "We do chicken right." This was one of the first times a minority agency had created an idea that became the mainstream slogan for a company.

Jones left the company in 1986 to work on her own; she formed Caroline Jones Advertising and developed an impressive list of clients that included American Express, Anheuser-Busch, McDonald's, Toys "R" Us, the U.S. Postal Service, Westinghouse Electric, and Prudential. She was widely sought to speak before business symposia, colleges and universities, and elsewhere, and she lectured on her struggles as a black woman in an industry that had been hostile to women and to blacks. She had become a role model, and others wanted to know how she rose from secretary to the pinnacle of the advertising world.

In 1994, Jones's company voluntarily filed for Chapter 11 bankruptcy protection, in an effort to overcome the $1 million client arrears accounts and to put pressure on many companies that owed her money. In that same year her company won an assignment to prepare a public service campaign to inform blacks how to file a claim against the parent company of Denny's Inc. The South Carolina restaurant chain had agreed to settle a racial discrimination lawsuit by paying $54 million. She also served emerging African governments by providing them with business strategies.

Outside of advertising, Jones hosted radio and television programs, such as *Focusing on the Black Women* and *In the Black: Keys to Success.* She endowed a scholarship in her name at her alma mater, the University of Michigan. Her memberships include the New York State Banking Board and the advisory committee of the Women's Bank of New York and boards of the New York City Partnerships, Eureka Communications, the Advertising Council, the National Association for the Advancement of Colored People (NAACP), and the National Urban League. Her recognitions were in advertising and business, from Clio, a Galaxy Award for Public Relations, a Cannes Film Festival Award, and an Obie Award.

A divorcee with one son, Anthony R. Jones, she died of cancer in New York City on June 28, 2001. Her son planned to continue the firm to keep her name and her legacy as a pioneer and successful African American woman in advertising. Jones is remembered as a polished, intelligent, and articulate woman who sought and achieved perfectionism in her work.

*See also*: Advertising and Marketing; Women and Business

**Sources**

Brennan, Carol. "Caroline Robinson Jones." *Notable Black American Women*. Book III. Ed. Jessie Carney Smith. Detroit: Gale Research, 2003.

Elliott, Stuart. "Caroline Jones, 59, Founder of Black-Run Ad Companies" (obituary). *New York Times*, July 8, 2001.

LaBalle, Candace. "Caroline R. Jones." *Contemporary Black Biography*. Vol. 29. Detroit: Gale Research, 2002.

Vagnoni, Anthony. " 'Role Model' Jones, 59, Dies." *Advertising Age* 72 (July 16, 2001): 4.

*Jessie Carney Smith*

# John Jones (1816–1879), Tailor, Civil Rights Activist, Politician

John Jones was one of the first African Americans to establish a business in downtown Chicago; his thriving cleaning and tailoring shop made him one of the wealthiest African Americans in the country. He was also active in civil rights and politics: He established his home as a terminal on the Underground Railroad; was vice president of the Colored National Convention of free black men; was president of the first Black Illinois State Convention held in Chicago; became the state's first black notary public; and as Cook County commissioner, was the first black elected to public office in Chicago.

Born on a plantation in Greene County, North Carolina, on November 3, 1816, Jones was the son of John Bromfield, a German, and a free mulatto woman named Jones. Her first name is unknown. His mother's status as a free black meant that John Jones was also born free. Fearing that Bromfield or his family might enslave her son, she protected his status by apprenticing Jones to a man named Shepard, who saw that he received training as a tailor. Later Shepard relocated to Tennessee, where he bound Jones over to Richard Clere, a tailor who lived in the Memphis area. He trained well and became an experienced tailor; when Clere's business became slow, however, he often hired out Jones to work with other tailors in the area.

In 1841 Jones met and fell in love with Mary Jane Richardson, daughter of Elijah Richardson, a free blacksmith in Memphis. The Richardsons moved to Alton, Illinois, while Jones remained in Memphis for three years to complete his apprenticeship and to become financially secure. Sometimes Jones used his father's last name, becoming John Bromfield. He obtained his free papers from North Carolina and then petitioned the Eleventh District court in Tennessee to free him from Clere's service and custody. By 1844, when he was age twenty-seven, he had saved approximately $100; with both economic and legal freedom, he moved to Alton and married Richardson. The Joneses decided to relocate to Chicago to work in a climate that was more favorable to blacks than Alton and to become active with the abolitionist movement. Although they were free, they complied with Illinois law that required free blacks and mulattos to obtain a certificate of freedom and to post a $1,000 bond for the privilege of traveling and living in the state. In March 1845 the Joneses, including their only child Lavinia, traveled by stage and canal and reached Chicago on March 11.

Jones became one of Chicago's first black entrepreneurs in March 1845, soon after his arrival in the city. His home at 119 Dearborn was the site of his business known as J. Jones, Clothes Dresser and Repairer. Some sources claim that at first they lived in a one-room cottage at Wells and Madison Streets and opened their business a few blocks away. A skilled tailor, he soon had a thriving enterprise and catered to many of Chicago's elite. By 1860 his business was called Clothes Cleaning and Repairing Room and, by his claims, was the city's oldest and best business enterprise. His wealth had increased from the mere $3.50 that he had when he reached Chicago to between $85,000 and $100,000. Although he lost money during the Great Chicago Fire of 1871, he continued to be recognized as one of the country's wealthiest African Americans. As well, from the 1850s until he died, Jones was undisputed leader of black Chicago.

## JOINS THE ABOLITIONIST MOVEMENT

Without formal education, Jones knew that he needed fundamental reading and writing skills to manage his business venture and to enable him to operate in the abolitionist's activities that he found appealing. Under Chicago abolitionist and noted lawyer Lemanuel Covell Paine Freer, Jones learned to read and write. Another Chicago abolitionist, physician Charles V. Dyer also befriended Jones and Freer and Dyer remained steadfast friends with Jones the rest of his life. Jones also became active in the abolitionist movement by opening his home, now at 43 Ray Street, as the second major station on the Underground Railroad—the first having been established at Quinn Chapel, Chicago's oldest African Methodist Episcopal church. From that station many slaves escaped to Canada for freedom. Jones hosted several abolitionists such as **Frederick Douglass**, John Brown, and Wendell

Phillips. Jones also had developed a powerful pen and voice and used these skills to lash out in support of the black struggle.

Jones distinguished himself in the black convention movement beginning August 7, 1848, when he was elected vice president of the Colored National Convention; Frederick Douglass was elected president. As a delegate to the Cleveland conference held in September that year, he supported their primary interest in equality for blacks. He saw mechanical trades, business, farming and other professions as appropriate for blacks and condemned menial labor except when it was the only means of obtaining a living. Jones was elected president of the first Black Illinois State Convention held in Chicago on October 6–8, 1853. He enlisted the support of the white abolitionist movement and the state Republican Party to protest Illinois' Black Laws that banned free blacks from entering the state. He led a long and successful campaign and finally saw the state ratify the Thirteenth Amendment to the U.S. Constitution on February 1, 1865, to become the first state to abolish slavery. He also saw the legislature repeal the Black Laws on February 7, 1865. He joined a committee headed by Frederick Douglass and went to Washington, D.C., in 1866 to urge President Andrew Johnson to grant suffrage to the newly freed slaves.

Political office soon attracted Jones. When blacks became eligible to hold office in 1869, Governor John M. Palmer appointed him a notary public for the state, making him the first black in that post. Later, in 1871, he was elected a Cook County commissioner, becoming the first black elected to public office in Chicago. After his one-year term was over, he was reelected for a three-year term and was defeated in the 1875 elections. While in office, however, he protested the segregated school system, resulting in school integration in 1874. Long before Jones died on May 21, 1879, he had become a prominent, wealthy, and important black leader of Chicago. His wife, Mary Jane Richardson Jones, and daughter, Lavinia Jones Lee, survived him.

**Sources**

Bontemps, Arna, and Jack Conroy. *Anyplace But Here*. New York: Hill and Wang, 1966.

Gliozzo, Charles A. "John Jones." *American National Biography*. Vol. 12. Ed. John A. Garrity and Mark C. Carnes. New York: Oxford University Press, 1999.

———. "John Jones: A Study of a Black Chicagoan." *Illinois Historical Journal* 80 (Autumn 1987): 177–188.

Smith, Jessie Carney, ed. "Mary Jane Richardson Jones." *Notable Black American Women*. Book III. Detroit: Gale Research, 2003.

*Jessie Carney Smith*

# Quincy Jones (1933– ), Composer, Producer, Media Entrepreneur

Quincy Delight Jones Jr. was born in Chicago, Illinois, on March 14, 1933, to Sara Wells and Quincy Delight Jones Sr. His early schooling was in

Chicago. In 1943, his father remarried and moved the family to Bremerton, Washington. It was there that his talents and development in music truly began. He started playing brass instruments including the French horn and trumpet from the age of ten, then in high school. He began playing in various bands with friends quite early, and at the age of fourteen he met Ray Charles, who was then sixteen years old. They became lifelong friends. Among his other musical acquaintances were Ernestine Anderson, Charlie Taylor, and bandleader Bumps Blackwell. Charles gave him his first instructions in jazz harmony and arranging. He also met Jeri Caldwell, whom he later married and with whom he had his first child, Jolie.

## EARLY TUTORING WITH CLARK TERRY

At this time things started happening quickly for Jones. Soon (in 1947) his father moved the family to Seattle, and Jones's acquaintances broadened, as did his opportunities. He was able to meet many major entertainers at events in the Seattle area, including Cab Calloway, Billie Holiday, Billy Eckstine, Lionel Hampton, Sammy Davis Jr., and Count Basie. Clark Terry, in town for an engagement, took a liking to him and saw his potential as a musician. Jones would wake him up early in the mornings after only a few hours of sleep following a late-night gig. Terry gave young Jones (then only about thirteen years old) trumpet lessons early in the mornings before Jones went to school and helped him work on his technique as well as on jazz phrasing and style. They became lifelong friends. In another interesting incident, Lionel Hampton, also in town for an engagement, invited him to play with his band and compose some arrangements, whereupon young Jones took this as an open invitation, packed up, and literally "got on the bus." Hampton's wife, Gladys, however, objected, insisting that Jones first "finish his schooling," which he did.

Jones continued to grow as a composer, writing a suite for orchestra, titled *From the Four Winds*, and a *Nocturne in Blue*. The suite was submitted and earned him a scholarship to Seattle University; the *Nocturne* was performed at a high school recital. After graduating from high school, Jones attended Seattle University for one semester, prior to being awarded a scholarship to the Schillinger House of Music in Boston, Massachusetts (now the Berklee School of Music).

Looking past the horizon, Jones saw a glimpse of his future. He left Seattle to make a new home in New York City, with his soon-to-be new wife Jeri to follow later. They soon married and got an apartment. Jones, however, went on to Boston to study at Berklee, commuting often to New York as the next step on his road to professional success in the music industry. The road took him to engagements as an arranger and performing musician in New York, tours of the United States, Europe, and South America, and eventually a career as a composer, producer, and media executive, working in the film and recording industry. During his long career he has earned numerous awards: Grammies, Emmies, Academy Awards, honorary degrees, and commendations in the United States and abroad.

## WORKS WITH LIONEL HAMPTON

Ironically, his first major engagement following his studies at Berklee was with Lionel Hampton, who reflected on his earlier offer and agreed that Jones was now old enough to join his band. After engagements in New York, the band went on a long tour of the South. He met many of the major musicians of the day, including Oscar Pettiford, Miles Davis, Dizzy Gillespie, Charlie Parker, Charles Mingus, and others. Pettiford, particularly, was helpful on many occasions. Jones prepared arrangements for him for recording sessions, and Pettiford was somewhat of an elder brother, providing housing and encouragement at times of need. Jones also made his first recording while with the Hampton band in 1951, a recording of his composition "Kingfish," on which he played the solo part.

On the Hampton band's southern tour, Jones got a taste of sequential "one-nighters," as well as a firsthand introduction to all the manifestations of racial segregation. The tour scheduled seventy-nine one-night stands in the Carolinas and numerous performances at various halls in Texas and the other southern states. His fellow musicians told Jones their interpretations of the social situation: This was the early 1950s, he was eighteen, and this was comparable to an open-registration college course in racism for him.

The Hampton band's next assignment was a tour of Scandinavia, beginning in 1953. Following their southern tour, there was only time for a brief respite before the plane left for Oslo on September 2. The tour was to include concerts in Oslo, Stockholm, and other venues, where they were met by sophisticated audiences who loved jazz. A group of recognized Swedish jazz instrumentalists was assembled for the concerts and for later recording sessions. Jones served regularly as arranger, working with Art Farmer, Clifford Brown, and the assembled musicians, producing a record titled *Quincy Jones and the Swedish All-Stars* (now a valuable collector's item). The record was received with acclaim by European jazz enthusiasts as well as by the press; it went a long way toward establishing Jones as an important jazz artist in Europe.

## DEVELOPMENT AS AN ARRANGER AND COMPOSER

The Scandinavian tour was a very busy one, with concerts often twice a day with extensive travel between dates. Jones used all the free time he could muster to compose and arrange new works. While they were in Paris, he participated in numerous recording sessions, composing works for a variety of combinations ranging from sextets to a seventeen-piece ensemble including both American and French musicians. It was while in Paris that he heard by phone from his wife Jeri, telling him of the birth of his new daughter, Jolie.

From Paris, Jones returned to New York, found an apartment, and took on more work focusing on freelance composing and arranging on assignment for several colleagues in the music field as his principal means of support for his new family. His next assignments in 1955 came in work for Tommy Dorsey's summer TV show on CBS and work for a variety of groups—jazz, gospel, R&B (rhythm and blues), and popular—from James Cleveland to Cannonball Adderley. Then, in 1956, another prestigious assignment surfaced: Jones was named to organize a tour group of well-qualified jazz and bebop musicians to give concerts in the Middle East, sponsored by the State Department and led by Dizzy Gillespie.

## STATE DEPARTMENT TOURS OF MIDDLE EAST AND SOUTH AMERICA

The tour of the Middle East was to begin in Rome, following the completion of a tour by Dizzy Gillespie in Europe with "Jazz at the Philharmonic." Congressman Adam Clayton Powell, the well-known minister and Harlem congressman, had shepherded the concept to fruition as a sponsored program to present public concerts in the Middle East. Jones served as music director. After assembling and rehearsing the group for about two months, Jones and the group met with Dizzy in Rome, where they had a few more rehearsals and left on their goodwill tour. The tour visited Karachi, Beirut, Damascus, Ankara, Istanbul, Belgrade, Zagreb, and Athens and proved an immense success. The region acquired an excellent opinion of the United States, jazz, and its practitioners. In fact, some Cypriot students had previously stoned the American embassy in a political protest, but the band's concert in Cypress was met with cheers and boisterous applause. After reviewing the immense success of the program, the State Department decided to continue the program and approved an extension. They decided to send the group to South America, where the band played concerts in Quito, Guayaquil, Buenos Aires, Montevideo, and several cities in Brazil. Jones remarked that the international language of music as well as the interracial composition of the band, including blacks and whites, men and women, accounted for their warm reception everywhere. Following these tours, Jones left the group and returned to New York to write and spend some time with his family.

In 1957 a job opened up for Jones in Paris, with Barclay Disque. He was named head of recordings and music for the company, associated with Mercury Records. This gave Jones an excellent opportunity to study with Mme. Nadia Boulanger, the famous French theorist and composer, with whom Aaron Copland and Leonard Bernstein had also studied. He also attended seminars conducted by Pierre Boulez and Jean Barraque. As a result of these studies, he developed further and experimented with new combinations and voicings. Mme. Boulanger was a leading authority on "French" harmonic sounds, as well as the supremacy of melody. She later said that he and Igor Stravinsky were her most distinguished pupils.

## ASSOCIATION WITH MERCURY RECORDS

In 1961–1963, Jones worked for Mercury Records, initially in talent development, then as head of its artists and repertory department. He returned to the United States and was named vice president, the first black vice president in the music business. His scoring of Ray Charles's hit song "I Can't Stop Loving You" rose to the top of the charts and earned him a Grammy in 1962. The next year he worked abroad for Mercury, in Holland, Italy, Japan, and Great Britain, and also recorded "Swinging at the Sands" with Frank Sinatra. In 1965 he left Mercury and moved to Hollywood, and his career blossomed in a new direction again. He scored the movie *Mirage* (1969) with Gregory Peck and a major feature film, *The Pawnbroker* (1971), directed by Sidney Lumet. Regular TV and film work followed: *Walking in Space* (1969), *Rodgers and Hart Today* (1971), *Ironside* (1972); he was named music director of *The Bill Cosby Show* in 1972.

## CHILDREN, WOMEN, AND SERIOUS HEALTH ISSUES

A major crisis in Jones's life occurred in 1974, when he suffered a painful attack of severe headaches, comparable to a stroke. He was rushed to the hospital for tests, and the diagnosis was an aneurism—a swelling of the aortic artery in his brain. Major brain surgery was needed to repair the artery. This could have proved fatal except for the skill of his surgeons and Jones's willpower. While convalescing, Jones got the news that the operation was only a partial solution. An additional operation would be necessary to excise an aneurism on the other side of his brain. Again, despite very unfavorable odds, Jones pulled through and made a full recovery. His wife, the former Peggy Lipton, was with him throughout the entire ordeal. Unfortunately, the stressful time as well as his "normal stresses" wore very severely on their marriage. They separated in 1986 and subsequently divorced. They had two daughters, Rashida and Kidada, born in 1974 and 1976. The breakup caused a severe depression for Jones, bordering on a mental breakdown. To recover, he took his doctor's suggestion and, with Marlon Brando's help, withdrew to a convalescence on the island of Tahiti.

On reading *Q: The Autobiography of Quincy Jones* (2001), one might gather the impression that he was somewhat of a predator where women were concerned, particularly in his youth. At the very least, one may certainly say that he had a constant series of close relations with women; seven children born to five women testifies amply to this. However, we also learn of a very giving father who dearly loved his children and who maintained a familial closeness at all times. Two points stand out in this regard in the warm and loving relationship with Jolie, his first child, born in 1953, and Quincy Delight Jones III, his son, born to Ulla Anderson in 1968. Jolie contributed a significant chapter to his *Autobiography*, as did his daughters Rashida and Kidada.

As for Quincy Delight III (or "Snoopy"), his father set him up in business and encouraged his full participation in Jones's *Back in the Block* (1990) album project, rehearsing, recording, writing lyrics, performing with his father, and generally contributing substantially to the final product. In preparing for the album, Jones introduced his son to a number of major rap and hip-hop artists, including Melle Mel, Ice T, LLCool J, and Big Daddy Kane, and encouraged a merging of talents. The release dovetailed with Jones's penchant for stressing a fusion of styles—a constant stream flowing from deep in Africa's past into contemporary black music. The album traced this flow and met with great success, earning Jones a Grammy for Album of the Year in 1988.

Continuing in the same vein, "We Are the World" was an attempt at a humanistic and cultural outreach to Ethiopia and Africa in general and its serious problems with AIDS (acquired immunodeficiency syndrome), civil war, and famine. The original concept stemmed from a suggestion by Harry Belafonte stressing the need for help by the world's richer nations in a time of a drastic crisis. The means was to be an effort by prominent artists to produce a musical work that could sell across the world, furnishing cash to quench this massive thirst. Lionel Richie and Michael Jackson were tasked with writing the lyrics of a passionate song. A group of forty-six artists of the world's best musical artists gathered in January 1985 for a massed single recording session in Los Angeles, directed by Jones, to give their best efforts to producing a finished recording. Amazingly, as Jones told them all to leave their egos at the door, an almost magical harmonious blending resulted, and the final tapes were cut by the group early the following morning. The artists included Michael Jackson, Lionel Richie, Diana Ross, Bob Dylan, the Pointer Sisters, Willie Nelson, Bruce Springsteen, Stevie Wonder, and others. The combined creative efforts of these artists resulted in a masterful product that was released by CBS Records, was immensely popular, and garnered more than $200 million in sales in the United States alone. Similar outpourings followed from other sources. The task of taking care of African refugees, as we know, still continues.

Other major projects undertaken by Jones included the *Thriller* (1982) album, produced as an output of a close collaboration between two committed artists, Jones and Michael Jackson, with some assistance from Rod Temperton, who cowrote some of the songs and participated in engineering and editing the final version. The finished product was the result of serious interplay between Jones and Jackson, listening to partial solutions along the way. They listened to segments many times, worked out various musical problems, retried voicings, harmonies, and accompaniments, working steadily on the product intensively over a period of about six weeks. The result was a masterpiece, acknowledged to this day as perhaps their finest work and one of Jackson's signature albums. It is still the all-time bestselling album, with sales of about $40 million and winning for Jones the award of a Grammy for Producer of the Year in 1984.

Another project for which Jones will be remembered for many years to come is the film *Color Purple* (1985), an adaptation of Alice Walker's best-selling novel. He, together with Steven Spielberg, masterminded this project to a success shared by principal actress **Oprah Winfrey**. The film, coproduced and with a musical score by Jones, gleaned a record eleven Oscar nominations and had a successful run in cinemas both here and abroad. It marked Winfrey's debut as a screen actress: She credited her triumph in this role to Jones's constant support.

Other recent achievements by Jones include the launching of *Vibe* magazine, in 1992, specializing primarily in news of urban popular music, and in 1998, *Blaze*, the first major publication devoted to hip-hop music and culture. For this and similar achievements, Jones was honored at the 67th Academy Awards in 1995 with the Jean Hersholt Award for Humanitarianism. He produced the 1996 Academy Awards show and telecast and received the MusiCares Award for philanthropic giving from the National Academy of Recording Arts and Sciences. In 1997 he became executive producer of the syndicated talk show *Vibe* and received the NAACP (National Association for the Advancement of Colored People) Image Award as Best Jazz Artist for his album *Q Live in Paris*.

Having produced "America's Millennium Gala" to usher in the New Year as well as the millennium, we can look forward to more from Jones in the coming years, for as he says himself in Linda Bayer's book *Quincy Jones*, he has seen what happens when people retire: "[T]hey just dry up."

**Sources**

Bayer, Linda. *Quincy Jones*. Philadelphia: Chelsea House Publishers, 2001.

Brow, Anthony. *New Grove Dictionary of Music*. Vol. 13. New York: Macmillan, 2001.

Gates, Henry Louis. "Interview with Quincy Jones." PBS and WGBH/Frontline, 1998.

Haley, Alex. "Quincy Jones: A Candid Conversation with Pop's Master Builder about Rock, Rap, Racism and His Thriller of a Career" (July 1990). *The Playboy Interviews*. New York: Ballantine Books, 1993.

Horricks, Raymond. *Quincy Jones*. New York: Hippocreme Books, 1985.

Jones, Quincy. *Q: The Autobiography of Quincy Jones*. New York: Doubleday, 2001.

*Who's Who among African Americans*. 18th ed. Detroit: Thomson Gale, 2005.

*Darius L. Thieme*

# Vernon Eulion Jordan (1935– ), Corporate Lawyer, Investment Firm Official, Organization Leader

As a protégé of the immortal Thurgood Marshall, Vernon Jordan emerged as a famous civil rights attorney whose impeccable skills would lead him on the front lines of desegregating the University of Georgia, directing fieldwork with the National Association for the Advancement of Colored People (NAACP), developing the United Negro College Fund and the National Urban League, and on to significant battle as a fund-raiser, negotiator, arbitrator, and all-around power broker. His direct influence through directorships is paralleled through his behind-the-scenes influence on numerous corporate boards at the highest level of national and international prominence. With a carefully tailored reputation, Jordan has earned the respect of colleagues and adversaries alike and positioned himself as one of the more widely recognized men of power in the world. This reality came to pass when Jordan became a household name to the average American citizen when he was characterized as former President Bill Clinton's right-hand man as the embattled president made sensational headlines during his tenure from 1992 to 2000.

On August 15, 1935, Vernon Eulion Jordan was born into middle-class, Jim Crow Atlanta, Georgia. Jordan interacted with upper-class whites of society but still experienced the undeniable sting of being black in a society that was defined by whites, for whites, and the perpetual state of such affairs. After graduating from **Booker T. Washington** High School in 1953, he embarked on an educational journey that ultimately led him to experiences marked by psychological adjustments. He was the only black in his graduating class at DePauw University, Greencastle, Indiana, in 1957; in 1960, he graduated from Howard University School of Law.

Jordan's passage through the rugged terrain of intimate contact within high levels of white society at DePauw and the rich tradition of civil rights law under the tutelage of the esteemed legal mind of Thurgood Marshall produced a dynamic professional life. He emerged as a member of the legal team that desegregated the University of Georgia in 1961; as field director for the Georgia Branch of the NAACP from 1962 to 1963; as executive director of the National Urban League from 1972 to 1982; as Washington, D.C. legal and political guru, power broker, and counsel member for Akin, Gump, Strauss, Hauer and Feld from 1982 to the present; as chief of the Transitional Team, political insider, and primary confidant for President Bill Clinton's administration from 1992 to 2000; and as senior managing director of Lazard Freres Investment Firm from 2001 to the present.

Throughout his career, Jordan has consistently nurtured networks and sustained communication within all levels of society. His ability to adapt to radical, conservative, and neutral camps has made him a most effective source of influence and power, all toward the greater good of black people in the United States.

His bold stance and literal escorting of Charlayne Hunter and Hamilton Holmes through hate-filled air of white mob nostalgia at the University of Georgia cemented his courage while still fresh from law school. His track record as executive director for the United Negro College Fund in 1970 solidified his credentials as a superb fund-raiser and efficient organizational force with which to be reckoned. Accordingly, his efforts propelled him to the National Urban League post as its leader. Jordan remarked in *Newsweek* for February 19, 1973, on the changing nature of civil rights and the process of attaining true equality in American society. He noted that people in leadership positions should not try to recreate the dramatic conditions of the 1960s because it was unwise. To further his claim, Jordan stressed that the era of street protests were over and the time was long overdue for delivery of services to the community. He made this point by using the analogy of trench warfare as a vehicle for bringing about meaningful change through job creation.

Immediate gains for black citizens were felt from Jordan's tenure as Urban League director, primarily because his work at the league helped integrate American businesses and provide economic and social support to the new and expanding black middle class. An On-the-Job Training Program provided work for upward of 70,000 people, and the Labor Education Advancement Program assisted blacks in securing work within manual labor crafts and unions in the mid-1970s under Jordan's watch. Additionally, his administration launched a Family Planning Program and a Street Academy and erected 2,500 public housing units for lower-income residents. Jordan, however, was not content to rest on the loins of the civil rights gains of the 1960s and refused to lose sight of necessity for group identification.

While under political attack in 1977, Jordan responded to criticism launched by staunch conservatives who felt that getting the right to sit on a bus should have ended the struggle for civil rights. By looking at blacks as a group, he pointed out that the critics marginalized the legitimate interests of blacks such as in issues other than formal, legalized segregation. For instance, Jordan hammered the issue of employment, where black jobless rates were double those for whites. Furthermore, among young people they were considerably worse. He furthered his cause and shook the baseless criticisms by suggesting that crippling effects of joblessness were rampant realities within the entire black community. Black representation in most professions was approximately 2 percent, according to Jordan. He went on to question the feasibility or responsiveness for black groups ignoring disadvantages aligned with racial discrimination and how their constituency could no longer be silenced on such matters. Rather than co-opt into white society in a fashion that abandoned his calling to assist his people's cause, Jordan worked within high levels of the corporate power structure to lobby and secure vital funding needed to advance efforts aimed at an egalitarian society for citizens.

A racially motivated attempt on Jordan's life occurred in 1980, but he survived. Into the 1980s he was a noted "mover and shaker" in political and legal circles because of his calm, yet firm savvy. Jordan attracted clients and handled business with a determined since of integrity. He is generally characterized as one who offers precise judgment, exudes confidence in his abilities, is personable, and has a manner about him that is warm and attentive. Such power broking would propel Jordan in 1992 to the role of President-elect Bill Clinton's Transitional Team chief. Longtime close personal friends, Jordan and Clinton would mutually benefit throughout Clinton's two terms in office. Jordan's cool approach and contacts from his Urban League years with leading corporate heads made him a valuable player.

Concerning his clout as an "insider" and priceless accountability as a centerpiece for influence, Clinton's association with Jordan raised some political eyebrows as possible conflicts of interests. But, to no avail, the pundits did not get their wishes met. Instead Jordan was noted as a "Rainmaker," or deliverer of legal business to the firm he represented. Seven of the twelve companies whose board Jordan served on were also represented by Jordan's law firm. RJR Nabisco, Union Carbide Corporation, Corning Incorporated, Revlon Group Incorporated, Xerox Corporation, Ryder System Incorporated, and Sarah Lee Corporation all were represented by Jordan on their respective boards and also as their lawyer in the 1990s. American Express Company, Bankers Trust Corporation, Banker's Trust New York, Dow Jones and Company, and J. C. Penny were other boards Jordan served simultaneously, but in a capacity as legal counsel.

What is readily apparent from Jordan's major corporation board involvement is that he carries tremendous weight in national and international affairs because he has positioned himself to be at the tables where decisive stands are taken, monies are allocated, and human conditions are impacted directly. Beginning in 2001, Jordan assumed responsibility as senior managing director of Lazard Freres and Company Investment Firm. Lazard has global firms representing the Americas, Asia Pacific, and Europe and focuses on financial advice, asset management, and capital markets. The year 2001 also produced *Vernon Can Read!: A Memoir*, by Jordan and Annette Gordon-Reed. In classic tongue-and-cheek mode, the title derives from the summer of 1955 when Jordan was home in Atlanta visiting on summer recess. His summer job was to chauffer a retired white banker who responded in amazement as his young black driver routinely read books while the elder statesman napped. He replied, "Vernon can read." Apparently he can do more than just read. He can analyze, interpret, and make tough decisions. Most important, though, is his demonstrated utility in sustaining bridges and not burning them, cultivating productive resource relationships and not letting them dry up, and always standing front and center at the door leading to equal access of opportunity for blacks in America. He is married to the former Anne Dibble and lives in Washington, D.C.

**Sources**

Goldman, Peter. "Black America Now." *Newsweek*, February 19, 1973, 29–34.

Grove, Lloyd. "Vernon Jordan: He's Doing Well, but Is He Doing Good?" *Washington Post*, National Weekly Edition, November 30–December 6, 1992.

Jordan, Vernon E., Jr. "Race and the Issues." *To Be Equal*, November 30, 1977.

Jordan, Vernon E., Jr., and Annette Gordon-Reed. *Vernon Can Read!: A Memoir.* New York: PublicAffairs, 2001.

Wortham, Jacob. "League Leader." *Black Enterprise* 5 (March 1975): 15–18.

*Uzoma O. Miller*

# Marjorie Stewart Joyner (1896–1994), Hairstylist, Inventor, Educator, Philanthropist

Born into poverty, Marjorie Joyner worked through life's obstacles to help shape America's black hairstyling industry. She played significant roles as a stylist, inventor, educator, and advocate. In her later years, she led community and political causes and raised funds for education and other philanthropies.

Only four of George Emmanuel and Annie Dougherty Stewart's thirteen children survived beyond infancy. Their daughter Marjorie entered the world on October 24, 1896. Her own life spanned ninety-eight years. George Stewart taught school, and the importance of education played a role throughout Marjorie's life. In 1904, the family moved from Monterey, Virginia, Marjorie's birth home, to Dayton, Ohio. Soon her parents divorced, and Marjorie lived with other families. In 1912, she moved to Chicago to live with her mother.

Her education required persistence because she often had to abandon school to work as a waitress, babysitter, or domestic. In 1924, she earned a certificate in dramatic art and expression from Chicago Musical College, but it took her until 1935 to complete high school. She undertook her college education much later in life, graduating in 1973 with a B.S. degree from Florida's Bethune-Cookman College, at the age of seventy-seven.

Her own family life proved much more stable than that of her original family. During her early years in Chicago, a young man named Robert S. Joyner roller-skated by her house and into her life. The two married on April 4, 1916. Robert became respected in the field of podiatry. They raised two daughters, Anne and Barbara, who became educators. When Robert died in 1973, the couple had been married fifty-seven years.

## BECOMES AGENT FOR MADAME C. J. WALKER

Joyner attended A. B. Molar Beauty School in Chicago and, after becoming its first African American graduate, opened her own salon in 1916. A bad haircut prompted her mother-in-law to sponsor her enrollment in a class with **Madame C. J. Walker**, a noted black beautician. Joyner soon became an agent for the Walker Company and worked closely with Madame Walker to build the company. By the time of Walker's death in 1919, Joyner had risen to the role of national supervisor over Walker's 200 beauty schools. Walker's "hair culturists" traveled door to door styling women's hair. Dressed in black skirts and white blouses, they carried black satchels containing a range of sixteen beauty products.

Joyner's own travels for the company took her to Paris, London, Rome, the Holy Land, the West Indies, and West Africa. Her clients included notables Ethel Waters, Marian Anderson, Billie Holliday, Dinah Washington, and Louis Armstrong. Through more than fifty years with the company, she taught 15,000 people and eventually was named vice president.

Throughout her career, Joyner created a number of hairstyling products. The Walker Company actively promoted her Satin Tress, a type of permanent that relaxed hair and made it easier to style. She invented and, in 1928, patented her permanent wave machine. The product was used widely within the company, but Joyner drew no profit from its invention.

Joyner helped shape the hairstyling industry in other ways as well. In 1924, she and two other women drafted Illinois' first cosmetology laws. After white beauty associations excluded her, she saw the need to establish an organization for black beauticians. In 1945, she and Mary McCloud Bethune founded the United Beauty School Owners and Teachers Association along with its Alpha Chi Pi Omega sorority and fraternity.

In 1954, Joyner took 195 black beauticians on a tour of Europe. The idea originated in 1932 as a result of being banned from participating in a contest because of her race. Then once she suggested the idea to others, it took five years to plan the trip. Paris and London, in particular, extended elaborate welcomes to the group. The ladies trained under master hairstylists and toured a variety of European sites. Robert Joyner and four other men accompanied the group.

Joyner's convictions about equality of the races led to political involvement. She developed a friendship with Eleanor Roosevelt. The two once faced down the Ku Klux Klan to attend a Bethune–Cookman College concert. In 1935, she helped found the National Council of Negro Women. President Franklin Roosevelt appointed her to leadership in the Democratic National Committee during World War II. She worked with the Works Progress Administration, the Civilian Conservation Corps, and the National Youth Association. Joyner came to know other presidents up through President Jimmy Carter's administration.

Joyner became active also in community affairs, especially in Chicago's annual Bud Billiken Parade. Sponsored by the city's only African American newspaper, the *Chicago Defender*, the parade has become the largest African American parade in the United States. Founder **Robert Sengstacke Abbott** began the parade in honor of his newspaper carriers. Joyner helped organize and rode at the head of each parade for more than sixty years. She also headed the *Chicago Defender* Charities, raising money and organizing food and clothing drives. She helped found and actively participated in the city's Cosmopolitan Community Church.

In her later years, Joyner engaged in fund-raising for the Bethune–Cookman College she had attended. Donors included Nelson Rockefeller and the United Beauty School Owners and Teachers Association. In the 1970s, the college named a residence hall for her.

Several other honors came her way. In 1975, Chicago named her Senior Citizen of the Year. A 1987 Smithsonian Institution exhibit featured Joyner's permanent wave machine and a replica of her original salon. In 1990, during the 44th National Council of Negro Women, participants honored the ninety-three-year-old as one of five recipients in their "Salute to Black Women Who Make It Happen." That same year, the *Washington Post* named her "Grande Dame of Black Beauty Culture."

Joyner continued to go to her office and to attend church regularly until a heart attack took her life on December 27, 1994. Throughout nearly a century, she made significant contributions to hairstyling, education, and community endeavors. Along the way, she also influenced how young African American people thought about themselves.

**Sources**

"Beauty Pilgrimage." *Ebony* 9 (August 1954): 38–44.

Flug, Michael. "Marjorie Stewart Joyner." *Notable Black American Women*. Book II. Ed. Jessie Carney Smith. Detroit: Gale Research, 1996.

MacDonald, Annie L. *Feminine Ingenuity: Women and Invention in America*. New York: Ballantine Books, 1992.

"Madame Walker Has New Hairdressing Treatment." *Ebony* 4 (January 1949): 62–64.

Manheim, James M. "Marjorie Stewart Joyner." *Contemporary Black Biography*. Vol. 26. Detroit: Gale Research, 1992.

Nelson, Jill. "The Fortune That Madame Built." *Essence* 14 (June 1983): 84–86, 154, 156.

*Marie Garrett*